D0895483

EXPLODING

THE HIGHS, HITS, HYPE, HEROES, AND HUSTLERS
OF THE WARNER MUSIC GROUP

Stan Cornyn
with Paul Scanlon

HarperEntertainment
An Imprint of HarperCollins*Publishers*

A Rolling Stone Press Book

Editor: Holly George-Warren

Associate Editor: Nina Pearlman

Assistant Editor: Jordan N. Mamone

Editorial Assistant: Andrew Simon

Editorial Contributors: Ashley Kahn, Kathy Huck, Wendy Mitchell, Kimberly Curry

HarperCollins books may be purchased for educational, business, or sales promotional use. For information please write to Special Markets Department, HarperCollins Publishers Inc., 10 East 53rd Street, New York, N.Y. 10022.

FIRST EDITION

Designed by Rhea Braunstein

Printed on acid-free paper

Library of Congress Cataloging-in-Publication Data has been applied for.

ISBN 0-380-97852-0

02 03 04 05 06 RRD 10 9 8 7 6 5 4 3 2 1

To Mo and Joe,

who opened the door
that let me play
for my entire working life

Also to the inventor of the secretary,
and his greatest hits:
Glenis, Jeannie, Laurel,
Nina, Helene, Carol, Gaynor, and Sue

Intro

Aᴛ Warner Bros. Records, my job in early years was to introduce new acts to people. To do this, I wrote ads with headlines like

STAN CORNYN JUST WROTE
187,000 NAUGHTY WORDS

that were supposed to arouse your interest.

Some thirty-five or so years later, I find myself repeating this ploy. Once I wrote *Exploding,* "they" in New York wanted Prefatory remarks from me.

I'd spent over three decades working in Burbank for music entities whose names began with the word *Warner.* Twice before during those decades, I'd gathered up book-length histories of the Warner Records Group—from its beginnings at zero sales; on to its becoming far and away the biggest records empire of the Seventies, Eighties, and Nineties; then to its decline. Those two never got into print. I saved the research.

The first nonbook was in the Sixties. As a label, we at Warner Bros. Records were exploding. My bosses let me spend money without question. I turned to a colleague's wife to research the background-up-to-now of Warner Bros. Records (and at that time, our new brother, Atlantic Records). She—Ellen Pelissero—did a good job, considering she used a typewriter, carbon paper, and other relics of the Machine Age of Writing. Ellen remembers, "You sent me to New York City to learn about the New York office, plus set up an interview for me with Ahmet Ertegun to talk about the Atlantic/WB merger and sneak up on the Maitland firing. I was doing fine until I actually got to the Maitland firing and he blurted out, 'Who sent you to do this?' Then promptly escorted me out of his office in a fury while simultaneously complimenting me on my Norwich City (England) Soccer bag. Said he was going to scream at you and Mo about it all. It was quite exciting, as I recall, but scared the hell out of me at the time." That first book pooped out about then, but I saved a typed copy.

The second time I researched this story came with a call in 1995 from WEA Distributing's Bob Moering and Jerry Sharell, who informed me that I was their second choice to write a commemorative book for the twenty-fifth anniversary of WEA (born 1971). I said sure, even though I knew the story was still controversial, considering the management mayhem the Music Group had just been through. Still, I wrote and wrote. Much research was done for a book so polite that Hallmark might have been its publisher. That book underwent gobs, pages even, of deletes. Unfortunately, WEA was just recovering from much of the turmoil of the preceding years, and Jerry later called me to say, "They just say they don't need this at this time." That book, called *Footprints,* died.

Two down. By now, as part of my endless restlessness, I was well retired from the record business, having again wanted new challenges in my life.

Finally, though, I decided: "Now or never. Do the book." Quickly, two publishing executives, ROLLING STONE's Jann Wenner, and HarperCollins's Tom Dupree, had the wisdom to say that magic word: yes.

So now, the third time, I began a book with a Schwarzenegger-like marquee: *Exploding.* Despite its Hiroshima-hot title, the book is not about any Big Bang. *Exploding* is a word the record industry just uses a lot, a synonym for "breaking out." Like, "Tracy Chapman's exploding on KSHE." "Exploding" is, in sales terms, a positive slang word for "just stand back and let it happen." It also means life is good today, so memorize the feeling. In that previous sentence, you may on my behalf substitute "three decades" for the word "today." My three-decades-plus at Warner felt good, and the feeling's memorized.

Nevertheless, I learned during my writing the history, that I had on my hands a mystery story. As close as I'd been to this history (and I spanned most of it, from Jack Warner to Val Azzoli), I kept ending up with puzzling questions:

- How could the 1990s go-Boom! have happened to such a great company?
- Who (or what) was at fault?
- Why is the whole record business sagging now?

To unravel *Exploding*'s mysteries, I turned to a few record-business colleagues, members of a group we now loosely refer to as the Montecito Book Club, for answers. You'll meet the club at the end of this book, as we try to unravel mysteries that still amaze many of us who've lived through the Rise and Fall of the Group.

For their assistance to my writing of the book, day after day, I'll quickly thank a few people: my faultfinder, Paul Scanlon, who tested my patience with corrosive comments like "Zzz" and "Are you ever going to learn that an apostrophe denotes present tense?" I felt great justice was enacted in the winter of 2000 when Paul's bathroom ceiling collapsed. But he was right enough to save my ass. At HarperCollins, copy editor Maureen Sugden, who cleaned up an amazing amount of goofs for us. At Rolling Stone Press, thanks to its fervent director Holly George-Warren, Andrew Simon, Ashley Kahn, Kathy Huck, Nina Pearlman, and Jordan Mamone (who corrected my comma faults and more). And to the ever-patient Sarah Lazin, the agent who connected us with better people skills than the Mayflower Madam's.

But I couldn't have done this without hours of talks with those who were in rooms I wasn't, and who told me what happened in them. Thanks also to those who lied the least, from Jack Warner to Mo Ostin and Bob Morgado (plus the two who talked but didn't want their names used). And no thanks to the five asses who refused to be interviewed by me; may they serve out their remaining years in Provo, Utah.

Among those interviewed: Beryl Adams • Paul Ahern • Fran Aliberte • Peter Asher • Ted Ashley • George Avakian • Brian Avnet • Val Azzoli • Russ Bach • Linda Baker • Ornetta Barber • Johnny Barbis • Mary Barna • Dave Benjamin • Georgia Bergman • Jason Berman • Bill Biggs • Victor Blau • David Braun • Bryn Bridenthal • Mike Bone • Jimmy Bowen • Dave Brown • Sonny Burke • Ken Buttice • Dorothy, Joe, and Kurt Bryer • Danny Buch • Phil Carson • Mary Cicio • Bob Clark • Dave Cline • Alan Cohen • Jim Conkling • Cory Connery • Hal Cook • Shelley Cooper • Dan Cotter • Terry Cox • Fern Cranston • Chris Crist • Bob Daly • Marvin Dean • Paul DeGennaro • Freddy DeMann • Lou Dennis • Tom Donahue • Tom Dowd • Henry Droz • June Droz • Don Dumont • Ahmet Ertegun • Selma Ertegun • Bob Evanik • Barb Evonits • Vic Faraci • Rudi Fehr • Oscar Fields • Lou Fogelman • Joel Friedman • Michael Fuchs • Gregg Geller • Lowell George • Manny Gerard • David Gersh • Eddie Gilreath • Murray Gitlin • Dave Glew • Jerry Gold • Danny Goldberg • Elliott Goldman • Irwin Goldstein • Ron Goldstein • Brent Gordon • Don Graham • Bob Greenberg • Jerry Greenberg • Larry Harris • Roger Helms • Bruce Hinton • Allen Hirschfield • Cecil Holmes • Jac Holzman • Keith Holzman • Jerry Hopkins • David Horowitz • Fran Howell • Bob Hurwitz • Elliott Hyman • Quincy Jones • Benjamin Kalmenson • Mickey Kapp • Carmella Kasoff • Chuck Kaye • Lenny Kaye • Arthur Kern • Ellen Kern • Ellis Kern • Dick Kline • Peter Knecht • Bob Krasnow • Nina Holzman Lamb • Dick Lederer • Ray Leong • Aaron Levy • Joanie Lowry • Jeannine Luby • Jeannie Lumley • Bruce Lundvall • Jim McAuliffe • Paul McDermott • Al McPherson • Lou Maglia • Mark Maitland • Mike Maitland • Tony Mandich • Nick Massi • Bob Merlis • Hale Milgrim • Bob Moering • Artie Mogull • Linda Moran • Bob Morgado • Jo Motta • Dave Mount • Murray Nagel • Claude Nobs • Helen Noletty • Mo Ostin • Randy Patrick • Marty Payson • Bill Perasso • Mel Posner • Bud Prager • Phil Quartararo • Jody Raithel • Steve Resnik • Annie Roëves • Mary Ann Romeri • Phil Rose • Ed Rosenblatt • Steve Ross • George Rossi • Mickey Rudin • Jackie Sallow • Norm Samnick • Al Schlesinger • Denny Schone • Carl Scott • Terry Semel • Francis Scott III • Jerry Sharell • Paul Sheffield • Allan Sherman • Mike Shore • Lou Sicurezza • Jim Silverman • Joe Smith • Neil

Speilberg • Charlie Springer • Larry Stanley • George Steele • Burt Stein • Teresa Sterne • Pete Stocke • Jim Swindel • Irving Taylor • Ted Templeman • Han Tendeloo • Ed Thrasher • Russ Thyret • Sheldon Vogel • Jim Wagner • Thelma Walker • Jack L. Warner • Lenny Waronker • Bert Wasserman • Steve Wax • Ron Weisner • Bobby Weiss • Ed West • Jerry Wexler • Rick Wietsma • Fred Wistow • and others I didn't keep track of.

Those and many, many more walked in the doors of the Warner Music Group and then out again, the richer for having spent years in the middle of the best party the music business ever threw. For me, it began with walking in around the time Jack Warner decided to have a second go at a record company. It was 1958.

1

JACK Warner walked briskly from his office at Warner Bros. Studios in Burbank, California, heading for lunch in the Executive Dining Room. Fresh from his personal barber's daily shave and hot towel, Warner moved past his personal steam room. He strode through the ferns-and-lawn-lined path to the private bungalow, where his personal chef prepared luncheons for Warner's favored executives, a dozen or so. Entering the room, Warner saw his men seated, suited, chatting, with water glasses, ashtrays, but no lunch. Not till Warner sat down, a steward behind, adjusting his chair for him. Then came lunch.

Warner, a swarthy sixty-five in 1957, ran his studio with decisive powers—his own. He'd been in Hollywood and Burbank now since 1918. First-generation Polish-American. He'd been born Jacob Warner, without a middle name, but Jack adopted one, "Leonard," believing that three names made him classier. Among the four "Warner Brothers," Jack had become the brothers' studio man—the one who *made* the pictures. Just one year before this lunch, his elder brothers, Harry and Albert, had sold their interests in Warner Bros. to a syndicate. Jack, too, had been expected to sell but had reneged. That ploy made Jack the Number One brother. He had power: over what movies got made, over who got hired, over women he laid, over his on-staff tennis coach, and over everyone's paycheck. He considered this land in Burbank his kingdom, and he thought that employee medical benefits were a Communist plot.

Warner liked his luncheons, where people referred to him as "J.L." and "Chief." The lunch menu—it's 1957, remember—was lamb chops with mint jelly, potatoes and gravy, cigars not cellophane wrapped. Before his attentive fellows at the long table, Warner sipped a Jack Daniel's and water and cracked bad jokes. When meeting Albert Einstein, for instance, Warner had commented that he, too, had a Theory of Relativity: "Don't hire 'em" was Jack's crack. Einstein didn't get it. (In the early 1960s, I spent some time with Mr. Warner, asking him about the past. "Somebody once called me a raconteur," he told me, "and I've got the tennis court to prove it." I, too, smiled at the raconteur's joke. I loved being in show business.)

Jack Warner looked like success, tanned to a tee, a pencil-thin mustache, his white teeth even across the bottom, looking like they'd been filed straight. After lunch, Warner lit up and introduced his topic for today: He's tired of seeing other companies, like Capitol and Columbia Records, license record rights of Warner's hit movies, then make a mint off selling records of Warner's music. Warner music should be Warner's mint. "So I'm thinking we need a record company," Warner said.

Among all the "Good idea, Chief" replies, one dissenter spoke up. "You forgotten Brunswick?" The room went silent. Hurling turds from the past was not what these luncheons were about.

Moving his personal mustard pot to one side, Warner leaned forward. "Yeah, I remember Brunswick Records. That was thirty years ago. What's that got to do with now?" The roomful just stared back at him.

Here's why.

In 1887, as the city of Burbank, California, was being founded, the Warner family's father, Ben, had sailed alone from Poland to Baltimore, Maryland. Ben went to work, mainly as a cobbler, in the Land of Opportunity. In his horse-drawn cart, his gold watch hidden in an inner pants pocket, Ben Warner moved where jobs might be found, and he scrimped. There was, in 1887, little entertainment like records. There were no radio, no movies, no television. The idea of preserving ("recording") a music performance was pretty much limited to player pianos, which were rare, novel, and voiceless. The phonograph, just invented, was intended to be a dictaphone. The music business, aside from live performance, had but one medium: printed sheet music to prop up on the family's piano. To make music, you had to make it with your own two hands, your own voice.

Before long, Ben Warner had scrimped enough to send for his wife, Pearl, and their two children. When Pearl got to America, apparently she was happy to reunite with Ben, because they soon started having children, one after another, ten in all. It may have been the lack of other home-entertainment devices. Of the dozen Warner kids, four of them became the Brothers of fame: Harry, Albert (they called him Abe), Sam, and Jacob (called Jack).

The Warner family eked it out with no running water in places like Youngstown, Ohio. As the family's kid brother, Jack, once characterized it, "There were no silver spoons in our mouths when we were born. If anything, there were shovels."

One of Jack's elder brothers, Sam, was the inventive Warner; he'd already introduced the first ice cream cone in Youngstown. Six-foot Sam had his deep-blue eyes focused on something new: a projector of moving images, called the Edison Kinetoscope.

Sam wanted a Kinetoscope bad. His father Ben felt it, and in 1904 he hocked his precious gold watch and chain from the old country; then he hocked Bob, the horse that pulled his meat wagon, all to buy a used projector for $150. Bundled with Sam's projector came one movie: twelve minutes long, called *The Great Train Robbery.*

Eldest brother Harry was the strictly business type of the clan; as a teen, Harry dated only girls within walking distance, so he didn't have to waste money on carfare. Harry had found in Youngstown a 180-seat hall (the Dome Picture Palace). Out front, the huge-handed second-eldest brother, stern-faced, barrel-chested Albert, dealt tickets for a nickel, while inside, third-eldest brother Sam projected the movie to full houses, for weeks in Youngstown, before the audience dwindled and the brothers took their only film on to the next town. Youngest brother Jack, age thirteen, using the alias Leon Zuardo, led the audience in singing "Wait Till the Sun Shines, Nellie" backed by slides of clouds and magnolias. "Little Brother" Jack's boy soprano was the "chaser," used to empty the audience for the next show.

Although a lifelong ham, Jack also heeded brother Sam's early advice: Never become a performer. "Get out front," Harry had observed, pointing to the ticket booth; do something that will "tie in to the box office. That's where the money is." (Much of the history of the music business has proved Harry's advice sound: Record companies *are* the box office, and they make more money, record for record, than do their singers.)

The Warner brothers turned filmmaking into their life stories. Harry, Albert, Sam, and Jack learned distribution lessons worth remembering: (1) that without good product, distribution fails; and (2) that big distributors can squash indies. The Warner boys were in their thirties; they were the kids rebelling against the big guys. To rebel successfully in this business meant (3) getting your own film-production company, so your pipeline stayed dependably full of new movies.

The Warner Feature Film Company started turning out quickies. These movies were meant to last as long as, say, a magazine issue. By 1918, the film*making* brothers—Sam and Jack—worked out of the Alexandria Hotel, on Olive Street in downtown Los Angeles. The Alexandria was office/home of agents, of actors "at liberty," of hookers, of theater bookers.

Back in New York, business head Harry Warner moved forward, in 1923 incorporating Warner Bros. Pictures Inc. The brothers kept 60 percent of the stock; they sold the public the other 40 percent. In Los Angeles, Sam and Jack made silent bombs with no stars, forgotten duds like *Ashamed of Parents* and *Parted Curtains.* Their first hit, *My Four Years in Germany,* grossed $1.5 million. Warner's net was $130,000. In any list of all the hot movie studios of the early Twenties, Warner Bros. finished near the bottom.

There were nineteen studios in Hollywood, with movies ranking the sixth-biggest industry in America. Amid all that boom, Warner Bros., on the corner of Sunset and Bronson, was a minor-league team.

From way down in Hollywood oblivion, Warners scrambled for hand-holds. Company treasurer Abe Warner—whom Jack once described as a man who, when he saw red ink, got "meaner than a cornered coon"—announced his artistic credo, which was "You don't need those overpaid, so-called stars. All you need is a dog." Abe meant Rin Tin Tin, who was Warners'. In film after film, he barked to warn his masters of Danger! "Rinty" was a star whose work habits the brothers admired deeply. That dog did not talk back, could not read its own reviews, never once asked for a raise or more close-ups or a new press agent or air-conditioning in his dressing room. Rinty didn't bitch about overtime either. The German shepherd became the brothers' "mortgage lifter," so popular that Warner hired eighteen stand-ins for the pooch.

In 1925, Harry Warner bought a Brooklyn movie outfit, Vitagraph, with its library and its fifty distributors across the country and overseas, for $800,000 and assumed debt of $980,000. Warners built theaters to show its films, since getting good opening slots was dicey, because Hollywood's "Big Three"—Paramount, Universal, and MGM—owned most of the country's theaters. Size mattered.

Also in 1925, Sam—young, still totally the enthusiast, proto-nerd—conned his elder brother Harry into visiting Bell Labs/Western Electric. The ten-by-twelve-foot room was darkened. A movie projector turned on. On the screen, an orchestra played. But this time, they could actually *hear* the orchestra playing music, too. And in sync.

Harry liked what Sam showed, but he went one better. In the darkened room, he whispered to Sam, "No wonder this thing hasn't taken hold. It hasn't been done with showmanship."

Electrical sound recording, with amplification, singing into microphones in the place of bellowing into horns, was now being used to make phonograph records. So why not movies with *electrically* recorded discs, playing their sound, synced with the picture?

The lights came up. Harry, nobody's fool, checked behind the screen to make sure no orchestra was hiding there. What he found was a sixteen-inch-wide, 33⅓ RPM wax disc, nearly two inches thick, which played from its center out to its rim. Gears connected it to the projector, for synchronization. Each disc was a one-take, ten-minute performance; if an error popped up, the whole ten minutes needed a fresh take.

Harry and Sam mused over the financial possibilities. They thought of all those theaters, of their owners who could ill afford one piano player, let alone a pipe organ or a big orchestra. Sam interrupted Harry's thoughts, saying, "But don't forget. You can have actors talk, too."

"Who the hell wants to hear actors talk?" Harry hushed back. He knew his marketplace was only 5 percent English speaking. "The music—that's the big plus about this." The Warners made a deal and got sound.

Having bought Vitagraph, Warners called the new system Vitaphone. Vitaphone music from Warner Bros. delivered a technological blow to the rest of the industry. They produced short subjects, like Caruso singing "Vesti la Giubba," Eddie Cantor singing as he rolled his banjo eyes, and Al Jolson, in blackface and overalls, coming at you out of a log cabin to sing "April Showers." These novelties, like singles, were at first slipped in between longer silent movies.

On Broadway in the fall of 1925, there was a new, semimusical play about a cantor's son who preferred singing jazz to chanting in the synagogue, and so set off for showbiz. But, realizing his errant ways, the jazz singer returned home on Yom Kippur, the Day of Atonement. Standing over his father's deathbed, he sang "Kol Nidre."

Harry Warner picked up his telephone and *The Jazz Singer*'s movie rights for Vitaphone. The Warners, refusing to meet the price of the show's Broadway star George Jessel, ended up casting Jolson in the lead.

When filming began, Sam, dressed as always in a three-piece suit, was chauffeured each morning in his Pierce-Arrow to the Manhattan Opera House. In that good sound "barn," he recorded material to sync with the film.

Al Jolson was supposed only to sing. As usual, movie dialogue would appear on screen on title cards. But Jolson, carried away while filming a new scene, finished singing "Dirty Hands, Dirty Face," then looked out at a pal in the audience and, over the applause, ad-libbed spoken dialogue: "Wait a minute, wait a minute, you ain't heard nothin' yet!" Then, as the cameras kept filming, Jolson topped himself before the audience of extras with "Toot Toot Tootsie."[1]

Sam Warner thought there might be something to Jolson's ad libs. More dialogue got added. Jolson sang and chattered while Sam recorded both music and talk onto film and disc. To tell the truth, people had *not* heard nothin' yet.

To finish the picture on time, Sam never left the studio. Meals sent in to him lay cold, untouched. Sam grew wan and listless. He ate aspirins by the dozen, with milk of magnesia chasers. By September, Sam, unsteady on his feet, would not leave until the picture was in the can.

On October 5, 1926, Sam Warner died of a cerebral hemorrhage. He was thirty-nine. The next day, October 6, *The Jazz Singer* opened in New York. Jolson's lifelike chat, captured on Vitaphone discs, brought

---

[1]Oddly, in his autobiography, page 177, Jack Warner claimed that the phrase "You ain't heard nothin' yet" was not in *The Jazz Singer*. Not true; the phrase is there. But Warner's book also neglected to mention his first wife and his son, Jack Warner, Jr.

movie-house audiences to their feet and sound to motion pictures. Audiences stood and cheered the Mick Jagger of his time.

The three surviving brothers, instead of attending that premiere, attended Sam Warner's funeral. They missed out on what the *New York Times* reviewed as "the biggest ovation in a theater since the introduction of Vitaphone." Sam, seizing on this new sound technology, had spoiled audiences for anything less.

Jolson fever swept the country. Jack Warner, the youngest, had now taken Sam's place: making the movies.[2] Warner Bros. cleaned up. Brunswick Records put out the Jolson songs from *The Jazz Singer.* Within three years, 83 percent of America's movie theaters, twenty thousand of them, were wired for sound.

Movie attendance—for both silent and sound films—exploded, doubling by 1928 to 95 million tickets per week sold. Warner stock went from $18 to $65 a share within weeks. A follow-up, *The Singing Fool,* came out, with even more Jolson (he now cost $150,000, which he wisely took in Warner stock). Brother Albert, heading distribution, sent out for more rakes. *Fool* made $5.5 million at the box office, the biggest take till *Gone With the Wind* came along.

The picture's hit song "Sonny Boy" was acclaimed the first tune to sell one million copies of sheet music. Stats like those grabbed Harry Warner right in the wallet.

Back in New York, Harry captained the surviving three brothers' manna bonanza, investing it with what Jack once called "the toughness of a brothel madam." In 1926, Harry had set up Renraw (Warner backward) as the three brothers' private company. By 1929, each brother's salary jumped up five times, to $500,000 a year. The three brothers controlled 300,000 of the 350,000 shares of Warners stock, which Harry used as collateral for his borrowings. Harry knew that Warner's lead in sound would soon be history. "If we stand still," he said, "we're walking backwards." Harry, whose business card read "President," needed more than the studio's revenues to fund his growth fevers. He borrowed hugely from Goldman, Sachs and Hayden, then added a bond issue for more. Wallet bulging, Harry went on a buying spree that would transform one year's profits into a corporation with substance to it. Real assets were bought, much as, decades later, Internet companies with huge stock values would spend their stocks to buy "real assets" companies.

Harry bought a piece of a California studio named First National,

---

[2]Sam Warner's will gave his 62,500 shares of stock (worth about $1 million in 1927) to his three brothers, keeping the brothers' control intact. Sam's actress wife, Lina, age twenty, got $100,000, plus $40,000 insurance money, and the household goods.

which Jack, now age thirty-five, got to run. First National was over the hill from Hollywood,[3] through the Barham Pass, over into Burbank.

Next, to make sure they got their movies played, Harry bought the Stanley Corp., which had 250 theaters in 75 cities, including the luxe Strand on Broadway. Into those theaters they hustled Vitaphone sound equipment. Running the theaters was brother Abe Warner, a massive, big-headed character beloved in his industry, a man unafraid of the dinner-table belch. Harry was deep into merger mania: Vitagraph plus First National plus Stanley Corp. Redundant workers were deleted as fast as the pen could cross the page.

Not one to spend a nickel when a penny would do, Harry hated a new line item on his ledger, a cost called "music royalty." He coveted cheaper music for his sound movies. The answer was owning a lot of songs yourself, so you wouldn't have to pay outside publishers. You paid yourself and got sheet-music profits, too. Warner bought up music-publishing houses, one right after another: in 1928, M. Witmark & Sons, Remick Music Corp., Harms Inc., and New World Music Corp.

The buying binge of newly affluent Warner Bros. Studio did not stop. What else could we do with this sound thing? Harry wondered.

The sound for Warner Bros.' talkies had come from those big sixteen-inch discs, manufactured by the Brunswick-Balke-Collender Company, which owned patents on the process, made records, and had its own record-pressing plant, not to mention record players, radios, pool tables, bowling alleys, and balls. In April 1930, Harry Warner bought all that, too, for $8 million. Brunswick, also a record label, was to become integral to the future of Warner Bros. Harry had its record presses, weighing tons each, shipped out to Warners' old Sunset studio. He sold off pool tables and bowling stuff, the company's moneymakers.

Brunswick Records had scooted up be to the third-largest record label in America. Its catalogue was hot, including Al Jolson's "My Mammy" (seven weeks on the chart in 1928) and "Sonny Boy" (nineteen weeks). Also in the catalogue: noncharted recordings by Duke Ellington, Furry Lewis, Uncle Dave Macon, LeRoy Carr, Scrapper Blackwell, Tampa Red, Georgia Tom, Memphis Minnie, and Kansas Joe.

Most of Brunswick's performers appealed to America's jazz-crazed youth, who'd had out-of-body experiences (high on bathtub gin), danced too

---

[3]The same hill with the home developer's sign HOLLYWOODLAND on it. That sign was built in 1923 with fifty-foot-tall letters and four thousand lightbulbs. It shut down in 1939, and all the lightbulbs were stolen. In 1978, without the LAND part, the sign was rebuilt, providing today's landmark. Over the hilltop and down the other side, there was then and is now Warner Bros. Studios and Records.

hot for their elders' tastes (Charlestons, in which couples alarmingly never even touched), and dressed to prove they just didn't care what Mom and Dad thought (flapper gowns with hip-high hems).

With Brunswick, Warner Bros. was in the record business. Or, as the studio's executives thought of it, Warner had added records to its studio music department, taking a place alongside publishing, soundtrack scoring, and composers.

To oversee Brunswick Records, Warner Bros. wanted a watchdog, the kind that saved used bones. It assigned Brunswick to its no-nonsense music-division VP, Herman Starr. Starr knew his job. He was a five-foot-seven executive who wore primly cut suits and black-rimmed glasses; poised, tough, but fair if you followed his own hard rules. He had first joined the studio in 1920 as an accountant. When Warner Bros. incorporated three years later, Starr was elected its assistant treasurer and a director. Starr went on to set up WB's European companies. He'd left to be president of First National Pictures. When WB bought that company, Starr became VP of the combined studios. Then, with the acquisition of Brunswick, Starr took over as president of recording, radio-set manufacturing, and music. Starr promised his boss, Jack Warner, that his music division (in particular, music publishing) would deliver to Warners a million dollars in profit every year.

Starr's diligence exceeded that of Inspector Javert. He disciplined better than vixens in leather. He kept nothing on his desk. If someone came into his office to ask a question, Starr opened his top left-hand drawer, took out seven to ten pages, paper-clipped together. He would turn to page two and give you *the* answer. He was testy, a man with a very long memory about anyone who crossed him. He did not compromise. Starr would run all music for Warner for the next two decades.

He kept Brunswick's Jack Kapp—who'd been hot with his Jolson records—as head of its recording work. Kapp, an effusive guy, had just issued Jolson's "Sonny Boy" over the objections of his New York bosses (who had complained, till Kapp wired them saying, "I'm here, and you're thirty-three hundred miles away. You'd better take my word for it.").

Kapp, who had the ability to put up with massive egos of the day, remained the production head for Warner's Brunswick label. The music trade blessed him with praise like "he's a man of no taste, so corny, he's good." He wore suede shoes and checked suits under a flapping polo coat. He half ran, half walked. Nearsighted, he peered through his glasses, looking quizzical. His thinnish, loving-cup face sported a narrow nose and away-from-the-head ears. In evaluating himself, Kapp said, "I know how to keep my pulse on the multitude." The newly elevated Kapp added Hollywood's Gloria Swanson, Noah Beery, and Harry Richman to make records. He signed America's hottest new star: Bing Crosby. Crosby became the first hit signing by a Warner label, recording three Number One hits—"Out of Nowhere," "Just One More Chance," and "At Your Command."

Music publishing plus your own record company—it made sense, if you could predict depressions. The business parlay Harry Warner bet on was market dominance: You now have the most music copyrights in the world, you have a movie studio to popularize them and a record company to make for sale copies, so you should own the rest—radio to "plug" the songs. Hence L.A.'s KFWB, which Sam had picked up in 1924.

By the 1920s, radio had also started to mean business, mean money. It seemed like a great way to promote movies and make some money, too. *Billboard* put it this way: "Five years ago a hybrid form of entertainment and frowned on by show business in general, the radio infant has grown within record time to the point where today it is second only to motion pictures as a gigantic industry in the entertainment business. And growing bigger all the time."

By 1930, Warner owned 93 film distributorships (exchanges), 525 theaters in 188 cities in America, a total of 51 subsidiary companies. Warner Bros. stock was worth more than $200 million. The company had 18,500 employees, who cost more than $36 million a year in salaries. But the Great Depression was taking hold. For all that, in 1931, WB's balance sheet showed a loss of $8 million.

Stockholders found that odd. They complained. The government caught Harry Warner green-handed. He had to confess to the U.S. Senate that the brothers' Renraw Corp. had been buying/selling Warner Stock (in a practice later called "insider training"), and in the process had skimmed an extra $7 million for Harry, Albert, and Jack. Stockholders sued and got back 100,000 shares of Warner stock that the brothers had transferred to the Renraw Corp.

The Depression deepened. The question in homes became "Why buy a phonograph, then have to spend even *more* money for records to play on it? Instead, let's just play our radio and get the latest tunes for free! Or go to the movies! Movies cost only a nickel."

By 1931, the record business damn near collapsed. Appliance stores sold records mainly as a barely profitable sideline, and *real* money came from washing machines and iceboxes; even fuses sold better. Consumers found records in stores like Hollander's Radio and Electric, Humboldt Park, Chicago, where Manny Hollander stocked records only if the labels protected him (guaranteed he could return any unsold stock). In Chicago, Brunswick sold through Hollander exclusively. Marketing of records in such stores barely existed. Records were filed behind counters, edge out, in rows of pigeonholes, not to touch, not to break. Discs came in brown or gray kraft-paper sleeves, no pictures on them. The only way a customer could browse was by catalogue, one per label. Impulse buying was not encouraged. Selling records was, for guys like Manny, kind of a nuisance, like selling tongs to go with your icebox.

Retail sales slipped, then nosedived, near to the point of death. In 1922, records sold $92 million. Ten years later, as Warner was just getting in, record sales had gone down to little more than a tenth of that, to $11 million.

In December, quickly Harry dumped his record business—Brunswick Records, including its Vocalion label—plus the pressing business. He found his fast buyer in the American Record Company, which advertised itself proudly as "Producers of bargain-priced discs sold by Woolworth's and similar chain stores." American Record Company bought it all: the Jolson masters, those new Crosby sides, plus Brunswick's A&R head, Jack Kapp.

On its venture into the record business, Warner had lost $8 million. Worse still, on the movie side, the original Rin Tin Tin had died. To honor his death, in 1932, Warners chopped its payroll by nine hundred humans. For Warner Bros., it was back to movies—Bogart, Cagney, Robinson (all short, feisty, underdog guys, like Jack Warner imagined himself to be), Bette Davis, Errol Flynn, and Paul Muni. And when it came to music, it was Busby Berkeley's musical extravaganzas. Berkeley, it was said, had in his phone book the numbers of five hundred on-call chorines.

But the money lost on this record business, this Brunswick business, left an indelible impression on Warner executives. Most affected was Herman Starr. The pain of this failure, for him, was acute. After the Brunswick sale, Starr returned to Warners. He swore never, ever again to risk the record business.

The Warner Bros. executives who stood one step lower than the brothers took this lesson to heart. Even Jack Warner—otherwise preoccupied with his movie lot; dressed to impress (white pants and blazer); cracking bad jokes; driving a yellow Jaguar; having flings with starlets, his prerogative as a studio head—even Jack felt the Brunswick pinch.

In 1935, the father, Ben Warner, died. The schism widened between Harry, the straitlaced president of Warners, and Jack, the younger, randier production head, who *knew* he deserved not answering to his New York brother who'd never made a movie in his life. Now on his second marriage (one that the family found abhorrent, and told him so), Jack wanted to be the Head Guy. Getting to be Number One took Jack Warner another twenty-three years.

The brothers' fighting was interrupted, thankfully, by World War II. Warners became 101 percent American. It made fervent movies with clean guys like Bogart, Cagney, and Reagan, stories to make even college pinkos salute, like *Pride of the Marines, Casablanca, This Is the Army, Destination Tokyo, Mission to Moscow.* It was like the Warners worried that Roosevelt might ship them all back to Poland.

The studio passed on expensive stuff, like the bestseller *Gone with the Wind,* which Jack Warner referred to as "some kind of Civil War crap, cast of thousands. We can't put up that kind of cash. We're not in the business of making big movies, we're in the business of making big money." Warner saw himself running a factory. His manner at the studio was overbearing, brash, a little dumb, and power aware. He bowed to no one. He referred to his writers as "schmucks with Underwoods."[4]

Warner felt the power and used the wealth that Bogart and friends brought his studio. He bought himself a villa in Cap d'Antibes. He built his Hollywood mansion, called "1801" for its address on Angelo Drive, of mosaics, parquetry, a four-hole golf course, a driveway fountain statue of Cupid riding a seahorse, a library whose bookcases abounded with leather-bounds of every script Warner ever made a movie of, a room with a movie screen that went up and down by water pump, and a viewing sofa whose back flip-flopped for a better view when the movie started. On 1801's twelve acres, Warner had his tennis court, where the phrase most frequent was "Good shot, Chief!"

In 1948, the U.S. Supreme Court ended the Golden Age of Moviemaking by decreeing that movie companies had to choose two of three areas of operation: production, distribution, or exhibition. That stopped the "guaranteed audience" parlay. Moguls grasped less power. They had to deal with such realities as their contract players' (actors') demands. Independent moviemakers could now sneak into the studios' game. Actors began going "indie." That year, Warners' profit fell 50 percent, down to $10 million. Warners got one Academy Award, a Best Actress Oscar for Jane Wyman in *Johnny Belinda.*

Losing their theaters was just part of it. For where radio had once short-sheeted Warners' record business, now television was doing the same mean trick to its movies. The number of TV sets in America went from six thousand in 1946 to 6 million in 1950—just four years. Movie attendance and movies made fell in half. Jack Warner forbade the sight of a television set in any Warner film.

Music publishing, which once ruled the business of music, faded away, ending up offstage. By the 1950s, sheet-music publishers and their song pluggers (who'd pitched songs to bandleaders) had fewer shots they could call. Song pluggers, largely irrelevant, were replaced by record companies' promotion men, who got *recorded* songs played. Publishing's execs— "professional managers" (who once picked the tunes-to-be)—now finished

---

[4]It seems odd to me, but I recognize that younger readers may find this reference to "Underwoods" obscure. An Underwood was a brand of typewriter, and the typewriter is, it seems, now an ancient artifact, obsolete along with other artifacts of that age such as the phonograph needle and the hot water bottle. The word "schmucks" remains fashionable.

third in clout. Second in clout were record companies' A&R men (who thought about finished records more than the underlying "tunes"). But first in clout was the mighty disc jockey, who decided which records got played and which did not. Even Herman Starr got it: "If it's not in the groove," he told *Variety* in 1953, "nothing will help, no matter how you knock yourself out and no matter how many plugs you land."

With production costs up, profits in decline, music blown off, and TV stealing audiences, Warner Bros.' business divisions limped like fifty-year-old marathon dancers. Bennie Kalmenson, Warners' head of distribution now, could and did change the movie-TV part. He made a deal with ABC-TV for an hour a week. It was survival time again. By 1956, Warner Bros. sold its entire pre-1948 film library for $21 million, everything the studio had made before 1948: 784 features and 1,800 shorts.[5] The buyer was Elliott Hyman, president of companies known as Seven Arts and Associated Artist Productions, a distributor of movies to TV stations hungry for cheap programming.[6]

Hollywood read this sale of WB's heritage to Hyman incorrectly: Was the whole studio being put up for sale? Jack Warner got a telegram from one his longtime stars, begging him, CHIEF—DON'T SELL! WHO WILL I FIGHT WITH?—ERROL FLYNN.

In 1956, the financial advisers who for years had backed the three brothers—moneylenders Charles Allen and Serge Semenenko—joined WB's board of directors. They'd had it with these old, warring Warners' antics. They now owned huge blocks of stock in Warners and were fingering the studio's finances. The two money men started making points to Harry, Albert, and Jack about "it's time" and "moving on." They nudged the three brothers toward a sellout, but the brothers liked their jobs, their tall chairs, their fief.

Harry Warner wanted no part of any sellout. Albert, he was okay with it; he was pooped and already spent his afternoons at the track. Jack was more of an enigma but was leaning toward sell. "Harry," Jack'd say, "what the hell else can we do? It's time to sit on our asses and watch sunsets. I want out, Abe wants out . . ."

Only three months after his having been reelected president of WB, pressure mounted on Harry Warner, now seventy-five. Harry finally made

---

[5]Before 1948 because after that year, guilds representing actors and musicians have payments, called "residuals," due their members on income from pictures.

[6]The purchase of WB's past by Associated Artists stayed with Hyman and company for two years. In 1958, Hyman sold his AA stock to United Artists, recouping his investment hugely. MGM bought UA in 1981. Ted Turner bought MGM in 1986. Time Warner later bought Turner. *The Jazz Singer* and Tweety Bird thereby flew back home.

this rule: Okay, I'll sell, but only if *all three* of us Warners sell our shares to-gether and leave together. All right. Let's sell. But we all go together.

The deal for the brothers was that they'd get $22 million in exchange for the 90 percent of outstanding shares (800,000) they owned. Harry remained nervous. He kept asking who was going to be the new president of their company. In reply, he got answers that wobbled. The day the sale took place on May 13, 1956, the brothers celebrated with a dinner at Perino's.

The next day, Hollywood gossipist Louella Parsons quoted Jack Warner as saying this deal didn't mean he was actually leaving as the studio's pro-duction head. "Serge Semenenko has asked me to remain, and I have every intention of continuing to head the studio."

When they heard Jack's line, the two brothers were flat stunned. They knew that Jack, like they, had sold his stock. What they did not know is that a side agreement between Jack and Serge allowed Jack, the next day, to join with Semenenko to buy back 600,000 shares, of which Jack would own 200,000. Jack would become what he always wanted to be, president. Fire-plug shaped, foul-mouthed Ben Kalmenson became executive VP. Sam Schneider, ex-assistant to Harry Warner in New York, would take over in Abe's old job, as treasurer.

Abe never spoke to his brother Jack again. Harry, reading the news, turned ashen, dropped the newspaper to the floor, and fell on top of it with a stroke. Semi-invalided, he lived for several years within a few miles of the studio, walked with a cane, deteriorated, but never forgave his brother's treachery. Jack clung to his closest cronies—his personal talent scout, Solly Baiano; and his two-hundred-dollar-a-week personal masseur, Abdul Maljan—the three of them, Jack, Solly, and Abdul, all men who knew the importance of an even tan. With them, Jack Warner shared his view of his triumph: He had finally won out over those brothers in black suits.

At the time of Harry's death in 1958, Jack could not hear what Harry's widow said: "Harry didn't die. Jack killed him." During the funeral cere-mony, Jack was far from hearing range. He was at his villa in Cap d'Antibes, whizzing the corniches in his Alfa-Romeo, "unable to attend."

Had he returned for the funeral, he would have avoided the auto acci-dent on the Riviera that cracked his skull, nearly took his life. When Warner was ready to return, across the entry drive onto the lot, its employees stretched a banner reading WELCOME BACK, JACK. Warner's car drove in, Jack L. nodding at the lot's security guards as the car passed. Up one flight to sit in his familiar office, into his leather chair, hand reaching forward to touch, one by one, his leather-bound calendar, his carved-crystal inkpots, his vintage-1940 wood-and-vacuum-tubes intercom, there by his left hand, ready once again to send out his orders and once again to hear "Right, Chief!" come back from it.

Warner had a to-do list. First, he had his son fired. An incredulous Jack

Jr., who'd been learning the ropes at the studio, was abruptly banned from the lot, a deed probably urged by the senior Warner's second wife, Anne, Jack's equal when it came to starting family fights. Anne had wanted to wipe out the earlier marriage of her husband, including his son. Jack Jr.'s banishment deprived all four Warner brothers of the only remaining male heir to the company's future.

With Jack back, the money men started to polish Warner Bros. like a Caddy convertible in some showroom. Among other goals added to Jack's to-do list was: "Warner should have its own record company."

In his executive dining room—an extravagance overlooked despite its loss per year of $60,000—Jack Warner fished for an answer: to buy a record label or to create one from scratch. For a net $1 million, Imperial Records on Hollywood Boulevard might be had; its owner, Lew Chudd, was asking $2 million, but he had $1 million in cash and the IRS hounding him. He also had Fats Domino, Slim Whitman, and Ricky Nelson hitting. Warner Bros. music-publishing exec Victor Blau brought the Imperial deal to Jack Warner, who gave a quick yes.

On contract-signing day with Imperial Records, the Warner team waited at the studio for Chudd to sign. Hours passed. Chudd did not show. Calls to Chudd's office went unanswered. The family-owned KFWB was playing Ricky Nelson's latest single, "Stood Up." Chudd had flown to Hawaii, to hide.

Next? In the executive dining room again came the question: "What would it take to start a record company of our own?"

No one knew. Herman Starr, heading Warners' music-publishing company, worried that Warners' owning its own record company would make other labels shy away from his Warner/MPHC songs. The debate was lame; Jack Warner wanted a record company. Finally, the stick-in-the-mud Starr conceded, "The only way I'd ever go into the record business is if I could get one person to run it. That person is Jim Conkling."

Others in the room hated the record-business prospect. They again brought up the awful Brunswick deal of thirty years earlier and its loss to the company of $8 million. "Brunswick, Schmunswick," Warner said and told his secretary, Bill Schaefer, "Call this Conkling," who lived about ten miles away. "Mr. Warner would like to see you tomorrow," Schaefer said.

Jim had no idea why, but "I'd always wanted to meet Jack Warner, so I went." A blond, husky, honey-voiced executive, he parked in the Warner studio's circular drive, before the putty-colored, two-story, Spanish-tiled exec building. He opened its double front doors, climbed up the stairs, walked past the secretaries, opened the door to Warner's office. There, he saw a second door just beyond. He opened the second door, moved down several steps into Warner's kept-fairly-dark, art deco sanctum, in which no dust escaped editing. It was a fair hike to Jack's black desk, sized big enough to store a grand piano. Conkling got to sit in a chair faintly smelling of saddle soap.

Warner was himself, which means he was Adolphe Menjou yearning to be Errol Flynn. He wanted to enlist Conkling, who had, for this job, a godlike résumé: He'd helped build Capitol as the big company to emerge from the indies of the Forties; then headed Columbia Records in the Fifties, where he marketed the LP and introduced record clubs; founded the Recording Industry Association of America (RIAA); first administered the National Record Academy. Now he was well off, semiretired, living in nearby Sherman Oaks.

Warner and Conkling chatted, a contest in mutual seduction. "I've been thinking about starting a record company," Warner told him. "I understand that your experience is good and that you're available. You interested?"

"Interested in what?" Conkling asked.

"The presidency. The first thing I want from you, if you're the guy I've been hearing about, is how much is this thing going to cost?"

Conkling asked Warner, "How much do you spend on one of your B movies?" Then he asked, "Do you always get all the money back? Best case: How much can you expect to make on that one movie investment?" Good logic. Back a movie, it goes out, collects for a few weeks, then dies in a can. Back a record company, you can get ROI (return-on-investment) forever.

Working quickly at his home, Conkling wrote up a budget to create a profitable new Warner Bros. Records. His document ran twenty-five pages. It detailed engineering, pressing, packaging, accounting, artist acquisition, recording, advertising, marketing, promotion. It focused on a nationwide (eventually worldwide) distribution system, wholly owned and operated. Conkling, ignoring that majors take years to grow large enough to support branches, envisioned the only business world he knew: that of a major label. His outline was a classic statement not of an indie record company but of a major born faster than any major had been born before.

His price tag to reach positive cash flow: $2 million.

After three days' homework, Conkling drove back to the studio. He pointed out that, even if Warners lost the whole $2 million, that would be like one bad picture. But if they eventually did break even, then the investment would pay off and yield dividends and payout gravy for years, decades to come.

Warner flipped back and forth through the proposal, but he was known at the studio for his hatred of reading. Instead, he listened. "Two million?" checked Warner. Conkling nodded. "I dropped that much on *The Spirit of St. Louis* [actually six million]. Last year we made twenty pictures. So this year we'll make nineteen."

"So who'll I report to?"

"You report to me," answered Warner. "I'll give you all the rope you need to hang yourself."

Significant Records by Warner Bros. Pictures' First Label, Brunswick Records

1930–1931

Al Jolson ("My Mammy" and "Sonny Boy") • Cab Calloway ("Minnie the Moocher (The Ho De Ho Song)") • Bing Crosby ("Out of Nowhere," "Just One More Chance," and "At Your Command") • Abe Lyman & His California Orchestra ("Just One More Chance") • The Mills Brothers ("Tiger Rag") • Red Nichols ("Strike Up the Band")

2

Jim Conkling was a Spencer Tracy type, a reassuring guy. When I first met him, I, like everyone, just knew he was the best. Knew this guy could hold up collapsing bridges, defeat Nazis, and win Best of Breed. Conkling knew the rules of the record business. He sounded like he'd played stickball with Tommy Edison and Ricky Caruso, and he talked to you like he had a piece of sweet sucking candy tucked in his cheek. When it came to a guy to start Warner Bros. Records, no wonder Herman Starr had told the Chief "that person is Conkling."

But enough. It was 1958, and the Chief had given Conkling eight whole months to get sales branches running, singers signed, and albums shipped.

To get WBR incorporated, Conkling and Warner had flown to New York. (Warner had no company plane; the two men flew propeller driven.) On March 10, 1958, Jack Warner became WBR's chairman, Jim Conkling its president, and Warner money watcher Bennie Kalmenson vice president. Conkling signed a three-year contract, with pay of a thousand dollars a week, plus profit sharing, plus stock options.

Returning to Burbank, Conkling showed up, the first Monday morning of it all, at the studio. One of Jack Warner's secretaries, an Irish bachelor-for-life named Matt Gilligan, showed Conkling to his temporary office. "I'd never seen anything like it," Conkling told me. "Here I was, supposed to be starting a first-class record company. I had no secretary. I had no file cabinet. I was given an office with a desk and a chair. In fact, the only things in the office besides the desk and chair were one lead pencil and a yellow pad of paper. That was it. That was Warner Bros. Records, Incorporated."

Conkling and Gilligan (who was appointed as Conkling's office manager) made lists. Then lists of lists. More important than knowing how to compile lists, Gilligan, who had years of service in Jack Warner's office, also knew how to steal studio office supplies.

Jim Conkling, you could argue, eventually accomplished more in the record industry than anybody. He was born in 1915 in East Orange, New Jersey. En route to Dartmouth, Jim was urged by his father, "Son, major in economics and minor in poli-sci." Jim spent more time playing trumpet in Dartmouth's Barbary Coast Orchestra. During summers, he played in cruise-ship bands.

Upon graduation, Jim married one of the Forties' singing King Sisters; Donna and Jim were Mormons, of all things, part of a vastly connected family of hospitable people roughly the population of east Utah. Both believed that the devil was alive and out there. Both were the kind of open-faced, openhearted, good people who looked you straight in the eye, interested in what you had to say. It is hard to remember Jim Conkling without seeing him with an attentive smile, looking back at your eyes and listening.

With World War II having peaked, and following a medical discharge (severe shoulder injury), Jim was hired by his former college and cruise-ship pal, the thoughtful Paul Weston, who was music director at a two-year-old record label called Capitol Records, out in L.A. In 1943, still in his navy uniform (discharge taking longer than expected), suddenly there Jim was, this crewcut sailor, age twenty-nine, producing a Stan Kenton big-band session at Capitol. That just looked odd. Kenton's agent, Carlos Gastel, didn't get it at all, and called the head of Capitol, Glenn Wallichs, demanding, "Who's this punk kid you've sent in here to conduct this session?"

Conkling stayed at Capitol for seven years, during which Gastel stopped shouting (about him). Those were years when Jim worked with older guys who knew things he did not, and years in which he absorbed their rules, particularly when they were yelled at him.

In the late 1940s, Capitol ran fresh and loose as growing companies can, before they clog up with things like requisition forms. The year after the war (1946), the singles chart (the only chart at the time) listed one dozen hits by big labels: Columbia had six (two Frank Sinatras, two Frankie Carles, a Dinah Shore, and a Kay Kyser), Victor had seven (two Perry Comos, two Freddy Martins, two Sammy Kayes, and a Vaughn Monroe), Decca had three (the Ink Spots, Bing Crosby, and the Andrews Sisters), Majestic sneaked in with Eddy Howard, and Capitol had three (Nat King Cole, Johnny Mercer, and the Pied Pipers).

Conkling rose up, managing the company's artistic and creative development ("product"), signing talent, hiring producers with their own styles: classical, children's, country, show tunes, pop. He scribbled a contract deal on an envelope for Les Paul, an electric guitarist when such a two-word phrase was as strange to the ears as "electric melon." Out of that came the change-your-ears-forever recording of Les Paul and Mary Ford's "How High the Moon," which Conkling would not release since it "had been overrecorded and no distributor would want it."

Conkling grew Capitol. He founded its two publishing houses, Blackwood Music (BMI) and Ardmore Music (ASCAP). Executives from the major labels in New York peeked over the Rockies, noticing how Conkling had been significant in turning their "Big Three" (Columbia, Decca, RCA) into a "Big Four." In 1951, CBS called, wanting Capitol's Conkling for Columbia Records to follow in the footsteps of Ted Wallerstein.

While flying somewhere over Kansas, en route to New York for a first meeting with CBS heads Bill Paley and Frank Stanton, Conkling studied the real numbers in the back of CBS's Annual Report. He knew how to impress a recruiter: know what you're talking about. At thirty-six, he was hired as president of all of Columbia Records, the majorest of record labels. (Leaving Capitol, Conkling, as a favor to Les Paul, said, "Okay, we'll put it out." "How High the Moon" was a huge hit.)

Columbia was the Class Act. It had branches, artists, producers like jazz expert George Avakian, classicist Goddard Lieberson, hits-maker Mitch Miller, and pop-star finder John Hammond. Between 1951 and 1955, Conkling rode Columbia's introduction of the 33 RPM long-playing record through the Battle of the Speeds (against the rival RPMs of 78 and 45). Conkling was in the president's chair when Columbia brought out Broadway albums like *Pajama Game* and *Kismet,* when it signed artists from Igor Stravinsky to Miles Davis to Lefty Frizzell. Conkling became an industry phenom; even Mormon Tabernacle Choir albums sold. He started the first record club, Columbia's, tiptoeing through the anger of retailers who filed "record club" in the same bin as shoplifting and infanticide. To make the club idea work, Conkling cut a discount deal with major music publishers, led by Warner Bros.' Herman Starr. Starr, who either liked you or didn't, had given Conkling a green light to try this club idea.

On the side, Conkling helped organize something record companies never had: a Recording Industry Association of America. The RIAA belatedly gave labels their first voice in Washington. Conkling's RIAA helped dignify records, belatedly giving the record companies some leverage against music publishers and radio stations. He became the RIAA's first president. More to the point, he was there when people with actual college degrees got jobs in a business that, till then, had just been part of "coin op" and had been represented by a nickel-in-the-slot trade magazine called *Cash Box,* a name evoking less of Beethoven, more of Wurlitzer.

But Conkling, tired of New York, wanted to move back home to California. In 1956, at age forty-one, he retired. He bought a home in Sherman Oaks on a big lot with a circular drive, trees out front, its lawn croquet ready. Alongside his buddy Paul Weston, he helped start the Record Academy at a time when most people thought starting a Record Academy was as useful as starting a Mafia Academy. Conkling was content, active, doing good, raising his children with Donna, working with his church. He'd turned down start-a-new-label offers from Bing Crosby and *Dragnet* TV star Jack Webb. "Naw," Jim'd say with that warm smile. Conkling knew another rule: You catch more flies with honey than with vinegar.

Then came, unexpectedly, that phone call from Warner Bros., from a bigger lot, also with a circular drive and trees out front, its lawn polo ready, a few miles to the east from Jim's. For Jim, it was a fresh new opportunity, well funded, and he liked Jack's rope.

With Matt Gilligan, Jim Conkling soon got the key to leftover space. Warner Bros. Records' first offices were set up "across the street" from the main studio, at 3701 Warner Boulevard. It had no circular drive, not even crabgrass. The offices occupied only the second floor of a two-story that once had been Warner's machine shop. From its every wall protruded ankle-high, two-hundred-volt electrical outlets that could propel aircraft. Linoleum hallways. Paint on each and every wall: Warners pale green.

Carpeting at Warner Bros. Studios was always the same: three-foot-wide strips, always dull green, stitched together so they could fit any size room. I figured the studio had a Carpeting Rule: It would be replaced only after it had burned to a crisp in a nuclear holocaust; short of that, carpets got patched.

Conkling drew together his team. Three came from Columbia: sales VP Hal Cook, recording engineer Lowell Frank, and pop-album director George Avakian. From *Billboard* magazine, an energetic, 5'7" hustle guy named Joel Friedman, to do merchandising and advertising. Controller was Ed West, put in that job by Jack Warner to watch his money. Warner enjoyed accountants who walked around all day picking nits.

I met Jim when I'd quit working at Capitol Records. I'd been there in my first showbiz job, writing the words for the backs of EP jackets for such as Carmen Dragon conducting the Hollywood Bowl Orchestra. That lasted one year, ended with my boss annoying me. While pointing out my comma faults, he tapped his shoe on his plastic carpet protector. It was more than I could stand. I believed that, when it came to Dragons, I was Number One. I upped and I quit.

Producer Dave Cavanaugh at Capitol called a friend at a new label just starting in Burbank. They said they'd see me. I combed my résumé for incorrect commas and other faults. I sat nervous as my short bio was scanned. Pomona College, Yale grad school in drama ("Well, at least he should be able to spell," I imagined they were thinking). First postgrad job as tech writer for some oxygen-analyzer company. ("Well, at least he should be humble") where I learned to tell paramagnetic from diamagnetic. A year living in Paris, trying to outdo Hemingway (he'd left) six feet tall, 125 pounds. And then Capitol Records.

During Q&A at my Warners interview, I told them bits of my early life, reared as a goy (not a word I then appreciated) in a small, right-wing California town. What I could *not* tell them—just could *not* confess to—was how I'd fallen in love with music in the first place. Couldn't tell them about this skinny child living in a white land called Arcadia, California, with Republican parents. Mom and Dad were easy on me. They either indulged my freedom or were neglectful; I prefer answer number one. Somehow I got an eight-inch-wide radio beside my bed. At bedtime, in the dark, I'd see the orange glow from the dial and turn the knob till I found a disc jockey named Hunter Hancock who broadcast from KGFJ over in the black neighborhood of Los Angeles, far from the hayfield across our street. On his shows, I heard screamin' and rompin' and honkin' tenor saxes, and it made joy in my skinny body. Under the sheets, I moved my feet in time to Louis Jordan and His Tympany Five, and the Trenier Twins. Eventually, all that widened to Basie and Ellington, Goodman and Jazz at the Phil. I had found the escape hatch out of Doris Day–land.

Music crept into my life and settled down in my heart. It provided relief from the day's regular demands, like getting my merit badge for tying complicated knots. I began to collect records. Ten-inch 78 RPMs, whose every riff I memorized.

The indulgence/neglect of my folks (I was their only) allowed me, once I was sixteen, to drive my mother's Plymouth into the night while they played bridge. I took mystified dates like Carol Weber to Los Angeles's Central Avenue, where we went up the stairs to the Blue Light Ballroom to indulge in sax. (Carol has never spoken to me in the half century since.) I'd drive an hour with friend Gene Cameron down to Balboa's Ballroom for Stan Kenton, watch great men blow in our faces—Shelly Manne, Chet Baker, Milt Bernhart, Bob Cooper, Laurindo Almeida—then drive back home, at 4:00 a.m.

I absolutely could not tell Warner Bros. Records about my life-to-date highlight: Bandleader Stan Kenton had once stepped on my hand.[7]

Through the rest of my life, whatever else came along, swing-jazz-gospel-boogie continued to amaze my body. To hear Mahalia Jackson the first time! Do I hear amen? To have my own copy of Benny Goodman's

---

[7]Stan Kenton had been walking on the bandstand, while I was standing against it. He'd bent down to say, "Sorry, son." I looked up and told him, "It's my honor."

1938 *Carnegie Hall Jazz Concert.* To sit in the balcony of Jazz at the Phil and hear Illinois Jacquet take one breath and blow us all away. I wanted it for *my* life, but all I could do was compose sentences.

Up till now, I'd followed several muses (theater was the other biggie), got that awful first job as a technical writer, off to a year in Paris on thirty-five hundred dollars, then back to—can this be real?—actual show business. To Capitol Records, where I got to write liner notes. And then had come that shocking revelation: I committed comma faults.

Which brought me to Burbank, to Warner Bros. Records. You must understand why I could never confess all this to the hiring judges sitting before me.

WBR made me editorial manager. I had no one to manage. I worked for Joel Friedman. I typed everything from album liner notes to order forms. When I once told him I wanted to rewrite some liner notes I was late turning in, Joel pulled the pages from me. He taught me I was in business. "Without product to sell," he said, "we're out of business." Joel always made sense. In business, he was my dad. Lunchtimes, I got to wander the studio lot alone, into soundstages, to gawk at movies getting made! I was, as my mom could see, "tickled pink." I really, really was so pink I could've fooled a flamingo.

Conkling held meetings off campus in a motel with fuchsia curtains and fake hydrangeas, called the Hollywood Hawaiian, down near Fountain Avenue. By April, his starter crew had the new company meticulously planned. Procedures got adopted: pricing structure, billing and collection, promotion, distribution, export and trademark protection, artist royalty structure, branch operation, location for the L.A. warehouse, discount structure, shipping, distributor and in-house advertising . . .

The new label had zero artists. Conkling got phone calls from the studio: Its TV and Movies divisions wanted *their* new record company to promote *their* pictures. They wanted their label to record studio contract artists, like Connie Stevens of its TV series *Hawaiian Eye.* Stevens's contract was, like contracts for most kids entering this business, clear. She cost no advance and got no royalties. "And," the studio tossed in, "*she* can really sing."

Warner's music-publishing head, Herman Starr, suggested that Conkling record only *his* MPHC songs from Warner motion pictures and television. "Anything Herman Starr couldn't sell to some other company," Jim said, sighing, "he'd want us to handle."

Conkling and company organized waves of bright ideas for repertoire. With no star power, concept albums would do. Such appealing product ideas had worked for him at Capitol and Columbia. The rule about creating a steady-selling catalogue was to issue albums that people had *always* bought, like Hawaiian, Dixieland, piano, dance, romantic instrumental. Since stereo was new and appealed to consumers with two ears, WBR could and *would* be the only company with a 100 percent all-stereo catalogue, the only company with "Polka . . . in Stereo!" while the older companies' polkas would suffer in their monohood.

It made a lot of sense. Warners trumpeted stereo louder than swans in heat: On the liners of albums, WBR printed a technical description of how well they had been miked. The first WBR paper inner sleeves showed an aerial photo of the Burbank studio, in color, with these words: VITAPHONIC STEREO—WARNER BROS.—THE FIRST NAME IN SOUND.

VP and Sales Manager Hal Cook was given three months to open Warner Bros. Distributing Corp. (WBDC), patterned after Capitol's CRDC. The full Warner catalogue, expected within a year to number over a hundred albums, needed a sales force, with branches in New York, Los Angeles, and Chicago. Elsewhere, WBR would use its strength to prevail with independent distributors. Cook pitched the indies on their need to carry "a line," meaning the full WBR stereo-catalogue concept. Cook had the indies sign long, boring contracts. The indies' reaction: "Just send us your records. We'll sell them. No paperwork, please."

WBR's first trade ad appeared on July 21, 1958. A row of empty theater seats with the headline:

> YOUR PLACE IS RESERVED FOR THE PREMIER.
> THE FIRST NAME IN SOUND.
> WARNER BROS. RECORDS.

Warner Bros. Records signed its first act: Tab Hunter, who'd served as a Warner Bros. movie teen, then had one hit at Dot Records, but could not carry a tune in an armored car. No Hunter hits forthcame at Warner Bros. Records.

The Warner label's debut was set for September 1, 1958. Months-to-go became weeks-to-go became days-to-go. When it came time to send out the press kit for the first release, controller Ed West suggested to Joel Friedman that "we send it out on July 31. Because one day later, on August 1, the price of a first class stamp will go from three cents to four cents."

On August 31, one day before WBR's "World Premier," came an accounting from Ed West: The company's expense-to-date had been $230,000. The accumulated sales: $0. By Jim Conkling's budget, WBR was right on schedule. Tomorrow come the sales. His plan, executed perfectly.

On September 1, the label offered its opening release of good, good music, a release that prophesied its releases for the next three years. If this "Catalogue Is King" release had been put out by Columbia Records, had been created by Columbia artists, its belief that "categories of music can sell albums" would hardly have been noticed; they'd strengthen the catalogue, supported by other albums by hit acts. In the big ponds of radio and retail, Warner's small fish soon sank. Painfully. That first release:

For Whom the Bell Tolls (re-creation of movie score)
Ira Ironstrings: *Music for People with $3.98, Plus Tax, If Any*
Warren Barker: *The King and I for Orchestra*
Jack Webb: *You're My Girl* (recitations)
Connie Stevens: *Conchetta*
The Warner Bros. Military Band: *Sousa in Stereo*
Irving Taylor: *Terribly Sophisticated Songs*
Buddy Cole: *Have Organ, Will Swing*

The label's first single was "The Star-Spangled Banner" (without Jimi Hendrix).

Shortly after that first release, a conference of Warner's distribution personnel was called in Burbank. Conkling urged the assembled to "write down your gut reaction to our first release and the success you've had selling it to the trade and public. You need not sign your name."

Conkling looked over the answers. One sheet stopped him. Conkling looked up and asked, "Who wrote 'crap'?"

Don Graham, a sharp, fast-talking promotion man from San Francisco, who, oddly enough, was honest, too, answered, "I did."

Conkling asked, "What's your name?"

Don Graham identified himself as "Graham/San Francisco/Promotion."

"What do you mean, 'Crap'?"

"Oh, I don't know. Ira Ironstrings. It's kinda funny, but . . ."

"Do you know *who* Ira Ironstrings *is*?" asked Conkling. "He's Alvino Rey!"

"So what?" asked Graham.

Conkling, with three brothers-in-law recording albums on the first release (Alvino Rey, famous for his "talking" pedal-steel guitar; Del Courtney, San Francisco bandleader; and Buddy Cole, pop pianist—all of whom, like Conkling, were married to King Sisters), gently told Graham, "Well, tell your accounts that Ira Ironstrings is Alvino Rey. Whisper it to them. Tell them we can't put his name on the album since he's still signed to Capitol."

"They don't care, Mr. Conkling. They're interested in hit records, and they don't care who records 'em."

An awkward silence followed. Graham, a kid, had convinced no one. The rest of the room felt sorry for him. He didn't know the rules.

WBR would continue to look for repertoire holes, then fill them, in stereo. There followed, in October, a "piano release," a dozen albums, all piano led, all in stereo. There followed, in November, a "dance release," a dozen albums, all for dancing, all in stereo.

Singles, too, were thought through by A&R head George Avakian. In an October memo to Conkling, Avakian described singles he was working on:

1. *The Chateaus*—We have four very strong sides by the Negro male quintet, which is like a modern version of the Ink Spots.
2. *Candy Anderson*—This is a girl who can be our Patti Page. "I'll Bet You She'll Kiss Me" resembles "Tammy" structurally, but also has some of the flavor of a "Tennessee Waltz" kind of song.
3. *Gene Bua*—I believe his area should be that of Jimmie Rodgers and perhaps Pat Boone.
4. *David Allen*—As soon as David Allen gets his release, I will talk to writers about doing a special song for him which will slant his first single directly at the teenage girl market. This will be a revised twist on the theme of "Born Too Late," in which David is the understanding old man who recognizes that a teenager's infatuation for him is deeper than mom and dad think. I am sure the teenagers still fall in love with Gregory Peck, Cary Grant, etc.

To the executives in Burbank, intent on Conkling's most practical of business plans, Avakian's ideas sounded like intelligent business. Not one of these executives thought much about the counterforce of independent labels scuffling out there; of the men (and a sprinkling of women now) who had embraced rock & roll; who scrambled for hit singles, not albums; who loved more dangerous music, whether that music came from Harlem or the Adirondacks; who made sure, any way they had to, that their records got airplay; who were of a feisty new, hungrier world; whose only rule was Get Paid.

Fran Howell worked at our Los Angeles branch. His job was to sell Warner Bros. albums to stores. A warm, honest chap, more used to selling books than records, a Mormon, too, Howell drove his car from store to store to show Warner Bros. albums and take orders. "The first week, I went to five stores a day and came back with three orders. Not multiple orders, but three records, for the entire week. The store owners would look at me and say, 'We don't need your product.' I was taking my lunch then," said Howell, "because my income had dropped so that I couldn't afford to eat out all the time. My wife, Margaret, would pack a lunch, and I'd buy a little carton of milk. One day, I pulled up and didn't have the money for a carton of milk. I thought to myself, 'What on earth have I done?' I couldn't sell the product. I was terrified."

Me, I was naïve about any problems at WBR, since I had no clue about selling albums. Now that I think back, it's odd that so little attention was given to singles and Top Forty. All these industry hot guys, who'd managed the mightiest labels, treating hit singles like they came nineteenth on some agenda, down near Warehouse Insurance Costs. My bosses, seasoned executives, were just dancing on quicksand.

*   *   *

While Warner Bros. Records was celebrating its first birthday in 1959, across the street in the big studio, the only candles our owners lit were in prayer. Instead of a skinflint operation, the records people under Conkling had raced their company out of the driveway at top speed, spent money on albums that were far from what the music guys at the studio expected. Worst of all, WBR was not behaving like a good subsidiary—obediently.

Jim Conkling, still the smiling expert in all this, often spent noontimes in that executive dining room across the street radiating optimism about "next month," pouring honey on bitter criticism from the old hands, some still able to remember Brunswick, when an $8 million loss really meant something.

Tab Hunter stood for "the youth market" at WBR, but "teenager appeal" . . . that was for those ragged little indie labels, like Chess and Liberty, Imperial and Atlantic. It was for labels that scrounged. The teen market, that Elvis thing, was just put up with because it made no sense: *Sha na na na Sha na na na na Dop Dip dip dip dip Dip dip dip dip Boom! Get a job . . .*

Only some, and hardly the majority, of execs in the record business across America were paying attention to such nonsense nonlyrics. Gibberish, to them, just another novelty, another fad, against the rules that paved the middle of the road.

Warner Bros., as a mainstream label, might dabble in rock, but deep down it knew better. Elvis had been in the army; Jerry Lee Lewis had married his thirteen-year-old cousin; hula hoops and sack dresses came and went. With keen ears, our established record executives simply stared at such music. They clung like Vatican cardinals to the prophetic hitmakers from earlier books.

Then into the label's life came a popular Warner TV series called *77 Sunset Strip*. In it, a young actor named Edd Byrnes made girls squeal with his screen habit of sloooowly combing back his greasy hair, first on the right camera side, then on the left. The studio's execs believed that Byrnes was exactly what the record company should be riding. Only one problem: Edd "Kookie" Byrnes could not sing. He was unable even to tap his foot decently. WBR, however, if ever it needed one album, needed an album of this hit TV series' soundtrack.

Warner Records' Irving Taylor composed a single called "Kookie, Kookie, Lend Me Your Comb." Taylor recalled, "Byrnes could not count, and he had no concept of meter. In making the record, I had to stand next to him and whisper the lyrics in his ear for him to get the phrasing correctly. Producer Karl Engemann stood on the other side of Byrnes, pounding on Edd's shoulder with one hand and snapping his fingers with the other so Edd could hold the beat. You can hear the finger popping on the record."

Into a second mike, Connie Stevens sang the song's plea, "Kookie, Kookie, Lend Me Your Comb." She supported Byrnes as he talked through 2:05 of constructed hip phrases, such as "the ginchiest" (greatest), "piling up the Zs," "keep the eyeballs rolling" (watch), and "play like a pigeon" (deliver a message).

EDD: What's with this comb caper, baby?
     Why do you wanna latch up with my comb?
CONNIE: I just want you to stop combing your hair and kiss me.
     You're the maximum utmost.
EDD: Well, I beans and I dreams goin'. I'm movin' right now
     'Cause that's the kind of scene that I dig . . .
     Baby, you're the ginchiest!

The next step was to get this crap played on radio. WB's candor-unchallenged Don Graham got a Radio KYA promo on Kookie going: "Send in your old comb, we'll send you a new Kookie comb free!" The mail count: Eighty thousand dirty combs arrived in San Francisco shortly after the song was released. Radio voters cast their votes: "Should Kookie cut his hair?" Five thousand no; fifty yes. For weekend after weekend, Graham took dirty combs out of one stack of envelopes and stuffed clean combs into another. When some disc jockey observed Graham handling this mail, Graham looked up and said, "I'm *sure* this is the record business."

Radio. To Warner Bros. Records' early business plan, it was incidental.

Graham was as close as WBR came to the new force in promoting and selling singles. His talent was undervalued. In the later Fifties, disc jockeys like the powerful Alan Freed had become the sine qua non megaforce in selling records. DJs had, of course, gotten even more and more important since the war ended.

Record companies soon became addicted to radio exposure, increasingly unable to sell records without disc-jockey play. With disc jockeys came men who got paid to get records played on the air: Promotion Men. Sometimes it took more than the record itself. "Favors" had always been there. "Payola," once a combination of "pay" and "Victrola," had become the trick phrase. Pay to get your record played.

To tighten that noose, station owner and broadcasting pioneer Todd Storz invented the "Top Forty" radio format: play only these hottest forty singles, rotating the same forty over and over. Other programmers, Kent Burkhart and Chuck Dunaway, created the first playlist for KXOL, Fort Worth, Texas: Either you were on that list or you just didn't get heard. Radio no longer tried to program "something for everyone." Stations researched what appealed to their target demographic, then programmed to it. By 1956, Top Forty became a radio epidemic, and records over Forty—who cared?

Teens, gene driven, used music to rebel, more than ever. They could find music on radio that was different from Mom and Dad's at home. New idols from smaller labels below Conkling's radar got heard and sold: Little Richard and Chuck Berry, Elvis, Gene Vincent and Eddie Cochran, the Flamingos . . .

"There were maybe forty or fifty important DJs on 'the pay list.' Most of them were honest," remembered Atlantic Records' Jerry Wexler. By "honest," Jerry meant "when they took money, they played the record." Radio-station management condoned payola; like tips in a restaurant, it supplemented the stations' low wages.

In Boston, Yale grad Joe Smith had started out jockeying discs. Early on, a fellow DJ took him to lunch, advising him, "This is how it works. Some guys take money. Some don't. Do whatever you want. Don't be ashamed. Just don't start undercutting anyone else." Smith became Boston's new voice. He captivated teen ears. On the air, he talked back to the records he played. "Hello, Fats!" Smith called out. "Is that you?" and the record sang right back, "Yes, it's me, and I'm in love again." Afternoon drive times and evening shows, when the kids tuned in, it was Smith. He adopted the name José. He had his own theme song. He rang bells and slapped the phone book. He gave away autographed pictures. For phone interviews, Joe could get Elvis.

"Radio is an aphrodisiac for a young disc jockey," Smith rejoiced. "You can't imagine the thrill of sitting in a control booth and saying, 'You want me to play something, call up,' and all the lines instantly light up. Or, 'Hey, if you don't like the way they're doing such-and-such, toot your horn,' and someone comes in and says, 'Wow, they're tooting their horns all over town!' "

Smith ran record hops, out in public places, playing 45s. Record labels sent in acts—Freddy "Boom Boom" Cannon or Billy J. Ward and the Dominos—to lip sync. Scream levels at record hops became a DJ's form of test marketing. For such out-of-studio experiences, DJs like Smith would pick up $150 to $500 per event.

The mike power of Joe Smith brought weekendsful of kids to Smith-run record hops, which riled adults. Smith turned to respectable charities to cosponsor his record hops, especially any charity attached to the powerful Catholic Church, led in Boston by growly-voiced Cardinal Cushing, who began calling Joe Smith "Smiddy." From the cardinal, that was a blessing, particularly when the newspapers earlier had run headlines like this one:

VENEREAL DISEASE ON UPSWING

POLICE CHIEF BLAMES ELVIS PRESLEY
AND ROCK 'N' ROLL DISC JOCKEY SMITH

Ignoring VD, the cardinal remained a regular on Smith's radio show, intoning ten minutes of the rosary. In 1959, the new record Joe rode was Kookie's "Lend Me Your Comb." Joe promised the cardinal that he'd get Kookie to show up at a Fenway Park hop, for Cushing's Catholic Youth Organization. Smith called Warners to get Edd Byrnes. Warners told him that Byrnes was, on that day, doing promotion in Baltimore. Smith told Warners, "Switch him to Boston. I have every disc jockey in New England plugging this show." Massachusetts Senator Jack Kennedy even arranged for an Air Force jet to fly Kookie from Baltimore to Boston and a helicopter to deposit the star onto the Fenway pitcher's mound.

The afternoon came. Smith's eyes searched skyward, for hours it felt like. Cushing was beyond prayer. He growled, "Well, Smiddy, what about the creep with the comb? Is he going to be here?"

"Kookie" never showed. Smith fired off a scalding letter to Jim Conkling. Furious about being stiffed, embarrassed in front of Boston, its cardinal, its teens, and its DJs, Joe Smith picked out his words by knife tip. He roasted WBR's staff. He wanted, his letter said, to see how far amateurism went at Warner Bros. To see if it reached all the way to the top, to Conkling, because it certainly touched with everybody else at Warner. Smith's letter tore into Herbie Dale, WB's Boston branch manager. It eviscerated WBR's regional sales head, Bob Summers. It zinged Jim Conkling. The reaction at the record company to Smith's letter was predictable. In the words of Bob Summers, "Who needs him?"

While in Boston, venereal-disease rates were closely watched; in Burbank, home of Concept Albums in Stereo, pop DJs like Smith were still nicely disdained.

Meantime, behind WBR's back, hops had swept all the major cities. Top disc jockeys cleaned up. DJ Dick Clark recalled, "We made seventy-five cents a head on the record hops. We used to buy rolls of quarters, take in a dollar from each kid, then give them a quarter back. "We'd take the boxes of money and stick them in a spare bedroom. Two or three weeks would go by, and then my wife and I would try to straighten out all these crumpled, sweaty, one-dollar bills. . . . It was a cash business, and we kept immaculate books. I was making a killing, racing around trying to get all the money I could. My tentacles went in every direction."

The sudden importance of Dick Clark on TV riveted record-company men who'd do anything to get theirs played on *American Bandstand.*

"Philadelphia was like America's jukebox. On Tuesday nights, when Dick picked the music, all the promo guys would show up there," remembered early music businessman Bob Krasnow. Producer "Morty Craft was a wild man who would throw these huge pussy parties. He'd eat fifty yards of 'carpet.' No class. No anything. He was a paradox, putting out squeaky-clean records, but a triple-X guy. He got the records played, though. He was a lowlife, using hookers galore and balling parties. The foundation for the sleaze era. It was very enjoyable, I might add."

Feeling their power, disc jockeys felt the need to convene. First had come a 1958 conference at Kansas City's Muehlbach Hotel promoted by the Storz radio-station chain, a leader in broadcasting the still-controversial rock & roll sound. DJs had, by now, divided into two camps. Like Southern Baptists, these record men all worshiped one god named Hit. Some testified for the noise of rock, some stood up for Steve and Eydie.

Columbia's powerful A&R head, Mitch Miller was lavish of goatee, famous for his "Sing Along with Mitch" albums, and absolutely antirock. Miller had plenty of company, not only at Columbia but also with his peers in A&R, men who believed that hits had nothing to do with bumping your hips. Rock, to men like Miller, was hillbilly plus R&B. At his luncheon speech, Miller bitterly attacked radio for letting itself be programmed by "baby-sitters and bobby-soxers . . . Rock & roll? It's not music, it's a disease." Many DJs at the conference stood and ovated Miller. Had the executives of Conkling's new Warner label been there, they'd have stood and ovated.

Later that afternoon, Mitch Miller's tirade was answered by radio programmer Chuck Blore. He defended using record sales as a criterion for what gets radio play "in spite of fulminations from prophets, bearded or otherwise." Blore's broadcast chain quickly banned play of any Columbia records.

Radio was tuned in to its listeners. Radio and record buyers determined what was a hit. Record companies rode in the backseat. Some, like Columbia (and Warner Bros.) waited for all this just to go away. Hungrier labels hired promo men.

The next year's DJ conference erupted at Miami's Americana Hotel. Divided as the rock and nonrock camps were, they did agree on Miami's agenda. Newspapers ran headlines about the get-together: BOOZE, BRIBES AND BROADS screamed the *Miami Herald*. Joe Smith remembered the convention as a one-way street: "Roulette Records would run roulette tables. You'd bet something, you'd lose, the croupier would pay you anyway. The guy'd just say, 'Take. Take.' For entertainment, one night, it was Count Basie plus Joe Williams plus Sarah Vaughan at a midnight barbecue. Unbelievable event." The conference oozed scandal. Women imported for the conference were not only prepaid, they were coached. "We would sit with the girls and prompt them," End Records promoter Artie Ripp recalled. "We really want to get this new Flamingos record on, so as you are fooling with this fella, it's real important to convey how much you love the new Flamingos record." Warner Bros. Records never fondled DJs in Miami. The company was a no show.

One year after the birth of Warner Bros. Records, *Billboard* ran a chart showing of each label's entire catalogue, what percentage of all those albums do stores actually stock. The percent-of-catalogue chart started out:

90 percent   RCA, Columbia, Capitol
70 percent   Decca
60 percent   London
45 percent   Mercury
30 percent   MGM, Dot
15 percent   ABC Paramount, Kapp, Coral
10 percent   Verve, Angel

Subangelic, WBR was listed at 5 to 9 percent. In real numbers, this meant that, of the 150 albums so far created by Conkling and company, on average, 7.5 of them would be stocked in any store. And 142.5 of them would not.

Warner Bros. Records' independent distributors slow-paid for all the albums that had been loaded upon them. They sent back the once-fresh, now-unsold, ugly merchandise in stale cardboard boxes, which arrived in Burbank as welcome as last year's sweatpants. By the end of the year, WBR just gave up on their do-nothing independent distributors, mutter mutter. In their place, with little alternative, WBR compounded its problem: It opened more and more of its own branches.

WBR's financial chief, Ed West, summed it up, after exactly 365 days in business: The label had spent $4.46 million, against sales of $2.93 million. Net loss: $1.53 million. The budget couldn't handle the avalanche of albums that WBR's distributors were returning as unsalable. The label's real loss was closer to $3.5 million. Or, to look at it another way, fast approaching what Warner had lost on its previous biggest turkey, *The Spirit of St. Louis.*

By the end of 1959, Conkling and West were summoned to New York, to meet with studio powers Ben Kalmenson and Herman Starr. Jack Warner was not there; he avoided confrontations. For the meeting, Conkling, West, and associate Hal Cook had planned ahead. They had their 1960 budget ready. They walked into Kalmenson's office, shook hands, and spread out their budgets.

Kalmenson opened: "Gentlemen, before we begin, I just want to say that Warner Bros. has become disenchanted with the record business. We want you to fold up your tent and get the hell out as quickly as possible. Liquidate."

Significant Warner Bros. Record

1959

77 Sunset Strip, including "Kookie, Kookie, Lend Me Your Comb"

3

A dead silence followed. They didn't look in the others' eyes but rather looked around this cold, cement-walled, twelve-foot-high room in a New York office building whose windows had not for some years felt a good wash. The persuasive Jim Conkling, his money-practical Ed West, and his sales-savvy Hal Cook sat stunned.

Before the trio had shown up in Kalmenson's New York office, Warner's Studio execs—Jack Warner, Ben Kalmenson, Herman Starr—had agreed to kill the damn thing. WBR showed not one sign of making money and was out of their control. Phone calls had gone out from Corporate, particularly from Starr, to record executives of other labels: "How many people you got working for you?" "Ten," the answer might come. Starr saw the number 130 on WB's employee list. "Thanks." Starr also knew that life's Greater Purpose was saving Warner money.

White-haired West, who had been with Warner Bros. Studio long before the record company's birth, who'd been sent over from the studio to watch the brothers' investment, spoke up: "That won't work, Ben." Using financial explanations—receivables to collect, inventory to sell off, finished product ready to release—West made a case to his studio-minded brethren: You're better off letting the company eke through the next few months.

After West made his arguments, Conkling, too, pled. He volunteered to go on half salary. "Hardly enough, Jim." At the end of the meeting, the fledgling record company, including its president, was placed in the intensive care of Herman Starr, the man who remembered, vein by vein, how he'd halted the Brunswick hemorrhage back in the Thirties.

Toward the end of the short meeting with Kalmenson, a little time reprieve was granted Conkling, Cook, and West. Only a little. WBR's philosophy, so optimistic two years earlier, was reduced to life support:

- Get rid of all expensive contracts.
- After finishing up fifteen albums, stop recording.

- Collect cash, whatever you can get, for the inventory.
- Close all the branches.
- Drop all excess personnel.
- Conkling may not make a move without Starr's approval.

Conkling, Cook, and West flew back to Burbank to face their colleagues, most of us now "excess." The morning of February 12, 1960, 130 employees started the workday for Warner Bros. Records; by dusk that same day, some 29 remained. One by one, loyal workers were phoned to report to the bosses' office. I kept seeing others walk down the hall, then return heavy-footed, back to tell with dry mouth that they'd been fired, then packing up their Kleenex boxes. Personally, I knew I was okay. I was too good to be cut. Besides, I was the company's leading speller.

The weary marketing head, Joel Friedman, didn't get around to firing me till late that afternoon. "I don't get it," I told him. I was doing good stuff for Warner Bros. I was costing them peanuts. Sobered by the personal anguish all about him, Joel told me his hands were tied. "You know what today is?" he said. "It's Lincoln's birthday. The day we freed the slaves."

In New York, Starr awaited Conkling's phone call to tell him the firings had happened. The call was placed. Starr did not say thanks. In six months, he believed, it'd all be shut down anyway.

That weekend, my office buddy, art director Ken Kim told me I should be a freelance writer. He guessed we could persuade WBR to let us use our offices rent free, getting whatever work there was from the label. Ken's plan got okayed. Monday morning we drove back to our desks. There was not enough writing to pay me, so I used my address on Warner Boulevard and took up faking hot fan-magazine articles about TV stars, like one in which childless "Connie Stevens Confesses 'Why They Won't Let Me Keep My Baby.' " My crap sold, at fifty dollars a pop. To Ken Kim and me, Warners felt like a long shot, even less stable than phony articles I'd concoct about topics like TV stars' ESP experiences.

One way or another, I stayed on at Warners for another three decades. What I saw, starting that Monday, was a different record company. In his windows-overlooking-the-parking-lot corner office, Jim Conkling, once president of mighty Columbia Records, began spending hours on the phone to New York, getting okays from Starr for his any and every move. "I never saw anyone get to Jim the way Herman did," Hal Cook told me. "He was the one man who could destroy Jim's cool."

Hal Cook closed Warner's distribution branches fast. "So much for *that* excellent idea," Starr said, sounding relieved that a big drain had been plugged. He conceded to a few new signings but insisted that *all* artist signings be cleared with him. A few cheap singles deals squeaked through, but they, in balance, meant not enough. This was utter retreat from Conkling's vision.

Then came the news: Nashville's Everly Brothers, who recently moved to the West Coast, were hunting for a better deal. Those good-looking, high-harmony boys, Don and Phil—with a string of hits behind them on the Cadence label—liked the idea of signing with a movie studio's record company. It could mean a movie career, just like Elvis got. To sign the Everly Brothers would cost a million dollars (a hundred thousand a year for ten years). The price made Warner's execs gulp. Buried in returns, strangled by Starr and Kalmenson, the label wanted those boys bad but could not write that check.

Conkling pled, but Starr challenged back, "If the Everlys are so hot, go get the signing money from your distributors." Cook called around to all WBR distributors, now all indies. From each, he got an advance against the Everly Brothers' first record. Cook lined up the whole hundred thousand, though the getting took forty-five days. With attorneys billing for their every minute, contract negotiations took more than three hundred hours, and the distributors had to pay for that, too. Starr had insisted on a zero-risk policy.

That April, the Everly Brothers' first Warner single—"Cathy's Clown"—exploded onto the charts, spending five weeks at Number One. In Britain, "Cathy's Clown" was released with the catalogue number WB1. It sold three million copies worldwide, two million domestic, and was their biggest hit. The Everlys were ready to be more than record-hop teen idols out of the sticks. Their desire—to become Hollywood movie stars, with starlet wives, no hay sticking out—overwhelmed common sense.

To the surviving few records execs in Burbank, "Cathy's Clown" was *not* just more of the same. It meant we-*can*-do-it. Conkling, one hit ahead now, knew what to do with the Everlys: broaden their appeal from the teen/country market. He called Lou Busch, worse known as Joe "Fingers" Carr, his stride piano *nom de disque,* but a fully schooled music man. Conkling suggested Busch find new, more broadly appealing songs for the Everlys, add strings so they'd sell in Seattle. Busch did just that. Their next album had other songs in it, songs like "Temptation." The Everlys' longtime publisher, Nashville guru Wesley Rose, who'd provided the Everlys' hit songs up to this, was shut out. Rose lost his temper. He shut down the Everlys' Nashville song sources. "If that's the way you want it, do it without me," Rose told Conkling.

For two years, the Everlys had hits with Warner Bros. But that was that. When they enlisted in the Marine Corps Reserve to do six months' active duty rather than be drafted, I got the job to drive Don and Phil to the base, riding silently to a bars-across-its-windows barracks, a place utterly unlike their Beverly Hills dream, and see Don and Phil walk out of Chart Land.

One hit by the Everlys did not release Starr's grip on Conkling's wallet. Conkling flew tourist class into Chicago, to Jim's only office there, WBR's cardboard-dingy warehouse, now an indy eight months pregnant with aged albums. Six in the evening. Outside the warehouse, in the dark, a city bus pulled up. Out stepped Robert Newhart, an unknown Chicago accountant who did solo comedy phone call routines, lugging his clumsy portable tape recorder. Conkling, fearing the worst, listened. From this short, thin kid, Jim heard revolutionary comedy. The next day, when Conkling called Starr to check out the signing, Starr's eyes still rolled toward heaven.

Starr hated the whole idea. He squeezed Conkling on costs. Newhart would get recorded, live, at his next gig by A&R man George Avakian. "Uh, just one thing," Conkling had to confess. "There *isn't* any next gig, Herman. The boy's unknown."

WB found The Tidelands, a club in Texas, to cut the album live. To get to Texas, however, required travel expenses, so still another call to Starr. Avakian laid out the cost: "Twelve dollars a night for the hotel room in Texas, air fare, and one show per night, two successive nights."

"George, it's a mistake," answered Starr, "spending all this money on a guy who can't even get a job. Comedy records don't sell." Later, when he heard the album, Starr didn't like it. But by July 31, WBR had its first Number One album: *The Button-Down Mind of Bob Newhart.*

BOB NEWHART: Hi, Abe Sweetheart! How are ya, kid!
How's Gettysburg?

It stayed on top for fourteen weeks. It spent more than a year on the charts. On Warner Boulevard, we'd never felt anything like this before; we felt like front-page headline news, where before, we'd been buried in the classifieds.

"The whole salvation of our company was having the Everly Brothers and Bob Newhart hit. They hit very fast," recalled treasurer Ed West. "All of a sudden, we were making money. Nobody ever asked us to close up shop after that. Nobody ever said anything again."

Distributor payments came flooding in. "It was then that Ed West learned that accounts receivable meant so much more," Cook remembered. "We were really in the record business for the first time." Having flown home from a Vegas record retailers convention, Cook and L.A. sales rep Fran Howell arrived in Pasadena, at Howell's home. That Sunday night in April, Cook got a phone call. His son had died. Howell drove Cook to the Hollywood Hawaiian hotel. Cook got his things, headed home, back east, telling Conkling, "I've just got to take six months and figure out what is going on with my life." Before that deadline, Cook decided to leave the record business.[8]

Conkling again looked good. Bob Newhart won two whole Grammys: Best New Artist and—can you believe this?—Album of the Year. Take *that,* Herman.

Thanks to the Everlys-Newhart one-one punch, Jim Conkling set two next goals: first, to get control of the label back where it belonged, in his hands; and second, to cash in his Warner Bros. Pictures stock options. Just that day, those options had ripened, and could be bought/sold for a major profit. Conkling cashed them in.

Jack Warner and his New York crew always watched the company's stock trades. Seeing Conkling sell for profit, to Warner it was as if Conkling had just picked his pocket for a million dollars. No matter how legal it was to do, no matter how justified Jim was, Warner became enraged to the point of spit. "Hell," he said, "Jim Conkling's lucky to be still standing!" Good employees waited, gratefully, for six months, a year to elapse before cashing in their stock options.

Whatever hope there had been for Conkling to continue running WBR, in that one commonsense transaction, it went splat. In private phone calls, the studio heads—Warner-Kalmenson-Starr—made up their minds: Get a new label head. They questioned Conkling's loyalty. Conkling saw no reason to apologize. He'd just followed standard business practice, the kind that was commonplace at, say, CBS. His words fell deafly on Kalmenson's ears. "We're going to make the change, Jim." Conkling, seeing no reason now to repent, volunteered to pick his own successor. It was resolved: "Jim, pick us a good one," Kalmenson said. To which Starr added, "Check him out with me."

Conkling quickly turned to another ex–Capitol man, one recently churned out onto the street in his own intracompany battle: Mike Maitland, a handsome former pilot. Maitland had risen within Capitol from branch sales to head of all sales.

He was fresh from swatting down the ungrateful Frank Sinatra, who had turncoated against Capitol to issue his new Reprise label's first release. Maitland had hoped to succeed Alan Livingstone as president of Capitol but had just been passed over. Conkling offered Maitland the presidency of WBR.

The Maitland appointment got approved by New York. Warner Bros.

---

[8]Hal Cook eventually returned to records as developer of Record Source International, in-flight music entertainment, and finally, as publisher of *Billboard* magazine. He retired in 1974 and enjoyed another quarter century in ease, living in Palm Springs. He died, at eighty, in 1999.

Records' few remaining executives—Joel Friedman, Ed West, Lowell Frank—were given no inkling about this Maitland.

From the perspective of one decade later, Joel Friedman would reflect back on Conkling's two years at Warner Bros. Records: "Those who were not involved will say, 'What a load of crap they created in those days.' It's easy to criticize, but I don't know what anyone else would have done. People do what they do at the time that they do it. When we started the company, there was nothing.

"There's an old story about Fred Allen and Portland Hoffa, who were doing a radio show. The sponsor came in at the end of the show and said, 'That really wasn't very funny at all.' Allen looked up at him and said, 'You son of a bitch, where were you when the pages were blank?' "

Thirty-four years later, at a 1996 testimonial for Jim Conkling, his wife asked studio head of postproduction Rudi Fehr, "Why did they fire Jim? He would never talk about it."[9]

Mike Maitland looked the part. If this were some Warner Bros. movie, he would be cast as the good guy. He was in his young forties, solid, slick black hair, a tan offsetting intense brown eyes. He moved quickly, surely. Determined and proper. He was from the street, from selling in Detroit. In World War II, Mike had flown airplanes, for the winning side.

Maitland moved from Capitol into a company that was now mildly profitable but had little in the way of "a line" to sell. Maitland's job—and Starr made this clear—was to give the company structure and substance, turn it into a business that could grow without blowing its positive cash flow. Mike made some changes, not by sending out a memo, just by the way he did things.

Warner Bros. Records was now committed—not that it had any choice—to the independent distributor. Conkling had found dealing with indies distasteful. Own your own branches, people don't hand you any crap. You told them, "Take ten thousand albums," and they took. Try that with Milt Salstone in Chicago, he'd say, "I think I only need eight hundred. You keep the rest."

Maitland felt the same way about indies as Conkling did, but Maitland

---

[9]After Conkling left Warner Bros., he turned to public service, at one point heading up the Voice of America for Ronald Reagan, then the Mormons' broadcasting network, the Nat King Cole Cancer Foundation, even trying to teach China how to form a record industry. He once called me, asking, "Can I get the rights to translate Allan Sherman's album into Chinese?"

In his later years, a victim of Alzheimer's, Conkling was not robbed of his willingness to command. Mornings at Sutter Oaks Hospital in Sacramento, Jim dressed for work, tie and jacket, briefcase, worked the hospital halls, firing all the nurses. After lunch, Jim rehired them at triple salary. Jim Conkling died at that hospital, age eighty-three, in 1998.

needed a job. He handled tough distributors with salesman charm. Maitland had been out on the streets, competing with the Salstones. He was prepared to start small, and he was prepared to scrap.

So a sales guy replaced a music guy. The sales guy cut down WBR's paperwork, got rid of those Advertising Request forms, those Return Authorization forms; got rid of salesmen having to break up records at plants, of salesmen having to destroy defective discs. All manufacturing was contracted to Columbia Records, which agreed not only to press the record but also to assemble the disc into its cardboard sleeve, store the inventory, and, when the order came in, ship to distributors as requested. At the time, such collating was unprecedented.

Maitland skipped over early WBR's "concept" albums. He looked for Number One hits that would set off smash albums. For Burbank, Mike's ideas were revolutionary. His most productive move, however, came in his hiring of someone strong to handle radio promotion. For national promotion, Maitland called ex–Boston DJ Joe Smith, to offer him the job.

Along with many noted DJs, Joe Smith had survived the payola uproar. Headlines about "payola" had begun grabbing attention. In 1960, the House Legislative Oversight Committee's hearings looked into payola, into bribes at stations like Boston's WBZ-AM and others. A big spotlight concentrated on Roulette Records' Morris Levy, who also ran New York nightclubs Birdland and Roundtable. On the side—and the gravel-voiced Levy had more sides than the Hope Diamond—he also managed Alan Freed, who at New York's WINS had become radio's master of payola. During his appearance at the Washington hearings, Freed reveled in his way of doing business and refused to tap-dance to government tunes. For his inquisitors, he was an easy target. His indiscretion not only got him fired, it also made him unhirable.[10]

Joe Smith was also summoned to the hearings. When Smith married Donnie, his society bride, the couple had been inundated with gifts from appreciative labels. He'd even got owner shares in record labels, with cozy notes inside, words like these, from promoter George Goldner: "It's about time I did something for you guys, time you built something for your future."

At the Washington hearings, Smith sounded contrite. He was, after all, ex–Yale. Smith told the truth in Washington ("paid taxes on it") but found his Boston radio career at an end. He and Donnie had moved out to California to seek a different fortune. When Maitland called, Smith, remembering the story titled "Kookie and the Cardinal," was hardly attracted: "I knew, as a

---

[10]Freed, down and out in Palm Springs, gradually gave up looking for DJ work. His son, Lance, recalled, "I think what crushed him the most was that people wouldn't call him back. I remember our phone being disconnected in 1964 because of all the long-distance calls he had made to his friends, to try to reenter, to get back in the business, to ask someone for some support, some help. And there were very few people who would call back." Freed drank himself to death by 1965.

disc jockey, that Warner Bros. was a laugh. They made a lot of bad records, and when a label has that reputation, you don't even open their envelopes. I never thought much of that company." Still, Smith *was* job juggling in L.A., promoting records for $150 a week, and this *was* a job with national scope— the supply side of the record business—rather than local hustle.

Smith knew what his first task would be: stop the label from being laughed at. In November, he set off into the snows of America to see, first-hand, about WBR in the marketplace and to hire some promotion men. At the time of his hiring, WBR was down to one regional promotion man affectionately called "Nutty Graham," the same Graham who'd called Ira Ironstrings "crap." Moving cross-country, Smith found that Warner's distributors, too, hated the label. "Our prices were higher than other prices. Our advertising allowances were onerous. Our distributors were jammed with records which had been shipped out to them on some ill-advised sales program. By the time I got to my folks' home in Boston, I had an ulcer. I called Maitland and said, 'I can't work for this company. It's horrible.' "

Maitland calmed Smith, telling him to assemble his early promotion staff. Five guys. To his new, permanent staff, Smith added pizzazz by hiring off-season sports celebrities, notably baseball umpire Ed Runge and the San Francisco 49ers' defensive end, the scary-looking Cedric Hardman, nicknamed "Nasty." Or as Joe Smith justified it, "These guys walk into a radio station, they're going to get seen. Immediately."

Quickly, Smith's new crew got its first challenge. A New York City cop named Saverio Saridis, who sang opera on his beat, cut a single. Don Graham, having been told to "go all out" for the Singing Cop, did just that. The single's A side was "Love Is the Sweetest Thing." Graham pitched his pal, disc jockey Bob Mitchell of KYA, that Saridis was Greek and so was San Francisco's mayor, George Christopher. Promotion men, they look for any connection. Don had found one. Mitchell went on the record. Graham threw a party.

"We had flaming oysters," Graham exulted. "Everything rolling out on carts. People were jammed into the Fontainebleau at the Fairmont. It was mandatory. You had to go. Mayor Christopher was there. [Columnist] Herb Caen was there. The cop sang. I promised Mayor Christopher that after Saverio got through at the party, he'd go over and sing for a Greek Orthodox thing the mayor had that night. I think the Fairmont party was the first check Joe Smith signed when he came to the company. He thought it was a telephone number."

Because of the Top Ten furor in San Francisco, other radio stations picked up the single. A phone call came to Joe Smith at the Fairmont. It was Jack Warner asking, "You got a singer up there? A cop?" "Yeah." Warner got to his point: "Well, get him down here, Smith." Warner Bros. Pictures signed Saverio Saridis to make a movie, paying him twenty-five thousand dollars. Total sales: twenty-seven thousand singles, nationwide. And then, as things happen, it all just went away. Radio liked it; people didn't buy it. Happens.

"Don Graham," Smith once told me, "was the greatest regional promotion man in the history of the record business." WBR was, however, still far from out of the woods. Its hits were occasional. About the company in Burbank, struggling in its leftover Warner machine shop, there was a sense of frailty, at best.

The staff remained small. Despite Newhart's three golden Grammys, two Everly Brothers, and one Singing Cop, Christmas 1961 arrived bleakly in Burbank. "In December," Smith recalled, "we had a negative month. We had more returns than sales. In addition to being my secretary, Monetta Woodhead used to keep all the sales figures for this company. Many days the distributor telegrams would come in: NO SALES TODAY."

The company Christmas party was held downstairs in the old machine shop, in a twenty-by-twenty cleared space. Two bottles of New York State champagne, Styrofoam cups. The small company stood around, twenty-seven of us, huddled. There were no bonuses, no gifts. Maitland turned to Smith and whispered, "Say something funny."

To help him run Warner music publishing (MPHC), Starr hired songwriter magnet Artie Mogull, a music-business mover whose appeal to past employers had been mixed. Mogull gambled; in Vegas, he'd be seen holding all the stools at a blackjack table, taking all bets with two-inch stacks of black chips on each. Loan sharks forced him to pay; he got money where he could. But in an industry whose hunger for good ears outweighed all, Artie Mogull could be described as charming, witty, clever, animated, liked, and well eared. But seldom fully trusted.

One afternoon in 1960, Mogull promised Starr he'd catch a group playing at the Blue Angel. That night, Manhattan turned into a blizzard, causing Artie's reasonable reaction: "Oh, fuck this, I'm going home." Without seeing the group, the next morning, Mogull walked into Starr's office and reported, "I saw the group last night at the Blue Angel, and they're the greatest goddamn folk group! They're great."

Starr and Mogull tipped Maitland, who happened to be in New York hunting talent, something hardly his specialty. The next night, by himself, in five-degree weather, Maitland headed to the Blue Angel. He was one of few customers, though the others there looked like men from Mercury Records, people like that. Peter, Paul & Mary performed their full repertoire on stage: six songs. Maitland noticed, "They were into detail even at that time, in a rather obscure club. The lighting was right. Their mike technique was already way ahead of anyone I'd seen. They understood the lyrics. I loved what I saw and heard. I went up to them after the show and told them so. They said we'd have to get together with Mr. Grossman."

Albert Grossman, sometimes described as the Floating Buddha, had become the most tenacious, best-known, and most successful artist's manager in the music business. He was a generation ahead of the old 15-percenters (his contract with Bob Dylan gave him 25 percent). He managed full careers, not just deals. On that Fifty-eighth Street sidewalk, Grossman demanded that WBR take a "hands off" on the recording process of Peter, Paul & Mary. Maitland shook on thirty thousand dollars for a five-year deal, "a lot of front money," he thought, "for an act that worked together about a week." Still, since Mike was unsure he even had the authority to make such a deal, he dared himself. Why not?

Starr, hearing of the cost, became furious. He hadn't been checked with! In a time when most albums took nine hours to record, PP&M would take months. In a time when most albums could be made for ten thousand dollars, *Peter, Paul & Mary* cost fifty-five thousand. But PP&M had control.

As PP&M's release date neared, Don Graham pasted stickers saying PETER, PAUL & MARY all over San Francisco. When an old man tottered up to him to warn, "Young man, you can go to jail for that," Graham answered, "Great! We can use the publicity."

Bay Area disc jockey Tom Donahue remembered, "Graham had this incredible hustle going on Warner Bros. Records. He was a great promotion man in his time, and he had drek to take around. He had Connie Stevens, a couple of those little boy singers, Joanie Sommers, Bob Conrad, and George Greeley. You'd lean to Graham because you dug him, so you'd give his records a chance. I watched Graham make Peter, Paul & Mary stars. They came to San Francisco, booked into the Hungry i, and nobody had any idea who they were. Inside the tunnel on Route 101, Graham had painted PETER, PAUL & MARY. He got all these students from the College of Marin standing in line for tickets and picketing the Hungry i to get PP&M to stay over for another week. He really hustled his ass off for that record."

At this time, album cuts didn't much get played on radio. Singles did. Graham liked an album cut: "Lemon Tree." He got four acetates made. Then he went to Oakland Top Forty station KEWB, and lied: "Here's the new single from Peter, Paul & Mary. Exclusive!" He gave exclusives to three other Bay Area stations.

In Burbank, Joe Smith saw an avalanche of orders from San Francisco for "Lemon Tree." He called Graham, excited that they wanted the album.

"No," Graham answered, "they want the single."

"There is no single."

"There'd better be," Graham told his boss. "Quick!"

Within months, the album was embraced. "Lemon Tree" bore gold fruit, the album spent seven weeks at Number One out of three full years on the charts. It might have been unstoppable on its own, but painting a tunnel never hurts.

He was soft, gentle, fat, Jewish, Chicago. Allan Sherman, comedy writer, composed song parodies as a hobby. He performed them at Hollywood parties, even at Conkling's farewell stag. Sherman had doozies covering the most familiar of songs, like the songs from *My Fair Lady*:

> *A piece of rye bread isn't very tasty.*
> *A slice of onion isn't such a treat.*
> *A slab of cream cheese tastes a little pasty, but—*
> *With a little bit of lox, with a little bit of lox,*
> *You got something very good to eat!*

Fine, except the authors of *My Fair Lady* were not about to have Allan Sherman kill their copyrights. Nor was Columbia Records.

Maitland suggested that Sherman do satires on public-domain songs. Sherman, then broke, thought, yeah, maybe he could. For making the deal, manager Bullets Durgom got a $1,500 advance for Sherman, more money than he'd seen on one check in more than a year. Bullets took his 10 percent; Allan Sherman got $1,350 and went crazy, writing night and day, in the shower, in the bed, in the car driving to unemployment.

On August 6, Allan Sherman recorded live in front of a hundred guests. A bar and hors d'oeuvres. He opened the session with a western ballad, "The Streets of Laredo," redone as "The Streets of Miami." Screams. Comedienne Pat Carrol laughed so hard she had to hit to the ladies' room four times during the forty-five-minute session. Then more: "Seltzer Boy." "Jump Down, Spin Around, Pick a Dress o' Cotton."

> *I'm singing you the ballad of a great man of the cloth.*
> *His name was Harry Lewis and he worked for Irving Roth.*
> *He died while cutting velvet on a hot July the Fourth,*
> *But his cloth goes shining on!*
>
> *Glory, Glory Harry Lewis . . .*

The album came out with no to-do. Warner Bros. Records salesman Reggie Tobin was doing his daily rounds at White Front Discount Department Store in the San Fernando Valley. He had a bunch of *My Son, the Folk Singer* with him. Tobin was trying to push the album on the buyer, who said what they'd all said: "I never heard of this record." A frenzied customer rushed up, saying, "I just heard something on the car radio. Something about Harry Lewis and the drapes of Roth. I've got to have this record. I laughed so hard I thought I'd have an accident."

Tobin pointed to the album. "That's what I've been telling you. 'Glory, Glory, Harry Lewis.' It's in this album."

"Okay," the buyer answers, "I'll take ten."

The album took off *so fast,* WBR could not print enough jackets. At Wallich's Music City, Sunset and Vine, the albums were sold in inner sleeves, with a note that you could come back later and get the jacket free.

Nine months later—September 1962—on Warner Bros. Records' fourth birthday, hits had happened: the Everlys' best, Bob Newhart, Peter, Paul & Mary, and Allan Sherman were a series of successful albums; a few singles had hit—"Al Di La" and "Let's Go" and "Johnny Get Angry"; soundtracks of *The Music Man* and *Gypsy.* We'd stepped in it, and this time it smelled green. Sales totaled $4.2 million. Profits, more important, became a plus: $505,000. Controller Ed West felt that inner pride that good accountants get but so seldom show. He had stuck with the record company, at some risk to his own future. Now this lifelong accountant was able to stroll, barely avoiding skipping, into Maitland's office with the news: "You'll be glad to know, I just sent the studio the statement. We've totally repaid its three million dollars."

In person, Maitland took the news to Jack Warner. "You know, kid," Warner told Maitland, "it always bothered me about that record company, that it hadn't been doing well. It's got my name on it." To Mike, the Chief sounded relieved. "I don't like anything with my name on it that isn't doing well."

From that point on, Warner Bros. Records was no longer controlled by Starr. Maitland got invited to play weekend tennis at the Chief's house. He was savvy enough not to win.

Life at 3701 felt good at last, but. Life usually includes a "but." But Maitland was not being told that the Chief was just now meeting with Frank Sinatra and Sinatra's *macher,* Mickey Rudin, men whom Maitland, back at Capitol, had angered with his anti-Reprise "twofer." The Sinatra-Warner meetings were about Sinatra making movies for WB. Down in Clause 93 came talk about Sinatra's idling record label, Reprise, maybe Warner Bros. taking it over. Jack Warner never thought to tell Maitland about those talks; in Warner's mind, the deal was mainly about movies, not records. Warner gave not one thought to how the talks could upset Maitland's applecart.

Significant Warner Bros. Records

1960

The Everly Brothers (*It's Everly Time!* and *A Date with the Everly Brothers*, including "So Sad," "Cathy's Clown," "Lucille") • Bob Luman ("Let's Think About Living") • Bob Newhart (*Button-Down Mind,* including "Abe Lincoln vs. Madison Avenue," "Cruise of the U.S.S. Codfish," and "Driving Instructor") and *The Button-Down Mind Strikes Back,* including "Grace L. Ferguson Airline (and Storm Door Co.)") • Connie Stevens ("Sixteen Reasons")

1961

Gone With the Wind soundtrack re-creation • George Greeley (*The Best of the Popular Piano Concertos*) • Bob Newhart (*Behind the Button-Down Mind*)

1962

The Everly Brothers (*The Golden Hits,* including "Crying in the Rain," "Ebony Eyes," "Walk Right Back," "That's Old Fashioned") • Bob Newhart (*The Button-Down Mind on TV*) • Emilio Pericoli ("Al Di La'") • Peter, Paul & Mary ("If I Had a Hammer") • Saverio Saridis ("Love Is the Sweetest Thing") • Allan Sherman (*My Son, the Folk Singer*) • Joanie Sommers ("Johnny Get Angry") • *The Music Man* and *Gypsy* soundtracks

4

OVER Barham Boulevard, down past the Hollywood Bowl, down curving Cahuenga Boulevard, across Hollywood Boulevard, three more blocks, second floor over a radio-parts store, another upstart label, Reprise Records, fought and grabbed for any percentage of the market.

Frank Sinatra, despite just having negotiated and then signed—in ink—a new, seven-year deal with Capitol, later in 1960 decided to screw it. He wanted to own a label. Not some vanity label, just for him, but a big label, one for him and his pallies. He'd had that kind of passion since he was a kid singer: get ahead, stay ahead, be the star.

This new label would be a haven for *his* artistic freedom. His freedom, however, was actually already real. For years, Frank had had contractual freedom to reject songs at Columbia. There, he could have killed release of the embarrassing "Mama Will Bark" he'd made with Mitch Miller and the blonde and bountiful Dagmar, but he didn't. He had the same control at Capitol but continued to feel owned. Although he'd talked up the "freedom" urge, other reasons went less declared: His own label would give him strutting power, no one to argue against him, a bigger piece of the pie.

But how to get out of his new deal? Frank knew. He grew hoarse.

In the MGM film *Can-Can*, Sinatra sang. When Capitol wanted the soundtrack album, Sinatra coughed. He had not too many cards to play against Capitol, but laryngitis was one. Aside from the *Can-Can* soundtrack, for Capitol, Sinatra would not sing. For ten months (1959–60), he whispered.

Turning Sinatra's label lust into reality became the job of Frank's attorney-who-makes-things-happen, Mickey Rudin, a man born to twist arms. Rudin was, in Hollywood, valuable, a power attorney with clients like Lucille Ball. Rudin was more than a lawyer; he was a guy who could get whomever you needed, from the president of the United States to the president of the Teamsters, on the phone, right now, first call, zip, right past any secretary.

Rudin was smart, out of the *Harvard Law Review* mixed with a Brooklyn upbringing. He also had a cruel streak. When a negotiation was going bad, Mickey would write devestating letters about the guy opposite him at the table, letters doing everything from questioning his math competence to suggesting he enter his ass in the Kentucky Derby. Then Mickey would send this letter to the guy's boss, with a carbon copy to the guy himself. And just wait for the guy's insecurity and pain to turn the deal Mickey's way. Mickey once told me one of his power secrets: "I get a lot of questions about Frank's Mafia connection." Then he smiled the smile of a guy who knew how to turn fear into a business asset. "But, you know, whenever people asked me about it, I just would smile and look wise. It never hurt I wouldn't deny it." Even in the way Rudin confided in you, he made you realize there was a lot he knew that you didn't.

Rudin had figured out how power works like he'd got an A in Intimidation 101. He smoked Cubans. Not just cigars. Gardeners, too. Rudin spent hours figuring each new deal like it was *The Daily Racing Form.*

Rudin reported to Capitol that, with Sinatra's attitude toward the label, his throat might never heal. Sinatra, though he could not sing for Capitol, could still yell at its president, Alan Livingston, "I'm going to destroy that round building! I'll tear it down!" he yelled. Capitol, furious right back, did the obvious thing: It negotiated. "We got the *Can-Can* album for them," Rudin recalled, "but in return we negotiated a nonexclusive contract for Sinatra."

Sinatra first tried to buy "Jazz at the Philharmonic" impresario Norman Granz's Verve label, but MGM made Granz a better offer, which he took and moved to Switzerland. Sinatra next decided to start his own, better label. To administer the label, he turned to an ex–Granz man, the hundred-dollar-a-week controller of Verve Records; a young UCLA graduate in finance; a man with glasses, a brain, curiosity, and a respect for talent. Despite these good traits, this young man was not well enough known to have his name correctly spelled by December 12, 1960's *Billboard:*

Moe Austin has resigned his Verve Records post to become the administrative head of Frank Sinatra's new recording company . . . Austin's appointment to the key position marks the first tangible indication that Sinatra is building his label's executive force . . .

Mo was born Morris Meyer Ostrofsky in New York, March 27, 1927. His family moved from New York to L.A. around Pearl Harbor Day (1941), when Mo was fourteen. He'd attended Fairfax High, where he achieved his first presidency, as president of the Fairfax High Music Society. In 1947, Mo moved on to UCLA in economics. He worked his way through school and had the good sense to marry a younger Fairfax High girl, Evelyn, in 1950. In the next apartment over lived a school fellow named Irving Granz. Irving's brother was Norman, of Verve Records. Introduced, Mo started out with Verve Records in 1953. To this day, Mo slides by telling about his youth, as if it lacked glamour. It probably did.

During his time with Norman Granz, the young Mo Ostin had learned how to deal with the high and haughty. Five rules: You listen to them, you ask lots of questions, you know who's boss, you wait your turn, and, in the studio, you leave them alone, let them improvise. Granz practiced such rules dealing with Flip Phillips, Ella Fitzgerald, Illinois Jacquet, and other of his "Jazz at the Philharmonic" recording stars. Mo practiced those rules dealing with Granz.

Granz could be imperious. I remember a red-leather-booth dinner with Mo and him at Chasen's. Granz is sitting powerful; it's nine at night and he's wearing dark glasses, sending back his osso bucco for tasting too something, acting the true bitch. I told him about my balcony seat at his Jazz at the Phil concerts. He did not look impressed. It felt like I was sharing a booth with Citizen Kane, Jr. But Granz held on to his jazz performers. He had an ego, but it was not located near his ears.[11]

Ostin never forgot those five "things you do." With Sinatra, he listened to, asked questions of, knew who the boss was, waited his turn, and let him do the signing. Post-Granz, Mo now dealt with a higher couple of haughties: Mickey Rudin (whose business card revealed him to be named "Milton") and Frank Sinatra (no card). Sinatra and Ostin talked about what kind of label to start. "Frank really wanted to build a record company," Ostin recalled, "what he called 'a better mousetrap.' He was vindictive about his relationship with Capitol. One day, when we were driving up Vine Street past the Capitol Tower, Sinatra pointed up at it and told me, 'You see that tower over there, Mo? Someday we're going to have one just like it.' "

Ostin became day-in, day-out administrative VP of the to-be-named new record label. Sinatra got to be label president. Ostin's responsibility was to build a major record company with three hundred thousand dollars. They chose the label background: a steamboat. Then, from a long list, they

---

[11]Norman Granz's imperious manner should not be confused with his contribution to the business. He made the first legit records of live jazz. He was more than important in Ella Fitzgerald's becoming a world star. He paid his artists better than average. He insisted on racial equality for all them. As Oscar Peterson once so vividly put it, "I can recall him standing his ground at the Houston airport when the sheriff pulled his gun from his holster and jammed it into Norman's stomach while telling him how he hated him more than he hated blacks because he was insisting that Ella Fizgerald be allowed to ride in a 'white taxi cab.' "

chose the label's name: "This is it! This is it! 'Reprise: to play and play again.' "[12]

Sinatra announced that Reprise artists would have a latitude previously unknown in the business of record-contract rules. Reprise artists would keep the ownership of their masters. (Few did.) His artists would own shares in the company. (Never happened.) Reprise artists would have complete control over their record sessions. (Happened.) Reprise artists could record for other labels when they wanted to. (Hardly.) "He divined that the thrust of this company should be its artists," Ostin recalled. "It all seems logical today, but back then it was truly revolutionary." But Sinatra's menu of artist rights never got followed. It was a list of ideals, the kind presidential candidates orate.

Free to record for himself while owing albums to Capitol, Frank did little to soothe feelings at the tower. He became expert at stiffing the bastards. Ostin would sit with Sinatra as he chose songs for his Reprise albums. "We'd go through songs, and if there was a lousy song, he'd say, 'Let's save that one for the Capitol record.' " Once, recording for Capitol under the new arrangement, Sinatra walked into Studio A wearing a necktie embroidered FUCK YOU.

In building his new label, Sinatra first wooed Dean Martin from Capitol. Capitol felt twice slapped. Sinatra failed to deliver the albums due Capitol. Capitol felt screwed. Its sales chief, Mike Maitland, knew how to handle that screwed-over feeling. Just as Reprise focused on putting out its first, anti-Capitol release, its Frank Sinatra album, *Billboard* ran a headline story: CAP TO LAUNCH PUSH ON SINATRA ALBUMS AS SINGER'S OWN LABEL BOWS FIRST SET.

Reprise took out a trade ad for Sinatra's new *Swing Along With Me* album. Holding his middle finger erect, Reprise PR man Mike Shore wrote ad copy: NOW—A NEWER, HAPPIER, EMANCIPATED SINATRA—UNTRAMMELED, UNFETTERED, UNCONFINED—ON REPRISE.

The tower sued. Two Sinatra albums headed to a showdown in the market: Capitol's *Come Swing With Me* vs. Reprise's *Swing Along With Me*. L.A.'s Superior Court quickly enjoined Reprise from using the two words "With Me" on its cover.

To make things tougher, Reprise was an indie while Capitol was a major. Capitol owned its own branches, which sales chief Maitland controlled. To counter, Reprise had little in the way of street-level marketing. Both Ostin and Reprise sales chief Jay Lasker had earlier traveled the country, looking for distribution. Ostin was remembered by indie Henry Droz of Detroit's Arc Distributing as coming by his house one morning in Southfield, Michi-

[12]Almost everyone pronounced the label "Re-preese." Frank, who was slow to forgive, was the only one to pronounce it "Re-prize," as in "reprisal."

gan, "in a stunning red raincoat, knocking on our door, and asking me if we'd handle one more line. I told him, 'Sure, Mo.' It was the first time I'd ever seen anyone in a red raincoat in Detroit." Many of Reprise's new indie distributors, used to Polka King and bebop albums, were hardly accustomed to LPs by an artist of Sinatra's stature.

On Valentine's Day 1961, Reprise issued its first single: Frank Sinatra singing "The Second Time Around" (which got up to Number Fifty on *Billboard*'s Hot 100). Reprise's first full album release occurred on March 27, including Sinatra's *Ring-a-Ding Ding!*, which eventually rose to Number Four on the charts. The release had an even stronger antirock bias than had prevailed across town at Warner Bros. and included stuff like Calvin Jackson's "Jazz Variations on Movie Themes," Sande & Greene's "Ol' Calliope Man at the Fair," "Primitive Percussion African Jungle Drums," "The X-15 & Other Sounds of Missiles, Rockets, Jets," and "Passionate Valentino Hits." Other than a Sinatra, no album in these early releases sold over twenty-three thousand copies, and that was high. Sinatra held firm: no rock & roll on Reprise.

The label moved from its temporary Beverly Hills headquarters in the William Morris office down to something less fashionable: 8330 Melrose Avenue in West Los Angeles, taking half a floor upstairs over a carpet company. The new space was big enough for eight or ten people tops. Production manager Mary Ann Romari remembered that "it was so small, nobody used phones. We just yelled back and forth to one another. You could hear just about every conversation going on in the building."

Unquestionably mean to Mo, Mickey Rudin added tension to daily life. Reprise was expected to become a big winner simply because of Sinatra. Mo bore the brunt of the criticism. If anything went wrong, Mickey was constantly on the phone to him complaining that he didn't know what he was doing.

Reprise's artist roster kept growing, looking, in the 1940s–1950s sense, stellar: Jo Stafford, Rosemary Clooney, Count Basie and Duke Ellington, Dennis Day, the Four Lads, the Hi-Los, Danny Kaye, the McGuire Sisters, Ethel Merman, Debbie Reynolds, Dinah Shore, Joey Bishop, Peter Lawford. Cronies aside, the list read like Sinatra's master's thesis on Good Music.

In 1961, the year Columbia signed twenty-year-old Bob Dylan, Reprise's roster might have been drawn from the phone book of Palm Springs, a place that had become home to the Dinah Shore Set. Reprise's were singers who, on weekdays, spent little time in recording studios and lots more lunching at the Racquet Club.

"The only thing that was meaningful at Reprise was the kind of music Sinatra had been involved in all his life," Ostin recalled. "I really had no strong A&R feelings at the time. My background was totally foreign to

A&R, and I recognized my inadequacies in that area and, under those circumstances, was open to any kind of suggestion from anyone I respected in terms of music. If Sinatra said rock & roll was dead, or had no future, or was ridiculous for us to get involved with, then I'd probably go along."

Based only on his experience at Verve and on Sinatra's love of jazz, Ostin signed jazz acts: Ben Webster, Mavis Rivers, Jimmy Witherspoon, Calvin Jackson, Eddie Cano, Barney Kessel, Chico Hamilton, Dizzy Gillespie, Shorty Rogers, Marv Jenkins, and a reissue of Django Reinhardt. They sold next to nothing.

Reprise again moved its office, to Cahuenga in Hollywood, this time taking the floor above a Pacific Radio store. Neil Hefti and Steve Venet were hired to be A&R. Money was burning, but no one panicked. To get Reprise Records' accounting straightened out, Ostin hired his college buddy, CPA Murray Gitlin, a man who on that day and each day since negotiated every single move in life, starting in the morning negotiating with his own feet over which would get to step on the floor first. Gitlin abandoned his own, more profitable accounting practice to take the job. He dug into Reprise's finances. In 1960, Reprise made $100,000, but in 1961, oops, it lost $400,000. Then first quarter of 1962: in the red $250,000.

The Sinatra/Capitol duel escalated into round two. Just as Reprise issued its recalled, repackaged, and relabeled *Sinatra Swings,* Capitol offered its *entire* Sinatra catalogue to its distributors on a twofer plan, two albums fer the price of one: an unprecedented 50 percent discount plan. Customers could snatch up complete Sinatra libraries at $1.99 per album. At $4.98—and able to offer only a one-fer—Reprise's newer product languished in bins. Soon Sinatra had thirteen albums on the charts. The bad news: twelve of the thirteen were on Capitol. Reprise's new album sold a humiliating 156,400 copies.

To cap off its first three years of so-so releases, Reprise came up with its most ambitious project ever: 1962's "Reprise Repertory Theater" series, four whopping big albums of Broadway musicals: *South Pacific, Kiss Me Kate, Finian's Rainbow,* and *Guys and Dolls.* Artists involved in the all-star recordings were impressive: Bing Crosby, Frank Sinatra, Dean Martin, Jo Stafford, Sammy Davis, Jr., Debbie Reynolds, Keely Smith, Rosemary Clooney . . . Cost of the albums was, for Reprise, enormous: a hundred thousand dollars each. It was a gamble that defied the marketplace. Only 17,900 real people ever showed interest in buying the series. It was Reprise's biggest gamble, its biggest disaster.

Ostin began to tiptoe into A&R judgments. When Sinatra brought to Reprise a Sinatra sound-alike named Frank Jerome, Ostin gingerly advised against it. Sinatra, finding Reprise fading, as interesting as last year's broad, took Ostin's advice. Ostin hired two new men for Reprise's A&R staff, replacing Venet and Hefti: noted arranger-gentleman Sonny Burke, and rock

& roller–turned–producer Jimmy Bowen,[13] who came in as a "catch-all" producer.

Control over Sinatra's finances had grown as wiggly as kindergarteners at nap time. Rudin knew that Essex Productions, which incorporated all finances of Frank Sinatra, was in trouble. One of Sinatra's ownerships, the Cal-Neva Lodge in Lake Tahoe, was getting redecorated: another major money drain. The lawsuits with Capitol, the mediocre albums . . . at Essex, the ledgers did not ring-a-ding-ding. When Reprise Records lost money, it lost Sinatra's own money, enough to dry his throat.

The single largest asset Essex could leverage for fresh cash was Sinatra's acting. He was hot from 1960's *Ocean's 11,* a movie he both starred in and produced for Warner Bros. It had cost $4 million, and grossed around ten. Jack Warner liked those kinds of numbers. When Warner wanted to ask Sinatra about a multipicture deal with his studio, he already knew he'd be dealing with Mickey Rudin.

Rudin drove out to Burbank to meet with the surviving Warner brother. It was 1963. Warner told Rudin he wanted to beef up his film-production schedule. Aware that Warner Bros. had a struggling label of its own, Rudin figured to himself maybe he could couple a movie deal in with the sale of Reprise Records, toss in Cal-Neva . . . Sitting down with Jack Warner, Mickey Rudin reached into his coat, pulled out a cigar, asked "Mind?" and clipped off the tip of another Cuban.

Giving up on Reprise bothered Sinatra not for a moment. He'd had it. With his quick passions, Sinatra had craved his own label—the same as he'd other times craved that broad over there, or his own leather booth and bottle of Jack. Quick passion: You do it, you forget it.

Draft One of the deal got memoed by Warner attorney Peter Knecht, who synopsized the Reprise part in one sentence: "What they are asking is that in exchange for all of the outstanding Essex stock, Frank Sinatra receive approximately 350,000 shares of Warner Bros. stock . . ." That deal had a value of about $5.25 million.

Warner balked. He didn't *want* the other stuff, like the Cal-Neva Lodge. He didn't want to co-own (with Danny Kaye) Essex's radio stations or residuals from old Sinatra pictures. As for Reprise Records, well, he didn't care one way or another.

But closed-door talks sped along, studio people to Sinatra people, all out of earshot of Mike Maitland or anyone at Warner Bros. Records. Unlike Sinatra and Warner, Maitland didn't *own* his company.

Ostin was the first to learn of the possible "merger" (nicer word, but it

---

[13]He'd made the first single (#4001) for Morris Levy's Roulette Records as Jim Bowen and the Rhythm Orchids ("I'm Sticking with You"). Also in the Rhythm Orchids was Buddy Knox.

still meant "sale"). Rudin needed to place a dollar value on Reprise Records, which took some adding up. A startled Ostin was commanded to evaluate the label: Add up the worth of the record masters, the contracts, the tables, chairs, paper clips—anything you could sell. Ostin pressed his own secretary, Thelma Walker, into service. Thelma was a bright and forthright black woman known for fighting for her boss, even if it meant her tromping down to the men's room, opening up the door, and yelling at the stall, "Mo, it's Mickey on the phone." Faced with all this inventory evaluating, Thelma recalled, "You can imagine my horror when I learned I was working that hard to maybe do myself out of a job!"

Ostin dutifully added up the assets, although he considered getting sold off to Warner Bros. a total ego slammer. With moments to go, he fought to make Reprise profitable, hoping that might save the label from being bought by Burbank.

Other folks working at Reprise woke up to what the lawyers were doing out in Burbank. If only, they dreamed, Reprise could get a hit, quick, before the deal was signed. If only . . .

In August, Reprise released *Trini Lopez at P.J.'s,* P.J.'s being the dance-bar–lounge–eatery–happening spot in Baja Hollywood, where ladies of the bar wore eye shadow that sparkled like crushed jewels. From Lopez's album came "If I Had a Hammer" (#11). Reprise employees kept gasping for more air. If only . . .

Mickey, it was known in town, had balls of brass. To make the deal with Warner, Rudin threw in a curveball idea. What if Sinatra got 50 percent ownership in the *combined* Warner-Reprise Records? Warner negotiated Rudin down to 33 percent.

Selling his two-thirds interest in money-losing Reprise, Sinatra got cash, plus a one-third interest in moneymaking Warner Bros. Records. Rudin covered up Reprise's loss facts with nine hundred thousand dollars' worth of tax-benefiting depreciation, reducing Reprise's cost to Warner to only six hundred thousand dollars. At the time, Rudin felt he'd made a *coup de deal.*

Fine print in the deal memo: If Jack Warner ever wanted to sell the labels, Sinatra got veto power. No problem; it was a toss-in line. Jack Warner just wanted Frank Sinatra. Sinatra would own a third of Warner/Reprise but not have to underwrite it financially. Warner did all the funding. At the last minute, Rudin threw into the contract that Sinatra would have the "ceremonial" title of Assistant to the President of Warner Bros. Studios, a title Sinatra loved. Exquisite negotiating, dragging out small points while the other guy's late for lunch. Shake. On his way to lunch, Rudin knocked off one more Cuban.

A meeting of the Warner Bros. board of directors got called in New York, a meeting again run by Jack Warner's tough business exec Benny

Kalmenson, the same slight, dapper, animated, cigar-smoking, bitchy-tongued man who'd told Conkling to "liquidate."

Kalmenson had his own style in running a board meeting. He opened the discussion by telling all present the expected decision of the meeting. "Before there is any discussion," Kalmenson announced, "I just want you to know that this is a deal that we're going into. We've had good success with Frank in the past with *Ocean's 11*. We feel we can make some good money out of this picture deal. As part of the deal, we're going to acquire the record company, and, in turn, we will allow Frank to buy a one-third interest. All of this is acceptable to Jack Warner. In fact, Jack wants the deal, and I want the deal. I expect each of you to vote in favor of the deal. Are there any questions?" Not a mouth opened.

At Reprise, while this was being said, artist Jack Nitzsche released an instrumental, "The Lonely Surfer," produced by Jimmy Bowen. It jumped twenty points on the singles charts. Pianist Eddie Cano had a hit with "A Taste of Honey." Lou Monte sold a lot of a novelty, "Pepino the Italian Mouse."

A call came to Ostin from Rudin in New York: Deal's done. Ostin was sick over it. "Terribly disappointed and had no idea what would happen."

Sinatra told all Hollywood about his new title. Hollywood speculated that Sinatra would someday be running all of Warner Bros. Hearing that, Jack Warner flipped, and Warner Bros. quickly reacted with a press release stating "there is no evidence or reason for speculation" that Sinatra was in line to take over Warner Bros. Studios. Sinatra stopped flashing the title.

Up Cahuenga three blocks, across Hollywood Boulevard, past the Hollywood Bowl, turn right over Barham, right again to 3701 Warner Boulevard, Reprise's remaining few drove out to Burbank's Warner Bros. Records. One moving van of their stuff followed.

No welcoming reception occurred out at Warner Bros. Records on that morning. Reprise's employees showed up. As Thelma Walker saw it, "Warner Bros. *had* a national promotion manager, Joe Smith. And they *had* a national sales manager, Bob Summers. And they *had* and they *had* and they *had*."

Upstairs, now running the newly merged Warner/Reprise, was Mike Maitland, the ex–Capitol sales head whose Sinatra twofer sale album had shat upon the debut of Reprise Records. Now Maitland would be chief not only of Warner Bros. Records but also of its resentful bride, Reprise.

The moving van with their desks, chairs, files arrived late. In his empty office at the east end of a dark hall, Ostin just stood there with his hands in his pockets. He had not forgotten what Maitland's Capitol had done to his baby, Reprise. And now, at one end of the hall, there was Maitland. Between the two, a dim hallway and sixty feet of linoleum.

Reprise Chart Albums

1961

Frank Sinatra (*Ring-a-Ding Ding!* and *Sinatra Swings* and *I Remember Tommy*)

1962

Sammy Davis, Jr. (*What Kind of Fool Am I, and Other Show-Stoppers*) • Lou Monte (*Pepino the Italian Mouse & Other Italian Fun Songs*) • Eddie Cano *At P.J.'s* • Frank Sinatra (*Sinatra & Strings*)

5

On September 3, 1963, Warner and Reprise financially and awkwardly amalgamated. The deal was signed before Mike Maitland and the rest at WBR had even heard about it. The deal disturbed Maitland, but getting left out was even worse. Maitland knew that Reprise had been losing money. The cost of buying it would again sink Warner Records back into red ink. That sink would be negative $1.5 million, not to mention, for WBR, a bigger payroll. Also not to mention an artist roster in need of crutches. And, of course, here he was, the head man at Warner-Reprise, with Sinatra owning a third.

Mo Ostin, accustomed to being Number Two (to Norman Granz, then to Sinatra and Rudin), behaved like a gent in the merger. He knew what was coming up: thinning down. Maitland involved Ostin in cutting Reprise's roster of sixty-two artists. Of that sixty-two, so far only one had amounted to anything commercial: Trini Lopez. So away they went, chop chop. Cut were Dodgers pitcher Don Drysdale, Arturo Romero and His Magic Violins, Art Linkletter, Alice Faye, Mavis Rivers, Nelson Riddle, Dinah Shore, Keely Smith, Jo Stafford, Count Basie, Les Baxter, Rosemary Clooney, Bing Crosby, Duke Ellington, the Four Lads, Danny Kaye, Ethel Merman . . . and a dozen jazz acts to boot. Would-be pop/rock & roll acts went: Debbie "Tammy" Reynolds, The Rev-Lons, Dorsey Burnette, Ral Donner, Thurston "Kansas City" Harris, Jack Nitzsche, Johnny Prophet, Del Reeves, and lesser-knowns. Ostin and Maitland worked cooperatively, buying out bad deals with WBR cash.

When he heard about the Warner/Reprise merger, pop-concerto pianist George Greeley, who'd (first) made fair-selling *The Best of the Popular Piano Concertos* albums for Jim Conkling, then (second) had been dropped by Maitland's new Warner Bros., only to be (third) picked up that April by Reprise, found himself, five months later (fourth), back at Warner/Reprise. Greeley did not look forward to (fifth).

For all the career killing involved in roster shrinking, the WB+R merger handed Maitland at least two other extra-strength headaches. First was, as could be expected, Frank Sinatra. He showed few signs of asking Mike over for tennis. In the coming years, he would never communicate with Maitland, the president of his own label. Sinatra talked only through Ostin. Maitland understood. He bided his baritone.

Maitland's second headache remained Herman Starr, who rode Maitland like a generic nag, despite WBR's recent successes. "Herman Starr was a very difficult man," remembered Maitland's New York head, George Lee. "He either liked you or he didn't like you. He didn't like Mike. He thought Mike was very frugal, that he was a sport, but he always thought Mike was not the big man he should be. Starr would send him nasty notes. He'd call Maitland 'just a salesman.' "

Starr phoned Maitland to inform him that Mo Ostin had two major flaws: (1) He'd been a bookkeeper for Norman Granz's Verve Records at the time when Verve was notoriously late in paying song royalties to Starr's MPHC; and (2) Starr blamed Ostin for the $1.5 million downside inherited from the Reprise buy. Starr gave Maitland strict instructions: "Get rid of this bum." Power, however, by now had shifted. Ostin's rationality, there through a messy start, appealed greatly to Mike. He ignored Starr's rant and kept Ostin off the "drops" list.[14]

For his part, Ostin realized that he must hold on to Reprise's identity, must defend his Reprise logo, his Reprise A&R staff. With those two assets, Reprise could make hits and maybe survive mergerdom. Maybe. Thelma got the "Reprise identity" hint. Starting that week, and for many, many years, long after the full merger of the two labels, Thelma would use only Reprise stationery to type Mo's memos. Every Monday, she would mark up the *Billboard* charts for Mo distinctly: red underlines for Reprise, blue underlines for Warner Bros.

Maitland set up side-by-side, equal labels. He had Ostin as Reprise's general manager; for Warner Bros. Records, in a similar position, he moved up Joe Smith from promotion head. To get WB into the singles market, Smith took over that slice of A&R. His early choices gave us no big hits but did bring acts reminiscent of the late-Fifties sound, when Joe had starred in Boston radio: Dick and DeeDee, Freddy Cannon, the Marketts.

Maitland, Smith, and Ostin found themselves behaving like gentlemen and having fun. Each believed he had a goal: to get the company out of the 1950s, away from music meant to soothe adults and excite teen lovers, but a music now best described with words that sound a bit silly, like catchy, cute, sweet, stirring, and toe-tapping. It had been good music, to be sure, but it started sounding shallow here in the 1960s, shallow and old hat. The three

---

[14]Herman Starr, a veteran of Warner Bros. since 1920, died the next year, in 1964, at sixty-six still holding the reins at MPHC. Upon Starr's death, not a ripple was felt at the record labels, not a wreath displayed.

leaders of Warner/Reprise were open of ear. They had to be. The stars of the Fifties still cost a lot to sign. The stars of the Sixties would cost a lot *not* to sign.

On a licensee-evaluating-trip through Europe, Maitland and newly appointed Joe Smith stopped at the office of WBR's France licensee, Vogue Records, run by Leon Cabat. There, they learned how business in France differs. Lunch? Up to La Tour d'Argent, with a view across the Seine of Notre-Dame's rosiest window, the waiters in tuxedos, not aprons over slacks: This midday, the businessmen ate, drank, and felt the extreme *joie* of the beyond-scrutiny expense account, clinking, sipping, and noshing for two hours. Maitland and Smith got buttered up. Back to the offices at three-fifteen, sunk deep into a down-filled chair, a fireplace hugging you in its warmth. Smith's challenge was to keep from passing out. Vogue Records A&R men demoed masters of French artists they hoped WBR would pick up for America. Most of the masters were songs in French, far from Fats. Vogue played one single by an English girl star, now in her early thirties. With dinnertime approaching, Joe picked up for American release the afternoon's only single that was sung in English, Petula Clark's "Downtown."

Smith knew that Warner Bros. Records was the world's "whitest" label. "In Burbank, they didn't really even know where the R&B stations were," summed up DJ Tom Donahue, Big Daddy in San Francisco radio. Wanting a black label for WBR, Joe Smith turned to Bob Krasnow, who'd worked at King Records and who knew James Brown personally. Even at twenty-two, Krasnow had developed four traits: a wry wit, an acute taste for fine living, an abnormally good ear for music talent, and an abusive intolerance when it came to anybody else's lousy work.

Smith defined a label to be called Loma and hired Krasnow to run the subsidiary. There, he could range wide, from sales to producing—anything, just so long as the category was R&B. Or, as Krasnow later summed it up, "I don't think Mike Maitland knew a black record from a pink record. But Joe certainly did."

With an energy that stayed revved up even in a hammock, Krasnow fit uncomfortably into Maitland's business culture. The company left him alone. When Krasnow needed attention, he found a way to get it. One day, he went into marketing head Joel Freidman's office, saying, "Joel, I gotta talk to you." Friedman pleaded, "Bob, look at my desk. I can't talk to you now." With one motion of his arm, Krasnow swept everything off Friedman's desk. "Now we can talk," he replied.

The first song Krasnow recorded turned out to be a Number One record, only not with his label. Loma released "Good Lovin'" by the Olympics, only to be beaten at radio by Atlantic Records' Ahmet Ertegun, who'd heard "Good Lovin'" on a trip to L.A. and quickly remade it with white vocal group the Rascals. When it came to a full-court press, Atlantic had better re-flexes than Loma, knew how to rush singles out to radio, knew what jocks wanted, and were better at trouncing.

Success eluded Loma, despite Krasnow's signings of Ike and Tina Turner and Redd Foxx. "We were all so young and so happy," he reminisced. "This wasn't a business. My parents used to ask 'What do you do for a living?' I'd tell them, 'I'm in the record business.' They'd say, 'What's that? There *is* no record business.' I didn't understand how profound that was. *Now* there is a record business. When I got into it, it was like getting into a sandbox."

Krasnow's first stay at Warner Bros. was well remembered. When, four years later, Randy Newman created *12 Songs*, the twelfth was called "Uncle Bob's Midnight Blues":

Goin' down to the corner, baby
Gonna have myself a drink
'Cause this shit that we been usin'
Sure confuse my thinking.

But by then Krasnow had felt that his life would be better elsewhere. He went off to join a label more filled with rapscallions, Buddah Records.[15]

For Warner and Reprise, general managers Smith and Ostin's jobs were focused: Keep shrewd ears open, and sign what will sell. Smith came up with deliberately barefoot, Cockney-sure girl Sandie Shaw (singles: "There's Always Something There to Remind Me," "Girl Don't Come," "Long Live Love," "Puppet on a String").

In his office down the dark hall, an office affording a clear view of a cow-size air conditioner sitting five feet away on a tar-paper roof, Mo also looked for artists to license. He arranged stacks of records on his desk. Some were already finished records by some overseas label, looking for a U.S. company. So much the better: Some other company had already paid the recording cost.

One day in 1964, Mo played one of the records from the stack for Krasnow. It went "Duh-DA-DA-duh-DA." As in "You Real-ly Got Me." Krasnow begged Ostin for the record for Loma, with no success. "Mo, that's your first Number One record." From that moment on, Ostin, a shrewd collector of

---

[15]Loma never did amount to much. WBR, certainly in those days, was inept at black music and black promotion. Another talented exec, Russ Reagan, came to revive (or maybe just to vive) Loma, but that ultimately pooped out. Both Krasnow and Reagan were the right guys; WBR was the wrong place.

extraordinary talent, always remembered Krasnow. But it was Mo who signed the Kinks, early and strong English Invaders. The Kinks made history not by being cute lads from London, dressed up in suits with big buttons. They made history by making thunderous rock sound and iconoclastic, sardonic lyrics, something fairly startling to ears that had grown up on Bill Haley–era rock & roll.

Both the Kinks' first releases, "You Really Got Me" and "All Day and All of the Night," hit their ceilings at Number Seven on the *Billboard* Hot 100. Both charted for months. It was a new sound for Reprise.

Sinatra uttered no contempt, even though he was no fan of "Duh-DA-DA-duh-DA." Sinatra was pure Reprise, thank you, and Loma was some Warner subsidiary. Sinatra ruled a world where "how good your voice is" mattered. Sinatra hung with his pack, Sammy, Dean, Lawford, Bishop. I flew to Vegas to take notes for an upcoming record jacket. For two nights, Frank recorded *Sinatra at the Sands* with the Count Basie Band and Quincy Jones out front conducting. Evenings at the Sands were electrifying, unmatched, pre–double knit, and I got to write down what I saw:

The house lights make us disappear, and a stage comes alive.

Tiny Sonny Payne, Basie's drummer, perches up near the back of the bandstand, whirling his sticks and thrashing his cymbals and snares like the man who invented drums. Three lines of unbuggable horn and reed experts gaze down at their well-worn charts. They've been traveling with this music for decades. Ask for "One O'Clock Jump" and they'll bring out a sheet of music that looks like a hunk of Kleenex after a flu epidemic.

During the wailing of the Basie band, those jammed, perched, squoze to the sides of the room can see an anxious figure peering out at the band from the stage wings. Catching the mood of the crowd, Frank Sinatra.

He just walks on. His pocket handkerchief folding in there nice. A bit of vest peeking out from under his tux coat. He pulls the hand mike out of the stand, glances up at the light booth where a thousand pounds of spotlight bear down on him. His shoulders hunch once, like they're absorbing the beat of Basie. He turns back to Quincy, Count & Co., smiling, extending the vamp. Go. Sonny Payne whacks his drums to stir up more groove. Then Sinatra turns back and sings. It looks effortless, the way he lazily loops the mike cable through his relaxed hands. But his face shows what he's singing. Eyes closed, head tilted, lips carefully phrasing and elocuting.

And Sinatra runs through his best. The songs are Sinatra's,

like "Come Fly," and "Crush" and "Fly Me to the Moon." Hip, up-tempo, wailing things.

And all the while, Quincy's at one side, setting the beat, Count's on the other making the beat, and Sinatra's center, demonstrating how wide and high the heart of a singing man can range.

Finally "My Kind of Town," starting deceptively with some talk about a nice city, then building choruses of mounting, modulating, upwards excitement. And then he leaves. Walks right off that stage, just like he was finished. But does the crowd want that? They yell no and more, one more, ten more, hell a lifetime more, they've got nowhere to go, dammit they want more of him.

Mr. Sinatra comes back and bows, not too low, but appreciatively. He makes "the dullest speech you'll ever have to listen to," thanking them, not for this one hour but for a lifetime of applause. He reprises "My Kind of Town." He does it with authority. Nobody follows that kind of finish, not even Frank Sinatra.

The waiters know it and start hurriedly distributing saucers with the tabs. The house lights force back up. It's like dawn, and you don't turn the sun back. Still, they keep applauding till the feeling gets hopeless . . .

The audience files slowly out into the smoke-choked casino, women adjusting their coats to the onrushing night air, to the silent walk down the concrete paths to an unenchanted evening's leftovers; men sitting down at the blackjack tables, where the waxen dealers take time during a deal to look up at their faces and ask, "You see the show?"

And the men answer, "Yeah. That Sinatra . . . he really puts on a show."

_____

And then I'd fly back to Burbank and type and retype such record liners. I once figured I'd written more than a thousand of them. I suppose, through all this, I was learning to write, though sometimes my fumbling got realized with a shock. I remember when we had Jim "Maverick" Garner come by the office (he was a contract player at Warner Bros. Television) to read part of some sales presentation for us. He looked over my script. I pushed the RECORD button on our office tape machine. He looked up and his first line was unexpected: "Who wrote this shit?"

But my life was otherwise low-budget and -stress. I lived in a little house in Studio City, collected dust balls in its corners, and had a twelve-foot-long wall just for my LPs in a custom browser box. Being a freelancer at WBR gave me freedom to roam. I dated college girls, usually one night and never again. Going to UCLA part-time, I got a master's degree, then started a doctorate at USC, which, due to a first marriage, I never completed. I told myself, "Stan, you're now making more money than your professors. So why bother?"

At work, they just let me romp. Fly up to Vegas for Sinatra? Well, I guess so. And there I dreamed about fitting right in with those Italian men wearing huge dark glasses, amusing cocktail waitresses who'd learned how to bend way over bringing me my free vodka tonic, and learning casually to say, "I'm with Frank."

For all of Vegas and tuxedoed nights, another sound was in the cards for Sinatra, and it had nothing to do with Vegas. His colleague Dean Martin had been having success with Reprise's new producer, Jimmy Bowen. Bowen drawled and shucked and jived and was your pal; he wore clothes that were too tight, or else he'd overeaten inside them. He wore aviator glasses with a beige tint and heard musical arrangements (not just tunes) in his head. He stayed up all night, drank Jack, and got hot girls. He never wore a pocket handkerchief. His drive: Just make hit singles.

He'd gone to work for Mo at Reprise, in the waning days of Reprise-before-Warner. Ostin had offered Bowen a $150-a-week salary to be Reprise's "youth A&R man." Bowen instead negotiated $100 a week and 1 percent royalty on records he produced. Mo saved the company $50 a week, so why not?

Bowen had earlier gotten a song under his skin while producing one of Dean's slow-drawl, boozy albums. He'd recorded a fitting, dreamy version of "Everybody Loves Somebody," sung soft and straight. After doing it for *Dream with Dean,* Bowen kept humming the tune. At two in the morning, after a long night of pool and beer, Bowen had turned to his housemate, Reprise sales manager Jack McGraw, and said, "I've got an idea, but I can't sing and play triplets at the same time. You play piano and beat out triplets, while I sing."

McGraw pounded out the triplets (a group of three notes performed in the time of two)—*ching*-ching-ching, *ching*-ching-ching—and Bowen sang against them. Sounded great. An hour later, Bowen called arranger Ernie Freeman, clearly a tolerant soul, and laid out his plan: They would record a new version of the song "Everybody Loves Somebody," with triplets. Martin was willing; he'd never had a hit with Reprise. Bowen next asked Ostin, who okayed the session with his typical comment—"If you feel that strong about it, go."

Triplets came to Reprise. In the studio, triplets were Ernie Freeman, an up-tempo arrangement, a piano going *klink*-klink-klink, thirty-five musicians, squeezed onto a four-track board by engineer Eddie Brackett, an exercise that caused him to sweat steadily for three hours.

Dean Martin went major, at one point becoming 20 percent of all

Warner-Reprise billing. "Everybody Loves Somebody" made it Dean Martin versus the Beatles (six Number Ones so far in '64) and the Supremes (three Number Ones in '64). Dean displaced the Beatles from Number One and went gold. Reprise had live triplets in its nursery and Kinks in its castle. The two gave Ostin what he needed most: his label's usefulness within the Warner/Reprise structure. Reprise was there to stay.

Seeing what Reprise did for Dino, Sinatra wanted his. Bowen promised Sinatra he wouldn't change a thing about how he sang but would dramatically change the music backing him, making it fit the "modern marketplace." Sinatra agreed, and they got started. Gingerly, a singles date was set at United Recorders in Hollywood. With "Softly As I Leave You"—promised to Bowen as an exclusive by its publisher—and arrangements by Ernie Freeman, musicians came in two hours early to get the charts and miking down by the time He arrived. Sinatra walked into the studio and heard two flutists playing triplets (*tweet*-tweet-tweet). From the control booth, Bowen, sweaty-palmed, watched Sinatra, who stared down at the flute players, then turned to Jimmy.

"What's that?" Sinatra asked.

"Them's triplets," Bowen answered.

"Oh."

Them triplets carried "Softly As I Leave You" to Number Twenty-seven. After that, where else do you go? To "Strangers in the Night," which got Sinatra his first Number One since "Learnin' the Blues" in 1955.

The evening before Sinatra-Bowen created "Strangers in the Night," Bowen had run into Kapp Records Vocalist Jack Jones at nearby pasta-to-the-stars restaurant, Martoni. Jones talked excitedly about a new single he'd just cut for his label: "Strangers in the Night." Bowen never flinched, but later one-punch-decked the song's publisher.

Learning of Jack Jones's leg up, Sinatra told Bowen, "I don't give a damn if *God* recorded it. I like the song, and we're gonna do it!" Bowen tacked Sinatra onto the last hour of a Dean Martin session for that night. He set up an all-night mastering session to follow Sinatra's recording. Sinatra called Ostin to describe plainly about how he'd broken his back to make the record and wanted it out. Now. Eight hundred dollars in twenties set aside for spiffs ("gratuities" to make sure things got done). Runners heading down to LAX, setting up "need a favor" courier duties with stewardesses heading off across America. For a twenty, they'd take a package with the Sinatra acetate in it to, say, O'Hare, where they'd be met with Reprise's Chicago promotion man. Another twenty and thanks and a cab to Chicago's Top Forty program director and hand over the package with "For you. From Frank." Jack Jones got leveled, flatter than the Death Valley Freeway.

Bowen's winning streak for Reprise continued for a few more years, but only a few. Sinatra led a double life, recording class albums with costars like Antonio Carlos Jobim, with white-haired producer Sonny Burke—a gent so distinguished he looked like he'd star in a bourbon ad—in the control room. Occasionally, Sinatra recorded singles with Bowen. To Sinatra, the Bowen singles, no matter how career important, were just low class.

"Frank never really enjoyed recording with Jimmy," Mo once told me. "He was never fully comfortable with that kind of music. After 'Strangers in the Night,' he would never perform the song. He ridiculed the song, made fun of it. He never thought it was a good song."

Bowen, not truly a company-man kind of guy, had now upped his producer percentage to 3 percent and was making huge bucks, maybe two hundred thousand dollars a year, living with Keely Smith, dating Nancy Sinatra, and still staying up till his eyes felt like corks.

Maitland's team of Ostin and Smith was paying off big. The offices at Warner Bros. Records now had *two* labels crowded into lousy square footage. One men's room served for all, and in that one room, one potty. Maitland, a regular man, hit that potty each morning at 9:12 sharp. Set your watch by it. Warner Bros. art director Ed Thrasher actually did.

One morning, Maitland found the potty occupied. Mike came back in five minutes. Still, somebody sitting in there. Third time. Looking very uncomfortable by now, Maitland was. Didn't want to pull any presidential rank but . . . Whoever was sitting there, he wore checked pants and two-tone shoes. (Mike finally went downstairs to pee.) Thrasher had set up a mannequin in checkered trousers sitting on the only stool in the room. Later in the day, he persuaded Murray Gitlin in finance to dress in the pants, then hang out in the halls for Mike to see.

The world at 3701 Warner had loosened up. Accounting paid for an impoverished secretary's burial of her newly dead husband; the funeral cost was allocated under "Personnel Relocation." The days were better. Nobody needed to tell Joe Smith to say something funny. A blessed, pretax adolescence was felt by all in that old machine shop in Burbank.

In the sizzle-soggy days of August 1964, setting a tradition of finding the hottest, most humid hotels to host sales meetings, it was Las Vegas and "The Wonderful World of Entertainment." Joel Friedman convened our North American distributors, two hundred owners, sales managers, and salespeople. For indie distributors, ours was now the Big One, not like some convention for two-bit Liberty Records where the best album might be *The Chipmunks' Greatest Hits, Volume 2*. For this one in Vegas, distributors showed up with polished shoes, as well-to-do businessmen. They, too, were At The Sands.

"The door to the suite opened, and Frank Sinatra came in," recalled

New York promotion man Marvin Deane. "At first, there was silence. I'll never forget the look on their faces . . . I remember being in the corner with Dean Martin and his manager when suddenly it was empty all around us, except across the room where they'd pinned Sinatra against the wall and were taking pictures."

At nine the next morning, the business session began with the introduction of WBR's new credit manager, "Jules Seder," a small, floppy-lipped guy with too little hair who assaulted the audience with vitriol. "Where's the distributor from New Orleans? What's your name? Henry Hildebrand? Saturday night in New Orleans; cut 'em down, Henry! You dummies are all sitting here and the company's going under. Sinatra knows. He's drunk upstairs. Dumb dago. Mike Maitland, where's he? Jewish fag. Joe Smith? Pain in the ass. That woman—what's your name, dear? Yeah you, in the trick-or-treat glasses. Look at her: sitting there like a nun, and two hundred guys in heat."

A yet-to-be discovered Don Rickles got a standing ovation.

New fall albums were introduced, maintaining careful division between the two labels. Showtime. Engineer Lowell Frank pushed the tape player's PLAY button, and the show started. I watched our script, pushing the NEXT FRAME button on words we'd circled. Art director Ed Thrasher watched the Dukane film strip projector show still after still. Up on the screen and out through the speakers, there were Peter, Paul & Mary, wow, then there was Allan Sherman, the audience convulsing. Ripping through Trini, Dean, Sammy, Cosby, Kinks, Newhart. Climax of the show, sound and slides, came with the about-to-be-released Sinatra-Basie "It Might As Well Be Swing," which did indeed.

Hit after hit, it felt like, ending with what Warner's Canada guy, Phil Rose, remembered as "the band wailing as Frank and the Count flew us to the moon. Touchdown! Pandemonium! The most dour of the distributors were waving, cheering, whistling. It was a sight I had not before encountered in the record business, nor since."

By December, Warner/Reprise had four consecutive months of more than $1 million in sales. The labels' executives, like the Yankees, had learned to hit homers.

Significant Warner/Reprise Albums

1963

Reprise: Count Basie ("I Can't Stop Loving You") • Trini Lopez (*At P.J.'s*) • Dean Martin (*Dino Latino* and *Country Style*) • Jack Nitzsche ("The Lonely Surfer") • *Sinatra/Basie* • Frank Sinatra (*The Concert Sinatra*)
Warner Bros.: The Cascades ("Rhythm of the Rain") • Jimmy Durante ("September Song") • The Marketts ("Out of Limits") • Peter, Paul & Mary (*Moving,* including "Puff the Magic Dragon"; and *In the Wind,* including "Blowin' in the Wind," "Don't Think

Twice, It's All Right") • The Routers ("Let's Go!") • Allan Sherman (*My Son, the Celebrity* and *My Son, the Nut,* including "Hello Mudduh, Hello Fadduh")

1964

Reprise: Bing Crosby/Frank Sinatra/Fred Waring (*America, I Hear You Singing*) • Sammy Davis, Jr. ("The Shelter of Your Arms") • The Kinks ("You Really Got Me") • Dean Martin ("Everybody Loves Somebody" and *Dream with Dean* and "The Door Is Still Open to My Heart") • Sandie Shaw ("Girl Don't Come") • Frank Sinatra/Count Basie (*It Might As Well Be Swing*) • Frank Sinatra ("Softly, As I Leave You") • *Robin and the 7 Hoods* soundtrack

Warner Bros.: Freddy Cannon ("Abigail Beecher") • Bill Cosby (*Is a Very Funny Fellow, Right!* and *I Started Out As a Child*) • Dick and DeeDee ("Thou Shalt Not Steal") • Bob Newhart (*Faces Bob Newhart*) • Peter, Paul & Mary (*In Concert*) • Allan Sherman (*For Swingin' Livers Only!*)

6

It was the picnic days of this business, when the sun over Burbank warmed many while few got burned—days when you were startled because some guy in your bank had learned your name, sir—during such days one Rule of Life applies. That rule goes, "You never know how good times are, till they be gone." It would take some years to have that rule make sense to us.

If Vegas '64 had been tingly, '65's convention was ecstasy. By then, bankers had indeed learned new names. For me, I realized these Sixties better when, on a road trip, I didn't have to sleep in a twin-bedded hotel room with Joel Friedman, WB's VP of Snoring. My own hotel room![16] Once I got an expense account, I measured rented rooms by their bathroom amenities: new soap, wrapped in paper, was a step up; then came the lotions eventually, lotions that nestled in woven baskets; then came the tiles of gold-wrapped chocolate on a fresh pillowcase, leading to the sweetest of dreams. The ultimate amenity, however, turned out to be European bathroom amenities, packaged in France, labeled in French. My favorite was a two-inch box labeled *"Bonnet de Douche."* Since I had lived a year in Paris, I was able to translate such labels for my fellow Warner Bros. travelers.[17]

At '65's regional distributor meetings, engineer Lowell Frank would play a stereo blast of "The Stars and Stripes Forever" to stir up the salesmen there gathered for more Sinatra and maybe a new Petula. Joe Smith indulged his colleagues with a Warner/Reprise company look. He'd driven into Beverly Hills, to the clothier Carroll & Company, and ordered a dozen snappy executive navy blue blazers, tailored to each colleague, compliments of the labels, thank you. On the breast pocket was stitched a double-logo patch:

---

[16]My early motel rooms were not big on fancies and were characterized by bathrooms with used green soap. It got so that I could sense upward progress in my business life by my hotel rooms. I had first known progress after college, when once a motel room had in it a bed with a vibrating mattress. "Magic Fingers," it was called. For twenty-five cents, it buzzed.

[17]*"Bonnet de douche"* is French for "hat of the shower."

WB+R. All blazers were identical, except for Smith's. As the arranger of this, he had his own blazer made with a splashy red lining, giving him a slight edge in any bullring. With pride, we executives referred to ourselves as the Men in Blue. Clad in our blazers, we strode into convention halls snappily, actually feeling 50 percent snappy, 50 percent foolish. Matching red-and-silver-striped neckties, too.

Some three hundred people attended WBR's August-September march-plus-album-presentation as we flew in from Los Angeles, Chicago, Atlanta, and New York City. This filmstrip promotion featured a strong line of comedy and romance, a script that dealt with three female spies from an organization called NASTY bent on stealing Warner's new release plans. *Billboard* noted that "especially effective was a scene of company president Mike Maitland stripping open his shirt in a phone booth to reveal his true identity: Superman."

Like Mom's butterscotch, future hits poured from us Men in Blue. The albums we showed were easy sellers: singers and comics you liked, words you understood, performers who dressed neatly. They were safe, entertaining artists, ones whom TV could frame full figure without fear of pelvic pumps, artists who got decent haircuts, artists whose idea of a power drug was Extra-Strength Anacin. The chart impact of these bestsellers brought to Burbank an aura of middle-class hip. Without blue blazers, one after another, in marched songs and comedy routines about "Downtown," "Lemon Tree," "Abe Lincoln," "Puff," "Camp Granada," "Windy," and "Houston."

To the studio, we felt so good and green: Jack Warner called up Maitland to tell him he now was a vice president of the whole studio, with a long-term (two years was forever for Jack Warner) contract. Warner's move indicated the larger, more successful status of its record company. Sales at WBR reached $20 million per year. Maitland, his organization succeeding as Conkling's had not, started lunching in Warner's nymphs-muraled Exec Dining Room, across the street, rather than dally with his own company execs, who often walked one block in the opposite direction to lunch at a Chinese deli wondrously named Kosherama, on whose menu egg roll and pastrami were created equal.

Yes, 1965 felt entirely different. So much so that I suspended my doctoral studies, went back on salary at WBR, and married a just-twenty-one sunshine blonde named Gail, who became instantly pregnant with son one, Christopher.

More a manager/grower of a company than a signer of talent—and he admitted that—Maitland fully delegated the music making to Ostin and Smith. Maitland looked into strengthening the labels on other fronts:

- He hired Phil Rose away from WBR's Canadian licensee, Compo, to move WBR into international markets.

- He named five vice presidents for Warner/Reprise, something the company had lacked since the departure of Hal Cook: Mo Ostin (GM/Reprise), Joe Smith (GM/Warner), Phil Rose (International), Ed West (Treasurer), and Joel Friedman (Marketing).
- He moved Reprise A&R man Sonny Burke, whose gentlemanly producing style was less in demand these days, across the street to be Warner Bros. Pictures' movie-music chief. Fewer than ever were acts using producers who turned out four songs in three hours in the Sinatra fashion.

Warner Bros. Studios, hearing something about me (hip young writer across the street in Records; got a couple of Grammys for Sinatra notes; wears his hair a little long), called me to write a screenplay of an obscure novel, *Night Moves*, about Beatniks, set in San Francisco. It was never made, but I got paid.[18]

As part of my screenwriter deal, the studio paid for a weekend in the city's North Beach, so I could walk the hills and get a feel for Beat Generation hangouts. But this was 1966, and though I stayed in a purple-colored motel, I found that the cool Beat Generation had fled 'Frisco some time earlier. I noticed squiggly-lettered posters for the weekend's rock concerts being staged by Bill Graham at the Fillmore and Chet Helms at the Avalon. I squinted at addresses on them, yellow letters on orange backgrounds, and went. I walked into screaming, an asylum filled with agonized noise, rock with no form, electric guitars feeling up speakers and the speakers screeching back "rape." This sensory assault to my eyes, my ears, dancers swirling around washtubs filled with dry ice that billowed up to the ceiling, black light turning white clothes into blue blazes, strobes hot enough to shock the blind, dazed dancers dressed in Goodwill velours, men in fringed vests who, perhaps to *some* music, twirled and twirled. I had stumbled into very early hippiedom. Acid-spiked wedding cakes. Middle-aged little old ladies wandering stoned through Golden Gate park. It was a kick. I took care to follow a new record business rule: Don't drink the punch.

I was told I should wander other streets, head south from North Beach, like over where Ashbury crosses Haight, where I learned that euphoria came from smoking banana peels. I browsed in what were later named head shops: beads, ankh necklaces, ZigZag paper, exotica for those who would be free at last from the tyranny of the bra. My personal mantra became "wow."

---

[18]The only screenplay I wrote that ever came out was for what one reviewer quite fairly has called "the worst movie ever." I never tell people that movie's name and excuse it by saying, "I didn't write the story, only the dialogue." (The dialogue was awful.) At a film festival many years later, this film was shown, and I was on a panel afterward. I explained to the audience that "watching this film for the first time in thirty years was the most embarrassing experience I can remember since my first marriage."

On my return to Burbank, I mentioned my weekend to Mo and Joe—especially the screechy-music part. Like every other label in America, by 1966, Warner and Reprise were agog about how the record world had divided into two parts: (1) the Beatles and (2) All Else. Like every other label, Warner and Reprise lacked Beatles, so we'd wavered. Our world had been overturned by Beatlemania. The lads had turned rock into music that adults, too, could accept. Some labels imitated the Beatles, but did so from afar, missing the point. Most other labels tut-tutted about mop-tops. Very few labels went to see, hear, and feel for themselves. None of us realized what was at stake: life or death.

Since Mo and Joe had been signing acts, they'd never invested in a whopper, like Johnny Mathis or Andy Williams, acts more suited to a deluxe company, not us in an old machine shop. Mo and Joe had to reach under that top level, had to experiment. They had the freedom to do a bit of it.

Mo Ostin and I did a weekend in San Francisco with our wives. I tour-guided us through streets far from Union Square. For Mo, the visit turned out to be an ear-opener. In Mo's way, hungry for the new and next, he returned to Burbank and listened even more to fresher voices, harked unto younger people.

Joe Smith had also been called to San Francisco by WBR promo man Walt Calloway. There he reunited with fellow DJ, sumo-size Tom Donahue, who had switched from Top Forty to Infinity. Donahue had opened a club called Mother's, in North Beach, the first psychedelic nightclub, designed like a giant womb. Before most radios could even tune in FM, Donahue played "freak 'n' roll" with no pimple-cream commercials. While he was dining one night at Ernie's, a phone was placed beside Joe's crêpes. "The Dead are at the Avalon," said Tom Donahue. "They want to meet with you. Now."

Joe in his suit and the missus with pearls walked into a ballroom that seemed make-believe but was not; where rock acts did not think about rhyme schemes; where rock singers replaced doo-wop lyrics with visionary images of purple oceans, words whose meaning was, to Smith, as clear as the taxi driver's Farsi. Wet colors oiled across stage-filling screens; the Mime Troupe whirled, then posed white-faced; old films mixed up your eyes (you were allowed up to three eyes per person); dancers moved to local bands, others sprawled on the floor, painting each other's bodies. Acid tripping. A next generation had come to rock, enough to freak out an Elvis, you bet.

Smith worried how he was dressed. Donahue answered, "No one will ever notice. You look like you're in costume."

Over the din, Smith yelled into Donahue's ear, "Tom, I don't think Jack Warner will understand this." But Smith believed in Donahue, and Smith took chances. The record-business economy works like a roulette table: You spread your bets. Smith signed the Grateful Dead, December 28, 1966, to an unprecedented contract. It wasn't so much the money (thirty-five hundred dollars to sign the contract, then sixty-five hundred dollars more against the first ten thousand units). Smith gave the Dead more control than Petula Clark or Dean Martin ever asked for: from the studio, to the producer, to the songs, to the cover art. For his work in putting together the deal, Donahue could choose either a flat fee or a percentage of the Dead's future sales. Donahue took the flat fifteen hundred dollars.

THE GRATEFUL DEAD:
Look for awhile at the China Cat Sunflower
Proudwalking jingle in the midnight sun
Copperdome Bodhi drip a silver kimono
Like a crazyquilt stargown through a dream night wind[19]

More than San Francisco called out to us. Closer to home, down two Los Angeles boulevards: one called Sunset, the other called Laurel Canyon.

"Laurel," as it was called, became a Reprise lode of gold.[20] The canyon had become home to guitar-playing songwriters, some who could sing their songs, others who stretched wide any previous definition of the word "singer." In the 1960s, the wood-sided, vine-covered shacks/houses in Laurel Canyon were homes to Los Angeles County's (a) *lowest percentage* of regular working wage earners, as well as the county's (b) *highest percentage* of living-room floors furnished with a mattress. In another age, maybe you'd call Laurel an "artists' colony." In this age, you'd call it "uh gee far mmm out." Hippies abounded.

Residents were a combination of the cream of West Coast musicians joined by atonal kooks. There was Barry Friedman, a.k.a. Frazier Mohawk, who'd drive his sports car dressed in a King Kong outfit. But there was also Andy Wickham, a too-thin, slight English lad in his twenties, articulate, honest, a cannabis puffer. Wickham lived in Laurel amid its songwriting singers. And, like them, he was awake odd hours. Wickham discerned some

---

[19]Lyrics by Robert Hunter, the Dead's lyricist, who claims strangers come up to him and say they understand "China Cat Sunflower." Every word.

[20]Laurel the street was steep, a narrow two-laner heading up from Los Angeles, into the Santa Monica Mountains. It once had been a dirt road that stopped before it reached over the mountain's top. After World War I, Laurel's streets had been built by a county service, apparently following three orders: (1) All streets must constantly bend, as if laid out by earthworms; (2) no street may lie flat; all must go up and down; and (3) all streets must be built out of concrete guaranteed to crack. At first, mainly weekend houses had been built there; then they'd fallen into neglect and after that into the hands of those who, for housing, liked it cheap.

of their music as better, some of it worse, but at least Andy could still discern. Mo Ostin—with no choice but to gamble on the fresh and unexpected, since his tried-and-true had pooped out on Palm Canyon Drive—liked Wickham's good, heady signing ideas. All such signings were small-money deals, spare change to Reprise.

Wickham became Reprise's A&R liaison to Laurel Canyon (and elsewhere). He would bring to Ostin a remarkable streak of signings: Joni Mitchell, Van Morrison, Jethro Tull, and more. Wickham had become Laurel Canyon's employment agency. By 1967, Reprise would at last become identified with the hippest of times.

After signing the Grateful Dead, Joe Smith sensed that "San Francisco was it. There were new bands everywhere, and each of them could be signed for a $20,000 advance. I went to Mike Maitland and asked for $250,000 to scoop up handfuls of them. He thought it was too risky."

If there ever was a vintage year to be San Francisco's leading, hometown record label, 1965 was it. Autumn Records had that hometown advantage. Autumn was owned and run part-time, by Tom Donahue and his DJ partner, Bobby Mitchell. In contrast to Donahue's three hundred pounds of sonority, Mitchell was diminutive and hilarious. Like Smith, both had left the East right after the payola hearings. It was move or be prosecuted, they figured, and the congressional committee lacked funds to investigate west of the Mississippi.

By mid-1965, Donahue and Mitchell had become top San Francisco DJs on KYA. They'd become entrepreneurs as well: They had a management/publishing arm run by a youngster named Carl Scott; they owned and ran the *Tempo* tip sheet (advisory to DJs); they put on major rock concerts at the Cow Palace, some produced by Joe Smith; they owned racehorses.

Autumn Records already had recording contracts with nineteen-year-old producer Sylvester Stewart (soon to become Sly Stone), plus artist contracts with the Beau Brummels; the Warlocks (to become the Grateful Dead); Bobby Freeman; the Mojo Men; the Vejtables; and the Tikis (to become Harpers Bizarre).

Autumn's master tapes were tied up in a recording studio. Autumn couldn't pay its bills, even enough to free its own tapes. Donahue and Mitchell had spent all the money coming into the company on themselves. They needed ten grand. Casually, Warners purchased Autumn Records—its acts and its debt—for $12,749.33, plus a 2 percent producing override to Donahue and Mitchell. On this deal, Joe didn't even have to call Burbank.

"They just pissed it all away," remembered their office manager, Carl Scott. "If we'd had our shit together, Autumn could have been the most devastating thing to come out of San Francisco. Those two guys—Donahue and

Mitchell—were unbelievable. We could have had what I think Joe Smith thought he was buying."

Once it was bought, Smith found our in-house producers too busy with bigger acts to bother with the leftovers of Autumn. He had to turn over the Autumn sort-out to a kid who'd just been hired to listen to unsolicited tapes and demos: a slight and ever-worried boy named Lenny Waronker.

Lenny's credentials were born in his bassinet. His father, Simon Waronker, invented Liberty Records (and was the "Simon" in "The Chipmunks" song, though don't you know that's not what he'd like being remembered for). As a teen, Liberty would become Lenny's second home. For him, it was a place, like the engine room of a ship, where you learned how this business worked. His childhood pal was from Hollywood's musical Newman family; Lenny and Randy summered together in Tahoe. Lenny never considered any other business. He studied music and business at USC during the mornings, at Liberty after school. Upon graduating, he'd become a song plugger for Liberty's publishing division.

In April 1966, Lenny moved over to Warner/Reprise's A&R department, handling overflow. Tagging along were his pals Randy Newman, Leon Russell, and Van Dyke Parks. "Lenny didn't even shave then," Bob Krasnow recalled, "not that he does now."

Deputizing Lenny to pare down Autumn, Joe told him, "You'll cut these groups. It'll be cheap. It'll be fast. But first you have to hear them." Waronker did not hear much to save. Warner/Reprise dropped Autumn acts like the Vejtables, the Styx, and the Casualiers. He divided up the acts they wanted to keep: WBR got the Beau Brummels and the Tikis. Loma Records took Bobby Freeman. Reprise got the Mojo Men.

"Lenny met with the Beau Brummels and he met with the Tikis," Carl Scott recalled. "Lenny holds that I sat on the desk behind him and glared at him, and he was peeing in his pants he was so nervous. The Brummels were heavyweights. They were the stars at the time. Lenny was scared to death in his little black suit."

"Lenny had on a suit and tie," recalled Ted Templeman, the leader of the Tikis. The Tikis had already covered "The Lion Sleeps Tonight" quite badly. "We were from a whole different school. I remember thinking how slick Lenny was. He had a gold ID bracelet and really looked the Hollywood part. But we were excited because he told us, 'We'll make a record and use accordions.' He said he had a song that would probably do well for us."

The Beau Brummels, three guys from San Francisco, fit nicely into the English invasion: They had Beatle-like haircuts; the group's name sounded hip, Carnaby Street–born; and people browsing in stores under "Bea" for Beatles would find a neighboring "Bea" for Beau.

The purchase of Autumn and its artists would, musically, turn Warner and Reprise 180 degrees permanently, ending any bias toward the middle-class-adult album act. The one who had the ears was Lenny Waronker.

In 1966, Waronker started recording with Harpers Bizarre, né the Tikis. Day one, with Randy Newman on piano, they covered Simon and Garfunkel's "The 59th Street Bridge Song (Feelin' Groovy)". The single exploded—Top Twenty. Smith made it very very clear: A full Harpers *album* was needed. Quick. To rush a Harpers album, Waronker leaned on his pals. Randy Newman agreed to toss in "Debutante's Ball" and "Simon Smith and the Amazing Dancing Bear," but only if he was allowed to write his own arrangements. Leon Russell wrote two tunes and arranged. Van Dyke Parks wrote "Come to the Sunshine."[21]

Waronker's style of producing was thoughtful. He took pains. His most-used answer, said wistfully, helplessly, was "Gee, I don't know." But he did. He created what's been described as "the Burbank Sound," the nimble delights that range from Randy Newman to Maria Muldaur.

Downstairs on A&R row (it took imagination to glorify four offices that way), a generation was changing. New kids gathered inside WB/R. They knew it was more than triplets. It seemed like in minutes institutions of the early-Sixties music business went poof-poof-poof. Weekly TV shows *Shindig* and *Hullabaloo,* both lip-sync hours catering to the Carnaby and folkie crowds, *poof.* Acts with huge musical talent, "good acts," Steve and Eydie, found themselves off radio and being booked suddenly only in Vegas lounges, *poof.* Record labels that believed deeply in the *best* in music—whether that music was like Dot, with Lawrence Welk, *poof.*

To follow up "Strangers in the Night," Sinatra became determined to put out a gag record—"Din"—a straight reading of Kipling's poem until, at the part where Gunga gets shot as he's blowing the bugle, the bugle whimpers away as Gunga dies. It was all supposed to be one *very* funny joke.

Sinatra would (or could) not listen to reason, no matter how Mo delayed putting out the single in hopes this turkey would somehow just waddle its way out of Reprise's oven. Sinatra got headstrong, which was no fun, and Ostin was caught on the eighth hole at El Cab, where a caddy rushed up to him, announcing, "Frank Sinatra's on the line!" Fortunately, on a tree nearby, management had installed a phone, perhaps for less-pressing emergencies.

---

[21]"Feelin' Groovy" easily in itself paid for the purchase of Autumn Records. Waronker became hot stuff around Warner Bros. Records for roughly thirty years, ending up as its president. Carl Scott, who'd come down to sort through Autumn's cartons, hid out, collected his salary, hoping no one would catch on. Even into Y2K, Scott continued to work the halls of WBR, no longer hiding. Teddy Templeman had a distinguished, thirty-five-year career as producer at WBR, responsible for such acts as the Doobie Brothers, Little Feat, and Van Halen.

"Yes, Frank?"

"How dare you countermand my instructions! I told you to get that fucking record out, and you were supposed to get that record *out*. I own this company!"

"Oh, it was held up? Oh, let me see what I can do about it. I'll attend to it immediately." After taking a nine on the par-three, Ostin told WB's production manager, Matt Gilligan, "Get that record out!"

Ostin had to report the reaction from radio to Sinatra, where even Sinatra's biggest supporters had unanimous reactions: "Worst piece of crap . . . embarrassing . . . going to hurt his image." Expecting the worst, using an office phone, Ostin called down to the Springs to report the word of mouth coming in on "Din." Sinatra was calm, as if nothing had happened: "Well, why don't you stop it and call it off the market?"

Ostin got better and better at dealing with artists. As for Sinatra, he was occupied otherwise. Frank married Mia Farrow in a five-minute ceremony in Las Vegas. Jimmy Bowen, who had dated Frank's daughter Nancy, instead married Keely Smith, ex-wife of Louis Prima. Nancy had been celebrated for "These Boots Are Made for Walkin'," her song of controlled aggression and Reprise's first domestically generated rock tune; then paired up with her dad for a *Billboard* Number One, "Somethin' Stupid." Both singles exploded. Gunga Din fell, to our relief, on his sword.

Not all Warner/Reprise signings sizzled. After "Din," Smith also dabbled in the tasteless. He issued "They're Coming to Take Me Away," recorded by Jerry Samuels with a drum, tambourine, and no other musicians, for a total cost of thirty dollars: Twenty-five went for the studio cost (ninety minutes), plus five dollars to rent the hand-crank siren for the ending. Samuels released it under the alias Napoleon XIV. Without a B side, out of desperation, the A side was played backward, listed in *Phonolog* as "Ah-Ah, Yawa Em Ekat Ot Gnimoc Er'yeht."[22]

Advancing this Battle of Taste, in 1967 Ostin responded by signing a group called the Electric Prunes.[23]

What all of us at WBR were doing had little to do with being distin-

---

[22]It became a #3 single, with album to follow. The album was all Samuels, but doing different voices, like a wee girl in "Twinkle, Twinkle Little Star," which opened with a celeste and bicycle bell, demurely, as the girl recites, "Thirty days hath September, April June and no wonder, All the rest have peanut butter, All except my dear grandmother." Original copies of this album have sold for $100.

[23]The Prunes' third album, *Mass in F Minor,* would be sung entirely in Latin and would be reviewed by new rock rag *Rolling Stone* as "sort of like having tone-deaf monks singing Gregorian chants. The instrumental work of the rest of the album is in an uncontrolled feedback bag, which means that after a tranquil 'Holy, Holy, Holy,' Jimi Hendrix on a bad night comes bombing into the silence."

guished or tasteful. We just felt around for Sixties kids. Didn't try to be respectable but did try being in touch. Even with goofballs like Napoleon and the Prunes, the odds for success seemed to tilt our way, toward Burbank. In restaurants, we executives began ordering wines from lists, using French words far loftier than "red."

As music was shedding its crinolines, the incubators that were Laurel and the Haight meant nothing to New York's financial set. Among Manhattan bankers, very few even paid attention to Hollywood studios, let alone to guitar-playing hippies. The same inattention was eminently true of Jack Warner, now age seventy-four, a man more comfortable with Bette Davis than Joni Mitchell, a king with a wall around his Burbank castle, immortalized by his name painted on its water tower. Warner used that as his argument ender, telling dissenters, "See whose name is painted on that tower?" From our offices across the street, we were about to see, in the years to come, that tower's name repainted again and again.

The two bankers in Jack Warner's life, however, saw the Burbank movie studio drifting, near idle. By habit, those two men had always stood in the shadows. East Coast financiers who bought, sold, financed, and squeezed. They represented just two investing companies: the First National Bank of Boston's Serge Semenenko, and New York's Allen & Company's Charlie Allen. Both men ducked photographers. Each presumed he was the *real* movie business. Allen and Semenenko believed that the folks out in Hollywood just worked for the East Coast's bottom lines.

In 1966, these two financiers decided that Jack Warner was an aging mogul, holding on too long. They saw his picture company now being funded by its record and music-publishing profits. To protect their investments from out-of-touch management, Semenenko and Allen decided to buy up and transfer Jack Warner's one-third share of WB's stock. Warner, they believed, needed to retire, like it or not.

Both Semenenko and Allen were investors who made sure their investments paid off, whatever it took. Charlie Allen, patriarch of Allen & Co., longtime buddy of Jack Warner, had been known in the trade for over a decade as the "Godfather of the New Hollywood." Allen was thin, his skin pale and dry. He lived on the phone and at the Carlyle Hotel, just a bit uptown from his financial colleague, Semenenko.

Variety once dubbed Serge Semenenko "the Medici of the movies." Vice chairman of Boston's First National Bank, Semenenko spoke in a heavy Odessan accent, result of his White Russian banker's family getting the hell out before the Reds took over. A 1920s M.B.A. from Harvard followed, and he'd joined First National as a hundred-dollar-a-month clerk in 1926 and stayed there for decades. His professional specialty was engineering complicated mergers to save ailing companies.

First National let Semenenko run deals the way he wanted: from his plush suite in New York's Pierre Hotel, from Acapulco, from the French Riviera. Where most bankers reminded you of starch, Semenenko reminded you of *foie*.

Like Charlie Allen, Semenenko was thought by many to have been a man who'd saved the slumping movie industry in the 1950s. From his industry-saving maneuvers, he had benefited personally, borrowing millions in a shadowy way from a charity he was involved with, then using those millions to buy, for his own account, enough stock in Warner Bros. Studios to make himself its second-largest shareholder. As an insider, Semenenko knew when to buy in and, more important, when to cash out.

At First National, Semenenko was on his own way to retirement but held his job long enough to manipulate one more coup: the sale of Jack Warner's stock. In 1966, Semenenko and Allen had started leaning on Jack L. Come to your senses, Jack. Conserve your assets, Jack. Do you want to give it all to Uncle Sam?

Warner finally told Semenenko and Allen that for him to sell, he needed three things: first, an assurance that the Warner name would continue; second, an assurance that key personnel would remain; and third, $32 million. Not necessarily in that order. That fit into the bankers' plans.

Just as Sonny and Cher were floating down Colorado Boulevard as grand marshals of 1967's Rose Parade, Semenenko and Allen were getting the price right for Warner's shares. With Jack Warner fixed on his buyout price, Allen and Semenenko were now able to do what they knew how to do: find a buyer they could control. It didn't take but a minute; they already had a buyer in their pocket. His name was Elliott Hyman, the TV syndicator whose 7 Arts company, back in the 1950s, had bought Warner Bros. Studios' backlog of films.

Since that buy in the 1950s, 7 Arts had been growing sideways, not up. The D-level company had been characterized in Hollywood as "producer Ray Stark, running up and down Wilshire Boulevard, making deals." Partner Elliott Hyman stayed in Manhattan, reselling used movies.

In 1960, five years after the TV buy, 7 Arts had *again* needed money, and it had turned once more to investment underwriters Allen and Semenenko. They took 7 Arts "public," changing it from a privately held company to an open-to-all-investors company listed on the American Stock Exchange.

For all the years and deals, Semenenko and Allen had never gotten their money back from their early loans. Now, a two-part deal could fix that. First, 7 Arts would buy Warner's stock low. Then, short pause, WB+7A would be sold for a high amount. This simple buy-low/sell-high maneuver would make Semenenko and Allen's investments pay fat.

The deal between WB and 7A—the final buying-out of Jack Warner—

got signed. 7 Arts Associated Corporation bought, "for investment, 1,573,861 shares of Common Stock of Warner Bros. Pictures, Inc., from Jack Leonard Warner." The purchase price was $20 per share. Jack Warner's 1,573,861 shares equaled 32.6 percent of the outstanding WB stock. Control of the studio, its record company, and its publishing company ended up costing 7 Arts and paying Jack Warner $32,477,220. Put another way, that castle and water tower in Burbank, and all the music attached to it, had a stock value of $100 million.

Jack Warner, cashed out, drove his Bentley away from Burbank, his unnaturally black hair slicked back, his mustache razor-cut pencil thin, his face evenly tanned, a post-tax $24 million in his pocket. Warner knew how it worked. He told his son, "Yeah, today I'm Jack L. Warner, but wait until tomorrow. I'll just be another rich Jew." And, in fact, that came true. Without a studio, Jack Warner no longer had people willing to show up for the weekend's tennis games, no one to call out, "Great shot, Chief."

Warner afterward produced independent films, including *Camelot*. He died of edema at eighty-six, on September 9, 1978, eleven years after the last of the other four brothers, Albert, who had died at eighty-three, in 1967. In 1978, Jack Warner's home was worth $15 million. In 1991, David Geffen bought 1801 Angelo Drive, from the Warner heirs, furnished, for $47.5 million.

Jack Warner's shares, however, constituted only one-third ownership of the shebang. 7 Arts wanted the other two-thirds. With its advisers, 7 Arts persuaded the other major shareholders of WB to sell out their remaining 3,376,191 shares at $5 each: $16,880,955. Still more banker help was needed. The full purchase of Warner Bros. Pictures, Inc., cost (rounded off):

To Jack Warner:	$32,000,000
Outstanding Shares:	16,900,000
Convertible Debentures:	33,800,000
New Common Stock:	42,000,000
Liabilities Assumed:	59,000,000

Elliott Hyman hardly had that kind of cash in his pocket. With the backing of Semenenko and Allen, however, the tail bought the dog. Cost of the studio: $184,742,000.

In August 1967, the record charts made it clear: Warner/Reprise was doing things right. The company had eighteen albums on the charts. Of those, seven were released that very month. For the first time in its history, WB/R had as many albums on the charts as the big guy, Columbia.

Maitland was called across the street to the main office, handed a pen, and asked to sign an "Amendment to the Certificate of Incorporation," changing the name of his record label. He signed. Starting now, Maitland was running the same thing; it was just renamed: Warner Bros.–7 Arts Records. An inflexible, yucky new logo—it looked like Germanic plinth—started to appear on all our album jackets. A rigid financial policy was imposed. Within days, a scaffold was hoisted up on the water tower and WARNER BROS.–7 ARTS was painted.

Elliott Hyman was not into studios forever nor water towers forever. With his son Ken in the studio chief's chair in Burbank, Elliott Hyman stayed up in his deco moderne New York office on Fifth Avenue, doodling out some next deal. Hyman told me he had a rule of thumb: "When I buy a company, I hope eventually I'll sell it for four times my buying price."

We in Burbank/Records seldom heard from Ken Hyman or anyone at 7 Arts, which was fine. We heard from bankers, most often through a younger-generation executive, Allen & Company's Alan Hirschfield, who'd been hands-on in doing the deal. Hirschfield was an impressive business type who, when he visited my office, made me feel simultaneously inferior and at ease. Hirschfield was good and smart. He dated stun-your-eyes beauties, but he lacked one thing: He was not Elliott Hyman's son.

While Seven Arts was acquiring Warner Bros. Studios (and Records), Hirschfield had been envisioning a grander WB-7A, to use his words, "a leisure-time conglomerate." He made frequents trips out to Burbank to build "corporate value," making WB-7A worth more *next* time it would be sold. The quickest way to build was to buy undervalued companies, add them to what you have, and make the two worth three. It was called "conglomeration," and it was all the business rage. Hirschfield saw another record company, Atlantic, as conglomeratable. The label had just turned down an offer from ABC Records for $4 million, even though $4 million meant a whoppo $1 million in cash in the pockets of Atlantic's three principles, brothers Ahmet and Nesuhi Ertegun and Jerry Wexler. Atlantic had balked not at the price but at a different ABC demand: indemnification against any lawsuits.

The Atlantic label had, however, revealed itself prone to seduction.

Within Atlantic, the prospect of cashing out and getting hard money for years of hard work held appeal. While flirtations like ABC's had come and gone, Atlantic Records stayed its course and built up its catalogue, even though its catalogue, in this time of music transition, hardly felt like an annuity you really could lean against. So where was the big payoff, where was the financial cushion for the brothers Ertegun and Jerry Wexler?

Atlantic had been half aroused when Alan Hirschfield and Elliott Hyman called. Sitting on the seller's side of the table, behind the ashtrays and yellow pads, were Atlantic's three owners and its longtime attorney, the considerate Ted Jaffe. Preliminary flirts between seller and buyer took place, learning what concessions each side might make, the autonomy conditions under which Atlantic demanded to continue operating, its selling price.

Then "we'll call you," followed by months of "thinking that one over" and "checking that out."

Elliott Hyman was uncertain about buying Atlantic. After all, Seven Arts already had one record label, two if you counted Reprise. He flew out to California, in charge. He'd moved Hirschfield off the field to accommodate his son, Ken, who was spooked by the Wall Street glamour guy. Elliott then passed by his son to huddle directly with Warner Bros. Records' Mike Maitland and Ed West. Based on Atlantic's outstanding year, West and Maitland had to agree: If WB-7A could afford it, Atlantic was a good buy. Hyman got back in touch with Atlantic's three owners and also talked to Frank Sinatra, who still owned one-third interest in Warner/Reprise, who'd have to say yes to the deal. That's all he needed. Maitland was no longer involved. To Hyman, Mike was just an employee, not an owner.

With his ducks a row, Hyman then called Atlantic. He was ready to deal. Were they?

Significant Warner/Reprise Releases

1965

Reprise: Dino, Desi & Billy ("I'm a Fool") • The Kinks (*Kinks-Size,* including "All Day and All of the Night" and "Tired of Waiting for You"; and *Kinda Kinks,* including "Set Me Free"; and *Kinks Kinkdom,* including "Well Respected Man") • Dean Martin ("In the Chapel in the Moonlight," "Send Me the Pillow You Dream On," "(Remember Me) I'm the One Who Loves You," "I Will," and "Houston" • Frank Sinatra ("September of My Years," "It Was a Very Good Year," and *A Man and His Music*) • Sonny and Cher ("Baby Don't Go")
Warner Bros.: Freddy Cannon ("Action") • Petula Clark ("Downtown" and "I Know a Place" • Bill Cosby ("Why Is There Air?") • Vic Damone ("You Were Only Fooling") • Antonio Carlos Jobim • The King Family • The Marketts ("Out of Limits") • Bob Newhart ("The Windmills Are Weakening") • Peter, Paul & Mary ("A Song Will Rise" and "See What Tomorrow Brings")

1966

Reprise: The Electric Prunes ("I Had Too Much to Dream (Last Night)") • Don Ho and the Aliis ("Tiny Bubbles") • Dean Martin ("Somewhere There's a Someone" and "Memories Are Made of This" and *The Dean Martin Christmas Album*) • Frank Sinatra (*At the Sands* and "That's Life") • Nancy Sinatra ("These Boots Are Made for Walkin'" and "How Does That Grab You, Darlin'")
Warner Bros.: Petula Clark ("My Love," "Sign of the Times," and "I Couldn't Live Without Your Love") • Bill Cosby ("Wonderfulness") • The Marketts ("Batman Theme") • Peter, Paul & Mary • Johnny Sea ("Day for Decision")
Loma: Lorraine Ellison ("Stay with Me")
Valiant: The Association ("Cherish" and "Along Comes Mary")

7

THE debate between the three owners of Atlantic Records—whether to sell to strangers or to stay independent—troubled Ahmet Ertegun most. He liked a life steered by his own hands. That meant not sharing the wheel with others, especially with men like 7 Arts' Alan Hirschfield and Elliott Hyman, who boogied not. Ahmet *never* wanted to work for somebody else. And in this 7 Arts deal, his instincts made him extra-wary of his suitor's other labels out by the Pacific.

By now, after almost twenty years at Atlantic, he'd traveled a long, laugh-happy road to be worth a million. In 1967, he was forty-four years old and had a record company that, in the morning, never called roll. Getting to this point had provided a life of amusements. "One of these days," Ahmet had told his officemate Jerry Wexler, "we're going to laugh ourselves right out of the record business."

Atlantic, in its earlier years, had been like a lemonade stand run by eager Eskimo kids. Starting in the late Forties, Ertegun had learned the record business by just walking in and stumbling through it. He believed that making records was the most fun anyone could have while dancing. But now, with millions of dollars dangled before them, the owners of Atlantic felt angst.

Let's take it from the top, when Atlantic began.

Newlyweds Herb and Miriam Abramson made their home in an apartment in New York's Greenwich Village. It was postwar Forties, a time when, if someone said "rock," you flashed first on Gibraltar. Right after World War II, small, independent labels exploded. Other early R&B indies paved the way, such names as Apollo, DeLuxe, Exclusive, Jubilee, King, Miracle, National, Philo (later became Aladdin), Savoy, Specialty. These start-up labels had expanded the records marketplace like a land rush. Herb Abramson wanted a part of the rush.

Brooklyn-born Abramson was by trade a dentist but by passion a jazz lover. People referred to Herb—well-combed black hair, trim face with strong bones—as dashing. His new wife, Miriam, was bright, caustic, and impatient with dumb guys; out loud, her mouth was some kick. The Abramsons' walls were 78-RPM vinyl discs, up to the ceiling. They'd moved from Washington to New York because Herb wanted no more of capping molars; he wanted to produce records, and for his *own* label. Miriam, as jazzy as chicks came, shared her husband's feel for the music.

From their childhood, Nesuhi and Ahmet Ertegun's family had moved from country to country. The family business was their father's, Turkey's ambassador first to one country, then to another, as Turkey's need arose. Even before they turned teens, Nesuhi and Ahmet had already lived in ambassadorial residences and gone to private schools in Switzerland, then in Paris, then in London, at each stop the boys picking up one more language: a privileged childhood in a family where no one needed to learn car driving.

In London one evening, the Ertegun lads fell in love with jazz and the records that let them hear jazz anytime. Occupying the Turkish ambassador's residence there, fourteen-year-old Nesuhi, already a jazz fan, took his nine-year-old brother one night in 1932 to the London Palladium. That evening, the boys experienced the heat-flash-and-mellow-thunder orchestras of Duke Ellington and Cab Calloway. That flash, that thunder of American jazz, amazed and changed those two boys.

Ten years later, the Ertegun family had moved to Washington, D.C.'s Turkish Embassy. The boys were raised as fine young men: private schools, including St. John's College, where philosophy was considered a practical major, where one learned the ins and outs of René Descartes and crab cakes. The Erteguns were the kind of boys who might, of their own free will, visit an art gallery. They'd made friends with a black ex-fighter named Cleo Payne, who opened doors for them to more American music. As they grew, secure, they spent hours in Washington's race-record shops, in particular in Waxie Maxie Silverman's frills-free, robust Quality Music Shop store,[24] where aisle upon aisle of 78-RPM records made from shellac could be browsed by tipping them forward in wooden bins, looking down at their vivid labels.

In their teens, the Ertegun lads had memorized the lore of New Orleans and of Chicago's South Side. Evenings, upright in the frontest row possible in the African-American Howard Theater, they felt the jazz being blammed from a high stage; after ten at night, at Washington's Negro night clubs, they leaned forward to hear the jive. Finally at bedtime, they tuned to radio stations with signals much fainter than the pop ones'.

When their father died, elder brother Nesuhi moved west, to work in a

---

[24]In the early years of records, sound was etched onto records made of wax, shellac, and vinyl. Hence, the name Waxie Maxie. There might also have been a Mac Shellac or Vinyl Lionel; one hopes so. However, I only ever heard of Waxie Maxie.

twenty-by-thirty-foot jazz record shop on Santa Monica Boulevard, Los Angeles. He taught a course in jazz at UCLA. He'd become an impassioned retailer of jazz discs, but as a business, his Jazz Man Record Shop was much
too selective, like a flower store that sold only begonias. I remember it; I
bought records there. It had bins of records filled with heavy black discs on
labels like Commodore and Jazz at the Phil: 78s, meant to teeter on your
changer's spindle, then clunk, one after another, into play for their three
minutes each. Nesuhi loved to move music, his music, into your hands. I
bought from him wobbly armfuls for under twenty bucks, everything from
King Oliver to Slim Gaillard.

Younger brother Ahmet, at twenty-one, despite his travels, his studies,
his brains, fit neatly into the category "unemployable." He'd made his way to
New York, figuring that in this Bigger Apple maybe he should consider doing something, thinking the record business looked like fun.

With what money he had left, this younger son immediately set himself
up to do record business out of his suite at New York's Ritz, which he'd decided was the best hotel in the city. Out on the avenues, Ahmet described
himself as a record maker. As such, he hung out in Harlem clubs. "I thought
the way to get into the music business was to make a good impression . . .
But although I spent all the money I had, I wasn't getting anywhere. After a
couple of months, I had had a very good time, but I hadn't come close to
making a record."

Post-Ritz, there in the summer nights of Manhattan, Ahmet Ertegun,
naïve, out of hotel-room money, still did not scramble for work. Scrambling
was not what ambassadors' sons did. Without much in the way of cash, Ahmet moved in with fellow Washington exiles, Herb and Miriam Abramson.
They speculated about a record label, went up to 125th Street after dark,
then back to the apartment to plan their dreams. Lying awake nights on the
Abramsons' sofa, the night warm outside, window open, taxi horns bouncing between village-height buildings, Ahmet visualized tomorrow's delights, of still other visits into spotlit Harlem clubs with their small stages,
of standing elbow-close to passionate men and enviable ladies, in clubs
where the cocktail glasses came not from matched sets but from "used"
stores. Ahmet Ertegun did not fret over money. Instead, he dreamed about
moving through life in shiny shoes.

Even with his Turkish complexion, Ahmet Ertegun was the whitest cat
in the place, because these were not fancied-up-for-white-folk clubs. In
these clubs, no girls with cigarette trays and gardenias approached you. Ahmet had stood at the bar, nursing a gin with one green olive, eager to start
making records. The Abramsons had food to buy, rent to pay, records, bills.
In a spell working for National Records Abramson had cut sides with boogie pianist Pete Johnson ("Atomic Boogie"), the Ravens, Billy Eckstine's

big band ("Prisoner of Love" and "Jelly, Jelly"), Dusty Fletcher (the joyous "Open the Door, Richard," arranged by Jesse Stone, a songwriter who would become part of Atlantic's unstructured family for years to come).

In the Abramson apartment in 1947, the three hopefuls fantasized as they talked business. Herb was thirty-one and had done lots. The more boy-ish Ahmet, at twenty-four, ad-libbed his Business Math theory: "If just one out of ten record shops in America were to buy just one of my records, I could make some money." Ertegun, however, had no idea how to record, to press, distribute, promote, or retail records, all of which, he figured, were just details. He instead brought love to the business: "I felt that I knew what black life was in America, and I knew what black roots and what black gospel music and black blues from the Delta that went on to Chicago and the Texas blues that went out to the West Coast—I knew what they were. And I loved all of that. So, in loving America, I thought I loved something more than the average American knew about."

Herb and Miriam were more practical. "The idea of a record company was really an outgrowth of the hobbies of all of us," Miriam recalled. "We were all jazz fans. We were interested in jazz, and we thought we could have a company that would specialize in the kind of music that was being largely ignored by the large companies."

To create Atlantic, the three decided they'd be partners. Abramson put up twenty-five hundred dollars of his own money. Herb was the one who knew how to get records pressed, how to find a lawyer to write contracts, how to get cheap studio time. Ahmet took the train back to Washington to ask his family dentist and friend to extend him a credit line. The dentist, Dr. Vahdi Sabit, established a draw account of ten thousand dollars. Ertegun later realized that Sabit's credit line "turned out to be one of the best invest-ments ever made. He didn't even have to put up the full ten thousand, be-cause by the time he came to put up the last part, he was getting money back from what we were making."

In 1947 (when many ex-GIs were creating their own labels) with little money, Atlantic Records began, not in the Ritz but in a two-room suite in Manhattan's cheaper Jefferson Hotel: the bedroom for Ahmet Ertegun and his cousin, a poet named Sadi Koylan, to sleep in, and the front room for an office. Herb was Atlantic's president; Ertegun was vice president. Miriam was fully in charge of all dirty work, whatever was needed to keep Atlantic running. Cutie became the company bad guy.

When Abramson and Ertegun found a performer they liked, they pushed back the furniture in the front room to make their place a recording studio. The repertoire they recorded was less than commercially defined, less than focused on black music. "We had very small budgets," Ahmet later recalled, "and we had to record whatever we could find. The first recordings we made were just terrible. I shudder now when I hear them."

In its first year, 1947, Atlantic recorded a total of sixty-five songs. It was too late in the year to release any. Of those sixty-five sides, twelve were by the Gospeleers, seven were by Tiny Grimes. Of those sixty-five, Atlantic would eventually release half. The others became learning experiences.

Of the eventual first Atlantic releases (all 78-RPM singles) in 1948, the first was "The Rose of the Rio Grande" by the Harlemaires, but most of them were by good jazz players, but not big-name jazz stars: sidemen not under contract to bigger labels, singles like bassist Eddie Safranski's Poll Cats: "Sa-Frantic" backed with "Bass Mood." Other jazz by Bob Howard & His Rhythm, by Melrose Colbert, by Tiny Grimes's Quintet.

There were four cuts by a long-forgotten Turkish humorist/storyteller named M. Baler: "Iki Karpuz bir Koltuga Sigarmi" backed by "Iltimas Etmeye Yare, Variniz Yalvariniz" and "Göden Cemalin Cün Irag Oldu" b/w "Taksim."

The years 1948 and 1949 brought on "Square Dance Party" by Burt Hilber & the Boys from Chubby's Headquarters (Chubby was Chubby Jackson, Woody Herman's bassist); and "The Complete Works of Shakespeare: Volume One—Romeo and Juliet," with real actress Eva LeGallienne. The project never made it to Volume Two.

Atlantic's first record that sold many: Stick McGhee's "Drinkin' Wine Spo-Dee-O-Dee," copied from the same artist/song already out on Mayo Williams's Harlem Records label. When "Wine" started to sell in New Orleans, nobody could locate the Harlem Records version. Atlantic sped into the studio with Stick and his brother Brownie, recut a custom order of five thousand copies for Atlantic's New Orleans distributor. It went on to sell forty thousand copies. Atlantic's first R&B hit (Number Three). Showing a remarkable lack of focus, Atlantic quickly followed up with its country version of "Drinkin' Wine Spo-Dee-O-Dee" by Loy Gordon and His Pleasant Valley Boys, which sold like roadkill.

To Miriam, her bad-guy role meant fighting record-pressing plants to get such records—good or bad—out to the market. "I was the one who had to talk to the factories, all the time, which I did. I yelled. Herb and Ahmet, they never had to yell 'But you *owe* me' at anybody, or 'But it was supposed to be here yesterday.' " Miriam would strut around, looking for a fight, screaming at singers who asked for cash advances. Her stinginess kept Atlantic open.

Herb found a kid in his twenties named Tom Dowd to help make records. Dowd knew this much about how to record: "The band would drive up to New York, go into the studio for three hours, get four sides down, and that was it. You put up one microphone and told the band to play louder or softer. 'Good-bye,' in and out in a day." Dowd's first recording job for Atlantic was by Frank "Floorshow" Culley, doing "Central Avenue Breakdown." Ahmet, seeing the boy engineer Tom Dowd in the booth, stormed out, saying he would not have this infant spoil his record. Dowd knew what he was doing, joined Atlantic, and stuck for thirty-five years.

Eventually, Atlantic focused its ears and its heart uptown, 'round 125th Street. Let the majors do what they want, thought Abramson and Ertegun. "The people in the music business did not understand where the *real* American taste was," Ertegun once recalled. "They—the major labels—were making songs for a bourgeois society that they imagined existed in this country. You know, the people at RCA Victor, they didn't know shit from Shinola. And they didn't know that 'I Want to Rock You, Baby' had more meaning than 'Putting on My Top Hat, Polishing My Nails,' which had no particular appeal to a longshoreman in Seattle or a cotton picker in Alabama."

Stick McGhee had been a one-hit artist (at a time upon which one hit was not to be sneezed). Not true of Ruth Brown, in 1949 Atlantic's first "career" (meaning longer than one shot at it) artist. Signing her to a contract, Atlantic hit its first stride—honest race music, just now being called "rhythm & blues" (R&B).

Ruth Brown was down to no cents at all, singing for meager money, maybe tips. Her singing idols were mostly blonde, sweet girls, the kind she'd seen in movies. Ertegun recalled telling his new artist, "No, you've got to sing like Miss Cornshucks.' And she said, 'I don't *want* to sing like Miss Cornshucks.' And I said, 'You'll never sell any records singing like Doris Day'." Ruth just nodded.[25]

On the way from Washington up to New York to record, Ruth Brown got into a car accident, mangling both legs. She ended up in the hospital for six months. During her stay, Atlantic brought to her hospital room a book on how to sight-read music, a pitch pipe, a tablet for writing down new lyrics, and a record contract to sign; it offered that Atlantic would pick up all the hospital charges that her insurance company would not. The deal made Atlantic's dollar-conscious Miriam Abramson complain, "Absolutely ridiculous!" Ahmet and Herb did it anyway.

In the hospital, Ruth Brown signed her contract without too much thinking. When she asked about the royalty rate—5 percent—Ahmet nodded encouragingly, saying, "At Decca, only Bing Crosby gets five percent." He was right. For the times, it was a deal better than many artists got. (At Chess Records, employee Muddy Waters not only sang, he had to paint Leonard Chess's house.) In the contract were Atlantic's other conditions: The 5 percent came only after Atlantic got back its advances (sixty-nine

---

[25]Little Miss Cornshucks (born Mildred Cummings) was briefly recorded right after World War II, starting at Chicago's Sunbeam label. After that, she recorded freely for many labels, including Columbia's black subsidiary label, Okeh. She was a combination country/R&B singer: a black woman in a Minnie Pearl straw hat, gingham dress, shoeless. She could rock like mad, though. Then, by the first of the Fifties, she was gone. Doris Day, however, kept going.

dollars for every side Ruth recorded), after all production costs (musicians, arrangements) for all records cut, whether issued or not, after cost of records used for promotion, and after a flat 10 percent deduction to pay for records that broke. These terms, which were not just Atlantic's but common throughout the industry, meant that few singers saw more than that first advance, that sixty-nine dollars per song.

Even the major labels, like Columbia and RCA, seldom paid royalties; artist royalties were hardly mentioned in deals. Instead, to dominate, the majors offered artists larger recording fees than any indie could come up with. Most lawyers, negotiating for their artists, preferred those bucks-in-the-hand deals. (Atlantic lost artists because, even though the label meant to pay royalties, the prospect for getting rich on royalties was slimmer at the smaller label, where distribution was shaky.)

The difference was the white guys who ran the labels lived their white lives—loving black music for its bounce and laughs, and taking their end of the money off the top. For the black folk, who sang and played, getting sixty-nine dollars for singing a song meant food money. Better than cleaning houses.

Atlantic had moved out of the Hotel Jefferson and into a walkup office at 301 West Fifty-fourth Street. When Ruth Brown came out of the hospital, with Herb Abramson in the booth producing, she recorded "So Long" at Apex Studio. It became Atlantic's first unstolen hit: Number Six on the R&B chart. Atlantic enjoyed that "we did it" feeling, like a kid's first successful bike ride.

Atlantic stayed Harlem-sensitive. In 1946, Abramson had cut records for National with Big Joe Turner ("My Gal's a Jockey"), a giant-size gent with one volume setting: loud. Turner was available again. In Braddock's Bar, Abramson and Ertegun urged him to record for them. "I know we can make hit records with you."

"Okay, if you pay me money," answered Turner.

"We can give you five hundred dollars," said Ahmet.

"Yeah, that's good!"

"For four sides," Ertegun added quickly.

Turner, who could not read, recorded "Chains of Love" with Ahmet behind him, whispering each next line. It spent twenty-five weeks on the charts, from June through December 1951.

Abramson and Ertegun had thus transformed a waning blues artist— this massive Joe, whose voice could loosen the putty around windowpanes, who could sing over a brass section's blare without benefit of microphone— into a hotter, more city-sounding vocalist.

In such a way, they began building a minority label, having touches of success, chart listings, but far from the earshot of the mass market. Atlantic succoured black-talking white disc jockeys, all bearing odd first names:

Atlanta's Zenas Daddy Sears. Buffalo's Hound Dog Lorenz. Cleveland's Alan "Moondog" Freed. Los Angeles's Hunter Hancock. New Orleans's Clarence "Poppa Stoppa" Hamman. Nashville's Hoss Allen. Del Rio, Mexico's "Bob Wolfman Jack Smith."

Atlantic's full tilt to R&B had come with a phone call from Waxie Maxie. He'd found five young men in Washington: the Clovers. From them came "Don't You Know I Love You." It set another Atlantic trend: the vocal group, all identically suited, stepping in precise patterns, arms and fingers in sync, voices in harmony with their souls.

"Don't You Know I Love You" was written by someone named Nugetre, which can be spelled backward. "I wanted to do real hip, funky music," Ahmet recalled. "So when I got the Clovers, I thought I couldn't get a song. You know the publishers; they didn't want to give us anything anyway, because they thought the little company out of a little hole in the wall—you know. So I forced them to record this song I wrote."[26]

Ahmet could not write down music. To demo his songs, he used a Times Square "Record Your Voice—25¢" booth to make a singers' demo. "Ahmet could write a lyric faster than some of the people we hired to write lyrics," recalled Tom Dowd. "Look at the hits that Nugetre wrote. I mean, it's frightening. What we were doing was having a good time. We'd lived through a hell of a time. We'd survived a war and every other fool thing. And here we were finally playing. But we were twenty- and thirty-year-olds—playing. And we're having a good old time making records and telling stories and communicating with people who were not the spoon-fed people that you were accustomed to hearing by the major record companies."

Herb knew a good lick when he recorded it, and he respected his VP's talent. Ahmet, he recalled, "wrote quite a few good songs [for Clyde McPhatter, Joe Turner, Ben E. King, Ray Charles]. He was 'hip to the tip' as we say. In other words, he was not a square. He was somebody who understood the idiom." How to make a hit began to sink in.

In 1952, Atlantic moved again to bigger offices: a loft over Patsy's Restaurant on 234 West Fifty-sixth. The building was a wood-framed brownstone, late nineteenth century. Atlantic's shipping room was on the fourth floor, its executives were on the fifth, on a floor that sagged and creaked. The sloped ceiling had a skylight in the middle, last cleaned during the reign of Charlemagne. The whole office was about nineteen by twenty-eight feet. Two desks, one for Ahmet, one for Herb, and a miniature piano for song pluggers. Dowd built in an eight-track recorder. When it came time to record, one desk still got piled on the other, chairs got brought in for the band, and that was the studio, for Big Joe Turner, for early Ray Charles.

---

[26]In June 1951, "Don't You Know I Love You" first appeared on *Billboard*'s R&B chart, slowly chinning its way up to, yes, Number One. For two weeks.

At this point, Atlantic needed a real financial controller. Sheldon Vogel, six foot three, had a voice that, when he had a point to make, boomed. Vogel replaced Atlantic's previous controller, who, according to Vogel (a legend disputed by Abramson), had "died on the job after Miriam Abramson yelled at him." Here's Miriam's version: "The people who were making records were like people who study the Torah. They had nothing to do with the guts of the business. There was *always* a financial bind. The people who were artistic were never really involved in it." Willy-nilly, Vogel decided accountants needn't know music; they had to know counting. Moving into his new job, now Vogel got yelled at by Miriam.

Looking at Atlantic's books, Vogel found a company that was not making much money. Enough to pay the bills, and what was left over from bills went for salaries. Those salaries were not high. Ahmet Ertegun, the company's most highly paid, was making twenty-five thousand dollars a year. Partner Herb Abramson matched Ertegun in élan: He was tall, dressed to the nines. But these people only *dressed* like dandies. Contrary to their silver-spoon looks, they could not afford wallets of genuine leather.

Swingtime Records' Joe Lauderdale needed money. After hearing a hit on the Swingtime label, "Kissa Me, Baby," Abramson and Ertegun paid twenty-five hundred dollars to buy out his Ray Charles contract, real money for a company originally financed on ten thousand dollars. For that, Atlantic expected some cooperation from its new star.

But Charles was the artist who was not dependent, in contrast to other Atlantic artists who worked "on cue," as in Ruth Brown's willingness to wail whenever Abramson asked her, "Gimme one of your patented screams here." Charles recorded it his way. "I tried to make Ray Charles make records like we were making hits with the Clovers. It didn't work with Ray Charles," Ertegun recalled. "He told us our way was not as good as what would happen if we didn't fuck around with him and let him do what he wanted to do. Because he got his shit together when he got his own band." Charles was not being difficult, just different.

To Ertegun and Abramson, it felt odd, their not being needed in the studio to get a record made. To their credit, they let Charles do his thing, as they eventually had to learn to do with most artists. Around now, artists began obeying their own instincts—Ray Charles, for instance, used R&B lyrics against a sixteen-bar gospel chord progression—began acting less like the tools of record-company bosses. Freedom didn't happen in one night or even in one year, but the time of the in-the-studio executive was waning.

It was February 1953, four years into Atlantic, when Herb Abramson got recalled into the Army and sent over to Germany, where the army needed his dentistry skills in the worst way. Miriam stayed back, alone in New York. In principle, Abramson retained the presidency of Atlantic Records, but Ahmet was left there with no one to tend the recording studio with him. Atlantic did not grow more productive. "Ahmet's working habits were not severe," Miriam summed up. She was being polite.

To fill the Herb void, Atlantic recruited a soul mate: Jerry Wexler, wearing horn-rimmed glasses, robust, vivid of character, fluid of mouth, working at *Billboard*. Wexler was a black-music aficionado who'd adopted as his own that new kind of roadside music that combined hot jazz, shouting blues, and gospel. Wexler's qualities fit well with Ahmet's: Both dug the same music, and both were literate. But there were other differences: Ahmet carried about him a European air; Wexler would have you think he ran juke joints. Wexler's education had consisted of just two years at City College, where no one ever heard of crab cakes. After World War II, Wexler'd landed a reporting job at *Billboard*, met New York's music guys, and felt brotherhood toward some, especially Atlantic's. Wexler's outspoken opinions, however, were more like Miriam's. It was a company where graciousness seldom made the Top Ten.

Just the year before, in 1952, reporter Jerry Wexler had turned down the job of running music publishing for Atlantic; he had argued for a percentage of the record side, and there was no deal. Ahmet now offered more: In this new job, Jerry could *make* records for Atlantic.

As Wexler recalled in his book *Rhythm and the Blues*, Ertegun then described to Jerry what *kind* of records Atlantic wanted to release: " 'There's a man living in the outskirts of Opelousas, Louisiana,' Ahmet had said. 'He works hard for his money. He has to be tight with a dollar. One morning he hears a song on the radio. It's urgent, bluesy, authentic, irresistible. He becomes obsessed. He can't *live* without this record. He drops everything, jumps in his pickup, and drives twenty-five miles to the first record store he finds. If we can make that kind of music, we can make it in the business.' "

"I still want to be a partner," Wexler replied.

After consulting with Herb, Ertegun let Wexler buy in. For $2,063.25, Wexler could own 13 percent of Atlantic: $2,063.25 was, roughly, about $2,000 more than Wexler had to his name. In place of the $2,000, Wexler offered to toss in his pickup truck. The truck was placed on Atlantic's books, valued at $1,000, the rest to be paid later.

Wexler started at $300 a week. The first day, Miriam Abramson dumped the mail on his desk, saying, "Go to work." Wexler's and Ertegun's two desks abutted. If an act came in to sign a deal, Ahmet might offer the act a 5 percent royalty. At this, Wexler would explode and insist that 3 percent was all Atlantic could afford. The act, looking on, unable to defend himself, would be relieved when Wexler and Ertegun finally compromised on 4 percent. Wexler and Ertegun, they'd shake hands: deal made. End of negotiation. No lawyers to mess things up.

Artistically, between Wexler and Ertegun, there was no veto power. If one of them wanted to record this song or that singer, it just happened.

Black music started going pop, a phenomenon in the business called "crossing over." White disc jockeys played black records for white kids. Although bigots called him "nigger lover," Alan Freed made it with the kids: He whooped and hollered on air and spun the records of indies like Roulette, Chess, King, Atlantic.

Then a hillbilly act that was experimenting with a jump-country R&B sound, Bill Haley cut "Crazy, Man, Crazy," though not for Atlantic. At Atlantic, they referred to this kind of music as "R&B that sells to whites." Freed named this music rock & roll and nailed its future: "Let's face it, rock & roll is bigger than all of us."

In 1954, to test if they could find this R&R market—while protecting their reputation in the R&B field—Jerry and Ahmet, in disguise, invented a subsidiary label, Cat Records, based on an early nickname for white R&B music. Cat had one hit—"Sh-Boom" by the Chords. "Sh-Boom" quickly got covered—copied—then buried by the Crew Cuts, white kids from Canada. As a label, Cat fast faded away. Atlantic stuck to R&B.

"People like our engineer Tom Dowd, as a freelance engineer," Wexler recalled, "were going over to Mercury Records or MGM, and recording [our] same song with a white artist, and our record would be on the turntable in the control room to get the exact key, the exact beat, the exact cadences, and to copy the record as closely as possible. They really wiped us out."

Big Joe Turner recorded "Shake, Rattle and Roll" for Atlantic, with background vocals by Ahmet Ertegun, Jerry Wexler, and lyricist Jesse Stone. "Shake, Rattle and Roll" nestled up but could not reach over that dividing line: the racial barrier, where black singers were broadcast on black radio stations, sold in black record stores, to black customers. Major (white market) record labels knew in their hearts and wallets that the black versions were wrong, lyrically and musically, for their market.

Big Joe Turner's "Shake, Rattle and Roll" got covered quickly by Bill Haley and the Comets, who made its lyrics safer. Radio stations for the white versions just could not play that black version.

TURNER'S VERSION:
> *Wearing those dresses, the sun come shining through*
> *I can't believe my eyes, all that mess belongs to you.*

HALEY'S VERSION:
> *Wearing those dresses, your hair's done up so nice*
> *You look so warm, but heart's as cold as ice.*[27]

---

[27]The song's white editors (Haley and his pianist John Grande) did not realize the meaning of another line and left in "I'm like a one-eyed cat/Peeping in a sea food store."

Atlantic's black-artist hits got creamed by white artists.

	On Atlantic By	Covered By
"Tweedle Dee"	LaVern Baker	Georgia Gibbs
"Shake, Rattle and Roll"	Big Joe Turner	Bill Haley
"Such a Night"	Clyde McPhatter	Johnnie Ray
"Mambo Baby"	Ruth Brown	Georgia Gibbs
"Oh, What a Dream"	Ruth Brown	Patti Page
"Sh-Boom"	The Chords	The Crew Cuts

The onset of rock & roll ended Big Joe Turner's streak. Ever congenial and mild-mannered, Big Joe took it philosophically: "I made all those things before Haley and the others, but suddenly all the cats started jumping up, and I guess I kinda got knocked down in the traffic." Atlantic's biggest, loudest, roaringest bluesman, Turner Shook, Rattled, and Rolled for years but never once cracked the Top Forty.[28]

Even without crossover rock & roll, Atlantic Records got hot. Wexler+Ertegun made hits, records with a strong hook, variety, a boom-di-bam bass, a singing melody. Atlantic's marketing style turned into a positive lust for hits. Wexler recalled, "We recorded four nights a week—only singles. We'd release three records at a time, every three weeks. To make the nut back in those days, we needed to do sixty thousand singles a month. We were lucky. All the records sold between two hundred thousand and three hundred thousand, but hardly ever more than that. But it was enough to get us going . . . This was a push, get-to-the-distributor, get-to-the-DJ, get-the-goddamn-song-on-the-air business."

Hearing that Clyde McPhatter had been fired as lead singer in the Dominos, Ertegun found shy Clyde and his angelic voice in a rented room in Harlem. McPhatter remembered how King Records' budget-conscious Syd Nathan had saved money by Nathan himself playing the drums on his recordings, and he gingerly asked Ertegun, "I hope *you're* not going to play

---

[28]Characterized by Ertegun as the only artist he ever signed who never needed a mike, Turner recorded nearly two hundred albums during his career. In the early 1960s, Turner was dropped by Atlantic. His recorded output shifted to over a dozen labels. His health began to fail, but he kept on singing, his huge frame sometimes on crutches or in a wheelchair, the voice always able to reach out the front door to the street. He died at seventy-four in 1985 in Inglewood, California. At the funeral, songwriter Doc Pomus spoke these words:

Joe, I know that heaven's a sweeter place now that you're going to be there. But the angels are going to have to sing a little louder to keep up with you, and the all-star backup band is going to have to keep on their toes. But they're all going to be really inspired now.

drums on my session." Atlantic promised a professional drummer. Ertegun urged McPhatter to do two things: form a new group and change his name (because Clyde McPhatter sounded, to Ahmet, like the name of a comedy sidekick in a western comedy). McPhatter took only Ahmet's first suggestion. The result was the Drifters. The resulting single, "Money Honey," became one of the biggest R&B hits of 1953.

The Drifters recorded a splash of hit songs, including "Such a Night," which got banned on Detroit's WXYZ after loud, angry moms called the station in fear that the single would ruin their daughters. They then recorded "Honey Love." Same thing again, except now the Mothers Who March were in Memphis. "Back then," Wexler remembered, "the words seemed to suggest something dirty, which was sexual satisfaction. This was so shocking that the police chief in Memphis banned it off the jukeboxes. Imagine being banned off jukeboxes in juke joints where the booze was flowing and the reefer and whatever! To me it was like an honor; it was like being on Nixon's enemy list."

Atlantic had hits aplenty: LaVern Baker, the Drifters, the Clovers, Ray Charles, Ruth Brown—all black. Atlantic execs bought themselves Caddys, had laughs, knew what it meant to feel like kings, relaxin' on the axis.

In April 1955, after his two years with the U.S. Army, back from Germany came Herb Abramson, with his German girlfriend. *Oops.* The new girlfriend was pregnant. "Oh, uh, hi, Herb."

Significant Atlantic Singles

1948
Tiny Grimes ("Midnight Special")

1949
Ruth Brown ("So Long") • Frank "Floorshow" Culley ("Cole Slaw" and "After Hour Session") • Stick McGhee & His Buddies ("Drinking Wine, Spo-Dee-o-Dee, Drinking Wine")

1950
Ruth Brown ("Teardrops from My Eyes") • Al Hibbler ("Danny Boy") • Laurie Tate & Joe Morris ("Anytime, Anyplace, Anywhere")

1951
Ruth Brown ("I'll Wait for You" and "I Know") • The Cardinals ("Shouldn't I Know?") • The Clovers ("Don't You Know I Love You" and "Fool, Fool, Fool") • Stick McGhee ("Tennessee Waltz Blues") • Joe Turner ("Chains of Love" and "Chill Is On")

1952
Ruth Brown ("5-10-15 Hours" and "Daddy Daddy") • The Cardinals ("The Wheel of Fortune") • The Clovers ("One Mint Julep"/"Middle of the Night," "Ting-a-

Ling"/"Wonder Where My Baby's Gone," "Hey, Miss Fannie"/"I Played the Fool") • Joe Turner ("Sweet Sixteen")

1953
Ruth Brown ("(Mama) He Treats Your Daughter Mean" and "Wild, Wild Young Men") • The Cardinals ("The Door Is Still Open") • The Clovers ("Good Lovin'") • The Drifters ("Money Honey") • Joe Turner ("Honey Hush")

1954
Ruth Brown ("Oh, What a Dream" and "Mambo Baby") • Ray Charles ("It Should've Been Me") • The Clovers ("Lovely Dovey") • The Drifters ("Such a Night"/"Lucille" and "Honey Love") • Joe Turner ("Shake, Rattle and Roll" and "Well All Right")

1955
Ruth Brown ("I Can See Everybody's Baby" and "As Long as I'm Moving") • LaVern Baker ("Tweedlee-Dee," "Bop-Ting-a-Ling," "Play It Fair," and "That's All I Need") • Ray Charles ("I've Got a Woman"/"Come Back" and "A Fool for You") • The Drifters ("Ruby Baby") • Clyde McPhatter ("Love Has Joined Us Together") • The Robins ("Smokey Joe's Cafe") • Joe Turner ("Flip, Flop and Fly" and "Hide and Seek")

1956
LaVern Baker ("I Can't Love You Enough," "Still," and "Jim Dandy") • Ray Charles ("Drown in My Own Tears" and "Hallelujah I Love Her So") • The Clovers ("Love, Love, Love") • The Coasters ("Down in Mexico") • Ivory Joe Hunter ("Since I Met You Baby") • Clyde McPhatter ("Seven Days" and "Treasure of Love") • Joe Turner ("Corrine, Corrina" and "Lipstick Powder and Paint") • Chuck Willis ("It's Too Late" and "Juanita")

1957
The Bobbettes ("Mr. Lee") • Ruth Brown ("Lucky Lips") • Ray Charles ("Swanee River Rock (Talkin' 'Bout That River)") • The Coasters ("Searchin' " / "Young Blood") • Ivory Joe Hunter ("Empty Arms") • Clyde McPhatter ("Without Love (There Is Nothing)," "Just to Hold My Hand," and "Long Lonely Nights") • Chuck Willis ("C.C. Rider")

8

HERB Abramson, Atlantic's president, had had his fill of dentistry and was ready to get back to record making. As house engineer Tom Dowd saw it, "Jerry was flying. Ahmet was flying. Herb stepped onto a wheel going at seven hundred miles an hour." Record makers Wexler and Ertegun, as hot as grits, knew there was no room in their office for a third desk. After a half year of awkwardness, for Herb, they invented a new label: Atco Records. Atco meant that Atlantic could get a second set of distributors alongside Atlantic's. That'd mean doubling their muscle promoting records.

The cast-off Herb Abramson signed to his Atco label a cocky, shiny-suited young Bobby Darin. No hits followed. Out in L.A., Abramson was about to give up on Darin; they'd found no formula. He called New York. Ahmet said he'd like a shot or two recording Darin before calling it off. The result—done so easily it makes you wonder sometimes—was "Splish Splash." Darin had written it, he claimed, "in twelve minutes." The song, plus two other sides, was recorded in less than two hours. To the beginning of the take, engineer Tom Dowd added the sound of some water splashing, then sent the acetate over to Atlantic's main office for evaluation. "It took the messenger ten minutes to deliver the acetate to the office," Dowd recalls, "and it took them two forty-nine to play; then they may have played it twice before they called and said, 'It's a smash. Master it right away, pull out all the stops, make masters for all plants, and get them out tonight!' "

Darin told a friend he was nervous. "You'll vomit when you hear it." The results: A hundred thousand were sold in a month; a million were sold overall; Darin became a teen idol; Atlantic had its first hit in the white marketplace.

Reaction within the company did not consist of jumping up and down. Jerry Wexler, tending a roster of twenty black performers, thought it "was utter garbage." Ahmet's success with Darin so affected Herb that he decided he was in the wrong company. His ego had been smacked hard. "After a while," recalled Abramson, "I couldn't take it, so I said, 'Buy me out.' It was the stupidest thing I ever said, but that was it." In December 1958, he was out.[29]

Darin, not abundantly modest, talked to the press about his ambitions, comparing himself to Sinatra: "I hope to pass Frank in everything he's done." When Sinatra heard what Darin had said, he went on record with his opinion: "Bobby Darin does my prom dates."

Through Darin and Atco, for the first time in its history, Atlantic in 1959 achieved a Total Pop Record hit: "Mack the Knife."[30] In the same year that Warner Bros. Records' best was "Kookie, Kookie, Lend Me Your Comb," Bobby Darin got Grammys for Record of the Year and Best New Artist of the Year. Ertegun came in to the office more often.

Darin was, for Ahmet, the wake-up call. Sales of Atlantic's staple, the R&B single, had slowed.[31] Singles started being for teens only (think Frankie Avalon's "Venus" or pop balladeer Guy Mitchell's "Heartaches by the Number"). For above-teens, the stereo LP became the top sales configuration (*Peter Gunn*; The Kingston Trio; *Flower Drum Song*). LPs made singles seem like foreplay. Very non-doo-wop. Record companies now sold twelve songs per sale, not just two, and enjoyed that.

Atlantic kept rowing its wobbly boat—R&B singles—and that meant crunch time. Its execs reduced their pay by fifty dollars a week. Atlantic's regular payments for airplay to DJ Alan Freed, delivered by Wexler on the first Monday of each month in a paper bag to the Brill Building's cloakroom, got tough to meet. "I was the bagman," Wexler recalled. "We paid Alan Freed six hundred dollars a month. One day I met with him and said, 'We can't keep up the payments. Can you carry us for a while?' He said, 'Gee, I'd love to, but it would be taking the bread out of my children's mouths.' "

---

[29]After leaving Atlantic with his buyout, Abramson continued to scuffle in the record business, with his own little labels (like Festival Records, with Butterbeans and Susie). He had his own A-1 Recording Studio in New York, where he made sides on spec. His biggest hit became Tommy Tucker's "Hi-Heel Sneakers" in 1964, on Checker Records.

In 1980, he moved to California, where he dabbled for one more hit. As of 1990, Abramson lived in a run-down house in Culver City, California. In the front room, a sagging divan where he'd sleep. Old car seats were turned into chairs. Crates of yellowing memorabilia from his founding of Atlantic sat in another room. He, in the words of Jerry Leiber, "hit the bottom of the well, after being almost at the very top." Herb Abramson died at age eighty-two in 1999, in Henderson, Nevada, survived by his wife, Barbara, three children, five grandchildren, and dozens of so-so tries at hits.

[30]Atlantic's label copy for the song's author, Bertolt Brecht, nicknamed him "Bert."

[31]The LP, in contrast, fueled a mighty growth in U.S. record sales (in millions of dollars):

1950	1951	1952	1953	1954	1955	1956	1957	1958	1959
$189	199	214	219	213	277	377	460	511	603

Atlantic scrambled. Maybe try R&B with strings? Songwriting team Jerry Leiber and Mike Stoller produced just that. In 1959, with lead voice Ben E. King replacing Clyde McPhatter's, the Drifters' massive hit "There Goes My Baby" became, for the ailing Atlantic, successful bypass surgery, a huge hit. Yet when he heard strings-with-R&B, Wexler, ever articulate, went bananas. He described the single "an excrescence," Wexlerian for "shit."

To increase its product flow, Atlantic started making "label deals," in which even littler record labels turned to Atlantic for the handling of sales, marketing, pressings, and the like. "Come by my house," Jerry Wexler would beckon to them, recalling such deals as "hog heaven," giving the little labels 10 percent deals (better than RCA or Columbia, which would come up with only half that). Atlantic's distributor in Florida, Henry Stone, a street rogue with a goatee and balls, had never met a rule he couldn't bend. After he'd handed some master over to Atlantic, the temptation for Stone was too great. He just kept on pressing, bootlegging his own record. Wexler recalled, "So we had an altercation, with his brand-new lawyer, Alan Grubman, who comes in, shirttail hanging out, belly hanging out." Wexler, whose tolerance for agents, lawyers, and leeches was nil, couldn't help himself, telling Grubman, "If you're going to be hanging around, Counselor, I'm going to start an industry petition to hyphenate your last name." The warning was too mild.

Atlantic found even better label deals than Stone's. Wexler was at the ready: "You never refuse to answer the phone. You never refuse to listen to a tape. You never refuse to listen to a record. Because you never know where your next million-seller is coming from." Buster Williams of Plastic Products, Atlantic's regional record presser in Memphis, on the phone: "Wexler, we got this record."

Williams had alerted Wexler to a tune by Rufus Thomas and his daughter Carla, " 'Cause I Love You." Its label, first called Satellite, then Stax, definitely small time, could not get distributed outside its own city. Stax's sister-brother owners, Estelle Axton and Jim Stewart (first two letters of each's last name), stuck up a sign in plastic letters reading SOULSVILLE USA on their storefront offices. So in the early Sixties had begun an amateur record company. Without distribution, Stax had promoted its records by filling its Chevy with a trunkload of 45s, then driving to as many radio stations as it could reach, to Tennessee, Mississippi, and Arkansas. Stax's sales area was as far as one could drive before turning back to work.

Wexler laid out a quick distribution deal: a thousand-dollar advance, a small royalty, a five-year option on sequels. The thousand dollars was the first money Stax had made. Atlantic's job: Take the record worldwide.

In what was an embarrassingly imbalanced (but again quite precedented) business arrangement, Atlantic's financial risk did not begin until the pressing and distribution time. Only then would Atlantic bring Stax's Memphis Sound—Booker T. and the MGs, Sam and Dave, Otis Redding (who, when first introduced to Ahmet, heard his name as "Omelet" and called him that), Rufus and Carla Thomas, the Bar-Kays—to the world beyond Tennessee. At Stax, the studio musicians known as Booker T. and the MGs made "Green Onions" and a million dollars for Stax/Atlantic.

In 1962, Atlantic grossed over $7 million, vo-dee-oh-dee, best year so far. Atlantic even got a Grammy for Best Rock and Roll Recording; it was for Bent Fabric's "Alley Cat." (Recording Academy voters believed that anything loud belonged in its Best Rock & Roll category.)

Artistically, however, Atlantic itself drifted through the early 1960s, sustained mainly by the Drifters and one of their emeriti, Ben E. King. Indeed, rural soul never would be again, though that was not yet clear to either Wexler or Ertegun.

Jerry Wexler's pursuit of the Stax-Volt sound helped sustain Atlantic Records over some stinging slaps:

- Ray Charles got a better contract offer from ABC Records. He showed its terms to Ahmet: 5 percent royalty plus a producer royalty plus eventual ownership of his own masters. Ertegun found the offer "a little rich for my blood" and wished Charles well. In 1959, soon after recording "I'm Movin' On," Charles was across town at ABC Records. Atlantic felt betrayed.
- In 1960, Leiber and Stoller created horror with their longtime label allies by auditing Atlantic's books. They found $18,000 in (disputed) payments missing. They demanded their $18,000. Atlantic flipped out, in the words of Miriam, who's remembered for pithy wisdoms like "I have to tell you that I was not in favor of giving anything away, ever."
- Second, Leiber and Stoller demanded a producer credit, plus a producer royalty, on the records they made for Atlantic. Such demands were unprecedented. To Atlantic, the feeling was "You don't trust your own parents?" To Leiber and Stoller, however, this was goodbye. They started their own record label.
- Next, Bobby Darin quit, heading for Capitol, which had been looking for a new Sinatra to replace the one who'd fallen hoarse from his lingering towerphobia. Darin wanted a Sinatra-style movie career, too.

Defections like these can shock a bottom line deeply, can siphon some of the fun out of things. This shock zapped Atlantic. But that feeling—of hits (Darin's "Mack the Knife" going Number One on the pop charts, a first-time-ever feeling)—felt so seductive to these R&B mavens. Hits, the holiest of holies. In the new, pop LP business, Atlantic began selling albums and learned another rule: From albums came bigger profits.

The change didn't happen overnight, and it certainly didn't happen to Jerry Wexler. He remained with ears facing South, remained indulged in R&B and his flip way of living. He made the world share *his* attitudes. When Apollo Records dropped Solomon Burke, Wexler just called him in and said, "Sit down. You're home. I can sign you today." They right away made a hit: "Just Out of Reach (of My Two Open Arms)."

Singers as good as Burke would stay for years, not just one single and out.[32] "At Chess Records, it was different," Wexler knew. "There, if somebody came in off the street with a song, they'd take that guy into the studio and cut that song with him. And that would be a one-record event and gone. At Atlantic, if somebody straggled in off the street with a song, we'd buy the song and save it for Wilson Pickett or Solomon Burke. We had a constant hunger for songs. A&R is high-flown verbiage for 'a singer and a song.' "

Atlantic embraced songwriters, because major publishers rarely came to Atlantic with a fresh hit. Atlantic latched on to writers themselves, like Jesse Stone, who'd begun in minstrel shows, grown up through the Cotton Club, arranged music at the Apollo, became in the early Fifties part of Atlantic's heart: writing, producing, arranging for Ruth Brown, Ray Charles, the Drifters, and Big Joe. "Shake, Rattle and Roll" was his. Wexler could hear a hit song, and writers like Stone always had places on the sofa in the hall.

Another? Polio-stricken Doc Pomus, responsible for the song that sent the Drifters' career soaring: "Save the Last Dance for Me," written by Doc with Mort Schuman. Doc was one of the top (and hippest) songwriters ever. A kind man, he'd had been confined most of his life to a wheelchair. And in this song, there Doc is, going out with his gorgeous blonde wife, watching her dance with other men. Doc stays calm, but you know those lyrics, they ache in him. Watching her dance, he's wishing to himself, "Save the last dance for me." The song is personal, confessional—everything songs should be but seldom are. When Wexler cut it with the Drifters, Doc's ache reached the world.[33]

More tension. Miriam, now remarried to the urbane, monocle-sporting music publishing exec Freddy Bienstock, had been running operations at

---

[32]Following his Atlantic years, Burke dabbled with many labels, then took up the Ghost by becoming a gospel artist. He also became operator of a mortuary chain; Spiritual Father of the forty-thousand-member House of God for All People; and father of twenty-one children.

[33]Atlantic got its first million-seller album, produced by Leiber and Stoller, with a special soloist: The Drifters' "On Broadway," with guitar solo by office hanger-on Phil Spector. "We used to put Phil [Spector] in these guitar sessions as a way of keeping him in money," Leiber and Stoller recalled.

Atlantic with a style that'd been tough, raucous, and free from undue grace. She'd dealt with all the issues that no man had patience for.

For all her worth, around the office, men like Wexler ground their teeth over Miriam. "She was a horror. I bore the brunt of it, because I was the daily operations man. She didn't report to me, because she was a partner. In her divorce, she'd gotten ten percent of the stock."

Miriam's style and Wexler's style collided like cattle in a closet. If he was trying to impress some English producer, Miriam was just as likely to bust into his office, no knocking, wave a sheaf of invoices, and demand, "Who the fuck okayed three thousand freebies for these guys?" On that very day, Wexler, not shy about his own opinions, just had it. He persuaded Ahmet, the company's waters-oiler, to face this fact: Miriam had to go. Buy her out.

The men asked Miriam, "What's your price to sell?" She named it. They gave her exactly that. Miriam Abramson Bienstock's 10 percent of Atlantic, from her divorce/child-support settlement from Herb, was bought out for six hundred thousand dollars. As she walked out the door for the final time, waving the check in her hand, she yelled back, "I give you assholes six months."

Like his brother, Nesuhi Ertegun was a man who could tell good from great, when he saw and heard and ate and sipped it. He had married three quick times during his L.A. life. He dressed for work the way others dress to attend weddings. His hands were eloquent. He used them to clap loudly when a waiter wasn't at attention. He used them to brush off dissent, as if someone's disagreement had dirtied his hands.

It was time for Nesuhi to join his brother at Atlantic. Nesuhi fit. LPs were happening, and Nesuhi loved art direction. Nesuhi knew the international market.

In the Fifties, Nesuhi had started his own indie record label: Crescent Records, named after the Crescent City, New Orleans. On its label he put a Turkish flag. Crescent was dedicated to authentic New Orleans Dixieland jazz, and Nesuhi recorded Kid Ory's band; Ory's trombone solos could make an elephant sound laryngitic. Atlantic in New York had not forgotten jazz. It had a good artist list, from Mary Lou Williams to Sidney Bechet. But to Nesuhi, jazz was the Meaning of Life. In touch with his brother, Nesuhi signed Shorty Rogers to Atlantic.

Wexler acknowledged that the arrival of Nesuhi "was one of the great moves that really elevated Atlantic into an all-around, eclectic record company." He recorded skinny tall men and round full ladies, musicians who laid down The Truth for Atlantic, singin' and boppin' jazz with no uncertainty. Nesuhi specialized in single-take music making, recording jazz miracles. Acts like the Modern Jazz Quartet and John Coltrane were

Nesuhi's. Not to mention Ornette Coleman, Charles Mingus, Rahsaan Roland Kirk.

But it was never *all* jazz. Traveling, Nesuhi too had stumbled on "white pop" in Atlantic's own Los Angeles distributorship, Record Merchandising. There, a young, energy-pushed Sal Bono was promoting the distributorship's records to radio stations. Sal wanted to rock himself. Because of his haircut plus his wife Cherilyn's aquiline looks, they called their duo Caesar and Cleo.

Caesar and Cleo had made a "singles only" deal with Mo Ostin at Reprise, which had released, "Baby Don't Go," a song Caesar had recorded on his own, for a borrowed three hundred dollars. That was followed by "Love Is Strange," but nothing much happened. Sal returned to promotion. Learning that Reprise had no contract with them, Atlantic signed Caesar and Cleo to its white-pop label Atco, letting them use their everyday first names: Sonny and Cher.

For Nesuhi, the signing was not natural to his ears. Nesuhi had risen above his own taste (or sunk below it, if you like that better) and tuned in to "what'll sell."

Atlantic stopped specializing. With Jerry facing south and Nesuhi facing west, Ahmet faced London, where group rock was growing like Midas in May.[34] Ahmet began to commute. Polydor distributed Atlantic in England and got first choice of Atlantic's signings for its UK market. Reciprocally, for North America, Atlantic got first pickings from Polydor. That simple deal carried Atlantic into hugeness. In London, Eric Clapton, already getting legendary, became subject of a graffito attack: CLAPTON IS GOD.

In 1967, recalled Atlantic engineer Tom Dowd, "Ahmet called me up and said, 'There'll be a group here from London tomorrow. They've got to be on a plane at seven o'clock Sunday.' We started on Thursday at eleven o'clock, and when the limousine driver came into the studio Sunday at five o'clock and said 'I'm looking for a group,' I said, 'They're ready.' And the three guys got on the plane, and they were gone. We did the album in three days." That band was Cream, which began its rise to the top.

Next, Ahmet signed a West Coast band named after a brand of steamroller. It was America's answer to the English supergroup, the kind designed to explode when touched on the ego. The steamroller was Buffalo Springfield (born 1967; died 1968), led by Neil Young and Stephen Stills.

As Jerry Wexler put it, "If you didn't have the Beatles in 1964, you didn't have anything." If only to survive, Atlantic had changed neighborhoods, left

---

[34]King Midas belonged in the record business. He was a king of ancient Phrygia whose finger's touch was said to turn all things to gold. The god Apollo gave Midas the ears of an ass as punishment for not liking his music.

R&B behind. London and L.A. it now was. The move wasn't announced, but old friends could feel it. Ruth Brown became one of those older friends. Articulate as were Ahmet and Jerry, what could they say now?

Several years earlier, sitting in the lobby of Atlantic's smart new offices at Columbus Circle, the label's first star, "Miss Rhythm," had been kept waiting. A long time, like maybe the buses had just stopped running. She recalled, "I sat out in the lobby waiting to see Ahmet. I sat outside for four hours. Ahmet's secretary, Noreen, now had her own secretary. You didn't get past the receptionist, and the door was closed, and everything was done on the intercom. . . . All of a sudden I thought, 'Well, they don't want to deal with me.' I realized that my days at Atlantic were numbered."

By 1965, Ruth Brown had found the only work she could: as a maid. She wrote a ten-page letter to Ahmet describing how she thought she should be getting money, which she needed for groceries. Atlantic's Sheldon Vogel and its attorney Mike Mayer looked up Brown's royalty report. She was buried under charges for promotional expenses from years back.[35] Atlantic sent her a mercy check for a thousand dollars.

Ruth Brown recalled what Bobby Darin had once told her. Before he'd left Atlantic, he'd checked its books. "I've been shortchanged, Ruth," Darin had told her. "All I can tell you is that if I were you, I'd push a little harder." Brown decided not to give up, not to stop.

Despite all this rock, Wexler held fast and true to the form-tested, three-minute single and the black belters who made them. Wexler also knew that Columbia's Mitch Miller had, up till now, been a bad guide for Aretha Franklin's career, recording her as if she were Judy Garland.

Aretha found in Wexler her kind of brother. "He invited me to his home in Great Neck. I spent long evenings out there listening to records and looking for material. It was evident that Jerry had the preparation. What's more, he was interested in getting my input and approval on everything." Wexler signed Lady Aretha.

To record, Wexler flew to Rick Hall's Florence, Alabama, Music Emporium (FAME) Studios in Muscle Shoals. The first session for the album was set to last a week. Producer Hall, knowing the importance of these sessions, had his studio and lobby filled three deep with musicians; if one could not cut the lick, he was fired and the next one would come on in.

Song One: "I Never Loved a Man (the Way I Love You)" was in the can, and they were cooking. Now, song two: "Do Right Woman, Do Right Man."

---

[35] Artist contracts often state that record labels can charge artists with a range of their expenses, from recording costs to cover art to tour support. The contracts, unless negotiated otherwise, permit this. Atlantic followed the Ruth Brown contract, doing all it allowed, charging her royalty account with all permitted expenses. The practice meant that royalties would probably never reach her.

Suddenly recording stopped. Yelling? Franklin's husband was having it out with a horn player. Husband stormed out. Aretha followed. Exit the whole damn session. Wexler, with 1.5 sides for a single requiring 2.0, lugged his 1.5 back to New York. There, using Aretha's sisters Erma and Carolyn, Wexler completed the other 0.5. "I Never Loved a Man" single topped the R&B chart for nine solid weeks. Aretha Franklin's first gold disc was there, real, yes, you could touch it.

Hits followed. Otis Redding's "Respect," redone by Franklin, spent eleven weeks upon the pop charts, followed by "A Natural Woman." By the end of 1967, Aretha got named *Billboard*'s Top Female Vocalist. It seemed like the whole world was listening. To Wexler, who'd felt a bit out of all this London/Frisco rock stuff, whose R&B had become as fashionable as black-and-white TV . . . ahh, the satisfaction.

Later, Jerry reflected in an interview for WHMM-TV: "There was such a thing as a 'Periclean Age' in Greek art. And I think there may have been a 'Periclean Age' in blues and rhythm & blues music. And the Solomon Burkes and the Otises and the Sam & Daves."

Even Pericles can get pooped. In the mid-Sixties, Soul Music (the next name for R&B) began a four-year decline. Wexler's art form got heard less on middle-class stations. In its place, psychedelic music rocked the minds of pop buyers.

"Atlantic didn't get big on black music," Wexler finally realized. "It thrived on black music and got healthy, but it didn't get large. It got large with rock—not rock & roll, but rock." Aretha Franklin—often chosen Female Vocalist of the Century in millennium closeout magazines—had been the climax, and then the end, of Atlantic R&B.

Franklin was just starting to sell for Atlantic when the phone had rung, and 7 Arts' Elliott Hyman had said, "Let's go." It was now time to face WB-7 Arts's offer for the label.

Atlantic's three owners decided to vote their shares on the issue. To Wexler, getting bought out meant getting some security cash to tuck away. At Atlantic, the possibility of selling, of converting two decades' work into cash, appealed most to Wexler, a restless man. His vote on selling: yes, for personal security.

Second to vote, Ahmet Ertegun, now living well in his town house on East Eighty-first. His decision on selling: no, for the sake of independence.

The decision came down to Nesuhi. For him, the question of selling Atlantic was broader than one of just money. Nesuhi also saw Atlantic's fellow indie labels failing. Of the R&B indies alone, many had closed their doors—Imperial, Old Town, King, Specialty, Duke/Peacock, Modern, Apollo, Savoy, Chess, Exclusive, Herald/Ember—all fallen in this now-strange world. Their old-time leaders—expert record guys, now sat together in red-leather booths in midtown bars at four-thirty in the afternoon, bull-shitting about the better old days, lying about how busy they've been lately, sipping drinks with huge olives from matching glasses. To Nesuhi, Atlantic's survival-through-size was the main issue. He did, however, have very mixed feelings. Nesuhi—mmm—decided—to sell: yes, too.

For Hyman, the deal, since the companies started talking, had been sweetened by Atlantic's cash position. It now had $7 million in the bank. The buyer owned that $7 million the day the deal closed.

These three shrewd men of Atlantic—men who for years had squeezed the nickels in recording contracts, in royalties, in costs—these three apparently had little clue as to what their label was worth on the marketplace. Instead, seeing around them the shriveling-up of other, indie labels, they persuaded themselves, half out of fear, to taste some of that cash stuff before it was too late. On walking back to the bargaining table, Wexler hustled the two Erteguns: "All their high-flown rhetoric about synergy? That's bullshit, man. This is the *real* American dream: capital gains."

Met again, Atlantic and 7 Arts sat down, chatted for forty seconds about the early snow outside, then got to the subject: the deal.

On October 1, 1967, in another Manhattan building, Warner Bros. Records' New York head, George Lee, got a phone call from Elliott Hyman. Lee was told, "Don't leave, because we're going to need you to sign some papers." Lee had his lunch brought in.

Then his dinner. To make all this work, Warner–7 Arts stayed up late. Lee just sat there, wondering what might be up. W7 had to make two deals. First, W7 had to exchange Sinatra's 33 percent of Warner/Reprise for a 20 percent interest in a still-bigger company: Warner/Reprise + Atlantic Records. That deal, made with Mickey Rudin, was simply done, to mutual advantage.

Later that night, Hyman's new, 80 percent–owned 7 Arts Record Group acquired "all the outstanding capital stock of Atlantic Recording Corporation and affiliated companies [meaning its publishing companies] for $4,500,000 cash, $3 million principal amount of unsecured notes [IOUs], and 66,225 common shares of the company [W7A]."

All that amounted to $17.5 million, for Ahmet Ertegun, Jerry Wexler, and Nesuhi Ertegun to divide. Discounted by Atlantic's cash, W7A's real cost was $10 million. Atlantic was now owned; its founders were *ex*-owners now. They were employees, albeit with goodly chunks of stock in W7A.

Somewhere around ten that night, George Lee was summoned, as an officer of Warner Bros. Records, to sign what he recalled as fifty thousand papers. The purchase of Atlantic Records was being made using cash from Warner Bros. Records' bank account. After that, Lee knew he had to call Maitland, to tell his boss what'd just happened, what he'd just signed.

Only with that phone call would Maitland learn again that, without telling him, his parents had adopted for him a second brother, this one named Ahmet. This was not like learning about Mo and Reprise. Neither of these two new siblings—Mike nor Ahmet—had ever excelled at sharing toys.

Later that month, W7A's studio music chief, Sonny Burke, drove over to Maitland's house, and then the pair headed from Encino to Palm Springs for a golf weekend. As they drove on, Mike's knuckles grew whiter. He was livid. "I think I'm going to get the hell out. I've had it with Hyman. There's no sense to try to continue. It's just one injury, one insult, one careless thing after another." Burke hypothesized for Maitland a different vision. He described a W7A music division, one that embraced its various record labels and all the rest of Warner music. "Divisions," Burke said, spreading his hands wide off his steering wheel, "you know, like they have at General Motors."

"If you establish one *division,* you're going to tie the whole thing up," Burke prompted Maitland. "Why don't you prove to Elliott Hyman and the 7 Arts people that you're really capable of coming up with something that's great for the company? For once, there would be cohesion between the arms. You've got me running the motion-picture music department. You have Mo and Joe running the two labels. You've got George Lee in New York, who's devoted to you. And now you've got Atlantic doing its part, too."

By the time they were halfway to the Springs, Maitland was making plans. First, clean up the publishing company. It was run by Victor Blau in the role of Scrooge, not only cheaply but with scared employees hand-posting numbers in big ledger books using pencils sharpened by knife. Another good step would be to consolidate duplicate support staffs ("noncreative," as if accounting were a science) between the two record companies. Distribution might be a good place to begin . . .

Shortly after buying Atlantic, Elliott Hyman called a meeting in Burbank, in WBR's closetlike, eight-foot-wide conference room. In that poor room sat Hyman and Alan Hirschfield; the Erteguns and Wexler; Maitland, Ed West, Mo Ostin, and Joe Smith, together on studio hand-me-down shabby sofas.

Maitland, knowing he was right, presented what he saw as the natural progression of business, talked about the labels' opportunities to save money together. He asked, why do we need *two* accounting departments, or *two* sets of international licensees, or *two* sets of distributors?

For Hirschfield, that first meeting had been "a tough, persuasive battle for me, because I had to eliminate enormous amounts of ego on all sides. Everyone had some objection to the plan." Maitland's idea of opportunity was doomed. Maitland got told, firmly, that in the buyout, Atlantic's autonomy had been guaranteed.

Smith sat quietly through the jockeying and saw his colleagues as they went on theorizing "grandiose schemes. Like we were going to use the 7 Arts' distribution people around the world to help with our records. It was a lot of crap. Nothing came out of it." The managers of the music area and their corporate owners envisioned just one plan. Hirschfield proposed that the labels could, together, buy five or six major indie distributors for between $10 and $12 million, getting into distributing that way. It sounded good enough, and it threatened nobody's turf. Hirschfield would start deal making. Ahmet Ertegun, never great at marching in formation, knew he had his buyout money. Now, he felt like just abandoning Atlantic altogether.

Later, during his trip to Burbank, Elliott Hyman suffered a heart attack. He was flown fast back to New York, to be hospitalized, then home to recuperate.

Hirschfield approached Chicago's Milt Salstone, owner of MS Distributing. "We had the deal made," Hirschfield remembered. "Salstone was dying to come in. We had the Schwartz Brothers in Washington and what eventually became some of the major Pickwick operations." In Chicago, the negotiators went to dinner to celebrate the buying of MS. The key deal—the Salstone deal—was then presented to 7 Arts' board of directors. The board didn't get it. "It would have catapulted those two record companies light-years ahead of their time," Hirschfield knew, "and it could have been accomplished within a six-month period." Futility.

Because of their innate need for autonomy, each of the labels stuck to its indie mind-set. The center of W7A's record business immediately shifted from Burbank to Manhattan. Maitland, who had been Jack Warner's money-maker, who had joined the Warner Bros. board and lunchroom gang, was immediately the outsider. He told me, "Decision-making moved back east. Probably because of a philosophy difference. For the first time, I was at the other end, away from the home office."

For his Warner Bros. Studios, Elliott Hyman had never felt a paternal love. By now, recovering from his heart problem, Hyman put 7 Arts' two-years-ago acquisition—Warner Bros. Pictures and Records, including Atlantic—into turnaround: a phrase that asks the question "What'll you give me for it?" Companies came sniffing to take over W7A: National General, a West Coast conglomerate run by Eugene Klein, was one suitor; Klein owned movie theaters. Commonwealth United, run by Milton Rozet, was a second; it owned Seeburg, the jukebox company. Steve Ross's Kinney Services became a third; in addition to parking lots, it owned a talent agency.

During this sniff-around, Hyman's tactic was to keep Warner-Seven's costs down and its sales value superhigh. Meanwhile, Atlantic's leaders, realizing that their $17.5 million payday had been way too cheap, gave 7 Arts their own proposition: They asked if they could buy back their company. They offered Hyman $40 million. He turned them down. Flat. Hyman was fishing; Atlantic was fine bait.

Feeling no allegiance to their buyers and having no employment contracts binding them, the Atlantic management told Hyman that, once their employment deals were up, they'd be moving on. Unless, of course, Hyman chose to resweeten the deal. He had to. He sweetened, extending their contracts.

In contrast, Warner Bros. Records got treated with less and less deference. Maitland was made to sit in the 7 Arts lobby for an hour, waiting for Hyman to be ready. To Wexler, the deference difference was clear: "7 Arts acquired Atlantic Records from the owners of the company, us, who continued to run it. Seven Arts acquired Warner Bros. from Jack Warner, who was essentially out of the picture immediately. Then they dealt with Maitland and his subchiefs, Ostin and Smith. They weren't as easy on Maitland or as courteous, because Maitland was 'only an employee.' We at Atlantic were the owners. That always conveys special cachet."

To the Warner execs, one of 7 Arts' more stunning economic moves was its 1967 turndown of its comedy-album star's—Bill Cosby's—contract renewal. Cosby had become a huge seller for us, album after album. We were stunned by 7 Arts' penury. "Let 'im go," we were told. The press release stated that 7 Arts management refused to meet "excessive demands for a renewal advance." Bill Cosby and his manager, Roy Silver, were enraged by the statement.[36]

Similar pinchpenny attitudes were imposed on Maitland in other areas of his domain. Smith and Ostin also wanted a better deal for *them*selves. After all, Mo and Joe were signing acts that would please the god Apollo.

Squeeze time.

Significant Records by Atlantic

1958

LaVern Baker ("I Cried a Tear" and "I Waited Too Long") • Ruth Brown ("This Little Girl's Gone Rockin'") • The Coasters ("Yakety Yak") • Bobby Darin ("Splish Splash" and "Queen of the Hop") • Clyde McPhatter ("A Lover's Question" and "Come What May") • Chuck Willis ("What Am I Living For?" and "Hang Up My Rock and Roll Shoes")

---

[36]Bill Cosby started his own record label but could not record for it; he still owed albums to Warner Bros. His new label was run by Roy Silver, plus Bruce Campbell, promotion man Marvin Deane, and VP Artie Mogull. The label's name, appropriately enough, was Tetragrammaton, which is Greek for "rip-off." Tetragrammaton caught its first hit with Deep Purple but was not to be long for the world. Marvin recalled the highlight of Tetragrammaton: "Magnificent offices in Beverly Hills with a full-time cook."

1959

Atlantic: Ruth Brown ("I Don't Know") • Ray Charles ("What'd I Say (Part I))" • The Coasters ("Charlie Brown," "Along Came Jones," and "Poison Ivy") • The Drifters ("There Goes My Baby") • Joe Turner ("Honey Hush")
Atco: Bobby Darin (*That's All,* including "Beyond the Sea" and "Mack the Knife")

1960

Atlantic: Ray Charles (*The Genius of Ray Charles,* including "Let the Good Times Roll" and *In Person,* including "What'd I Say") • The Drifters ("Save the Last Dance for Me") • Ben E. King ("Spanish Harlem")
Atco: Bobby Darin (*This Is Darin,* including "Clementine," and *At the Copa,* including "Dream Lover" and "Won't You Come Home, Bill Bailey")

1961

Atlantic: Solomon Burke ("Just Out of Reach (of My Two Open Arms)") • Ray Charles (*The Genius After Hours* and *The Genius Sings the Blues* and *Do the Twist*) • The Drifters ("Save the Last Dance for Me") • Ben E. King ("Stand by Me") • Carla Thomas ("Gee Whiz (Look at His Eyes)")
Atco: Bobby Darin (*The Bobby Darin Story,* including "Artificial Flowers," "Early in the Morning," and "Queen of the Hop") • Jorgen Ingmann & His Guitar ("Apache") • Ben E. King ("Spanish Harlem")

1962

Atlantic: Ruth Brown ("Mama (He Treats Your Daughter Mean)") • The Drifters ("Up on the Roof") • Ben E. King ("Don't Play That Song (You Lied))" • Mel Tormé ("Comin' Home Baby")
Atco: Acker Bilk ("Stranger on the Shore") • Bobby Darin ("You Must Have Been a Beautiful Baby," "What'd I Say," and "Things") • Bent Fabric & His Piano ("Alley Cat")
Stax: Booker T. & the MG's ("Green Onions")

1963

Atlantic: Solomon Burke ("If You Need Me") • The Drifters (*Up on the Roof,* including "Save the Last Dance for Me" and "There Goes My Baby") • Ray Charles ("Let the Good Times Roll") • Barbara Lewis ("Hello Stranger")
Atco: The Drifters ("On Broadway") • Ben E. King ("I (Who Have Nothing)" • Nino Tempo & April Stevens ("Deep Purple" and "Whispering")
Stax: Rufus Thomas ("Walking the Dog")

1964

Atlantic: The Drifters ("On Broadway" and "Under the Boardwalk") • The Vibrations ("My Girl Sloopy")
Atco: The Beatles ("Ain't She Sweet")

1965

Atlantic: Solomon Burke ("Got to Get You Off My Mind" and "Tonight's the Night") • The Drifters ("Saturday Night at the Movies") • Barbara Lewis ("Baby, I'm Yours" and "Make Me Your Baby") • Wilson Pickett ("In the Midnight Hour") • Joe Tex ("Hold On to What You've Got" and "I Want To (Do Everything for You)") • Willie Tee ("Teasin' You")
Volt: Otis Redding ("I've Been Loving You Too Long (to Stop Now)" and "Satisfaction")

1966

Atlantic: Wilson Pickett ("Don't Knock My Love," "Land of 1000 Dances," and "634–5789 (Soulsville, U.S.A.)") • The Young Rascals ("Good Lovin'") • Percy Sledge ("When a Man Loves a Woman," "Warm and Tender Love," and "It Tears Me Up") • Joe Tex ("Sweet Woman Like You") • The Troggs ("Wild Thing")

Stax: Eddie Floyd ("Knock on Wood") • Sam & Dave ("Hold On! I'm Comin'") • Carla Thomas ("B-A-B-Y")

Volt: Otis Redding ("Fa-Fa-Fa-Fa-Fa (Sad Song)" and "Try a Little Tenderness")

1967

Atlantic: Bobby Darin ("If I Were a Carpenter") • Aretha Franklin ("I Never Loved a Man (The Way I Loved You)," "Respect," and "A Natural Woman (You Make Me Feel Like)" and *Aretha Arrives*, including "Baby I Love You") • Wilson Pickett ("Everybody Needs Somebody to Love," "Funky Broadway," and "Mustang Sally") • The Young Rascals (*Collections*, including "I've Been Lonely Too Long" and *Groovin'*, including "A Girl Like You," "How Can I Be Sure," and "You Better Run") • Sonny & Cher ("The Beat Goes On") • Flip Wilson ("Cowboys & Colored People")

Atco: Bee Gees (*1st*, including "New York Mining Disaster 1941 (Have You Seen My Wife, Mr. Jones)" and "To Love Somebody") • Buffalo Springfield ("For What It's Worth (Stop Hey What's That Sound)") • Arthur Conley ("Sweet Soul Music" and "Shake, Rattle and Roll") • Cream (*Fresh Cream* and *Disraeli Gears*, including "Sunshine of Your Love") • The Fireballs ("Bottle of Wine")

Stax: Booker T. & The MG's ("Hip Hug-Her") • Otis Redding & Carla Thomas ("Tramp" and "Knock on Wood") • Sam & Dave ("Soothe Me" and *Soul Men*, including "I Thank You" and "Soul Man")

Volt: The Bar-Kays ("Soul Finger"/"Knucklehead") • Otis Redding (*History of Otis Redding*)

9

INSIDE Warner Bros. Records, around 1967, the executive look grew slightly shaggier. Atop executives, those craving entente with their artists, heads of hair were less frequently harvested. Beards sprouted like an epidemic of ragweed.

I kept knocking out liner notes for acts I could comprehend, like Petula Clark:

Used to be, girl singers rode on buses, undressed with the door ajar, drank liquid gin, swore good. Were equal parts pretty paint, swinger, porter, promoter, and hooker. Most had bad arches. Plus six teal blue ball gowns with ripped hems. No more.

Like many of us at Warner Bros. Records, I was straddling two worlds of music. I, too, had grown my beard and let my hair get an inch longer than business barbers recommended. I looked terribly hip and wore a Nehru jacket. Pet Clark asked me to write her screen test (for *Finian's Rainbow*) and I wrote a mod (vs. hippie) scene. For liner notes, I was nominated for a third Grammy. At the ceremony, sitting next to Petula, when my name came up, she put her hand on mine. When I lost, she took her hand back, nicely. I also spectated at the year's Sunset Strip riots ("There's a man with a gun over there") along with my neo-hippie-looking first wife, Gail, and our two-year-old son, Chris, up on my shoulders. This was not, however, the Rose Parade. A sheriff with a large baton stared at us and said, "What are *you* doing here?" He batoned Gail in her stomach. I rushed us to UCLA Med Center in my new green Jaguar XKE covertible, top down. We at Warner were working two worlds.

Still attending Frank Sinatra record sessions, still writing down what I saw. Over the past several years, Mr. Sinatra noticed me but never called me by name. At first I felt slighted by this. Then I understood why. Sinatra was jealous of me. I was thinner than he, I realized, and I could type.

But by 1967, the end of such liner writing was near. I'd graduated within the company to the status of "young and hip." Once Joe signed the Grateful Dead, I'd met them at their house on Ashbury, near the intersection of Haight. The living room was stunning; on its west wall hung a five-foot-high photo of a nude woman sitting astride a nude man's lap. I appreciated the art, as college had taught me to do.

At our first Burbank meeting with the about-to-record-in-Hollywood Grateful Dead, they stunned WBR's beloved writer of album notes by insisting that, instead of my prose on *their* album's liner, *they* wished instead to put a picture of a two-masted sailing ship flying toward the viewer through clouds. They thought liner notes were dumb and used the word "exciting" excessively. I caught the Dead's drift and quickly shifted to other exciting outlets within WBR.

Following that meeting, the Grateful Dead entourage moved, with vans, old ladies, kids, and two dogs, down to L.A. to record its first album, which it did during periods when its members were not passed out on the studio floor. The Dead were deeply inspired in ways that those of us not stoned could not comprehend. For instance, they sensed that, on the blank recording tape that producer Dave Hassinger was using, the silence hissed. Raising his head, one of the Dead ultimately spoke a cure: "What we ought to do is record thirty minutes of air in the summertime, when it's hot and smoggy. Thirty minutes of heavy air. Then we could go to the desert and record thirty minutes of clean air. Then mix the two together, get a good sound, and record over it."

Once packaged and ready, the Grateful Dead's album got its 1967 San Francisco debut party at Fugazy Hall. Joe Smith and I flew up in our Men in Blue blazers. We entered a hall and saw a big tin tub in the center of the floor. In that tub, floating in water, was some starchlike stuff. I was informed that this was a "feely." Girls stood near that feely moaning, "Ohh! Yeah." I passed on the feely, avoided drinking their punch, and continued to smoke machine-made cigarettes while all about me smoked the Dead's music, right down to the blazing roach.

San Francisco, which had so blessed Burbank, was viewed with little reverence by Joe. He was of the opinion that "the biggest bullshit was the San Francisco bullshit. That was the flower children and love and 'for the people.'" Meanwhile, the Dead's lawyers treated them like they were pro-football draft choices. "You know," Joe recalled, "they need thirty thousand dollars to say 'Maybe,' and another twenty-six thousand dollars to go into the studio. They need twenty-two thousand dollars to . . . well, it's all bull-shit." Neither Joe nor Mo turned his back to the BS. They stuck with the movement.

Wearing his red-lininged blazer, Joe Smith climbed onstage, DJ-friendly like this was still Boston and this was Freddy Cannon Night, to say the customary, innocent thing: "I just want to tell you all, Warner Bros. Records feels privileged to take the Grateful Dead out to the world." The

Dead's manager, Rock Scully, shirted in tie-dye, leaped onto the stage, took the mike, and added, "The Grateful Dead feel privileged to introduce Warner Bros. Records to the world." 'Twas the last night I wore my blue blazer, other than to bed.

Live ballroom music had returned to America, in a way not seen since the big bands of the Thirties and Forties. Haight-Ashbury had become the hippie epicenter during the Summer of Love. The Fillmore and Avalon ballrooms became the Palladiums and Paramounts of the Sixties. In New York, Bill Graham echoed his San Francisco light-show ballroom with dance concerts at the Fillmore East. Behind the stage screen, on a twenty-foot-high catwalk, I stood beside a USC grad-school buddy, Josh White, as his Joshua Light Show projected oily experiences onto movie screens for dance-floor freakin'. Discoordination of the senses—sound, sight, taste—exploded in the heads out front. Dancers kept the beat with their hearts, felt the air move across their bodies, and found "where" and "when" irrelevant. The physical experience of music, however, took place on such evenings with an intensity equaling Bach's, its sound waves reaching out for more than thirty years.

In Greenwich Village, "head" retained its earlier meaning: a place to think. Still searching for signables, Ostin found three Greenwich Village intellectuals, about whom the words "tattered and unkempt" barely covered it. The Fugs sang songs like "Coca Cola Douche" and "Kill for Peace." In New York, Mo's signing of the Fugs passed for an intellectual fashion statement: Reprise was on the side of rebels. Onstage, the Fugs gave the finger freely, spoke "fuck" and "shit" like they were pronouns, and were hip, honest, and pacific to the point of outrage. For Reprise, the Fugs became the tails side of the coin. Heads, it's Frank; tails, it's Fugs. In signing the Fugs, Ostin had opened doors to offbeat heroes of the new, underground generation, acts like the Stooges, MC5, and the Mothers of Invention.

However, do not search 1967's charts for such Fugs, whose performing career may have peaked with their unsuccessful attempt to get behind the Iron Curtain in Czechoslovakia to masturbate in front of invading Russian tanks. Such signed singers were obscurities, beneath charts still buried by Beatles.[37]

Warner Bros. had changed with the Dead. Reprise had changed from the Kinks on. It was now Mo untethered, exercising his belief in how Reprise best ran: He signed contracts with musicians who believed in themselves, he matched them up with the best producers, he handed the result over to hot marketing execs, and he avoided press interviews. Mo hired the

---

[37]In contrast to their earlier deal with EMI, in 1967—amid the record industry's first billion-dollar year—the Beatles resigned with EMI for 17 percent of wholesale royalty in the United States, and 10 percent for the rest of the world.

best people and gave them more than enough rope, endless rope, it felt like. Reprise became, Quincy Jones later told me, "like walking into a whole different planet."

Often Mo and I would walk the pavements of New York after dark.

One night we had taxied down to the Village to meet up with Albert Grossman, who had redefined the term "artist manager" in building the careers of Peter, Paul & Mary and Bob Dylan. To me, Grossman appeared extraordinarily well fed, full as a Thanksgiving turkey. His hair, long and gray, was tied into a ponytail. He wore granny glasses. He smoked in an orginal way, his cigarette held between his ring and little fingers, the rest of his hand curled into a smoke chamber, inhaling with big pulls through the hole between his thumb and first finger. This I saw as the epitome of pot-hip culture.

As the three of us headed through the Village toward some down-three-steps, black-walled nightclub to find an act, Albert was engrossed in what he was telling us, so much so that when, from a second-story window, an egg was tossed at him (hip old men still being outlaws in parts of our culture), Albert did not pause in his pitch. The eggshell crunched, unnoticed by him, onto his shoulder, then onto the broken sidewalk. We just moved on, intent on catching an act more important than some old egg.

A&R had changed. Texas rock & roll sounded as corny as Roy Acuff. Jimmy Bowen—whose triplets had hoisted Dean and Frank to the singles charts only a few years earlier—noticed the change. Bowen left Reprise to start his own company, Amos Records, but that went nowhere. WBR's traditional A&R men, Dick Glasser and Jimmy Hilliard, finding their well-crafted recordings as dated as Danish Modern bedrooms, both left WBR. Nancy Sinatra and her boots walked on out, too. All that "mod" business gone, in a couple of years' time, brushed to smithereens by Laurel Canyon, the Haight, the Village.

In came the next. Lured by Andy Wickham, Joni Mitchell signed with Reprise after rejecting a "slave labor" contract with Vanguard. David Crosby produced her album. It got no AM airplay. Mitchell's kind of music became known as "underground," a euphemism for "heard only on FM."

At Warner Bros. Records, the underground challenge felt, to us, like a holy war. We figured we were headed in the right direction (left), but the market had yet to bless our turn. By now it was our label's tenth anniversary. We crusaded to a Hawaiian island called Kauai. Lights down. Slide projector on. Roll the tape, but this year's stars did not remind their audience of Vegas, nor of ring-a-ding ding:

NEIL YOUNG:
Everybody knows this is nowhere
Every time I think about back home

RANDY NEWMAN:
Seven ships without a sail.
Seven cats without a tale.

Our convention impressed even native Hawaiians, so accustomed to nudity but shocked when, one evening during the cocktail party, our professionally tanned San Francisco promotion man Pete Marino walked up from the warm surf, into the luau; a WB logo tattooed on his arm, butt naked.

The convention in Kauai felt euphoric. Warner/Reprise distributors and licensees, who'd flown in, some from Paris and beyond, experienced new signings, attention-getting talent.

1967: The Fugs • The Jim Kweskin Jug Band with Maria Muldaur • Kenny Rogers and the First Edition • The Jimi Hendrix Experience • Miriam Makeba • Van Dyke Parks

1968: Arlo Guthrie • Tiny Tim • Joni Mitchell • Randy Newman • Neil Young • Frank Zappa, with Bizarre and Straight Records • Eric Andersen • Charles Wright and the Watts 103rd Street Rhythm Band

Warner/Reprise's signers, Smith and Ostin, used the signings above to make up for their less-remembered signings, artists with the longevity of clouds, though each of these artists hoped its label would treat him or her more like a cathedral:

Joe Smith's Worst Sixties Signings:

Louise Huebner, the Singing Witch: *Seduction Through Witchcraft*
Uncle Dick's Old Time Singers: *Swing Along with Uncle Dick*
Nikita the K & Friends of Ed Labunsky: *Go Go Radio Moscow*
Sidney Poitier: *Poitier Meets Plato*
Rod McKuen and Rock Hudson: *Love of the Common People*

Mo Ostin's Worst Sixties Signings:

The Paris Sisters Sing Everything Under the Sun
Arthur Writus & the Nagging Pains
Mephistopheles: *In Frustration I Hear Singing*
Wilderness Road: *Sold for the Prevention of Disease*

Despite such turds, despite company execs who dressed more and more like Indian scouts, the financial industry viewed and blessed Warner's record labels, revering them as that noblest of animals, the cash cow.

One night in New York, Mo suggested we stop at a West Side club called The Scene to hear some country act. While we were waiting, a most embarrassing thing happened. A gangly tramp in makeup, carrying a shopping bag, stepped up to the mike and sang in falsetto, "Tiptoe Through the Tulips." While I crawled under our table in embarrassment, Mo signed Tiny Tim. Good shot, Chief.[38]

In a young man's game, Tiny was already forty-five years old. He'd already been through his real name (Herbert Khaury) and p.k.a.s (Larry Love, Julian Foxglove, and Emmett Swink). He preferred not to be called "Mr. Tim" and indeed called us all by our own first names, like "Mr. Mo" and "Mr. Stan." Once for a Christmas party at my house, Tiny's producer, Richard Perry, asked if Tiny could be invited. Tiny brought his uke and for more than one hour sang Christmas, Valentine's, and Groundhog carols, while forty guests politely squirmed on my living-room floor. Tiny's "Tiptoe Through the Tulips" sold around a quarter of a million singles, then about the same number of albums. In a time of fear over menacing longhairs, America embraced Tiny Tim as its "lovable" freak.

Radio, however, ignored our odder artists, from Van Dyke Parks to Frank Zappa. We looked for other avenues to get the word out. For our "fringe" artists, we took out ads in papers. Ads had become my job, handed me one day in 1969. My entire training in advertising consisted of my boss, Joel Friedman, going on work sabbatical to study for his bar exam. He came into my office with this guidance: "Here, you do it." So, till my boss got back, I wrote full-page ads to run in the trades (music-business weekly magazines) and what we called "the underground press," a euphemism for a loose bunch of non-sched opinion papers, left-winged to the extreme, occasionally intelligible, and, with their ads costing like seventy dollars a page, dirt cheap. For seventy dollars, why not? Soon label heads Ostin and Smith started getting a few, then many, compliments on my ads. Artists liked their candor. Our ad style was a "what have we got to lose?" approach, addressed to the trade ("We're really batting zero on this album") and consumers ("You don't like our records, send in for a free Baggie of Laurel Canyon dirt").

Following the lead of rock-music-intense *Crawdaddy!,* a new rock journal, more movement intense (as well as more clearly printed) called *Rolling Stone* snuck onto hippie newsstands in late 1967. Their ads cost little, no one without a bongo bought them, and their circulation was a few thousand. Warner/Reprise took out ads in both. For the labels and me, it was a chance to wail.

At Warner/Reprise, we enjoyed "the movement." We accommodated artists who behaved with gall. Joe, a social whiz, and Mo, a modest kid, catered to their newly signed acts, many of which made a specialty of gall.

---

[38]I later learned that Mo had not acted spontaneously; Peter Yarrow of Peter, Paul & Mary had tipped Mo to look for Mr. Tiny.

Singers were no longer called "singers." They and guitarists and bands were now "artists." Artists seized power from art departments, chose what their packages would look like, eliminated prose in favor of their songs' (often unintelligible) lyrics, plus personal thank-you lists whose thankees ranged from the artist's cousin Louie to God Almighty. To us, this was like some guy at Kellogg getting to thank his mom and teachers on the backs of cereal boxes.

In recording studios, artists indulged their time, sometimes without finishing anything we could release. Shockingly, at least to us, our artists didn't give a damn. Hey, that's just the way it crumbled. Don't give a shit what's written down on that piece of contract paper, we'd get told. You get it when *we* think it's ready.

Accommodating such behaviors was a lesson learned by some labels, though not by labels with a death wish. Artists brought in their own hand-drawn album covers; I often had to retrieve the eyes of our art director, Ed Thrasher, after they'd rolled to the ceiling. But like it or lump it, we learned to accomodate.

One after another, my new kind of artist-loving ads (and posters and buttons and inscribed toilet tissue) rolled out of Burbank. Recently divorced, I wrote this stuff on weekends when, alone with my yellow tablet and too much time on my hands, I self-amused.

- For the Grateful Dead, WBR ran a contest centered on the music's scruffiest keyboard man. Headline: THE PIGPEN LOOK-ALIKE CONTEST.
- When Joni Mitchell felt chagrined at a series of my sexist ads—JONI MITCHELL TAKES FOREVER, followed by JONI MITCHELL IS 90% VIRGIN—I promised I'd never repeat such headlines.
- When time came for a trade ad for Sinatra, I wanted to complain about how little airplay he'd been getting. I knew a good headline: FRANK SINATRA IS 90% VIRGIN.
- For Reprise's revolting-to-the-eye group, the Fugs, the headline was WIN A FUG DREAM DATE COMPETITION. Contestants wrote back letters why they wanted/needed such a date with one of the Fugs. The winner:

Dear Sirs (or whoever you are):
I would like to go out with Tuli because I would like him to fuck me.
　　　　　　　　　　　　　　　　　　—Barbara
P.S. Even if I don't win, I would still like it.

To get attention via such ads took no hard work. Record-company advertising all looked like Vic Damone's glossy under a headline like ROCK-

ETING UP THE CHARTS! Ad reps for the underground press began to sit in the office of my English secretary, Jeanie Lumley, waiting to see me to get an ad while watching her hot pants. Jann Wenner's *Rolling Stone* page rate was three hundred dollars. Wenner hadn't been getting any (ads). He, too, sat, waited, and watched agog. I obliged Wenner. When Randy Newman failed to sell well, Reprise took out an ad in *Rolling Stone* offering to give away the new Newman album free.

WBR's Van Dyke Parks issued a 1968 album (*Song Cycle*) that critics called "a milestone in pop" and "the most important, creative, and advanced pop recording since *Sgt. Pepper*." Plus a few votes as Album of the Year. The album moved out of stores like a stone unable to roll. I composed a pissed-off trade ad for *Billboard,* lamenting HOW WBR LOST $35,009.50 ON THE ALBUM OF THE YEAR.[39]

Some years later, Joe Smith, talking about our ad style, said, "Out of it, I think, [came] the whole philosophy of our company . . . [Our] advertising has been a major factor in attracting artists." Then he recalled the pain of certain ads: "Van Morrison with a black mask across his eyes, saying, 'This man scored last night.' Van was not happy about that. But in the end, every manager, attorney, or artist sits down . . . and they talk about our advertising. Tell me another company where people talk about their advertising. Not how much, but the quality of it. And on the general bottom line, our advertising is far more effective than ineffective, and we get a lot more hits out of it than we do misses. And if Joni Mitchell is unhappy with the ninety percent virgin line, it's for personal reasons, not that the ad was ineffective. It was a damn good ad; she was just maybe not happy with the connotation that she was a virgin."

When Joel Friedman, after flunking his bar exam, returned as marketing head of WBR, Mo stepped in to inform him that they'd decided I should continue to do the advertising. In fact, they handed my department a new title, a fancy term—Creative Services. All of a sudden, I got a staff. I could now splatter my flippancies across Warner's Publicity, Artist Relations, Art, Merchandising, and other stuff.

Through all this, I got my own office. It was ten feet by ten feet; its best feature may have been that it had a ceiling. In this private cave, I could shut the door to neck with my typewriter. I became startled when, one day, Mo escorted somebody good, somebody like Neil Young, down the hall, opened the door to my office, pointed at me, and said with pride, "*That's* Stan

---

[39]One of the longest-careered artists (and earliest industry video exec) with Warner Bros. Records, the erudite Parks lives in Los Angeles, does movie scores, and has, over three decades of recording, made six albums: *Song Cycle, Discover America, Clang of the Yankee Reaper, Jump!, Tokyo Rose,* and *Orange Crate Art.*

Cornyn." Then gently closed the door and walked away. I felt that my writing career had just peaked. It may have.[40]

In north San Francisco, above a street called Broadway, where in the late Fifties there used to be dim-lit coffeehouses where beatniks read paperbacks bought at City Lights, the raw-wood bookstore, now in the late Sixties there were topless bars with neon signs featuring blinking tits. Down Broadway toward the bay, there was also a little radio station up on a second floor. An obscure radio station, in the morning it broadcast in Chinese but in the evening, when through the city many lights had gone out—even the tits lights—and most people slept, others stayed up to hear a new kind of radio.

Those who stayed up lived where rents were low and dreams were high. In their flats, often furniture free, they slept low to the floor. In the fog-diffused darkness, they lay there, tuned in. Their essential utensils of life were three: a short candle, an AM-FM radio, and a tambourine.

A different spirit whispered through the night banks of fog. Something we learned to call "underground radio" began with, once again, Tom Donahue, now moved over to KMPX-FM in San Francisco. Rid of Autumn Records, rid of KYA-AM, a turned-on Donahue invented a new radio form—his voice reassuring you softly in basso confidences, he was there, musically transported, for intelligent fans. He programmed music that didn't push you around but led you higher, as if you were among uncharted artists gathered at a strangely peopled party, artists from Country Joe to Erik Satie to P. J. Proby. No station jingles intruded on your night, no screaming commercials to flicker your candle, no hard-talkin' DJ jive. Sets of songs without talk segued on and on, sometimes full half-hour trips without a word.

In a few months, KMPX-FM became the most successful FM station in the country. That wasn't saying much, financially; AM, the yelling side of the radio dial, still was 90 percent of the action. But FM fit us. At first, we all called it "underground radio," but that evolved to "freeform" with leather-fringed DJs (then into "progressive" and "album-oriented" as the times' jargon evolved). Los Angeles followed with KPPC, New York with WNEW-FM, and even Wolfman Jack played "high" music. Warner Bros. Records felt attuned. FM played our odd records. We liked their other choices. Felt right. At other labels, like Dot Records, this underground radio went as unheard as some ten-watt college station in North Dakota. Within a year, Dot Records was dead, while in low-rent rooms in San Francisco,

---

[40]Around this time, my art director, Ed Thrasher, had a cartoon of me drawn: body of a Pepsi can, holding a typewriter, etc. With typical modesty, I used it to imprint my holiday gift to many, a sweatshirt with the cartoon and the headline I KNOW STAN CORNYN PERSONALLY.

candles burned on until, across the hills to the east, the sun rose fresh as ever, a new day whispered you awake, and you reached for your tambourine.

In his office at the back east end of the hall, still overlooking that roof air conditioner and, beyond it, the butt end of Technicolor's hulky building, Mo Ostin again scanned 1967's English trade paper *Melody Maker,* fishing for hits that had no U.S. labels. One artist's name had been catching his eye. He sent for the single. As usual, he checked with his network of hip ears. Mo never claimed he heard hit music, but he really heard hit heads: Lenny, Andy, a dozen more. Mo Ostin remained hushed about his interest in this one single. He knew that Atlantic had a first-refusal deal with British Decca (Track Records). Finally, Mo heard, Atlantic had turned it down with the comment that he sounded like "a second-rate B. B. King." Ostin signed the Jimi Hendrix Experience by long-distance phone.

He brought the single into our weekly "new releases" meeting, asking for our opinions. "When Mo brought in Jimi Hendrix," Reprise accountant Murray Gitlin remembered, "I thought, 'Oh, my God, we're paying forty thousand dollars!' We listened to the tapes. Nobody, *no*body could understand. It was a bunch of screeching and screaming. We looked upon Hendrix as one of the strangest things to happen."

In June 1967, three hours south of Haight-Ashbury, the Monterey Pop Festival sprawled out from a wide stage, its main audience sitting row upon row, flat out before it, with tiers on each side for lesser-priced seats. But for these three days, any seat was worth more than a kilo. Before this world spotlight crowd came acts, many still provincial in appeal but who soon enough would emerge into popularity's glare: The Association—with its unprecedented voice blends by Clark Burroughs and producer Bones Howe[41]— Buffalo Springfield, the Grateful Dead, the Jimi Hendrix Experience, Mike Bloomfield, the Paul Butterfield Blues Band, the Beach Boys, Booker T and the MGs, the Byrds, Otis Redding, Paul Simon, the Who—all to end up artists for our eventual conglomerate—dominated the three-day-and-mostly-night event.

Jerry Wexler, who'd known Hendrix since he'd played backup guitar with King Curtis, was backstage with Otis Redding. Hendrix was dressed in

---

[41]The Association, previously on WBR-distributed Valiant Records, now had been bought by Warner Bros. Records from Valiant's owners, Barry DeVorzon and Billy Sherman. Their festival-opening song was "Enter the Young." After leaving Warner Bros. Records in 1972, the Association continued as a performing act into the 1990s. In 1990, BMI announced that the Association's "Never My Love" and Paul McCartney's "Yesterday" were the only two songs in the last fifty years to have received over five million plays.

purple velvet, a pink boa, feathers. Passing Wexler backstage, he told him in a whispered aside, "It's only for the show."

The Jimi Hendrix Experience came on and turned up the amps so their buzz could reach the San Diego Zoo. Hendrix was an electrical storm, plucking his Fender Stratocaster's loosened strings with his teeth, behind his back—all the tricks he'd learned from guitarists on the chitlin' circuit. Hendrix's guitar screeched and whined as he caressed it, shoving it between his legs and humping it.

Two bands were known for destroying their guitars on stage (they flipped a coin to see who'd get to destroy first and who'd get to immolate his guitar). First, the Who'd destroyed guitars in a fit of speaker bashing. Hendrix could top that. He pulled out a can of Ronson lighter fluid, squirted, lit; his guitar blazed. He smashed the body of his still-amplified, shrill-shrieking, flaming guitar into the amps, then flung its limbs into the audience.

"Wild Thing" ended his set with a long, high-whistling whine and the biggest, *tha-wack* of a chord since Hiroshima. Ostin, having signed Hendrix unseen weeks earlier, actually saw him for the first time on that stage, that night. He told me he was a little embarrassed by the lighter-fluid spectacle. But the feedback, the eerie modulations, those changed rock the way *The Rite of Spring* changed classical.

The Monterey Pop Festival introduced to a "pop" audience such underground acts as Janis Joplin. With Big Brother and the Holding Company, she taught the audience a passionate, R&B song style. Otis Redding followed her and became the festival capper. Following a stirring warm-up by Booker T. & the MG's, on came Otis. "I was apprehensive, very leery of exposing Otis Redding to the thousands of flower children," said Jerry Wexler. "Here were the Jefferson Airplane. They looked like they were playing with twenty-foot Marshall amps. And the Grateful Dead doing their long boogies. And here comes Booker T. & the MGs, and they've got their little Sears Roebuck amps and this tiny sound."

Out strode Otis Redding in his too-tight suit, mod and passé. He peered out into the California night, through the blinding arc lights, and called out to the thousands of love children out there, dressed in beads and leather, "Y'all are the love crowd, right?" Thousands roared. "We all love each other, don't we?" Downbeat for "Shake," then "I've Been Loving You Too Long," top that with "Try a Little Tenderness."

A few months after his awakening appearance in Monterey, Otis Redding headed for another appearance in Madison, Wisconsin. His private, twin-engine Beechcraft plane crashed into a Wisconsin lake. He and his band died.

For the Jimi Hendrix Experience, however, little known, debuting in

America, Reprise had lucked out, arranging a national tour for the trio. The tour's first date would be Atlanta, where the Experience would open for the teen/cute act the Monkees.

That tour-opening night, Hendrix wafted onstage with trio members Mitch Mitchell and Noel Redding. Hendrix, his hair erect, frame all in paisley and velvet, boa flowing, his eyes peering into another dimension, afloat, wailed "Purple Haze." Midteen girls, there for the Monkees, there for titillation, experienced little arousal from these weirdos. For seven concerts on the Monkees tour, the Jimi Hendrix Experience tolerated little girls screaming "We want th' Mon-kees!" In Forest Hills, halfway through his set, Hendrix finally flung down his guitar, gave the audience the finger, leaned into the mike for a mellow "Fuck you," and walked off. Watching from the wings, one awestruck Monkee turned to another: "Good for him."

Reprise shipped Hendrix's first album, *Are You Experienced?* into its independent branch system. Reception to this new Experience was cool. In Detroit, for instance, distributor Henry Droz ordered 175, with 25 of those free. Charlotte distributor Burt Fleishman ordered 6. Plus 1 free. Mo Ostin remembered Charlotte's opening order, that 6+1 ("for every six you buy you get one more free"), that caution. This . . . this was not what Reprise needed, building a company. But distributors like Fleishman, they ran their own shows. If ever there was one moment that becoming a major label, that having your own branch outlets across the country got Mo pregnant, it was that 6+1 initial order from Charlotte, North Carolina. What was needed, Ostin knew, were enough hits to fill an all-Warner pipeline—enough to make a branch cost effective. He felt closer.

For pop record labels, the trades called the music of '68 "bubblegum," personified by the Archies. Warner/Reprise moved its New York office out of the picture company's dingy distribution offices into brighter (though still linoleum-floored) offices in the Look building, 488 Madison Avenue, opening it on June 5, 1968, the day Robert Kennedy was shot.

For R&B record labels, 1968 turned into trauma, a turning point in black music. Otis Redding, dead in a plane crash. Race riots charring Detroit. Berry Gordy moving Motown to Hollywood. And suddenly, Martin Luther King, Jr., shot dead. The R&B world stopped its jive, cold. Those background singers doing syncopated steppin', over, done with.

The Stax empire had gone down. Sam & Dave's records got little play. Don Covay and Ben E. King left Atlantic. As did Solomon Burke, who recalled, "I had a very funny feeling in my bones when we were in the height of all of this (and I even told Ahmet). I said, 'I have a strange feeling that maybe we're going to come to the end.' " Rhythm & blues, which had been the mainstay of Atlantic Records, was virtually exterminated. Burke's final record was "I Wish I Knew How It Would Feel to Be Free."

Black turned to "funk," the right word for the right time. Black artists stopped worrying about "crossing over." Instead, they made a statement on their own turf, talking and singing about their *own* identities, their own independence. James Brown preached, "Say It Loud: I'm Black and I'm Proud."

In Miami that year, Wexler was to be honored with two awards in front of the NATRA convention of television and radio announcers. Unexpectedly, the black civil rights movement no longer behaved nicely. At this year's NATRA, a black posse calling itself the Fair Play Committee took the convention hostage. Strong arms and guns prevailed. Al Bell of Stax was kidnapped, not seen for weeks. Booker T. was told not to play in a mixed-color band. When Wexler arrived at the hotel, he heard that a man with a gun had walked through the auditorium saying, "I'm looking for Wexler." King Curtis hustled Wexler to safety. Black power was, for a moment, in the hands of shakedown artists. Wexler got his awards by parcel post.

Atlantic's Wilson Pickett covered the Beatles' "Hey Jude," while the original was still on the charts, and did so decently. He turned himself into a world-touring act, regularly reporting in his successes to Wexler: "Jerry, those fucking English chicks have got to be crazy. Man, one after another, they come up, think they're gettin' my johnson for nothin'! Nobody wants to pay! What's the matter with these women?"

"If we hadn't traveled out into white rock," Jerry Wexler admitted, "we'd have gone out of the business, like every other of our fellow R&B labels. They all died."[42]

Back from the validation of Monterey's axis-shifting festival, the majesty of my new position—I was no longer in Editorial, now in charge of Creative Services—grew in my mind. Our attitude became, How can we break rules? Hal Halverstadt, Judy Simms, and Pete Johnson joined. We had total license to make up new ways to promote product. At noon, we'd take over the semiprivate street called Warner Boulevard outside our offices, playing our own version of football, in which one art director, stoned, going long for a pass, slammed at top speed, arms outstretched, into a lamppost, and may still be hearing his ears ring. Weekends many of us roamed places like Jerry Hopkins's early head shop in Westwood, tarting ourselves up by wearing turquoise pins and macramé bras, hanging drawings of Indian

---

[42]After 106 singles and seven albums and little success, in 1969 WBR officially deactivated its would-be R&B label, Loma Records. Behind, it left managers Bob Krasnow and Russ Reagan and A&R talent like Jerry Ragovoy. And one memorable cut: Lorraine Ellison's "Stay with Me."

gurus on the odd wall, and smoking eccentric pipes. (Rebounding from a timely first divorce, I found girls less inclined to push me away, perhaps because on first dates I'd stopped singing the Gene Krupa solo in "Sing, Sing, Sing.") But mostly we just kept thinking of new ways to get outrageous attention—radio spots that played the wrong music, anything we could invent—for Mo and Joe's new signings. Among record companies, our Creative Services barged into an industry, giggled, and performed like some circus come to town.

Thirty years later, I reflect on what happened: A bunch of us who loved to act fresh were allowed by our enlightened bosses—particularly Mo and Joe, bless 'em—to play creatively. Time and again, I'd get called to New York, to be paraded in front of Wall Street analysts as if Creative Services had found the divining rod to a whopping new market.

Nowadays, such marketing play seems to have become unthinkable. When I meet those still working at a label like Warner Bros., their reaction is the same: a hug and a whispered, "Stan, it's just not like it was. Now it's just about money and covering your ass." But those years of the Sixties and Seventies, our Creative Services was about fresh music and uncovering all kinds of balls.

Another thing. We went into the magazine business, publishing a weekly freebie called *Circular*, which promoted WB/R product while doing anything but hard selling. *Circular* wrote anything it wanted, sent thousands of copies out within the record/retail/radio worlds. It included specious want ads:

CLASSIFIED ADS

QUALIFIED GIRLS: Major record company now interviewing girls to be used in a series of paternity suits to bring fame to some of our less fortunate artists. Send scatological résumé of past experience to Box 5949, Columbus, Ohio.

Other record companies looked at our odd doings, so attractive to (most of our) artists, with envy. Or maybe it was nonenvy. Atlantic's tall treasurer, Sheldon Vogel, kept wondering "where Warners got all that money to throw around." The answer was, like early Atlantic, Creative Services never understood the concept of a budget. Ostin and Smith let us just happen.

Artists told their managers the good vibes they felt about Warner/Reprise. More and more, I heard, their managers called up the two men we had named the Gold Dust Twins. Mo and Joe started doing office tours with would-be signees, entering the office doors in Creative Services, pointing at our group, now saying, "*That's* them."

With AM radio blockading singer/songwriters—unknowns like Randy Newman—WB/Reprise came up with its $2 for 2 LPs Sampler albums. We sold them as utter bargains to consumers. Send in a coupon with two bucks, back came a double LP with our best. Without consulting music publishers—"Look, we'll just call these nonprofit promotional things and not have to pay"—the Creative Services group issued *Songbook,* the first in a string of such.

Other labels, hip to the WB/Reprise attitude, went on an insouciance-emulation drive. Mercury and Buddah Records made their own two-dollar sampler, but they lacked Ostin/Smith signings to fill the disc. Nice try. Inside, their jacket was, according to *Entertainment World* magazine, "virtually identical to Warners'. Advertising for the Buddah set is a direct acknowledgment to Warners' success, reading in part, 'For almost a year now those clever fellows at Warner/Reprise have been offering impossibly delicious bargains.' " The sampler string went on for four years, until FM did the job for artists like Randy Newman.

So loose was the mandate for Creative Services that we were even allowed, on occasion, to sign and issue our own albums. Satirizing an onslaught of "supersession albums" in which big-name rock stars jammed together, boringly, endlessly, *Rolling Stone*'s Greil Marcus, posing as writer T. M. Christian, inserted this bogus review in the magazine, by now the country's must-read music bible.

Set for release late this month, the Masked Marauders' two-record set may evoke an agonizing, tip-of-the-tongue, lobe-of-the-ear recognition to some, or cries of "No, no it can't be true" in others. But yes, yes it is—a treasured, oft-Xeroxed sheet of credits (which for obvious contractual reasons will not be reproduced on the album), and the unmistakable vocals make it clear that this is indeed what it appears to be: John Lennon, Mick Jagger, Paul McCartney and Bob Dylan, backed by George Harrison and a drummer as yet unnamed—the "Masked Marauders."

Produced by Al Kooper, the album was recorded in impeccable secrecy in a small town near the site of the original Hudson Bay Colony in Canada. . . .

Based on reading this fake review, I phoned Mo, lunching in the studio commissary called the Green Room. "We can make a fake album for thirty thousand dollars." Mo answered, "For that amount of money, don't even call me. Just do it." An album was created, for special release on the credited label, Deity Records. It was, I guess, the first album ever recorded to match its review:

. . . an indescribable twelve-minute John Lennon extravaganza, James Brown's "Prisoner of Love," complete with a full ten-minute false ending; Dylan shines . . . displaying his new deep bass voice with "Duke of Earl"; and Mick Jagger's new instant classic, "I Can't Get No Nookie."

Record stores kept getting calls asking to buy the album. Other publications picked up the story, seriously. I put together a standard "Master Purchase Agreement" memo about the forthcoming single from the Masked Marauders, titled "Cow Pie." While waiting for the album to be ready, our *Circular* magazine told all that it could:

> Contractual nebulousnesses with Deity forbid us from naming names Marauders-wise, but we can say that the "group" comprises five, six, or seven of the biggest names in contemporary popular music, each displaying totally unfamiliar facets of his particular genius . . . Here's a little clue for you all: One of the Marauders once named Eydie Gormé as his favorite protest singer; a second one got himself into a lot of hot water public morality–wize by displaying his privates on the front cover of a far-out experimental avant-garde arty electronic-music album; a third is currently rumored deceased . . . [and] the gentleman who produced the album quite candidly considers himself one of the heaviest talents to ever set foot in a super-duper-session.[43]

Every department in WBR stood straight-faced. Industry trades *Cashbox* and *Record World* made "Cow Pie" their Pick Hit. *Billboard* printed Deity Records' press releases verbatim. Ultimately, WBR ran a teaser ad: DO NOT BE FOOLED BY OTHER MASKED MARAUDERS.

The album, released in November, sold forty thousand copies. Creative Services, easily bored, planned no follow-up.

Frank Zappa, then a fringe bandleader who identified with Dada and MOMA, came to Burbank in 1969 with his label Bizarre, to be distributed by an increasingly bizarre Reprise Records. Besides his own artistry, Zappa (with manager Herbie Cohen) brought Captain Beefheart, Tim Buckley, Wild Man Fischer, Lenny Bruce, Alice Cooper, and the GTOs and Plaster Casters.

The Creative Services Department dealt agreeably, even fondly, with the weird, like the Plaster Casters. Zappa had found it/them in Chicago and brought Casterdom west. On the Sunset Strip, the Plaster Casters costarred

---

[43]Marcus and fellow *Rolling Stone* critic Langdon Winner brought together a group of obscure San Franciso musicians to create the parody. "It came out rough," Winner remembers, "but we were happy."

with the queen groupies of Los Angeles, Pamela des Barres's GTOs (for Girls Together Outrageously). They costarred as well on Frank Zappa's Bizarre release *Permanent Damage.* The Plaster Casters were little known as singers, but better known for the plaster casts they made of rock stars' erect pricks. Their leader was Cynthia, a nineteen-year-old student at the University of Illinois, who "got this class assignment from my college art teacher on the same weekend that a bunch of rock bands were due to come into town for a big *Dick Clark Caravan* show. Back then I was just a teenage virgin dying to meet rock stars. When the teacher suggested we go out and make a plaster cast of something hard, I knew exactly what I wanted to do."

Lead Caster Cynthia delegated the job of arousing their models to her fellow coeds, while she prepared the casting material (at first plaster of paris; later a tinfoil/hot-wax combination; finally an alginate product used by dentists). Cynthia made anatomically precise statues of Jimi Hendrix, Young Rascals' lead Eddie Brigati, MC5 guitarist Wayne Kramer, even singer/songwriter Anthony Newley. Eventually, when her home was robbed, Cynthia turned the casts over to Zappa's manager, Herb Cohen, for safe-keeping.

The heretofore more stable Atlantic Records began acting strange:

- The Young Rascals took the year off to drop the "Young." They succumbed to the Summer of Love. Felix Cavaliere, group guru, adopted Swami Satchidananda as his own Indian guru. Even better, the entire group signed up with the swami's Integral Yoga Institute. Then, being ready, the Young Rascals dropped one word from their name. In so dropping, they stopped selling records.
- Since they'd previously brought in Sonny & Cher, then Buffalo Springfield, indie A&R team Charlie Greene and Brian Stone once again approached Atlantic. This time they offered still another California group, further out, druggy, called Iron Butterfly, just because. Okay.

  Led by Doug Ingle, Iron Butterfly was verifiably spaced-out. Its members slept inside the notorious nightspot (drug raids guaranteed semiweekly) called Bito Lito's. Five shows a night, six nights a week. Atco caught the Butterfly, which became famous for one song, whose title, "In the Garden of Eden," turned unpronounceable for Ingle after three days with no sleep plus one gallon of red wine. "In-a-gadda-da-vida" as recorded, filled a full LP side: 17:04. For airplay, Atlantic cut out fourteen out of those seventeen truly expendable minutes. Including a 2:30 drum solo. Result: a 3:08 single.
- Buffalo Springfield, after one year of squabbling, split into pieces. In grief, Atlantic signed Buffalo's sister, Dusty. No, that's a rotten joke.

Really: Ahmet Ertegun deputized Los Angeles manager David Geffen to follow up on Stephen Stills's newly forming group, going through all the contractual processes to assure that Stills's new trio (with Graham Nash and David Crosby) could be Atlantic's.

- Cream dissolved after a pan in *Rolling Stone*. Ginger Baker and Eric Clapton went on to form Blind Faith, with Steve Winwood and Rich Grech. Quicker than a high-school romance, Instant Supergroup! yelled the music press. Ahmet Ertegun, always frenzy's fan, signed up Blind Faith. The group's debut was set for Madison Square Garden.

The Men in Blue had hid their blazers, and by 1968 had begun traveling to sales conventions sporting muttonchop sideburns. Presenting their product before their still-suited-up European licensees, the Monterey-look Mike Maitland, Phil Rose, and Joel Friedman showed our new strip film: "Turn On, Tune In." Acts from deepest underground blared feedback. Licensees from Denmark and Italy heard The Jimi Hendrix Experience and wondered what was happening to NATO.

Art Director Ed Thasher and I created a massive billboard to stand above the Sunset Strip, with the faces not those of record acts but of Mo and Joe, whom we labeled The Gold Dust Twins. Pure self-pride. WHY ARE THESE MEN SMILING? was our headline. After a month, to the Twins' relief, down came the board. Thrasher hoisted its better parts above the roof of our two-story offices across from the Warner lot. Employees arriving Monday morning found themselves gazed down upon by the twelve-foot-high faces of Mo and Joe on the roof.

The emergence of a profit-sharing and pension plan for employees from 7 Arts stunned us, at least those on the West Coast, because Jack Warner had always regarded employee lunch breaks as indulgences. Suddenly, under 7 Arts, key employees got stock options, profit sharing, and—can you believe this?—medical benefits. Nobody had even asked.

Employee plans, though welcome, were hardly enough for Ostin and Smith, who were red-hot. Other labels could not understand why, within the Warner/Reprise structure, these two guys were only "second tier" vice presidents. Rival record companies went after Mo and Joe like they were freshmen coeds from hick towns. Aware that W7A was on the block, Ostin and Smith had no real sense of loyalty. They had no contracts with Warner, no stock, and each still had a home in Encino with a forty-thousand-dollar mortgage on it. Smith and Ostin were not getting greased.

Mo and Joe's phones were ringing with offers from other labels. Their attorneys had been talking to Maitland about better deals for their two clients, but nothing got done. Ostin had been offered lead roles with the labels owned by ABC and MGM. Maitland, knowing that his job was to run this ship tightly, put off and then put off longer any good deal for his two general managers. "We were really up in arms!" Smith recalled. "It wasn't feathers that had to be soothed. We were planning to walk. To tell them, 'Screw you! We're not part of this package. Go run it on your own.' "

Wexler became aware that unfinished renewal-contract deals for Mo Ostin and Joe Smith sat, unattended, on Maitland's desk. Executive flight by Smith and/or Ostin now would affect Atlantic's own profits. Wexler told Ahmet about the unsigned deals, and Ahmet told Elliott Hyman, and Hyman told his secretary to get Maitland on the phone.

Mike and wife, Carmel, were traveling to Greece. They'd gotten as far as the airport in New York when he was paged: an urgent phone call. Hyman demanded to know why contracts with Ostin and Smith sat unsigned. Hyman didn't really want to hear any explanations. He explained out loud, "Do not get on that airplane until those contracts are signed."

Mr. and Mrs. Maitland returned from JFK into Manhattan. Phone calls zinged back and forth between Maitland and Ostin and Smith's attorneys, all day, all night. Mike conceded every point to Smith and Ostin. Mike could now go to Greece.

And Elliott Hyman, he had two more pieces of fine bait under term contract, dangling for some big fish. Preferably a fish named Steve.

Significant Releases by Warner Bros. and Reprise Records

1967

Reprise: The Electric Prunes ("I Had Too Much to Dream (Last Night)" • Arlo Guthrie ("Alice's Restaurant") • Jimi Hendrix ("Are You Experienced") • The Kinks ("Sunny Afternoon") • Miriam Makeba ("Pata Pata") • Dean Martin ("Welcome to My World") • *Francis Albert Sinatra/Antonio Carlos Jobim* • Frank and Nancy Sinatra ("Somethin' Stupid") • Nancy Sinatra ("Sugar Town" and "Jackson" with Lee Hazlewood)

Warner Bros.: The Association (*Insight Out*, including "Windy" and "Never My Love") • The Beau Brummels • Petula Clark ("Don't Sleep in the Subway" and "This Is My Song") • Bill Cosby (*Revenge* and *Silver Throat* including "Little Ole Man (Uptight-Everything's Alright)" • Grateful Dead • Harpers Bizarre ("Come to the Sunshine" and "59th Street Bridge Song (Feelin' Groovy)" • Van Dyke Parks (*Song Cycle*) • Peter, Paul & Mary ("Leaving on a Jet Plane," "I Dig Rock and Roll Music") • *Camelot* and *Finian's Rainbow* soundtracks

Loma: Linda Jones ("Hypnotized")

1968

Reprise: The First Edition ("Just Dropped In (to See What Condition My Condition Was In)") • The Fugs ("It Crawled Into My Hand, Honest") • Jimi Hendrix (*Axis: Bold as Love* and *Electric Ladyland*) • Dean Martin (*Greatest Hits*, volumes 1 and 2) • Frank Sinatra & Duke Ellington (*Francis A. & Edward K.*) • Nancy Sinatra & Lee Hazlewood "Some Velvet Morning" • Tiny Tim ("TipToe Through the Tulips with Me") • The Vogues ("My Special Angel," "Till," and "Turn Around, Look at Me")

Warner Bros.: The Association (*Everything That Touches You* and *Greatest Hits*) • Petula Clark ("The Other Man's Grass Is Always Greener," "Kiss Me Goodbye," "Round Every Corner," and "You'd Better Come Home") • Bill Cosby (*To Russell. My Brother. Whom I Slept With* and *200 M.P.H.*) • Grateful Dead (*Anthem of the Sun*) • Peter, Paul & Mary (*Late Again*) • Mason Williams ("Classical Gas") • *Bonnie and Clyde* soundtrack
Loma: Redd Foxx (*Foxx-a-Delic*)
Tetragrammaton: Deep Purple ("Hush")

10

STEVE Ross was six-foot-something tall (I never asked him how tall he was, but to me it looked like his height was about six feet plus one cantaloupe). In 1954, at age twenty-six, Steve had wowed the daughter of and married upwardly into the family funeral business, New York's Riverside Chapels. Ross sold caskets with a smile so genuine, with caring so persuasive, that the bereaved felt salved by his every word, even if that casket *was* a bit beyond the budget. In the velvet hush of Riverside's display room, Ross listened to what people wanted, then gave them more—seven-foot mahogany boxes ornamented with genuine Bavarian hardware, looking like they should last at least forever.

Assuming you don't count wand-bearing fairies, Steve's ability to feel your need, to make good things happen for you, was unparalleled. He'd confess, if you asked him, what he'd learned about people in the funeral business, describing it as "a service business. You learn about people's needs and feelings at an emotional time for them, a funeral. You service their needs." And as he told you that, you could feel Steve's hand on your shoulder.

Ross itched to be rich. Among all New York funeral businesses, Riverside Chapels had a 10 percent Share of Casket. To Ross, 10 percent felt measly. He pestered, warmly warmly, his in-laws about Riverside's growth, about merging, about "going public" on the stock exchange.

It took what seemed in the world of chapels like an eternity, but less than one decade later, in 1962, the Rosenthal family, including son-in-law Steve Ross, became the principal stockholders, officers, and directors of Kinney Service Corporation. Then, in 1966, with an even larger tribe, of Kinney National Service. By 1968, Steve Ross was no longer the son-in-law. He was forty-one and chief executive officer.

In fifteen years of merging and buying, Ross had led a growing tribe of companies/employees/industries to hugeness. He ruled everything from office cleaners to parking lots to Wonder Woman.[44]

---

[44]Over these years, cited here for the list-craving, Ross & Company had acquired Kinney Parking Lots (synergy: funeral limos in the day, theater limos at night); car-rental ser-

The Sixties had become, in American business, the Age of Conglomeration. To conglom, sharp companies bought other companies, because in buying the other company you got to mix its sales and profits in with those of your own, a practice called "pooling of interests." This often meant you got to trampoline your company's revenue numbers, which in turn upped the market value (earnings per share) of your stock. Buying a company without using hard cash but with "Chinese paper"—new stock flotations whose value was based more on promise than on past performance—that kind of deal made you a Wall Street *macher.*

For Ross, conglomerating had come as naturally as had selling coffins to widows, but now at a more lively address: 10 Rockefeller Plaza.

Steve's conglomeration of pawns alone don't win chess games. To checkmate, Ross needed knights, castles, rooks. In late 1967, Steve found his first knight, and a white one at that.

Ted Ashley owned and ran Ashley Famous, a Hollywood talent agency. It packaged TV series ranging from *Get Smart* to *Dr. Kildare;* it represented talent like Burt Lancaster, Sean Connery, Tennessee Williams, and Sidney Lumet. Ashley was a bold if short achiever (following some rule about Hollywood's top agents never being tall). Ted heard that Steve wanted to talk a deal. To Ashley, the idea of getting his agency scooped up by some janitorial/parking-lot conglomerate, one that—dear God—minored in funerals, that for Ted smelled sweet as Lysol. Then Ashley and Ross, a pair both expert at the schmooze, finally sat down in one room. Ross, as he'd learned to do, slouched in his chair, so as not to intimidate with his height. Ross dreamed aloud. Three hours later, Ashley Famous, the second-largest talent agency in Hollywood, had been bought. Ross, his arm around Ashley's shoulder, was the difference.[45] In showbiz, where schmooze is 51 percent of the game, Steve Ross had worked higher than a volleyball spiker.

That summer, Ross flew a selected crew of his execs to Miami. None of his old parking-lot guys got invited. Steve Ross asked, "What's our next move?" During the sweltering days, Ross's new top staff—Ted Ashley and Spencer Harrison from Ashley Famous, Bill Sarnoff from publishing, attor-

---

vices; cleaning and building maintenance services; two printing companies; the Frankel family's National Cleaning Contractors. Ross conglomerated with Hackensack Trust, bought for "paper" (adding Hackensack's $150 million in assets to the cash drawer); eight more traditional service suppliers plus *Mad* magazine and National Periodicals (owners of Superman, Batman, Green Lantern, Wonder Woman); Licensing Corporation of America (if you want your product to have James Bond or NFL logos on it); and Panavision, for Hollywood lenses and cameras.

[45]With this acquisition came Ashley's strong, showman executives, especially Ashley's Number Two Spencer Harrison. Both got along well with their new boss, Ross. Cost of this acquisition: $13 million. In its *Annual Report*, Kinney National Services announced a fifth new "service category": call this one Leisure Time Communications.

ney Allan Ecker—chose their goal: either a movie studio or a TV network. Three candidates: MGM, ABC, or Warner–7 Arts. Ted Ashley flew back to L.A. with *his* bait, to see which of the three might bite. Ashley's choice quickly became Warner–7 Arts. On first visiting the Burbank lot, Steve Ross observed, perhaps from habit, "If nothing else, Warner would be a nice parking lot."

An analyst of the entertainment business, the fast-talking, gum-chewing, hyperalert Manny Gerard, was working on Wall Street when his phone rang loud. Steve Ross came to Gerard's office to ask about buying Warner–7 Arts. Gerard cut through: "It's not a movie company, it's a record company. Essentially, all the earnings come from the record business." Gerard was hired by Steve Ross to help with the acquisition. Moves began to be made.

Competing, growth-minded companies had already started runs at buying the teetering Warner–7 Arts: Commonwealth United, National General, Chris Craft Industries. From 10 Rock, Ross had kept close watch on the rival suitors. He added team members—Felix Rohatyn of Lazard Frères and Paul-Weiss tax lawyer Alan Cohen. Ross and Cohen invented a new stock security with enough muscle to clear the deal. It was a less-than–Fort Knox security called "Preferred C" stock.

One by one, WB-7A's other suitors dropped out.

It took Ross months to assemble the deal. His Kinney team studied who owned the W7A shares and then targeted them. The team pitched major shareholders on the tax benefits of capital gains. One shareholder, Carroll Rosenbloom, owner of the L.A. Rams pro football team, remained unpushed. Alan Cohen described it: "The deal [we set up] with Carroll was 'stuffing the stock.' To guarantee a price, you couldn't guarantee the cash, obviously, because that would kill the bankers. You guaranteed a price over a certain period of time. If the average stock price of Kinney didn't meet that guarantee, we'd then have to stuff additional stock in."

Steve Ross took flights to Miami to persuade Rosenbloom to sell, succeeding only when Rosenbloom's wife, Georgia, worked out Ross's astrological chart, then decided the sell signs were auspicious.

Ashley kept busy in Hollywood: "I talked to Elliott Hyman. I talked to Jack Warner, who, though he sold his business, he's still Jack Warner, and tried to deal with as many of the board members or build relationships."

The whole ball of wax—cash, paper, and long-term payables—added up to $400 million. Part of Ross's problem, however, was that 20 percent of the Atlantic and Warner record labels were still owned by Frank Sinatra. That 20 percent had to be bought out, too. Ross and Alan Cohen faced off against—guess who—Mickey Rudin. "Mickey asked me for the world," Cohen recalled, "and ended up getting nine-tenths of the world. They had a tremendous position. Sinatra really had veto power."

Rudin and Ross held the final negotiation over veal chops in a private room at La Reine restaurant. Rudin's throat had just hemorrhaged; he'd been advised not to speak till it healed, so he negotiated by writing notes on paper napkins. Smelling a rat, Ross wrote back on his paper napkins. It became the most silent negotiation in Hollywood history. Napkins took wing.

In early 1969, the deal was struck. Frank Sinatra and his two partners, Mickey Rudin and Daniel Schwartz, owned 107,500 shares of W7A. Sinatra sold his remaining 20 percent of Reprise Records for $22.5 million. His price for 20 percent of the record company was only $9.5 million less than Jack Warner's price for his 33 percent share of the entire studio two years earlier. Besides 25,000 shares of Kinney stock, Mickey Rudin got a finder's fee of $1.5 million, to be paid out over ten years.[40]

For tax reasons, Sinatra and Ross signed the papers in New Jersey. The signing took place in Fort Lee, over a major Italian dinner at the home of Sinatra's mother, Dolly. Sinatra had told Ross about her habit of trying to squirrel away any of her son's money that she could get her hands on. After closing the deal, Ross held out the check. Dolly grabbed it but snared only a decoy check for a thousand dollars. The real money got handed over separately, out of Mama's sight.

With Warner/Reprise and Sinatra in hand, Ross was concerned about Atlantic Records, too. Sure, Atlantic was owned by Warner–7 Arts. But, once this deal closed, would Atlantic's management stick? Or walk? Ross moved to get Ahmet Ertegun as a team member. Ahmet, however, after experiencing life with 7 Arts, had endured enough of running his old record company for some conglomerated guy who knew not riffs. Like Hyman, Steve Ross was another one, even if his hand felt warmer to the touch. Still, Ertegun itched to move on.

Ross casually met some family friends, one of whom—the friends' son—was bored with Warner's picture company but enthused about its records side, particularly Atlantic and its new act, Blind Faith. The boy told Ross, "Blind Faith's Stevie Winwood on the organ, plus the old Cream, and they haven't cut a record yet, but they've sold out Madison Square Garden. Isn't that fantastic?" Ross, having no clue what the boy yammered about, asked Manny Gerard, more of a rock fan, to coach him.

Ted Ashley tried to persuade Ahmet Ertegun to meet with Ross. Ertegun had no interest in meeting with this funeral-parlor cat, either in Ross's office or in Ertegun's. Didn't need to. You know how hot Atlantic was? Three of America's Top Ten albums:

---

[40]Rudin's annual $150,000 payment appeared on the budget of Warner-Reprise Records for a decade, mystifying us executives who were trying to squeeze expenses. Mo Ostin would just wave his hand when that line was scrutinized, saying, "Oh, don't worry about it."

6. Aretha Franklin: *Lady Soul*
8. The Rascals: *Time Peace/Greatest Hits*
10. Cream: *Wheels of Fire*

—and four of its Top Ten singles

4. Otis Redding: "Sittin' on the Dock of the Bay"
5. The Rascals: "People Got to Be Free"
6. Cream: "Sunshine of Your Love"
10. Archie Bell & the Drells: "Tighten Up."

Ashley, in his habitual "what you have are two choices" way of talking, leveled with Ertegun: "Ahmet, this is no way to behave. What you think or you don't think about where you should or should not wind up, it's happening. I think it's in your own interest as well as my own that you should get out and talk to him."

Then Ross himself called Ertegun and invited him to dinner at '21,' a restaurant with hamburgers the price of used cars. The meal took place in a private room. Ross, as always, knowing his audience, opened, "Ahmet, we leave you alone, that's our pledge."

Ertegun had heard that same noninterference pledge from 7 Arts. He was frank: not really interested in his new owner, a nice enough guy, but a man who didn't know diddly about records. Ertegun did know Diddley. All Ross knew was funeral parlors.

After six hours of discussion, impasse. It was 12:45 in the morning. The attending waiter stood by, estimating his tip. When Ahmet mentioned his newly signed group, Ross blurted, "You mean the one with Stevie Winwood on the organ, plus the old Cream, and you haven't got a record but you've sold out Madison Square Garden?"

Ahmet, whose eyelids congenitally drooped at half mast, raised them to three-quarters. Steve Ross knew of Winwood, of Cream? On that remark, Ertegun decided he might give Kinney a chance. Yes.[47]

After many months, Ross had all his ducks a row. On leaving '21' that morning, their waiter, after glancing at his tip, thought about a down payment on a new home.

On June 30, about three weeks before Neil Armstrong would stroll on the moon, our big headline ran KINNEY NATIONAL BUYS WARNER–7 ARTS. The deal

---

[47]Atlantic's three heads would get rich in stock options. According to Kinney National Service's Prospectus dated January 7th, 1971, they had Kinney Stock coming: "an aggregate of 121,185 shares of Common Stock is issuable by Kinney to Ahmet Ertegun (50,134 shares), Gerald Wexler (40,391 shares) and Nesuhi Ertegun (30,600 shares) through September 16, 1971 . . ."

was final-final. The long-term attenders to Warner Bros.—the guys named Semenenko and Sinatra, Allen and Ertegun, Wexler and Hyman, and others behind those men—finally all of them had gotten theirs, their dreams richer even than the waiter at '21.'

Only hours later, it felt like, a scaffold got hoisted to the top of the water tower, the same tower Jack L. Warner used to point to so boastfully. Before sunset, the logo for 7 ARTS was painted over. The word KINNEY was not painted on.

The euphoria that Steve Ross and other Kinney cats must have felt in graduating from scrubbing floors, where assets might be counted in hundreds of mops, that euphoria was short-lived. Taking over the studio, Ashley reviewed the movies in the pipeline. He was appalled. What was there, what had been paid for at the studio, was largely worthless. He phoned Ross, telling him, "We're going to lose over $59 million." In September, Kinney's board announced "provision for unusual loss resulting from the write-down of the asset values of the motion picture films . . . and story properties of W-7A." The write-down came to $59 million before estimated present and future tax benefits ($27 million after taxes).

Every year, Chapter One of Kinney's Annual Report had been given to the hottest division, then next hottest, next, next, ending with "Funeral Homes," which ended up in brief paragraphs back on a page like thirty-two. So, for the past several years, it often had been "Parking Lots" that'd been Chapter One. This year, 1969, against previous priority instinct, even Warner Bros. Pictures got downgraded, listed as Chapter Two, because among Hollywood's Top Eight Movie Studios, Warner Bros. had finished a near-death last, its hits as rare as panty hose at luaus. The only movies mentioned were John Wayne's *Chisum;* a sci-fi drama by George Lucas for executive producer Francis Ford Coppola, *THX1138*; and *Woodstock*.

Steve's drive to buy W-7A quickly resulted in a heavy feeling, like the feeling guys might get importing a mail-order bride, sight unseen, from Samoa. Kinney's stock was worth only half of what it had been the year before. Those who'd taken Chinese paper instead of cash were sick about getting taken. For Kinney Service's 1969 Annual Report, the editors pushed records and music up front to Chapter One. There its writers struggled with the language of the late Sixties:

———————

Records and music have stirred young people around the world. In the billion-dollar-a-year record industry, your company is represented by many leading artists under the Warner Bros., Reprise, Atlantic, Atco, and Cotillion labels. All of these labels have moved rapidly into the distribution of fast-growing 8-track stereo cartridges and cassettes, new ways of marketing recorded music.

> Concentrating on pop music ranging from the middle of the road
> to the "underground" variety.

Waiting for the elevator in the Warner building, engineer Tom Dowd turned to Ahmet Ertegun and said, "Atlantic is going to change." To which Ertegun replied, "Tom, Atlantic has got so big it wouldn't matter if you and I died. There would still be an Atlantic."

At Kinney's first budget review with Atlantic that very October, both sides suffered attitudinal whiplash. "Budget? Man, we never had a budget," answered Jerry Wexler to Kinney's financial head, Bert Wasserman. "Never had a recording production budget, a promo budget, a publicity budget."

In the "get acquainted" style that Steve Ross and Ted Ashley employed, new faces down inside the Burbank record labels were sought out. Ashley suspected that Maitland might have be downplaying the company staff, hiding them away. Hiding *us* away, I mean.

By now we in Records knew the politics. Ross and his two labels were no different from Hyman and his two labels. "Ahmet was still concerned about Mike ultimately becoming more powerful," Mo recalled. "Mike equally was concerned about Ahmet. On a chart, they were equals. Joe and I were down the ladder a step." As for me, I'd been flattered by visits from Manny Gerard, Alan Hirschfield, Kenny Hyman, and others but had no idea how my ads giving away Randy Newman LPs for free related to the Dow-Jones Industrial Average. Apparently they did.

Mo later told me, "What happened was that Ahmet, in his manipulative fashion, after convincing Hyman, subsequently convinced Ross and Ashley that the real strength of the record company was not Mike Maitland but Joe and Mo."

With the informal blessing of both Warner and Atlantic Records, Warner's droll international head, Phil Rose, had set off for Australia with mandate to set up a joint international sales company. On his arrival, Rose learned that Atlantic, "in complete defiance of a program we'd laid on the table in a joint meeting—had gone out and renewed four-year licensing deals with their licensees a week before, which was a slap in the face, to Warners and particularly to Mike."

Maitland blew what was left of his stack. He phoned Ahmet directly, to find that the politicking—especially directed at Ted Ashley—was heavy. Atlantic Records clutched its sales receipt, the one with the word "autonomy" all over it. Mike's big plan for that music division had already been discredited. As he often did, Jerry Wexler nailed it: "We had a category in our minds for figureheads (like Maitland). We called them 'Presentable Gentiles.' I say no more."

To make "who rules whom" clear, Kinney issued a press release announcing that Ahmet Ertegun had been elevated to Executive Vice President—Music Group of Warner Bros., Inc. It explained that Ertegun would "serve as liaison among the record, music publishing, television and motion picture divisions of Warner Bros., Inc." In this role, Ertegun reported to Ashley. So did Maitland, but Ahmet's title sounded lots bigger.

At its January 1970 Palm Springs sales meeting, Atlantic Records splurged, showing off fifty-five albums. A Niagara of label deals was represented: albums from San Francisco Records (Bill Graham and David Rubinson), the Robert Stigwood Organization, Sun Flower Records (Dave Kapralik and Sly Stone), and Capricorn Records (Phil Walden and Frank Fenter). Sonny Bono personally worked the room.

Ashley and Ertegun wanted insurance that Ostin and Smith would stick in their jobs. While at the conference, Ahmet (in his new role) called Mo in Burbank, two hours to the north, to set up a meeting. He told Mo that Kinney wanted to talk to him about a new contract. Mo replied that he didn't want to sign another contract, one that would begin two years from now. Why should he, perhaps too early, sign away his future?

After that, in Beverly Hills, talks between Ashley, Ertegun, and Ostin went on, but contract signing did not. Ostin and Smith were men who in two years (1969–70) signed Black Sabbath, Doug Kershaw, Jethro Tull, Gordon Lightfoot, Van Morrison, James Taylor, Fleetwood Mac, Ry Cooder, Deep Purple, Alice Cooper, and Small Faces with Rod Stewart, a spurt of prescience heretofore unknown in the record business, I'd say.

After a few days of talking, Ertegun and Ashley asked Mo their Big Question: Would you sign if we made *you* president of Warner Bros. Records? Ostin refused. He wanted no part in deposing Maitland.

Outside the meetings, Mo and his lawyer, Werner Wolfen, discussed ethics. They discussed Inevitability Theory. Ostin protested: It seemed unfair. Maitland didn't deserve this. Wolfen's legal counteropinion was "Don't be a schmuck."

Mo went home to Encino to discuss it with Evelyn. Guilt was the prominent emotion: What would happen to Mike? Evelyn and Mo agonized over it all night long. Later, Evelyn, who simply melted any new acquaintances with the warmth of her eyes, got almost angry because Mo and she could not delight in the good that was happening to them, looking only at what they felt was this terrible tragedy about to happen. The next day, Ostin told Ashley and Ertegun that he would take the job. "See my lawyer," he said.

The degree to which Atlantic was responsible for the downfall of Mike Maitland is, historically, a bit slippery, even now. Ashley told me it was he who made the decision. Others, deal analyst Manny Gerard among them, thought differently: "I can't believe, knowing Steve Ross, that he would have made the decision, naming Mo and Joe, without sitting down and spending some time talking to Ahmet about it. Now what I have to believe is that Ahmet said, 'You're crazy. You've got to go with Mo and Joe, because that's the way to go.' Which it was, absolutely. So Ahmet at least had to be asked, I think, and had to give the opinion that that was the right way to go."

Out in Beverly Hills, Friday lasted a long time. Joe Smith's office phone rang with an urgent summons to the Beverly Hills Hotel. He strode across its lawn, one worthy of Rodeo Drive's finest furriers, into one of the hotel's private bungalows erected to challenge expense accounts. When Smith walked in, Ashley spoke the news: Joe would get to run the Warner Bros. half of WB/Reprise.

"How would this work?" Smith asked. "What's Maitland going to be?" Ashley danced back, "Don't worry about Maitland."

Joe leaned forward, for once in his life unsure how to phrase something. Then he asked, "Are *we* really going to run this company?" Ashley and Ertegun both nodded. Joe caught his breath. Maitland was going to go. A meeting for Smith plus his attorney was set up for the next day, Saturday.

On Sunday, January 5, Ashley called Maitland at his Ventura beach house, an hour north on Route 101. Without tantrum, Maitland accepted the decision, quietly, with dignity. He said he thought they were wrong, but he saw no way to fight it.

Ashley phoned Ostin to tell him, "It's done. Maitland is aware." Quaking, Ostin knew he had to phone Maitland. "I told him that I felt terrible, that it was nothing I had any part in. He was great. He said, 'I know it wasn't your fault. I know you had nothing to do with it'."[48]

Warner/Reprise's new top two executives had no chance to call any company meeting, no chance to reassure their troops. Monday we all split up, out in teams on the road doing product presentations: East, Midwest, West, South. During the week, as the word seeped out, astonishment flooded in. I called back to Burbank, making sure the world heard the truth.

Next Monday, *Circular,* our weekly newsletter to the world, reported:

Guerrilla bands swept through the corridors of the Warner/ Reprise Burbank headquarters, raping accountants and knifing and shooting officials of the dying regime, their roughshod feet slipping slightly on the unfamiliar texture of linoleum . . . The coup (pronounced *coo*) had succeeded.

---

[48]The appointment of Ostin and Smith to their supreme roles (president and executive vice president, respectively) at Warner Bros. Records left their fond colleague, Joel Friedman, feeling underaccepted. Friedman confessed as much to Ostin and Smith. They sympathized and remembered that only two of the Musketeers just got ceremonial swords.

Significant Releases by Warner/Reprise

1969

Warner Bros.: Petula Clark (*Portrait of Petula*) • Bill Cosby (*It's True! It's True!*) • Grateful Dead (*Aoxomoxoa*) • Rod McKuen (*At Carnegie Hall*) • Peter, Paul & Mary (*Peter, Paul and Mommy*) • The Watts 103rd Street Rhythm Band ("Do Your Thing" and "Love Land")

Reprise: Sammy Davis, Jr. (*I've Gotta Be Me*) • Kenny Rogers & the First Edition ("But You Know I Love You," "Ruby, Don't Take Your Love to Town," and "Ruben James") • Arlo Guthrie (*Running Down the Road*) • Jethro Tull ("This Was" and "Stand Up") • Dean Martin ("Gentle on My Mind") • Joni Mitchell (*Clouds*, including "Both Sides Now") • Frank Sinatra ("My Way") • The Sinatra Family (*Wish You a Merry Christmas*) • The Vogues (*Till*, including "No, Not Much") • Neil Young (*Everybody Knows This Is Nowhere*) • *Laugh-In '69*

Bizarre: Frank Zappa (*Uncle Meat* and *Hot Rats*)

Straight: Alice Cooper (*Pretties for You*)

Tetragrammaton: Deep Purple (*The Book of Taliesyn*)

11

Aﬀter our three-day trip for sales meetings, we got back to our desks by
that Thursday, a bit wide-eyed at what'd happened but ready to sell more albums, not mourn.

I was startled on Friday morning when Mo came into my office and
asked me if I'd like to be a vice president of Warner Bros. Records. I was
thinking, "Doesn't Mo have anything more important to do?" but I had
enough poise to appear thankless. "Of what?" I asked him.

Mo answered, "More Creative Services," and said I'd VP over this bigger bunch of areas, including Editorial, Art, Advertising, Artist Relations,
Publicity, Merchandising. I did not have a very good idea of how to do many
of those jobs, but they all sounded to me like "get attention for our albums."
Sounded like a cinch.

Mo was moving down to Maitland's larger, view-of-the-parking-lot office, so I could have Mo's old view-of-the-air-conditioner office. My new
office was twenty by ten feet, ideal for canoe storage. My VP-ship felt all to
the good, except for my being boosted over my strip-film buddy of some
years, art director Ed Thrasher. I felt awkward about being the one getting
promoted. I was never able to talk with him about that.

Of Kinney's two record companies, it was Atlantic that ruled the British
Empire. Jerry Wexler got a call tipping him to an act called the New Yard-
birds, an update of the old Yardbirds who'd been on Epic Records. This New
Yardbirds was an act on paper only.

Wexler was in charge of hard bargaining. The New Yardbirds and Atlantic made a five-year commitment: $75,000 for the North American
rights. Wexler then got another call. Would Atlantic like the rest of the world
for only another $35,000? Well, maybe, let's see if we can lay off $20,000 of
that for UK rights. United Kingdom said no. Oh, well, we'll do it anyway.
The group, signed, changed its name to Led Zeppelin. It was Atlantic's first
big reach—a *world* signing, not just a North American–rights signing—for
an English band.

In looking back on it all, singer Robert Plant would recall that this signing with Atlantic had been, mostly, peer pride: how proud he'd feel to be on
the label that had Cream and Buffalo Springfield. "And besides that," added
Plant, "that I got eight thousand pounds was even more amazing."

In January 1969, Led Zeppelin opened an American tour for among
others, Iron Butterfly, who became so unnerved by the crowd's reaction to
Plant and Company that the Butterfly refused to go onstage. By October,
less than a year later, Led Zeppelin toured as headliners in New York's
Carnegie Hall, the first rock group to play there since the hall had banned
rock in 1965, following a Rolling Stones recital.

Led Zeppelin was led by Robert Plant's whip-it-up stage presence. After
watching Plant onstage, the Rolling Stones' Keith Richards commented, "I
could never get along in a band with a posturing, posing lead singer."

Such late-Sixties signings changed Atlantic internally. The old system
of record promotion—cut singles and get 'em played, whatever it takes—
now had to adapt to an album market, to FM radio. Adapting, when you're
good in one kind of promotion, when you know certain program directors'
unlisted phone numbers, when you've learned the steps to more than one
hustle, adapting to a new radio business came hard. For faster hustling, Atlantic found younger men.

Wexler's schedule of administrative and production work got as heavy
as the buy-off wad, several million thick, in his pocket. Nobody had asked
Jerry to work so much, but he'd been workaholicking from eight in the
morning till ten at night. Ahmet, never an administrator, was more the
company's seductive front door. The hits, they were coming from afar, not
from Muscle Shoals. Wexler, less in the studio, now mostly made deals.
For relief, he brought a hot promotion man in from New Haven—Jerry
Greenberg—and installed him in Manhattan. Greenberg went to his first
meeting at Atlantic, surprised to hear Wexler tell the conference room,
"This is my assistant."

"Wexler was a maniac, but a great maniac," Greenberg said. "Learning
the business from him was like going to boot camp on Parris Island. You
came out either a man or a corpse. He *never* stopped working deals. Once he
called my house on Yom Kippur, wanting to discuss an urgent business matter. My wife said I was in synagogue. 'What's the number there?' he wanted
to know. 'I'll have him paged.' "

In the back of his mind, Wexler was thinking: Miami. A boat. The good
life. No more dealing with what he called "Rockoids"—those white kids,
those English bands. With black artists less and less important at Atlantic,
Wexler could clearly see all that sand in front of his house, sand reaching
down into the sea. "The idea was I could go south and have a boat in my
backyard. It was time to go. We didn't own the company anymore. I don't
know what I had in mind. I thought I could phone it in." Still, Jerry had no

intention of leaving Atlantic. He just wanted the kind of freedom that, say, Ahmet enjoyed.

Greenberg moved from being Wexler's assistant up to pop promotion director, and Dickie Kline moved from the South up to New York to help handle promotion. Kline recalled, "We became real close buds, since we were the only young people in the organization. It was still the pioneering days. The bottle of Jack Daniel's in my suitcase never left."

Kline knew the good ol' rules of promotion: "You had to bribe your distributor's promotion man to get *your* record put on top of *his* pile. Local promo guys used to come into stations with fifty records at a time. Whoever ended up in the first three on *top* of the pile were the ones that'd be worked for the week. Everyone had their own little game going."

Kline was reflecting on promotion as it *had* been. "I'd be at the station at nights, with a bottle of whiskey and a sandwich, getting my add [addition to the playlist]. The next morning, I'd go to the record store and sell them a box of records, based on the fact that I had got the station's phone lighting up at night."

Up in New York, Kline discovered big-city differences: FM radio. The pot scene. The Woodstock Generation. "Eighteen forty-one Broadway. We had two floors. We had six promotion people in one room. Mavis Barton, who was head of production at the time, we'd get her crazy. We would have singles on the street within seventy-two hours."

Kline was pulling down a fast $135 a week. But "very good expenses." He liked the money, and he loved the perks. "I partied like everyone else did. This was two-fisted drinking, two-fisted fighting, two-fisted screwing around. There were no two ways about it. That was the original way to do business. The *way* to do business—we're talking about the *roots* of the business—the whole concept is to get somebody to do something for you. You are, in turn, trying to put your hands in their pockets. They, in turn, are trying to get something back. A good time is had."

One late evening, Kline got an unexpected phone call from Ahmet Ertegun, back in New York, home from London, doing what he used to do, *making* records, not licensing them. Ertegun was down in the studio. It was the eve of the Jewish holiday. Atlantic offices, empty. When Ertegun got back to the offices from a record session, Kline and Greenberg had to hear this new cut, even if it was the eve. Ertegun asked, "What would you do if I told you that Tom Jones is in the studio covering 'Take a Letter Maria' right now?" Atlantic's version was actually by newcomer R. B. Greaves. Kline answered, just like this was ten years earlier, "Cut me twenty dubs right now, twenty acetates." Done. The mailroom got invaded. One hour later, the Greaves acetates were in the mail to the top DJs, first-class mail, with PERSONAL on the envelopes.

Monday morning. Kline got his first phone call, from Chuck Dunaway, program director at WIXY, Cleveland. "This record sounds like a smash," Dunaway said. "It *is* a smash," answered Kline. Dunaway asked, "So who the fuck is it? There's no label on it." Kline, in haste, had sent out twenty unidentified acetates to twenty major radio stations across the country. Off the blind mailing, they got four "adds." Label copy to follow.

By 1969, though, such hot single-promotion antics were becoming pretty much history. This was a new age, rule-breaking time, as Ian Anderson (Jethro Tull) once viewed it, a time that "coincided with a boom in FM radio . . . You could break all the rules that had ever been written, never even release a single, and still have a Number One album."

In order to survive, Atlantic Records learned how *that* worked, too. The rulebook had not yet been updated, but promotion survival was something more now than good-buddy-ism. Like records, radio had become a better, hotter business, run by new kinds of owners who watched audience ratings as intently as puppies watch little lizards.

Into the record business now came David Geffen, who dressed like he never even owned a business suit, and that was fine with him. Geffen had been born about twenty years later than many of his about-to-be colleagues, in 1943, growing up in Brooklyn with a view to getting out of Brooklyn. He'd faked his way into the music department in the New York office of the William Morris Agency, where his intensity got him ahead. Geffen climbed up by telephone, incessant phoning, a skill as essential in the agency business as stealing home is in baseball. He learned the agency business morals, of which there are far fewer than Ten Commandments. He looked for business openings. Mostly doing music, which in Agencyland meant that young David was rare, an agent who worked with people his own age. He repped rockers inside big movie/TV agencies that were much more interested in movie and TV stars. David stood out.

In the Morris music department, Geffen worked the hang-out-all-night schedule. He hung with what he could afford: undiscovered kids in small clubs where the tables teetered. He signed the Association, Jesse Colin Young. Older agents, men better at pinning on a boutonniere, began seeking David's guidance in Youth Market matters. Geffen's ego was of good size, but not channeled into "look at me." Not into "see my car" or "love my furniture" or "feel my jacket." Instead, Geffen used his balls for external goals, becoming a guy you loved because of his fervor for some artist. He had little life outside his business, his work, which were his ego.

Geffen's all-consuming talent signing had been a young singer/songwriter, Laura Nyro. He worked for Nyro through thick (her record contract with Columbia Records) and thin (less-than-magnetic on stage). By bonging away at Verve Records, Geffen got her out of an old record deal. As talent manager Larry Marks once said admiringly, on Nyro's behalf David Geffen had "yelled at the wind, and eventually the wind changed direction."

In 1968, Geffen had been working at Ashley-Famous in L.A. Once Kinney bought W7A studio, the law said it could no longer also own Ashley-Famous. Owning both an agency that sold stars and a studio that bought stars violated antitrust laws. Geffen, an Ashley-Famous asset, wanted to move on, up. He demanded his freedom, even before the deal to sell Ashley-Famous had been closed. To free himself from the agency, Geffen had to promise both Ross and Ashley that he would not compete with its buyers, had to swear he'd stay out of music management and not work for a rival agency. Promise accepted. Ashley-Famous was sold off. Within a few months, Geffen unpromised, going to work for a rival outfit, CMA (Creative Management Agency).

For his word-breaking sin, Hollywood's temporary disdain followed David for a bit, though hardly a lifetime. Or, as David once said, "In Los Angeles, they don't want you to fail. They want you to die." This did not include Ross and Ashley. They'd sold the agency and felt the thunder in this intense young man.

By 1968, Geffen was learning what made himself tick: making not good deals but making *huge* deals. When a colleague from his William Morris stint, Elliott Roberts, asked David's help in putting together a group around Roberts's client—the Byrds' David Crosby—Geffen shifted into maneuver, a gear that became his specialty. Geffen left CMA. He and Roberts created a cahoot. They set it up in Phil Spector's ex-offices at the west end of the Sunset Strip—at 9126, a building that was, to oversimplify, a Greek-columned, French-chateaued mountain lodge earlier owned by Hoagy Carmichael. Roberts saw a trio: Crosby + Stephen Stills + Graham Nash. All three musicians were contracted to different labels. It was, for David, a deal huge enough.

To add Stills + Nash to Crosby, Geffen needed two deals: (1) Get Stephen Stills from Atlantic Records and (2) get Graham Nash (part of the Hollies) from Epic Records. In return, Geffen had nothing to offer either label but the nerve of a young man. He flew to New York, there to meet first with Atlantic's in-house deal maker, Jerry Wexler.

When young David Geffen came in to get a release for Stephen Stills, Jerry flat-out refused. "Why should I?" Wexler shouted. Geffen recalled that Wexler just "threw me out of the office." David's eyebrows, which easily reveal incredulity, showed how hurt he was by Atlantic's refusal even to *talk* about Stills's joining Geffen's yet-to-be-named dream group. David gossiped Wexler's crude treatment all over town. (Geffen believed he would never get hurt speaking his mind, out loud, frankly.)

The day after Jerry evicted David, his hotel room phone rang. It was Ahmet, who sensed that tossing out young blood like Geffen was not shrewd. Geffen might be someone who could move, free of any burden of what *had* been great. Ahmet knew that the record world was changed. For Atlantic, Geffen could be new ears, always a blessing.

When Geffen came back the next day, Ahmet, looking across at the compulsive young man opposite him, made a new offer: David could have Stills, but only if the resulting group—C+S+N—ended up on Atlantic. There are the shrewd, and then there are the shrewder. Next came Graham Nash. Geffen traded Richard Furay to Epic, which owned Nash as part of the Hollies. C+S+N, done. Stills later realized that neither Nash nor Crosby could play guitar well. He schemed with Ertegun and manager Roberts to lure Warner Bros. Records' Neil Young into the group. (Many years later, when Atlantic wanted to reform CSN&Y, Geffen Records would refuse to give Atlantic a release on Geffen artist Neil Young. Proving that shrewder is a learnable skill.)

Geffen started connecting with Ertegun over the management of Crosby, Stills, and Nash. He memorized Ahmet's phone numbers and called them regularly. "When I first met him," Geffen acknowledged, "if there was any excuse to call him up, I would. He would always pick up my phone call. It made me feel very important." It got to be, whether either man realized it, the father-son relationship both had lacked.

With the first Crosby, Stills, and Nash album came the hits "Marrakesh Express" and then "Suite: Judy Blue Eyes," which Stills had written for his girlfriend, Elektra's Judy Collins. "David, Stephen, and I were in love with each other during the first album," Nash recalled. "Musically, we ate, drank, and slept together every night. I was with Joni, and that was flowering. Stephen was with Judy, and that was flowering. David was with Christine, and that was flowering. Within a year, it had all changed.

"My relationship with Joni had turned sour, Stephen had stopped going with Judy, and David's girlfriend, Christine, had been killed. We were knocked for a loop. We were all romantic people, and our love lives were in shambles. Then bring in Neil and plug in to his insanity, and it's amazing *Déjà Vu* ever got recorded."

Having assembled Crosby + Stills + Nash + Young in 1970, Geffen pushed for more at Atlantic, looking to sign another of his management clients—Jackson Browne. Ertegun 99 percent refused. "Ahmet, look," protested Geffen, "I'm trying to do you a favor by giving you Jackson Browne."

"You know what?" Ertegun answered. "Don't do me favors."

"Seriously, you'll make millions with him."

Ertegun had become an expert at fine collectibles, and he had his eyes on an original Geffen. "You know what, David?" Ahmet answered. "I've got millions. Do you have millions?" Geffen shook his head. Ertegun went on, "Why don't *you* make a lot of money? Why don't *you* start a record company, and then you'll have millions, too. Then we can *all* have millions."

David, as he would, pressed on. Ahmet held tight, warning, "You know, a soldier is sometimes *too* good a soldier. Whatever happens, I'm your friend and I love you, but don't squeeze the juice out of every situation." Such advice was hard for David to hear; he'd trained as an agent.

But about a label deal, Ertegun was indeed serious. Atlantic would henceforth depend on young, white ears, and David's stood out. Atlantic would finance and distribute a David Geffen label. "You can have my label so long as I get it back," Geffen dealt. A three-year deal was made. The label's identity, from the beginning, was fueled by Geffen's philosophy: to protect his *artists* from the rest of the world. This was an identity in vivid contrast to the more exploitive behaviors of older companies. To artists, Geffen's company would offer asylum.

Woodstock had come and gone. "I was basically on about a triple acid trip," recalled John Sebastian, albeit vaguely, "right when they asked me to play at Woodstock. Which answers the question: 'Can a man still play his own songs when he couldn't find his car?' "

Atlantic quickly signed the recording rights to the festival, even though the label had only one act on the bill: Crosby, Stills, Nash, and Young. Rights were set, with clearances to be sorted out later. Warner Bros. Pictures picked up the movie rights. At Warner Bros. Records—a place where Warner Bros. movie soundtracks had always gone—shock was felt. Atlantic's having *Woodstock* felt like your kid brother got a bike, too. "From a corporate standpoint, it didn't matter who put the damn record out," Manny Gerard told me. "It said to the label people, 'We're all on the same team. We don't have favorites. We don't play the game that way.' "

An age of edgy brotherhood began. Kinney tiptoed like this was the 1770s, when States were barely United, had their Rights, and were leary about Federating into any whole. The resulting three-disc *Woodstock* ended up a Number One smash on Atlantic's new Cotillion label, at $14.98, and went a long way to proving to Atlantic that, now, as a label, it would not always be Number Two.

Harmony between the opposite-coast labels was beginning to gel, bit by bit. Defenses between them, once up to the eyebrows, sank to about ankle level. Decisions that were impossible a month earlier, now, with the perceived "threat of Maitland-izing" gone, were made with greater ease.

With Maitland's exit, with indie distribution faltering, Atlantic's defenses against branches were fewer. Even Wexler now said what he'd never brought himself to say during the rivalry era: "The worst branch distribution is better than the best independent distribution." Still, for Atlantic executives, leaving their lifelong companions—the indies, those street guys they'd been dealing with for decades now, guys who knew which doors to knock on when it's one in the morning—leaving them would hurt. With indie distribution, Atlantic's CFO Sheldon Vogel thought, "We had lots of clout, and little in bad debts. We could run the show, dictate to them because of our size and power. Under a Kinney branch system, Atlantic would no longer have that clout. We couldn't pull the line [go to some other distributor]. We were somewhat against going branch, but not violently so." Mo's dream—branches of your own—began growing on Atlantic's trunk, too.

On a day in 1969, when Ross was visiting Warner Bros. Studio to meet with Ashley, Elektra Records' Jac Holzman got pulled into meeting them. The pullers were Mo and Ahmet. Ross, perhaps out of habit, asked if Jac was interested in selling Elektra; Holzman answered yes, "but only if we're going to have our own distribution." After that meeting, tall, thin Jac waited and waited, but his phone did not ring.

A decade was about to fade out: the Sixties. During this decade, American record-industry sales had about tripled. Warner Bros. and Atlantic no longer backstabbed each other. But we were still thinking like plantation owners, far from thrilled about constitutional convening.

Significant Releases by Atlantic

1968

Atco: Bee Gees (*Horizontal*, including "(Lights Went Out in) Massachusetts" and *Idea,* including "I Started a Joke") • The Buffalo Springfield ("Last Time Around") • Arthur Conley ("Funky Street") • Cream (*Wheels of Fire,* including "White Room" and "Crossroads") • Iron Butterfly ("In-a-gadda-da-vida") • Otis Redding ("Happy Song (Dum-Dum)" • Vanilla Fudge ("You Keep Me Hangin' On")

Atlantic: Archie Bell & the Drells ("Tighten Up" and "I Can't Stop Dancing") • Clarence Carter ("Slip Away" and "Too Weak to Fight") • The Drifters ("Dance with Me," "I Count the Tears," and "I've Got Sand in My Shoes") • Aretha Franklin (*Lady Soul,* including "Ain't No Way," "Chain of Fools," "Natural Woman (You Make Me Feel Like)" and "(Sweet Sweet Baby) Since You've Been Gone") and *Aretha Now,* including "I Can't See Myself Leaving You," "I Say a Little Prayer," "See Saw," and "Think") and *Aretha in Paris* • Wilson Pickett ("She's Lookin' Good," "Stag-o-Lee," and "I'm a Midnight Mover" • The Rascals (*Once Upon a Dream,* including "It's Wonderful") and *Time Peace,* including "A Beautiful Morning") • Percy Sledge ("Take Time to Know Her") • The Sweet Inspirations ("Sweet Inspiration") • Joe Tex ("Skinny Legs and All")

Stax: Booker T. & the MG's ("Hang 'Em High") • Eddie Floyd ("I've Never Found a Girl (to Love Me Like You Do)" and "Bring It on Home to Me") • Sam and Dave ("I Thank You") • Johnny Taylor ("Who's Making Love")

Volt: Otis Redding: "(Sittin' on) the Dock of the Bay"

1969

Atlantic: Archie Bell & the Drells ("There's Gonna Be a Showdown") • Crosby, Stills & Nash ("Marrakesh Express" and "Suite: Judy Blue Eyes") • Aretha Franklin (*Soul*, including "Gentle on My Mind" and *Aretha's Gold*, including "House That Jack Built") • King Crimson ("In the Court Of") • Led Zeppelin ("I" and "II") • Wilson Pickett ("Hey Jude") • The Rascals (*Freedom Suite*, including "People Got to Be Free") • Sam & Dave ("I Thank You") • Dusty Springfield ("Son of a Preacher Man")

Atco: The Bee Gees ("Odessa" and "Words") • The Buffalo Springfield ("Retrospective") • Cream ("Goodbye") • Iron Butterfly (*Ball*) • R.B. Greaves ("Take a Letter Maria") • Otis Redding ("Love Man")

Stax: Booker T. & the MG's ("Time Is Tight")

12

Jac Holzman's fever—to cash in Elektra Records after nearly two decades of labor, then to hammock in Hawaii, to change his life before he ended up in one of those old-timers' bars at four-thirty—focused him. Elektra was no longer the precocious, college-feeling toy he'd started. It was now a mature label in a world where maturing was a drag. This change—for both Elektra and Jac—began when Holzman had visited the Sunset Strip in the mid-Sixties and become fascinated with a club crowd there that smoked and swallowed drugs, wore granny glasses, and heard inaudible messages in music. To the best of my knowledge, Jac never wore granny glasses. The rest of his life, however, had changed. He'd drunk the punch.

Unlike other record-company presidents, Holzman had never boogied in a recording studio, had never stuck his name on a song, had never, in fact, paid a lot of attention to promoting or selling his records. He'd come into the record business mind first, toes last.

On the streets of New York back in 1951, when Jac decided on "records," recorded music was changing: Atlantic was there, just beginning with Ruth Brown. Sinatra was fading out at Columbia. To such singers, Holzman was oblivious. He loved tubes, knobs, soldering irons.

In record studios, change had come from magnetic tape. It brought in men who used razor blades to cut and splice tapes with Scotch. Multitrack recorders gave editors after-the-session control of different mikes, so they could fix a bad baritone days after he'd slept it off. The result was better than the old one-take acetate disks, which had made editing almost impossible. Producers could re-re-re-record the bass drum till it thumped to their ears' content. The Ampex Model 200 tape recorder became every nerd's delight. As nerd as has ever been born was tall, skinny, nearsighted Jac Holzman.

The year 1951 also brought a change for consumers. In 1948, Columbia Records had advertised a tiny, red-and-black plastic box, really just a turntable, for $29.95 (later, only $9.95). Using your radio's amp and speaker, this box played a new, thinner, shinier, flexier, wider record. It held narrower grooves (called "microgrooves," around 250 spiral tracks to the inch, versus the old singles' 85). The new record seemed to play on and on, maybe twenty-three minutes on each side, without the every-four-minutes *kerplunk* break of heavy disks stacked on a changer spindle. Columbia called this a Long-Playing record (LP™). These LPs had virtues: Because they flexed, Columbia called them "unbreakable." LPs didn't sound as noisy as 78s. They didn't take up as much shelf space. The price seemed reasonable, too. In stores like Sam Goody's on Manhattan's Forty-ninth Street, ten- and twelve-inch LPs sold for $4.85 in stores.

America already had fifteen million owners of 78-RPM players, not to mention their collections of favorite 78-RPM records. But by 1951, LPs had caught the ear of those who cared. Unlike many "technological breakthroughs," in the LP's case, people could hear the difference, could hear basses thump and cymbals go clannnnngg. Growing up in Arcadia, California, I remember the day I put my 78s into our wheelbarrow and rolled them to Eugene's house down the block. Bye-bye. LPs had trounced a rival 45-RPM speed sponsored by Victor, and people bought the new turntables to play this sleek, slower-speed disc.

Using this new, long-playing record for his front-of-the-store merchandise, Sam Goody introduced a better record store: "full-line merchandising." Everything any record company made, Goody stocked. Goody also came up with in-store promotions and discounting, pioneering much that became the retailing revolution in subsequent decades.[49]

Countless young men—to be eligible for this sentence, it helped if, like me, you wore glasses and couldn't land hot dates—became addicted to LPs and their castles, the hi-fi sound machines.

Up in tall buildings that people claimed could scrape the very sky lived "the majors"—RCA, Decca, and Columbia. In this year, Jim Conkling was taking over Columbia. These big companies recorded good, good music—from Percy Faith's strings to Perry Como's croons—records for play on all-American radio known for only one bandwidth: AM. Mono. Records for home consumption.

Down below those skyscraper majors, where people scraped for every nickel, lived smaller record companies, indies, exploring fringe music because . . . well, who could afford string sections? Between 1949 and 1954, the number of independent record labels grew from eleven to almost two hundred.

And then there was Jac, with all the prerequisites—black-rimmed

---

[49]With all that, Goody eventually ran into credit problems. When a creditors committee was formed to oversee Goody's climb up from bankruptcy, committee member Jac Holzman of Elektra spoke endorsements for Goody, helping save his company.

Later, when Holzman needed cash to buy out his partner, Goody would remember Holzman's words.

glasses and a soldering iron—the kind of youngster who worshiped fidelity, the sort heard in audio fairs, where woofers, housed in black boxes the size of Frankenstein's coffin, rumbled earthquake-sounding music.

Jac was born Jacob Holzman. He'd grown up verbally self-assured, an intimidating quality that he was never able (and perhaps never wanted) to defuse. In 1950, in their junior years, Holzman and a buddy, Paul Rickolt, dropped out of the Great Books college St. John's to indulge in "hi-fi" full time. Rickolt was the gregarious one of the two, a bit fat, a shank of blondish hair, loved to play canasta all night. The two had bet they could record an LP of better quality than any of the major labels. With six hundred dollars, Rickolt and Holzman formed a fifty-fifty partnership record company: three hundred dollars from Rickolt's Navy Vets bonus and three hundred dollars of Holzman's bar mitzvah money.

Although it had no doors to open, on October 10, 1950, Elektra Records faked it, using an Annapolis tobacco store called Wally's for its business address.[50]

In almost every way, Elektra 1950 was utterly unlike Atlantic 1950. Singles were beneath Elektra; at Atlantic, singles were a way of life. Both labels were lost in their first choices of what to record. Elektra picked a recital of mostly German and Japanese poems that had been set to music by New York composer John Gruen and sung in English translations by soprano Georgianna Bannister, a concept that hardly had "hit" writ all over it. The resulting ten-inch LP came out in a type-only jacket. The initial pressing order for ELK-1 was five hundred copies. Of those, ELK-1 sold extremely few. But ohh! the adrenaline just making that first one.

The need dawned on Rickolt and Holzman that out of their six hundred dollars they not only had to *make* records but also afterward had to *sell* copies of them. These men had, after all, college-grade minds. The partners each put in another two hundred dollars. Holzman paid his bills by doing hi-fi installations. Time for ELK-2: Jean Ritchie, a singer of Appalachian mountain ballads, *Sings Songs of Her Kentucky Mountain Family.* Folksingers had many appeals. They required no musical arrangements to be bought, no orchestra to hire, in fact, no producing talent at all. What they required was setting up a single mike, often in someone's living room, recording authentically, not creatively, on a binaural Magnecord tape recorder. Total album production cost: one reel of magnetic tape. Folk music (which had recently been popularized by the Weavers' "Goodnight Irene" on

---

[50]Rickolt and Holzman chose the name Elektra under the mistaken impression that there existed an Elektra who was Greek goddess of all the muses. They spelled their Elektra with a K since Holzman (perhaps because of his Germanic streak) felt a K looked more big businesslike than a C. Pinching each nickel, to make the logo Elektra look really Greek, they did not order a special K. They simply tipped over an M.

Decca) fit Elektra's viewpoints: intellectually elitist and commercially aloof. And folk songs themselves, being in the public domain, cost nothing.

In 1952, Jean Ritchie signed a contract with Jac Holzman that paid her twenty-two cents an album. She got three copies free. Ritchie's contract made her responsibility clear: "Self-accompanied singer will perform the folk songs before a recording machine and the party of the first part." Ritchie's album sold about a thousand copies through Elektra's original "national" distributor, Harry Lew over on Ninth Avenue, and made back its cost in five months. Ah, so *that's* how it works!

Partner Paul Rickolt got tagged with army duty in the early Fifties. Jac bought out his share of Elektra for a thousand dollars, then moved Elektra from his dorm room to the back of a sheet-music shop at 189 West Tenth Street—you know, the place next to the Chinese laundry?—where every year for a few years he released three or four ten-inch albums. To distribute his new LPs locally, Holzman hand-delivered, riding New York streets on his stylish new Vespa motor scooter, discs strapped behind him. Each day, Holzman's goal was that of any early-twenties bachelor: earn enough cash to (a) cover Elektra's bills, with enough left over to (b) go to the movies that night.

After three years, Holzman moved Elektra to 361 Bleecker Street, a cheap location filled with forty-foot-wide restaurants decorated outside with hanging salamis and squatting mamas to hold down their doorsteps.

Holzman then approached another classmate from St. John's, a debonair, rich kid named Leonard Ripley, who invested ten thousand dollars. Not only could Ripley engineer, he could also hear music. A bon vivant and Continental traveler, Ripley was less than a dependable office-worker, but he contributed. Greater contribution came from Holzman's new wife, Nina (best man: Ripley). Soon Nina was working at Elektra (Jac took out hundred dollars a week in pay; Nina took out fifty-five dollars). Nina Holzman attempted to update her husband's diet, which, prior to the nuptials, had consisted of tomato soup and vitamin pills.

Time slogged by without threat. Army-McCarthy hearings on TV. Rickolt, back from the army, worked part-time. Holzman dipped again and again into folk music—it was now 1954—with Elektra's first "name" star ("name" because Susan Reed had once made a record before for some other company). She also owned the antique shop down the street. Her album sold well into the low thousands.

The actual selling of records was not the highest of Holzman and Ripley's priorities. Marketing skills like radio promotion, charts listings—those were for other labels, beneath this one. For Elektra, selling was done by guys you licensed your records to, guys who drove Plymouths from city to city, stayed in hotels without working elevators, but made a living. For many record labels, K. O. Asher was such a man. A "Mittel European," the kind who usually ran the one-man candy store down the street, K.O. covered the

Midwest, from Chicago down to Texas but, if a real good order came in, from Arizona to New Hampshire. Each night Mr. Asher took all the blank stationery in his hotel's desk, cut off the hotel's letterhead, and, with a rubber stamp, stamped his own name and address at the top of the somewhat shortened paper. K.O. paid his accounts on time, exactly thirty days after receipt. Exactly. For a Christmas present, Holzman once gave K.O. Asher some new, professionally printed stationery. K.O. found this an offensive extravagance.

Among all the folk- and world-music signings Elektra made during its long infancy was Theodore Bikel, who later got to be called the Man Who Built Elektra. On Bikel's first album, the title—*FOLK SONGS OF ISRAEL*— appeared REALLY BIG, while the name of the artist was really tiny: THEODORE BIKEL. Bikel's name size did not stay small. Exotically Viennese by background, Bikel sang, acted, performed, and supplied much of Elektra's income into the 1960s, recording folk songs anyplace you asked him to (in some living room—"more comfortable than one of those uptown studios"— for under a thousand dollars). Elektra's main job, in doing the recording, was to avoid getting ringing phones and taxi horns in the background. Holzman recalled once having "to record out on Long Island in competition with a parakeet, a duck, the Grumman jet air base, a chiming clock, four children, a noisy water heater, and twelve chickens." But no studio costs.

By 1956, Elektra was making a tiny profit. Fortunately, about this time, Elektra discovered that two activities, stereo and sex, both worked well in pairs.

Canadian Ed McCurdy, a tall, tough-jawed Village roamer with a burly voice, worked concerts with his guitar, appeared as "Freddy the Fireman" on local TV, and scrambled for any buck. He came up with an album of bawdy Elizabethan poetry that Elektra set to any music they could think of. The eyebrow-raising result: *When Dalliance Was in Flower, and Maidens Lost Their Heads*. (Elektra liked to cram as many jokes as possible into its album titles.) *Dalliance* was Elektra's first hit; horny college boys loved lyrics like:

Let her body be tall, let her waist be small,
And her age not above eighteen.
Let her care for no bed, but here let her spread
Her mantle upon the green.

Elektra enjoyed the thrill of its first profitable year, even if that meant to Rickolt and Holzman becoming a sex-song factory.[51] Elektra could afford

---

[51]Many sex album follow-ups ensued: *Dalliance 2*, including "Uptails All" and "A Virgin's Meditation" • *Dalliance 3*, including "She Rose to Let Me In" • *Son of Dalliance*, including "The Fornicator" and "The Miller's Daughter."

another employee, a just-out-of-the-army-without-two-nickels-to-rub-guy named Mel Posner. His job, before the term "gofer" was coined, was shipping, billing, and floor sweeping. He was kept downstairs in the basement. Posner would stay with Elektra for twenty-six years, ending up in the Number Two spot at the label.

Mercilessly, Elektra extended its bawdiness, adding other singers to its roster:

> Cynthia Gooding: *Faithful Lovers & Other Pleasures*
> "The Bailiff's Daughter" • "The Derby Ram"
> Tom Kines: *Of Maids and Mistresses*
> "The Brisk Young Widow" • "Ye Maidens of Ontario"
> Paul Clayton: *Unholy Matrimony*
> "The Wooden-Legged Parson" • "The Old Wife Who Wanted Spunk"
> Bobby Burns's *Merry Muses of Caledonia*
> "Nine Inches Will Please a Lady" • "Lassie Gathering Nuts"

On the cutting edge of tedious smut, Elektra was more than breaking even. Folk music, meanwhile, until now a very marginal category, had suddenly emerged as something huge. Out in California, in '58, three young, non-trad (tieless) men recorded "The Ballad of Tom Dooley," with *whing-ding* harmonies and high presence. They recorded in studios, richer in sound, echo chambered. The Kingston Trio made "authentic" and "documentary" folk records (by Elektra, Folkways, Riverside labels) sound under-zippy. The Kingston Trio broke folk music open big, but did so for Capitol Records. The Village's recording folkies got left way, way behind.

The Kingston Trio sent larger American record labels scrambling for their own folk groups. Any three guys with guitar, banjo, bass, and shirts with fat stripes got signed by the majors, which hoped their copycat signings would be equally eaten up by the public. Elektra and like labels had neglected commerciality—forsaken hiring hit-sounds producers or arrangers for the music-recording studios with echo chambers, full-color, photographed album covers, all the stuff others labels used to attract the masses. Before long, bigger, more commercial labels strode Village sidewalks like overweight Midwesterners striding through some Chinatown, looking for souvenir singers to take home.

The Limeliters, a trio led by Glenn Yarbrough's honey of a voice, had to tell an eager Elektra that, golly, love you guys, but we want to be on a *big* label, and it's going to be RCA. RCA was taking its time, so the Limeliters asked Jac, "By the way, could you lend us two thousand dollars?" Elektra lent it and in return got a one-record deal. Following the success of RCA's album, half a year later, Elektra's one Limeliters album could actually be heard over the radio. A mixed pleasure, as an Elektra album had finally reached Number Forty on the *Billboard* chart, ten years after the label had entered the record business but six months after losing the act.

In 1955, Ripley married a belle from the South named Alexandra.[52] Three years later, amid the 1958 folk music din, Mrs. Ripley objected to the terms of her new husband's business arrangement with Holzman. Ripley had put up *more* money than Holzman, for which he got only a *minority* share of the company? Alexandra figured her husband should have been in charge, and Holzman was bleeding Elektra. The Ripleys sued.

Holzman's lawyer concocted an auction plan to settle this suit: Let Leonard Ripley name any price he thinks either partner's share should be worth. If Holzman could pay Ripley that named price, then Ripley had to sell Holzman his shares in Elektra. But, if Holzman could *not* pay the price, then Ripley had to pay that amount to Holzman, and Ripley would own Elektra. The question got put to Ripley. "How much, Leonard?" Ripley, not wanting to overpay, and knowing how small was Holzman's stash, named $25,000.

Phew. Sam Goody, remembering Holzman's early kindness during his 1954 bankruptcy as a record-store owner, heard of Holzman's need for buy-out money. The fast-talking, scrappy, balding Goody was about to become 5 percent of the entire record business. He advanced Holzman $10,000 (against records yet to be delivered) of the $25,000 needed. Jac's father lent him $7,500, and, even though Elektra owed its suppliers $90,000, a bank agreed to put up the final $7,500, collateralized against all of Elektra's masters. So Holzman bought out Ripley, becoming 100 percent owner. (Soon thereafter, Holzman sold 5 percent of Elektra to Theo Bikel for $20,000. Bikel later would recall this $20,000 as an investment that, when Elektra eventually was sold, would return him $500,000.)

The mildly ribald "Dalliance" series was followed up with a second series led by another collector of songs, disc jockey Oscar Brand. Brand had previewed for Holzman a group of songs supposedly being sung by our pilots in Korea, an album idea that appealed to Jac because he, too, liked to pilot planes. The songs were parodies set to standard folk melodies, like "Barnacle Bill the Pilot." With six musicians, no rehearsals, and no arrangements, Brand made an album called *The Wild Blue Yonder,* aimed for sale at air force bases.

"Then one morning as Mel and I were opening the mail," Holzman recalled, "we came upon a thick envelope from the Army and Air Force Exchange Service: a bundle of papers in quintuplicate tumbled out with an order for ten thousand units. I was in shock." Elektra kept shipping, by the thousands. Trained earlier how to dally in a series, Elektra backed up its

---

[52]Alexandra Ripley, decades later in 1991, wrote Warner Books' *Scarlett: The Sequel to Margaret Mitchell's Gone With the Wind.*

Yonder albums with a new series: songs for the navy (*Every Inch a Sailor*), then *Tell It to the Marines*, then another pilots' album, *Out of the Blue* (featuring "Will You Go Boom Today?"), then *Songs Fore Golfers*, others for boaters, sports-car drivers, even an album for the Army Medical Corps, called *Cough*.

Elektra also stayed true to its engineering bent, putting out sound-effects albums (which sold lots, surprisingly) and quick to market after Columbia's first stereo album by Ray Conniff with Jac's less-than-equivalent artist, the Neue Deutschmeister Band, oompah-ing in stereo. Once again (just as, in Burbank, young Warner Bros. Records was issuing *Polkas in Stereo*), Elektra's technogroupie fascination was part of the bloodstream. Like the LP and hi-fi before it, stereo now took off. For consumers, this meant buying (or wiring up their own kits) *two* amplifiers wired to *two* speakers in boxes bulky enough to overwhelm whole living rooms.

Elektra had by now moved up to 116 West Fourteenth Street, getting in the move five thousand square feet of studios and offices. Its staff now numbered nine (one-tenth the number Jim Conkling was hiring this same year to launch Warner Bros. Records), and the label, now distributed by Decca, was beginning to act commercial.[53] Maybe. Its new singer, Judy Collins, looking (and acting) both folkie and seductive, gave Elektra's releases a more pop appeal (Ritchie remembered Holzman describing Collins as "Jean Ritchie with balls").

With the waning of Appalachian folk music, though, Holzman felt rudderless, felt it time to move. In 1962, he'd sensed that "something" in music was about to happen in Los Angeles, land of the hip, land of Boss Radio, so Elektra opened an office in West Hollywood. While five or six people kept things going in New York, two or three people (including Holzman) ran Elektra West Coast. By moving, Holzman ended up in exactly the wrong place at the wrong time, missing the New York emergence of Bob Dylan. In effect, Elektra missed the birth of protest rock, just as, three years earlier, Jac had missed the start of pop-folk with the Kingston Trio, then decided he couldn't afford to compete for the Limeliters. Twice in a row hurt. Holzman brooded for a year, then shut down Elektra L.A. and headed back to the Village, marking time, releasing albums by younger singers with fresher messages: John Sebastian, Geoff Muldaur, Maria Muldaur, Dave Van Ronk, Phil Ochs, Tom Paxton, and now stalwart Judy Collins.

One year later, when either you were a Beatle or you were "all other,"

---

[53]Commercial folk groups—like Peter, Paul & Mary, the Brothers Four, the Chad Mitchell Trio—had squeezed all life out of "They Call the Wind Mariahhhh." Some, like PP&M, managed the transition to pop.

Elektra was not a Beatle.[54] Elektra's dedication to traditional, singer+guitar folk music was put to the test. It was 1965, at the annual reunion of traditional folkies, the Newport Folk Festival. In a setting that revered the acoustic guitar, an "electric blues workshop" had been scheduled.

Instead of the usual couple of hundred shuffling music-history buffs in hand-hewn sandals, a thousand or so crowded in and stood to hear, hoping to see their idol—Bob Dylan—wearing Iron Boy overalls and singing about purple mountains of Appalachia. But this was Dylan toting an electric, plugged-in guitar, like some rock kid, Dylan in black, skintight jeans and a polka-dot orange shirt, backed by Mike Bloomfield, Al Kooper, the Paul Butterfield Blues Band, and General Electric.

Alan Lomax, a good old folkie, disparagingly introduced this electrified session by young white boys. He taunted, "Let's see if they can play this hardware at all." He asked if the audience would "mind putting up with this anyway."

Dylan performed his previously acoustic "Maggie's Farm" before a wall of Loudspeakers from Mars. Bloomfield's *wa-wa*-ing guitars burned the air. Electric amps spat out at the audience. Hatred spat back. The folkies, those in the back, booed and booed. Watching it all, Paul Butterfield fan and producer Paul Rothchild told himself it was "the beginning of another era . . . another turning point in America's music direction."

For an encore, Dylan returned onstage solo. He played on his D harmonica, "It's All Over Now, Baby Blue," then walked off. At the time, in Elektra's 175-album catalogue, 90 percent of the albums were acoustic old folkies. To change, plugging in would be tougher than Atlantic's leaving R&B. Unsure of itself, Elektra gingerly established the Bounty label (named for the English candy bar), for singles it feared might be "too commercial."

After Newport, Holzman fell into an evening chat with that young producer from Cambridge, Massachusetts, Paul Rothchild, who knew more than Jac about where folk was heading. Holzman did not intend to miss another boat. Later, Holzman called that evening's conversation the most important of his life.

---

[54]With Capitol's Beatles stealing every moment of attention, other labels responded, each in its own hippest way: Warner Bros. Records issued *Dance to the Hits of the Beatles*, a thrown-together studio album, made in haste by Jack Nitzsche with a no-name band. Elektra released its *Baroque Beatles Book,* which became Elektra's fastest seller. Artist was the Baroque Ensemble of the Merseyside Kammermusikgesellschaft, conducted by Joshua Rifkin. Atlantic Records released an old Polydor album by the Beatles, *Ain't She Sweet,* on Atco.

Significant Elektra Albums

1952
Georgianna Bannister and John Gruen (*New Songs*) • *Jean Ritchie Singing Traditional Songs of Her Kentucky Mountain Family*

1954
Ed McCurdy (*Sin Songs—Pro and Con*) • Susan Reed (*Old Airs from Ireland, Scotland and England*)

1955
Theodore Bikel (*Folk Songs of Israel*)

1956
Josh White (*At Midnight*) • Ed McCurdy (*When Dalliance Was in Flower, Volume 1*)

1957
Gordon Heath and Lee Payant (*An Evening at l'Abbaye*)

1958
Glenn Yarbrough

1959
Oscar Brand featuring the Roger Wilco Four (*The Wild Blue Yonder*)

1961
The Limeliters

1962
Ed McCurdy (*The Best of Dalliance*) • Judy Collins (*Golden Apples of the Sun*) • Judy Henske (*Judy Henske*)

1964
Judy Collins 3 • *The Even Dozen Jug Band* (John Sebastian, Maria Muldaur, Joshua Rifkin) • *The Blues Project* (John Koemer, Dave Van Ronk, Mark Spoelstra, Geoff Muldaur, Bob Landy (pseudonym for Bob Dylan) • Phil Ochs (*All the News That's Fit to Sing*) • Woody Guthrie (*Library of Congress Recordings*) • Tom Paxton (*Ramblin' Boy*)

13

WHEN it comes to racing into any new technology, the record business finishes just ahead of the Amish. To get to the front of the pack, it takes fresh-born ears. The new ears at Elektra belonged to Paul Rothchild, hired by Holzman to handle this amplified-rock business. In three areas, Paul was cutting edge: in clothes, engineering, and drugs. Rothchild, at twenty-seven, was years younger than Holzman, dressed like a businessman—suits and ties—and smoked widely. Give him a studio, though, and Paul differed from Elektra's others: With performers, Paul was a co-creator of the sound, not just a documenter of it. In a quick run of years, Paul transformed Elektra from cerebral to gut. Because of him, Elektra would find a real market, one far beyond those albums of traditional and mock folk, those songwriters with hollow guitars who had sustained the label through music's Age of Wood.

Rothchild had just produced thirteen albums for Prestige's Folklore series in three months. Speedy. To Elektra, Rothchild brought with him artists like Tom Rush, younger musical pals who'd never seen the dust bowl nor felt a dulcimer. He signed Paul Butterfield and his band of amplified anarchists. Elektra's electricity bill went straight up.

Holzman, who'd loved twisting dials, now focused on starting a tasty, low-priced classics label, Nonesuch. To feed it, Elektra licensed records from obscure European classical labels, repackaging them for America. It was like paperback books: cheaper. In either mono or stereo, these albums cost what college kids could afford: $2.50, half the price of normal classical LPs. Nonesuch had it easy: no recording costs, 5 percent royalties (about a dime), $500 advanced to the leasing label, no copyright payments owed Mr. Vivaldi. Gross margins were around 50 percent. Break-even was down around 2,000 units. Ten Nonesuch titles a month flowed out, at one point becoming 40 percent of Elektra's annual sales, enough to fund rock and drown out Dalliance.

After many years in the mailroom, Mel Posner climbed out of Elektra's basement. He'd been promoted to sales. He traveled America, calling on distributors, showing slides and cover slicks. "I was on the road all the time," Mel recalled. "We had the highest-priced records. Our price for a four ninety-eight record was two thirty-seven, but with no returns, only exchanges. Jac did not believe in taking back returns. I was writing orders for albums: fives, tens, fifteens, and twenties. Unless it was Nonesuch, when it was twos, threes, and fives."

Paul Rothchild recorded the loud bands. He did the Paul Butterfield Blues Band, redid it, then redid it again to get rock to sound close: first, at Elektra's studio; then second, live at Howard Solomon's Bleecker Street Café à GoGo. The third version was cut in Mastertone Studios, with Ampex 4-tracks, up close as applied mascara. That third try made, in Rothchild's recollection, "the electric blues a viable form for popular music, made it possible for hundreds of American performers to play electric music." Like tape, the amp had won.

On *Billboard*'s chart, the triply indulged album reached only Number 123. Butterfield got five tracks on Elektra's early electric-rock compilation, *What's Shakin'*. Others in *What's Shakin'* read like a list of don't-you-wish-we'd-signeds: the Lovin' Spoonful, Tom Rush, Al Kooper, and an Englisher: Eric Clapton, leading his group called the Powerhouse. Powerhouse was not put under contract. Clapton had formed a secret new group, called Cream, signed for everywhere but America to Robert Stigwood's Reaction label. For America, Clapton had already been picked up by a guy uptown, Ahmet Ertegun, for Atlantic.

As he flew out to Los Angeles, Holzman must have felt creamed by this third missed-the-boat-again event. With positive cash flow, he dug down once more for L.A. roots. In effect, he left folk music behind. Left behind the once-acoustic Bob Dylan. Left behind Phil Ochs, an attractive activist-folkie whose songs jumped for your jugular. A banner waver, Ochs once tried to organize folksingers as if they were stooping farmworkers. Frustration over aloof audiences and industries tormented Ochs. Ochs hated what was happening; he dreamed of martyrdom. In 1966, Elektra released *Phil Ochs in Concert*, but no one's heart was in it.

For $69,000, the label bought its own building on La Cienega Boulevard, about two blocks down from the bowling alley that in a few years would be turned into the world's first roller disco. Inside its new building, Elektra created a studio ready for amped-up music.

Jac hired Suzanne Helms to handle the West Coast's business part. She, like most financial execs, considered wasting money less fun than we normal people do. Helms was the kind of person who wept with joy when LP content went from twelve songs down to eleven, next settled on ten, thereby saving Elektra four cents per LP in songwriter royalties. Suzanne just proved that not *all* of Elektra was wigged out. "Suzanne Helms was a strange, bizarre character," remembered Nina Holzman. "A big smoker. She lived with three German shepherds, who one day turned on her." By comparison to what was about to barge in Elektra's front door, however, Helms was vanilla.[55]

Jac Holzman worked his bicoastal offices. When arriving in Los Angeles, he'd pick up the *L.A. Free Press* to find out what the nights might hold. One was the dive ("nightclub" was too glorious for this joint) on Selma Avenue called Bito Lito, which Holzman later described as "a large pressure cooker like the black hole of Calcutta, but with a cover charge." On its tiny stage played an electrified band that had nothing better to call itself than Love. It starred Arthur Lee, a man who helped define the style of the hippie band. He wore one Indian moccasin (keeping one foot bare), triangle-lens sunglasses (one lens red, the other blue), striped trousers, a leather vest. The group lived in a single hotel room of little neatness.

(Later, Love's home would become a Laurel Canyon house once owned by Bela Lugosi. Its façade was made of riverbed stones cemented together. Half the swimming pool came, on purpose, into the living room. There, sunk into a beanbag chair, Arthur Lee would ramble his life's and art's philosophies, both of which sounded utopian until you tried to figure out what he really meant. His philosophy was Incoherence-ism.)

Holzman was learning that the economics of the Sunset Strip were unlike those of a college quad. Up to this point, Elektra had used a mildly humanistic standard contract with its artist. It had clauses like "Label agrees to treat artist with love and affection; artist in turn agrees to treat executives of label with a modicum of respect." But that was then, and now was lawyers. So Holzman signed Love, even though the signing broke Elektra's rules two ways: (1) It was a rock signing, and (2) the label paid real money: $5,000 cash in advance, and a $17,500 recording budget to be recouped by Elektra from Love's 5 percent royalty stream.

Lee focused not on the 5 percent but on the $5,000 cash. After signing, Holzman agreed to meet Lee the next day at the bank, where he grabbed the $5,000, said "bye," then ran off to buy a new harmonica and, for $4,500, a gold, two-seater, gull-wing convertible. The rest of the advance, now about $400, Lee let his band split equally. The convertible, he explained to them, was a *business* expense, the band's bus.

In its history, Elektra had issued maybe fifteen singles, roughly one per year. To the old Elektra, the word "marketing" sounded Madison Avenue. In 1966, Love's "My Little Red Book" became the sixteenth. After driving away from a board meeting at St. John's College, Holzman tuned in his car radio. On came the single. For Jac, this was the first time in fifteen years he'd heard an Elektra record on the radio. He pulled over to the side of the

---

[55]Suzanne Helms later moved to Switzerland with a bass player. She has stopped smoking.

road, listening in awe. Elektra had tripped into the pop world. Promotion man George Steele marched through the halls of Elektra blowing a bugle.[56]

Powered by "My Little Red Book," the Love album sold about 150,000 copies, becoming Elektra's biggest seller to date. "I really thought when I first heard 'Forever Changes' by Arthur Lee that I was listening to anthems," said Led Zeppelin's Robert Plant later. "I really thought the whole social structure was going to shift, naïve little boy that I was."

Elektra's La Cienega employees appeared to have been cast by Dalí. Billy James, a combination artist finder ("ears" guy) and publicist ("hugs" guy) headed the office. Guys like James (and Warner's Wickham) were categorized, to their amusement, as "company freaks," since they smoked dope and dug screech. James had worked in Artist Development for Columbia on the West Coast. To his bosses back east, James had forwarded a series of signable, we-have-an-option-on California acts: Frank Zappa, the Jefferson Airplane, Lenny Bruce, Tim Hardin, and an art-rock quartet called Rick and the Ravens. James had been unable to persuade Columbia to sign any of these acts, including keyboard player Ray Manzarek's Rick and the Ravens.

After five months of nothing, Rick and the Ravens got its option release from Columbia. The quartet had read books about new worlds, and, by ingesting small tablets, its members had experienced them. The band rehearsed for months, renaming itself the Doors after a description of a mescaline experience in Aldous Huxley's *The Doors of Perception,* then setting off for its debut gig at a Hollywood club appropriately named London Fog.

The Doors landed house-band status at the Whisky A Go-Go, a cramped, popular club on the Sunset Strip. Overhead, befringed dancers twisted in cages suspended from the ceiling, above the sweating singers on the stage below. Watusi-ing to the Doors proved taxing, even if you were Rhonda Lane, the club's shimmy pro, up in her cage, in her fringed dress, go-go boots, and bikini top. To the rhythms of the Doors, it was tough to do a decent Frug.

On the sidewalk outside, an endless strand of the young weaved and wandered at a spacey pace from the Strip's east end (that border guarded by a twenty-foot-high plaster Bullwinkle) to its west end (that border ending with a sign reading, as if to warn you, BEVERLY HILLS). The twenty-somethings, many of whom were unclear as to where they'd sleep that night, were beyond being bothered by that. Among them all, whether on the sidewalk or under the go-go cage, there was this feeling of having landed in Oz,

---

[56]Arthur Lee later renounced Love's contract with Elektra because he'd signed it as a minor, then renegotiated, asking for 10 percent, because Love was next going to have ten members. Holzman argued back that, based on population logic, the Mormon Tabernacle Choir should get a 100 percent royalty. They settled for 7.

where sex was now good to do, where loud was now good to hear, and where out far was good to be. All this was felt. I believe that in what was felt on those neon nights there was some truth.

Billy James had touted the Doors to Holzman. So had L.A. music attorney Abe Sommer. So had Whisky publicist, actress, and rock-group manager (for both Them and the Doors) Ronnie Haran, who one night had picked up Holzman at the airport, driven him to the Whisky, sat him down, and made him listen. Jac did not get it.

How to hear this, this different music? Or was what they were playing just what it sounded like: noise? For people who'd been in the business long enough that they got to be company presidents, hearing the new, that gets tougher every year. Had Joe Smith felt shivers on hearing the Dead, or had he just *seen* how Jerry Garcia's endless feedback worked on the stoned? Had Ahmet Ertegun responded with his gut to Clapton? Had Nesuhi's jazz instincts really responded to Sonny and Cher? Or had these presidents made lucky, inexpensive guesses?

I once asked Mo Ostin about this. We were driving to the Forum to hear some loud thing, and I asked him, "Mo, if it were just you, at home, and you wanted to hear just music that you really liked, what would you put on?"

"Oh, Andy Williams maybe," he answered.

More tellingly, perhaps, Ostin on another occasion said that on the day he and Evelyn were married, when they got home, the newlyweds watched *Your Hit Parade* on TV, with hit songs sung by Russell Arms, Dorothy Collins, Snooky Lanson, and Gisele MacKenzie.

Many years later, Ahmet Ertegun explained it differently: "You have to develop a second ear. The first ear is your private taste, which is what moves you personally. The second ear is one that, when you listen to a piece of music and you personally think it's terrible but it's a hit commercially—the second ear has to say, 'This is great!' The second ear, if it's good, is in tune with the taste of the public."

After five nights going back again and again to hear the Doors—"I just had to *understand* what they were"—Holzman ultimately signed them to a guaranteed three-album deal. Cost: $5,000 advance against 5 percent royalty, plus Elektra got 25 percent of the publishing income. The next night, the Doors were fired from the Whisky for performing Morrison's oedipal freak-out, "The End." They packed up, drove down the wandering stream of Sunset's stoners, turned up Laurel Canyon, and were heard from again.

Paul Rothchild was young enough, had the discipline, knew the psychology, and had the magic to produce the Doors' first album. A year back, he'd even had his own drug bust and done jail time. For nine months, behind bars, he had the freedom to listen uninterruptedly to rock radio. Paul had then moved to Laurel Canyon, to become another Elektra West Coaster.[57] With nineteen-year-old engineer Bruce Botnick, he captured the already-erratic Jim Morrison and group in a recording any way but traditional but, in every new way, musical. Rothchild recalled recording one of the takes they made of "The End,"

... where the acid started peaking. [Morrison] had these vespers and he started reading from it and tearing it up and got into "Kill the father, fuck the mother."

We were halfway through, and I got chills top to bottom. I said, "Bruce, do you know what's happening out there? That's history. Right at this moment. That's why we come here." It was one of the few times you turn and say to somebody, "Pay attention, this is it." I remember it so vividly, and at the end of the take I was drained as anyone out in the room from the experience.

The result, according to Holzman, "was and is a masterpiece of pristine production—a beautifully realized album that I hoped for in my head but could not flesh out myself. That first record and the five other Rothchild-produced Doors LPs that followed helped Elektra to enter its rapid-growth phase."

"Light My Fire," shortened from the original, nearly-seven-minutes-long album track, became Elektra's first Number One single. In 1967, Buick asked to use it in its TV commercial; the band turned down its $50,000 offer. The band appeared on Ed Sullivan's TV show where, despite his promise that he'd change the line in the song, Jim Morrison sang without change, "Girl, we couldn't get much higher." Afterward, Morrison's explanation was not an apology. He told Sullivan, "I am interested in anything about revolt, disorder, chaos, especially activity that seems to have no meaning."

Elektra erected a first-of-its-kind billboard above the Sunset Strip. The slogan—THE END WAS A BEGINNING—puzzled drivers more accustomed to billboards where cowboys smoked filtered. Other rock acts, bereft billboards, felt cheated, began to think ill and iller of their stingy labels, then demanded billboards in their contracts.

To be sure, transcendence ended when it came to getting your piece of the action. Promo rep Ronnie Haran sued Elektra. She claimed it was she who brought the Doors and Holzman together. Haran claimed that Holzman had promised her a continuing percentage of the Doors' royalties.

---

[57]Later, when his Laurel Canyon home's couch was sold at a rummage sale, Rothchild's son Dan recalled that couch had been sat on by "Janis Joplin and the Full Tilt Boogie Band, Jim Morrison, Ray Manzarek, Robby Krieger and John Densmore, Joni Mitchell, John Sebastian, David Crosby, Stephen Stills and Graham Nash, Paul Butterfield, Glenn Frey, Linda Ronstadt, Jackson Browne, and another dozen butts of distinction."

Holzman countersued, saying she was promised 1 percent, and only on the *first* album. Looking back on it, Holzman believed that his stance "demonstrated that you *could* boogie and think at the same time; it's very, very true."

Agog with the new depths of experience, Holzman and some of his colleagues were lured by Judy Collins into an encounter group. Such all-hold-hands seances had become the rage. The assumption was that couples and solos could sit in a circle, lower their defenses by lighting candles, hum "aummmmm," thus liberating suppressed feelings. Truths got expressed ad nauseam. At his first session with the group, Jac heard Judy reach down into herself and ask why he thought it fair that he made more money out of her records than she did. Holzman reached down into his soul, fell back on politeness, but found no words to answer her.

It seemed as if most of Elektra now tried to transform a bag of rare weed into the Meaning of Life. Its offices avoided three-dimensional limitations, as if Timothy Leary had descended into Hollywood, smoked some shit, and opened his paint box.

- The new Los Angeles offices on La Cienega discarded desks in favor of a bar, food, even removable arms on the couches in a lounge to facilitate a little friendly sex play after hours.
- In her West Coast office, the assistant to publicist Danny Fields insisted that she would answer only to the name Tinkerbell.
- Fields himself once described life with acid there as an experience of "watching the rug turn into the universe." To the office, he wore denim pants with flowers embroidered near the pockets.
- Producer David Anderle's office was decorated like an Arabian tent. Visitors sat on pillows, inhaled incense, and listened to Anderle envision.

Elektra also decided to fund a commune for recording artists, off in the wilderness of 1967. Depending on whom you talk to, the place was called either Paxton Lodge, or the Recording Farm, or the Fantasy Orchestra Ranch, or, occasionally, Operation Brown Rice. The commune leased a rustic ex-sanitarium for alcoholics up in the Feather River area near Keddie, California (get out your atlas). Its purpose was for "rest and rehabilitation . . . making it possible for people to move around in various combinations without being bound by highly restrictive recording agreements." Running the commune was the man who, once named Barry Friedman while traveling Laurel Canyon as King Kong, had now, to avoid creditors, renamed himself Frazier Mohawk. The ranch stretched any IRS definition of "legitimate business expense."

- Girls living at the ranch paraded into town in their leopard capri pants, high heels, and shades, scaring the Keddie locals (not hard to do). Inside the ranch, nudity was normal. Naked girls liked giving musicians (and guests) baths.
- Girls, boys, and visiting execs indulged in the box in the living room filled with pot and hash strong enough to cause whiplash.
- Drummer Sandy Konikoff achieved fame by recording (naked except for his shades) with a slim mike, wrapped in plastic, covered with lotion, and shoved up his rear end, making him appear, in the words of Ned Doheny, "like an electric rat." To transmit good rhythm, Sandy would slap himself, leg and chest, like some Irish jigger, producing drumbeats for his anal mike. Konikoff's invention was later called a SphincterPhone.
- Holzman, envisioning himself as "an equipment-happy Virgo," spoke of the "water signs at the Fantasy Orchestra Ranch."[58]

In L.A. one night in 1967, while lounging in their 100 percent candlelit home, Jac stunned his wife, Nina, by telling her he was going on a long Trip Around the World, with no idea when he'd return from his "Journey of Discovery." Holzman realized that his record label had gone out of his control and had gotten beyond even his influence. Employees were on their own trips, and Jac could not (and would not) restore reality. Jac's self-prescribed antidote was to "get away" on his own trip. He asked Nina to take over running the label, then embarked on the SS *President Roosevelt,* heading for Hong Kong. First stop, Hawaii. Nina found him there and persuaded him to come back home to their children. Holzman returned but with a new outlook. He decided to rid himself of administering Elektra, hoping to float back to Hawaii and hammock it out under purple sunsets. During his absence, Elektra had managed to issue only one single.

Hawaii in mind, Holzman cornered Jerry Wexler and Mo Ostin whenever he could, urging Ostin to set up Warner's *own* distribution, hoping Elektra could be part of any branch operation. He offered the presidency of Elektra to Mo, trying to induce him over with a 10 percent share of the label. Mo "respectfully declined." Holzman slicked up his act. He dressed businesslike, trimmed back the sideburns. "I dolled myself up and danced around until somebody got the idea to approach me."

As part of that financial seduction dance, Elektra got visited by *The Wall Street Journal*, which made note that office "conversations are likely to be sprinkled with 'monsters' (smash hit records) or 'needs more of a beard'

---

[58]Barry Friedman later moved to Puck's Farm in Ontario, Canada, where he has successfully sold ad space on the sides of his cows, so passing train passengers would have living billboards to watch.

(instrumentation could be heavier). The staff is partial to fashionable boots and to various items from smart leather jackets to paisley bell-bottom trousers. The artists may be long-haired, somewhat 'unorthodox' types."

After his first meeting with Steve Ross way back when, introduced by Ahmet and Mo, Holzman's Ross hot line had never rung. He felt what single girls experience after first dates, when boys say, "I'll call ya."

Finally, 2,213 hours later, at Wexler's house, Holzman asked his host, "What happened? I had this terrific meeting with Ross and I haven't heard a peep since." Wexler, agreeing it was weird, said he'd look into it.

In late June, Jac got a call from Ahmet, arranging a second date with him and Kinney's executive vice president, Alan Cohen. Accompanied by Jac's lawyer, Irwin Russell, Holzman, Cohen, and Ertegun met. When asked what he wanted for Elektra/Nonesuch, Jac responded with certainty: $10 million. "At that point," to quote Holzman, "Ahmet continued to buy and sell a rug." Kinney's offer started at $8 million. By the end of the day, the number rose to $9.5 million. Holzman said, "It's ten dollar million, and that's it." Down the elevator he went.

The price—$10 million—was a figure based on Elektra's current net earnings of about $1.2 million, times eight years, rounded upward. One reason the Kinney people were dickering was that, to avoid going to the Justice Department for clearance, if the price of a deal stayed under $10 million, you wouldn't get your deal searched by the government. The next day, Kinney and Elektra avoided federal frisk by dividing one deal into two: $9,800,000 for the record labels, and $200,000 for its accompanying publishing company.

Ross liked his Kinney Music Group becoming tri-labeled: Warner + Atlantic + Elektra. "Steve had this saying," Kinney CFO Bert Wasserman recalled. "If you had one office with three doors, you wouldn't have grown as fast as having three offices with doors located in three different buildings." In the record business, Ross believed decentralization made more money.

Within three weeks, signatures got signed. On July 22, Elektra became one more part of Kinney. Ross, Prince of Leveraged Buyouts, paid his price using $7 million in cash, the rest in convertible debentures. The deal cost Kinney nothing. It bought Elektra out of the label's own cash flow.

Holzman believed that the fertile Sixties were over, that Seventies life was about to be different. He quoted a saying by skier Jean Claude Killey: "Every man should have at least three occupations in his lifetime." Jac prepared for reincarnation. But despite his desire to enjoy retirement now, in the middle of his life, instead of in "the golden years," Holzman was trapped. As part of its purchase of Elektra, Kinney had insisted that he sign a continuing-employment agreement, with options, binding him to the company. Jac's suit stayed buttoned. The hammock hung empty.

The next years became less enjoyable for Jac. He was bone tired. After taking care of vet employees Mel Posner, Bill Harvey, and country-music head Russ Miller, plus a share for now-ex-wife Nina and long-ago investor Theo Bikel, Holzman netted $5 million for his label.

The energetic Rothchild had watched Elektra turn tougher, particularly in its business/legal regimen. Paul, who thought he knew his value to Elektra, asked Holzman for more than his producer royalty (1 percent if you were salaried at Elektra). When asked "How much more?" Rothchild replied, "Oh, maybe a million dollars." As graciously as possible, Holzman told Rothchild he was worth *much* more than that, then let Paul go out on his own. Holzman recalled Rothchild as "part martinet and part broken-field runner." Others saw Rothchild as the man who made Elektra commercial. Either way, in a costly clash of valves, their marriage of convenience ended then and there.

Significant Elektra Albums

1965
The Paul Butterfield Blues Band • Judy Collins (*Fifth Album*) • Leadbelly (*The Library of Congress Recordings*) • Love ("7 and 7 Is" and "My Little Red Book") • Joshua Rifkin (*The Baroque Beatles Book*)

1966
The Paul Butterfield Blues Band (*East-West*) • Love (*Love*) • Judy Collins (*In my Life*)

1967
Tim Buckley (*Goodbye and Hello*) • The Doors (*The Doors*, including "Light My Fire" and *Strange Days*, including "Love Me Two Times" and "People Are Strange")

1968
Judy Collins (*Wildflowers*, including "Both Sides Now") • The Incredible String Band (*The Hangman's Beautiful Daughter*) • The Holy Modal Rounders

1969
Bread ("It Don't Matter to Me") • Judy Collins (*Recollections*) • Delaney and Bonnie and Friends (*Accept No Substitute*) • The Doors (*The Soft Parade*, including "Touch Me") • MC5 (*Kick Out the Jams*) • Nico (*The Marble Index*) • The Stooges

14

As Warner Reprise grew, three executives—Ostin, Smith, and Friedman—shared East Coast ancestry. They now lived in the same town: Encino, in an area they'd renamed Warner Heights. Mo, Joe, and Joel had synagogued together. Saturday mornings at Art's Deli, they egged-and-pastramied together.

When it came to outlining how a branch system for Warner and Atlantic might work, Mo had turned to Joel, trusting in his friend's addiction to memoranda. Joel had typed up a plan.[59]

"Let's get going," called Ted Ashley in 1970, assembling Kinney's label heads—Atlantic, Warner/Reprise—and now Elektra—in a bungalow of the Beverly Hills hotel. Ashley and Ross had their list of goals that would make their labels greater, much as W7A's Alan Hirschfeld had tried before. Ross asked Mo if he'd bring up this first notion. Distribution was at the top of Ostin's list; he'd already committed to creating Warner/Reprise's own system, having suffered for years the inertia of independent distributors who'd been kicking Mo's albums around. If you didn't have your own branches like Capitol, Columbia, RCA and MCA did, it was like playing pro ball for the Keokuk Eagles. W7 Arts deserved major league status.

The problems of starting a branch system were two: Would the guy in charge be an Atlantic or a Warner nominee? And how much of our clout would we *labels* have to give up to some new distribution company? Despite that Jimi Hendrix 6+1 business in the Carolinas, labels like Atlantic and Warner were now very used to being biggest fish in their respective ponds.

Ostin passed out originals and carbons of Joel's two memos, one about how branch distribution worked, the other about how distribution should be administered by Kinney's labels: how it would run, what it would cost. One

---

[59]In the 1950s, the first distribution organization owned by a record company (the "tree") was created by CBS's Bill Gallagher. It got called a "branch system." Branches had changed record selling in the same way that radio play had changed it in the same decade. The essentials of marketing records got down to just two: Get it on Top Forty and get it into stores. Besides those two essentials, ads and other buyables meant little.

key recommendation by Friedman: Each label would keep its own unique and separate identity, and the distribution branch would not interfere. "Why detract from that identity by centralizing advertising or other functions?" Friedman's memo read. "Surely you could save enormous amounts of money. But the way each company did things individually had to be preserved." Much yes-nodding all around.

Ostin endorsed the plan as common sense. It meant that in local markets, with our own employees, we labels could call our own shots, not have to compete against other indie labels, like A&M and Motown and a hundred more, each of those hundred others demanding airplay, each of them expecting their stock to be properly laid out in stores, each of them at the mercy of indie distributors who ran their territories in their own interests.

Questions about indies vs. branches were asked by Ross and Ashley. They knew little about record-business jargon, little about how promo men handle spiffs (greasing through better giving), little about returns policy and product dumping. Their questions were easily, if impatiently, answered. Soon Ross and Ashley just sat back, listened to their record guys. WBR's plan made sense, even if it meant, mostly to the three men from Atlantic, abandoning longtime allies in the record-business marketplace, meant pulling away from colleagues who spent decades roistering with the goateed Stone in bars, restaurants, radio stations, and hooker joints, decades of doing anything that needed to get done to sell records.

"Things like what?" asked Ashley.

"You don't want to know," answered Smith.

The question came to *who* would run this new Kinney Distributing. Ostin and Smith suggested Friedman. Silence. Clearly, Atlantic was still leery of Burbank. Elektra, worth only 20 percent of the whole, having suffered for years for its sin of smallness, just wanted to ride this wave, not make another one.

Another issue—foreign distribution for three combined companies— was also raised. Warner Bros.' international head, the lanky, wry traveling man Phil Rose, was already setting up outposts. With Ostin's okay, Rose had set up WBR in Canada (already working), and had been to Australia to do the same.

Atlantic's Nesuhi Ertegun was known to covet the International job. Silence. "So who'll run International?" was asked. After ten minutes of hem and haw, "Look," Smith said, "if you'll accept Joel, then you can name the head of International."

That quick, the deal was struck: Joel and Nesuhi. Smith later recalled it as "the day we sold out Phil Rose."

The labels themselves, not Father Kinney, would own their American distribution company. Joel's new company would report to the three labels and for its work receive a fee: Each label would pay Distribution 16 percent

of its records' sale price. That, they figured, was about break-even for Distribution, and a good deal less than the bite indies had been taking. Profits
from Joel's new organization would come straight back to the labels.

Still one more condition: Joel would get bossed. As intent as the labels
were about their artist-signing presences, so were they intent in controlling
this new company. By 1972, the labels had set up a "grip" group of three
strong overseers. In "Grip," the G stood for Dave Glew, running sales for Atlantic; the R for Warner's most recent hire, sales manager Eddie Rosenblatt;
and the P for Elektra's first employee/sales manager, Mel Posner.

Davey, Eddie, and Mel had all begun in records in the 1950s, when
record distributors' areas were divided on maps and regions named for their
central cities, like Philly. Glew, Rosenblatt, and Posner—sales guys—had
seen retail grow from the early Fifties, when a town's record store had listening booths forty inches wide—just big enough for one—a few records for
listening, and an ashtray the size of a hubcap. In the years since, these men
had experienced change, as concentrated radio play and bigger jukeboxes
came along, when people would've heard records before they went into
record stores, when listening booths disappeared and records stopped being
blamed for lung cancer. When records could be bought in Sears.

In the 1960s, Dave Glew, working for independent Seaway Distributors,
had gotten the call from Atlantic offering a home-office job, which Dave accepted fast as a contestant on *The Price Is Right*. As a label guy, he now
traveled short plane hops, from distrib to distrib. There, about four in the afternoon, Dave would fit its salesmen into rooms so narrow the word "conference" could hardly fit. He'd pull out Atlantic's "slick books" (collections
of new albums' covers), play a track or two from the latest releases, take the
branch's opening order, throw in some freebies, then take them all out for
dinner to some place with cloth napkins, a place whose name ended in
"-io's," ordering Italian *con* Schlitz, where Atlantic picked up the tab. They
all—Dave and Mel and Eddie—did this, night after night. I came to think of
those guys as the keels of our boat, while the rest of us frolicked on the main
deck.

Like Glew, Rosenblatt had come out of independent distribution. He
had made his mark serving as manager at a Cleveland distributorship, Mainline. When rack jobbing[60] came along, Eddie threw off territory limits like
Spartacus throwing off his chains. He became fearsome on the phone,

---

[60]Rack jobbing was a another way of selling records. The sellers didn't own stores; they
leased space (racks) for records in bigger stores, like department stores. But they didn't
staff the space with their own clerks. Customers picked up what they wanted from the
rack of records there and bought it from the store. The rack jobber just kept his inventory
up to date, without all the costs of running a store. Becoming rack jobbers, distributors
could sell records two ways: to stores and, via their own racks, direct to consumers.

selling records far beyond Cleveland. Seattle? Ed had the number. He dialed remarkably fast.

Authoritative of voice, Eddie Rosenblatt had then been hired to move to California, first by A&M Records. He flew to Los Angeles in December 1966, and as he got off the plane from snowbound Cleveland, he walked to the terminal throwing off his cap, his overcoat(s), his galoshes. He toured sunny Los Angeles in a rental car, looking for a home. His wife, Bobbie, hurried out to join her husband, driving past possible neighborhoods and schools. Bobbie commented on all the black children in one schoolyard. Eddie assured her, "Bobbie, those are not blacks. Those are Jews, with tans."

After a short stay at A&M, Rosenblatt reached Warner Bros., adapting to a new universe. "One of my first memories of Warner Bros. Records," he recalled, "was sitting on the floor in Stan Cornyn's office with half a dozen gorgeous young girls who worked in Creative Services. There may have been some men in the room, too. Anyway, I sat there thinking, 'I've died and gone to heaven.' I also remember how surprised the Cornyn crew were when some album started selling off radio play, before their ads had run."

Glew, Rosenblatt, and Posner were sales vets. They understood indie distributors and their problems: getting too much inventory. Record-label sales managers always pulled one side of the tug-of-war rope: Their job was to call thirty distributors and shove merchandise down their throats. Distribution's end of the rope was keep the labels happy while selling stores tons of what was *already* selling.

Against the instincts of the sales guys, GR&P had to keep the new distribution plan in the bag. The existing indie distributors, if they learned they were terminal, would flip. So, very quietly, in July, the lawyers secretly incorporated a new company, SHHH, short for Kinney Records Distributing Corporation.

Utterly unlike what had happened a decade before in Conkling and Cook's attempt at distributing, this set of company-owned branches would be gassed up by a no-lead catalogue of premium hits. Mo Ostin's secretary, Thelma Walker, had enlarged her earlier underlining habit: Now she underlined *Billboard*'s charts in four different colors, One for WB, another for Reprise, another for Atlantic, a fourth for Elektra. She knew what was coming—one branch system for all. Thelma Walker's count—her criterion was any label's album that made the bestseller chart during its year issue— would add up to a whopping start for Kinney Records Distributing: 442 chart albums was the opening ante. 442. That was more like it.

The day after we'd heard that Joel was chosen to head up Distribution, I saw him on the stairs of our offices. He was just coming in, so it was around nine, and he was charging up the stairs, loosening his tie, and saying to himself, "Shit, what a day." Joel's job was to tumble the first dominoes toward a fully operating, eight-city branch operation, and do it all in under two years, before any distributor guessed we were leaving. No easier than answering "What's that lipstick on your collar, dear?"

That July 1970, Atlantic's L.A. inventory, formerly handled by Merit Distributors down on ratty Pico Boulevard, moved out to Burbank, to share room with WBR's already working distribution center. (Elektra was still niggling with its L.A. indie.) Over that hot weekend, trucks hauled cartons of albums from Atlantic, around the mountain pass, over Barham, into the San Fernando Valley. Sunday night, the Atlantic albums snuggled against the Warner albums, Ben E. King being introduced to Pet Clark. The next morning, clerks opened and shelved carton upon carton of Atlantic's bonanza:

Bobby Darin • Ray Charles • Ben E. King • Mr. Acker Bilk • Bent Fabric • Aretha Franklin • Booker T & the MG's • Nino Tempo & April Stevens • The Drifters • Rufus & Carla Thomas • Otis Redding • Solomon Burke • Wilson Pickett • Joe Tex • The Young Rascals • Percy Sledge • Sam & Dave • Bee Gees • Buffalo Springfield • Arthur Conley • Cream • Flip Wilson • Iron Butterfly • Blind Faith • Archie Bell & the Drells • Crosby, Stills & Nash • King Crimson • Ginger Baker • Eric Clapton • Delaney & Bonnie Bramlett • Mott the Hoople • Dr. John • Donny Hathaway • Led Zeppelin

L.A. branch up; seven to go. Friedman needed help. His first hire was Liberty Records' Mike Elliot. Elliot, too, had grown sick of indies, sick of consigning albums and never getting money for them, sick of having his line cherry-picked (a term meaning buying cherries [or albums] one by one, rather than by the bunch). In his new job, Elliot, a patch over one eye, glasses on top of that, got the title National Director of Branch Administration. Which meant that Elliott wrote, he nudged, he thought, he pipe-puffed, he got it done. The problem solver. As a memo typer, he ranked up near Friedman. A separate line in the Kinney Distribution budget was needed for carbon paper. Elliot, who never got the recognition he deserved ("without him, no company") was exacting, like this paragraph in his seven-page, forty-points-deep memo with advice to branches like . . .

4. As we discussed, please have the DJ mailing room set up for both singles and LP's, indicating the stations to be serviced. I think it's imperative that a log be created to indicate when a particular record arrives, when it was shipped, how, and to whom. The same type of log should be instituted for display material.

To calm its existing indie distributors, Kinney lied, announcing it had decided *not* to "go branch." Well, maybe just "two or three big cities," Friedman typed for a press release. He'd hardly pulled the paper out of the type-writer when his phone rang. It was Atlantic's Glew. "Seaway's in deep shit" was his message. "We gotta open Cleveland, and fast."

Opening Cleveland meant "pulling the line" (taking your distribution away) not only from Atlantic's Seaway but also from Warner and Elektra's Mainline, run by Bill Shipley. Friedman and Posner flew in to tell Shipley, who had his answer ready: "Okay, but I want my money back."

"What money?" asked Joel.

Knowing it was all a game, Shipley bluffed Friedman: "The money I paid for the franchise. I paid Maitland." Mainline's sales manager—tough, no-bull, honest, totally Italian Mike Spence—was hired out from under Shipley to head the new Kinney Music of Cleveland.[61]

Soon Joel Friedman felt like some boarding-school lad who'd been plunged into a jungle of mean men. Jackie Presser, for instance, one of the most devious and greediest men ever to have lived, was heading up the Teamsters Union #107, prior to filling Jimmy Hoffa's cement shoes. Presser came to Mike Spence's Cleveland branch, ready to organize. Spence, the sweetheart, became deeply pissed. He called Kinney's labor expert, Norm Samnick, a sizable lawyer with a wrap-you-in-his-arms persona and a love for laughter. Samnick took on the case with Presser.

At first it was threats. The Teamsters sent in guys with names like Fas-ciano and Samino, guys with big collars and gold chains. Guys good at graphic explanations of how they could handle things, like "or we could throw you out this window." Spence explained how he needed his employees to do *more* than one job in the warehouse. To explain, he emphasized hered-itary bonding: "Let's say we get this new *Sinatra* record in . . . you know, by *Frank* Sinatra . . . because *Frank Sinatra*, he records for *us* . . ."

A "unionize/not unionize" vote was held. Even after the Teamsters lost the vote at Kinney Distributing, Presser still called Samnick to ask when the two of them could sit down to do the contract. Astounded, Samnick replied, "Hey, Jackie, you guys lost the election. You were voted out!"

"A mere technicality," Presser countered.

"You're kidding."

"I'm not kidding," Presser replied. "We're serious."

"Jackie, tell me," Samnick asked, "what would you do if the Teamsters won the election and I called and used the 'mere technicality' line on you?"

"I'd tell you, 'Norm, go fuck yourself.' "

---

[61]Spence picked awful quarters: nine thousand square feet on the third floor of a sixty-five-year-old building where the once-little-known Stearns auto had been made. To get there, you either rode up its one freight elevator or drove up a three-story spiral ramp. On opening day, seventeen workers made it up the ramp. On opening year, Kinney Cleve-land's total year's business was $13 million, 60 percent in LPs, 20 percent 8-tracks, 15 percent singles, and 5 percent cassettes.

"Jackie, go fuck yourself." Samnick hung up, then peered out his window, weighing his chances.

Joel's small crew and the three "GRPs" groped for answers—like how many loading docks they'd need—while still keeping wary eyes on each other. That's why there was this committee, right? Atlantic guys didn't trust their own mothers. Elektra's Posner constantly fought against getting pushed around ("Elektra was ten percent of the sales and ninety percent of the noise," recalled GRP Ed Rosenblatt). So Friedman had two of three partners who didn't trust him. Sometimes three.

Logistics, like picking branch sites, confounded these novices. "We were ahead of our time," Rosenblatt put it. "We created seven new branches, to serve greater areas. It was a first of its kind. Columbia had it set up differently, because they were manufacturers. They used the plant as the warehouse. They'd manufacture, then move records to the other side of the plant, and that became the branch."

The Friedman-GRPs group made repeated trips, city after city, shopping for a branch manager and financial guy at each, staring at vast cement floors in empty spaces, trying to sound savvy to real-estate agents who saw right through them. The Friedman gang members realized they were just kids in a world of Teamsters and even had no clue about what question to ask realtors.

"Do you have sprinklers here?" they'd ask.

After the first couple of branch cities got set up, every indie distributor knew that his day came next.

For years, indie owners had studied Scamming for Dummies. With Kinney pulling its labels, that was time for their final exam in Scam. They wrung the last dime out of their divorces. In an exercise that Mel Posner termed Creative Writing 101, the indies sent the labels mountains of Charge Back forms. They demanded huge amounts of after-the-fact payments, their paperwork ranging between shenanigans and theft. They pulled stock out of stores to return to the labels.

The three labels' savvy financial officers, men trained like unusual dogs to sniff out fact from phony—Atlantic's tall Sheldon Vogel, Warner's wiry Murray Gitlin, and Elektra's fat Jack Reinstein—took on all their old distribs' nonsense like divorcées fighting over who should get the blue napkins. Scrambling to avoid getting killed, the three labels had to get through the planned two-year transition in nine months. The race had begun.

Through this eventful year—1970—Mo's secretary, Thelma, had meticulously continued to underline the charts each Monday, using her rainbow of pens. Her scorekeeping will, in this book, henceforth, be known as Thelma's

Tally. For 1970: Warner had 37 chart listings for the year + Atlantic 35 + Elektra 7 = WEA's 79.

You may underline in this book.

Billboard's "1970 Year End Review" proclaimed that the year's top *label* was Columbia. That really pissed off Mo. However, the top *corporate group* of labels was . . .

Kinney (albums)	18.4%
CBS	15.3
Capitol	8.3

All that work, all those years of work before branches—showing up in Detroit on Saturday in a red raincoat, looking for distribution; hanging on to Ruth Brown for a year when she went into the hospital; speeding across Manhattan on a Vespa with your tape machine strapped on—added up to a catalogue of albums and a know-how about what sells. In this, its season of birth, Kinney had gone to Number One.

Which really pissed off CBS.

According to its 1970 Annual Report, brand identity preoccupied Kinney:

> We feel that by using the Kinney name on millions of company products, from TV and movie trailers to record jackets, publications, advertisements and stationery, more people will begin to recognize our full range of services. This program also encompasses a proposed corporate name change to Kinney Services, Inc.

Kinney's Leisure Time Group was now viewed by Ross and Ashley, at least, as the future of their corporation. The two men discussed it in their own ways: Ashley setting up clear alternatives with phrasing like "We have two choices, and one of them isn't going to help," Ross keeping more to himself, smoking one cigarette after another, occasionally switching to nibbling one cuticle after another. Together, the two men learned to speak new words, hip-culture words like "youthquake" and the "Now Society."

Ashley, busy running WB Pictures, had little time these days for records. Ross turned to one of his top aides/negotiators, Alan Cohen, who'd dealt with Jac's sale of Elektra. Cohen became senior vice president of Kinney. Ross handed him Records to look at. Ross and Ashley tended to the movies, selling half the Burbank lot to Columbia Pictures, once again raising the painters' scaffold. The water tower now read THE BURBANK STUDIOS.

The next year, 1971, Kinney executed a Full Caterpillar, completely losing its Lysol-smelling past. Shedding its vacuum-cleaner and parking-lot

cocoon turned Kinney into a Wall Street Butterfly. Kinney first sold its funeral chapels for $35 million, half in cash, half in paper.

Ross then divided the rest of Kinney into two piles. All real-estate operations were moved to the right-hand pile, together with a hundred thousand
mops. Call that pile National Kinney Corporation. National Kinney sold
that half of itself to the public as a new company, with separate management, separate shareholders, and no Steve.

Into the left-hand pile Ross and friends moved sexy stuff. They called
the pile Warner Communications, Incorporated. Into WCI all the music-
business properties of the corporation were lovingly put. And movies, magazines, cable. Plus money: As one of this pile's assets, WCI kept the half of
National Kinney it hadn't sold to the public, but only for money's sake.
From this arrangement WCI got a bunch of cash to use buying its way into
the cable-television business. The WCI Butterfly flew off in its first corporate jet labeled—right there, on its tail—Warner Communications.

Riding the company's jet was for me, of course, a peak experience, but
a mixed blessing. By now some of us automatically rode first class anyway,
and for me that meant often on American Airlines, which had two virtues:
cute stewardesses and, after dinner, hot-fudge sundaes. Between marriages,
I was seldom disappointed with the two choices offered by American Airlines. The WCI jet, however, had neither hot fudge nor hot stewardesses,
though it did have a small candy drawer in the bar area, where I could
pocket candy bars for free.

Following Corporate's image change from Kinney to WCI, calling our
new branch system "Kinney" seemed stupid. But calling the new distribution company "Warner" also seemed unfair to two labels with different
names.

The label politicians met in high summit, serious, as if they were renaming Jerusalem. For a name, they decided on the first letters of each label,
A, E, and W. Next, they pondered, should we list the three in alphabetical order? AEW? No, that sounded like you just smelled something bad. Ahmet,
perhaps relieved simply to see his A survive, relaxed. "I don't care," he conceded. "A can go last." So how about EWA? Nesuhi spoke up. EWA would
"cause pronunciation problems in Europe." Thus, a new, Warnerized word
was coined: WEA. Both distribution companies—U.S. and International—
became renamed.

With WEA on new stationery, Friedman, Mike Elliot, financial head
Jack O'Connell, and the GRPs kept running. Joel confided in Glew, Atlantic's newly appointed VP and director of marketing, his secret goal for
the year: "I want to see us sell a hundred million dollars."

Publicly, Joel had been masquerading, having to pretend "we love our
indies." In April, when the WEA group finally came out of the closet and
confessed the formation of a full branch system, it was to no one's surprise.

Considerable cold-shouldering came from those lame-duck indies still quacking for us. Warner Bros.' Rosenblatt stopped in the Washington indie distributorship, armed with slick book and a tape to play sample tracks. He had good goods: a new Jethro Tull, James Taylor's *Mud Slide Slim,* Deep Purple, all future platinum releases. He was into his pitch fifteen minutes, when he saw "the guys were already throwing beer cans at me. They didn't give a fuck. They were losing the line. I told them, 'Look, this is very simple. We have a great release. Sell the hell out of it, and WEA takes back all your returns next year.'

"I had an eight-minute meeting in Philly, a seven-minute meeting in New York, and in Boston we went out with our distributor and got bombed. It was very sad leaving those guys." It was our old crowd. The sales guys at Alpha in New York, wearing their yarmulkes to work, sharing pizza that Rosenblatt had brought by.

The passing of the label-indie relationships had its downsides, in particular losing those road shows, when label execs would move from city to city doing one-nighters, showing new releases in some hotel auditorium, with steak and booze to follow. After that, guys like Harry Apostoleris of New York's Alpha Distributing had other amenities ready. At the Plaza Hotel, for example, there'd be a two-bedroom suite. In the main room, a couple of his sales guys plus a couple of women wearing nothing above the waist. Label execs would be shoulder-tapped, then led, one by one, up to the suite and introduced to Lorna (but not to Sherry, who was already in one of the bedrooms). After a full twenty-second introduction ("Where ya from?"), Lorna'd right away invite the guy into the other bedroom.[62]

This system, now sounding antique, I guess, passed away with our indies. The Golden Age of Amenities was replaced in the 1970s by free sex, which had much less tingle than twenty minutes with Paula.

For New York, there was no clear candidate to become WEA's new branch manager. Friedman interviewed for two solid days before visiting the soon-to-be-ex-distributor Harry Apostoleris. When Friedman walked in, Apostoleris told him, "Don't sit down." He opened his desk drawer, pulled out a lead pipe, and slammed it on the desktop, yelling "Why are you here?" Friedman said, "I want to go out to dinner." At six, Apostoleris and Friedman went out, got drunk, moaning about fate and the partings of friends.

City after city, WEA branches opened. Bad and good branch bosses were picked. Bad bosses got changed fast, like babies with the runs. Good bosses turned out to be strong, self-assured guys who ran branches their

---

[62]At the Playboy Club on some lake in upstate New York, there was a girl named Paula, who gave blowjobs with her mouth full of seltzer water. (I *think* this is what footnotes are for.)

own way, autonomously, and got results. Which brings us to our Question for 1971: In which WEA sales office was sexual intercourse first found objectionable? Answer below.

In every city where WEA hastily opened a branch, one common phenomenon occurred: Salesmen became astounded by the quantity of albums they sold. The focus on *one* company's albums to sell, not the old hundred indie labels' releases, was working. Six plus one was unthinkable. New York's Paul DeGennaro, who for years had been squeaking out good enough orders for years, wrote an order for thirty thousand dollars on his first day out selling for WEA. Right away, he started thinking about buying '21.'

Beyond its branches, WEA established local sales offices (no warehouses) in big cities, markets like San Francisco, where one was opened at the Wharfside, a classy brick-and-skylights building at 680 Beach Street, with ten employees under sales-office manager Bill Perasso. Inside the offices, right away, a dispute broke out over who'd get the bigger office, manager Perasso or promotion man Pete Marino, whom you may remember wading up out of the Hawaii surf butt naked. A large space was divided between the two, with Perasso getting the slightly larger chunk. That, however, was not final victory.

The flamboyant Marino, WB tattooed indelibly on his arm, created an office unlike others in WEA. Pete imported his furniture from Mexico, including credenzas, velvet chairs, chandelier, and candelabra. And more: a replica of King Tut's throne, a jukebox, a hand-carved desk. The swarthy Marino drove San Francisco in his vintage Rolls-Royce with two phones (front seat; backseat). You sensed he wasn't doing this on four hundred dollars a week.

San Francisco's open-house party was organized as a genteel affair for an invited group of fifty. Guests of honor were Liberace (then on WBR) and the J. Geils Band. Press, radio, and television came out in full force, filming the party for *News at 11*. Marino and Liberace tried to outjewel one another, bauble for bauble, ring for ring.

In the end, the guest quantity exceeded fifty; some five hundred people crowded in. The next day, the building manager sent Perasso a concerned letter:

Gentlemen:

   I understand your party of the other day was a great success. Apparently the number of guests was quite large.

   The party has prompted some problems which I must call to your attention:

1. The party overflow into the corridors caused the walls adjacent to
   your office to be dirtied to the extent that they will require a complete

repaint job. We must bill you for the painting required, since this area of the building had recently been painted.

2. *The carpet was stained by the great amount of champagne which was spilled all over the corridor. We will need to send you a bill for the shampooing required afterwards.*

3. *One of the offices was burglarized during the party and a $1,000 calculator had been stolen.*

4. *The behavior of some of your guests was unfortunately adverse to the standards we must maintain in the building. Specifically, there was sexual intercourse in at least one instance in one area of the corridor . . .*

With pride and using oversize nails, members of the San Francisco office hammered this letter to the wall.

Through all this, Atlantic, Elektra, and Warner Bros. Records never stopped fighting it out in A&R and promotion, with WEA sitting in the middle, ducking. When WBR and Atlantic recorded competing versions of Carole King's "You've Got a Friend," to duck got tough because two labels had the same song to promote. Atlantic's version was by Donny Hathaway and Roberta Flack. Atlantic jump-released its single before Warner could get out its version by James Taylor.

"In addition to the natural desire to win—which is another way of saying our dedication to healthy competition—there is a matter of responsibility to your artist," Wexler told *Billboard,* which covered this Duel of the Singles. "We plan an all-out promotion and advertising drive on the Hathaway-Flack single."

When the "You've Got a Friend" race between Atlantic and Warners ended, the result:

First Place Winner: James Taylor (Number One, fourteen weeks)
Definitely Runner-Up: Hathaway-Flack (Number Twenty-nine; twelve weeks)

As a result of this race, no one got killed exactly. *Billboard* called back Atlantic for a comment. Ahmet publicly explained away Atlantic's loss with this statement: "Atlantic was distracted, fighting Warners to sign two artists, Tony Joe White and the Rolling Stones. Warners ended up with Tony Joe White."

Atlantic, after all, was the label dominating the London acts-to-sign market. Since the mid-Sixties, Ahmet and Nesuhi, Jerry and Jerry (Wexler and Greenberg), had become addicts of such deals. They had flown frequently to England, set up alliances with British labels (Polydor in particular), and hung with the tuned-in music men (like Bert Berns, the ex–Atlantic producer who'd pointed Wexler toward Led Zeppelin). Since the "British Invasion," Atlantic had made London a second home. The Erteguns co-bought a Kensington town house. Ahmet had traveled endless nights with the Stones, it seemed, while in the inside pocket of his designer blazer he kept a six-albums-in-four-years deal. "I would marvel at Ahmet," recalled Jac Holzman. "He had the stamina of a rhino, could work all day, party all night, lock his legs and fall asleep standing up for fifteen minutes . . . then wake and pick up in the middle of a sentence."

Ahmet had by now spent, it felt like, the better part of a decade, perhaps two, chasing around Europe, to untold numbers of resort islands, and across America as Mick Jagger's close-close pal. Drinking into the night in maroon-leather booths, Ertegun's lidded eyes lowering, heavier, heavier, but still there enough to tell the next amusing tale. In the end, the bon vivant–ism of Ertegun, plus Ahmet's willingness to stand shoulder to shoulder at a row of urinals to pee along with Mick, paid off with the band's new label Rolling Stone Records' distribution union with Atlantic. In money offers, Atlantic had come in only third, but Jagger liked Atlantic because Ahmet talked music.

At WEA branches, the Stones became cherries on their sundaes. Designed by artist Andy Warhol, the Stones' first Atlantic LP cover featured the crotch of a man's well-occupied jeans. On the cardboard cover, the jeans zipper would really zip and, having unzipped, a red balloon would flop out. Such was Warhol's notion. Atlantic compromised: zipper yes, balloon no.

Each of the three labels now began competing for attention with branch promotion men. Despite Ahmet's "Tony Joe White" shrug, promotion races among the labels touched nerves. Promo people in smaller markets got known as "two-baggers" (people who represented two labels' suitcases) or even "three-baggers." They were criticized when they got one label's single on the air but the other label's was stood up. Bitter incidents arose over how many "baggers" were needed in a city. Labels fought WEA, pounding Joel's desk for "my label only" promotion people. Friedman held them back, the labels thought, pinching pennies so he'd look good. His attitude particularly affected the shortest of the labels, Elektra. "The biggest challenge I had," Elektra's Posner recalled, "came from WEA's mentality that it was okay for Elektra to be repped by a three-bagger, or a two-bagger."

In Greenwich Village, a group called the Chapins debuted at the Village Gate, performing Harry Chapin's story songs. His songs spun out as long narratives. One of them—"Taxi"—was the tale of a pot-smoking cabbie from San Francisco who picked up his first love as a rainy-night fare, then had to deposit her at the home of her wealthy husband.[63] "Dogtown" told a multicharacter saga of a New England fishing village where the husbands left for months at a time, their women back home with no companionship but their dogs.

Several other record companies, including Atlantic and Columbia, went after Chapin. Columbia's Clive Davis showed Harry a printout of how many copies his branch system had sold of other artists' albums. Its sales numbers were staggering. Holzman, without a WEA printout to impress the singer/songwriter, felt impotent to counterattack. Chapin told Jac he'd decided on Columbia. Good as branches were, WEA's were not *as* good, it looked like, as Columbia's. In Burbank, Holzman described for Joel about how humiliating it was, having to look at Columbia's numbers. Friedman answered, "That's bullshit. You want to see the *real* numbers?" Joel had in his desk drawer a true Columbia printout, illegally got. The numbers on Joel's *actual* printout were considerably less impressive than the one Davis had showed off.

Printout in hand, Holzman red-eyed it back to New York. At six on Sunday morning, he banged on Chapin's door. Woke Harry up, walked in with the *real* numbers, and would not let go. To get some rest, Chapin's path of least annoyance was to sign a nine-album deal with Elektra, for a $40,000 advance plus free studio time. Holzman rewarded himself. He got a personalized license plate for his silver Mercedes; it read EARS.

By 1971, schlock rock, in which acts added wooziness to their charms, started attracting fans. Take Alice Cooper, who once summed up his career, "The thing that really turned it all around for us was when we realized that we were not into peace and love. We were the *National Enquirer* of rock & roll." Let me put that another way: Take the story of Alice Cooper and how I learned to bend over.

I had been in curious awe of Alice ever since the Toronto Peace Festival, when someone in the audience had thrown a live chicken onstage. It was clearly an improvisational moment, which Alice recalled this way: "I'm from Detroit. I'm not a farm kid. I figured a chicken has wings, it'll fly away. So I took the chicken and threw it, and it didn't fly. It went into the audience. Blood everywhere. The next day, everybody's reading, 'Alice Cooper rips chicken's head off, drinks blood.' To this day, wherever I'm booked, the ASPCA is usually there, too."

Alice Cooper had a new album being released, called *School's Out*. Alice's manager, sharp Shep Gordon, had decided that instead of Warner's usual white paper inner sleeve, the *School's Out* black-vinyl disc should be

---

[63]When "Taxi" was released, the song ran 6:37. Too long for most radio. Elektra simply changed the label copy, asserting the length was 4:69.

sleeved inside ladies' disposable paper panties. Pink ones. I found all kinds of reasons my record company could not tolerate such expense; Shep overcame them all. When U.S Customs stopped the pink panties coming in from Israel, where they'd been made ("too flammable"), secretly I rejoiced. For an interview with the *Washington Post,* our PR man, Bob Merlis, decided our best tactic would be government humiliation. He prompted the reporter. The reporter interviewed a Customs rep, asking "This is the same material that's used in surgical garments, correct?" "Correct," he answered. "So if you were to put these panties over your head and face, they would be okay?"

In the meantime, Shep Gordon sneaked carloads of pink paper panties in through Canada. I immediately saw why Mo had decided I was right for Creative Services—I had learned to bend over.

In the field of rock excess, Alice was hardly alone. Touring, WB's act the Faces were, in their own words, "the ultimate heavy-driving band." They were barred from so many hotels—the entire Holiday Inn chain, for one—that many times the group had to check in under the name Fleetwood Mac.

Recalling the Faces, lead vocalist Rod Stewart did not attribute their behavior to genius or excessive masculinity. Rod's recollection: "We were scared shit, and we didn't think we were very good. We were all big drinkers, so that is how we got our image." He recalled Faces Firsts: "We were the first band to trash a hotel. We were womanizers. We came along at a point when everything was extremely serious. Marc Bolan was topping the bill at a big outdoor festival, and everyone was taking music extremely seriously. Marc's head was down as he played. Then we came along, blind drunk and laughing."

By late 1971, the three WEA labels had made it across their first finish line: eight distribution branches, up and working. At holiday parties, across America pride-filled workers, newcomers to show business, toasted one another. Even if your job was loading LPs into cardboard boxes, pouring plastic peanuts in, then slapping wet brown tape over the lids, and that was your whole job description; and even if you weren't invited to Mick's wedding to Bianca, or to hang out with Ahmet; even if those were not in your cards, by George, you *were* in show business, which is a damn sight better than being in tire sales, any day. Friedman still made a point of remembering the names of your kids. For what had been erected, WEA, Friedman felt pride, several times repeating to me one of his father's sayings: "Son, think of what footprints you're leaving."

And looking back on that year of branch building by Friedman, Glew, Rosenblatt, and Posner, it seems a good thing that all those men were *record-label* guys, not distribution guys. WEA got built to sell their records, which they did not call "units," to sell hit music, not "product." In time, soon enough, the language would say "units" and "product." In time, WEA *would* know Shinola about sprinklers and loading docks. Just not yet.

It was an age when, say, one record guy was stopping by another record guy's office before they headed out for lunch, and the second guy would come out with a line like "Wait a second, first you just gotta hear this new dub we just made." And the two men would pause to play it, to listen, and to groove to the music. This would change, within twenty years, to "Wait a second, first I gotta tell you about this new deal I just made." Twenty years later, on the way to lunch, men would stop and chuckle and groove over money.

But, for now, an intensity to promote our music captured both home offices and sales offices. For a new album by the rock group White Witch, indefatigable promoter Pete Marino chose Daphne's Funeral Home in San Francisco to throw Witch's coming-out party. At the door, the ceremonious funerals manager asked, "You are here for . . . ?" And the guest would answer, "White Witch." Food and drinks were served from caskets. Over five hundred people showed, some getting all mixed up with others who were at Daphne's for-real funerals.

Earlier in the afternoon, Marino had released two hundred white doves from a casket above a downtown record store, part of his White Witch promotion. Unfortunately, the doves' wings had been clipped. Who knew? The birds, disoriented from spending the day inside the coffin, were unable to fly. They plopped onto the street below, where they were trampled by the crowds, run over by cars. Marino fled the rooftop, the Humane Society in hot pursuit. WEA later got a bill from City Hall for hospital care of the birds. An irate Marino, waving the bill for boarding the doves, charged into City Hall: "Where the hell did you keep them for that kind of money? The Fairmont Hotel?"

In the end, WEA San Francisco had to pay the bill, and that meant Friedman's budget getting nicked. WEA's medical plan did not cover plopped doves. Hearing about the cost, Joel slammed down the phone and whined loud at his secretary, Sheila, "What do they think we *are* here, Fort Fucking Knox?"

The doves were one of many backbreakers for Joel's fixed promotion budget. The three WEA labels sided, by nature, against Joel and for promoting their albums, even at the cost of dead birds. Within a year or so, the euphoria of having your own branches had come down to "Who's in charge here?"

Rosenblatt spoke right up: "I got very frustrated with Joel. I told him that we had to stop this sharing of Promotion people. It was just getting crazy. Joel would put me off and put me off because he ran that thing like it was his money. I got unbelievably frustrated and I went to Joe Smith,

Joe spoke to Steve, and before you know it, Ross called a labels-heads meeting."

At the swans-in-the-pond, mock-elegant Bel Air Hotel, in California, the group assembled. The meeting started at ten. Joel was asked to arrive at ten forty-five. Friedman waited in the hotel lobby, which was big enough even for the aggressive pacing of a frustrated Musketeer.

At ten, into the meeting room strolled Ross, our presiding judge. He unfolded his tall frame into the empty chair next to a nervous Rosenblatt. About a dozen label execs were there. The first major agenda point would get talked about without Friedman in the room. Ross turned to us in the room to ask, "Well, shall we fire Joel?"

Four measures of silence, tacit.

No one had even dreamed of that. Ross asked it so easily, I remember thinking, like he could just toss it out so simply, then light his cigarette. Made me wonder. Joel's head was not on the labels' guillotine, despite their anger. Atlantic's Greenberg recalled, "Not everybody was in agreement, but Joel made the cut."

At ten forty-five, Joel got called into the meeting. A rule was announced. WEA was to be a *service* organization, responsive to the labels, which will dictate WEA policy.

Friedman listened. He got it: His role was to be less than czar of distribution. There would *not* be a Big Four—three labels and his distribution— just a Big Three. Friedman's creed was "family"—*hamish*. He stood still for it. More single baggers would get packed into WEA.

With Joel facing stricter rules (for a while, anyway), the labels could now get back to their primary business, which was to bicker. Unable to submerge its identity to the threesome, in 1972 Warner Bros. Records insisted that it would allow "No Traditional Fall Discount" on that year's albums. Atlantic and Elektra didn't like that. Fall discounts were as traditional as red leaves. So the meeting agreed, "Okay, on *Warner* product, no discount. On ours, we still give a discount." That fall, standing alone, Warner Bros. Records' sales got clobbered. Gitlin and Rosenblatt learned: It's all together from now on. You can split personalities, but not policies.

Promotion costs continued to run wild, in Friedman's mind. He could give you such a list! Parties, m'gawd, the parties!

Not all, however, was lost. On behalf of the release of Randy Newman's *Sail Away*, Marino and Perasso arranged for two thousand wooden airplanes to be launched off the roof of San Francisco FM station KSAN, located downtown, at noon. Local officials applauded WEA's change from live doves to balsa wood.

Significant Releases

1970

Atlantic: Clarence Carter ("Patches") • Crosby, Stills & Nash (*Déjà Vu*, including "Woodstock," "Teach Your Children," and "Our House") • Roberta Flack (*First Take*, including "First Time Ever I Saw Your Face") • Aretha Franklin (*This Girl's in Love with You*, including "Call Me," "Share Your Love with Me," "Son of a Preacher Man," The Weight," and "Eleanor Rigby" and *Spirit in the Dark*, including "Don't Play That Song") • Led Zeppelin (*III*) • Les McCann ("Compared to What") • Wilson Pickett ("Sugar Sugar" and *In Philadelphia*, including "Don't Let the Green Grass Fool You," "Don't Knock My Love," and "Engine Number 9") • The Rascals ("Carry Me Back") • Dusty Springfield (*Brand New Me*) • Stephen Stills ("Love the One You're With")

Atco: Ginger Baker (*Air Force*) • Bee Gees ("Lonely Days") • Eric Clapton/Derek & the Dominoes ("Layla") • Cream (*Live*) • Iron Butterfly (*Live* and *Metamorphosis*) • Otis Redding ("Tell the Truth")

Cotillion: Brook Benton ("Rainy Night in Georgia") • Lord Sutch & Heavy Friends • *Woodstock*

Little David: Flip Wilson (*The Devil Made Me Buy This Dress*)

Elektra: Bread (*On the Waters*, including "Make It with You") • Judy Collins (*Whales & Nightingales*, including "Amazing Grace") • The Doors (*Morrison Hotel*, *Absolutely Live* and *13*) • Mickey Newbury ("An American Trilogy")

Warner Bros.: Black Sabbath • Deep Purple and the Royal Philharmonic Orchestra (*Concerto for Group and Orchestra*) • Grateful Dead (*Live Dead*, *Workingman's Dead*, and *American Beauty*, including "Truckin'") • Van Morrison (*Moondance* and *His Band and the Street Choir*, including "Blue Money" and "Domino") • Peter, Paul & Mary (*10 Years Together*) • James Taylor (*Sweet Baby James*, including "Fire and Rain") • Charles Wright and the Watts 103rd Street Rhythm Band ("Express Yourself")

Reprise: Fleetwood Mac (*Kiln House*) • Norman Greenbaum ("Spirit in the Sky") • Jimi Hendrix and Otis Redding (*Monterey Pop*, including "Wild Thing" • The Kinks ("Lola") • Gordon Lightfoot (*Sit Down Young Stranger*, including "If You Could Read My Mind" • Joni Mitchell (*Ladies of the Canyon*, including "Big Yellow Taxi" and "Woodstock") • Neil Young (*After the Gold Rush*, including "Only Love Can Break Your Heart")

Bizarre: Frank Zappa (*Burnt Weeny Sandwich*)

Deity: The Masked Marauders

Straight: Tim Buckley (*Blue Afternoon*)

1971

Atlantic: David Crosby (*If I Could Only Remember My Name*) • Crosby, Stills & Nash (*4 Way Street*, including "Love the One You're With" and "Ohio") • Aretha Franklin (*Live at the Fillmore West*, including "Bridge Over Troubled Waters," and *Greatest Hits*, including "Spanish Harlem") • Led Zeppelin (*IV*, including "Stairway to Heaven") • Graham Nash (*Songs for Beginners*) • Stephen Stills (*2*) • *All in the Family* Soundtrack • J: *The Way to Become the Sensuous Woman*

Atco: Bee Gees ("How Can You Mend a Broken Heart?") • Delaney & Bonnie ("Never Ending Song of Love") • King Curtis (*Live at Fillmore West*)

Cotillion: Emerson, Lake & Palmer (*Tarkus. Woodstock II*)

Capricorn: Jonathan Edwards ("Sunshine")

Island: Traffic (*The Low Spark of High Heeled Boys*)

Little David: Flip Wilson (*The Flip Wilson Show*)

Elektra: Bread (*Manna*, including "If" and "Let Your Love Go") • The Doors (*L.A. Woman*, including "Love Her Madly" and "Riders on the Storm") • The New Seekers ("Look What They've Done to My Song Ma" and "I'd Like to Teach the World to Sing (in Perfect Harmony)") • Carly Simon ("That's the Way I've Always Heard It Should Be" and "Anticipation")

Warner Bros.: Black Sabbath (*Paranoid*) • Alice Cooper (*Love It to Death*, including "Eighteen") • Les Crane ("Desiderata") • Deep Purple (*Fireball*) • Faces (*A Nod Is As Good As a Wink . . . to a Blind Horse*, including "Stay with Me") • Grateful Dead • Little Feat • Van Morrison (*Tupelo Honey*, including "Wild Night") • Paul Stookey ("Wedding Song (There Is Love))" • James Taylor (*Mud Slide Slim and the Blue Horizon*, including "You've Got a Friend") • *Billy Jack* soundtrack

Reprise: Fleetwood Mac (*Future Games*) • Jimi Hendrix (*The Cry of Love*) • Jethro Tull (*Aqualung*) • Gordon Lightfoot (*Summer Side of Life*) • Joni Mitchell (*Blue*) • T-Rex: "Bang a Gong (Get It On)"

15

Coupled with Warner Bros., Atlantic, and Elektra's decision to "branch with Joel" had been the decision to "go international with Nesuhi." As small labels, our three companies had so far done little about what we at the time shrugged off as "the rest of the world." Our overseas ambitions usually were two: Get the best licensing deal for our albums outside America, and license foreign acts, cheaply, that we could sell domestically. Anything more, from Norway to Siam, was just dabs of gravy on the far side of our plates.

International excursions back in the 1960s had been, for me, limited to semiannual product shows for Phil Rose's licensee group. Most memorably, Phil set these up on the Spanish Mediterranean island resort of Majorca. There we felt the patronage of a gravel-voiced international-licensing rep named Charlie Brady, who sold tons of goods, from auto tires to condoms, to American PXs around the world. He tossed in Warner Bros. Records "for fun." Brady paid army buyers on the side, whatever it took, just get his goods on their shelves. On Majorca, next to a deluxe hotel called Son Vida, Brady built a mansion complete with fifteen-foot ceilings, huge terraces, and two nifty daughters who failed to appreciate my wit.

It was hard to believe that actual business got done at such meetings. One soft afternoon, back earlier in the Maitland era, circa 1970, we had gathered at sundown in Phil Rose's hotel suite, awaiting the appearance of jet-lagged Maitland and Smith. On their arrival, we laughed through a cocktail party at Brady's mansion, then went back to our hotel for more. By now, Smith and Maitland had gone three days with little sleep, fueled by booze. From the balcony of Rose's suite, Smith waved to those below like the queen of England, palm up. The patioful of record execs mistook the wave as an invitation. Soon Phil's suite overflowed with conventioneers. Room service was called but would not hear. Maitland's eyes fell shut. Smith finally ran down to the kitchen, waving his Diners Club card to prove that he was a qualified doctor, then led a procession of one fruit-bearing waiter (the only employee working that late, he put on a waiter's jacket) back to the suite. We acclaimed the headwaiter, stood him on a stool, crowned him with bananas, and sang "Guantanamera."

The phone rang, and it was "Ted Ashley for you, Mike." Maitland had passed out, facedown on the floor. We shook him awake, then hushed as Mike listened to this important call from Burbank. Finally, he looked up at us, groggily, and asked, "Who the hell is Tom Jones?" then passed out again. Smith hurriedly ended the call from Ashley. Wine and fruit mixes flowed. We all laughed at antics that were not funny, dazed to be where we were, neglecting sleep, kings of commerce. I somehow remember informing the room, "Hey, my chair has pockets!"

Through all this, the record business spun its discs and made its money, Ross and Ashley thought we were smart, and Tom Jones signed somewhere else, *gracias*. And on this Spanish island, lying flat on the floor, answering international phone calls seemed a grave intrusion on our festivities.

Warner had begun setting up its own pre-Kinney foreign companies in the late Sixties. First, in 1967, a juicy start was a WBR/Canada company in Phil's own homeland. Before that, Warner's onetime Canadian licensee, Compo, had sent back 12½ percent of suggested list (minus tax) for all its sales of WB albums. Our Burbank label had enjoyed only that percentage and paid its record artists out of it; Compo kept three times that amount. After Warner opened WBR of Canada, the new company sent not only the same 12½ percent to Burbank but also *all* of WBR/Canada's profits, a goodly amount. WBR/Canada started making money after one month in business.[64]

In 1969, Warner Bros. opened its own London shop, appointing the suave, ex-bandleader/charmer Ian Ralfini its managing director/president. Appropriately, offices were secured at 69 New Oxford Street. American artists flew over to visit Ralfini, among the first of them Clarence "Frogman" Henry, who arrived at Heathrow Airport with a frog on his shoulder. Henry never could understand anyone's name, and he called Ian Ralfini "Iffen Ralfnic." Those with long memories in the record business still call Ralfini "Iffen Ralfnic."

Based on maintaining a strong, thirty-person office in London, Warner Bros. Records now offered English acts more than the North America–only deals previously made. WBR could kinda claim, "We'll sign you for the whole world." First to fall for this line were Fleetwood Mac and the Small Faces with Rod Stewart.

Across London, pre-Kinney Nesuhi Ertegun plugged for Atlantic's *own*

---

[64]Warner Bros. Records–Canada in short order became renamed Warner–Seven Arts Records, then Kinney, then back to Warner Bros.–Canada, then to WEA. Because of the frequent name changes, the company was investigated by the Canadian government for tax evasion.

presence: He signed up a bright marketing energy bundle (and part-time bassist) named Phil Carson, who was about to become marketing head for Danish Bacon. Over tea at the Connaught, Nesuhi seduced the twenty-two-year-old Carson to Atlantic. "For the bacon-company job," Carson recalled, "I was going to make twenty-eight thousand pounds a year and get a car. Nesuhi says I'm going to make a huge mistake. He was going to double that money, but there were two conditions: One was that I say 'yes' right now, and the other is I don't come to him for a salary raise for three years."

Carson signed and became a torrid presence on the cool English scene. He picked up Virgin Records for three years. The fee was $125,000 for Mike Oldfield's *Tubular Bells.* He called New York repeatedly, but soon Jerry Wexler just began taking Carson's word for things. He became the first rock & roll musician running a label in London. Acts like Australia's AC/DC got signed by Carson during an English afternoon while setting up a tour for an act called Rabbit, repped by an Australian gal named Carol Browning. "This must have been 1976," Carson thought back. "She came in, and I thought she was beautiful. All I wanted to do was, you know . . . in true Atlantic style. Anyway, she showed me AC/DC, and we made the deal." The first AC/DC album was delivered for $25,000 and that only if they could "come to England to do a promotion tour at their cost." The deal, including options, ran to fifteen albums. AC/DC outsold both Rabbit and Led Zeppelin.[65]

Carson rampantly partied with rock stars through Europe. On the birthday of Peter Rudge, the Rolling Stones' tour manager, Phil threw a party in Germany's Tiango nightclub. "That club was one where you could hang your coat and hat or all of your clothes. There were rooms you could go to. If you fuck a chick on the floor of the place, it's free. If you want a room, you have to pay. I end up with this girl, mind you, and as I'm doing what I'm doing, I suddenly see a group of people come in. The first person I see is [Ahmet's secretary] Noreen Woods. The second person is Bianca Jagger. The third is Ahmet. I am in flagrante on the dance floor, and Noreen said, 'Well, I thought it was you, but I couldn't see much of your face.' Noreen picked up the check."

London as a font of rock bands had become one huge hatchery. We Americans had begun acting like reverse colonizers. This time, we had flown overseas to tax London. There we'd found rock stars who yearned truly to be "signed for the entire world," not just picked up for North America. Signing for the world we could do only if we had our own companies *throughout* the world.

---

[65]Carson occasionally played bass with Led Zeppelin when they toured. When asked how he'd become so good at seducing women, Carson answered, "Having a gold American Express card and standing very, very close to Robert Plant."

Empowered to launch Kinney International in 1970, Nesuhi Ertegun, five foot five, and Phil Rose with his 13CCC-size shoes formed a team. Nesuhi—a man inclined to insert superlatives into any sentence—laid out their operating rules: "Phil, you're the best international executive in the business. Of *course* we'll work well together. If we don't agree, I'm the boss, and that's the way it will be."

Rose knew that wisdom lay in agreeing with Nesuhi even if, after that first sentence, Phil's empowerment did seem to shrink. Like some sixteenth-century pope, Nesuhi divided up the world by drawing a line down the Atlantic Ocean: Europe and Brazil would be his, while Phil's would be the rest of the Americas wrapping through Japan all the way to Southeast Asia. Countries like China, India, and Russia, filled as they were with copyright scoundrels, would remain *terra piratica*. Kinney International ignored these masses; if they wouldn't pass a copyright law, what police could Kinney call? Besides, Nesuhi put it, they don't like jazz.

Both men knew the world's record companies. From the early 1960s, Nesuhi had handled Atlantic's international alliances, just as Phil had handled Warner Bros.' Atlantic and Warner had different licensee deals in almost every country.

Warner's Canada and London companies became the first legs of the new Kinney Records International. One difference from our U.S. distribution with Joel: With Nesuhi and Phil, the profits stayed inside Kinney International, a new profit center within Kinney's music group. The U.S. labels that risked their profits and losses by signing, funding, producing, and promoting the albums used to start those companies' businesses got less than an ownership share. The rationale was that keeping the profits inside the selling company—Kinney of Germany, for instance—would supply Germany the funds to record local talent. "Greece needs Greek albums" became the excuse. Contention over "who deserves how much" of the profits from U.S. label albums sold overseas would continue between the American labels and International for years to come.

The trilateralization of Kinney/England, however, proved to be even worse: a dozen years of turmoil ahead.

In April 1970, the corporation moved its three labels into WBR's New Oxford Street offices. The conversion to Kinney/UK was headed by Warner's Ralfini, with Atlantic and Elektra joining in as soon as they became contractually free of previous deals.

Predictably, the American labels resented being Kinneyized in London. Rivalries immediately arose. Labels acted like bulls, it was mating season, and there was just one cow.

Ralfini reported to Nesuhi and Phil, but when it came to talent, he answered to the U.S. label presidents, which gave Ian five bosses to juggle, not counting Frogman Henry. Later in 1971, when Atlantic became free to join

WEA/UK, a system of label managers was set up, each label manager—WB's Martin Wyatt, Atlantic's Phil Carson, and Elektra's Clive Selwood—reporting to Ralfini.

Phil Carson, knowing that Kinney was coming, had already steered his latest discovery, the trio called America, away from Polydor and over to Ralfini. To Carson's shock, Ian signed America to Warner Bros. Records, worldwide. Carson, still on Atlantic's payroll, had assumed the act would be that label's. It was like three children in the family, and one kid decided to eat the whole refrigerator.

Ian turned as circumspect as any dapper, funny guy can. In 1972, he threw a party for Elektra Records, when it joined Kinney in London. A yard-high cake was ordered, topped by an Elektra butterfly made of sugar. The frosting order specified that the cake top would have four logos: those of Kinney, WBR, Atlantic, and Elektra. When the quadra-labeled cake arrived at the banquet table, Rose said, "Turn it around." The cake was turned, then turned. It had a Kinney logo, an Atlantic logo, and two WBR logos. Rose, a quiet Canadian, felt his heart pump. No Elektra logo! Rose started eating the icing. Like some starved wildebeest, Phil gobbled, the whole side of the cake, destroyed the other logos, so he could claim he had enjoyed Elektra the most.

Much as we label execs concentrated on London, Nesuhi and Phil were opening companies in the rest of the world. Kinney exec Alan Cohen went along on some of their races to sign up top local executives and remembered the three days spent with his wife, Nesuhi and Phil, in Milan. Cohen's missus sat at the hotel's typewriter, typing a three-page contract on a keyboard that did not work like an American version, so when you typed in "royalty" it would come out something like "rõ&a£t&." But out of those chaotic three days came Kinney of Italy.

Bonding between Phil and Nesuhi had begun after their first working-together negotiations got interleaved with chaotic runs for trains and planes to some next country. Nesuhi was a master at getting whatever was needed. He was fluent in English, French, Turkish, and Jive. After those chaotic three days and an out-of-breath exit from Milan, Rose and Ertegun found themselves, exhausted, in a shared compartment on the train to Frankfurt, the shorter Ertegun in the lower bunk. As Rose nodded off, he heard Nesuhi's summation from below: "Phil, you know, yesterday we negotiated our first deal. Tonight we ate off the same plate. And now we're sleeping in the same room, practically the same bed. Yes, I think it's working out."

Both men spent years on the road, prospecting for gold executives and signing up strong national leaders who, like France's Bernard du Busson, also knew lots about burgundies and once played piano with Dizzy. Country heads were music lovers, much as Nesuhi loved jazz, much as Phil loved fresh Singapore crab.

The countries we learned about in History of Western Civ classes— European countries—more or less behaved well (satisfied *our* business needs), paid their royalties, respected copyright laws, and jailed crooks. Countries in Asia and steppes beyond obeyed their own rules (and our needs were not of particular interest to Asian businessmen or political systems). In their own lands, Asians behaved to *their* custom, and Kinney (by now translated into WEA International), was congenially nodded at but not paid money. We Americans, involved in making a profit, found Asia to be a pisser. The attitude there resembled another of those record-business sayings spoken by New York rascal/label head Morris Levy to his long-suffering artists: "Royalties? You want royalties? Go to England!"

Alongside commercial piracy of the audiocassette had risen do-it-yourself cassette recorders that civilians could buy, for "home taping." Rose had seen one of those recorders first in the 1960s, in one of Hong Kong's ten-foot-wide electronic-gizmo stores. It was a Philips cassette recorder, the first model, with a plug in it so people could copy LPs onto magnetic tape. To his escort, Hong Kong distributor T. K. Whang, Rose pointed out, "You see that red button, T. K? Where it says RECORD? That button can put us out of business."

"Pirated cassettes," we called them, none of them earning the record labels one red-white-and-blue cent, flooded world markets. College dorms and high-school neighborhoods became cottage industries of freely "shared copies." What had been impossible with 78s in my boyhood was now— during my second marriage[66]—possible with cassettes.

"Private copying" was about to slam our business. Tape-to-tape copying reduced the fidelity of the original. For the few, fidelity remained of interest. For the many, getting it free became a Top Ten pleasure. "Private taping" took off like a blight out of hell.

Our royalty concerns remained of little interest to our Southeast Asian would-be allies, let alone to their larger neighbors who scoffed at capitalism and promoted communism as socially the fairest of all. In countries like the Philippines, we American execs may have enjoyed even unfootnotably naughty pleasures our licensees would provide at night, but the next morning we would turn aghast ambling sidewalks past table after table of obvious copies of our precious cassettes, from the First Edition to Aretha Franklin, sold in Manila for the local equivalent of a buck.

The frontier of the Asian world was wild as our West's had been, except here we had no John Wayne. England, for all the elbowing in our companies,

---

[66]Not to get too autobiographical, but I had now remarried. Her name was/is Theodora, and her credits included introducing *The Jackie Gleason Show* as a boffo fourteen-year-old slinky model with boa; being WBR's image model (album covers and ads, she with sheath dresses and boas); and more beautiful than a Heismann. This marriage lasted nearly two decades, blessed with the second son, Thomas Guy Cornyn II. Now back to our show.

was terribly more fun. Coming into Heathrow, our plane gliding down over the Thames and the castles, we knew that a major treat was minutes away. His name was Dennis Goodman. To Ahmet and Nesuhi he was known only as "Goodman." The rest of us still called him "Dennis." He was the company's chauffeur and had at first been the Erteguns', attending to them at their town house. Goodman, too, soon became WEA-ized, though.

Goodman drove the company Bentley out to Heathrow to pick us up, said "sir" believably, and turned service to us all into an art form. Goodman was bemused by our behaviors but handled us with aplomb. Three quick examples:

- During a Top Ten London downpour, Phil Rose and some other execs were exiting Mr. Chow's, "the" Chinese restaurant in London, and were cabless, just as Ahmet pulled up for dinner at the same restaurant, driven by Goodman. Seeing Rose's plight, Goodman volunteered to drive the Rose group back to its hotel, then return to wait for Ahmet. The next day, Goodman told us Ahmet had fired him for leaving without notifying anyone. The firing did not, of course, last. "You Americans!" He chuckled.
- One evening, the sun still up at nine, Mo Ostin, me, eight of us, left a world-class dinner in Covent Garden to find Goodman waiting (as he did) to drive us crosstown back to the Dorchester Hotel. We decided to take a bit of a stroll first. Goodman maneuvered the Bentley at stroll pace behind us. Euphorically, we strolled, on and on, with Goodman testing low gear behind. We got to the front door of the Dorchester, turned, and thanked Goodman. "You Americans!" He smiled.
- During one visit to London, my family and I had been invited by George Harrison to his estate home. Goodman, of course, drove us up, parking out by George's awful collection of lawn gnomes. Harrison spent a few hours of his day with us, even rowing my sons through his estate's underground grotto/lake, complete with stalactites. We showed Goodman our souvenir Polaroids. "You Americans," he said.

England made us forget Manila and Bangkok, Hong Kong and Shanghai. In London, we got to stroll King's Road (mod dress shops clerked by emaciated girls who looked like they'd just come from a mascara tournament). We got to dally in private nightclubs (velour booths, drinks with perfect ice cubes, six-foot-wide dance floors).

In America, with a 1972 promo theme called "Bundles from Britain," Atlantic had opened its year with Emerson, Lake and Palmer's *Pictures at an Exhibition,* King Crimson, Mott the Hoople, Yes, and Screaming Lord Sutch and Heavy Friends, all acts licensed Atlantic's release in America from Ertegun's England connections. Beyond that January album release, Atlantic was now handling labels named Rolling Stone, Clean, Embryo, Chimney-ville, Capricorn, Win or Lose, and Pelican. To handle the influx, Atlantic established a custom labels division under Johnny Bienstock, brother of Miriam (Abramson) and music publisher Fred Bienstock.

This cornucopia of hits was purely Atlantic's-for-America. It was in no mood to spread this "fairly" with Warner and Elektra. No one expected Phil Carson to spread, at least during business hours. To Ralfini, trying to administer England equitably, the task became impossible. Despite a top staff, he was destined to fall from such a tightrope. Atlantic believed Ian still had a Warner Bros. air about him. Phil Rose had to tell Ian that a new managing director "was being considered" and that Ian might take his severance and retain his sanity. In 1974, he did just that, leaving to start his own label, Anchor Records, removing from us his style and wit.

After three years of WEA-izing in England, the three labels decided to act naturally; they set up their own offices: Phil Carson for Atlantic, Jonathan Clyd (replacing Clive Selwood) for Elektra, and ex–Beatles publicist Derek Taylor for Warner Bros.[67] The three labels and their signings got wild again. (WEA International reestablished its overall business control in the UK. Distribution was still run by WEA, but out of sight. The three labels remained otherwise autonomous.) For us at Warners, Derek Taylor chose quarters in Soho's Greek Street, in a downtrodden walkup, twelve metres wide, sandwiched in with the area's falafel and porn shoppes.

By 1975, in its Annual Reports, WCI decided to reveal its sales by division, challenging CBS (without saying such words aloud) to do the same. We figured the published numbers would reveal the might of our U.S. labels but, more significantly, show the growth that Nesuhi and Phil's WEA International had come up with:

	U.S. Labels (in millions)	*International* (in millions)
1971	$144.3	$18.2
1972	170.0	35.1
1973	174.9	49.0
1974	217.1	60.8
1975	220.7	75.4

In five years, WEA had made those old, 12½ percent royalties look like pennies; income from International was up 400 percent. By 1977, WEA had

---

[67]Later, when Taylor moved to Burbank to take over Creative Services for me, he was replaced in our London offices in Soho's shoddy Greek Street by the late Ron Kass, married to an actress, therefore known to us, unfairly, as "Mr. Joan Collins."

organized its world. It was down to opening WEA/Austria. When I asked Phil, somewhat travel weary, he put Austria in his perspective: "We spill more." Phil and Nesuhi's growth surge had matured. Now it *was* up to these individual countries, like Greece, to make Greek hits.

By 1977, after three years' more zigzagging, the WEA labels again became ready to reorganize as one. The elbowing had subsided. Nesuhi took on this chore, pulling the three U.S. label offices together with one hand and running WEA International with the other.

For the rest of the world outside North America, the Rolling Stones ignored WEA and signed with EMI. The question got louder: Wasn't WEA International good enough to sign the stones for the whole world? Was this a rejection of WEA International? There remained that distance. For all those profit gains, International was hardly a major leaguer, not like we'd become in the United States. Europe-entrenched companies like PolyGram and EMI were giants in country after country. WEA just squeaked, like pips do . . .

Using the back cover of *Billboard* for three months, country after country, I created an international Big Button campaign. The concept was Our Power Execs who, if one wanted a hit, all he had to do was push that big button on his desk. The first ad showed Nesuhi Ertegun, eyes looking into the distance, like some Alexander the Great, pushing an eighteen-inch gold button marked around its base, WARNER • ELEKTRA • ATLANTIC. The ad copy showed what WCI was driving at: We got power.

NESUHI ERTEGUN
HAS HIS FINGER ON 88% OF THE WORLD

In the beginning there were only licensing arrangements. The world tended to be a confusing place.

Today there is a vast and speedy organization called Warner Elektra Atlantic International. From the start in 1971, WEA International has come to span 88% of the globe.

WEA International chief Nesuhi Ertegun (pictured above with the Biggest Button in the Business) was in at that beginning. He hand-picked its executives. He settled for the very best. WEA in England now has as Managing Director, John Fruin, the very best record executive in England.

John Fruin joins eleven other World Class Presidents working for WEA in eleven different countries.

They are not tired men, these WEA Workers. They go to the office on Saturdays. Their wives barely get to see them.

They know how to get it done.

Next week's ad headline covered Germany's head man: VISIT COLORFUL SIGGI LOCH. And so on.[68]

Then, abruptly, John Fruin left as head of WEA/UK. Something about his conflict of interest (he'd sold WEA's cutouts and "faulties" to another company he owned).[69]

In 1980, Nesuhi had temporarily resumed running WEA/UK. He cast so widely for a replacement that one evening during one of my visits there, he had Goodman pick me up from St. James Club, where I stayed, and drive me a few blocks to join Nesuhi at Poon's, a super Chinese restaurant in Soho. There, to my utter shock, Nesuhi offered me the job: Run England. I was flattered and asked for the night to think it over. The minute I was back in my room, I knew better. The next morning, I stopped first at WEA's offices to tell Nesuhi, "Thanks for your generous offer. I'm flattered, but I . . ." Before I could get half a sentence out, Nesuhi clapped his hands together dismissing the whole subject, saying, "I've been thinking about it, too, and you're not right for it."

"Nesuhi, please!" I protested. "Let me get out my entire first sentence before you reject me!" Nesuhi and I became even better friends.

Later, Goodman, driving with Nesuhi in the front seat and other WEA leaders in the back, was questioned by Nesuhi.

"Goodman," Nesuhi asked, "you remember who played saxophone for Ted Heath?"

Goodman knew the answer: "Ronnie Scott and Henry MacKensie, sir."

"See, *you* know about music. Those other people know nothing! All right, who played baritone sax for Ellington in 1954?"

"Harry Carney, sir."

"Look at those guys in the back of the car," Nesuhi told Goodman. "They haven't a clue. But *you* know, don't you, Goodman?"

Upon halting at a stoplight, Goodman gentlemanly turned to Nesuhi. "I'm not taking the job, sir."

---

[68]Eighteen-inch-across gold buttons were manufactured for show-off. We had one even larger, a yard-across button displayed under a glass case in the lobby at an industry convention, guarded by Brinks. We considered a Big Button float for the Rose Parade.

[69]Cutouts are overstock of albums that are "remaindered" by publishers, who don't want to sell them anymore. "Faulties" are British for defective records.

16

As an adult, Mo Ostin was never good at sitting in a bus, taking a backseat with someone else behind the wheel. Deep down, like most of us, Mo wanted to steer. By the early 1970s, he'd gotten Warner/Reprise seated up front. Owning its own distribution, that was more like driving a tank. He could steer, and his new tank—WEA for the world—would turn at his command.

By now the letters WEA stood forth on buildings in letters bolder than a bank's. For the immense results of his tenacity, indeed for any personal results, Ostin made no outward show of his pride over all this, not ever. He just kept on challenging easy assumptions with door-opening questions that behaved like land mines: "Why should we do it *their* way?"

Quietly as ever, Mo had survived through the Sixties. He'd used his brain. Survived with his hands in his pockets, waiting for his desk to arrive in Burbank the day Reprise had been shut down, welcomed at Warners like some soap salesman, no one saying much of a hello, let alone a "need anything?" Survived alienating the glam-tribe of Sinatra pallies to sign the Kinks and Hendrix and Zappa and the Fugs, while stronger labels stood safe behind their Perry Comos. And survived outspokenly pushing for company-owned distribution—alone at first in L.A. and Canada—before his fellow labels caught on and up.

By the end of 1971, WEA, still being called by some "Kinney Distribution," had sped past everything in America. *Billboard*'s chart for 1971 showed (via number of albums, in parentheses) the year's corporate (as distinct from label) chart share:

Kinney (156)	22.6%
CBS (131)	15.0
RCA (59)	6.4
Capitol (72)	6.2
A&M (36)	5.9

That figure, 22.6 percent, amazed us. The day we opened *Billboard* and saw that number, we felt something even Columbus hadn't. We weren't just some hip little island. Shit, we were now a whole continent. That Number One ranking, that sudden bigness—to be sure, it had been accomplished by Joel and three labels, but the drive to get it started, that had been the drive of Mo Ostin. Being Number One became addictive. And for Mo, controlling his tank would remain his quiet obsession.

Over the heads of his label leaders, Steve Ross spun financial incentives like a lamé lasso. Ross's general rule was if one of his labels made a million dollars in profit, WCI would take half of it, but would leave the other half for the label to divvy up among its execs. The label's chief exec got to do the divvying, but he could take a maximum of half (a quarter million) for himself. The other quarter million was spread over the company's employees. Ross's generosity fell over many of us, in particular over WEA label chiefs.[70]

Ross believed in autonomy, and Mo believed in Ross. Both men, while asking if you'd like another coffee, would be doing lightning arithmetic in their heads. While other men chose to strut, both Ross and Ostin preferred to bargain. Both used aides to deliver bad news. Ross knew about the A word—autonomy—and assured his chiefs of it, with only one proviso: You bring home good profits. Do that, and the world is yours.

The money got bigger than any of us had been used to. Soon the phrase "stock options" murmured its way into our lives. In my memory is a December day I was called into Mo's office. Mo and Joe sat there, giving out holiday bonus checks. I took mine in hand, thanked them. Raised to be polite, I merely peeked down at the check, then smiled back at them and blurted, "Holy shit!"

My word selection pleased them. My check was for half my total annual salary. I'd been expecting, oh, five hundred dollars. Instead, my check was for twenty-five thousand dollars.

Mo's devotion to Number One–ness at first confused me; I couldn't figure out *why* he was so determined. To me, our company was a giggle still. And to me, this was not some contest for Olympic gold.

One day Joe Smith faced my "why?" with his easy wisdom. "It doesn't

---

[70]Ross knew how to lavish. He sent a postcard to top executives just before Thanksgiving, alerting them they'd be getting a present: a turkey by mail, for Thanksgiving cooking. A card came to me. Theodora asked me, "How *big* is the turkey?" I told her, "I dunno. Call Steve." WCI chairman Steve Ross put Theodora on hold for thirty seconds, then came back on the line. "Sixteen pounds, Theodora," he answered. She thanked him, but only a turkey's worth. She understood: Steve was a suit. Her husband was not. Suits, if you were in the record business, you took them for granted. One week later, our turkey, well over twenty pounds, showed up.

matter how important the contest is, Stan. It's always better to win than to lose."

In Burbank, Ostin was clearly the business head of the WB+R set up, while Smith had a different vital, joyful energy with good signing instincts. Smith's signings were a bit more middle of the road; Ostin's often had an edge. Both men worked together and betrayed no friction. Smith did not angle for Mo's job, and Ostin appreciated the value of Smith. When a few years later Smith was offered the presidency of Capitol, Steve Ross rushed in to enforce Smith's WBR contract, which had four good years yet to run.

Ostin had seen WEA "Corporate" win at 22.6 percent. He'd seen his Burbank labels, WB+R, deliver more cash to Steve than either E or A, so he'd won there. Where he had not won was WB+R against every other *label,* to get known as the Number One greatest label in America. Who remembers the *second*-highest high jumper?

Looking over *Billboard*'s 1971 market share, by label, Mo did not like the ranking of Warner's slice—actually divided into two slices, counting Reprise—of the pie:

Columbia (100 listings)	11.92%
RCA (53)	5.78
Warner Bros. (33)	5.50
Atlantic (30)	5.33
Capitol (57)	5.27
A&M (31)	4.75
Reprise (34)	4.75

None of this had become obsessive to the eye. We talked about it in passing. This was still the early 1970s, when ranking higher than stock options on most of our agendas were hot pants. But I think, around this time, Number One became his life's gasoline to Ostin. Blocking the track ahead of him and us, since as long as most of us could remember, had been that dudelike company in New York, that label named Columbia, where guys wore perfectly knotted ties made of cloth that shone. Columbia, however, was disarrayed, having fired its president, Clive Davis, over expense account overreach.

Adding together our two labels—Reprise + Warner Bros.—would move us up to Number Two. Mo started asking around. "Maybe we should take all of Reprise, and stick it into Warner Bros. Then we we'd have over ten percent."

In 1972, with yet another color pencil, Thelma Walker began creating a new "us vs. them" list each week. "Them" was Columbia. Reprise would be for Sinatra only. And "us" would jump up.

Beyond all the awards and rankings, Mo and Joe also decided that WBR itself needed more substance. Big rival labels, like Columbia, might be derided as fat guys, and sometimes fat was what they were. But Columbia also had big muscle: diverse artist-support capabilities, get-it-done-ness, things WBR's ultrahip style and signings couldn't compete with. Big-time managers of acts that Mo and Joe wanted to sign reminded them about that difference and also said in passing that our dim linoleum halls were no help.

In the next two years, Ostin and Smith grew their company. Especially to Ed Rosenblatt in Sales and Promotion and to me in Creative Services, they gave practically a blank checkbook to bulk up WBR's marketing, to create ways of making their company State of the Seventies. Our growth plan was simple: "Let's try it."

Artist Relations, traditionally a record-company nicety devoted mainly to making sure there were flowers in touring artists' hotel rooms, had been headed at WBR by Warner's hoarse-voiced, affable Walt Calloway. Tour support had been looked after by ex–Autumn executive Carl Scott. "We realized that the degree of talent out there in the management of our artists was terribly lacking," recalled Scott. "We knew we'd have to become more involved with the artist on a very personal level. You're talking about lives here, not just records. It is perhaps more emotional than your average insurance salesman's career."

We'd seen our no-name artists go out on scroungy tours to little clubs in towns like Mobile, Alabama. Maybe their records got played in Mobile, maybe not, but they were playing on behalf of their careers, and somebody needed to make something happen in Mobile that weekend. Captain Beefheart, for instance, was not a performer whose career direction had the clarity of, say, a Johnny Mathis or Frank Sinatra. Beefheart, a wiggy performance rocker name Don Van Vliet, needed more than a bouquet delivered to a Mobile motel. Between reality and Beefheart lay miles of disconnect. I am able to prove that. Among Captain Beefheart's Quotes of the Year:

- "Everybody's colored, or else you wouldn't be able to see them."
- "If you give ants sugar, they won't have to eat the poison."
- "There are only forty people in the world, and five of them are hamburgers."
- "I don't want to sell my music. I'd like to give it away, because where I got it, you didn't have to pay for it."

Singers like Beefheart were not the kind one casually lets go out for the morning paper, much less let out alone on tour. We came up with "Artist Career Development," another part of the growing Creative Services glob. I knew we'd found the right guy to run it when six-feet-four-inch Bob Regehr, from the Hollywood PR world, came to my office with his résumé and a deck of cards.

An affable, mumbling, and brilliant publicist, Regehr knew a world different from the record business. His aide, Carl Scott, described him as "a remarkable guy who could lie on a couch and think of a beginning and end but needed people in the middle to fit it together."

Regehr put together an eager team eager to assist WBR artists. Artist Relations' first big coup was Alice Cooper. Regehr once told me, "In one meeting I remember Joel Friedman said, 'Alice Cooper. Her record is really doing well.' " Perhaps, Regehr figured, Alice could use a coming-out party.

The stuffy Ambassador Hotel's ballroom was rented, while acts were hired that would startle any lobby. "You want me to sing naked?" asked one of them, a huge black lady called TV Mama, during a phone call. "I'm three hundred and some pounds, and I sing either topless or dressed. I get a hundred fifty dollars with the clothes, two hundred dollars without." Hired. Weighing the question, $150 or $200, Regehr answered, "Well, maybe both."

As the pre-party events built, Regehr got a call from Joe Smith, just, uh, just asking. The party bills were already up to seven thousand dollars. Bob told his assistant, the bumptious Shelley Cooper, "Hide the bills. If it's a success, they're not going to worry."

On Bastille Day, in the Ambassador's lobby, normal, elegant hotel guests mingled as usual in their chiffon minigowns, the men in business suits with lapels wider than grown ducks. On cue, the evening's straight band, tuxedoed, struck up "Pomp and Circumstance." Gradually, these fashionable guests became aware of even stranger people parading through them to get to the Venetian Room.

Through the lobby, the Cockettes began the procession. They were a satirical transvestite troupe from San Francisco. Most had beards. One came dressed as a cigarette girl with an old-fashioned tray around her neck, offering "Cigars . . . cigarettes . . . Vaseline . . . ?" Cockettes threw roses at everyone. Later in the evening, their trays offered complimentary dildos.

The lobby parade continued. A dog pushing a baby buggy. Rod McKuen[71] was there, his date's face made up like a psychedelic poster.

Earlier in the evening, Mo had called Regehr to explain that he and his wife would be late to the party. It was Evelyn's birthday dinner, with Ahmet, too. They missed the parade, but when the Ostins arrived, they got a good table, down front. A guy in a gorilla suit presented Evelyn flowers. TV Mama sang "Happy Birthday," then dropped her top and shook her size-100 yayas in Evelyn's face.

---

[71]Joe Smith, who had a useful ear for middle-class appeal, had signed Rod McKuen. If poetry is the grand banquet of writing, then at this banquet, the poetry of Rod McKuen was its Pop-Tart. For Warners, McKuen recited his lo-cal imagery against strings, for albums like *The Earth,* which sold well enough to embarrass some of us.

The GTO groupie who'd been told to stay crouched inside the cake decided she hated this confinement. Pissed off, she burst out naked and started throwing icing. "What the fuck am I doing here?" she yelled. Icing fire was returned.

The Ambassador's manager turned hostile. One of our guests, that fellow in the tuxedo there, the one standing on the dinner table, he was taking down all the crystal dangles from the hotel chandeliers! Oops, it was our pop poet, Rod McKuen.

Alice Cooper sang while his boa constricted. The band had indeed come out. The traditional trade press, more accustomed to mainstream parties, still learned to pair Alice Cooper and the word "he."

In the morning, Shep Gordon called to tell us that Warner Bros. Records was in trouble, however, with Western Costume Company. The gorilla suit was gone. One of the Cockettes was last been seen in it at six in the morning, running, miles away, up the Sunset Strip.

When it came to Artist Development, Regehr had been able to expand the term "legitimate business expense." Frank Zappa, label chief over Alice Cooper, organized his own weird parade, with drum and bugle, GTOs and freakhorns, to march and tootle down Warner Boulevard, stop before our humble offices, and bow in salute.

Into trailers parked at the side of WBR's small building, jammed in like a refugee camp, operations like Friedman's WEA and WBR's fast-growing Artist Relations crew worked, being jarred only occasionally by Ostin's poor skill at parking his car.

Inside WEA, Joel's team had its own muscle-building program under way. His first distribution pro, Mike Elliot, had fallen ill to a stroke. For support in building a big-time organization, Friedman, knowing he was just a label guy, turned to distribution-talented men.

WEA was learning to handle the growth of mass merchants—stores that outreached branch territories, that bought albums in one city but sold them across the land. To handle that mass, Handleman's VP Henry Droz moved from Detroit out to the Encino Heights, getting his home with its own swag-chain chandelier.

To develop WEA's marketing, Friedman turned to Chicago's branch manager, Vic Faraci, once a big-band leader,[72] now turned engaging marketeer, an enthusiast who could make you *want* to buy a broken water cooler.

For Faraci and Droz, the style in Burbank offices widely differed from

---

[72]Vic Faraci found it hard to be both a bandleader and do promotion for indie MS Distributors. The Vic Faraci Orchestra had been getting $550 a night, split among Faraci, fourteen sidemen, and a girl singer. They did about thirty-five gigs a year, making records for RCA's Vik label, and for the X label: "Vic's Boogie" (written by Porky Panico) and "More Brothers."

their old sidewalk hurly-burly. For Joel, meetings were the day's meat. "We'd generally have two or three or four meetings *about* the meeting we were going to have," Faraci said, "before we actually had *the* meeting, where we'd go through an incredibly long day of discussing very, very heavy kinds of topics, because we were, virtually, writing the book.

"Then, five or six o'clock would come around, and Joel would say, 'Let's go to dinner,' and we'd all go to dinner, and then he'd say, 'Okay, let's go back to the suite and play cards,' and he'd be the last one to leave the damn parking lot at night."

The challenges to Friedman's organization were tough. Distribution was never polite inside businesses using names like "coin op." I hate using clichés, but this one just might fit: "cutthroat." New Jersey's Teamsters now arm-twisted WEA's staff, even getting an extra nickel-per-man-hour spiff direct to the Teamster organizers. WEA's Jersey billing clerks had learned to wink, learned to blink away "nobody says what that is" items on invoices.

It stank, and even worse, it cost a lot. Friedman sent Droz to New York to clean up one such mess. After one day, Droz retreated to the Sherry-Netherland, downed four quick vodkas, and announced, "I wouldn't be president of this organization for all the tea in China." To do the full makeover, WEA brought in straight-no-bull Philly branch manager George Rossi; he took one look—perhaps it was the forklift lowering a skid from the fourth floor, seeing it wobble, and finding a drunken shipping clerk on a twelve-foot-high pile of cartons—and George slammed the doors, promising to move everything from Jersey to Philly.

Which, of course, tripped Atlantic's fear button—no local branch?—so Jerry Wexler demanded, "Why don't you do this to Warner Bros? Close L.A. and ship out of Vegas?" Then Rossi moved the branch's Promotion and Sales staffs into the WCI building, next to Atlantic's space there. Elektra and Warner Bros. now worried *they'd* be outhustled by Atlantic.

By 1972, records by WEA labels got more gold awards than any other company's. Fifty of the year's 180 certified million-selling singles and albums went to the Warner group's artists. WEA itself, however, received no gold records, so our distribution arm just manufactured its own. A photographer was called to record WEA awarding itself a gold album.

WEA Sales:
1971: $144,000,000 • 1972: $170,000,000

The Thelma Walker Tally for 1972: Warner/Reprise 26 + Atlantic 25 + Elektra 11 = WEA's 62 of the Top 200.

Ostin's hand held another card to play.

OPEC was raising the cost of crude oil, alarmingly (assuming you didn't own your own wells). America's cars lined up around the block to get gas. Record labels lined up at pressing plants to get another petroleum-based product: vinyl. Costs to make LPs went up 60 percent. Label execs, flying around in WCI's gasoline-powered corporate jet, bitched about petroleum costs.

For years, WBR had dealt with Columbia's pressing plants for the making of all its records (while Atlantic and Elektra had played the field). Now, Warners suspected, when pressings were getting rationed, Columbia's plants had been serving Columbia's needs first. Now, Mo reasoned, if Warners pulled out of Columbia plants, Columbia Records would have fewer profits, less risk capital to use against Warners in rock-act bidding wars.

Ostin planned switching WEA's pressing-plant work over to Capitol, which operated underused plants but, more important, was nowhere near Number One-ness. The deal suited both labels. It got made in one hour. Columbia viewed the deal as treason, a moment remembered.

Ostin and Smith pushed for more, to be like a major label. Results:

- To strengthen WBR's sales efforts, Ed Rosenblatt stationed district sales managers in each WEA branch. Decisions that had previously gone through Burbank now got made on the spot. Rosenblatt's staffings were edgy. He moved black district sales manager Eddie Gilreath to Atlanta, where the Caucasasian branch controller walked around in see-through white pants under which he wore briefs featuring, inter alia, the Confederate flag. Gilreath stuck to business, outclassing and outdressing them.

- To investigate a then-little-known marketing area—long before the rest of the world used the phrase "music video" (or, for that matter, even the word "video")—Ostin endowed the amusing Van Dyke Parks, who possessed articulate-beyond-normal ears, to make "artist films," a perceived waste of money in the years well before MTV. Vaguely, there was TV and, in London, *Top of the Pops*, but the use of these films was not critical. Parks commissioned art films for the music of Ry Cooder, Little Feat, Joni Mitchell, Earth Wind & Fire, Randy Newman, and Captain Beefheart.

  The Beefheart-Parks collaboration entitled "Lick My Decals Off, Baby" made Dadaism look like a Kellogg's commercial. Starting with Beefheart's surreal, free jazz, its visuals included close-ups of a woven basket, over which a deep-voiced announcer spoke of California cities and their real and imagined people: "In Encino, it's Zoot Horn Rollo." Other visuals: Beefheart's flicked cigarette butt hitting walls with huge thuds; revolving flour sifters and eggbeaters; band members strolling the streets sideways. Little public play came from the video, although it's now in the Museum of Modern Art's collection.

- The arrival of the T-shirt—ads for people to walk around in—brought a new word to my vocabulary: "Swag" (for "stuff we all get") the tchotchke, a term now translated on eBay as replacing a "collectible." T-shirts, posters, stickers, belt buckles, zipper jackets, baseball caps, all overprinted with album hoopla, then sent from us over to WEA. About half of all this clothing managed to reach its goal: the AM and FM programmers. The first half stuck in the hands of WEA's employees. Closets, like those of San Francisco display manager Hale Milgrim's, became overtchotchked. Twelve-step programs were planned for people addicted to inscribed baseball jackets. Only A&R man Andy Wickham, in his English accent, held the line: "I do not wear clothing which carries advertising."

We weren't the only ones changing. Some undiscovered economic law—let's call it the Law of Ringo—made radio play fewer records than it did the previous year. Too soon, the time of FM just playing anything it felt like went *poof,* in favor of the Top Forty Formula, now concentrated not on singles but on the Top Forty albums. The first of such stations—actually a Top Thirty albums station—WPLR was born in New Haven, Connecticut. WPLR (and soon many other stations) challenged the Sixties' share-a-toke FM promotion style. Spacey promotion men, who once boasted about feeling at one with infinity, no longer got records played. Now they had to feel at one within thirty. WEA promotion men trimmed their sideburns and stashed their ankhs. For guys like Rosenblatt, who'd worked radio before it had turned formless, back when promotion was about favors, relationships, and what's selling, this Top Thirty albums format felt like home again.

But overall, for us, this remained an age of freedom. If we could imagine it, we did it. We invented ways for our company to act like a big guy. Doing all this, it cost a cow.

Each October, the three labels attended separate confessions before their bosses—Ross, Cohen, and WCI's financial head, Bert Wasserman—to present the year's results and the next year's budget. In budget meetings, Cohen recalled treating each WCI label differently. Elektra, that was a quick meeting; "small" was his summation. Atlantic, Cohen regarded as tightly run, with high profit percentages, run by guys like Sheldon Vogel, who treated Atlantic's money, out of habit, like it was their own and the last they might ever see. Cohen liked Atlantic. Then there was Warners.

"I remember having some real, roll-up-the-sleeves times," Cohen recalled. "Warners was spending too much money in promotion and advertising." Even though WBR delivered the most *cash* of the labels, in the end, its profit *percentage* was lousier.

This year's budget-meeting parishioners—Mo Ostin, Joe Smith, Ed West, finance administrator Murray Gitlin—listened to Cohen's sermon,

often feeling the heat under their seats. Ostin defended his whole haber-
dashery, down to the last belt buckle. "This," Ostin said, looking directly at
Ross, "is the way to build a company." It took three hours, but corporate let
us keep abuilding. Even smiled about the Cockettes.

Cohen himself was on a hot seat. He was dealing with our autonomous
labels, labels with the right to tell him no. Even as Number Two at WCI, Cohen had all the responsibility for his divisions with as much authority as a
Second Lieutenant. Patiently, I'd guess, Cohen began holding presidents
meetings, in hopes the label heads would share "signing ideas." Cohen recalled, "I'm at one of our meetings and Jerry Wexler mentions he's discussing a new deal with Aretha Franklin. Wexler's presenting his numbers,
saying things like 'The last two albums she's done, she's sold nine hundred
thousand, and with our deal, all we need to make out is four hundred thousand, and so this deal's no risk.' To which David Geffen, who regarded diplo-
macy like others regarded leprosy, cut through with 'Jerry, the minimum
number of albums any artist can sell, including Elvis Presley, is zero.' "

By 1973 and 1974, Warner had seen its late-Sixties rage, the "underground"
singer/songwriter, turn into bestsellers, the bulk of the business. In February
1973, WBR released sixteen albums. Within two months, ten were on the
charts. That felt heady. Lenny Waronker had a good producing year: Gordon
Lightfoot's *Sundown* (Number One); Maria Muldaur's *Midnight at the Oasis*
(Number Four); Randy Newman's *Good Old Boys*; Ry Cooder's *Paradise
and Lunch*. Lenny earned a WBR vice presidency. He was toasted with
champagne in glasses made of genuine glass.

The singer/songwriter had become, for Warner/Reprise, as important as
rock bands, with Top Twenty hits from:

Jethro Tull • Arlo Guthrie • T-Rex • Neil Young • America • Black Sab-
bath • Alice Cooper • Deep Purple • The Doobie Brothers • Seals &
Crofts • James Taylor • The Allman Brothers • Maria Muldaur • Faces
• Van Morrison •

I was stunned by an event unthinkable five years earlier: In 1971, James
Taylor appeared on the cover of *Time* magazine. That stuck in my mind. It
documented that underground music had climbed up and commanded the
earth. I felt a little sorry for Peggy Lee.

In year-end 1973, at WEA's Los Angeles branch, its employees experienced a month like never before, pumping albums like weightlifters on up-
pers: more than a million dollars in one month. Just . . . exploding! Branch
manager Russ Bach told his merchandising head, Bob Moering, "Go out
and get three or four cases of beer." The beer was put on a packing table in
the back. Work stopped a half hour early that day. Moering got up on the

table to tell about forty packers, "I just want to say 'Thank you.' Here's a very small token. Have a beer on me."

By early 1974, WEA had 110 salesmen, calling on 4,500 accounts. The impact those 110 were creating became a wake-up call at the record business's annual National Association of Record Manufacturers (NARM) convention of retailers. Joe Smith delivered the keynote address at NARM, which was held at Miami's aging melange of velvet and plastic, the Diplomat Hotel.[73] Showing off its flair for the catchy phrase, NARM that year chose as its theme "Partners + Professionalism = Profits."

Smith commented how the "uncomfortable and unforeseen events" of the past year—material shortages, spiraling costs, investigations, and the "agony" of CBS (over the dismissal of Clive Davis)—should have demonstrated to manufacturers and sellers alike that the only friends we in this auditorium could rely on were each other. "But, through all this nastiness," Smith observed, "one thing persisted: hostility between manufacturer and merchandiser."

From NARM, Smith traveled to New York, where a gold album was to be presented to Black Sabbath. Receiving it was the group's leader, Ozzy Osbourne, who had his name—O-Z-Z-Y—tattooed on his knuckles. (Smith later told publicist Bob Merlis, "That's how he remembers how to spell it.")

Smith recommended to NARM who its next year's opening morning speaker should be: He offered up me. Driving to work one day, I phrased out what I thought was my message, that selling records should not depend so on radio play, that radio owed us no favors. My speech I called "The Day Radio Died." It hit some nerve in this convention of record sellers. Hey, *Billboard* said I titillated the opening session with my wit:

. . . regaled his audience with some fantasizing on what might happen "the day radio died" with lines like "Kal Rudman sent fifty white labels to the Mayo Clinic" and "Gary Owens cupped his hand to his ear and heard nothing." But it was when he came up with concrete recommendations to bolster business that he added heavy applause to the laughs . . .

On a professional level, I meant what I said: Why was my record business—records you listened along to—at the mercy of some other business—radio—which had its own market goals? That meant records had to be made to fit radio's needs, and I found that wrong. (Still do.)

---

[73]Compared to Joe, Mo hardly ever spoke publicly. He dreaded the experience. Even touring the branches, sitting in two chairs like some talk show called *The Mo Joe Show*, just mikes, a few notes, and a small table with water pitcher between them—for Ostin that was agony.

On a personal level, my addressing the whole record business sitting out there felt really, really good. Underneath all the vice presidency of me was still the kid who in high school had entertained his dates by singing notable drum solos. Now, after my speech, out there in front of me, were two thousand fat-ass rack jobbers, big-time dealers, and Mo and Joe, standing, applauding. I felt, personally, arrived. Downstairs in the hotel garage, I had my own Jaguar, valet parked. As I drove home that afternoon with my glam wife, I felt more adult than I had that morning.

Warner Bros. Records took on Neil Bogart's Casablanca Records for distribution. Bogart, his hair done about his head in a three-inch halo, had the face of a cherub. His eyes twinkled like they'd come from Disney. His enthusiasm could hardly be interrupted. He was as mod as we'd seen. Neil had pushed music all his life. At labels like Kama Sutra/Buddah, he'd become known as the Bubblegum King, for his teen-cute singles by acts like the 1910 Fruitgum Company and Ohio Express. He'd also become known as extravagant. If it wasn't a hit yet, spend money on it. "Bogart's antennae were always up," Joe Smith knew. "If some people start running through rooms naked, Bogart's out there first with a song called 'The Streak." But he was a drug user, stoned all the time. And could they spend money? I visited their offices on Sunset. I took one look at the parking lot and asked, 'What is this, a branch of Stuttgart? All Mercedeses out there? The worst car in the lot's a BMW!' "

We turned up at a private Casablanca concert at the Century Plaza Hotel to witness Kiss, a four-man act that wore more makeup than a sixty-year-old madam. A group whose drummer rode a forklift overhead, whose drumsticks spurted sparklers, whose lead singer revealed a tongue rivaling a lively python. Kiss's first single, "Kissin' Time," brought together the full force of Ostin and Smith's new WBR—with video, artist development, district sales managers, merchandising forces, all at their peaks. Miami promotion man Eddie Pugh had started off the record by holding a radio-station contest, calling it a "Kiss Off." Pugh became a Casablanca hero. Faster than herpes, Kiss Offs spread across America.

When Kiss debuted in New York, Neil Bogart's introduction from onstage involved his telling the press that his personal numerologist, a Puerto Rican lady, had predicted the group's success. To avoid giving away the real faces of the group, New York publicist Bob Merlis arranged interviews for the quartet under hot towels at the Georgette Klinger facial salon.

Kiss's debut got attention. "One night when I breathed fire," group member Gene Simmons recalled, "my hair caught on fire. One of our roadies put it out, but everybody thought it was part of the act. The mania happened so suddenly. We didn't have a chance to react. All of a sudden we're fucking our brains out every single day of our lives and doing two hundred ten, two hundred thirty shows a year. It was ten months on the road, four weeks to make a record, then back out. And we did that for eight years."

Kiss's Paul Stanley summed it up, "We're the McDonald's of rock. We're always there to satisfy, and a billion served. . . . I remember one time my parents came to see us at Madison Square Garden, and there I am on-stage playing game-show host to eighteen thousand people, and I'm wearing tights and high heels and playing with a guitar between my legs, stroking the guitar. I remember saying to myself, 'My God, my parents are out there absorbing this. They're watching eighteen thousand people watching their son, and their son is in makeup and high heels, and he's jerking off a guitar.' "

Kiss and Casablanca Records' stay at Warner Bros. was short, however. Bogart's "more, we need more" pressures became insatiable, while "no" was not a word Bogart understood. A year after it began with Warner Bros. Records, the Casablanca deal ended deep in the red, despite Kiss's flamboyance. Casablanca's promotion head (and Bogart's brother-in-law) Buck Rheingold taped WB's weekly phone call, called the "Promo Hot Line," and heard our promotion head, Gary Davis, tell his troops to give more attention to WB product than to the distributed labels, like Casablanca, Capricorn, and Chrysalis. Major goof.

When Bogart faced Ostin with this, his executives admitted it. Ostin, embarrassed by Davis's gaffe but relieved to end this deal-beyond-human-control, let Bogart take Casablanca elsewhere, assuming Bogart would someday, as he promised, repay its $750,000 indebtedness to Warners. (He did.)

In time, talented singer/writers with fair but honest voices would themselves become answers in trivia games. Already this had happened to Warner Bros. Records' *first* singer/songwriter. This man's singing and songs had, in the early Sixties, supported our little label when our chair had no legs. Just nine years earlier, it had been an album whose title, as if spoken by a proud Jewish mama, was *My Son, the Folk Singer*.

Joe Smith once reflected on what nine years can mean: "Even more than Peter, Paul & Mary, at that time, Allan Sherman became The Moment. You must understand The Moment because The Moment is very important: You're The Moment for a short time; then you're not The Moment anymore."

Nine years later, in 1973, Allan Sherman was anything but The Moment. He was broke, divorced, sick, and unshaven. In the decade since *Folk Singer*, the pain of becoming less than The Moment—personal, professional pain—had ruined his life. He had tried to sing well, to lose weight. Before that, Allan was fat and roly-poly, and people found him cuddly. But now, as his original music director Lou Busch told me, "If ever I saw success ruin a guy, it was Allan. He blew the wife, the kids, and eventually, the money, too.

He got difficult." His books failed. His Broadway musical failed. Even at golf-tournament banquets, he bombed. And now his crew cut had grown gray and long, and he stayed home, wearing only his boxer shorts, laughing gleefully as he talked his thoughts about Man and Sex. He was impotent.

A feeling man, Joe Smith re-signed Allan Sherman as an artist, paying him a $5,000 advance for an album of golf routines. On November 20, 1973, about 5:00 p.m., engineer Rudy Hill from Warner's recording studios received a call from Sherman, who wanted a copy of what he'd recorded so far. Rudy took a copy up to Allan's house in West L.A.

As Sherman began to eat some cabbage soup, he suffered a sudden, massive heart attack, caved to the floor, his head hitting with a clunk. Hill was alone with him. "I called the doctor and began to give him mouth-to-mouth resuscitation. He regurgitated in my mouth, and then he died." When the paramedics arrived, they began pumping his heart. They worked for twenty minutes until, finally, one of them said, "Let him go." They laid him back on the floor. He was forty-nine.

"It was so cold," Rudy remembered. "I'd never seen anything so cold. His family was supposed to be coming over that night, but nobody ever showed up. It was unreal. I felt that I was in this other world. But there he was, that fat, obese man who'd made so many people happy, lying there on a cold floor.

"The paramedics put a sheet over him, and after awhile I walked over and pulled the sheet back and kind of started talking to him, because it was so weird. 'Hey, man,' I said, 'I was just talking to you.' I killed a quart of J&B Scotch that night to kill the taste in my mouth."

Seventy-six Saul Cohens in the country club,
And a hundred and ten nice men named Levine!
And there's more than a thousand Finks
Who parade around the links—
It's a sight that really must be seen!

Significant Warner Bros. Releases

1972

Warner Bros.: America (*America,* including "*Horse with No Name*") • Black Sabbath (*Vol. 4*) • Alice Cooper (*School's Out*) • Deep Purple (*Machine Head,* including "Smoke on the Water") • The Doobie Brothers (*Toulouse Street,* including "Jesus Is Just Alright" and "Listen to the Music") • Grateful Dead (*Europe '72*) • Van Morrison (*Saint Dominic's Preview*) • Seals & Crofts (*Summer Breeze,* including "Hummingbird") • Little Feat (*Sailing Shoes*) • Small Faces with Rod Stewart ("Stay with Me") • James Taylor (*One Man Dog,* including "Don't Let Me Be Lonely Tonight") • Tower of Power ("You're Still a Young Man") • Neil Young (*Journey Through the Past*) • *A Clockwork Orange* soundtrack

Reprise: Captain Beefheart (*The Spotlight Kid*) • Fleetwood Mac (*Bare Trees*) • Arlo Guthrie ("The City of New Orleans") • Jimi Hendrix (*Hendrix in the West*) • Gordon Lightfoot (*Don Ouixote*) • Randy Newman (*Sail Away*) • T-Rex (*The Slider*) • Neil Young (*Harvest*, including "Old Man" and "Heart of Gold") • Frank Zappa (*Hot Rats*)
Bearsville: Todd Rundgren (*Something/Anything?* including "Hello It's Me" and "I Saw the Light")
Bizarre: Frank Zappa (*Just Another Band from L.A.*)
Brother: The Beach Boys (*Pet Sounds*)
Capricorn: Duane Allman (*An Anthology*) • The Allman Brothers Band (*Eat a Peach*)
Chrysalis: Jethro Tull (*Living in the Past*)
Raccoon: Jesse Colin Young (*Together*)

1973

Warner Bros.: America (*Hat Trick*) • Alice Cooper (*Billion Dollar Babies* and *Muscle of Love*) • Deep Purple (*Who Do You Think We Are!* and *Made in Japan*) • The Doobie Brothers (*The Captain and Me*, including "Long Train Runnin'") • Faces (*Ooh La La*) • Little Feat (*Dixie Chicken*) • Van Morrison (*Hard Nose the Highway*) • Carl Reiner & Mel Brooks (*2000 and Thirteen*) • Seals & Crofts (*Diamond Girl*, including "We May Never Pass This Way Again") • Tower of Power ("So Very Hard to Go") • Uriah Heep (*Sweet Freedom*) • "Dueling Banjos" from *Deliverance* soundtrack
Reprise: Fleetwood Mac (*Penguin* and *Mystery to Me*) • Maria Muldaur ("Midnight at the Oasis") • Frank Sinatra (*Ol' Blue Eyes Is Back*) • Neil Young (*Time Fades Away*)
Bearsville: Foghat ("What a Shame")
Brother: The Beach Boys (*Holland* and *In Concert*)
Capricorn: The Allman Brothers Band (*Brothers and Sisters*, including "Ramblin' Man") • *The Marshall Tucker Band*
Chrysalis: Jethro Tull (*A Passion Play*)
Sire: Focus (*Moving Waves*, including "Hocus Pocus")

17

For WCI label heads, being Number One held a second meaning. It also meant not getting threatened by some ambitious Number Two guy working under you. No need to share, whether that was decision making, spotlight focus, bonus pools, the word "and," or office size. Back in 1966, when Kinney had acquired National Cleaning Contractors, Steve Ross had promised NCC's head, William Frankel, that Frankel would remain chairman of the merged companies. The move meant Ross had to demote his own father-in-law, Ed Rosenthal, to vice chairman, and Ross would get to be only Number Two (as president of the new company, Kinney National Service). Contractually Number One, chairman Frankel's ego was at peace. He let Ross run NCC with no interference.

Three years later, when Kinney National acquired Warner Bros., part of the deal was Ross got to rise up and become co-CEO with Frankel. Then, two years after that, Ross had made both Frankel and Bill's son and presumed successor, Pete, disappear. At WCI, Ross was now clearly Number One, with only one "runner-up" under him.

Alan Cohen, who'd been supervising Kinney's record-business holdings, became Ross's executive vice president. With the death of Frankel, Cohen offered his services to Ross, telling Ross he was willing to be president of WCI, willing to be Ross's Number Two.

Ross suspected Cohen of maneuvering to take over his new Warner Communications. Ross sidestepped by creating a structure that would serve him several times over the coming years: a management team who, a bunch of Twos together, would occupy an oddity called the Office of the President. Into those chairs Ross first sat both Cohen and former agent Ted Ashley. Cohen argued this wouldn't work; Ashley was busy running the studio. A few months later, in a meeting with competing conglomerateur, grumpy Charles Bluhdorn of Gulf & Western, the wary Ross dropped his hint: "You can take any of my guys, I won't hold it against you. But the *one* guy I cannot do without is Alan Cohen."

Very soon thereafter, Bluhdorn hired Cohen to run Madison Square Garden. Without him, WCI's record business interests had, for that moment, no corporate watchful eye. The three label heads hardly noticed.

Now successfully alone as both chairman *and* president, Ross announced new appointments. To oversee the music group, he reached out for a gentlemanly lawyer named David Horowitz, who'd represented Columbia Pictures in creating the co-owned Burbank Studios (up the water tower went the painters' scaffold again). For months thereafter, Horowitz remained stockpiled at WCI, waiting in a job with no duties. Now, into the mix of executives who were clearly subordinate to one chief, Horowitz found "Records" his given domain.

From Atlantic headquarters, Nesuhi Ertegun was absent; he was out staffing up his own domain, WEA International. Jerry Wexler was now living his winters in Miami, attending to America's southern music, leaving his one-time assistant, the sharp and hyper Jerry Greenberg, to handle details in New York. With Nesuhi and Wexler gone, that left only one of last year's three Atlantic chiefs, Ahmet, in charge in New York, and he was next-to-never at the office till after a quality lunch. If he'd show at three in the afternoon and ask why *this* or *that* had happened, it took tact to explain that others had been at both this and that since nine. Ahmet Ertegun had a splendid reason for his tardiness. He'd been doing what for all his business life he'd been doing: staying up late, carousing with Capote and company, booth-slouching with society's fun folk, and attracting new music stars, like oh, Bette Midler. Try finding the Divine at nine.

And often as not, Ahmet was off in London, there with his London friend Robert Stigwood, whose temperament matched Ahmet's. Both were dandies, though a generation apart. Stigwood, at age twenty-three, had come to London from Australia with thirty shillings. Within eight years, he had $10 million and lived in a fifteen-room Tudor mansion, hidden in thirty-seven acres of gardens within London. The short, dapper bachelor wore longish brown hair. He toured London in his white Rolls. He was polite to the point of sugar. For his U.S. excursions, he rented a $700,000 Manhattan townhouse on East Seventy-eighth, three blocks down from Ahmet's. Dinners at Ahmet and his wife Mica's—I'd attended a couple—impressed me, boy, oh, boy. Four tables-of-six dinners, where I'd sit with people I'd only read about. I tried to behave. But I realized that even if I lived to be a hundred, I'd never know as much as Mica about fine napkin rings.

Working at first as the agent for music acts, Stigwood soon grew interested in producing their records. He became one of England's pioneers in indie record production. He made millions with such groups as the Bee Gees, Cream, and Blind Faith. Atlantic got them all, for America. In 1973, when his acts were marshaled onto the RSO label (for Robert Stigwood

Organization), for three years RSO became distributed by Atlantic. It was a Bee Gees bonanza.

Ahmet and "Stiggy-poo," as Ertegun called him, prankstered. In Los Angeles, when Stigwood rented a house with bad statues out front, Ahmet took the chance, in the depth of night, to spray-paint them pink. On a transatlantic flight, while Ahmet was asleep, Stigwood replaced Ahmet's passport photo with one of a girl giving some guy a blow job, raising eyebrows at Heathrow's Passport Control. Ah, the fun days.

With WEA label heads Ostin, Ertegun, Smith, and Holzman frequently gone off to London scratching for hit acts, it was as if, for the fifty States of America, David Geffen's Asylum Records picked up the slack.[74]

Geffen had taken his time. He'd announced Asylum as a haven for record acts. *Billboard* had headlined it GEFFEN TO BOW LABEL; ACTS TO SHARE IN PROFIT. In the first year of his distribution deal with Atlantic, David released zero records. Many within Atlantic became Asylum sceptics. They preferred siding with the Aretha Franklin–Roberta Flack sound, and held on to a "Shit, all we need here is one more record label" attitude. Wexler was the only label head who still worked in a recording studio. But within the Warner music group, "distributed labels" had become rife.

(To become "distributed" by WEA, as Island, Capricorn, Swan Song, and now Geffen Records had, one rule applied: The outside label could get WEA distribution only by first making a deal with one of WEA's founding three labels. It came down to who risks the money and who reaps the rewards. If a label like Asylum had a bad year, the loss went through the label [Atlantic] on up to WCI, but that loss cost the label getting distributed [Geffen's Asylum] nothing that year, nothing for all its A&R, marketing, manufacturing, and distribution costs—nearly the whole kaboodle. If, on the other hand, a label had a hot year, it often gave up 50 percent of its profits. After such a distribution deal is over, when it's walk-away time, who keeps the masters created during the deal? To David Geffen, *that* was the most sacred point of all. By retaining his masters after a deal was up, Geffen would eventually grow the record industry's largest personal kaboodle.)

Year One. As Geffen spent money, month after month, Atlantic held its breath. Year Two at Geffen began big. Out came a pouring of albums to Geffen's taste: the West Coast laid back, country inflenced sound of Jackson Browne, Linda Ronstadt, the Eagles, the Byrds. Then Joni, over from Reprise in 1972. Hit albums.

---

[74]Asylum, early on, was David Geffen plus secretary Linda Loddengaard, publicist Lita Eliscu, promotion man Paul Ahern, gofer/mailboy Steve Baker, and a receptionist. Downstairs, Elliott Roberts, Geffen's ex-partner in management.

Geffen learned hard what running a record company was like. Company running was far from Laurel Canyon, far from lounging the day away in beanbag chairs. "David was on the phone with a major program director," his promo chief, Phil Ahern, recalled. "I remember seeing the expression on David's face when the program director told David that he didn't like this J. D. Souther record and was not going to play it on his station."

Geffen already knew that dealing with temperamental artists was a drag. Especially the Eagles.

In Washington, D.C., promoting the Eagles, its stars, Glenn Frey and Don Henley, were doing an on-the-air interview. Halfway through, the DJ asked Henley why *he* wasn't talking much. "Why the fuck should I do the talking?" Henley answered. "Glenn's the one who got laid last night."

In his life, Geffen never trashed a hotel room, never threw a refrigerator out a window, never vomited in a limo. He found some behaviors exasperating, wastes of time.

Geffen appointed Clevelander Jerry Sharell as Asylum's general manager. Once again, Sharell (like Rosenblatt, like Glew) had become "coastal," no longer having to hit secondary stations in the boonies in his Chevy Nova. He'd done his time.[75] For his first interview, Sharell showed up dressed in splendor: brown gabardines, brown suede shoes, tan turtleneck, and a Rafael jacket. Geffen grabbed him by the lapels and pulled him into his office, closing the door. He asked, "Holy Christ, do you always dress that way? Your clothes cost more than Jackson Browne's car!" Within the Warner labels, Sharell started getting attention for his new trademark: bow ties. He showed the rest of the world how to dress. (Sharell was particularly beloved for his desire to be a crooner. He got a personalized license plate for his car that put him into the near-Sinatra league. It read OLBRNYZ.)

Sharell quickly saw in his boss what others did: "David Geffen was a positive panic to work for. He was totally driven, quick to read a situation, and insatiable. He only knew Number One, and he wasn't happy being Number Two or Number Ten . . . He sucked up knowledge and used it. He absorbed life. He had great faith in his acts and his judgments. He loved it that David Blue's song made the charts. It killed him that Ned Doheny never made it."

Year Three 1973. Atlantic's distribution deal had one more year to run. Geffen knew that Atlantic had no option for more years. Ross approached Geffen about selling his label. How much? Ross asked. Eager and greedy

---

[75]In Cleveland in the 1950s, Sharell had to be friends with Leo Mintz at the Record Rendezvou, since Mintz talked to the trades and the labels. At ten in the morning, Mintz told Sharell, "Let's have breakfast across the street." Mintz orders two double Cutty Sarks. Sharell's visits with Mintz got cut back. Too bad. Mintz next took on a protégé: a young DJ from WAKR in Akron named Alan Freed.

(as Ahmet once described David), Geffen blurted out "the biggest number I could think of": $7 million. A mistake; in such negotiations, never name *your* price first. Quickly, Ross stuck out his shake hand, said okay, then phrased it his own way: $2 million in cash, plus $5 million in WCI stock. Shake. Asylum became a fully owned part of Atlantic Records. Geffen also had to sign a seven-year employment agreement, meaning he'd run Ross's Asylum for seven years for $150,000 a year. In a matter of months, Geffen's $5 million in WCI stock shares, worth $45 a share when the deal was made, sank to $8 each. His $7 million payday had sunk to $3 million. Before taxes. Such sinking displeased Geffen. He soon wanted out of this deal to run what was now someone else's label. And Geffen was a man who knew how to make his unhappiness heard.[76]

The $7 million buyout also displeased the Eagles, who by this time felt they'd become "family" at Asylum, partners in its success. When Geffen got his buyout, the Eagles got zero. They remembered Geffen's motto and that *Billboard* headline about "acts to share in profit." David's keeping it all became the end of "family" between Eagles and Geffen. The Eagles took on in-your-face manager Irving Azoff who understood based on his own earlier employment at Geffen/Roberts the conflicts of interests that came from Geffen/Roberts working both as the Eagles' record company and as its managers. With Azoff, the Eagles started building bank accounts all on their own.

At Elektra, management had changed. Top executives worked with elbows stuck out like lances. Holzman, outwardly focused, had left his hands off the company's inner management. He later told me he believed that appointing no successor was the biggest Elektra mistake he'd ever made. Managerial turf battles arose between Bill Harvey and Mel Posner, between Bill Harvey and Mickey Kapp, between owl-eyed lawyer Larry Harris and financial head Jack Reinstein. Inside Elektra, once-charming ingestions of pot-for-world-peace had turned into snortings of cocaine. Elektra's butterfly, its logo of love, had expired.

Having sold his label to Kinney almost three years earlier, Jac's first employment-contract option was due for WCI pickup. Holzman waited for the pickup letter, knowing it would bind him to another two years of serving Elektra.

WCI never sent the letter. A month after the contract deadline had passed, Holzman wrote to Ross, explaining he was leaving Elektra for Hawaii. Ross asked Holzman to become a WCI consultant in technology,

---

[76]Jac Holzman took advantage of WCI's stock decline, sold his debentures back to WCI for $1 million, bought about 100,000 shares of WCI at $9, and waited, profitably, for the stock to rise again.

because, as Ross put it, "No one around here knows how to screw in a light-bulb." Holzman agreed, intending to explain how to screw one from a hammock in Maui.

Ross quickly approached Geffen about running a new double-label setup: WCI's Elektra combined with Atlantic's Geffen-run Asylum. Geffen pondered. He'd seen Elektra losing money and "heading for oblivion." Elektra's promotion head, George Steele, recalled, "I think that it was a reluctant move on David's part, but one that he knew he had to make. David didn't want to run a big record company. He was happy with that little family of six at Asylum." Knowing how low WCI's stock had sunk and what effect that'd had on Geffen's buyout net, Ross sweetened his offer. David's salary would go up to $1 million a year. Plus, every year for five years, WCI would pay Geffen 20 percent of the difference between $40 and the stock's current price. That should get David even again.

Geffen swallowed Ross's bait. Now thirty years old, he took over both Elektra and Asylum, technically becoming chairman and CEO of each company for WCI. In turn, he promoted Elektra's Mel Posner from executive VP/general manager to be president of the two labels. Geffen asked Posner to move Elektra out to California. Posner countered, "Let's try a year of bi-coastal." Geffen put up with that structure for a year.

David's first step in the merger was "refreshing" Elektra's staff. He fired Bill Harvey, Elektra's ranking officer, together with all of Promotion, Publicity, and Production. Step two in the merger was dropping the old regime's loser artists, trimming the roster from forty-five down to thirteen. *Kerplunk* went artists of anonymity, like Alasdair Clayre. "Let's put it this way," Geffen later reflected, "over time, eighty percent of everything you sign turns out to be shit. That's pretty much the industry average."

He believed that Elektra was both (a) overly technology devoted ("I'm not sure what . . . technology excellence does in the record business. Engineers are like bringing in a plumber to fix your toilet") and (b) overly intellectual ("I was not a person who would say I was in this for the music. I used to be offended by people who would tell me they were in it for the music who were just trying to make tons and tons of money. It's all self-serving crap, one way or the other. Jac took the money and left, so what can I tell you? I think Jac got a very poor price for it. We can simply look at where I am in the world today and where Jac is").[77]

---

[77]Ex–Elektra producer Paul Rothchild, speaking as a free spirit, reflected the other viewpoint toward what David was saying. Geffen had outmaneuvered Rothchild when it came to signing CSN&Y, to which Rothchild's retort had been "When David Geffen enters the California waters as a manager, sharks have entered the lagoon. And the entire vibe changes. It used to be 'Let's make music; money is a by-product.' Then it becomes 'Let's make money; music is a by-product.' "

The merger press release, as always, highlighted the artists considered hot. Unlisted artists lost sleep.

Asylum list: The Eagles, Jackson Browne, Joni Mitchell, Jo Jo Gunne, The Byrds, Linda Ronstadt
Elektra list: Carly Simon, David Gates & Bread, Judy Collins, Mickey Newbury, Ian Matthews, Harry Chapin

Elektra's forty-five artists, with Geffen scything his way through the roster, stared into the Pit of the Has-Beens, or Never-Got-to-Be's. Newly signed Queen, stuck in fog at JFK, phoned Elektra in Manhattan, nervous because no one had come out to say hello. Karin Berg, just hired by Geffen as an Asylum publicist, decided it was up to her and taxied out to the airport alone.

According to Carly Simon, the merger—with a new man there—caused "mayhem." "Who is this kid?" David was so different. He wore T-shirts. He spoke his mind. Simon felt like "an ugly stepdaughter, that suddenly I was thrust upon David Geffen and his associates, and nobody really knew me, and they had to take me on. I felt kind of ousted—not ousted, because I wasn't kicked out, but it was like being a stepchild.

"Geffen," Simon went on, "did not respond to several calls, was of course identified with Joni Mitchell, whom he co-managed . . ."

Hardly missing a morning edition, David, fresh from taking over Elektra, talked next to Ahmet about a "supermerger," in which his Elektra/Asylum would next be merged with Atlantic. Two reasons for Ahmet to say yes: (1) Ahmet was faced with losing Asylum's sales volume. In the Thelma Walker Tally for 1973, Atlantic/Asylum had outshone WBR: Atlantic/Asylum 36 + Warner Bros. 35 + Elektra 5 = WEA 76. And the E, it was exploding. Any Atlantic-Asylum-Elektra combine would dominate the whole Warner group. (2) Ahmet had always said he liked others in his company who would do the work. Ahmet immediately agreed to the merger with Elektra/Asylum. It looked salvational.

In the resulting A-E-A, Ertegun and Geffen would remain the co-chairmen. Wexler would become vice chairman. Greenberg, Vogel, and Posner would be co-presidents. Sounded fine. WCI put out a press release headed:

ATLANTIC, ELEKTRA/ASYLUM
MERGE FIRMS: AHMET ERTEGUN, DAVID
GEFFEN, JERRY WEXLER NEW CHIEFS

Ertegun and Geffen left the thousand details to their lieutenants. Atlantic's Jerry Greenberg flew out to Los Angeles to meet with Elektra/

Asylum's Posner. Lists were made: who'd stay, who'd go. "When it got down to the L.A. office," Greenberg told me, "we discussed Tony Mandich, Ahmet's driver. Mel said he has to go, because we don't need an 'Ahmet's Driver' position."

Greenberg placed a call to Ahmet, who was awake (he was in Germany). With that phone call, the supermerger of Atlantic + Elektra + Asylum ended, went away, within twenty-four hours, killed by (1) Wexler's dislike for Geffen, to whom he'd never report; (2) the sacrifice of autonomy by Atlantic; and (3) Ahmet's need for a driver in L.A.

Months earlier, both Wexler and Geffen had individually and publicly vowed to sign Bob Dylan, who'd said he was leaving Columbia. Wexler and Geffen waged a two-man "sign here" war, each in his own way. Wexler, by persuasion and by personal reputation, envisioned for Dylan and the singer's attorneys a career-growing change. This would not be a question of *how* big a deal either. Atlantic would *match anything*.

For lawyers, Wexler's "name your price" line had turned him into a sitting target. But for Jerry, signing Dylan would be career icing. The bearded Wexler, wearing Buddy Holly black-rimmed glasses, a gray turtleneck, and Village cords, began whispering into Dylan's east ear.

Though uncommonly liberal, Wexler's approach was still gentlemanly and discreet. Which is to say, he followed the rules of signing acts: We, as the record company, accustomed to the driver's seat, write up the first draft. We then negotiate with you, the artist's manager/lawyers. As if to say, "There's lots of talent out there, and our company, while it likes the way you sing, will make *our* kind of deal with you. Here are the rules of such a deal." And then, with the to-be-signed artist looking on hopefully, a negotiating dance—"We'll give you fourteen percent, but you have to pay packaging costs out of your end . . ." —leads to a contract. These contracts run longer than Leviticus and include even more mentions of potential *artist* sins. Page after page spells out gloomy contingencies for which the artist must financially atone. (Few clauses mention the possibility that the record company might screw up.)

That is how the game's played, how it's always been played, and how Wexler assumed that the Courtship of Bob Dylan would be played: slowly, stately, a polite wooing like the ones upper-class boys and girls of Victorian England played out, traditionally, kicking one another's shins, but with manners.

Lawyers and shin kicking were not Geffen's game. An ex-agent and an ex–artists' manager, David didn't look at artists' deal points, he looked into their eyes. Night and day. Geffen got home phone numbers. He'd call at ten-thirty at night to get an update or deliver one. It was like David was suddenly there, woven into your life.

His approach to Bob Dylan: Take Dylan's side but never try to *be* Dylan. He talked about a new way an artist like Dylan could work: He'd be in charge of his own record career and not at the mercy of some big machine like his former employer, Columbia. The two would work together, taking on the world. Instead of being Dylan's label boss, he would be Dylan's fighter/manager.

Geffen had been sharing housing with Joni Mitchell. House visitors moved fluidly in and out, as if the living room were a dorm foyer. Bob Dylan became a houseguest, day and night. That made it easier when it came to ten-thirty. No need to phone up your intended if he's hanging out in your kitchen.

So during this wooing period, Joni Mitchell had been creating her newest album. "I was so excited the night I finished *Court and Spark*," Joni remembered, "I brought it back to the house to play it." At the end of her playback, silence. Dylan had fallen asleep. Geffen wondered aloud about its commerciality and had many suggestions. Mitchell, shaken, headed for bed. The guys hung out downstairs.

Dylan signed with Geffen.

Around now, the relationship between the Stones and Atlantic took a bad turn. When label staffers unwrapped and played the Stones' 1973 album master, murmurs of "Oh, shit" spread rapidly through the company. The album, *Goats Head Soup*, had on it a song called "Starfucker."

"With *Goats Head Soup*, they wanted to exclude 'Starfucker' altogether," Mick Jagger recalled. "They got the complete horrors and screamed 'We're gonna be sued!' and everyone else got the horrors. And I said, 'I don't mind if I'm sued.' I mean, I just fought and fought and fought . . ."

Ertegun fought longer, finally getting Jagger to change the title "Starfucker" (repeated sixty times in the song) to "Star Star." Atlantic relaxed. The Stones headed off across America, building up to touring with a forty-foot rubber penis for a stage prop (called "Casper the Friendly Ghost" by one wishful writer).

Wexler got a new itch. He signed Willie Nelson. Success in country music had escaped the WEA labels. Elektra had fumbled it with Michael Nesmith (an ex-Monkee) and Russ Miller (no longhair hippies make it on Nashville's close-cropped turf). Warner Bros. had done little under its first country heads, Chips Moman, then Norro Wilson and Andy Wickham, who had left Laurel Canyon to hang out with fellow right-wingers in Tennessee. There had been isolated hints at country rock (The Eagles, Gram Parsons, Emmylou Harris), but not enough to construct custom offices in Nashville over; our involvements were truly short-term rental.

For Atlantic, Nelson's album *Phases and Stages*, made in the magic studios of Muscle Shoals, produced no scratch. Wexler blamed his label for "no push on the album." As analyzed by Atlantic's money watcher, Sheldon Vogel, after twenty months in operation, Atlantic Nashville—its overhead and albums—looked like a financial sinkhole, $600,000 in the red. With some disgust, Wexler told Nelson, "Willie, we're gonna have to cut you loose." Wexler also saw that his working self-exile in Miami was *not* working. After five years, Jerry returned to the office, to New York. Quickly, he found that the Atlantic staff could get along without his meddling in every-day decisions. Wexler recalled, "The kids had taken over."

For its twenty-fifth-anniversary convention, Atlantic convened with WEA at Le Meridien Hotel in Paris, did a solid ten minutes of business, then headed off for lunch at Lasserre. Joel Friedman handed twenty dollars to a streetsweeper, bought his beret, and wore it for the rest of the convention. WCI, pleased with its profits, closed its eyes to excessive truffling. (The only directive from WCI that I ever got in this era was to "fly Air India." WCI had money tied up in India that it could use only through trade. I tried Air India once but got nervous when I realized that its pilots believed in reincarnation.)

By the early 1970s, all my fellow executives at Warner Bros. Records lived in Encino, a-bit-better-than-middle-class ramble of houses all running about forty thousand dollars. I think there was an Encino city ordinance that all dining-room lighting fixtures had to hang from the ceiling on swooped brass chains.

Joe Smith was the first to escape the Encino homes-three-blocks-from-the-deli category. The Smiths—well-raised wife, Donnie, and two outgoing children—moved across the low but chisel-topped Santa Monica Mountains, over into another world called Beverly Hills, where, perhaps through a different city ordinance, chandeliers never could come from Sears. Their new house—once home of the bug-eyed singer comedian Eddie Cantor—stood impressively on North Roxbury Drive. Helluva lawn. The place cost the Smiths the amazing amount of a quarter million dollars, which came up in conversation more than you'd think.

At Smith's mighty home, following the Parisian outing, the WEA group's three record labels (and even I, at times) convened with two from Corporate: Ross and Ashley. I recall vividly one such meeting to "iron out differences." This Tuesday morning, the executives moved easily up Joe's long redbrick driveway, lawn to the left, Englishy-looking two-story manse ahead. The front yard had mature trees whose branches arched and drooped with grace, as if Smith's gardener were Vidal Sassoon. Inside the house, the woodness of paneling, the deepness of carpeting, the fullness of furnishings felt specially chosen, as if the rule had been "Thou shalt not import one stick from Encino." Joe, ebullient as a kid in his first tree house, conducted mini-tours, showing even his "wine attic," where his new hoard of bottles got stored, uniquely reached by a pull-down stairway above the master bedroom.

In the dining room, Donnie Smith had laid food, ready for any meeting break. These were no doughnuts and coffee. She began with a salmon centerpiece, red-pink and moist. In the school that surrounded the superstar salmon reposed all things and more we execs might want, from lime wedges to designer pretzels.

In the living room, our tribe of record and business moguls chatted the latest gossip, waiting for the last to arrive, who would be, by nature and need, Ahmet. Ertegun, the one in any room most likely to have professionally buffed fingernails, was driven places by his Los Angeles driver, the safely unmerged Tony. Eventually, Ahmet entered, apologizing briefly for his tardiness, enough to make sure you heard it but not enough to make you feel he was *really* sorry. He wore made-exclusively-to-his-feet black-velvet slippers from one of those London shops on Jermyn Street, the kind that had a crest over its front door ("Exclusive to Her Majesty and Ahmet"). His slippers, too, had crests with letters in them. Much of the day, I squinted to read the slippers' letters, but I knew that getting down on my knees to stare at them was wrong; I'll just believe those gold letters read AE.

Once seated, men demoed brotherhood with slaps on one another's knees. Banter abounded. Spritzing was easy, until David Geffen began to lean too heavily on his spritz-spigot. Geffen the Lad wore sneakers without crests. He started after Jerry Wexler, digging in a bit heavily about his recent Dylan-signing victory.

His banter turned edgy. Wexler held back, but Geffen *rubbed* it in, like a prosecuting attorney. He said he figured that Wexler lost the Dylan race because he ran out of steam in the home stretch. Chuckles. Wexler saw no humor. Geffen zinged about "Atlantic's Old World attitude," and Jerry lost it. His face red, neck veins near popping, he yelled, "David, why don't you just shut up? You don't know a thing about music. You're nothing but an *agent*! You'd stick your head in a bucket of pus to come up with a nickel in your teeth."

I glanced up from Ahmet's slippers. The gathering had stopped cold, with several quarter-second peeks over at once-an-agent Ted Ashley, who pressed back into his sofa cushion, contemplating Joe's coffered ceiling.

Ross, ever the enabling good dad, shrunk from this conflict and excused himself from the room. Ahmet looked amused, but if it came down to choosing between Wexler and Geffen, both men he'd had a hand in nurturing, he'd remain impartial.

Joe Smith, ever the raconteur, quickly changed the subject, pointing through his leaded windows to the tennis court across the street, identifying it as "Rosemary and Jose's house, Clooney and Ferrer, and they like us to use their court anytime."

In the uncomfortable mood of the room, Geffen, a disciple of est (self-interest) therapy, who personalized nothing, who exuded innocence—after all, this *is* just business, right?—moved seamlessly ahead. A bathroom break seemed in order. Outside the room, but within earshot, Donnie fretted how all this might affect her salmon mousse.

During the break, I felt puzzled by the change in the room. What was different, my feelers wondered? Was it David, who seemed to bring an odd attitude toward what we did, who seemed to care less for the boogie and more for the cash? So soon, a new generation of record label heads, just when I . . . ?

Or was I being a child again, thinking that rich wall coverings and wine attics just happened to us when we were good at our jobs, and that when *we* dived in, we didn't have to concentrate on the nickel?

Here I sat, sunk into Joe and Donnie's fat new furniture. For me, it felt great, felt Big Time, Big League. Maybe I should have known better.

Nothing more got said about the Geffen-Wexler exchange.[78]

After the pee break, no one observed that, with his Dylan-signing methods, David Geffen had changed the way record deals worked. Once it had been a company-vs.-artist imbalance. Instead, Geffen had pushed *for* the artist. He'd taken the artist's side at a time when artists were demanding artistic control. David evangelized that record companies (like his own) were to *serve* their artists. The agenda of artist courtship in the record business (if not the actual who-gets-how-much-money division) had shifted. Artists became, in appearance at least, kings, queens, tyrants, though (so far) very little the richer for it.[79]

The rest of the day's agenda flowed in spirit. As the Bob Dylan fight proved, our three labels were stumbling over one another, bidding artist prices up among ourselves.

The meeting came up with a rule about which label gets to sign the artists. It would be "the man who got to the artist first." That rule eventually would not work either. It led to Smith's observation: "It was what I called Atlantic's 'The Girl in England' approach. Atlantic would always say, 'I

---

[78]Jerry Wexler, who sometimes refers to himself as a "Wandering Jew," years later produced Bob Dylan's album *Slow Train Coming,* the first of Dylan's "Jesus Era" albums during his conversion to Christianity. Wexler became converted to Dylan but not to Christianity, nor to any religion, for that matter.

[79]Geffen later grew to believe that it was *all* about money. "Most of the artists were trying to make a living, trying to get laid, trying to figure out who they were," he recalled. "They weren't trying to change the world. That's what other people put on them. I knew all those people. I knew them all, intimately and well. Bob Dylan. I would say that Bob Dylan is as interested in money as any person I've known in my life. That's just the truth."

once met this girl in England. She later got married and had a son. That son . . . is the head of this group we're both after.' "

Later, the men moved toward the Smith dinner table, elegantly displayed for them, candles now lit. Dylan was just history now—hell, he was whole *hours* ago, all of it swept under the wall-to-wall carpet.

Only later did I realize that this day had been spent with no talk about music. Of the executives in that room, only one still spent time in studios producing music, and that day he, Jerry Wexler, had felt the least comfortable. Among these men of purpose, opportunity and spritzing, only Jerry Wexler had, for the moment, lost his way.[80]

By the time David's combo-company Elektra/Asylum grew one year old, its volume had grown 150 percent. Two thirds of its releases had hit the charts.

Mel Posner, now president of Elektra/Asylum Records, moved to Los Angeles, his year of bicostalism at an end. David had his world all in one place: 962 North LaCienega, where only a year before, Elektra had stood alone.

The early Seventies was a time, with Steve Ross as the good king, that his barons could still taunt and rattle one another but not slaughter. Where grown men could sit in one room, slap knees, and work things out. This time would end. Slaughters would come. But in these early years, we all knew: There would always be another artist to sign and mousse enough for all.

Significant Atlantic and Elektra Records

1972

Elektra: Bread ("Baby I'm-a Want You") • Harry Chapin ("Taxi") • Judy Collins (*Colors of the Day*) • Carly Simon ("You're So Vain")

Asylum: Jackson Browne ("Doctor My Eyes") • The Eagles (*Eagles,* including "Take It Easy," and "Witchy Woman") • Jo Jo Gunne ("Run Run Run") • Joni Mitchell (*For the Roses*)

Atlantic: Graham Nash/David Crosby • Donny Hathaway ("Where Is the Love") • Aretha Franklin ("Day Dreaming," "Rock Steady," and "Amazing Grace") • Robert John ("The Lion Sleeps Tonight") • Bette Midler ("Boogie Woogie Bugle Boy") • Spinners ("I'll Be Around" and "Could It Be I'm Falling in Love" • Stephen Stills (*Manassas*) • Yes (*Fragile* and *Close to the Edge*)

Atco: Bee Gees ("Run to Me") • Derek and the Dominos ("Layla") • Donny Hathaway

Big Tree: Lobo ("I'd Love You to Want Me")

Little David: George Carlin (*FM & AM* and *Class Clown*)

London: The Rolling Stones (*Hot Rocks*)

---

[80]Let's not get too sentimental. Jerry was in business, and he loved to sell records. He once observed, "I've made hundreds of legendary records that people talk about that didn't sell."

Signpost: Danny O'Keefe ("Good Time Charlie's Got the Blues")
Stax: The Staple Singers ("Respect Yourself")

1973

Elektra: Bread (*Best of*) • Harry Chapin (*Short Stories*) • Judy Collins (*Cook with Honey*) • Queen
Asylum: Jackson Browne (*For Everyman*) • Eagles (*Desperado*) • Linda Ronstadt (*Don't Cry Now*)

Atlantic: Billy Cobham (*Spectrum*) • Roberta Flack ("Killing Me Softly with His Song") • J. Geils Band ("Give It to Me") • Led Zeppelin (*Houses of the Holy*) • Spinners ("One of a Kind (Love Affair)") • Stephen Stills & Manassas (*Down the Road*) • Yes (*Yessongs*)
Atco: The Allman Brothers Band (*Beginnings*) • Black Oak Arkansas (*High on the Hog*) • Blue Magic ("Sideshow") • Dr. John ("Right Place Wrong Time")
Bell: Tony Orlando and Dawn ("Tie a Yellow Ribbon Round the Ole Oak Tree")
Big Tree: Brownsville Station ("Smokin' in the Boys Room")
Island: Traffic (*Shoot Out at the Fantasy Factory*)
Little David/Atlantic: George Carlin (*Occupation: Foole*)
Manticore: Emerson, Lake & Palmer (*Brain Salad Surgery*)
Rolling Stones: The Rolling Stones (*Goat's Head Soup*)
RSO: Bee Gees ("My World") • Eric Clapton and Others (*Eric Clapton's Rainbow Concert*)
Stax: The Staple Singers ("If You're Ready (Come Go with Me)")
Virgin: Mike Oldfield ("Tubular Bells")

18

COMPARED to the Kmart towns where our customers often lived, towns in which a midnight's high might be finding a taco stand open, midnight in New York was wide-open nightlife flambé. After dinner, we strolled or taxied to Manhattan's midnight-plus clubs, finding there men and women out to kill—for a kiss, a quart or snort, a couple of hours. A new generation of midnight killers had begun to dance with their backs turned to our previous love—that generation of singer/songwriters—as if they'd been just some high-school fling.

It took us time, took years, until many of us, emphatically most at Elektra and Warners, realized that there could be more to happiness than singer/songwriters. Ours had been acts who used their real names, ones we could have a fun dinner with. When they got shoved off center stage, we, too, felt displaced. We'd gone from concert halls to disco balls.

At the core of this shoving war was sex. The war's battlefield was the dance floor. Its gunmen painted their bodies silver. Its medals were standout nipples. Its infantry ranged from Rollerina, who dressed in a tutu, and with magic wand danced his nights on roller skates, to a seventy-year-old party mom we called Disco Sally, who on the dance floor loved to leap up and wrap her legs around the waist of a passing man. This war's rocket's red glare was the disco ball. Victories were celebrated in massive clubs, often behind unlisted doors.[81] Singer /songwriters had been besieged.

The discotheque's ancestor had been, way back, the juke joint. But now, instead of a Wurlitzer, a live disc jockey played records. Doormen now banned beer bellies. To get in, a certain chic about you had to be recognized. Leather helped. Looking like a peacock helped. Once inside, you danced; you danced with your head back, with your eyes nearly shut, feeling the beat

---

[81]The most interesting closed door of the disco era was Plato's Retreat, a "couples only" sex club farther uptown. There, two or more adults could screw in public. Despite all my research, I have few stats about Plato's, other than that its most-played record was Donna Summer's appropriately sized twelve-inch single, "Love to Love You, Baby."

in your bones, your bunions, your bladder. Sex was this year's mantra; disco was not about giving peace a chance, but about getting a piece by dance. Its beat pounded you in 4/4 time, the bass drum pounding out Me! Me! Me! Me! Unlike in Haight-Ashbury, here a new kind of stone freak came to dance, all night, till on the disco's walls you could touch the sweat.

Time ran an article titled "Sex Rock," which pointed out that Casablanca's Donna Summer hit, "Love to Love You, Baby," possessed "a marathon of twenty-two orgasms." The article was solid journalism, including mention that a Tallahassee preacher's "poll of North Florida high schools revealed 984 of 1,000 unmarried girls sampled had become pregnant listening to pop songs." Is it any wonder why, in a church bonfire, parishioners burned albums by the Stones and Elton John, just as in '56 they had burned Elvis and Jerry Lee?

Out west, talent manager Jerry Brandt, a friend of David Geffen's back in 1973, convinced E/A to release an album by a gorgeous young singer Brandt had in hand. Jobriath, a model of a man, was, alas, a clunk of a singer. So what? In this age of disco (Brandt had pitched Geffen), "It's gay time, and I think the world is ready for a true fairy. The only thing that's keeping us alive is sex. I'm selling sex. Sex and professionalism." The advance was $300,000 for the first album.

Jobriath's debut show took place in Illinois, at a place called the Rush Up Club. At show time, six people showed up. It fell to E/A promotion rep Burt Stein to work the street, dragging people in on the promise of a free drink, free eats. Nothing worked. Jobriath went on, performed bad music.

> JOBRIATH:
> I maman
> So I'm an elegant man
> I'm a man
> Clara Bow and open toes
> Are what I am.

For Bert Stein, Jobriath was just one more night in showbiz.

After Jobriath's first album disappeared, producer Brandt parlayed. Without asking Elektra, Brandt hired the entire London Symphony Orchestra to back Jobriath singing a song named "Scumbag." Another awful record. Brandt couldn't pay the orchestra bill. Geffen paid for the session on one condition: Brandt was never to ask Geffen for another cent.

Jobriath was thereafter promoted by a forty-three-foot Times Square billboard of him in the near-nude, followed by a $200,000 stage debut at the Paris Opera House in which Jobriath mimed inside an eight-foot Lucite cube that grew into a forty-foot phallic Empire State Building thing, Jobriath crawling up it like King Kong. In interviews, Jobriath called himself "a true fairy," becoming one of the rare openly gay rock pioneers of the Seventies. This sold no records. Jobriath just about vanished.[82]

Even without Jobriath, Geffen's Elektra in 1974 had *Billboard*'s Number One, Two, and Four top albums: Bob Dylan's *Planet Waves*, Joni Mitchell's *Court and Spark*, and Carly Simon's *Hotcakes*, all making it tough to remember the Elektra of two years earlier. Since Geffen had taken over, two out of three of Elektra's releases had hit the charts. Of course, Geffen again felt restless.

Overall, Elektra/Asylum now ranked fifth in singles, eighth in albums, eighth in combined. At its offices on La Cienega Boulevard in Los Angeles, the label built out its new second story while keeping things going down below on the street floor. Geffen looked for a way out, telling Ahmet, "Everyone else is so stupid. Let's just take over everything: films, music, the lot." He may have meant it. David, who, in the opinion of Jac Holzman, "could outsmart and outscream even Ahmet," was once more on the move.

Signaling that Joni Mitchell's 1972 defection to Asylum Records was not being blamed on those "90% Virgin" ads I'd earlier run about her, Mo Ostin and Joe Smith promoted me to WBR's Number Three spot: senior vice president, adding more administration to my fave folly, Creative Services.

It quickly became clear to me what the real duties of a senior VP were when I got a call from Neil Young's office. There'd arisen this certain knowledge within California's after less-scientific hippie community that, during the upcoming weekend, the state's San Andreas Fault would spasm once again, plopping western California (including Beverly Hills, Burbank, and Neil) into the Pacific Ocean. Neil was, he said, very scared. As senior VP, my job was not to laugh. Neil wanted to ride out the quake, but he would feel most comfortable if, over the weekend, he could park and stay in his trailer (its inside a marvel of ornately carved filigree redwood) on the movie lot's Western Street, the very street on which Clint Eastwood and the Maverick brothers had shot it out. "I'll get right on it, Neil," I replied.

This involved a call to the studio police. "No way," they answered, explaining that Neil would fall into the category of property hazard. My second call was up the ladder to the studio production manager. "No way," he answered, claiming with all the insight of a DMV clerk that a lack of toilets on Western Street violated OSHA rules. My third call was to Frank Wells, who administered the whole damn studio. "Frank," I said, "we have a contract with Neil Young, who brings to Warner Bros. Records maybe thirty

---

[82]He used several other names (Jobriath Boone, a.k.a. Bruce Wayne Campbell). Born in 1939, he'd been part of the Aquarius Theatre Tribe, and failed through his record career. He died of AIDS in July 1983, while living in a pyramid cottage atop New York's Chelsea Hotel, alone and forgotten.

million dollars in sales a year. I permit no questions to follow what I'm about to say. I need Neil Young in his trailer on the back lot, Western Street, this weekend. Will you do it?" Frank got my point. I called Neil back with the directions. This, I later saw, was what senior vice presidents do.

In 1975, even without earthquake damage, Warner Bros. Records had finally fled its old machine shop at 3701 Warner Boulevard. It had served us poorly for seventeen years, but we'd overwhelmed it. Our new redwood-and-glass home was ready at 3300 Warner Boulevard, on the corner of the Burbank Studios lot where once had been the studio's "jungle." For our move, we'd issued an instruction sheet on new building standards. These instructions struck at least one of us, our newly promoted promotion head, Russ Thyret, as overly rigid. The morning of move in, Thyret showed up in the lobby dressed for a formal party—tie, black shoes and socks, tux jacket, boutonniere, no pants.

The signings of Ostin and Smith had found the heart of the market (or perhaps the heart of the market had found them). One signing that Joe came up with we found most odd: very "old-fashioned," we told him. He took a poll of the executives. The score was 9 to 1 against. Smith signed the Four Seasons anyway and had some hits. I grew to like this trait in Joe. He believed in freedom of singing. Years earlier, he'd gone against our liberal culture by signing a pro-Vietnam singer, Johnny Sea, and got "Day for Decision," another hit. When we protested, Smith simply asked, "Don't you believe in freedom of speech?"

Mo Ostin reached back for another hit provider, to the gent who'd started Loma Records for us in the early Sixties, stylish Bob Krasnow. Krasnow and Loma had parted, with Bob heading off to join friends at the start-up of a new label, Kama Sutra–Buddah. These friends turned out to be, in Krasnow's words, "your worst nightmare": Artie Ripp (whom Krasnow referred to as "the Jew the rest of us take the rap for") and Neil Bogart. Kama Sutra–Buddah, despite having the Lovin' Spoonful, lasted only a few months.

By 1973, Krasnow was running his own label, Blue Thumb Records, then selling it to Gulf&Western. He was now well off and afloat in Brentwood, indulging himself (a Krasnow art form) in a home with a professional kitchen, stoves capable of incinerating eyebrows.

Bob thought he was rich. Mo kept tugging at him: "You're too young; you gotta go back to work." Luring him, Ostin promised, "It won't be like you're working for anybody. We'll give you an exotic title." Ostin and Krasnow settled on "Executive Without Portfolio." "You can do whatever you want to do, *and* you'll share in whatever you bring in," Ostin offered.

Krasnow drove his red Jaguar into WBR Career Two on January 2, 1975, and started power signing, based on a vast set of relationships he'd built, whether or not the artists were contractually free. Krasnow's artists were black but hardly old-school R&B: Chaka Khan, Bootsy Collins, George Benson,[83] and George Clinton's Funkadelic.[84] It had been Clinton, I felt, who had most clearly discriminated between old R&B and the newer rock. "In rock," he'd said, "the singer gets the pussy."

Krasnow ran by his own loose rules. In my days as senior VP at the label, the nearest I ever came to an out-of-body experience was signing off on Bob's expense accounts, including one where he'd hired a limo to go pick up a Mont Blanc pen at a jeweler's. We took in stride Bob's remarkably corrosive critiques about everything we did, from stupid artist signings to sub-MOMA album covers. We knew a Krasnow deeply dedicated to the best: in music, food, furniture, and pens. To that list of bests, I was able to add jewelry. For my birthday, I'd skipped over the clunk-heavy watches like Rolexes in favor of a smartly designed Parisian watch from Hermès. With pride, I showed it to Krasnow, who looked it over and pronounced it a good "starter watch." I complimented him on his diamond stud earring.[85]

It was not all neo-black at Warners. Ostin made his own retro-white deal with Mike Curb. With the Bellamy Brothers, Shaun Cassidy, and Debby Boone, Curb lit up Warner's singles life as never before. He produced hits. When we called an "appreciation" lunch for Debby Boone, she was escorted by her father, Pat, who was seated next to me. As an opener, I told him he must be very proud of his daughter today. "Which one?" he asked back. I didn't know how to take that.

Curb, politics aside, was our right-wing hit finder, specializing, like Jim Conkling, it turned out, in Mormon hitmakers, singers without facial hair,

---

[83]George Benson was signed by Bob Krasnow as a pop artist while Benson was still under contract, recording jazz for another label, owned by Creed Taylor. Benson, however, wanted to be a singer; no one else thought that a hot idea. Krasnow met up with Benson while he was playing in Chicago. Krasnow began his hip bribe. The hotel had a Gucci shop. Benson and Krasnow stopped by, Krasnow with unsigned deal in hand. "George, that coat looks great on you. Sign here. And I'll make you a big star. And you can sing, too. And the coat looks great."

Little was said about the other recording contract. Benson signed, got the coat, and sang "Masquerade."

[84]A man of many bands, singer/producer Clinton not only supplied his bassist, Bootsy, to the world but ran other variations on his forty-member Parliament/Funkadelic Thing, a corporation that also gave us the Brides of Funkenstein and Horny Horns.

[85]One of my jobs was to make up the agenda for our annual, prebudget meetings at the Mauna Kea Hotel. Mo remembered fondly one of my items having to do with how to stop Krasnow and his "naughty, naughty ways." (Krasnow would not stay, for instance, with us at the Mauna Kea, which was not good enough for him; he flew in for each day's meeting from the Kahala Hilton.) For all of this, Krasnow was of great value to Mo and us, and Mo knew talent when it worked.

thin kids who caused shivers on teen-magazine covers sold in towns with feed-and-seed stores. Their fans bought their records. Curb had then (and has had for the decades since) an ear for hits, either country or middle of the road. (Boone's "You Light up My Life" was 1977's Number One song). With Curb handling that, we could boogie with Bootsy all night, which we did.[86]

This wide range of releases, from Bootsy to Debby, challenged the company. Our core of workers arrived, some as early as 9:00 a.m., to get these records exposed in new ways. Send promo copies to Christian radio? Seems a natural. Linda York, a young, blonde, lean, smart lady, worked in WBR's Artist Relations. Her phone rang.

"This is Mick Fleetwood."

"This is Linda. May I help you with something?"

"We've decided we want a billboard on the Strip. How fast can we get one up?"

"Your album's been out four months already."

"Yeah, I know. But we'd still like the billboard."

"It takes months to put one of those up," Linda told him. "There's the art, they have to be hand-painted, and they cost five thousand dollars and the only people who see them are driving home to Beverly Hills and probably get their records free anyway."

"Well, we'd really like the board."

"Look," Linda said, "the single is starting to get some action. Why don't we take the five thousand dollars and put it into secondary radio? Call me back in a week and we'll see where we stand." Linda York spent five thousand dollars on secondary radio ads. She just winged it, nervously.

One week passed. Linda read an industry trade, *Radio and Records.* Fleetwood Mac's "Over My Head" was listed all over the sheet as "Pick of the Week." Her phone rerang. It was Mick Fleetwood.

"I think I'm in West Virginia, Linda. That's right, isn't it? There is a place called West Virginia?"

"You're all over the fucking radio, Mick!" Linda screamed in her phone. "*All* over the fucking radio! On your next album, you won't even have to *ask* for a billboard!"

Coming next was *Rumours*. Thirteen times Platinum. Thank you, Linda. It is more important to remember Linda than to tell more record-business stories about throwing up in the backseat of Vic Faraci's Lincoln Continental.[87]

---

[86]Soon after his successful singles at WBR, Curb ran for and, to our astonishment, won the post of lieutenant governor of California. That shocking interlude lasted four years, and then Curb got down to business again.

[87]Faraci had moved his car with him when he left Chicago, where, Vic said, you had to have *big* cars since you might have "unexpected visitors" occupying the backseat from time to time.

By 1977, Atlantic Records was drifting some. Stigwood, having set up his own label, RSO, for real, was no longer in need of Atlantic/WEA. In fact, Stigwood was on the phone from his suite in Paris's Plaza-Athénée, negotiating with Mick Jagger (who was registered at Paris's Hotel Georges V as "Mercedes Benz") to sign the Rolling Stones. Jagger would write down Stigwood's offers, then relay them out to Beverly Hills, where the Stones' business manager, the stuffy Prince Rupert Lowenstein, leveraged up Stiggy's offers to squeeze more and more out of Ahmet, also out in 90210. Finally, Stigwood gave up and sent Ahmet a bottle of Louis Roederer champagne. But RSO and its disco successes had moved on.[88]

"We had cooled off," said Atlantic promotion head Dick Klinc in 1975. "For the past year and a half, every project we started, from Night Crawler to you name it, everything turned to shit. There was nothing that Ahmet had signed or Greenberg had signed that had materialized into anything substantial. By then, Atlantic was quite a huge company . . . over two hundred employees."

Jerry Wexler knew syncopation when he felt it. Inside Atlantic, he could no longer feel it. He'd made a reasonable deal for the Jacksons, the source of the then-younger, Afro-haired Michael Jackson: $1 million for five years and, for the group, a decent royalty (the Jacksons' Motown royalty had been 2.7 percent). On Shelly Vogel's desk, Wexler's deal just sat, unsigned. Wexler felt second-guessed by "the kids" running around. "I just didn't fit into the company. Everything had changed. My apparatchiks had gone elsewhere."

He approached Ahmet, complaining about Atlantic's new *three*-man decision group (Ahmet, Jerry, and newly made president Jerry Greenberg). The three were to be the decision makers, working as a troika. When Jerry asked Ahmet how the company felt about him, Ahmet's answer to his two-decades colleague was blunt: "Ahmet informed me that I was viewed as abrasive, derisive, and cynical, a maverick at meetings, a flaunter of my quick sales of option stock, an undiplomatic critic." Wexler conceded his own discomfort at being someone's subordinate, dues paid when one gives up ownership for money. When you're an employee.

It had been twenty-two years, but now even Ahmet saw Wexler working only with artists *he* liked, in a world where Ahmet was dealing with managers, lawyers, and acts of retail value. Jerry couldn't get used to a company that he did not run, a label whose priorities were set by others, including consumers. After all the turmoil, the pain, the Bob Dylan, the Willie Nelson, R&B forgotten, his inability to regain command, Jerry Wexler knew the conclusion: Retire from Atlantic. Forever and ever.

---

[88]No sad songs need be sung for Stigwood. He rode "Disco Duck" to "Saturday Night Fever" and became, in the late 1970s, the man who owned not only disco in Hollywood but selected Caribbean islands as well.

Wexler approached Sheldon Vogel about finding some way that he could *really* retire. WCI worked out the deal. Jerry quit Atlantic, dividing his life between two homes, East Hampton and Florida, concluding, "I'm left with a ballroom full of ghosts."

Ahmet, observing his longtime colleague, the man who partnered with him to success, the man at the other desk in the single office back in the Fifties, Ahmet watched Wexler go, understood the sadness, and understood that "the music to which he gave his life [was] no longer important . . . It is a mistake to invest the music we recorded with too much importance . . . It isn't classical music, and it cannot be interpreted in the same way. It's more like the old Fred Astaire moves: They're fun, but they're not great art. And they shouldn't be seen as great art."

In 1975, combined as one entry, Elektra/Asylum got respect in *Billboard*'s chart analysis.

Atlantic (74)	5.4%
Warner Bros. (64)	5.3
Elektra/Asylum (54)	4.6

Even at a heady 4.6 percent, David Geffen had decided now, completely, and once and for all, to leave Elektra/Asylum Records. He flew to Steve Ross's Long Island home, East Hampton, and resigned. Ross would not accept the resignation. David gave Steve one of his challenging shrugs. "Well, in that case, I'm going to leave the job." David wanted to make movies now, working with Ted Ashley at the studio. He summed up his view of the new Elektra, after a year or so with him in charge: "I built it into a very, very profitable, successful record company, which, by the time I left, had the highest net profit of any record company in the world and the largest amount of successes per release of any company in the history of the record business." Immodest, but probably close to true.

With Geffen half out the door, WCI's Record Group leaders convened with Ross to figure out "what next?" Ahmet revived the merger possibility: Atlantic would take over Elektra and Asylum. Mo made another point clear to Ross: The tri-label WEA structure should stay in place. Big Elektra might absorb little Asylum—that was fine; but Atlantic should not absorb it all—that was not fine.

Joe Smith, part of Steve's "what next?" committee, recalled, "We went through the list of candidates to replace Geffen—and I sat in on those meetings—and we couldn't come up with anybody." The short list came down to one: Joe Smith.

"Mo and I had it worked out very well, but maybe he really wanted to try it on *his* own, totally. And maybe I wanted to try it. We never expressed that. If the Elektra thing never came along, I'd have been absolutely as happy . . . The logical thing was to go where we had a duality of leadership, neither one of us having to relocate."

In December 1975, Joe Smith became chairman of Elektra/Asylum. His office in Burbank was left vacant as Mo took over both titles: chairman of the board and president, a situation at first attributed to the abruptness of Smith's exit. "The general idea [was] that my work area," Joe said, "which mainly dealt with artists and custom labels, will be divided among the Warner vice presidents . . . It would be physically impossible for Mo, or anybody else, to carry both his full workload and mine."

At transfers of power, comments get made. Geffen had looked at the Elektra he'd taken over and used words like "shambles." Less easy, now, for Smith, taking over from full-steam-ahead Geffen, but Joe still had improvement on *his* lips: "The blackest artist we had at Elektra was Joni Mitchell." Succinctly, that's the style difference between Geffen and Smith. Both could be blunt. Joe had learned delightfully stone-blunt humor, as blunt as David's but with such a sense of "over the top" that you loved Joe, cringed at David, but were impressed by both.

Joe Smith knew one thing foremost: Elektra had to reach out. Topping Joe's shopping list were black music and country music.

The first half of the 1970s had seen the king-and-barons structure firm up throughout WEA. Perhaps it began with Ross, who first had bypassed Alan Cohen, who wanted more clout up top at WCI in favor of Steve's "office of the president" grouping. With Wexler retired, Atlantic was completely king'd by Ahmet. At Elektra, Joe had become the one and only. At Warner Bros. Records, with Joe gone, Mo let Joe's office stand vacant for months thereafter. He'd named me his executive vice president, but I was no threat, to put it mildly.[89]

For the first time the Annual Report–writers effused over WCI's music execs with paragraph openers like "The glitter of all that gold drives music executives to wear dark glasses"—Thelma Walker's Tally for 1975 showed an all-time high: Warner 55 + Atlantic 36 + Elektra/Asylum 13 = WEA 104. Elektra Asylum had made it into *Billboard*'s list of Top Ten album companies. And the *Guiness Book of Records* decided which was The World's Loudest Band: Deep Purple.

---

[89]As executive vice president, I thought I should put somebody in the role of Creative Services, while I exec-VP-d. We lucked out by getting the Beatles' publicist, urbane, witty, totally charming, and (when it came to getting much done) utterly unstructured Derek Taylor.

Significant Releases
1974

Atlantic: Abba ("Waterloo") • Average White Band ("Pick Up the Pieces") • Billy Cobham (*Crosswind* and *Total Eclipse*) • Crosby, Stills & Nash ("So Far") • Aretha Franklin ("Until You Come Back to Me") • J. Geils Band ("Must of Got Lost") • Daryl Hall & John Oates ("She's Gone") • Richard Harris ("The Prophet by Kahlil Gibran") • Herbie Mann ("Hijack") • Graham Nash (*Wild Tales*) • Spinners ("Mighty Love," "New and Improved" and (with Dionne Warwicke) "Then Came You") • Yes (*Tales from Topographic Oceans* and *Relayers*)
Atco: Genesis ("The Lamb Lies Down on Broadway")
Manticore: Emerson, Lake & Palmer (*Welcome Back . . .*)
Rolling Stone: The Rolling Stones (*It's Only Rock 'n' Roll*)
RSO: Eric Clapton (*461 Ocean Boulevard,* including "I Shot the Sheriff")
Swan Song: Bad Company ("Can't Get Enough")

Elektra: Harry Chapin ("Cat's in the Cradle") • Queen (*Sheer Heart Attack*) • Carly Simon (*Hotcakes,* including "Mockingbird" (with James Taylor))
Asylum: Jackson Browne (*Late for the Sky*) • Bob Dylan (*Planet Waves* and *Before the Flood*) • Eagles ("Best of My Love") • Joni Mitchell (*Court and Spark,* including "Help Me") • Traffic (*When the Eagle Flies*)
Nonesuch: Piano Rags by Scott Joplin, performed by Joshua Rifkin

Warner Bros.: America (*Holiday,* including "Lonely People" and "Tin Man") • Black Sabbath (*Sabbath Bloody Sabbath*) • Alice Cooper (*Greatest Hits*) • Deep Purple (*Burn* and *Stormbringer*) • The Doobie Brothers (*What Were Once Vices Are Now Habits,* including "Black Water") • Little Feat (*Feats Don't Fail Me Now*) • Van Morrison (*Veedon Fleece* and *It's Too Late to Stop Now*) • Seals & Crofts ("Unborn Child") • James Taylor (*Walking Man*) • Tower of Power (*Back to Oakland*) • Jesse Colin Young (*Light Shine*)
Reprise: Gordon Lightfoot (*Sundown,* including "Carefree Highway") • Maria Muldaur (*Waitress in the Donut Shop,* including "I'm a Woman") • Randy Newman (*Good Old Boys*) • Neil Young (*On the Beach*)
Bearsville: Foghat (*Energized*)
Brother: The Beach Boys (*Wild Honey & 20/20*)
Capricorn: Dickie Betts (*Highway Call*)
Casablanca: Kiss (*Kiss* and *Hotter than Nell*)
Chrysalis: Jethro Tull (*War Child*) • Robin Trower (*Bridge of Sighs*)
Little David: George Carlin (*Toledo Window Box*)

1975

Atlantic: ABBA ("I Do, I Do, I Do, I Do, I Do" and "SOS") • Average White Band (*Cut the Cake,* including "Pick Up the Places") • The Jimmy Castor Bunch ("The Bertha Butt Boogie—Part 1") • Alice Cooper (*Welcome to My Nightmare* including "Only Women") • Roberta Flack ("Feel Like Makin' Love") • Ben E. King ("Supernatural Thing—Part 1") • Herbie Mann ("Hijack") • Spinners ("They Just Can't Stop It (Games People Play)") • Yes (*Yesterdays*)
Atco: The Rolling Stones ("Metamorphosis") • Roxy Music (*Siren*)
Big Tree: Hot Chocolate ("Emma" and "You Sexy Thing")
RSO: Bee Gees ("Main Course") • Eric Clapton ("There's One in Every Crowd" and "E.C. Was Here")

Rolling Stone: Rolling Stones (*Made in the Shade*)
Swan Song: Bad Company (*Straight Shooter,* including "Feel Like Makin' Love") •
Led Zeppelin (*Physical Graffiti*)

Elektra: Judy Collins (*Judith,* including "Send in the Clowns") • Tony Orlando and
Dawn ("He Don't Love You") • Queen (*A Night at the Opera,* including "Bohemian
Rhapsody") • Carly Simon (*Playing Possum*)
Asylum: Eagles ("One of These Nights") • Joni Mitchell (*The Hissing of Summer
Lawns*) • Orleans ("Dance with Me") • Linda Ronstadt (*Prisoner in Disguise,* includ-
ing "Heat Wave")

Warner Bros.: America (*History* and *Hearts,* including "Sister Golden Hair") • Deep
Purple (*Come Taste the Band*) • The Four Seasons ("December, 1963 (Oh, What a
Night)") • Bonnie Raitt (*Streetlights*) • Rod Stewart (*Atlantic Crossing*) • James Tay-
lor (*Gorilla,* including "How Sweet It Is (to Be Loved by You)") • Gary Wright (*The
Dream Weaver*) • Jesse Colin Young (*Songbird*)
Reprise: Fleetwood Mac ("Over My Head," "Rhiannon," and "Say You Love Me") •
Neil Young (*Tonight's the Night*)
Bearsville: Foghat (*Fool for the City,* including "Slow Ride")
Brother: The Beach Boys (*Spirit of America*)
Capricorn: The Allman Brothers Band (*Win, Lose or Draw*) • The Marshall Tucker
Band (*Searchin' for a Rainbow*)
Chrysalis: Jethro Tull (*Minstrel in the Gallery*) • Robin Trower (*For Earth Below*)
Curtom: The Staple Singers ("Let's Do It Again")
DiscReet: Captain Beefheart (*Bongo Fury*)

19

BEFORE Atlantic's 1975 budget presentation for Corporate, the label's financial boss, Shelly Vogel, felt as good as it gets, at least for financial guys. Walking into the twenty-ninth-floor boardroom, Vogel had it down: Atlantic showed great profits for the year, plus hits in the oven for a repeat in 1976.

Three hours later, Vogel walked to the elevator, muttering, "It's like, if this year I walk in with a thirteen-inch dick, twelve months later they expect me to show up with a fourteen."

WCI's bosses constantly fixated on what they called "double-digit growth." "Double-digit" meant next year do at least 10 percent better, since 9 percent or under, having only a single digit, does not impress Wall Street. To wage this double-digit campaign on the stock market, Corporate had impressive ground troops: three hot labels plus music publishing, WEA distribution, and WEA International profit centers. We felt fit for battle.

I have told my sons all too little about how to live life. One line that I have said to Chris and Thomas is this: When, maybe once or twice a year, you realize just how good this moment is, how amazing this day feels to you, and how you today are so better off than many others, sons, memorize that moment, capture that day, close your eyes and impress that realization in deeply. Because that feeling, that smiling moment, is bound to fade, maybe sooner than you think, then drop away like pirates off a plank.

We in the Warner music area had no idea when and where the plank we walked would end. We gave it no thought. Who says it's not an endless highway we're on? It was difficult not to just keep walking—to accept our blessings, our profits, our Number Ones in platinum, as deserved.

WCI's part of the record market jumped, like a frog on steroids, higher and higher. Ross lent us his jet. We dined at restaurants where the menus were big as doors. Our business life got like one of those supermarket shows on TV, where contestants have two minutes to load their shopping carts with tons of truffles. Surely it was our duty to exploit this market that clearly loved us like we were gods of the New World. All modesty aside, our dicks just kept growing.

In WCI's every-October budget meetings, David Horowitz's watch-'em areas were two: WCI's interests in cable and records. The soft-spoken Horowitz phrased slow questions, avoiding giving us dictation. He carried no big stick. I remember Mo once cautioning me for inviting Horowitz to sit in on one of my meetings at WBR. Mo liked turf limits. Horowitz, no matter how benign, was a "them," not an "us." To his credit, David handled well the frustration that came with being in the office of the president yet not being able to behave presidentially. Of all the division barons he dealt with, Horowitz said he felt closest to the feisty, energetic Joel Friedman and to Joel's branch execs, street guys like Philadelphia's Pete Stocke.

The Teamsters never gave up. Finally, they won an election. To sign a contract, branch manager Stocke and WCI's wry, a-lot-to-hug lawyer Norm Samnick, met three Local guys with no necks and waxed-back hair in a New Jersey motel. The union reps were led by a Teamster heavy named Charles Cimino. He opened the meeting by holding up a poster that Stocke had had printed for election day. The poster read, "Don't vote for the union because it's run by thugs and crooks like Charles Cimino." Cimino asked, "One of you's Pete Stocke?" Samnick quickly pointed out his partner across the room. From across the table, Cimino slowly leveled his forefinger at Stocke's head. Samnick fast-changed the subject to WCI's contract with the union. A second Teamster asked about a phrase on page seventeen: "force majeur." Samnick explained that meant "act of God." The Union fella demanded, "Take out that word. This is an American contract, and we only want English words in it." For reasons difficult to explain, Stocke survived the motel meeting.

Such realities, however, seldom rose to the top of the Office of the President, where David's main job was to watch for icebergs. Horowitz, too, stared in awe as the record industry, led by WEA, was exploding. That Christmas, record retailer Sam Goody ordered $1 million worth of albums from WEA, then astonished the industry with a seven-consecutive-pages ad spread in the *New York Times*. The RIAA decided that gold records (for $1 million in sales) were as common as pizza coupons and came up with the platinum record (for one million *units*). The Eagles' *Their Greatest Hits 1971–1975* crossed this new platinum line first, on February 24, 1976. Eagle Glenn Frey recalled, "In some ways, success took a lot of the fun out of it. Putting pressure on ourselves also took a lot of the fun out of it. I think Henley took some of the fun out of it for me, and I'm sure I took some of the fun out of it for him. Looking back, I think the band lasted a couple of more years than I thought it would." Even fun was now measured by platinum standards.

In 1976, WEA scored forty-four gold albums and eleven platinum albums (versus CBS's thirty-two and eight). That left only one stat that annoyed us: CBS got three platinum singles, while WEA got zero. For almost ten seconds, that really hurt.

At Atlantic, selling singles had never left the consciousness; they'd built their R&B business on it. But 180 degrees away, in total contrast, was Elektra, which for decades had believed that singles were toys for tots. To get a stronger hand in singles, Joe Smith, just moved to Elektra, reenacted his own career path by moving Elektra's promotion head, Steve Wax, up to exec VP. At Warner, gold singles between 1967 and 1975 had made a skimpy list: only twelve in nine years. Russ Thyret moved over from sales to promotion, packing his leadership dynamic with him. He restaffed and inspired confidence.

I saw the New Vigor while sitting in a promotion meeting along with Thyret's group. We were waiting for one of Russ's new guys, Dave Urso, who was on the phone getting close to a major add on a record with some radio PD. Thyret sent his assistant, Carol Hart, to tell Urso, "Russ is holding up the meeting for you." Dave told her, "I'm getting the record added. Tell Russ to wait." Minutes later, Carol came back to Urso's office a second time, saying, "Russ is getting very pissed." Same answer from Urso; he was *really* working this guy on the phone. Three minutes passed. Thyret walked into Urso's office with a pair of scissors, cut Urso's phone line in two and, just to make sure, took Urso's phone back with him into the meeting.

A lack of platinum singles hardly entered WEA's minds. WEA was five years old. To celebrate, Joel Friedman's crew ordered a cake the size of a yak. At one that afternoon, Friedman worked the entire office, remembering everyone's name. Behind Friedman trailed white-gloved waiters carrying trays of champagne and desserts. Accountants put aside their Bob Cratchitt-size ledgers. Friedman's top execs chipped in for a gift for Joel, so often the butt of their jokes about being out of shape: an Exercycle. Friedman, excited by the toy, took it home to Encino and had it set up on his back porch.

In this five years, WEA proudly announced, its seven hundred employees across America had sold over $1 billion worth of records. The '76 album charts recap showed each label's percent of all listings for the year.

WEA (307 albums)	24.2%
CBS (194)	16.1
Capitol (117)	8.3
RCA (101)	7.5
A&M (80)	7.0

Columbia Records glowered in second place. Their story to would-be artists became "You'll get lost inside WEA."

In interviews, we got defensive over our success. I certainly did, telling

Billboard: "Those of us who have been with this company a long time pre-fer to think of ourselves as the innovators who shook up the industry by signing Tiny Tim or the Fugs. If we can still get a Hot 100 single in 1976 with something as off-the-wall as 'Popsicle Toes' by Michael Franks, or sell more than sixty thousand units of the first album by an offbeat neo-folkie like Leon Redbone, then we don't have to feel like we're the Board of Gen-eral Motors around here yet."

This string of fortune—to be growing fastest inside of America's fastest-growing pleasure, records—led to acting as if we were infallible. We grabbed every hot artist we could reach. The whole industry grabbed. The mid-Seventies saw "signing fever." But unlike the old days, when we'd found Tiny Tim in a cellar club, now our staff signers had little time for cel-lar hopping. Instead, we dealt secondhand, working with "ears" guys, with managers, and mini-labels that had the time to stay up late.

During 1976, the three major labels—CBS, WEA, and Capitol—signed more than 200 new artists. Seventy of those 200 were established acts, just switching labels, while 130 were newcomers. CBS led, signing eighty new acts in the year. WEA signed 56 artists—from Firefall and Warren Zevon to where-are-they-nows Jelly and Impact—each act intent on making it, each thinking, "Hey, now I'm with WEA! Big Button, here we *go!*" Looking at it from the other side, Big Button labels were expected to break 56 artists, break a new one faster than once a week.

Absent from those 56 was the latest scurvy force to challenge American music: punk rock.

Feeling like the Thomas Paine of punk, New Yorker-to-a-fault Seymour Stein was the head of and whole staff of Sire Records, a label almost invisi-bly distributed by ABC Records. Stein loved records more than music and music more than sleep. At punk rock, Stein's eyes bulged forth. He stam-mered, his speech unable to keep up with his fervor. Men like Stein are te-dious to deal with but great at hearing records.

Seymour had started as a thirteen-year-old gofer at *Billboard* for editor Paul Ackerman and charts handler Tommy Noonan. He could tell wondrous stories about two of the earlier days' scroungiest, Scroogiest labels. First, he'd worked for Syd Nathan at King Records, a man who dealt with his fists, trusted no one, and managed, somehow, to thrive in Cincinnati. Second, Seymour had talent-scouted for Leiber and Stoller at George Goldner's Red Bird Records, a gig Seymour would slyly call "a further learning experience."[90] He and pro-ducer Richard Gottehrer had been introduced by a lady named Roberta Gold-

---

[90]Goldner was beholden to Morris Levy, a shadow power in the record business, who had on his wall a needlepoint that read, "Yea, though I walk through the Valley of Darkness I shall fear no evil, for I am the meanest son of a bitch in the Valley."

stein, whom Seymour once described for me as "the girl who, many believe, together with her partner in crime, Melinda Rogers, was the original prototype of the modern-day groupie." The two young men founded Sire on "less than a shoestring" when Seymour was twenty-seven; its name came from the "S and E" in Seymour plus the "R and I" from Richard, and Sire meant someone who was servant to a King (Records). SE and IR scrimped to survive. One distribution deal after another. Rent was $315 a month. "Stingy" was the adjective most often hung on wheeler-dealer Stein by street record guys who made up sayings like "Seymour Stein, See Less Money."

For eleven years, Seymour Stein had eked out a living mostly by licensing Eurorock for American release. He spent hours in narrow stores that had more old wax for sale than the candle shop at Lourdes, fingering single discs, obscure 45s in this age of albums. In New York, he frequented the down-and-dirty ex–wino bar CBGB in the bowels of the Bowery, discovering new "talent." Stein then promoted his acts, like Talking Heads and Ramones, acts that sounded to many like musical typewriters and looked about as much fun. Their common denominator was this ugly word "punk." The word seemed well chosen, covering those stark, two-minute singles, with only three chords to learn, bands playing in dives, places without disco balls, with walls of grime, music with silly lyrics and thunderous amps, soothing as a bikini wax.

Sire's distributor, ABC Records, had bellied up. Stein had his own mailer printed. In it, he spelled out his tiny label's manifesto. Our intention is to break down, he wrote, radio's resistance to punk rock. He likened the present to an earlier era, when radio had a "closed-minded attitude toward rock music . . . The term 'punk' is as offensive as 'race' and 'hillbilly' were when they were used to describe rhythm & blues and country & western music thirty years ago."

In desperation over ABC's folding beneath him, Stein called a fellow ex-writer for *Billboard*, Jerry Wexler. Both men knew the sound of sidewalks. Stein stammered to Wexler, "Could you find me something?" Jerry now felt like an outsider from WEA. Though he knew their barons like brothers, rejection from Atlantic still bothered him. "I was always friends with Seymour," Wexler explained. "But I'd resigned. I didn't feel welcome. I thought, then I took the Sire label to David Horowitz. Let *him* face rejection. I told Horowitz, 'This is Fort Knox. Take it.' "

Horowitz called Ostin. Warner Bros. Records took over distributing Sire, plunging us into a kind of music, led by Ramones, that felt to many of us like narrow streets in a Dickens novel, the kind with open sewers running down their middles.

"What could go wrong?" became our business motto. Even better than "*selling* platinum" became a new phrase: "*shipping* platinum." Sweating

Perrier through every pore, Elektra shipped its new Linda Ronstadt *Hasten Down the Wind* "double platinum": 2.1 million copies, actually. Elektra now stood life-size, shoulder to shoulder beside Atlantic and Warners. Even Elektra got accused, to its astonishment, of "too big–ness."

October became the label's biggest month ever. Smith and Company had outsold Geffen! By the end of 1976, Elektra/Asylum had four albums in the Top Ten: Jackson Browne, Joni Mitchell, Linda Ronstadt, and a new Eagles. Never mind these were all Geffen holdover signings. Smith just got there. In three days in December, WEA shipped more than a million copies of the new Eagles release.

From the minute the prospect of running the label dangled before him, Smith had seen opportunity at Elektra. He clearly saw it expanding beyond its white, tree-lined music, beyond neighborhoods filled with singer/ songwriters like Joni and Jackson, beyond white vocal groups like the Eagles even, all of which had built one hell of a market but were not all of the label's potential. For a trade ad, Elektra posed Smith sitting in his office chair on the curb outside the E/A building:

We have a few select artist openings for 1977. So let's talk business. Here's what's happening. Columbia is offering you a fat deal you can't turn down. Capitol is spinning on its axis and The Tower is leaning your way. A&M has found you a special spot in the parking lot. The MCA guard has been ordered to smile as you walk through the door. Warners takes you to lunch in the Blue Room. You're walking on air and Ahmet's got the WCI Jet—the trans-Atlantic pick-up. Limos and domestic champagne flow like the future's yours. And it is. The choice is up to you and everybody's offering you just about the same deal. So why choose Elektra/Asylum? *Are we any different . . ."* Sure we are.

The ad picked up on the year's gospel: Record companies should handle acts hands on, in person, like octopi in love. Joe got out his Rolodex and Steve's checkbook and expanded.

Joe's search for deals turned first to black music, where Dick Griffey's Solar Records looked hot. Smith romanced him with Lakers tickets and Wicky Bird (executive slang for "WCI-bird") jet rides. The size of the Solar deal surprised others within Elektra. "I told Joe," said Oscar Fields, representing black music within WEA, "that deal is probably worth about $8 million. Those groups on Solar are not platinum-selling groups. The Whispers, groups like that? Joe ended up paying about sixteen million. And WCI erected a building for Solar on Cahuenga." After Solar, Smith hired Don Mizell away from A&M's Horizon label to start a jazz thrust, signing major deals with Grover Washington, Jr., Dee Dee Bridgewater,

Lenny White, Donald Byrd, and Patrice Rushen. "The deals that we made were outrageous," Mel Posner recalled. "We were paying over the top on jazz artists who had already peaked. Suddenly, when we started signing all these things, it started to go the other way. All those deals were problems."

Faced with a floundering country operation in Nashville, Joe built with enthusiasm. "When I came to Elektra/Asylum," Smith said, "there was some indecision as to whether to continue [in Nashville] or merge with Warners or something like that." Smith added country promotion and sales, new A&R, and a Nashville general manager.

Joe's signings were confident and played the industry odds.

The Thelma Walker Tally for 1976: Warner Bros. 50 + Atlantic 24 + Elektra/Asylum 15 = WEA Total: 89 albums made the charts. Of the industry's Top Ten Albums, with pleasure WEA sold 50 percent:

2. Warner Bros.: *Fleetwood Mac*
4. Asylum: Eagles' *Greatest Hits 1971–1975*
6. Warner Bros.: Gary Wright's *Dream Weaver*
8. Elektra: Queen's *A Night at the Opera*
9. Warner Bros.: *America's Greatest Hits*

But the real *real* stat, for Mo Ostin, was that *finally*, finally, Warner Bros. Records had become America's Number One *label*. Columbia had split off its second label, Epic. Its salesmen, Columbia's Jim Urie remembered, "felt we were suffering, with heavy sales quotas on every album, we felt burdened, imagining what *we* could do if we only had *their* repertoire." Warner/Reprise edged up, one-tenth of a percent above Columbia.

WB's Bugs Bunny ruled. At the CBS convention, the other guy blinked. Sales chief Jack Craigo stirred his troops, rumbling slurs like "I always hated that fucking rabbit." Walter Yetnikoff, now heading Columbia, unfurled a banner that read FUCK WARNER BROTHERS. Wall posters proclaimed FUCK THE BUNNY. Yetnikoff had, as he recalled it, "all the troops rallying around the flag, using the excuse to go in and steal artists under the banner of 'Fuck Warner Bros.' It was a way to create an army, a rallying point for a company that was floundering a bit at the time . . . It worked."

Yetnikoff had an almost insatiable anger toward the man in his pen sights: the quiet Mo Ostin. In his office, Walter had a circus muscleman doll that he could make quiver. On it, he'd taped a sign: THE MENSCH WITH SPILKAS (the Yiddish, "the man with jitters"). To swayable visitors, he'd say it was a Mo Ostin doll. Walter needed to win. With CBS's checkbook in hand, he snuck up on one of Warner's most heartfelt artists, James

Taylor. Meantime, in the studio, Columbia was warming up Michael Jackson.

Double-digiteers were delighted with 1976. Our labels turned out around "up 30 percent," enough to make Wall Street applaud for 364 more days.

Acapulco became, for us at Warner Bros. Records, a year after year joyride. During the day of his promotion men's conventions, Russ Thyret evangelized the single. Once known for albums only, Warner had found itself. Russ had hired thirteen specialists just to promote singles.

Unofficial gold records ("unofficial" really meant we could make up framed phonies for $120 each) were passed out at the convention in quantity, becoming ego emblems for promo people to cart back home to Phoenix or Mobile. Evenings, Thyret—tarted up in a pale blue tux with dark blue satin trim, wearing his extra-large glow-in-the-closet vest, his bow tie the size of an American eagle—worked the open-air lobby of the Acapulco Princess hotel, welcoming the ocean breeze while looking after his staff's needs, whatever or whomever those might be. San Francisco promo man Pete Marino, whom you should still remember from the Hawaii luau of 1963 and the San Francisco dove toss, "married" a fellow promo man, "Little Pete" Natchez from Florida, one night. That evening, Marino dressed as the bride, flowing white gown and veil; Little Pete was tuxed. Convention nights became truly fulfilled when you got dumped, fully dressed, in the hotel pool but carefully drank no drop from it.

Wet or dry, there was much to spout about. In October, WEA had one, two, and three of the top singles (Debby Boone, Carly Simon, and Shaun Cassidy), with Boone and Cassidy both coming from Mike Curb's all-American market sense. Full-line retail record stores—the kind that stocked a huge variety of catalogue albums—helped make the industry fat. Virtually every major new shopping center, most of the malls being built, they all seemed to have a chain store that sold records. More and more places stocked inventory that could, at the store's discretion, freely be returned to WEA's new national Returns Center, an industrial cemetery soon referred to as the Elephant's Graveyard.

But so what? Early during the sale of the Eagles' *Hotel California*, Elektra just upped its price, from $6.98 up to $7.98, knowing that, with a hit, the public bought. The price of each recorded song on an album was now up to 80 cents apiece, even if you didn't want them all. Elektra's press release explained its dollar-up move as "commitment to the proven concept of selective pricing." Not mentioned was the underlying theme of "whatever the market will bear."

When Mo Ostin learned that the Sex Pistols were in trouble with A&M Records, where legend has it they'd stood and peed on the desk of company head in London, he sent two emissaries across the Atlantic to meet with this born-to-say-fuck "group."[91]

Bob Krasnow, our Executive Without Portfolio, and his Artist Relations pal Bob Regehr flew to find the Pistols in London. The address they had went down below the city surface. Krasnow said he'd never been this low before, which meant something. He referred to it as Journey to the Center of the Earth. It smelled. Krasnow knew that these were no longer his kind of people. Below, he and Bob found a room with torn mattresses, paper everywhere, a few amplifiers, and whacked-out (though not drugged-out) boys. When the Pistols saw Regehr and his cigar, they spat fast vulgarities. They offered Regehr and Krasnow slugs from the same bottle they'd been drinking from, a mix of beer and Scotch. Krasnow noticed that they had "things" in their belly buttons. Had words scrawled across their chests. Krasnow asked them to play. "It was the worst shit I'd ever heard, horrific," he recalled. "The music was a train wreck. They weren't even all playing the same song!"

VOICE: They wanna play "Johnny B. Goode" while you sing "Through My Eyes."
JOHNNY ROTTEN: God! Awright, then.
VOICE: Ready? Go!
JOHNNY ROTTEN: If you could see . . . oh God, fuck off . . .
    Ayan Louisiana ya-ya New Orlean
    I was a bada baby an' a little key
    Ayinananananananana Johnny B. Goode!
    A-gogogogogo Johnny B. Goode!
    A-gogo, go Johnny, gogogogogo
    I don't know the words!
    Gogogogogogogogogogogyogyuh
    Ayayayaya-strah yaya-strah-uauaua
    Ayayayaya-strah anda banayaya
    I wanna wanna bay, yayayaya
    Let's gogo, ago Johnny gogogogo
    A-gogo, go go go gogogogogogogogogogogogogogogog
    Go, Johnny, go, go
    Go! Johnny B. Goode
    Ayayayayayayayayayayayayag-wuah
    Oh, fuck, it's awful!
    Hate songs like that!
    The pits
    Eeeeeeeyayayayay eeeee!

[91]The Sex Pistols had previously been dropped by England's EMI Records for (figuratively) doing likewise to Queen Elizabeth II with their ribald "God Save the Queen."

Warner Bros.' first recording star, Al Jolson (left), with Brunswick Records head Jack Kapp, in the early 1930s.

(Courtesy of Myra Kapp Levitt)

Jack Warner with Capitol Records founder Glenn Wallichs and Jim Conkling (from left).

(Courtesy of Donna King Conkling)

Conkling (center) with Phil (left) and Don Everly,
right after he signed the Brothers to Warners.

Ahmet Ertegun, record store owner Max "Waxie Maxie" Silverman,
Miriam Abramson, Nesuhi Ertegun, and Jerry Wexler (from left).

New York's St. Nicholas Arena, circa 1954: (standing from left) R&B artist Buddy Johnson, Cashbox's Norman Orleck, Ella Johnson, Big Joe Turner, Lou Willie Turner, and Mrs. Alan "Jackie" Freed; (kneeling from left) Jerry Wexler, Alan Freed, and Ahmet Ertegun.

Bobby Darin and Wexler in Atlantic's New York office on West Fifty-seventh Street, circa 1960.

Frank Sinatra and
Mickey Rudin.

"The Men in Blue"
in front of Warner's
first building, including
(front row, from left) Stan
Cornyn, Joel Friedman,
ball carrier Mike
Maitland, Joe Smith,
and Lenny Waronker;
(back row, second, fifth,
sixth, and ninth from
left): Phil Rose, Ed West,
Jimmy Bowen, and Ed
Thrasher, circa 1966.

(Stan Cornyn collection)

Jac Holzman after he tidied himself up to sell Elektra to Kinney.

Mike Maitland congratulates Mo Ostin (standing) with a gold record for *Sinatra: A Man and His Music*, with Ed West (second from left) and Stan Cornyn (far right), 1965.

(Courtesy of Holzman Family archives)

Cornyn's second Grammy, handed to him by singer Joanie Sommers,1966.

(Stan Cornyn collection)

Elektra producer Paul Rothchild at artist manager Albert Grossman's Bearsville, New York, home, 1965.

WBR Creative Services crew, circa 1969, including (in the back row) Cornyn (wearing glasses), Hal Haverstadt (with rocket), and Ed Thrasher (with three fingers raised); middle row includes Jean Lumley (miniest of skirt), Judy Sims (plaid suit), and Pete Johnson (whitest pants).

A "Coming Out" party for Alice Cooper: (standing) Theodora and Stan Cornyn; (seated) unidentified guest and Rod McKuen.

Neil Young manager Elliott Roberts, Graham Nash, David Geffen, and Young (from left).

Cornyn (left)
celebrates his
promotion to
Senior VP with
Joe Smith, Mo Ostin,
and Lenny Waronker.

Bette Midler
lassoing Sheldon
Vogel of Atlantic.

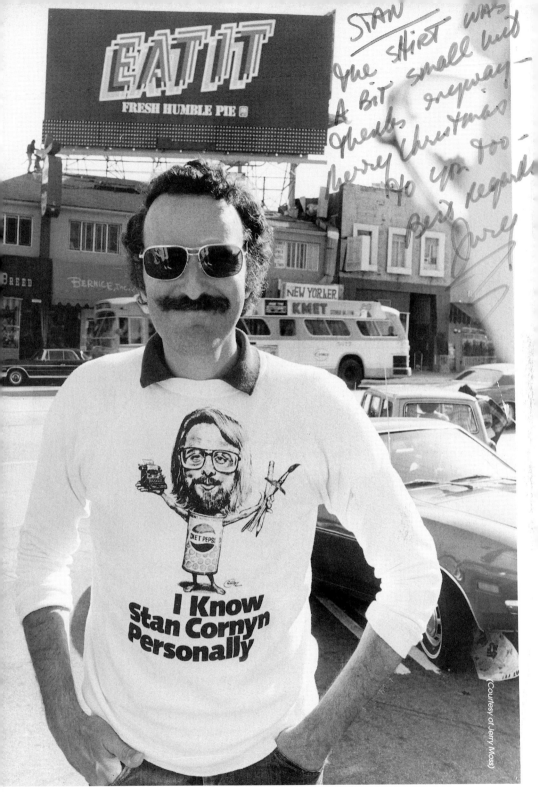

A&M Records' Jerry Moss modeling his Cornyn sweatshirt—
a priceless collector's item today.

WEA convention speakers (from left) Ahmet Ertegun, Joel Friedman, Joe Smith, Stan Cornyn, and David Horowitz.

The VGRs: Vogel, Gitlin, and Reinstein.

Mo Ostin, George Harrison, and Stan Cornyn (from left), posing with Harrison's gold record for *33 1/3*, 1977.

Rod Stewart hangs on Linda Baker at the Joe Louis Arena on Superbowl Sunday, 1982.

In the Wicky-Bird (seated, from left): Stan Cornyn, Chrysalis Records' Terry Ellis, Mo Ostin; (standing, from left): Russ Thyret, Joe Smith, and Chris Wright of Chrysalis.

Elektra's Mel Posner and WBR's Ed Rosenblatt embrace.

Happy Birthday, Stan. Can

At Stan Cornyn's fiftieth birthday party, Cornyn grins as Phil Rose talks, 1983.

(Stan Cornyn collection)

WCI Chairman Steve Ross busses WEA Chief Henry Droz at the WEA convention, 1986.

(Courtesy of Henry Droz)

YOUNGBLOODS

we keep the bodies?

In 1983 *Billboard* Magazine reached back about a decade to an old Cornyn ad (featuring WBR's execs with faked bodies and carefully positioned new album releases) in a tribute presented at Cornyn's fiftieth birthday party.

Jerry Levin (with mustache) and Marty Payson.

Bob Krasnow, Nesuhi Ertegun, and Mickey Kapp, circa 1970.

New Year's party with (seated) Michael Klefner, Sheldon Vogel, Phil Carson, Mel Lewinter; (standing) Dicky Kline, Jerry Greenberg, Dave Glew and date; looking for Vogel's credit cards.

Late 1990s leaders: WBR's Phil Quartararo and Russ Thyret; Time Warner's Jerry Levin; Elektra's Sylvia Rhone; Atlantic's Val Azolli and Ahmet Ertegun; Warner Entertainment's Bob Daly and Terry Semel.

(Photograph by Larry Busacca)

Bob Morgado.

Former WBR exec Danny Goldberg.

(Courtesy of Artemis Records)

Former Atlantic and Warner Music-US head Doug Morris (right), with rap impresario Russell Simmons, 1999.

(Courtesy of the Rock & Roll Hall of Fame)

A pair of WBR's celebrated "ears": Mo and Stan.

*   *   *

Clearly, Krasnow reflected, "they had *some*thing. Attitude, that's it. I told Mo I didn't like them."

True to form, Mo signed the Pistols. He accepted the group's evident hatred of record companies, how they'd revolted their companies, had made those labels want to give up their cash advances to the Pistols. Accepted that group's public-relations spokesman, Johnny Rotten, not only spat, but also spoke spit: "I don't listen to music," he'd say. "I hate all music . . . The only thing that keeps half the people alive in factories is the fucking radio on all day."

The eventual meaning of the Pistols was, at this stage of things, easy for us all to overlook. Keith Richards yawned: "It's a real feeling of déjà vu. They puked at the London airport. We pissed in the filling station." Neil Young said something a bit nice: "I've never met Johnny Rotten, but I like what he did to people."

The Pistols didn't make many records. They failed to appear as scheduled for their shot on *Saturday Night Live* (Elvis Costello replaced them). The show's producer, Lorne Michaels, felt it was "very strange that a group that prides itself on representing the underground turns us down because we don't pay them enough." The Sex Pistols broke up shortly after making Warner's Artist Relations department feel like Humphrey Bogart covered with leeches.

Among different, suddenly wealthy WEA groups, good mixing was not confined to recording studios: "It was during this time that I had my brief affair with [Fleetwood Mac's] Stevie Nicks," Eagles Don Henley recalls. "I remember the Eagles were on tour, and so was Fleetwood Mac. These were the extravagant days. One time, I chartered a Learjet and ran her to where I was, and for weeks I got a lot of shit about that from the band. If she had a couple of days off, she'd come over and go on the road with us for a while, and then I'd fly her back in time for wherever Fleetwood Mac was supposed to be. We coined the phrase 'Love 'em and Lear 'em.' "

In 1977, the ultradisco, Studio 54, opened. From its ceiling hung a brightly lit man-in-a-crescent-moon. An automated spoon moved up and down to the man's nose. Our labels' sales rose higher than the spoon. Atlantic's Jerry Greenberg and John Kalodner signed Foreigner, which during its career sold an astonishing 47 million copies (or "units"; when you got over 100,000, you now called them "units"). Warner Bros.' Fleetwood Mac issued *Rumours*, and that *one* album started a surge that eventually sold over 17 million units.

The platinum, million-unit standard had been well passed. The Eagles sold like someone had stolen the OFF knob from the salesroom shower. Sales just poured over us. Elektra's Eagles sold twelve times platinum of *Their*

Greatest Hits, then nine times platinum of *Hotel California*. The term became "multiplatinum."

When Joe Smith had taken over Elektra, he had to meet with the manager of its best-selling Eagles, the tough, six-foot-minus-one-soccer-ball-tall Irving Azoff. At the meeting, Azoff had slapped Smith's desk with demands, threats of Eagle laryngitis, his whole repertoire. Smith had the answer. "Irving," Smith said, "you can't threaten me. I'm already rich. I don't need this, and I don't need you." Azoff retreated.[92]

In Smith's first year, the Eagles made Elektra look great or greater. For the Eagles themselves, though, their job felt done. Touring became vacationing, with somebody else covering any damage. Elektra promotion man Lou Galliani remembered "Joe Walsh turning a hotel room into a suite by chain-sawing through the wall and knocking a door through."[93]

Then, to Joe's distress, the Eagles nested, abandoning recording. For three years. Off mike, the Eagles partied on. Miss those Eagles? Sure. Was life over? Nope. Here came Queen.

Queen was the glitterest rock group from Britain. Its leader, Freddie Mercury, appeared onstage in costumes ranging from women's gowns to stormtrooper outfits. Mercury concocted the camp bestseller "Bohemian Rhapsody," a song that became so familiar it got its own nickname: "Bo-Rap." With over 180 vocal overdubs, "Bo Rap" became a bizarre mock opera, with a wailing chorus intoning pidgin Verdi about "Beelzebub," "Galileo figaro magnifico," "Mama mia," and "Scaramouche." The nearly-six-minute single became Top Ten. Queen sold over a million units of *A Night at the Opera* in four months. Queen had by now become one of the top-selling groups in America, with two new Top Ten albums in 1976. Queen's tour pranced across America, wilder than some herd of gay buffalo. A major fight ensued at a Holiday Inn in Detroit. Queen was late for a flight, but Freddie Mercury wouldn't come downstairs. He was accusing Brian May of stealing his eyebrow tweezers.

In 1978, Queen came up with an album called *Jazz*, with the single, "Bicycle Race/Fat-Bottom Girls." The album's inner spread photo was an

---

[92]The next year, movie producer Azoff cast Joe Smith as a radio exec in the movie *FM*, about an FM station's last days before turning Top Forty.

[93]Irving Azoff considers this to be the second-best Eagles story. His first-best was the night Eagle Joe Walsh led colleagues in knocking out the windows of Joe Smith's top-floor suite at Chicago's Astor Towers. The windows had to be destroyed, Walsh reasoned, so they could shove the suite's grand piano out into the night air. Walsh, along with Elektra's Steve Wax, Kenny Buttice, Burt Stein, and others heaved and ho'd. Lou Maglia watched as the grand piano flew out and down twenty-two floors to land on the hotel manager's Cadillac. The cause of the incident, Walsh later explained, was that the hotel's restaurant would not let him in without a tie.

ass-focused rear view of sixty nude women on bicycles, the result of a bike "race" that Queen had staged in London. Nudes on bikes rapidly became the band's standard motif. At a Madison Square Garden concert, the audience cheered half-nude women wheeling across the stage during the band's performance. To draw even more attention to "Fat-Bottom Girls," Elektra tossed what may well have been, to climb out on some limb, the most ribald rock party ever held in public view.

Elektra rented the city of New Orleans, or so it seemed. The party theme was obvious: Really Fun Women. The party became a $200,000 exercise in debauchery, even by French Quarter standards. When Elektra asked its guests of honor to attend . . . well, the only possible, the only *conceivable* way for Queen to get to that party was to fly there via a private jet. With a bedroom in it. With a shower. With a glass door on it.

Queen disembarked from the rented plane, leaving behind its satin sheets and fur spread for a bed with no seat belts. That night, Queen met the Quarter. Both boogied through the humid night. Sweat melted shirts and blouses until most anything above the belt became free to rub.

Through this all-night romp roamed hired hermaphrodite strippers. Topless waitresses bore trays of condoms, K-Y Jelly, and herpes antidotes. Rock reverberated through cobblestone streets more used to Dixieland parades playing "St. James Infirmary." Amped-up rock deafened streets named Bourbon and Desire. The Quarter's old-timers bent over iron balconies, agog at behaviors no Mardi Gras had ever seen on parade. Stoned secretaries, whirling their arms, spun themselves dizzy, opening themselves freely to anything. Hired escape artists did their Houdini tricks. Freelance dwarfs, some hired, some not, tugged on people's pants, yelling up obscenities. Crowds flocked to see the woman who was smoking cigarettes from an orifice that precluded any possible concerns about lung cancer.

In the meantime, women's-rights groups like Women Against Violence Against Women were growing dissatisfied with WCI labels' deaf ear to their protests over women being mishandled (on album covers). They called on the Feminist Studio Workshop to set up a mini-theater production on Sunset Boulevard, near Tower Records. There, ladies dressed as roosters symbolized cocky record-company executives. The set was a money-laden office complete with the WEA Big Button, album covers, marching women, and gold records.

Women-who-march proclaimed that WEA was *the* most offensive company, its ads depicting "women being abused, raped, and gang-raped implied by the use of suggestive poses, whips and chains," cited their leader. "Very rarely is a woman portrayed as a human being." They urged a consumer boycott of WEA-distributed product, citing the covers of Average White Band's *Cut the Cake*, Montrose's *Jump on It*, and the Stones' *Black and Blue*. These shouting women stunned and confused us. *Our* wives didn't shout. If they wanted to protest our attitudes, our wives shopped. We label execs bucked all this up to Corporate, which gave the women expert lip service.

Women were not the only ones we offended. We also angered people who, a few years later, might be called "altitude disadvantaged." Randy Newman just called them "Short People." They also turned out to be "humor disadvantaged." While on a concert tour in Memphis, Newman received his first death threat about this new song. He played the concert hunched over the keyboard, making himself a small target. Journalists, hearing of the stir, apparently serious, called upon Randy to defend himself against his "blatant expression of prejudice." He tried to be serious, which to Randy never came naturally. To answer journalists' questions, he tried to offer rules. "A short person?" he'd reply. "Let's say three feet seven inches. No, that's too timid. Anybody under five feet six inches. No. That'd mean some little karate guy is likely to kick the shit out of me . . . Actually, I don't expect this record to be a big commercial success in Japan."

For Warner label execs, flying in the Warner jet had become an executive perquisite. Riding it wasn't just for singers; it also was for *signers* of singers. The privilege turned into a need. Doting parent Warner Communications, the guys in Manhattan who owned these private jets and loved golden eggs, their job was to steady the basket under us golden geese.

Those who actually distributed the albums—Warner's pick-pack-and-ship distribution centers—never flew in private. WEA workers also got overlooked when the invites went out for Queen's party/orgy in New Orleans. WEA workers lived in places you never had to go to, like DeKalb, Illinois, and were on no A List.

In this heady sell-'em-by-the-ton age, *bubeleh* Joel Friedman was caught between his own conservative sense of the market's feeling oversold and his responsibility to the labels' ship-out-more euphoria. When it came to making how-many-to-ship policy with the labels, Joel remembered a few years before, at the Bel Air Hotel, when he'd been taught to speak his piece, then shut his mouth.

After six years of working out of sight, back in the record group's kitchen, Friedman still only rated flying first-class commercial. No WCI jet. Still not a full-fledged Musketeer. The corporate jet . . . well, if you were a back-in-the-kitchen kind of guy, you *knew* not to ask. If you did ask, you knew they'd answer something like "Clint Eastwood," and, if you were just a distribution guy, you'd answer back "Sure." And wait your turn.

Friedman had soldiered on. Like others in this business, Joel worked a lot of nights and weekends to midnight, ate every meal with extra marinara, and halfway through most meetings had to empty the ashtray. In an up-all-night crowd, Friedman became legendary for his drive. At La Costa sales meetings, if it was tennis break, he'd be out on the court, four-eyed, bandy-legged, big-bellied, gold neck chains bouncing off his chest, yelling across the net at younger, fitter opponents, "That all you got?"

By 1977, just six years after its birth, WEA felt formidably flush. Rather than its save-a-buck regional conventions—the kind where employees stayed home and a few executives traveled from branch to branch—this year, the distribution arm decided to convene all its infantry, over seven hundred of them, in one major convention. There, in a darkened auditorium in the Diplomat Hotel near Miami, for the first time, the seven hundred looked up onstage where a banner proclaimed (who knew what this thing meant?) THE FUTURE IS NOW.

Joel's distribution company had been elevated to glamour status. Couldn't you just see? Right there, in the auditorium's front row, sat the Very Big Guys from New York: WCI chairman Steve Ross, and David Horowitz, and WEA International's head, Nesuhi Ertegun. Validation: These men had actually flown down to be with their Golden Goose!

Friedman got his turn to come into the spotlight. At the mike, he announced his opening hurrahs:

- Each year for the past six years, WEA's sales have risen more rapidly than anyone else's in the industry.
- WEA labels have earned more RIAA-certified gold and platinum awards than any other company in the business.
- Fleetwood Mac's *Rumours* and the Eagles' *Hotel California* have sold five million each. Once, such sales (such as Carole King's *Tapestry* and the original Tijuana Brass) were a freak occurrence. Now they've become a commonplace fact of life.
- Last year, more than seventy-two Warner artists sold in excess of one million units in the U.S. alone.
- Last year, WEA sold one of every four albums sold in America: a 24 percent share. (Nearest rival Columbia, at 17 percent, felt gall.)
- "We haven't even scratched the surface," exulted Friedman. "We hereby predict a new level of award: the titanium album, for ten million unit sales!"

Rock stars like Queen got shipped in to perform for the convention. Onstage, these acts flailed, their guitars swinging aloft, their shirts unbuttoned in deep Vs, directing your eye to the bulging Wonder Jocks that promised triple-A pricks. Meat onstage performed for Row A, where sat Money.

During one such courting of the sales force, down in the darkened auditorium, the puffs-after-climbing-three-steps Joel Friedman stood next to his

Number Two exec, Henry Droz. Suddenly Friedman seized Droz's arm, whispering, "Hold me. I can't see." Droz steadied Friedman. Within a minute, Joel recovered. In the dark, he pooh-poohed, "I'm okay now." Hey, Joel, maybe too much celebrating last night?

The week following the Miami convention, up in Manhattan, Joel Friedman shook hands with Horowitz on his new contract, one that gave Friedman that "equal Musketeer feeling." Now, at long last, doing as well as his former colleagues Mo and Joe. On American Air back to his home in California, Friedman munched his Rolaids and leaned over to his seatmate, a promo guy from Atlantic. He could not hide his got-it-made excitement. "Well, kid, I can't believe it. They gave me everything I wanted. I got so much money coming in, I don't know what's going to happen next."

He paged through the week's *Billboard*, with glee. Of the Top Five albums in the country, WEA distributed four:

1. Fleetwood Mac: *Rumours*
2. Linda Ronstadt: *Simple Dreams*
4. Foreigner: *Foreigner*
5. The Rolling Stones: *Love You Live*

And eight of the Top Twenty! He turned to the promotion man. "That's forty percent share!" And, with a couple of Jack Daniel's down, Joel Friedman, the third Musketeer, drifted off to sleep. From fifteen years earlier, I knew Joel to be a ferocious snorer. But let the man be, feeling so good about this year, with all its jets with showers and asses on bikes.

At home that evening, Friedman told his wife, Shirley, about his new deal at WCI. How he was now as big a guy as the three label heads. "Finally," Friedman told her, "it feels like I'm one of the Big Four." The next morning: right into another ferocious workday, tie loosened, impatient, looking for more. Later that night, as he left the office, Joel stubbed out the workday's last Parliament, shook his head, and told Henry Droz, "I gotta stop with these."

On November 8, early morning, Joel Melvin Friedman woke at 4:00 a.m., complaining of chest pains. Though paramedics rushed to the scene, they couldn't save him: Friedman's aorta had ruptured. He was fifty-two.

The next day, work colleagues gathered at his Encino home, just to be there. They stood in groups in the backyard, not wanting to let Joel's presence escape. They told stories of late-night poker games with Jack Daniel's on the table. They spoke of their up-from-Brooklyn kinsman. They revisited stories of the endless nights of restaurant-made pasta with meatballs and cornball jokes. In that backyard, this was a day when, instead of laughing at those good old jokes, you could only nod yes, I was there, yes, I know.

On the back porch, this assembly of colleagues noticed Joel's Exer-

Cycle, the holiday present his staff had given him just one year earlier. WEA executive Vic Faraci walked over to the machine. To the others, Faraci read off the mileage meter: "Six."

Significant Records
1976

Atlantic: ABBA (*Greatest Hits,* including "Fernando") • Average White Band ("Soul Searching") • Firefall ("You Are the Woman") • Aretha Franklin (*Sparkle*) • The Manhattan Transfer ("Coming Out") • Bette Midler (*Songs for the New Depression*) • The Spinners ("The Rubberband Man") • Ringo Starr ("A Dose of Rock 'n' Roll") • Stills-Young Band (*Long May You Run*)
Atco: Genesis (*A Trick of the Tail*) • Roxy Music (*Viva!*)
Big Tree: England Dan & John Ford Coley (*Nights Are Forever,* including "I'd Really Love to See You Tonight")
Rolling Stone: The Rolling Stones (*Black and Blue*)
Swan Song: Bad Company (*Run with the Pack,* including "Young Blood") • Led Zeppelin (*Presence* and *The Song Remains the Same*)

Elektra: Harry Chapin (*Greatest Stories—Live*) • Carly Simon (*Another Passenger*)
Asylum: Jackson Browne (*The Pretender*) • Keith Carradine ("I'm Easy") • Eagles (*Their Greatest Hits—1971-1975* and *Hotel California,* including "Life in the Fast Lane" and "New Kid in Town") • Joni Mitchell (*Hejira*) • Orleans (*Waking and Dreaming*) • Linda Ronstadt (*Hasten Down the Wind,* including "That'll Be the Day," and *Greatest Hits*) • Tom Waits (*Small Change*)

Warner Bros.: America ("Hideaway") • George Benson (*Breezin',* including "This Masquerade") • Elvin Bishop (*Struttin' My Stuff*) • Black Sabbath (*We Sold Our Soul for Rock 'n' Roll*) • Bootsy's Rubber Band ("Stretchin' Out") • Alice Cooper (*Goes to Hell,* including "I Never Cry") • The Doobie Brothers (*Takin' It to the Streets* and *Best Of*) • Manfred Mann (*The Roaring Silence,* including "Blinded by the Light") • Leo Sayer (*Endless Flight,* including "How Much Love" and "You Make Me Feel Like Dancing") • Candi Staton ("Young Hearts Run Free") • Rod Stewart (*A Night on the Town,* including "Tonight's the Night") • James Taylor (*In the Pocket,* including "Shower the People," and *Greatest Hits*) • Gary Wright ("Dream Weaver" and "Love Is Alive")
Reprise: Michael Franks ("Popsicle Toes") • Emmylou Harris (*Elite Hotel*) • Gordon Lightfoot (*Summertime Dream,* including "Wreck of the Edmund Fitzgerald") • John Sebastian ("Welcome Back")
Bearsville: Foghat (*Night Shift*)
Brother: The Beach Boys (*15 Big Ones*)
Capricorn: The Marshall Tucker Band (*Long Hard Ride*)
Chrysalis: Jethro Tull ("Too Old to Rock 'n' Roll/Too Young to Die") • Robin Trower (*Live*)
Dark Horse: George Harrison (*Thirty-Three & 1/3,* including "Crackerbox Palace")
ECM: Keith Jarrett (*In the Light*)
Island: Bob Marley & the Wailers (*Rastaman Vibration*) • Robert Palmer (*Some People Can Do What They Like*)
Sire: Climax Blues Band (*Couldn't Get It Right*) • *Ramones* • Flamin' Groovies (*Shake Some Action*)

1977

Atlantic: ABBA (*Arrival,* including "Dancing Queen" and "Knowing Me, Knowing You") • Average White Band ("Person to Person" and "Benny & Us") • Chic ("Dance, Dance, Dance (Yowsah, Yowsah, Yowsah)" • Crosby, Stills & Nash ("Just a Song Before I Go") • Emerson, Lake & Palmer (*Works*) • Firefall (*Luna Sea,* including "Just Remember I Love You") • Foreigner ("Cold as Ice," "Feels Like the First Time," and "Long, Long Way from Home") • Leif Garrett ("Runaround Sue" and "Surfin' USA") • Bette Midler (*Live at Last*) • The Trammps ("Disco Inferno") • Yes (*Going for the One*)
Atco: *Peter Gabriel* • Genesis ("Wind and Wuthering")
Big Tree: England Dan & John Ford Coley ("Gone Too Far" and "It's Sad to Belong")
Island: Grace Jones ("Sorry") • Bob Marley & the Wailers (*Exodus*) • *Steve Winwood*
Rolling Stone: The Rolling Stones (*Love You Live*)
Swan Song: Bad Company (*Burnin' Sky*)

Elektra: Bread (*Lost Without Your Love*) • Queen (*A Day at the Races,* including "Somebody to Love" and *News of the World,* including "We Are the Champions") • Carly Simon ("Nobody Does It Better")
Asylum: Andrew Gold ("Lonely Boy") • Linda Ronstadt (*Simple Dreams,* including "Blue Bayou" and "It's So Easy")
Warner Bros: America (*Harbor*) • George Benson (*In Flight,* including "This Masquerade") • Debby Boone ("You Light Up My Life") • Bootsy's Rubber Band (*Ahh . . . The Name Is Bootsy, Baby*) • Shaun Cassidy ("Da Doo Ron Ron") and "That's Rock 'n' Roll" and *Born Late,* including "Hey Deanie") • Alice Cooper (*You and Me*) • The Doobie Brothers (*Livin' on the Fault Line*) • Fleetwood Mac (*Rumours,* including "Don't Stop," "Dreams," "Go Your Own Way," and "You Make Loving Fun") • Emmylou Harris (*Luxury Liner*) • Steve Martin (*Let's Get Small*) • Van Morrison (*A Period of Transition*) • Randy Newman (*Little Criminals,* including "Short People") • Bonnie Raitt (*Sweet Forgiveness*) • The Sanford/Townsend Band ("Smoke from a Distant Fire") • Leo Sayer ("When I Need You" and "Thunder in My Heart") • Sex Pistols (*Never Mind the Bollocks, Here's The Sex Pistols*) • Rod Stewart (*Foot Loose & Fancy Free,* including "Hot Legs," "I Was Only Joking," and "You're in My Heart")
Reprise: Neil Young (*American Stars 'n Bars* and *Decade*)
Bearsville: Foghat (*Live*)
Brother: The Beach Boys (*Maharishi International University Album,* including "Rock and Roll Music")
Capricorn: The Marshall Tucker Band ("Heard It in a Love Song")
Sire: Ramones (*Rocket to Russia,* including "Sheena Is a Punk Rocker") • Talking Heads (*Talking Heads 77*)
Whitfield: Rose Royce (*In Full Bloom*) • The Undisputed Truth (*Method to the Madness*)

20

THE question of who would be chosen to replace Joel Friedman atop WEA caused, for once, no debate. David Horowitz checked out one name—Henry Droz—with the label heads. Horowitz suffered no resistance, and within a week changed his offer to Henry from "pro tem" to "official." Henry was from the street, from Detroit, and knew how to sell the most units for the least cost. He'd been in distribution, it seemed, since the Forties, starting as a Decca branch manager. Henry looked like he'd never actually lifted a card-board box. His hands were executive smooth. He once reminisced with me about one of our co-idols, the Mount Everest of jazz, Louis Armstrong.

Decca had assigned Henry to escort Armstrong around Detroit to record stores and radio stations. Henry's main stop was with DJ Jack the Bellboy on WJBK. "Jocks with their own shows did more for the business than anything and anybody at that time," Droz recalled, "but in those days, black stations only played black records. Jack once got heat because he played 'White Christmas' by Sister Rosetta Tharp."

Droz had asked his secretary to get Armstrong a room at the Statler. Reservation clerks knew Armstrong's color. No rooms. Try the Sheraton, then. No rooms. Negroes stayed at the Gotham. Droz encountered a 1952 Detroit Reality. He picked Armstrong up at the Gotham at eight in the morn-ing, and the two of them, working out of Droz's '50 Chevy, pulled twenty hours straight, till four the next morning. Even up into Canada, where there was an all-night jock good for an interview. Armstrong did not complain. At 4:00 a.m., Henry Droz dropped Louis Armstrong off in front of the Gotham Hotel. He watched from his car as America's greatest jazz artist walked away, his shoulders slumped, looking beat and tired, quietly disappearing into his solitude, into the only hotel in Detroit that would have him.

After managing Decca's branch, Droz had opened his own indie distrib-utorship, called Arc, financed by Droz with crosstown distributor Johnny Kaplan and disc jockey Robin Seymour. Henry started wearing a tie to work. Like his Windsor knot, his timing was top-knotch. Arc attracted dozens of emerging labels, including Elektra.

But like indie stores and labels, independent distributing began to teeter. By 1961, huge sellers like Korvette's and the Handleman Brothers' rack jobbing octopus rode into town after town waving banners that said "Efficiency" and "Cheaper." With "functional discounts" (labels sold albums cheaper to racks), they undercut middlemen such as Droz and Kaplan. Their racks had made stand-alone rock and pop record stores seem like overpriced little toy shops.

Thanks to functional discounts, Handleman bought cheaper and sold records cheaper, with no costly clerks. Droz's Arc cut its own prices for a $3.98 album by 10 percent, from $2.47 down to $2.25, even without a "functional discount," so his accounts might compete against the big guy. Droz's Arc then merged with Atlantic Records' local distributor, John Kaplan, who put it this way: "It's an effort to maintain some sort of dealer picture in this city."

Ultimately, Droz and Kaplan gave up. They sold out to Handleman. The big guys won. When asked why, Kaplan answered tersely, "Anything is for sale if the terms are right." Both men left independence behind to become vice presidents in the big guys' giant cement barns. Record labels turned glum, realizing that this huge rack jobber Handleman had become, literally, a national distributor, one that might *not* pick up the phone soon as they called.

At Handleman, Droz joined a penny-pinching world born out of Depression-trained minds. All cookies remaining after a meeting were stashed away for the next. If an employee left at four on Saturday, he got asked why he'd put in only a half day. Employees were openly blasted for infractions, humiliated in front of others.

So when Joel Friedman had approached Henry Droz, asking if he'd like to move to L.A. and have some WEA fun, Droz had answered quickly, with a hug.

The Monday after Joel's memorial service, Henry drove from Encino to the WEA headquarters, then on the ground floor at Warner Bros. Records' new building. Nothing felt "as usual." Sheila Hafner, Friedman's secretary going back to the early 1960s, moved over to fill the same role with Droz. At year's end, still not moving into Friedman's office, uncomfortable about doing that, president Droz appointed Vic Faraci as his executive VP/director of marketing. Up from the Los Angeles branch, he brought in the bright-faced, savvy M.B.A. Russ Bach as his VP of marketing, under Faraci.

Replacing Russ Bach in his ex-job as Los Angeles regional branch manager, Droz appointed street veteran George Rossi; the man who'd "fixed" New York was being rewarded with a job in the sunshine. "The difference between West Coast and East Coast," Rossi learned, "is people on the West Coast try to sell better, and the people on the East Coast try to buy better—how they can get an extra this or an extra that. Which is the major difference in the two cultures." Los Angeles became Rossi's third branch to run. In the Los Angeles branch, merchandising continued under young Dave Mount, who tried adjusting to Rossi's New York style—work fast all day, then at six head over to Leon's Steak House for sirloin and booze.

Droz and his new team started 1978 without a wobble. Steve Ross bought a second jet, a helicopter especially for Fridays to beat the traffic out to the Hamptons, an executive villa in Acapulco, with a view of New Zealand. Holiday turkeys did not grow large enough. January opened with five of the Top Ten:

1. Fleetwood Mac: *Rumours*
2. Rod Stewart: *Foot Loose & Fancy Free*
5. Linda Ronstadt: *Simple Dreams*
6. Shaun Cassidy: *Born Late*
8. Queen: *News of the World*

Fleetwood Mac's longevity amazed even *Billboard*. *Rumours* stuck at Number One for more consecutive weeks than any album in two decades.[94]

After a few weeks' delay, Henry moved a bit uncomfortably into Joel's office. He added little to the Joel decor, just a couple of Chagall prints and a rope macramé mirror. He and his staff met to figure how to handle the growth predicted by indicators that pointed up and up.

WEA's own building was coming. It would be fifty-four thousand square feet in a four-story wood-and-glass (and platinum) design, meant to hold not only WEA but also the West Coast, Phil Rose–led offices of WEA International. Joel's widow, Shirley, and son, Mike, posed with golden shovels at the groundbreaking ceremony for the new headquarters at the corner of Hollywood Way and Olive Avenue.

Droz drew up expansion plans for double WEA's volume. Faraci planned for doubling to sixteen shipping points by 1983. Home-office staffers prepared for avalanches, like having to pack and ship 175,000 ABBA T-shirt decals.

"Send out for more zeroes," called the accounting staff.

Across America, WEA branches met under the new banner, WEA MAKES IT HAPPEN. Addressing his troops, Droz, in his twangy but thoughtful way, told them, "Our industry is on the verge of a complete explosion. In recent years, we were pleased with our marketing efforts when one person out of

---

[94]All-timers at Number One, till then, had been two Broadway cast albums, *South Pacific* and *West Side Story*, and Harry Belafonte's *Calypso*.

every four hundred purchased a particular album. Today we have a realistic target of selling one person out of every ten. This is mind-boggling . . ." So it felt.

Holiday Inns in Pop. 20,000 towns set up discos in their breakfast rooms. Roller rinks became discos. Casablanca Records, having left Warner Bros., sat astride the disco world with the Village People. In 1978, radio once again changed, almost overnight. Contemporary Hit Radio (CHR) played only hit album cuts. Disco became a must for any label west of Deutsche Grammophon. Four out of five of the top singles originated in disco. In albums, it was the same: The Rolling Stones and Donna Summer bringing home the thump-a, thump-a.

Two albums, both Robert Stigwood's (though no longer Atlantic's), became the biggest sellers: *Saturday Night Fever* and *Grease*. This duo alone made up about 9 percent of U.S. record sales in 1978. One out of five American homes had a copy of *Saturday Night Fever*. Among Johns, Travolta was bigger than Denver. Thump-a, thump-a.

Even Atlantic, now age thirty, stayed up later. The year before, label president Jerry Greenberg had overruled his staff and signed Chic, a group that in an earlier, pre-disco incarnation had called itself Allah and the Knife-Wielding Punks. Jerry believed in the act. After Chic's disco single, "Le Freak," its leader Nile Rodgers recalled, "Within twenty-five to thirty minutes, we had the biggest hit record of our lives." (Number One for six weeks, and eventually topping four million, becoming Atlantic's best-selling single.)

The Rolling Stones, having undergone "Starfucker" censorship by Atlantic, would no longer be tamed. In 1978, for their new album *Some Girls*, they came up with a cover of a lion atop a woman. Sheldon Vogel, praying never again to be Atlantic's censor, called up WCI's top lawyer, Marty Payson. Payson, a man whose mouth raced so fast he neglected to finish half his sentences before racing on (he may have taught Joe Pesci how to say "Okay? Okay?"), helped Vogel. "I told Sheldon," Payson recalled, " 'Just tell them we said you can't do it, that . . . this crosses a certain line that as a corporation we can't . . .' You know what?" Vogel marveled. "They accepted it."[95]

Some Girls' cover was, however, only part of Atlantic's worry. The album's title song had the line "Black girls like to fuck all night." Atlantic issued the album. Thump-a, thump-a.

By 1978, the employee count at the Warner Music Group had grown to over 2,000; a dozen years earlier, that number had been closer to 200. Of these

---

[95]The next cover of *Some Girls* had photos of Lucille Ball, Raquel Welch, and Farrah Fawcett-Majors in a mock wig ad. That cover was changed after the threat of lawsuits. Another rock collectible, born for eBay bidders.

2,000, 170 employees were dedicated to just one task: getting our records radio play. These 170 killer promoters flew coach. They worked out of WEA warehouses. At WCI, they never rode elevators higher than Floor Four. To this 170, "double digits" meant flipping up both middle fingers. They kept the company out in front, leaning on DJs while rock acts were tossing refrigerators out hotel windows. Let label execs in Tokyo get massaged by giggling geishas. This 170 got Picks to Click. They loved their music. Their jobs felt fresh as heaven.

One of these 170 was Linda Baker, still fresh from college, filled with energy and agog over being in rock, even as an inventory clerk. Linda was twenty but looked twelve, a wide-open, outgoing enthusiast when in 1978 she first entered the WEA branch system in Detroit, working for Gil Roberts, a strong, cigar-chomping Italian; and for fifty-something, red-haired office manager Chickie Harris. Gil and Chickie had "seen it all." Linda Baker had not. She loved it when "Boogie Till You Puke" by Root Boy Slim and the Sex Change Band got airplay. She wrote in her diary:

Nov. 15, 1977. I'm starting as a rookie, banished to department store stockrooms and record store basements to write up over-stock and defective returns. Nearly as often, I'm involved in as-sisting our merchandiser Charlie Cates in creating displays. On Mondays, I work the phones, acquire store reports. Sometimes the hype and the *tsatskes* work to get our record added.

The Atlantic rep, Ron Counts, starts acquiring his store re-ports on the Sunday before, usually from feeling intense label pressure to produce positive sales figures. We worked over the clerks at Harmony House, Korvette's, and Full Moon Records. The freebies like the Warren Zevon picture discs, Steve Martin life-size cardboard stand-ups go a long way in establishing rapport.

Comp tickets go even a longer way. The clerks love the meet-and-greets, and after the concerts, bands like Van Halen know how to charm the Music Directors' girl friends or assistant sales managers.

Other notes from Linda Baker's 1978 diary mentioned "Backstage passes in Detroit for Cheech and Chong (smoking herb on the bus with them, while Cheech watches porno movies). • In store with the Ramones after their first concert date, with Joey hiding in a stockroom in Ann Arbor, too nervous to shake hands. • Dinner with Jackson Browne's drummer, Jim Gordon, during the *Running on Empty* tour, then being astounded when, in '84, he's convicted of stabbing his mother to death after claiming that voices told him she was evil. • "Todd Is God" groupies for Rundgren in long black pea coats at Harmony House. • Promo God Rich Wolod pulling over on the freeway to throw up while driving Thin Lizzy's Phil Lynott around for an interview, because Phil stinks so bad. • Detroit's radio W4 with rookie DJ Howard Stern letting kids play their bands' tapes over the phone, then critiquing them. • The Tubes *DramaRock*, with large phallic props and tilt-a-whirl girls. • The Talking Heads visiting Linda's house where, as she put it, "we hung."

Linda Baker was just one of 170, within a company of 2,000, in love with music and backstage passes.

Joe Smith's campaign to move Elektra out of its "white, folky" confines picked up measurably when he hired Jimmy Bowen back into WEA. From his Sinatra-Martin days, Bowen had gone off with his own label, Amos Records, then over to MCA Records to run country for Mike Maitland. On a Nashville trip, Smith had baited his hook and brought in Bowen to create Elektra Country. "You have to understand how Jimmy Bowen operates," Smith once told me. "It's not a gentleman's club. Jimmy knows angles. He bends rules, looks for soft spots. I was frank. I said, 'You pick up a little bit of publishing for yourself, okay, that doesn't hurt Elektra. But if you pocket any discount on studio rates, that's larceny, that hurts Elektra, and that's off limits. But if you can get this division into profit by three hundred thousand dollars, you can start making real money.' "

Bowen set to work: Eddie Rabbitt, Johnny Lee, Conway Twitty, Mel Tillis, Hank Williams, Jr. Country became a major success for the Smith-run Elektra. Something Joe talked about on the twenty-ninth floor.

David Horowitz read the sales swell as well. David believed in "vertical integration" (acquiring your own suppliers). Warner's current pressing contract with Capitol Industries would expire in mid-1982. David's plan: Be self-sufficient before that. He bought the Warner Group its first pressing plants. Olyphant, Pennsylvania (Pop. 5,864), was home of four churches, no disco, and sixteen manufacturing business, one of which was named Specialty Records. WCI bought Specialty from its owner, Richard Marquardt.

As far back as 1916, when his business was known as the Scranton Button Company, grandfather Frank Marquardt had developed a sideline, manufacturing recordings for customers, even for Mr. Edison over in New Jersey. In 1951, Frank's son Roy opened a new business with three employees, pressing 45-RPM records on one floor of a square, three-story building previously a dress factory. LPs followed 45s. Employees made a decent wage, even though pressing records was "hot and tough": Heat up a black piece of stock vinyl and cover it with a piece of Teflon. After it melts, put it into a press with a label for each side. Push the press cover down, wait sixty seconds for the record to form, take it out, lift the lid. Do that two hundred times a day.

By the time Atlantic's Sheldon Vogel called Specialty with orders for two fast-moving LPs—Cream's *Goodbye* and Led Zeppelin *II*—Specialty had automated presses, and had became a steady supplier for WEA. By 1978, its third-generation owner, Richard Marquardt, was willing to cash out. Horowitz bought, then bought another: Allied Record Company, in Los Angeles. Allied occupied a 60,000-square-foot building but could expand to one five times that big, it was so large. Olyphant got upgraded to 240,000 square feet, plus cassette duplication in nearby Scranton. Sales were good. Planning demanded capacity.

Every one of us, from David Horowitz south, behaved like a boys' soccer team—we just played all offense, never mind defense—never thinking we had enough square feet, never never thinking we had too many.

Mo had moved me next to him into "Joe's" office in the executive end of our building. I got to redecorate my new place, which, with its fifteen-foot ceiling, was big enough for indoor volleyball. My "executive" vice presidency allowed me perks like two secretaries, black leather couches, a fully mirrored wall, a customized Cadillac convertible (our company handyman, Jimmy Rowe, called it "the pimpmobile"), and no job description. Between our two offices, Mo and I shared a bathroom. It had a shower. I never found a reason to shower during work and seldom opened the door to see who was peeing.

On the other side of the wall, Mo had the spiffiest office of all. His was three feet wider than mine, about thirty by thirty feet, walls covered with tan fabric, real wood floors, carpet to make Ali Baba turn green. Mo's desk, too, gleamed: It was an inverted U of molded blue plastic, and it came from no catalogue.

One day, I heard Mo's phone ring. The call was succinct. He walked through the bathroom into my office to say, "Columbia Records is signing James Taylor."

That I simply could not believe. *Ours* was the company that talent wanted to be with. We had never been divorced by a singer; we always got the best prom date. James, leaving? It was like the end of innocence, and just when I'd moved next to an executive toilet. The news confounded me in ways no two secretaries could help with. Mo made quick calls to James and his manager Peter Asher. Profoundly hurt, Mo, Lenny, and A&R's hot-with-Doobies Ted Templeman flew with Asher to New York, to Carly (Simon) and James's apartment at the San Remo. Mo & Company presented their case, to no avail. After the meeting, James rolled up into a ball and started to cry, not wanting to hurt anyone. Mo thought their appeal might work, but it did not.

Back home, the initial shock of this abandonment turned to anger. The word on the street was that Columbia's Yetnikoff had met with Bonnie Raitt and written an alluring number on a napkin. "Well, we'll show *them*," we decided. Plans got thought up.

Bidding wars for hot acts like James, and especially supergroups from England, had become hotter than pizza ovens on Super Sunday. When managers Dee (Peter Frampton) Anthony and Brian (Yes; Emerson, Lake & Palmer) Lane spread word of *their* new supergroup—a killer act named Scorpio—many of America's label heads swooped in for quick acquisitions.

Scorpio was, however, a prank—a wholly fictitious band that Anthony and Lane had concocted to test how high label heads would bid—sight unseen, ear unheard—for such an act. At a B'nai B'rith dinner honoring Ahmet, the Scorpio buzz captured the ears of hot signers like David Geffen, Clive Davis, Robert Stigwood. Master of ceremonies Joe Smith commented on Scorpio from the podium, as he ran down the dais, besmirching the honor of all he intro'd: "Not content with ripping off the bands they already have, Brian Lane and Dee Anthony are going to start ripping off this new band, Scorpio."

Doug Morris and Dick Vanderbilt sent their lawyer over to the Lane-Anthony table with an advance offer of $250,000 if their label, Big Tree (distributed by Atlantic), got Scorpio. Anthony rejected the deal money, politely implying it was too low. Following up, Ahmet insisted, in the weeks following, that Scorpio be on Atlantic. Contracts were actually drawn up by lawyers, despite no band-members' names being attached to the fictitious group. Signing pens were uncapped. Only as the pens hovered over contracts did the "managers" of "Scorpio" confess their deception to Ertegun. Ahmet thought this over, then commented dryly, "Hysterical."

The Thelma Walker Tally for 1978: Elektra/Asylum 15 + Warner Bros. 48 + Atlantic 20 = WEA's yearly total of 83. In 1978, WCI sold off its stock in its own parents—National Kinney Corporation, all those mops and Lysol—sold its 47 percent of the company for $8.2 million, barely over its carrying value. Kinney was a footnote, now forgotten. Bye.

In bigger type, WCI preached that its record group's revenues were up double digits again, by 16 percent, reaching an all-time high of $617 million worldwide. In the last two years, WCI's music group had doubled its revenues.

Hot as we were, during 1978's Corporate budget meeting at 10 Rockefeller Center, I noticed that our bosses—Ross, Horowitz, Wasserman, others—now began excusing themselves to take phone calls from Sunnyvale, California. Those October budget reviews once had been rituals in feel-good, where we record guys strolled in like rich nephews, over for Thanksgiving dinner with appreciative Uncle Steve. Starting in 1979, Corporate eyed its favorite nephews a bit more critically, as if, yes, we *had* graduated, but without honors.

The "budget" room we met in was about thirty by twenty feet, dominated by a round table with a heavy blue plastic top, twelve feet in diameter, atop a huge aluminum pedestal. Under the tabletop hung, every four feet around its perimeter, telephones to bump your knee into. Corporate sat around one-half of the circular table, facing its division execs on the other side and, behind us, the windows over Rockefeller Center. We division execs got less of a view, just of corporate execs and the coffee cart. As much as the table dominated the room, Bert Wasserman, WCI's chief financial officer, dominated the meeting. He carried with him four-inch-thick accounting printouts. In them, he knew where to find the saddest numbers. Kind of a Jewish Spencer Tracy. He had a gentle sense of humor, did not swear, never shouted.

By 1979, our numbers had unexpectedly turned sadder. Expenditures were holding down our balloon. When we'd returned from our October retreat at Hawaii's Mauna Kea, we pink-slipped 8 percent of our personnel in a move we called "streamlining." Bert already knew that. He treated us well, asking questions but not recommending answers. Off to one side, Ross hunkered, looking thoughtful about it all. But this year's inquiry felt less casual, less tolerant. When asked why, why this new attitude after so many laughier years, Ross answered, "You're like a car going up a hill. The first time you go into neutral, you're going backward."

For the defense, Mo described our company differently, trying to dispel New York's financial throat clearing. He talked not about profits but about signings, our total Grammys, anything but our total profits. To which Ross finally spoke up, tapping his IBM printout. "The name of the game, Mo, is performance." I wrote down that bit of wisdom. But this year the air in the room felt like the air on the faces of those ice-skaters, scooting below on Rockefeller's rink.

Ostin responded to Ross's economics lesson. He remained politely intent on building his company, not cutting off its limbs. His vision: The best company was not something built in a day, nor was it staffed by talent easily replaced. Quincy Jones's Qwest Records was being added. WBR already had Albert Grossman's Bearsville label, Chris Blackwell's Island, Curtis Mayfield's Curtom, George Harrison's Dark Horse.

When asked the next day in Atlantic's financial meeting how his label intended to reverse this "low-profit situation," Ahmet made the answer simpler. He looked over at Ross and just said, "Make more hits."

The year 1979 subdued us. *Thump.* Flying back home from budget meetings, night flights back to the Coast, we stared out the jet's windows, down at clusters of lights from towns like Amarillo and Joplin. We thought about success, wanted more of it, but were not sure how to make it "go" on. Thought about James Taylor and Scorpio, wondered if it all had peaked, if the end of the plank was at our feet. Still, like other success-addicted men, we all had no intention ever again of being what we had once been: short people.

Significant Releases

1978

Atlantic: ABBA (*The Album*, including "Name of the Game" and "Take a Chance on Me") • Average White Band (*Warmer Communications*) • Ashford & Simpson ("Is It Still Good to Ya") • The Blues Brothers (*Briefcase Full of Blues*) • Chic (*C'est Chic*, including "I Want Your Love" and "Le Freak") • Foreigner (*Double Vision*, including "He Got Blooded" and "Blue Morning, Blue Day") • Genesis (*And Then There Were Three*, including "Follow You Follow Me") • The Trammps ("Disco Inferno") • Yes (*Tormato*)

Big Tree: England Dan & John Ford Coley ("We'll Never Have to Say Goodbye Again")

Rolling Stone: The Rolling Stones (*Some Girls*, including "Miss You")

Elektra: The Cars • Queen (*Jazz*, including "Bicycle Race" and "Fat-Bottomed Girls") • Carly Simon (*Boys in the Trees*, including "You Belong to Me")

Asylum: Jackson Browne (*Running on Empty*) • Joni Mitchell (*Don Juan's Reckless Daughter*) • Linda Ronstadt (*Living in the USA*) • Warren Zevon (*Excitable Boy*)

Planet: Pointer Sisters (*Energy*, including "Fire")

Warner Bros.: Ambrosia (*Life Beyond L.A.*, including "Biggest Part of Me," "How Much I Feel," and "You're the Only Woman (You and I)" • George Benson (*Weekend in L.A.*, including "On Broadway") • Black Sabbath (*Never Say Die!*) • Bootsy's Rubber Band (*Bootsy? Player of the Year*) • Devo (*Q: Are We Not Men? A: We Are Devo!*) • The Doobie Brothers (*Minute by Minute*, including "What a Fool Believes") • Funkadelic (*One Nation Under a Groove*) • Emmylou Harris (*Quarter Moon in a Ten Cent Town*) • Chaka Khan (*Chaka*) • Nicolette Larson ("Lotta Love") • Steve Martin (*A Wild and Crazy Guy*, including "King Tut") • Van Morrison (*Wavelength*) • Prince (*Prince—for You*) • Leo Sayer ("More Than I Can Say") • Rod Stewart (*Blondes Have More Fun*, including "Da Ya Think I'm Sexy?") • Van Halen ("You Really Got Me")

Reprise: Neil Young (*Comes a Time*)

Bearsville: Todd Rundgren (*Hermit of Mink Hollow*)

Capricorn: The Marshall Tucker Band (*Together Forever*)

Curb: Exile ("Kiss You All Over")

Curtom: Linda Clifford ("If My Friends Could See Me Now")

Island: Grace Jones (*Fame*) • Bob Marley & the Wailers (*Kaya*) • Robert Palmer (*Every Kinda People*)

Scotti Brothers: Leif Garrett (*Feel the Need*, including "I Was Made for Dancin'")

Sire: The Ramones (*Road to Ruin*) • Talking Heads (*More Songs About Buildings and Food*, including "Take Me to the River")

Whitfield: Rose Royce ("Love Don't Live Here Anymore")

1979

Atlantic: ABBA (*Voulez-Vous*, including "Does Your Mother Know") • AC/DC (*Highway to Hell*) • Chic (*Risqué*, including "Good Times") • Foreigner (*Head Games*, including "Dirty White Boy") • Bette Midler (*The Rose*) • *The Muppet Movie*, including "Rainbow Connection" • Spinners ("Working My Way Back to You"/"Forgive Me, Girl")

Atco: Blackfoot ("Highway Song") • Roxy Music (*Manifesto*)

Cotillion: Sister Sledge (*We Are Family*, including "He's the Greatest Dancer")

Island: Robert Palmer (*Secrets,* including "Bad Case of Loving You (Doctor, Doctor)")

Swan Song: Bad Company (*Desolation Angels,* including "Rock 'n' Roll Fantasy") • Led Zeppelin (*In Through the Out Door*)

Elektra: The Cars (*Candy-O,* including "Let's Go") • Queen (*Live Killers*) • Carly Simon (*Spy*) • Grover Washington, Jr. (*Paradise*)

Asylum: Eagles (*The Long Run,* including "Heartache Tonight," "I Can't Tell You Why," and "Long Run") • Joni Mitchell (*Mingus*) • *No Nukes*

Warner Bros.: The B-52's ("Rock Lobster") • Dire Straits ("Sultans of Swing" and "Communiqué") • Fleetwood Mac (*Tusk,* including "Sara" and "Think About Me") • Funkadelic (*Uncle Jam Wants You*) • Rickie Lee Jones ("Chuck E.'s in Love") • The Marshall Tucker Band (*Running Like the Wind*) • Steve Martin (*Comedy Is Not Pretty!*) • Monty Python (*Life of Brian*) • Van Morrison (*Into the Music*) • Randy Newman (*Born Again*) • Prince ("I Wanna Be Your Lover") • Bonnie Raitt (*The Glow*) • Rod Stewart (*Greatest Hits*) • Van Halen (*II,* including "Dance the Night Away") • ZZ Top (*Degüello*)

Reprise: Neil Young (*Rust Never Sleeps* and *Live Rust*)

Capricorn: The Allman Brothers Band (*Enlightened Rogues*)

Dark Horse: George Harrison ("Blow Away")

Sire: Talking Heads (*Fear of Music*)

21

Every day, WCI's CFO Bert Wasserman juggled numbers. His was a world different from the record business, where we lived and breathed singers and bands, records with hooks, and plagues. All those, in Bert's world, were simply causes. He was in charge of financial effects.

We got along well because all Bert really wanted to know about anything was "What'll it cost us?" or "What's the upside?" He asked outstanding questions, like "Why is tour support costing you so much more this quarter?" He always had his other two labels to compare us to.

It came to me that Bert's life in Corporate must be dull, maybe like life in pro football must be for the guy who chalks the stripes. Bert, however, never showed dull. He always showed jovial interest, acting as if he'd really like it if you asked him to lunch. In 1980, though, I did notice that Bert started tilting forward a bit more when asking us questions, then follow-up questions. My metaphor for him changed from football-stripe guy. I now saw Bert acting more like a forest ranger who hoped that flickering speck of red he saw ten miles away was under control.

In early 1979, the record industry asked me, again, to do the keynote speech at NARM. The trades had noted uglinesses: an avalanche of returns, and over two hundred record executives had recently lost their jobs. I'd read about that, but WEA's cuts had been silent ones, just twenty-five people, which is small—unless you're one of them. I was truly not wired into the "doldrums" in the rest of the record industry until I reached the lobby of NARM's Miami hotel. There, my eyes opened. In the lobby were long-timers, suited up well, often sales and promo execs, now in their later forties. Guys you could name by the first name and everyone knew whom you meant. In the lobby, those execs who'd been cut were glad-hugging their colleagues, ears open for what they called "the next career step."

In my pocket was my high-minded speech about how we in the industry should give back to music a little bit of the riches that it had given us. It was titled "Take a Little, Leave a Little," after an accounting rule I'd once heard from the fast-moving artist/publishing scamp Artie Mogull. Artie seemed never permanently employed. He darted in and out of companies like a teenage girl trying on dresses at the May Company. "Take a Little, Leave a Little" was Artie's rule about how to handle money, as it flowed through your hands on its way to artists. You shouldn't steal it all. I liked the Damon Runyon sound of Artie's skimming rule and laughed over his amoral attitudes; he compulsively lived for the deal, not just the music. But my innocent keynote speech about doing Good Things felt, this morning, morally pretentious.

Onstage, I hastily ad-libbed a few paragraphs of empathy about the job seekers out in the lobby, then launched into the least timely speech of my life—not counting my marriage proposals. I still remember, though, the anxieties of grown men working the crowd, looking for a job. It was like spotting some high-school friend a few years after graduation, and he's sitting there on a sidewalk begging with a bowl.

But within the Warner Group, life was nowhere near begging. Maybe, in early 1979, after every business lunch we'd swallow one more Rolaid. Maybe, looking back, I'd have truly had to be senseless to not see what was happening. But to the press and to Wall Street, the Warner Group denied that a sales depression had begun. We just flat-out lied.

Our best lying got directed at Wall Street analysts, guys who affected WCI's stock prices. For analyst meetings, Horowitz imported his glibbest guys. At the moment, those included Droz, Nesuhi, Smith, and me. Our concessions to reality were minimized; we were there to sell the stock. Horowitz once admitted to Wall Street that WCI's Records division's "first quarter will be flat." Asked to amplify, Horowitz blamed the recent revisions in the copyright laws, the price of using songs having gone up. Oh.

Like Horowitz, Droz knew his audience. He spoke warmly of the price hikes for certain new albums, up from $7.98 to $8.98. Faced with a slow year, WEA's labels had their always-comfortable answer: Raise list price.

Switch the topic. Talk about . . . growth! New investment. Building our own pressing plants. Smith spoke at a Beverly Hills seminar for the banking community. He corrected perceptions: Hey, 1979 was not really a "bad" year for the industry, it was an "off" year, compared to the phenomenal year of 1978. Smith estimated that perhaps only four hundred people in the record business had lost jobs. "But the press equates that with General Motors laying off seventy-five thousand," Joe said. "The record-industry slump has gotten more coverage than the pope's visit."

Other record executives made eloquent excuses for the "leveling off" of sales: Atari games were distracting their kid audience. Counterfeit product was coming in from everywhere. Home taping of the newly popular cassettes and all that blank tape. Those we termed "plagues."

What we could not call a plague were our returns. We called them "inventory correction," but our sales excesses, our "shipping platinums," were coming back at us, big. WCI started putting out a *Financial Fact Book*, containing what it called "real numbers." One number was that 16.8 percent of albums shipped to retail get returned. Which came down to this: For every $769 million of albums we sold, we'd get "only" $128 million returned to us. At the time, those numbers were meant to console.

Even WCI's Annual Report, that publication of optimism, was now forced to confess, "It appears that the industry is in transition from its remarkably high growth years of the mid-Seventies to an upcoming period of steady if moderate revenue growth . . ."

Returns became 1979's hottest topic. To make sure our albums were buyable, in depth, everywhere, the record business had turned to near-total consignment. Stores paid only after albums sold. Albums that sat were simply sent back at bill-paying time. Our hope was that the percentage of returns would be under 20. The platinum-dazzled industry had stopped obeying one of Joel Friedman's cautionary sayings about overshipping and overstocking shelves, which went "Volume has killed more Jews than Hitler."

WEA returns centers were getting buried in unwanted product. WEA executives, after winding up a four-city, traveling exec show at the Hyatt in L.A., got cornered by *Billboard* magazine. Droz & Company pooh-poohed any talk about changing WEA's return policy. The following Monday, *Billboard* published its own opinion: "WEA is lying." A tough return policy was being written up as Henry misspoke. *Billboard* knew it, and blew it for WEA.

RIAA estimated that returns were costing U.S. record labels $200 million a year (less 10 percent income from recycling all that gooey black vinyl). Other than in the trucker-intense South, 8-track tapes stopped selling, and those clunky devils came back to Central Returns big time, making a hollow roar as they poured onto tables specially designed to sort turkeys.

As a phrase, "shipping platinum" began feeling as inspiring a slogan as "enjoying alcoholism." Album cover printers like Ivy Hill's chairman, Lew Garlick, a man who always paid even the biggest restaurant checks with crisp hundred-dollar bills, got quoted as saying, "Business is at the lowest ebb yet in relation of capacity to production. Any jacket orders we take today would involve product due for release within thirty to sixty days, but we're just not getting major orders."

So we 'fessed up a bit, using euphemisms like "sobering year" and "year of self-examination." *People, Time, Newsweek,* the *New York Times,* and the *Los Angeles Times*—all published stories about what, one year earlier, might have been a new dance craze: The Slump. Some reporters looked upon us as showbiz guys and used verbs that sneered. It was the kind of year when you didn't want to memorize how all this felt.

MCA startled the business when it actually reduced list prices for some albums: $5.98 became a revived price category. Then Phonogram-Mercury, then Capitol, then CBS all followed suit.

WEA went the other way, stunning the trade with another price increase: singles up from $1.29 to $1.49. Album prices, too, up 3 percent, still believing that if you're under budget, you just raise your prices. Retailers reacted vehemently. For WEA albums only, L.A.'s vengeance-minded record chain Music Plus pushed its list price up to $8.98.

WEA quickly wised up. First, Droz quoted Friedman: "When you are up to your ass in alligators, it's difficult to remind yourself that your initial objective was to drain the swamp." WEA announced a revised returns policy, one that rewarded or penalized a retailer depending on its performance. If a retailer returned *under* 18 percent, the price it paid WEA was less. If it returned *over* 22 percent, that cost it extra. The pennies-per-sale returns policy worked. For WEA anyway, it destroyed the illusion that growth always took care of soaring costs. Expansion for the sake of expansion seemed as dated as colonialism for the sake of more colonies.

Again and again, David Horowitz called the few of us into New York to address the financial community, make promises. Nesuhi would speak of opening companies in Ireland, Taiwan, Zimbabwe, and would observe that "returns are not a problem in the international world, except for Japan. That is probably the best news I will give you this morning." Nesuhi symbolized Growth: 1978–79 growth percentage for WEA International had been up 31 percent; 1977–78's percentage had been 63.5 percent. WEA International became the record division's fourth big profit center. Me, I talked about fighting home taping by offering "a scientific cash award for the development of a device or tone which would prevent recording off the air, and from home stereos." Back in the Seventies, when our notion of a really scary epidemic was herpes, I had no idea how impossible blocking home taping would prove. (I still hear such "watermark" suggestions today and know their folly.)

David stated 1979's numbers. "The disc industry sales have lagged but haven't sagged," he said. "Sales of the industry declined six to ten percent from 1978." He noted that WCI "far outperformed the record industry in 1979. That's the good news. The bad news is that earnings declined twelve percent." Finally, Droz would list upcoming releases in a world where a hit would wipe away all ills: The Rolling Stones, the Doobie Brothers, Paul Simon, Rod Stewart . . . At the end of such analyst sessions, there was not a wet eye in the house.

These were not like the old days, nor even last year. The Big Button which had grown from WEA Intenational into a Mo-and-Joe-and-Ahmet too emblem, was pooped, dated, and retired. When Wasserman later added up the real numbers, our decline had been down not the 12 percent that David had announced, but 18 percent. We would survive.

These days, though, the WCI jet was a wee bit less available. It was often in Sunnyvale, California.

* * *

In 1976, when break-dancers spun on their backs, WCI had bought a small video-game company based in Sunnyvale, a flatness in Silicon Valley. The name of the buy was Atari, which I think of as Japanese for "jumping bean." WCI's kinetic Manny Gerard had seen an Atari coin-op game—Pong, or move the paddles to keep the bouncing ball from going off the screen—and Steve Ross had done a calculation. The machine cost $4,500 and was taking in $250,000 a year. "Now, that's my kind of business," Ross said. Atari became WCI's first acquisition in four years. It cost $12 million in cash, plus $16 million in debentures (paper). Headed by Nolan Bushnell, Atari had revenues in 1977 of $39 million and profit of $3.5 million. Ross's offer looked good to Bushnell.

While the Records Division had been puffed up by Queen, ABBA, and Christopher Cross, Atari had grown from Pong to Pac-Man to Space Invaders to Missile Command, and a cash rush of unprecedented proportions poured at the feet of WCI. Atari was no longer just coin-op in lounges and arcades. It sold home-op machines for teen boys to substitute for homework and home rock. To music people, Atari seemed fine, if lamentably audio-anemic. We didn't even distribute the game cartridges. Years ago, hadn't we moved beyond "coin-op"?

The reality shock to us Annual Report page-one types came with WCI's next report. Moving onto page one—and shoving us back ten pages like we were now some, oh, some floor-mopping company—was the new Consumer Electronics and Toys Division, meaning Atari. Sales there doubled in one year: from $238 million to $513 million. If you liked ramps that went up, Atari was heaven bent:

Revenue ($000)	1977	1978	1979	1980
Atari & Company	127,500	177,900	238,000	512,700
Record Group	282,000	394,500	400,000	445,900

Although not given the third degree at Elektra's previous budget meeting, Joe Smith was aware that his labels' new signings had so far produced little. His first line of defense was quips, which Bert enjoyed as often as possible. Joe was also aware that royalty-rich artists were slow with new product: "Jackson Browne makes a record every time Halley's Comet comes around, and the Eagles, who "spent three years making their last album."

Linda Ronstadt went off to Manhattan to star as Mabel in the Gilbert and Sullivan operetta *Pirates of Penzance* and didn't make a new album. Carly Simon left Elektra for Warner Bros., petulantly but purposefully. "I was signed in Elektra by Jac Holzman in 1970 and made my first record in 1971," she said. "Jac left the company in 1972 or 1973, and then I was with David Geffen, who brought in Asylum Records. All of a sudden I didn't get the same attention I did with Holzman. Then Geffen left, and Joe Smith came along. You begin to feel like a stepchild, once removed, and then twice removed.

"What is a company," Simon asked, "but the people involved, and you sign with a company because of the people. And if the people leave, it's like being orphaned."

To invigorate Elektra, Joe hired the recent ex–head of Columbia Records in New York, Bruce Lundvall, a tall, engaging, pure music man. Lundvall had left Columbia, where he headed its U.S. operation, in part because he disliked its bureaucracy, in part because a "deputy president," Dick Asher, had been slid in between Lundvall and the boss, Walter Yetnikoff. But more than avoiding politics, Lundvall wanted to run his own jazz label, spend more time at home, stop making convention speeches, and avoid thirty-first-floor meetings. He skipped the big-time job to stick with the music.

Lundvall became Elektra's East Coast general manager, senior VP, and "international presence." Joe promised Bruce that he'd get to start two more East Coast–based labels: Elektra Metropolitan (for pop) and Elektra Musician (for jazz).

Smith continued doing what he did best: signing more. The Stray Cats, Helmet Boy, and (on Planet) the Cretones and Sue Saad & the Next—acts identifiable now only by their dental records, but at the time riding the wave of skinny-tied, New Wave bands whose record careers lasted as long as ice cubes in August.

Bert Wasserman saw that Elektra was losing two tons of money. He recalled how to subtract.

While WEA was modifying distribution, the label executives made their own moves. Seymour Stein sold his remaining 50 percent of Sire to Warner Bros. Records. Included: the Ramones and Talking Heads. For Stein, what he got was real, secure money. He continued working at WBR, with a half-point override on any act he brought in.

Jerry Wexler hated the impotence of retirement. In 1977 Mo asked Jerry if he could help out Warners, and he was put in charge of our New York office. Jerry told us the last thing he wanted was to meddle. He meant it. Wexler's roots brought us albums by Etta James and Allan Toussaint. Neither album took hold.

Jerry Greenberg and brother Bob left Atlantic to start their own Atlantic-backed and -distributed label called Mirage. Jerry's idea: "We plan to do in the 1980s what David Geffen did in the Seventies."[96]

---

[96]For five years, Greenberg would sign acts and Atlantic would release albums. Greenberg's best-selling signing would be Whitesnake. But at the end, Mirage was not what Asylum had once been. And Jerry Greenberg, whom Geffen had once called "what held Atlantic together," was gone once more from Ahmet's label.

In Greenberg's place, Ahmet appointed two men: Sheldon Vogel as vice chairman and Doug Morris as president. Doug, whose own label, Big Tree, had been attached to Atlantic for many years, had in 1978 sold the label to Atlantic, then taken over running Atco. He'd gotten known as a straight-in-your-eyes guy, whose taste ran to singles of the 1960s sort. "Of all the people I've worked with," Ahmet commented, "Doug is the straightest person I've ever known. He does not have what the French call *arrière-pensées*—hidden thoughts. It's incredible, but in all the years I've been with Doug, we have never had an argument and we have never left the office without hugging one another."

But others within the company felt a difference. Jerry Greenberg had always kept his door open, knew everyone in the company. He treated his VPs and the trash man the same way. Doug Morris was increasingly a door-closed loner. He had a policy of not returning phone calls. He kept his privacy; few in the company even knew he was a grandfather. Atlantic's home-office, open-door continuity swung over to Vogel, tall, straightforward, a little loud at times. But at least Shelly returned phone calls.

In February, Geffen, ready to dis-retire after years involving a mistaken cancer scare, casual teaching at Yale, and an appointment to the Board of the University of California, finally wanted back in records. He phoned Ostin, ready to be backed now a third time running a new label. Mo loved talent magnets like Krasnow, Geffen, and Waronker. He collected them like his wife, Evelyn, collected fine scarves. By the end of this one phone call, the Geffen deal was roughed out. Warner Bros. Records, co-owner of the new label, would distribute. Profits would be fifty/fifty. Geffen got to pick his label's international distributor; if Geffen chose other than WEA International, that new distributor would have to send half its profits back to WBR. The distribution clause was a bit odd, but for WBR, this way international profits became win/win and hardly a sticking point.

Plans were announced to grow Geffen Records into "Warner Communications' fourth record company." David viewed the record business of 1980 with typical hauteur: "The problem . . . is not counterfeiting, which is illegal, or home taping, which is a fact of life and going on for years. What's wrong with the business is incompetence, a lack of commitment, and insensitivity." The Plagues of David.

After I'd been put in the second-largest office at WBR, and given the Number Two title in the company, Eddie Rosenblatt, wanting his own path to the top, left WBR after nine years and moved over to Geffen as its COO. The connection promised well: Geffen Records was depending on WBR for promotion, and Rosenblatt was well known at Warner.

Geffen again opened offices on Sunset Boulevard, with used furniture, his offices casual as a trailer park. He dressed in his classic Reeboks, jeans, a flannel shirt over his T. Three deals were quickly signed: the reborn disco-

Christian Donna Summer, Mr. and Mrs. John Lennon, and Elton John. To sign Geffen's first hair band, he'd hired a guru with an eighteen-inch beard and a white suit. John Kalodner had earlier worked at Atlantic, moving up from publicity (1974) to finding Foreigner for Jerry Greenberg there. Kalodner became David's A&R connection to the 1980s. Kalodner could actually hear this music. He signed Asia. When he recommended signing Genesis's Phil Collins, David overruled him in favor of the hairier Peter Gabriel.

For Geffen Records' international rights, WEA International offered a $1 million advance for three years. But Geffen was free to deal. His lawyer, Allen Grubman, landed Geffen Records a three-year, $15 million advance from CBS International. In exchange, CBS's Walter Yetnikoff could, for three years, give WEA International the finger. That $15 million advance, while unpatriotic, saved Mo's Warner Bros. from bottom-line grief during the Geffen label's start-up. WEA International's face turned redder than a Peruvian parrot.

MTV began. First the record business yawned. It was just a takeoff on Warner Cable's "music videos" show called *Pop Clips,* which had been hosted by ex-Monkee Mike Nesmith. Warner cable exec John Lack had thought, "Hmmm, twenty-four hours, round-the-clock music videos." He made a demo for a full-time channel called Music Television.

Horowitz introduced MTV to WCI's record labels in a carefully planned "presentation," the kind of meeting to which no grouch gets invited. We had been flown or limoed into New York, to be shown a fifteen-minute promo for the channel. The promo was talked over by Warner's John Lack, introducing his idea of the new venture, Warner AmEx Satellite Entertainment. During the presentation, staring at us were Steve and the project's co-financier, American Express chairman James Robinson. After the video, when asked, Robinson said, "I guess we have a few million we can spare for the project."[97] Asked what we label execs thought, we realized this was hardly time to get sordid. "Fine," we'd all nod, then leave, to limo and fly right back home. Why such "meetings" at Corporate happened I never really understood.

Within weeks, Lack's assistant, Bob Pittman, visited me in Burbank to explain why Warner Bros. Records should spend its good money making videos that he, for no payment to us, would show on his TV channel to very few people. "Fine," I lied.

---

[97]WCI had borrowed around $175 million for cable programming, and wanted to erase that debt. AmEx bought in, for $175 million, and got 50 percent of what was called Warner Amex Cable. WCI had the other half, now for free. By 1985, facing more financial pain, Warner wanted to unload it all, including MTV. In the unloading, both WCI and AmEx made a bundle or two, but so did the cable company's buyer, Viacom, which ended up with MTV.

By 1980, I had become weary with my job at Warner Bros. Records. Earlier, Mo had asked why I didn't just keep doing Creative Services, rather than handing it over to others, like ex–Beatle publicist Derek Taylor. In retrospect, Mo was right. Creative was what I did. And by now my executive-VP job seemed much more routine, like deciding who got little refrigerators in their offices.

I got an ulcer, the hole from stasis anxiety. I was no longer interested in lying to acts about how a poster would make their album a hit. I found my business—the record business—faced with larger issues. They interested me more.

Horowitz had all these Plagues to contend with: production facilities; packaging, testing, and launching new products (including videos); new product configurations (including digital records); statistical and consumer projections; antipiracy; home taping; expanded marketing methods. That list he offered to me. I took Mo to dinner at our neighborhood French restaurant, La Serre, and there, under hanging ferns and over trout amandine, I suggested I'd like to work on these larger issues for the whole WCI Record Group. Mo understood. Perhaps because I had shown so little interest in shower sharing, he told me I could keep my office. Soon enough, I was on Corporate's payroll, as a WCI senior vice president under Horowitz, with a list of challenges to tackle. I stayed put in Burbank, my ulcer disappeared, and I got ready to lick the 1980s.

Significant Releases

1980

Atlantic: AC/DC ("Back in Black") • Chic ("Chip Off the Old Black" and "Real People") • Genesis (*Duke,* including "Misunderstanding") • Bette Midler (*Divine Madness)* • Spinners (*Dancin' and Lovin'*) • Yes (*Drama*)

Atco: Gary Numan ("Cars") • Roxy Music (*Flesh + Blood*) • Pete Townshend (*Empty Glass,* including "Let My Love Open the Door")

Cotillion: Stacy Lattisaw ("Let Me Be Your Angel")

Island: Marianne Faithful (*Broken English*) • Bob Marley & the Wailers (*Uprising*) • Robert Palmer (*Clues*)

Rolling Stone: The Rolling Stones (*Emotional Rescue,* including "She's So Cold")

Elektra: The Cars (*Panorama*) • Robbie Dupree ("Steal Away" and "Hot Rod Hearts") • Queen (*The Game,* including "Another One Bites the Dust" and "Crazy Little Thing Called Love," and *Flash Gordon*) • Eddie Rabbitt (*Horizon,* including "Drivin' My Life Away" and "I Love a Rainy Night") • Neil and Dara Sedaka ("Should've Never Let You Go") • Carly Simon (*Come Upstairs*) • Grover Washington, Jr. (*Winelight,* including "Just the Two of Us")

Asylum: Jackson Browne (*Hold Out,* including "Boulevard" and "That Girl Could Sing") • Eagles (*Live,* including "Seven Bridges Road") • Joni Mitchell (*Shadows and Light*) • Linda Ronstadt (*Mad Love,* including "How Do I Make You" and "Hurt So

Bad") • Warren Zevon (*Bad Luck Streak in Dancing School*) • *Urban Cowboy* soundtrack

Full Moon: Johnny Lee ("Lookin' for Love")

Planet: Pointer Sisters ("He's So Shy")

Warner Bros.: Ashford & Simpson (*A Musical Affair*) • George Benson ("Give Me the Night") • The B-52s (*Wild Planet*) • Christopher Cross ("Sailing," "Ride Like the Wind," "Never Be the Same," and "Say You'll Be Mine") • Devo (*Freedom of Choice*, including "Whip It") • Dire Straits (*Making Movies*) • The Doobie Brothers (*One Step Closer*, including "Real Love") • Fleetwood Mac (*Live*) • Larry Graham ("One in a Million You") • Emmylou Harris (*Roses in the Snow*) • Al Jarreau ("This Time") • Chaka Khan (*Naughty*) • Little Feat (*Hoy-Hoy!*) • The Marshall Tucker Band ("Tenth") • Prince (*Dirty Mind*) • Paul Simon (*One-Trick Pony*, including "Late In the Evening") • Rod Stewart (*Foolish Behaviour*, including "Passion") • Van Halen (*Women and Children First*) • *Zapp*

Reprise: Frank Sinatra (*Trilogy: Past, Present, Future*) • Neil Young (*Hawks & Doves*)

Bearsville: Utopia (*Adventures in Utopia*)

Geffen: John Lennon (*Double Fantasy*, including "(Just Like) Starting Over," "Watching the Wheels," and "Woman") • Donna Summer ("The Wanderer")

Sire: The Pretenders (*Pretenders,* including "Brass in Pocket") • Ramones (*End of the Century*) • Talking Heads (*Remain in Light*)

22

WE'D take the morning Warner jet cross-country to budget meetings feeling optimistic for the year. But in that room with the big blue table, we now learned that just *leading* our industry was not enough. All WEA's changes and cuts, long overdue, had helped, but only some. The problem, I started to realize, was the odd way the record business itself had become structured. On one long corporate jet trip, between my raids for free candy bars, I made a yellow tablet list. OUT OF CONTROL, I headlined it optimistically. I underlined my observations about our business, though none of us had a clue how to fix the way our industry rattled on. Here's a paraphrase of that list:

- SALES of our product are *out of our control.* Retailers, each year larger and more powerful, handle our product only on consignment, then return it at will, paying only for what they sell. We record companies pay for everything from manufacturing to retail ads. We beg for floor space, while retail, our central avenue to the customer, works by its own rules.[98] Central Avenue has broken down (my reference to Lionel Hampton's "Central Avenue Breakdown," c. 1940).
- PROMOTION of our product is also *beyond our control.* Radio has not died; it has divided and multiplied. Program directors choose which record of ours to play, and we don't. We pander to them. Radio follows its own priorities; ours come second.
- ARTISTS' DEMANDS have also gone *beyond our control.* Artists demand freedom to create, a demand that gets coupled with their other freedom: to screw around. Artists get both freedoms, based on their clout and our hungers. More and more, they push for control. They aren't wrong. But the product—music—is less in our hands.

---

[98]Record clubs were hardly a factor in making records sell. From them, we got advances, mainly from Columbia's record club, but paid no attention to its choices. Record clubs were like income from Ecuador.

- MANUFACTURING COST of our product is still *beyond our control.* Arab oil makes decisions about what manufacturing costs.
- VALUE of our product is *beyond our control.* People can now make free duplicates, millions of them, and we don't get paid.

Try starting some new business with a list like that, I thought, and you'd get laughed out of Harvard Business School. Right then, the business all felt out of my and our control: Who could fix retail, promotion, artists, home taping, even OPEC? My list . . .

Beginning in the early 1980s, we all handled things a bit less invincibly. Our market behaved about as controllably as a greased pig. To start 1981, Atlantic had five of the Top Ten albums on the charts. Felt good. When the year ended, it was Warner that had five of the Top Ten. Felt good. At Elektra, Joe had been signing like mad. And the three labels that owned WEA also distributed a major banquet of forty-three other labels.

Just one problem: The charts did not reflect absolute sales, only relative popularity. Our problem: record buyers stayed home. WEA's hottest items got to be Jane Fonda's buns-bulging videos. Felt ugly.

Murray Gitlin was waving at me. It was my turn at the plane's backgammon board. I stuffed my list into my aluminum attaché case, snap snap.

In 1971, at the outset of shared distribution, our labels' money men—the always-audible Sheldon (Shelly) Vogel of Atlantic, the sly and quick-to-object Murray Gitlin of WBR, and the round and buddylike Jack Reinstein of Elektra—had formed an "oversight committee" to settle shared business questions. This financial committee was called "the ViGoR Committee," after V for Vogel, G for Gitlin, and R for Reinstein. Accountants, who infrequently get chosen "Most Popular" at proms, soon found us renaming their VGR troika the "VulGaR Committee." Either way, when sales went south, the VGRs' job was to cut cut cut. In 1981, as numbers got redder, Shelly, Murray, and Jack cut faster than paid-by-the-piece sweatshop workers.

Among themselves, the VGRs fought about which of their three labels should pay for what, an expensive version of "Now, who was it ordered the shrimp cocktail?" They'd go like this: "Well, your contribution should be consistent with your percentage of the business." So Reinstein from littler Elektra would answer, "Fine, I'm in for ten percent." Then Gitlin would come back with, "But you represent twenty-four percent of this year's business!"

Profits kept retreating, only single-digit now. The labels' mood was white knuckled, despite those five of the Top Ten spots we held on the charts. One day, I learned one of my own life lessons. I was sitting next to Eddie Rosenblatt in the conference room of WBR when he leaned over to say, "When sales are good, that's when guys like *us* get our way. When they're bad, the *money* guys take over."

In the early-1980s bear market, lunch dates with our nervous CFOs was about as appealing as eating fried feathers.

Meanwhile in my new Corporate job as Stan the Plagues (home taping and co.) Fighter, I'd called an all-labels meetings at Las Hadas, a glitzy Mexican resort starring the gleaming white walls and tile floors seen in the movie *10*. (We execs were not yet asked to cut back on our expense accounts, despite a wobbling industry.) There, following margaritas, we developed naïve Plague Plans, like gluing noncopyable stickers onto cassette boxes, so we could spot phonies by peering at any stickers through pen-shaped scopes; phony stickers would be quickly spotted.[99] We proclaimed market-expanding cures like promoting records as better holiday gifts than chocolates or flowers, citing our research that "five times as many people would rather get a Gift of Music than candy." We lobbied Washington to give us an anti-home-taping law. (I learned that senators were like radio program directors. Donations got you in the door. It could remind a guy of payola.) All of our high-minded Plague cures felt feeble.

Our Number One Plague was the recordable audiocassette, which we called "The Maxell Medfly." Coupled with the Walkman, cassettes gave people what LPs never could: truly portable music, albums for joggers. Now every album was coming out as both LP and cassette. But . . . cassette recorders *plus* blank tape, that got very scary. We speculated about college kids buying one new Foreigner album plus ten blank tapes, and suddenly eleven dorm rooms had our new album, but Atlantic had collected for just one.

With taping raging, once again, NARM bravely asked me to keynote its convention, whose theme was "Plan to Be There."[100] Correcting any optimism I'd shown a couple of years earlier, my new speech was called "The Seven Plagues of Sammy Ricklin." (Ricklin was a made-up name, but to me Sammy sounded like a guy who might own a one-stop somewhere.)

I described Plagues aplenty, leading with news tidbits:

- Counterfeiting: How in a raid on Hot Cakes Music and Federated Record Company in Newtonville, Massachusetts, our missing-stickers gizmo had turned up six thousand illegal cassettes.
- Piracy: How for the year, the International Federation of Phonograph

---

[99]Our pursuit of phony cassettes netted few felons. We found mostly swap-meet fakes. Killing them off was more trouble than it was worth.

[100]I never understood the mottos or themes of conventions, either NARM's or WEA's. I kept wondering, "What does this mean?" WEA's fall-program slogan for the year was "Fantastic Incredible Program."

Industries estimated that our worldwide loss from "commercialized taping" (piracy) was $915 million.

- Home Audiotaping: How it was costing the record industry $2.85 billion a year. How RIAA president Stan Gortikov estimated "for every album sold, one is taped." He claimed, "In our henhouse, poachers now almost outnumber the chickens."

Home taping, via the Betamax Case (MCA v. Sony), which aimed to ban home copying machines for movies, had reached the Supreme Court. We (the copyright business) again lost. Blank tape, the nine Supremes in their black robes decided, was no more dangerous than blank paper.[101] Our record industry felt only slightly affected by the judgment about *video*tape, but talked as righteous as ever. The RIAA's Jay Berman put it plainly: "American music is something the rest of the world wants to listen to. Our job is to make sure they pay for it." We spent little time at that job.

With dizzying speed, Henry and the VGRs (first) had raised our list prices to $8.98 an album, then (second) added a midprice tier for older albums at $5.98. Now, (third) we raised the price of the lower tier from $5.98 to $6.98, and (fourth) kept nudging up wholesale price, squeezing dealers with each increase.

Time, Newsweek, the *New York Times,* and *The Wall Street Journal* all ran stories in the early Eighties about the woes of the record industry. CBS Records talked about eliminating 30 top executives, but its real total was 375 jobs and the closure of ten branch locations. Capitol and CBS closed their California manufacturing plants. Atlantic dropped regional promotion reps, then 6 lower-level West Coast personnel. Warner Bros. Records "staff reduced" 29 employees and shut its merchandising warehouse. Elektra cut 22, including several VPs.

WEA fired Rich Lionetti, who'd replaced Vic Faraci as head of sales. Lionetti was a polished dude, a bit too polished for his fellows in sales. He pushed cassettes at all meetings, relentlessly predicting they'd take over recorded tape configurations. He was right, but tediously so, which made him wrong. "The really famous Lionetti line," Russ Thyret recalled, "was 'One degree of difference—the degree between hot water and boiling water, one degree of difference.' I heard that speech so many times . . . I mean you got really tired of it." It was the polished part that made Rich distinctive and, I guess, vulnerable. And one day, he was gone.[102]

At Atlantic, as the old ways seemed to fail, the archetypal recording

---

[101]Even blank paper hurt, as Xeroxing had done to the sheet music business in the Sixties.

[102]After being fired from WEA, Rich Lionetti struggled for a good job for several years. He never connected, really. One day we learned he'd just gone into his backyard, tossed a rope over a tree branch, and hanged himself.

engineer of our labels, the bearded Tom Dowd, looked around, felt Atlantic was not Atlantic anymore. Dowd chose to retire. He moved to Miami. My favorite line of Tom's, spoken late in his career to some young act out in the studio: "You guys are not playing or sounding like your lives depend on this!"

With minimal help from its sagging Records division, in 1981 WCI enjoyed its biggest profit year ever. Income—up 50 percent, to $3.2 billion—astonishing Bert Wasserman. Net income was up 65 percent. Such numerical thrills came from Atari. That division had grown not by double but by *triple* digits: from $512 million in 1980 to $1.2 billion in 1981.

Had Atari been one company unto itself, it would have come in around 300 on the Fortune 500. In two years, Atari had grown from three thousand employees to ten thousand. Atari game cartridges sold through WEA, but only for music-store distribution. Pac-Man, the Bambi of the Eighties, went twelve times platinum. We relaxed. As long as Atari was doing that kind of business, we could.

Mo named Lenny Waronker president of WBR in 1981. When Lenny and I discussed the news, he insisted that I should stay put in my big Number Two guy's office. "Don't be ridiculous," I insisted back. Down the hall forty feet, we carved another big office out of two regular ones, installed a new wall of mirror, and I moved and used the company latrine. Lenny redecorated my old office: glued tacky leather on the walls in place of my chic mirror. Privately, I thought it looked like a *Good Housekeeping* redo of Versailles, but I've held my tongue until this very sentence. Waronker did, however, make one important addition to his office furniture. For the first time in the history of Warner Bros. Records, up to its top floor came a piano.[103]

Though people liked Lenny, he was at first viewed by many in the industry as an odd choice for president; all he knew about was music. This was a time when the music business's executive ranks were filled by graduates from marketing and legal backgrounds. No major label had named an executive from the music-recording sector since, at least, the early 1960s. Mo, however, knew better: "I don't believe the problems of this business can be solved by businesspeople," he said. "I think the problems must rest with the music and will be solved by music people. If you believe in the future of this business, you've got to bet on the music."

---

[103]Lenny's piano might have been viewed by some as an antique. Only the year before, Warner artist David Lee Roth had observed that "rock & roll is not so much a question of electric guitars as it is striped pants." Whether symbolic or functional, Lenny's piano meant something.

Waronker and Ostin had seen some of WBR's "career artists"—Joni Mitchell, Neil Young—drift over to David Geffen's label. Geffen would tell them, "Look, if you go with Warner Bros., you have Mo Ostin. If you come with me, not only do you have Geffen, you have Mo and the WEA organization, too. So why not do it all? And besides," Geffen would add, "we'll *really* kill for you. We don't have that big of a roster."

But in its first two years, Geffen Records had underwhelmed. Donna Summer and Elton John were, at first, Geffen losers. Enterprising executives who once had said they wanted their new labels "to be the Geffen Records of the Eighties" switched examples. Geffen's records were not getting picked at stations. Rosenblatt visited Thyret at WB HQ. Trusting his old friend, Thyret pulled out his "nonexistent" priorities list, and that week's Geffen single was down at sixth in importance. Rosenblatt understood Thyret's reasoning; it worked right for Warners. Eddie returned to tell David, "We're gonna die." David set out to fix that.

Elektra's venture into new repertoire areas was slow in paying off. Picking brighter sides of his streets, Smith cited the success of Queen, even though the act was heading for Capitol-EMI worldwide. Country (Eddie Rabbitt, Hank Williams, Jr.) turned profits. But jazz fusion turned awful. Posner saw that its "artists were falling between the cracks. They weren't accepted by R&B stations or by jazz audiences."

Tiring of the record-business routine, in 1981 Joe Smith had asked Steve Ross about "trying something else." He wanted out of his contract, which had three years to go, saying he'd "lost the fire." Ross did not want Smith free and out on the market and answered, "No, you're family." The two men talked vaguely about a WCI sports division. Ross dreamed: "We could buy some teams." But what, then, would become of Elektra? Smith suggested names. Nothing became final; just, for now, talk, shared in the backseats of limousines.

Danceteria was a popular Manhattan disco where an ambitious young singer of evolving hair colors hung out. Club DJ/remixer Mark Kamins gave a demo tape he'd made of Madonna to Sire Records executive Michael (son of Eddie) Rosenblatt. Michael said he'd sign her, subject to the boss's okay. His boss, Seymour Stein, was in the hospital that week, recovering from heart surgery. "Can this wait?" Having waited all her life, it seemed, Madonna sighed. "Sure."

Stein, bored in bed, heard the tape. His instincts clicked; he was still a musical opportunist, a grown-up who still stood on chairs at concerts. He told Rosenblatt to bring the singer to the hospital. Now. *Right* now. Seymour shaved and put on a robe that didn't smell. Madonna entered. "I want to sign you," said Seymour. "Who's your manager?" Madonna had no answer.

Stein called artist manager Freddy DeMann, recently dismissed by the Jackson Family and Michael Jackson. "Got a new act for you, Freddy. Called 'Madonna.' Would you take a meeting?"

"No," answered DeMann.

"Freddy, oh, my God, do yourself a favor and do me a favor, this one is going to be a star."

"Seymour, what do you know about stars, you and your rock & roll bands? What's the name of this act?"

"Madonna."

"Okay," said DeMann. "Send them over."

While Jane Fonda's buns had become hot items, hotter even than they was TV's Richard Simmons, an ebullient, boyish personality who owned only two wardrobes: exercise tights and tuxedos. "I need nothing in between," he once explained to me. Simmons seemed fully at home within his market niche: overweight women. Elektra, in an apparent coup, signed Simmons to make an exercise-motivating album.

Excitement built over *Reach*. Elektra decided the album could get $10.98 list. WEA would stock not only record stores but also drugstores, health and beauty-aid departments, sporting-goods stores, and supermarkets. Television ads were story-boarded. Cross-promotion set up with Warner Books, publisher of Simmons's *Never Say Diet*. Counter display boxes, stand-ups, mobiles, and banners were printed.

Elektra's promotion guru, David Cline, arranged for "Simmons—Onstage at NARM!" to get rack jobbers up on their feet to tighten those buns! At NARM, Simmons led a fat-guys audience in a few minutes of aerobics. They actually stood up and loved it.

Following the industry's artist-freedom policy (through which stars since the late Sixties just cashed in their advances, then disappeared somewhere to record their albums far from their labels' studios and staff producers), the artist Richard Simmons did just that. He cashed and disappeared. His behavior was not unusual. Talent like Neil and Joni, Metallica and Foreigner, just wanted labels to pay the bills and, when they were through, sell their albums. A&R men had long ago stopped being the finders of songs to pair with artists—they were simply A men now, rarely sitting in their label's control booths to make hits. Many labels had even given up owning their own recording studios.

To the utter shock of Elektra, Simmons's album, once he handed it in to the label, had nothing to do with reducing ladies' thighs. Simmons had decided he would be a singer, performing songs like "Don't Tell Me" and "What Are You Waiting For."

During NARM, in every buyers' meeting, Elektra's focus was Simmons. Advance orders piled in. Vic Faraci, who'd left WEA to do marketing at Elektra, and who had actually heard *Reach*, nervously edged back the opening orders by 50 to 70 percent. Dealers, sensing Buns of Cash, expected Elektra to ship *three* million. *Reach* shipped platinum.

As those million copies shipped, little was said about the content of the album, any more than movie preview confess to a new film's tedium. After all, Richard Simmons was still the hottest guy in television.[104] His fame would wag this dog. Chicago's Central Returns, the site of flooding in 1978, watched again as its parking lot of snow melted into a lake, one that rose three inches an hour. Water rose up through the warehouse floor, turned waiting rooms into wading rooms. Shipping clerks wore fishing boots. Management, however, was ready for this flood. Quickly, workers hauled albums down onto the flooded floor, with highest priority given to Richard Simmons, Alex Haley, and similar stinkers. Tens of thousands of albums became soaked and unusable. Quick thinking brought WEA a flood of insurance payments.

After the build-it-up years at Elektra, Joe Smith felt he'd got it right, and still wanted a life fuller than the demands of running a label. He wanted to enjoy success. He announced that he and Donnie now, finally, were able to take that trip around the world, getting away from everything for sixty or ninety days. Releases were scheduled for artists who'd been lately absent: Linda Ronstadt (paired with Nelson Riddle), Queen, and Joni Mitchell in the first six months; Jackson Browne and the Eagles (individually or together) in the second six.

Despite and because of Joe's vigor, Elektra had been building faster (spending more money) than its sales justified. Bruce Lundvall, in from New York, gave Joe a piece of advice: Move your office down to the first floor (Joe had the isolated chairman's office upstairs). "There's stuff going on here that you don't even see," Lundvall said. A lot of white powder being used. Smith, a believer that what turns cold eventually turns hot again, did not hear Lundvall. Joe saw his company from its eyebrows up.

At WCI, Wasserman and Horowitz had begun to wonder. Smith told Horowitz, too, that he wanted out. There came no answer. Smith distracted himself with his attic of wines, his front-row Lakers seats. As for the label's now gangling artist roster, up to more than a hundred names, Smith's heart was not in it. His world vacation began.

---

[104]Much the same phenomenon—a TV hit should equal a record hit—happened at Warner Bros. Records following the success of Alex Haley's *Roots* series. We got ourselves into a total lather over a spoken-word album of Haley reading from his novel. Eddie Rosenblatt arranged a company pool on how many we thought we'd sell. Enormous. A reception for Haley at NARM! Huge! Within days of the album's release, it was suggested that we create a new pool on how many we'd have to take back.

Sales head Vic Faraci recalled, "While he was gone, we were faced with major artists who were supposed to deliver projects, who weren't delivering. Projects were being pushed back to later in the year. The projected numbers we had on paper—we didn't even come close." Elektra financial head Jack Reinstein knew that things looked bad. He did the company-loyal thing: He did some cosmetic accounting so the numbers would look better.

In New York, Wasserman realized that not only were Elektra's numbers dipping too low, they also looked unreal. Elektra accounting was overlooking liabilities, ignoring bad receivables, not writing down inventory . . . Bert sent non-Elektra accountants over to straighten out the label's books. Elektra's reliability was slammed hard. Reinstein, who'd tried to fool Corporate, was let go.

In two years, the label had lost $27 million. The cause: grand contractual commitments, like funding Solar's office building, and newly signed artists who'd failed to earn back their advances. A guy in promotion noted, "It seemed like we had a hundred and twenty accountants. With no beans to count, that's a lot of bean counters."

For WCI, Elektra's sputter was neither life nor death. Thanks to Atari, Warner's stock value had soared and, with it, our stock options' value. David Horowitz took on added duties, overseeing the new MTV.

Elliott Goldman, ex–CBS and Arista Records, well-tailored and opinionated, joined WCI to assist Horowitz·in records. Elliott worked with the vigor of a financial guy. He would forward me memos with items circled and "F.U." written by them. It took me a couple of memos to realize that the F.U. was not a personal insult; it meant "follow up."

With Goldman aboard in New York, Horowitz now could divide his concerns into three piles: (1) Cable programming he kept for himself; (2) the Plagues he left to me; and (3) any worsening situation within the labels he left to Goldman. Atop Warner and Atlantic Records, the general opinion on Elliott ranged from "nice enough guy but obviously don't need him *here"* to "great cufflinks." Looking at his options—meaning finding someone who might even *listen* to him—Goldman concentrated first upon Nesuhi Ertegun's International.

On March 29, 1982, in the conference room at the Belair Beach hotel in St. Maarten, came together WEA International's national managers, one per country, U.S. label International executives, along with Corporate's Horowitz, Goldman, and me.

While we were sitting through a discussion of some relatively minor issue, Nesuhi expounded like the lovable autocrat he was. In what Phil Rose saw as an attempt to impress his superior, Horowitz, Elliott Goldman interrupted Nesuhi, apparently assuming that his opinion was worthwhile. Goldman began with "Look, when I was at Arista, I . . ." I was immediately alerted by the sound of Phil Rose sucking his teeth. Rose had realized that Elliott had just made a fatal error: going up against the boss, Nesuhi.

Nesuhi's explosive response cut Goldman short. With an irate, Middle Eastern flip-off, he told Goldman that Arista was a *very* tiny company and you, sir, were only a tiny *part* of that tiny company.

Elliott would shift his attentions from International to Elektra.

By the fall of 1982, the Atari balloon had lofted WCI's stock up thirty times over its price of six years earlier. For seven years now, Wasserman's numbers had purred in Wall Street's ears their good song: "This quarter exceeds the same quarter last year." Bert had a favorite saying: "The thing I take pride in is avoiding surprises. People say WCI has too many financial reserves. And I say you can never have enough reserves for a famine."[105] Unneeded profits he'd squirreled away like acorns into lines like "reserves against future returns" on WCI's financial sheets. Bert's reserves helped shield our group's doldrums.

For 1982, U.S. label shipments declined another 8.5 percent. Record labels released 18 percent fewer new album titles. WEA was up, suddenly selling an unprecedented 39.1 percent of all records in the United States. Exclamation point. Trailing, at 16 percent, was CBS. But market percentages bought less than actual sales dollars.

Our labels, selling that 39.1 percent of all, felt huge. Then, in early 1983, WCI revealed the relative size of its divisions in 1982. Record people found themselves only one-sixth the size of Atari, only half the size of Warner Bros. Studios.

WCI was making over half a billion dollars, but Atari brought in more than 60 percent of it. Ross, buddying up to Steve Spielberg, wrote him an Atari check for $23 million (actually a guarantee against royalties), just to get video-game rights to Spielberg's hit movie, *E.T.* For Atari, *E.T.* turned into one lousy game, made in haste, too tame for the market, since, while Atari characters shot to kill, Spielberg characters warmed the heart. Steve Ross's $23 million shot—reminiscent of some of Joe Smith's gambles at Elektra, though Joe's were far less expensive—demanded that, to break even, Atari ship four million *E.T.* cartridges. Three and a half million got returned, later to be buried, rumor had it, as some small mountain in Arizona.

Then, far from Atari's mania and Wall Street's euphoria, Henry Droz noticed something odd. Atari cartridges in WEA warehouses were standing still. Droz told Manny Gerard and Steve Ross his warehouses were filling

---

[105]This was a corporate philosophy. Steve liked to say, "No one ever went to jail for understating earnings."

up; he got ignored. Manny, who knew Wall Street better than he knew Pac-Man, at first failed to read the truth about the company he was paid to supervise: Atari's game-business franchise was no longer a monopoly. Sales were down, very down. At first, Gerard tried to manage the illusion; he knew very well what telling the truth to Wall Street could cost. Ultimately, though, WCI had to fess up. On December 9, a Thursday, one sentence in one press release said this:

> Atari is experiencing "disappointing" sales of its video games cartridges during this Christmas period.

And that was all it took. A single sentence opened the trapdoor and WCI's value—its stock—went into free fall. Shares down $16.75 on one afternoon, 33 percent of WCI's value wiped out. The next morning, WCI was not $52 a share. It was $35, and it fell, then fell more. It bottomed at a single digit, at $7. Manny Gerard, who was the Atari guy in WCI's Office of the President, the forest ranger looking for red glows, sat stunned, seeing "a business that disappeared in twenty minutes, like the Hula Hoop."

Atari had shipped quintuple platinum. The company became a craze that lasted shorter than disco nights.

Amid all this, Ross, who regularly downed steak and eggs for breakfast, had developed in 1980 what WCI publicists called "a back problem" that laid him up. What really had occurred was a heart attack. It took weeks to recover from, weeks in which Ross hid from conflict, hid from old cash deal problems, hid even from his top executives like Gerard and Wasserman, who were struggling with Atari.

Against Atari's collapse, Wasserman's reserves proved inadequate. His managed stairsteps disappeared in one night. Wall Street's reaction nearly collapsed WCI, damn near bankrupted the whole corporation, and, with it, nearly killed WCI's former cash cow: its record business. For the first time, we record executives felt how Big Debt could affect lives. Corporate money hunger strode into our lives like Serbian rapists. I'd been caught in the middle of converting my three thousand square foot Colonial into an eight thousand square foot Splendor, to be paid for from my stock options. Two sons, two stepkids, and down at the street, a mailbox that, when opened, spoke throughout the home's stereo: "The mail . . . has arrived." Feel sorry for me. Please. I was stashing bills-to-pay in my bedside drawer.

Stock in Ross also went *kaboom*. Steve went from *Ad Age*'s "1981 Adman of the Year" to the *Gallagher Presidents' Report*'s "Ten Worst CEOs for 1982." Fellow executives with stock options called their real-estate brokers, canceling offers on that beach house.

From Rockefeller Center, weekly forays of corporate realists flew out to Sunnyvale, home of Atari, first to plug holes, then to patch dams. Among the hole pluggers was a newish executive at WCI, Bob Morgado, a no-nonsense political aide who'd come to New York from, of all places, Hawaii. Morgado had handled messy situations. In 1975, he'd been troubleshooter for New York Governor Hugh Carey, handling New York State after it nearly went bankrupt. Then he was Carey's campaign finance co-head. By 1982, when Ross was writing many-zeroed checks to Governor Cuomo, Steve had reached into politics to hire useful talent, like John Lindsay's deputy mayor, Richard Aurelio, who helped sign WCI cable franchises in outer-borough New York City.

Ross also had hired Morgado, known as "Bobby" by such pols as Richard Parsons, later to become Time Warner's president, then AOL Time Warner's co-COO. "Bobby" he may have been, but Morgado had also become the second most powerful man in New York State government and a man who seemed invigorated by tough challenges. He had impressed Ross. His skill disposing of dead wood filled Steve's bill. A man schooled in politics, where, unlike the record business, people do not have lifetime careers. They only have terms in office, then get moved on.

As Morgado once put it, "Steve knew that we had to downsize, and he was looking for someone to make it happen. He asked me."

Significant Releases

1981

Atlantic: AC/DC (*Dirty Deeds Done Dirt Cheap* and *For Those About to Rock We Salute You*) • Phil Collins (*Face Value,* including "I Missed Again" and "In the Air Tonight") • Foreigner (*4,* including "Break It Up," "Juke Box Hero," "Urgent," and "Waiting for a Girl Like You") • Genesis (*Abacab*) • The Manhattan Transfer ("Boy From New York City") • *Concerts for the People of Kampuchea*

Cotillion: Stacy Lattisaw ("Love on a Two Way Street") • Sister Sledge (*All American Girls*)

Modern: Stevie Nicks (*Bella Donna,* including "Stop Draggin' My Heart Around," "Leather and Lace," "After the Glitter Fades," and "Edge of Seventeen (Just Like the White Winged Dove)")

Rolling Stone: The Rolling Stones (*Sucking in the Seventies* and *Tattoo You,* including "Start Me Up," "Waiting on a Friend," and "Hang Fire")

Elektra: The Cars (*Shake It Up*) • Patti Austin ("Baby Come to Me") • Queen (*Greatest Hits*) • Eddie Rabbitt (*Step by Step,* including "Someone Could Lose a Heart Tonight") • Lee Ritenour (*Rit,* including "Is It You") • Grover Washington, Jr. (*Come Morning,* including, "Just the Two of Us") • Hank Williams, Jr. (*Rowdy* and *The Pressure Is On*)

Asylum: Lindsey Buckingham ("*Law and Order*") • Joe Walsh (*There Goes the Neighborhood*)

Planet: Pointer Sisters (*Black & White,* including "Slow Hand" and "Should I Do It")

Warner Bros: George Benson (*Collection,* including "Turn Your Love Around") • Black Sabbath (*Mob Rules*) • Ry Cooder (*Borderline*) • Devo (*New Traditionalists*) • Emmylou Harris (*Cimarron*) • Al Jarreau (*Breakin' Away,* including "We're in This Love Together") • Rickie Lee Jones (*Pirates*) • Chaka Khan (*What Cha' Gonna Do for Me*) • King Crimson (*Discipline*) • Prince (*Controversy*) • Leo Sayer (*Living in a Fantasy,* including "More Than I Can Say") • Rod Stewart (*Tonight I'm Yours,* including "Young Turks") • Van Halen (*Fair Warning*) • The Who (*Face Dances,* including "You Better You Bet") • Gary Wright ("Really Wanna Know You") • ZZ Top (*El Loco*)
Reprise: Neil Young (*Re-Ac-Tor*)
Bearsville: Jesse Winchester (*Say What*)
Dark Horse: George Harrison (*Somewhere in England,* including "All Those Years Ago")
Geffen: Elton John (*The Fox*) • Yoko Ono (*Season of Glass*) • Quarterflash ("Find Another Fool" and "Harden My Heart")
Island: Grace Jones (*Nightclubbing*) • Steve Winwood (*Arc of a Diver,* including "While You See a Chance")
Sire: Climax Blues Band ("I Love You") • Brian Eno–David Byrne (*My Life in the Bush of Ghosts*) • The Pretenders (*Extended Play* and *II*) • The Ramones (*Pleasant Dreams*) • Tom Tom Club ("Genius of Love")

1982

Atlantic: ABBA (*The Visitors,* including "Winner Takes All") • Laura Branigan ("Gloria") • Phil Collins (*Hello, I Must Be Going!,* including "You Can't Hurry Love") • Crosby, Stills & Nash (*Daylight Again,* including "Southern Cross" and "Wasted on the Way") • Foreigner (*Foreigner Records*) • Genesis (*Three Sides Live*)
Atco: Pete Townshend (*All the Best Cowboys Have Chinese Eyes*)
Cotillion: Sister Sledge ("My Guy")
Rolling Stone: The Rolling Stones (*Still Life*)
Swan Song: Bad Company (*Rough Diamonds*) • Led Zeppelin (*Coda*) • Robert Plant (*Pictures at Eleven*)

Elektra: Queen (*Hot Space,* including "Body Language") • Eddie Rabbitt (*Radio Romance,* including "You and I") • Patrice Rushen (*Straight From the Heart*)
Asylum: Eagles (*Greatest Hits, Volume 2*) • Glenn Frey (*No Fun Aloud*) • Don Henley (*I Can't Stand Still,* including "Dirty Laundry") • Linda Ronstadt (*Get Closer*)
Planet: Pointer Sisters ("American Music" and "Should I Do It")
Solar: Shalamar (*Friends*)
Warner Bros.: The B-52's (*Mesopotamia*) • Marshall Crenshaw ("Someday, Someway") • Dire Straits (*Love Over Gold*) • Donald Fagen (*The Nightfly*) • Fleetwood Mac (*Mirage,* including "Gypsy," "Hold Me," and "Love in Store") • Michael McDonald (*If That's What It Takes*) • Van Morrison (*Beautiful Vision*) • Prince and the Revolution (*1999,* including "Delirious" and "Little Red Corvette") • Richard Pryor (*Live on the Sunset Strip*) • Bonnie Raitt (*Green Light*) • Roxy Music (*Avalon*) • Simon & Garfunkel (*The Concert in Central Park*) • Rod Stewart (*Absolutely Live*) • The Time (*What Time Is It?*) • Van Halen (*Diver Down,* including "Dancing in the Streets" and "(Oh) Pretty Woman") • The Who (*It's Hard*) • Zapp (*II*)
Chrysalis: Toni Basil (*Word of Mouth,* including "Mickey")
Full Moon: Chicago (*16,* including "Hard to Say I'm Sorry")
Geffen: Asia • Peter Gabriel (*Security*) • Sammy Hagar (*Standing Hampton* and

Three Lock Box, including "Your Love Is Driving Me Crazy") • Elton John (*Jump Up!,* including "Empty Garden (Hey Hey Johnny)") • John Lennon (*Collection*) • Donna Summer ("Love Is in Control (Finger on the Trigger)")

Sire: The Pretenders ("Back on the Chain Gang") • Soft Cell (*Non-Stop Erotic Cabaret,* including "Tainted Love")

23

SHOULD we have seen it coming? It was a shocker—the worst year in our sales history—and no more predictable than the U.S. basketball team's losing in the Olympics. For 1983, WCI's record labels had a year with *no* Top Ten albums and *no* Top Ten singles. For the first and only time since its founding, WEA came in second in sales polls, losing out to rival CBS, whose Michael Jackson had walked the moon, Thrilled the entire known universe, sold more than any album in history, and humbled us.

Corporate, too, got its head held underwater. Atari ended up losing $539 million. That loss was five times the size of the music group's profits. It was as if without warning they'd canceled our life insurance.

Atari wiped itself right off the balance sheet. For WCI, it was hang-tough time. Corporate tolerance for bad "performance," to recall Steve's word, grew short.

To "restore Atari to healthy, profitable growth"—press-release talk again—WCI hired an executive from Philip Morris, James Morgan, to be Atari's new chairman. While WCI's stock kept going down, getting him into the boss's chair in Sunnyvale took what seemed like forever. First, Morgan had to leave the land of nicotine; he then took vacation before moving west. Atari, meanwhile, emulated Atlantis. In the end, Atari was beyond saving.[106]

Within WCI, CFO Bert Wasserman, coatless, lugged nine-inch-thick P&Ls from office to office. Bailing began. WCI assets like Knickerbocker Toys and Warner Cosmetics got sold off.

Atari laid off 25 percent of its staff in Sunnyvale alone: seventeen hundred employees. Executives' kids were pulled out of private schools; mistresses were fired. Bob Morgado moved from his temporary chair at Warner Cable over to full-time Warner Communications, where he earned repute as

---

[106]James Morgan stayed with Atari for a short term, then was out, with a (for then) parachuteful of cash. He later returned to Philip Morris and eventually became its CEO, able to testify, under many oaths, that "I have never seen a market strategy for any of our brands that suggests targeting people under age eighteen." Nor did he ever find one for Atari.

the company's Hatchet Man, so quickly that movie studio heads Daly and
Semel called up their boss, Ross, and insisted Morgado not set foot on *their*
lot. Other corporate wise men flew to Silicon Valley to assist with "trimming." They closed whole divisions. The count rose to four thousand employees gone, and still not through. By 1985, the employee count would drop
to 70 percent. Atari dropped any dealers served by WEA, switching to exclusive deals with forty indie games distributors. Other than that, the Record
Group was insulated, despite our weak performance. "I have to give Steve all
the credit for isolating the record group," Wasserman later said, "so that the
Mo Ostins of the world were able to continue doing their thing. By and large,
they did a fantastic job."

Corporate hunters felt Ross out, hoping what was left of WCI could be
had for cheap. First to feel was Australian media mogul Rupert Murdoch,
who in August took a run at WCI, buying 6.7 percent of its stock. To halt
Murdoch's raid, Ross had found a white knight by year's end: Herb Siegel,
chairman of Chris-Craft.[107]

There was little the Record Group could do to help resuscitate Atari,
whose market share had plunged from 95 to 55 percent. I remember one
meeting, where Steve asked for our cooperation, like "could Atari's R&D
work on home taping?" "Well, not really, Steve." Later, we caught the spirit
and came up with a one-dollar-off coupon deal on Atari's new Dig Dug
game cartridge. But the Record Group had its own problems.

Geffen Records, for example. Through four long years in its deal with
WBR, David's label sank. In his Asylum days, David had been den mother
for singer songwriters and California harmonizers, from CSNY to the Eagles. Now a different David had just filed a law suit *against* Neil Young,
claiming that he had delivered "uncommercial albums." Years before, David
had fought *for* Neil's "artist rights." Priorities had changed.

Geffen's successes, such as they were, were "hair bands"; by 1983, Gef-
fen's Kalodner had discovered Asia, mostly, and there were Quarterflash and
Sammy Hagar.[108] They were not enough to make Geffen Records profitable.
David, though young, was feeling musically dated.

On August 17, 1982, at another of those "just raise your hand and say
'amen' " meetings like the one that had started MTV, David Horowitz once

---

[107]Murdoch dropped out at WCI but went on to bigger media ownership. He had the fore-
sight, for example, to buy the publisher of this very book, which—who knows?—might
make the man a millionaire.

[108]Hair-wise, through 1983, Warner Bros.' crop included Black Sabbath, King Crimson,
Van Halen, Rod Stewart, and (from chin down) ZZ Top. For hair, Elektra came up with
Mötley Crüe. Atlantic, led by bald Ahmet Ertegun, led in hair with AC/DC, Foreigner,
Bad Company, and Led Zeppelin.

more called his records-division chiefs to Manhattan, to sit once more around the blue table. Facing us—Mo, Ahmet, Joe, Henry, Nesuhi, Goldman, me—Horowitz spoke as gently as a fully tenured prof at a liberal-arts college. He said that WCI had committed to support a new technology. This one was called "the digital audio disc." We glanced at each other. For *this* we'd flown to New York? He held up this little flying saucer. We'd be getting our saucers made by one of the CD's inventors, the Dutch label PolyGram, in its German plant, so we didn't have to buy new saucer presses. "Any questions?"

Our label heads had by now been through enough music configurations—from 78s to 45s to 4-track tapes to quad-sound LPs to microcassettes—to have perfected a tolerant shrug at such news. Whatever this CD's advantages—forever clean and clickless; seventy minutes long—they didn't mean much to executives concerned with weightier issues. There weren't even CD players out there. No one asked what "digital" meant, or cared.

Horowitz asked if I'd take over getting Warner Communications into CD Land. I nodded. "With pleasure." All I knew about digits were the five I had on each hand. My fellow execs seemed relieved it was me, since I was "a labels guy" who wore neither lace-up shoes nor threatening cufflinks. After the room emptied, David and I walked back to his office. His secretary, the wise, plump, and saucy Michele Von Feld, whose laugh gurgled down in that range where cellos play, signaled us to "stop/hush." We waited a moment outside David's door. White knight Herb Siegel was being shown through WCI's offices by Ross's attorney, Arthur Liman, and at this moment both stood in Horowitz's artistically decorated office. David had hired a high-tech decorator/artist who'd reconstructed his office's west wall into a set of yard-high, yard-deep, sculptural stadium steps that reached up to the ceiling. Possibly for seating, though to sit on them seemed like sitting in some amphitheater waiting for Act One of a Greek tragedy. Inside the office, we could hear Liman telling Siegel, "This is David Horowitz's office. He is in charge of the record business. He is not the CEO. If this office bothers you, you can't do this deal."

Siegel replied, "It won't bother me. I'm betting on Steve, and if he feels this is the kind of office David Horowitz should have, fine. I'm betting on Steve."[109] And out Liman and Siegel went. Once inside, David called Holland to speak to the head man at PolyGram Records, Jan Timmer. His call went straight through. Spelling my name slowly, David informed Timmer that I'd head up our CD efforts. When could I be there? "How about next week?" I answered. It was a take-charge answer, which they appreciated. And that was it. I flew back to Burbank on the Wicky Bird, scoring three Mounds bars.

I knew how to run this CD evangelism like I knew how to drive my car;

---

[109] I later read that this remodel of David's office had cost $750,000, a staggering sum for what I saw. I wouldn't have paid a penny over $650,000.

I steer well, but don't ask me about under the hood. I held tight to my my little staff's tech maven, the constantly underrated Al McPherson. Our job was to start making and selling these odd new digital discs. "Al, what's a digit?" I asked. We looked at my little sample disc. It looked odd, felt too small, came in a plastic box that was a bitch to open, and did not smell like petroleum. It didn't even have grooves. None of this mattered to Horowitz whose job had turned into a search for salvation for his Record Group. The compact disc was one prayer; for us, it became temp religion.

Born a label guy, I knew how to get this done: The way to get CDs from our labels was (1) to make it all cost the labels nothing, and (2) to do everything out of their way. We did just that: We took on all the work and charged nothing to their bottom lines.

My trip to Baarn, Holland, along with my tech arm, McPherson, his lieutenant, George Lydecker, and my manufacturing head, Tony Muxlow, was a trip into Oz. PolyGram's welcoming committee consisted of an affable Belgian named Hans Gout (pronounced "Howt") and our tech escort, a lean, lovable Dutchman named Han Tendeloo. Good guys, both funny. We got embraced like fresh NATO troops. Gout and Tendeloo felt lucky WCI was there, to join their digital crusade. Together, we walked softly through manufacturing plants that were free of clanking, where workers dressed in white gowns with masks over their noses and mouths, where we watched through glass windows as workers moved like nervous surgeons amid high-tech incubators. They peered down at baby discs through microscopes.

Philips saw the CD as very desirable (in appearance, accessibility, and sound quality). It was also, at that time, expensive to make. For pressings, they would charge us two dollars each. Philips reasoned it wanted a healthy (40 percent gross margin) mark-up on this new product. They figured a CD could sell for twenty-five to thirty guilders, about twice the list price of an LP. After consulting their country heads, they set a premium price for a premium product. WCI, like the rest of the record world, was pleased to accept. Part of my job was to figure out how all this was going to make financial sense for the Warner labels. Gout said that he couldn't legally tell us how to price our CDs, but PolyGram was going to ask $18.98 apiece.

Back in our hotel, when I got into my best thinking position—on a bed, belly down, with a yellow pad—I tried getting the numbers to work profitably. I started off with my guess: With luck, we might sell three thousand or so of a title. The pressings-and-packaging costs (doubled), the up-cost of artist royalties (double list price meant double artist's percentage)—those costs made CDs a drag. Despite the $18.98 price, it still didn't compute. When I mentioned that the next morning, Gout avoided restraint-of-trade but implied that PolyGram had decided to pay *its* artists only at the LP rate, about 50 percent of my percentages. "Aha!" I hoped, we'd just have to beg our artists' managers for the same forgiveness. Most artist managers, brushing aside CDs like small potatoes, forgave. While our business-affairs heads amended contracts, adding this New Technology deduction, our financial heads foresaw, in the distance, a deluxe New World. To see this New World in 1983, however, required deluxe squinting.

PolyGram's Hans Gout attended the NARM convention in Miami to show off the new Compact Disc packaging. He held high the five-inch plastic box like an Olympic torch. No time spent on the acceptability of the doubled price for this unidentified flying disc. Instead, a parade of advantages tooted its way past the conventioneers' ears: 72 minutes without interruption; players pouring in from Sony, Philips/Magnavox, and others; discs with no clicks or pops; no sound degredation, no matter how many times it got played; pocket-sized; long boxes fit into 12-inch browser boxes . . . Gout sold the CD as the Disc Eternal. NARM simply sat there, seeing this as one more, odd-shaped tech. When no bar code appeared on the sample package, NARM's president, John Marmaduke, could only lecture Gout: "If you expect us to sell CDs, you better get with the bar coding."

The ho-hum was huge. Wilfried Jung, EMI's Central Europe director, said, "I don't think there is any chance that the CD will replace the conventional LP. It will achieve some penetration and exist as a super sound carrier for hi-fi fetishists . . . but the black disk will continue to be the Number One sound carrier for many years to come." (So much for Wilfried's future.)

Publicly, Henry Droz cautioned against obsolescence for either the LP or the cassette, citing "damage to consumer confidence." Warner sales chief Lou Dennis saw no need for the CDs; he knew, with papal finality, that two configurations were enough. It was not as if David Horowitz's mandate—get behind the CD—was being disobeyed. CDs were put up with, like body fat.

Sounding like some desperate promotion man, Timmer predicted that in six years (in 1989), people would be buying fifty/fifty, LPs and CDs; and then, in ten years (1993), the vinyl LP would be gone.

Month after month, my crew shrank LP art into CD booklets and, as far as I was concerned, killed "liner notes" by copying them into wallet-size booklets, where they lurked like fine print in a loan document. Ah the shame of it. The Warner group of labels brought to CD marketing the most crucial selling factor: We brought hair-band hits onto the U.S. market, balancing PolyGram and Sony's less-compelling chamber classics. CD players, led by technology owners Sony and Philips, charged into the market at $999. Still, the day the first Doobie Brothers became a buyable CD in stores, that marked the day the CD got serious.

For the next two years, my small group sweet-talked our labels into clearing album rights for us, then transformed sound waves into numbers— forty-four thousand wave-height measurements per second—recorded by a Sony-made digitizer that we'd taken over, used, for four thousand dollars from Elektra. None of us wondered what the digitizing of sound waves would mean to our business: how fidelity degradation, which had held back some from making free tape copies, would no longer be a factor once sound waves got turned to digits. That the tenth, the hundredth copy of a CD sounded fresh as the first. Digital sound, being so casually accepted into our world, was free to cause an epidemic. It would make data copying easy, clean, free, and something that felt about as immoral a killing an ant.

We had more-obvious concerns. The Arkansas Senate passed a bill requiring that albums containing hidden backward messages be so labeled by record companies. The bill was sent on for signature to Governor Bill Clinton.

In 1983, Ruth Brown's campaign to rescue royalties from Atlantic surfaced once more. Accountant Mel Lewinter, assisting Shelly Vogel at the label, mailed Atlantic's attorneys' reply across town to Ruth Brown's attorneys. The letter talked tough. It made clear the label's position that "the Statute of Limitations protects companies . . . from having to bear the extremely costly and genuinely impractical burden of answering for every accounting and payment over long periods of time." The label had done exactly what its Ruth Brown contract said it could: charged her for promo records; charged her 10 percent for breakage, a policy somewhat hard to take in these days of unbreakable vinyl discs; charged gobs of costs against her royalty account, leaving her continually in the red.

Her attorney, Howell Begle, could not "believe what I'm hearing. They say you owe them money? And that the total sales of your stuff both home and abroad amounts to just seven hundred bucks over twenty years?"

Atlantic, back in the Sixties, had skipped crediting royalties-from-foreign to its artists. When an artist was dropped, as most Atlantic R&B artists had been in the mid-Sixties, Atlantic had just classified them as impossibly "in the red" and stopped crediting any sales of their records. Eleven years of data were missing. Brown's foreign royalties had become, like grades from your tenth-grade geography tests, simply untraceable. Begel realized that even though Atlantic knew that its data were gone, the label continued sending his client statements that pretended up-to-date accuracy.

Artists Joe Turner and the Clovers joined Brown's complaint, finding in their royalty accounts item after item that defied logic (if not contracts).[110] Atlantic felt exasperated. All this ancient history! The label had been more generous than other indies in the beginning, paying up to five cents a record when many others paid two cents, or nothing. But those two-cent labels had disappeared. Atlantic stood alone, attackable.

---

[110]The Clovers had been paid only twenty-five hundred dollars in total since 1969, an average of twenty dollars per Clover per year.

To put an end to it, Ahmet authorized payments of conscience. "Remastering charges" (costs charged to artists for changing songs from 45s to 33s) or into compilations were erased. Atlantic paid for Big Joe Turner's funeral and his widow's mortgage. The label upped its royalty rate from "foreign rate" to the twice-as-big domestic rate. It wasn't good enough. In the next three years, from testifying in Washington to lining up with Jesse Jackson, Ruth Brown and her colleagues hounded Atlantic. They got testimony from just-fired royalties head Gerry Bursey, detailing how Atlantic had been charging back to artists the payments it made to the musicians' union (AFM) pension funds, finding any excuse to move costs over to the artist's debts column, and on and on.

Vogel and Lewinter's penny-pinching policies became a political embarrassment for WCI. Both men were pardoned from further negotiating meetings between Ruth Brown's and Steve Ross's factions. Meetings now took place with smoother schmoozers: Steve himself, attorney Marty Payson, and Bob Morgado.

With her big, brown, wised-up eyes, Ruth Brown observed these non-Atlantic men. She watched as her side's Jesse Jackson went up against Steve Ross, whom she saw as "well briefed, a great listener, an altogether formidable opponent. He was the consumate CEO, bluff yet concerned, conciliatory yet strong, serious yet capable of producing sudden shafts of humor . . . Payson came over as smart and watchful, Morgado polished and bright, an impressive corporate executive."

In the end, WCI/Atlantic contributed $1.5 million to sustain a Rhythm and Blues Foundation, but nothing to Ruth Brown herself. Left out were bitter 1960s cats who felt cheated by what they now called "plantation accounting." At least, as songwriter Doc Pomus once observed, it could have been worse: "Ahmet was not Morris Levy." Pomus was right on.

Largesse. That's what it came down to. Despite the business's tight times, largesse still had its place, but this hard year, it also had limits. Joe Smith had been on a largesse spree at Elektra; when push became shove, if it took "your own building" to sign a Solar, abuilding we had gone. Now even Joe cut back. Mo also had limits, but he gave artists every bit of largesse they asked for, until his inherent calculator computed "the end." At that point, wisely, Mo just stopped the largesse and simply said, "We are not willing to lose money on this deal." And Ahmet, the best of all our executives when it came to feeling the flow, both musical and corporate, who wore custom clothes (I suspect even tailored socks), empowered his execs like Vogel, Morris, and Glew to watch Atlantic's bottom line. At stingy, they were good.

When the time came once more for a Rolling Stones re-signing, Ahmet was up against Columbia's Walter Yetnikoff, who'd by now become an increasingly overweight and often-peevish label head. Yetnikoff took the Stones from Atlantic at a cost of $28 million ($6 million each for four albums, plus $4 million for publicity). To recoup that advance, Columbia needed to sell three million copies of each album, high above the Stones' average. Signed in Paris, appropriately enough at the Ritz, the Stones-Columbia contract vaulted to a new world record: the richest in the history of rock. To the rest of the industry, the Stones deal looked like a sure loser. The group's Bill Wyman analyzed it coldly: "By that time, all the companies were the same, so [which label] didn't really matter." Stones negotiator Prince Rupert Lowenstein felt it was fatigue: "I don't think Atlantic was all that enchanted with the next contract, and I don't think the Rolling Stones were all that enchanted with Ahmet." Familiarity had actually bred contempt. Shelly Vogel was sober, too: "We hated losing them, but the numbers they were asking just didn't make sense." So, all around, it was no longer hanging till dawn, no longer lounging together on Bermuda. It was, as Shelly would say, "numbers."

By 1983's end, WCI's music group numbers felt about knee high. In describing the decline, WCI's Annual Report struggled like an M.B.A. in a lying bee:

If sales of 325 million albums estimated lost due to home taping in 1983 were added to reported industry revenues this year, retail spending on prerecorded music would be at an all-time high, suggesting that the market for music has never been larger than it is today.

Watching "his" Asylum "going nowhere" under Joe Smith, David Geffen felt a mixture of nostalgia and disgust, but he sensed a fresh target. He pushed, for months, a new pressure point at WCI: He offered to run both "his" ex-labels—Asylum (which he no longer owned) and Elektra (which he viewed as a hanger-on to Asylum)—*plus* Geffen Records (of which he owned half). Put the three together, argued David, and he'd split the total operation with WCI, fifty/fifty.

Smith had wanted out of Elektra but had no timetable, no place to go, so he lingered. Ross and Horowitz saw a stalled label with poor profits but didn't know where to turn. Geffen kept calling Horowitz and Ross, over and over, bugging them to hear his offer. Horowitz found Geffen's proposal below belief, but he knew that Geffen would not let up. Horowitz told Ross that Geffen was "trying to steal Elektra." Ross agreed.

Horowitz felt pressure. Joe Smith was not a go-go chairman; even Smith would have agreed to that assessment. Elliott Goldman viewed Elektra as a country club, guys too easily available for golf games at Riviera, guys driving around in hand-waxed Mercedes. He wrote Horowitz a long memo about restructuring. Horowitz pondered where he could turn with Elektra, other than Geffen. He and Ross solicited cures.

New presidential possibilities for Elektra got mused over. Mo Ostin suggested Warner Records' Bob Krasnow. Horowitz called Krasnow on a Thursday afternoon, just after New Year's, inviting him to lunch in the executive dining room. Horowitz told him WCI had decided to replace Joe Smith. Would Krasnow be interested in the job? "Whatever the shortest measurable amount of time is, that's how long it took me to say yes," Krasnow told me. "I was having a great time at Warner Brothers, and I was working for a man I admire—Mo Ostin—but I wanted my own company. I wanted to put *my* imprint on something. This was my opportunity, and I wasn't going to let it pass." In secrecy even from Joe, Krasnow signed a five-year deal to run Elektra.

Horowitz and Krasnow next met in the home of Mo Ostin, hammering out Krasnow's contractual release from WBR. Mo had a shopping list whose star item was a simple trade: Exchange Bob for Elektra's country division. "Knowing that Bob didn't have much interest in the country field," Mo justified, "I suggested that they put the Elektra Nashville branch under our wing." Agreed.

In New York, Bruce Lundvall, running Elektra's Musician label, was viewed as Number Two to Joe. Bruce received a Friday-morning phone call from Horowitz at the Beverly Hills Hotel, saying, "I want you on a plane this morning."

"May I ask you what this is about?"

"No. Just be here."

Lundvall made it to the Beverly Hills. He waited in his room till 1:00 a.m., when Horowitz called to say, "We'll do this in the morning." At nine the next day, Horowitz told Lundvall, "We're making some major changes. Joe Smith is going into a new division of Warner Communications. It's going to be a kind of a sports division. Elektra is in bad shape. We're losing a lot of money. I've appointed Bob Krasnow the chairman, and I'd like you to be the president. And we want to move the company back to the East Coast." Though he hardly knew Krasnow, Lundvall accepted. "Why don't you go up to his room," suggested Horowitz, "and talk."

Lundvall and Krasnow met. Bob ran down the changes: the move east, the roster . . . He and Lundvall would stay in L.A. for a while, and "we're going to have to end the Musician label." Lundvall's quick answer: "No. One of the reasons I came here was to do this jazz label. It's doing fine; we're not losing money with it. I'll put it on hold, but . . ."

At lunch, out by the pool, Horowitz also insisted on dumping the Musician label. Lundvall again refused. "Look," he said, "this morning you asked me to take this job and I said, immediately, yes. We haven't discussed money even. But I'm not giving up something I have a contractual right to, and one that's doing okay."

Horowitz said he was going for a swim and asked Lundvall to think it over. Horowitz went underwater. Lundvall knew the difference between a label that *bought* talent (CBS under Walter Yetnikoff had become a "deals" label) and a label that *developed* talent (more of a WEA trait, and one Bruce wanted for Musician). Once he surfaced, Horowitz asked him, "Have you given this some more thought?" Lundvall answered, "Yeah, I'm not giving it up." Lundvall's persistence paid off; his label survived.

Krasnow and Lundvall next dived into details. Whom to cut from the roster, and how.[111] Modify the Solar Records deal, which was expensive and not yet rewarding. Employee situations: people who would not be needed in New York.

Moving Elektra to New York—where both Krasnow and Lundvall wanted to live—would act as balance to the huge Warner Bros. Records on the West Coast. Atlantic was viewed as more "narrowcast" in the kinds of signings that Ahmet and Doug Morris had been doing. Additionally, in Elliott Goldman's view, the ability to combine two New York labels' background services (accounting, order service, computer operations) would be a clear economizer.

All this time, Elektra/Asylum chairman Joe Smith had been in the hospital, recovering from exploratory surgery. On Sunday evening, Horowitz, Lundvall, and Krasnow visited Joe. Horowitz told Joe that he was being appointed to run WCI's new Sports Division, a convenient face-saver which, though true, lacked a corporate pocketbook. All this would be announced in Elektra's conference room the next morning. Joe, they insisted, of course must be there.

That same evening, Elektra employees at a Solar showcase heard about an all-company meeting called for nine the next morning. The buzz was pessimistic.

Horowitz spent early Monday on his hotel phone, calling the rest of the Record Group's executives, Ahmet, Henry, and others, to tell them about Krasnow. One he called was David Geffen, who confessed to speechlessness but asked if they could meet for lunch. Later, at noon at Le Dôme restaurant on Sunset, Geffen yelled wildly at Horowitz as he approached the lunch table, shrieked about how his own company, Asylum, had been stolen from him. Geffen, a black belt in shouting, spewed curses. Horowitz, never having even sat down, said, "Well, I guess we're not having lunch today," and walked back out, back to work.

---

[111] Among those dropped was Irene Cara, managed by Al Coury. Quickly, Coury made a deal with Geffen Records, and out of it came "Flashdance." Coury used the single as his passport, claiming, "I personally made on that record over a million bucks."

At nine Monday morning, Horowitz told the employees jammed into Elektra's conference room what was happening, including the move to New York. At ten, Joe Smith arrived via ambulance. He came in, obviously sore, walking like those old guys on Miami sidewalks, their legs out too wide. Joe told his employees the facts he'd learned only the evening before. He spoke with as much animation as his postoperative energy allowed. "I've decided not to go with the company," Joe told them. "Bob Krasnow is going to take over. Anyone who is interested in making the move to New York, Bob and Bruce are going to be here for two days, so I suggest you make an appointment through my office to see them, to sit down and talk about what your future might be following Elektra Records to New York."

"Joe looked frail," Mel Posner recalled, "and I was floored." Joe the Quipster had no quips. A couple of the girls fainted. Others cried. Joe, recalling it later, told me that "the only thing I blame David Horowitz for is the way he handled it, with no warning. I was absolutely ready to go. It was his suddenness that wasn't right. That's the only part that hurt."

While Smith rode the ambulance back to the hospital, Krasnow made a rah-rah speech to a silent audience: "Come on, we gotta get going, we gotta turn this company around." Repeating Joe Smith's theme of the past years, Krasnow hoped "to expand EA's musical base, specifically by getting more involved in black music." When asked why this move was being made so suddenly—with so little preparation—Bob answered, "Quietly laying groundwork in the record business? The only quiet thing I've ever heard in this business is the B side of a bad record." Krasnow itched to scratch a label of his own. He knew there were a lot of ways to run a record company. "I wanted," he told me, "to have a record company with ethics."

Krasnow began operating out of Smith's office on the second floor, using Joe's desk, Joe's wines, Joe's cigars. "It's my office now," he said. Lundvall got a call from Donnie Smith. She'd heard how Joe was being talked about—his removal from Elektra. In tears, Donnie asked him, "What are they doing to my Joe?"

Krasnow and Lundvall went over Elektra's finances. "I didn't think Elektra was losing that much," Krasnow said, "until I opened up the books." They saw that the Country Division, just given away to WBR, accounted for 40 percent of the revenues. "When I got to Country, I said, 'Oh, my God. I've given Mo the only thing here that meant anything.' "

Now working again for Warner Bros. in Nashville, Jimmy Bowen rolled his Elektra country into WB's country operations. But he knew he wouldn't be long working for Mo. "If I'd wanted to stay, I wouldn't have left Warners in the first place, back in '68. I have good friends at Warner Bros., but it wasn't my kind of place. It's a gentlemen's club, and I'm not. So I knew I'd be moving on. I told this to Jim Ed [Norman]. He could be head of A&R and in a few years take my place. But things got a little speeded up."[112]

Within a few weeks, Krasnow and Lundvall moved Elektra back to Manhattan, to its former offices in the Rolex Building. Atlantic, for a fee, took over accounting. Thirty in Elektra accounting were fired, then another twenty in its Country Division in the merger with Warner Bros. Artists were cut, with Krasnow negotiating deal endings: "We're moving the company to the *East* Coast. We're out of these Linda Ronstadts and Jackson Brownes." Dick Griffey defended the future as "bright" as rumors swirled about Solar Records having a questionable future. Krasnow "categorically" denied it.

Joe Smith reminisced: "There were no deep problems at the company; '82 was the only rotten year Elektra really had. I think that, given a lower nut to meet, and by controlling costs and continuing with the artists they have, with any kind of breaks, they can have a good year."

Joe quickly moved into WCI's sports world, a new division with no assets to manage. "Things won't change," he promised. "It's just that now I'll be emceeing sports banquets. I'll be able to use a lot of the same material on these guys; they've never heard some of these lines.

"I wish the music business great health. It's very important to me. I own a lot of stock in Warners!" Smith's move came at the least opportune of times. With the chaos of Atari's collapse, WCI was hardly looking for new investment, and buying sports franchises was the wrong move, period. "Warner Sports" would last about a year, with Smith giving it his best try, but WCI's sincerity about building a sports division was as substantial as eyebrow glitter. Joe Smith moved on.[113]

WCI's 1983 Annual Report, ever scanning the clouds for gold beams, noted that Atari, once bought for $27 million, actually had earned $284 million, even after the year's loss. Sounded good; felt awful. Another chart said, after 1983 was all added up, WCI had just lost $417 million, an amount almost seven times the "Recorded Music and Music Publishing" group's profit of $60 million.

To WEA and the three labels, the events of the six years following the death of Joel Friedman had reversed the company's fortunes. The Plagues

---

[112]Seeing in Jimmy Bowen the kind of country producer he needed at MCA Records, that label's head, Irving Azoff, romanced Jimmy while the paint was still drying on Bowen's parking space sign in Nashville. Coyly, to the trades, Azoff whispered, "Bowen Records would be a big priority for me if we could get him." Irving Azoff got his man. Warner Bros. kept the Elektra country roster.

[113]At first Joe established temporary offices at Paramount Studios, to put together deals. Soon he was announced as the new head of NARAS but gave up that deal to become head of Capitol-EMI.

had visited, then moved in, squatting in room after room in a house we'd once run with Brady Bunch innocence. With costs and debt up, there was less money to play with. Sales, both in units and in dollars, behaved like that car in Steve Ross's story—having suddenly popped into neutral, now slipping back down the hill.

Significant Releases

1983

Atlantic: AC/DC (*Flick of the Switch*) • Laura Branigan (*2,* including "How Am I Supposed to Live Without You") • Crosby, Stills & Nash (*Allies*) • Genesis (*That's All!*) • Bette Midler (*No Frills*) • Zebra (*Zebra*)

Atco: INXS ("One Thing") • Pete Townshend (*Scoop*) • Yes (*90215,* including "Owner of a Lonely Heart")

Es Paranza: Robert Plant (*The Principle of Moments,* including "Big Log")

Modern: Stevie Nicks (*The Wild Heart,* including "If Anyone Falls" and "Stand Back")

Rolling Stone: The Rolling Stones (*Undercover,* including "Undercover of the Night")

Elektra: Mötley Crüe (*Shout at the Devil* and *Too Fast for Love* • Peter Schilling ("Major Tom (Coming Home)") • Carly Simon (*Hello Big Man*)

Asylum: Jackson Browne (*Lawyers in Love,* including "Tender Is the Night") • Linda Ronstadt (*What's New*)

Planet: Pointer Sisters (*Break Out,* including "Jump" and "Neutron Dance")

Solar: Midnight Star (*No Parking on the Dance Floor*) • Shalamar ("Dead Giveaway")

Warner Bros.: The B-52's (*Whammy*) • Black Sabbath (*Born Again*) • Christopher Cross (*Another Page,* including "All Right," "No Time for Talk," and "Think of Laura") • The Doobie Brothers (*Farewell Tour*) • Al Jarreau (*Jarreau*) • Rufus Featuring Chaka Khan ("Ain't Nobody") • Paul Simon (*Hearts and Bones*) • Rod Stewart (*Body Wishes,* including "Baby Jane") • ZZ Top (*Eliminator,* including "Legs")

Bearsville: Todd Rundgren (*The Ever Popular Tortured Artist Effect*)

Duck: Eric Clapton (*Money and Cigarettes,* including "I've Got a Rock 'n' Roll Heart")

Geffen: Asia (*Alpha*) • Berlin (*Pleasure Victim*) • Irene Cara (*What a Feelin',* including "Breakdance," "Flashdance," and "Why Me?") • Peter Gabriel (*Plays Live*) • Jennifer Holliday (*Feel My Soul*) • Elton John (*Too Low for Zero,* including "I Guess That's Why They Call It the Blues" and "Kiss the Bride") • Madness ("Our House") • Ric Ocasek (*Beatitude*) • Oxo ("Whirly Girl") • Quarterflash ("Take Me to Heart") • Neil Young (*Trains* and *Everybody's Rockin'*)

Qwest: James Ingram ("Yah Mo B There")

Sire: Madonna ("Borderline," "Holiday," and "Lucky Star") • Talking Heads (*Speaking in Tongues,* including "Burning Down the House")

24

From a podium, Henry Droz spoke much like Jack Benny: dry wit and looking a bit surprised you didn't see it his way. It was almost a takeoff on pomposity. In 1984, Henry told his colleagues, "When units were declining, we blamed the weather, we blamed the Jewish holidays, we blamed the economy, we even blamed poor little Pac-Man. Now, with unit sales increasing, we all know it's because of our sound business judgment and practices."

The year 1984 started brightly enough. Christmas and New Year's sales had been the strongest since 1978, a year that felt more like decades ago. Albums even continued to sell into January.

The worst felt (temporarily?) over. If you had to choose one individual within the Warner Group for green-lighting a future with "more" in it, my choice would be the lawyerly, paternal, gentle David Horowitz. While letting the record labels sell their records, and while letting still others clean up past messes, David looked for new growth.

One of David's clear calls had been to "get into CDs." He understood, more than any of us, what those shiny little devils might also do: double a label's profit on each album sold by turning $8.98 into $18.98, higher than even WEA's maestros of the markup could dream of.

At first, in '82, most folks in the American record business had figured that the CD was some kind of foreign trick. Example: For the first time, we labels would have to pay royalties to the disc's inventors, Sony and Philips. *Why?* demanded label execs. We never paid a cent for cassettes! Never did it for LPs! Why now? PolyGram's Hans Gout answered, "What they forget is that development has taken many years and several hundreds of million dollars." Labels dug in, so Philips-Sony shifted the license cost (three cents per disc) over to pressing plants. That way labels wouldn't have to see it.

The LP had been dying on its own. By 1984, cassettes had become 53 percent of the "record" business. CDs were maybe just 1 percent of the business, hard to find in stores filed somewhere under "Audiophile." When CDs first showed up in stores like J.C.Penney, Target, or Montgomery Ward, store managers treated them as alien Frisbees.

I hosted a meeting at WBR for the six major labels, where we answered what *Billboard* called "one of the burning issues": retailers' angst over buying new browser boxes, since CDs in LP browser boxes behaved like gophers. Henceforth, little CD boxes would be reencased in boxes—kazoom!—one foot high. It was a waste of cardboard and money, done only in America, but, with little regard for forest demolition, another retailer objection was hushed.

By midyear, with the growth of CDs amazing the trade, our industry stopped treating the little discs like oddities. Retailers found it amazing how some people came in and bought ten at a time. WEA cut both suggested list and wholesale prices on its entire catalogue from $18.98 to $15.98. The CD, previously for Vivaldi and Bach snobs, became prized by rock snobs. By November, 250,000 CD players had been sold, and 5 million CDs. Two months later, those sales had doubled.

Around then, Warner Bros. Records creative services director Adam Somers, seeing my little corporate group doing the conversion-from-LP digitizing and repackaging, finally asked, "Wait, isn't this something the *labels* should be doing?" My answer was ready: Go to it. In December 1984, WBR and WEA became the first label to sell a new title simultaneously in three formats: LP ($8.98), cassette ($8.98), and CD ($15.98) versions of Madonna's *Like a Virgin*.

That Christmas, CDs became a splurge. WEA labels ran out of stock. Every pressing plant in Europe and Japan was over capacity. The only active U.S. plant—CBS's in Terre Haute, Indiana—was supposed to produce 300,000 discs a month. Its output was closer to 30,000 a month. Making CDs had proved harder than baking vinyl pancakes.

Label financial officers—Gitlin, Vogel, and Elektra's Aaron Levy—found it hard to keep straight-faced about the CD. The labels' business-affairs heads had talked most artists/managers into accepting CD royalties at their LP rate. A rush of rich back-catalogue was okayed for release. The profit this new configuration could bring to their business was too good to believe; it was like this week your paycheck got doubled; it was like "whee!" Everything about CDs cost like LPs: the same cost to record, the same cost to market, soon even the same cost to make.

By the end of 1984, WCI's record division showed a 48 percent profit boost. Among his peers at 75 Rock, David Horowitz sat in the coolest seat, while those coping with Atari and other emergencies sat hotter. At budget meetings, our labels needed fewer excuses.

Hoping to avoid a cataclysm of LP returns, Droz spoke out: "A million turntables are not going to fold their arms and needles and slip quietly into the sunset." As if.

To sell off the twelve-inch records still in the bins, WEA execs pulled out charts to show how the LP decline had leveled off. Despite such suckin' in the wind, regulating the changeover became the most serious business of the day. Insurers had become flood-damage savvy. Droz spoke louder: "If the LP drops precipitously and CD demand goes up, we're in trouble." He began sounding less like Jack Benny.

Within months, it seemed, two thousand Kmarts were selling CDs. So were Walden Books' 980 stores. Henry, without enough CDs, was caught in a rare monosyllabic moment. He confessed, "Our fill is the pits." LPs were turning DOA.

WEA labels, which had (like all labels, really) been paying CD artist royalties at LP rates, now had to change their economics, and they kind of did. Royalties became 80 percent of CD wholesale (actually 100 percent, but with a whopping packaging deduction taken out).[114] The "new technology" clause got added to contracts. Nine Sinatra CD holdouts came out in October.

Just before its offices closed down for 1984's Christmas break, WEA wiped out all back orders for CDs, to start fresh in January (with no unfilled orders and at 10.8 percent higher wholesale price). Come January, retailers noticed that WEA's fill on CDs improved dramatically. Once-tough-to-get CDs by artists such as Madonna, Dire Straits, U2, and Bob Marley showed up more plentifully at the higher price.

Before long, people started replacing favorite LPs in the CD format. The flood of LP returns never happened. This was more a rise in the whole river, a rise that threatened no executive lawns. Catalogue sales reached their highest total ever.

All this good news just disguised the latest bad: Unit sales were down. Our market for recorded music—total unit sales—had simply stopped growing. Baby boomers, born after World War II, were now forty-year-olds with thinning hair. Boomers were not hair-band fans. We discovered that the world was flat.

Geffen Records, coming free of its international-distribution deal with CBS, was again up for negotiation. David went at it.

His Warner-financed label had spent its childhood losing money, first from CBS's $15 million advance but, after that was gone, more of Warner Bros. Records' millions. In contrast to Mo's earlier and easier transfers of Neil Young and Joni Mitchell over to Geffen Records, when Mo asked

---

[114]Warner Bros. Records business-affairs head, Dave Berman, did new math. His car's vanity license plate had, for a few years, read 10 on 90, meaning he wrote contracts that paid artists 10 percent of 90 percent of income, or 9 percent. The new CD math was 80 percent of income. Still, 8 percent on $15.98 was better than 9 percent on $8.98, so artists' managers objected lightly, if at all. Both labels and artists showed little moral regard for any "fair" price beyond "whatever the market will bear."

David if Geffen's Sammy Hagar could move to WBR to become Van Halen's lead singer, David screamed, he *geschreied*.

But Mo had faith in David; he wanted to renew with Geffen Records. And David, though free to move on, also needed to continue on with Warners; otherwise he had debt to pay back, and assuming his label's debt would appeal little to other possible distributing labels. Still, like most in the business, David wanted more (a trait shared by all labels this side of Gandhi Records). What David imagined was, five years from now, his own—I mean 100 percent his own—label, unshared with papa WBR. To turn 50 into 100 percent, Mo was David's obstacle, a businessman who would find giving up WBR's partnership share inconceivable. It didn't take an M.B.A. to figure out you don't subsidize a start-up label, continue paying its bills, then give it away.

David realized that dealing for his future with Steve Ross in New York would be much easier than dealing with Mo. He had to get over the Mo Hurdle. He met Evelyn Ostin for lunch at a Beverly Hills, under-the-umbrella, seventeen-dollars-per-salad place. Over lunch, David rattled on, pouring out gossip, revolting Evelyn by "sharing" snicker tales about Mo. A long, cold silence quickly fell between Geffen and the Ostins. The no-talk lasted the needed months for David to negotiate his next deal directly with Ross.

David had told Steve that "Mo won't talk to me," which was so. David asked Steve for $5-million-a-year profits advance. Just which profits *are* those, David? From where any rational man stood, Geffen Records' future looked bleak. The $5 million advance got turned down. Geffen next offered to trade his next five years' foreign distribution to WEA International for full ownership of Geffen Records after those five years, in 1990. Elliott Goldman, reviewing Geffen Records' poor sales numbers, all that red ink, told Ross, "If Geffen wants a hundred percent, give it to him. At least the international income might be worth something."

In the end, Ross did just that: he opted to get the international income stream today in exchange for iffy ownership five years down the road. Geffen could have his 100 percent in 1990. The shift of international rights from CBS to WEA relieved even Yetnikoff. Mo heard of the deal and was stunned. Warner Bros. Records, which had taken the five-going-on-ten-years of funding and man-hours to get Geffen Records going, objected but went unheard. If it had been Mo's to do, he'd have gone the other way and bought out Geffen Records at this point.

Next, Geffen pulled even one more step back from WBR (even though it still footed the Geffen label's expenses). At Geffen Records' holiday party at Chasen's, David approached the outstanding promotion head, Stigwood's Al Coury, and asked how many promotion people would it take to start his own Geffen Records team. Ten. Geffen and Coury made a deal, including key points like Coury's insistence on getting Fridays off for golf. Geffen told his financial officer, Jim Walker, "Jim, give Al all ten promotion men. Al's going to start his own team." No more depending on Warner people. Because of its boxes of goodies for electronics-deprived radio program directors, Coury's promotion staff would soon be known as "Circuit City."

To celebrate joining up with PolyGram to support the CD, Elliott Goldman and Jac Holzman had, in 1982, joined Jan Timmer at some schloss near Hamburg for a venison lunch. Timmer, a bald Boer of a man with a wrestler-thick neck and an agile mind, ranted about the inefficiency of his international-distribution system. Goldman and Holzman started kicking each other under the table. That evening, the WCI team proposed to Timmer merging his international-distribution system with WEA International.

To Timmer, a merger like that made good sense. Other than in classical music (where PolyGram owned 50 percent of the business), his labels bled red. Neil Bogart's Casablanca, now a PolyGram label, had become *Cash-ablanca*, suffering major losses. Serious questions had been raised as to whether PolyGram would even survive.

At midnight, schloss time, Goldman and Holzman called Horowitz in New York. Merger with PolyGram? A captivated David told his boss, and Ross even speculated about unloading some of WCI's own Atari "assets" onto Philips as part of the deal. Combining U.S. labels was also figured. The prospect of another "Number One"—this time Number One in the whole world—felt graspable. No longer would getting up there depend on Nesuhi's slow-building our own national organizations. Easier was Number One in one snappy deal.

Our international execs, like Phil Rose, hated the prospect. They knew that merger would mean PolyGram's country heads around the world shoving aside WEA's people.

The PolyGram-Warner merger deal was agreed to in principle.[115] Governmental okays would be a cinch, especially in America, where the Reagan administration was beloved by business for its rubber-stamp tendencies toward such activities.

At a merger celebration in Steve's three-stories-tall apartment at 740 Park Avenue, Ross romanced PolyGram's top execs. Jan Timmer and I discussed our interest in interactive, audiovisual CDs. I also concentrated on the free caviar and Steve's big-windowed views. Gracious foreigners

---

[115]PolyGram was owned, fifty/fifty, by Philips (of Holland) and Siemens (of Germany). The merger deal called for WCI to buy out Siemens's half interest in PolyGram, then WCI would transfer all of its record business (for legal reasons) to Warner Bros. Records. PolyGram would transfer all of its interests to Chappell Publishing. The two fattened-up companies would then merge into Warner-PolyGram, and issue new stock.

roamed the floor, using flattering words, comparing Steve's art collection favorably to the Louvre's.

CBS Records' Black Rock headquarters was just down the block from WCI. Once the word about the merger got out, its records head—the shameless (an adjective not exclusively his, although, among the people in this book, he'd surely make the Top Ten) Yetnikoff once again blew his stack, mind, and own horn. What he hated about the deal: it would mean CBS losing its final Number One–ness to WCI, whose corporate halls had already become filled with Walter-alienated, ex–Columbia executives, like Harvey Schein, Bruce Lundvall, Elliott Goldman, and Dick Asher.

Walter was "a character" in an industry that found foul-mouthed effrontery fun. A lawyer by background, as label head Walter grew into a hammer of a negotiator, afraid of offending no one, not even his most valuable artists. He ran CBS as a sheikdom. Walter was utterly tone deaf, except to the sound of a dropping coin. He played angles better than Willie Mosconi. You had to love Walter. You just never wanted to work for him.

In July 1983, Walter blasted off against the merger. "Everyone I've spoken with seems to think it's patently illegal—you're talking about laws in foreign territories and about regulations within the Common Market that are taken very seriously there. I can't see how the government can permit this," Walter pronounced.

Yetnikoff fought the merger on antitrust grounds, aiming at the Federal Trade Commission, thinking he had a chance. "If the government *does* permit it, they're giving me the green light to set up an auction block and say, 'Who wants to sell?' " Walter threatened tit for tat, invoking the possibility that CBS would go on a buying spree itself, narrowing the companies in the marketplace. WCI matched CBS attorney for attorney. Briefs, petitions, and market projections, print outs as thick as elephant thighs got Xeroxed, stapled, piled into boxes, the boxes piled onto pushcarts, all wheeled south toward Washington, D.C. Advocates, like economist Dr. Alan Greenspan, were hired to fight for us.[116]

Phil and Nesuhi's execs from Sydney to Stockholm convinced themselves that PolyGram execs in their countries would take over. In a deep funk, Phil Rose moved down to Palm Springs, not even bothering much to come in to Burbank. The whole feeling inside WEA International was "Who needs this?" T-shirts reading SCREW THE MERGER were worn widely within WEA International offices.

In Pasadena's Ninth Circuit Court of Appeals one Monday morning in

---

[116] I cherish one moment when six of us, including the eminent Dr. Greenspan, were lunching. During our talk, I piped up in recordese, "Look, Al . . ." only to see Greenspan's head jerk back in a kind of startled whiplash at being called "Al." I quickly corrected myself, calling him "Doctor" for the rest of the meeting. However, once out of that meeting, and ever since, to me he's just "Al."

July 1984, attorneys battled over the merger[117] for two hours. The FTC's arguer, Howard Shapiro, predicted monopoly, noting that the two companies combined would have a 26 percent market share. If this "floundering" PolyGram company (which claimed it was losing $300,000 a day) really needed to be merged, better with Capitol or MCA, both of which had said they'd be willing to head for the altar. When the FTC's lawyers suggested *that,* Jan Timmer exploded.

Two months later, the Ninth Circuit Court of Appeals agreed with the FTC injunction. No merger. To the corporate pushers of the deal, Horowitz and Goldman, its collapse was a major defeat.

Nesuhi Ertegun, age sixty-six, stuck to his guns, though they now seemed of smaller caliber, hoping, to use Mo's words, "to hang in there." Phil Rose, his interest in WEA International now completely shot, resigned after fifteen years or, as Phil calculated it, fifty-eight hundred days; he mailed in his resignation from Palm Desert, California. No replacement was even contemplated.

In a few months—call it mid-'83—MTV, cheerleading "I Want My MTV," had grown from pipsqueak to giant. It became the only music video game in the country; Discovery Music Network disappeared; Ted Turner's Cable Music Channel lasted thirty-four days. MTV ruled.

It did for records what no radio station could: It exposed them simultaneously all across the country, did it all day long, did it all night long. Radio, that was only single-city promotion. And MTV was heading for *world*wide. Nielsen, the rating service, found 60 percent of MTV's audience saying that the cable channel had a bigger influence on its buying than radio or retail ads or concerts or anything else on television, for that matter. Which really mattered.

Sensing heat, David Horowitz left the WCI music group to become president/CEO of MTV Networks, Incorporated (formerly the Warner Amex Satellite Entertainment Company), of which WCI owned one-third. Running his own company attracted David, and anyway, Steve's "Office of the President" was being quietly dismantled. David left, also quietly. He had known how to deal with difficult people, and he'd bent well. He'd regarded music executives as artists. Only once, in a moment of unguarded reflection, did he share with me this question: "You think David Geffen was easy? Ahmet Ertegun was easy?"

I, too, became only partially sponsored by WCI, starting up my own company, called The Record Group, without "Warner" in front of its name

---

[117]Legally, the merger was going to be a fifty/fifty joint venture between WCI and PolyGram's corporate dad, N.V. Philips Gloeilampenfabrieken (pronounced "Gloeilampenfabrieken," which could well be Dutch for "lightbulb makers").

(scary moment) since TRG was backed by both WCI and PolyGram. "My own company" felt to me as fun as bungee cord, as I'd spent all my work years pushing products (albums, mainly) that others had come up with. But Warner chose to let invent-for-invention's sake. With a staff small enough to fit into one lifeboat, the Record Group ventured into the sea of make-whatever-you-can-dream-up.

Thus blessed, I continued to disregard a thing business folk called "the bottom line." At the Record Group, we developed more uses beyond just music for the CD's digital data. We struggled to turn the data into both music *and* pictures, something not done before; the idea of watching a CD of the German-language opera *The Magic Flute*, and seeing on a monitor its words translated into your choice of language while the full CD sound pours out at you, that we believed was neat. (Still do.) We agonized over inventing our own tools to encode such discs, since the picks and shovels of "applications" did not yet exist. Bill Gates came by my office, saw our work, and pretended to be interested. I realized he'd never make it in show biz.

Next for the Record Group came more glitzes, like CDs that people could interact with on computer screens. The result of such never-before discs emerged, two years later, variously being called CD-ROM, CD+Graphics, CD+MIDI (CDs that would play music synthesizers), and on and on. Many of these products still amaze (and have not yet been marketed). Creating them gave us childlike joy, even if our budget crammed us into a Burbank motel-turned-offices owned by Dick Clark. We issued our hyper-CDs, a few dozen of them, but with no business push to make them famous. However—since our productions were more technology than chart hits—our creations meant little to our sponsors, two adult record companies busy chasing hit acts.

Eventually, Philips decided to throw its weight behind CD-i, a proprietary CD-ROM technology they'd come up with (sound + pictures + click here). CD-i was shepherded by another Philips company. It, too, was ignored by the real world (Microsoft and Sony). With Philips, we were through. Steadily, we lost money. I imagined gory graffiti on The Record Group's walls, and nervously made us look useful again to the Warner Music management.

As an entertainment medium, CD-ROM faded to a vehicle for games featuring lance-bearing ogres, with which our Mozarts did not compete. Our cord felt bungier than ever, and Dick Clark did not accept IOUs. Nervous-time.

Label heads Ahmet and Mo, Steve as well, having sampled the worldwide might of PolyGram, looked at Nesuhi's setup and again felt what they did not like to feel: Number Two, or smaller. Nor did they warm to Nesuhi's chosen next leader for International, their European star Siggy Loch, despite his good jazz instincts, blond hair, and good tailoring. Siggy's English was perfect, with one exception. He kept referring to compilation albums as "copulation" albums.

With Horowitz gone, WCI's real Record Group was, for now, overseen by Elliott Goldman, plus the logical and precise Dick Asher, over from CBS.[118] But Goldman, like Horowitz, restively wanted to move from his "staff" job ("staff" is where you have king-size titles but no armies to obey you) to a "line" job (where you appear further down the titles list, but get to run your own baronies and their armies). Goldman wanted his own division to command.

At a select meeting, Steve, David, Ahmet, and Mo had earlier agreed to look for a Nesuhi successor. He would be neither Goldman nor Siggy. Mo Ostin was asked to cast the successor or, to the best of Mo's recollection, "maybe I just did it." He'd been impressed, as had Steve, with PolyGram's leader in England, Ramon Lopez. PolyGram's Timmer had offered Lopez a new label, one to be part-owned and run by Lopez along with fellow Poly-Gram executives Roger Ames and Clive Swan. Mo persuaded Lopez to come to Warner instead, citing tempting growth (ergo, profit-sharing) factors: the upsides in Warner's limited operations "overseas," plus the CD profit jump.

Not realizing that Mo was already talking to Lopez, Elliott eyed WEA International. He proposed to Steve Ross that its management become Nesuhi Ertegun, chairman; Elliott Goldman, president; and Dick Asher, executive VP. Goldman found himself not invited to meetings. Deals he set, like distribution of Clive Calder's Jive/Zomba label, got passed on. When he asked Mo why this was happening, Mo advised him to just drop it. Ultimately, it was Morgado who told Goldman how things were going to work: International would be based in London under Lopez *and* Nesuhi; Goldman could be its administrative VP. Crushed, Elliott returned to his office. Sitting there was Ostin, there to break the news more gently, clearly. Mo asked, "Is there anything we could talk about?" Goldman was touched but knew that decisions had been made behind his back, and he went home knowing that his prospects had gone *poof.*

At Krasnow/Lundvall's Elektra Records, rumors swirled. Krasnow had his hands on everything. He wanted a better-looking label. He threw away the old E, and made a new E that balanced on one leg. He changed the company's name to Elektra Entertainment. He did not endear himself to Geffen when he dispensed with the word "Asylum." In open-jawed awe, Elektra's new head of promotion, Mike Bone, noted that Krasnow "destroyed the artist roster, completely dismantled it." Much as Geffen earlier had ejected

---

[118]At an industry dinner, Joe Smith's sensitive line about Dick Asher: "Truth be known, six months ago Dick thought Bon Jovi was a red Italian wine."

New York folkies when he'd taken over Elektra, now, under Krasnow, Elektra went from 150 acts down to 40, this time really getting rid of that *Hotel California*, singer/songwriter image.

Early on, Krasnow and Lundvall got lucky, with help from the Linda Ronstadt/Nelson Riddle *What's New*; the capture of Howard Jones's hot new "New Song" in a lightning raid into London by Bruce and Mike Bone; and with Solar's Midnight Star record *No Parking on the Dance Floor.* New signings started with Teddy Pendergrass, whose solo career on Philadelphia International Records had been cut short by a 1982 auto accident that left Pendergrass paralyzed from the neck down but left his soul and voice unhurt.

Feeling good, Krasnow had plans drawn to redecorate the entire office. Shown the blueprints, Bruce remarked, "Bob, I'd bet it's going to take a few million dollars to do what you want to do. Wouldn't it be better to wait until we're really in profit?" On the spot, Krasnow ripped up the plans and told Lundvall, "Man, that's why you're here. That's great, man." To which Lundvall replied, "It's not exactly profound, you know?"

Knowing that Krasnow really *still* did not want his Elektra/Musician jazz label, Bruce started meeting his artists away from the building. Bob wanted Bruce to be his head of marketing, even though Lundvall had told him that he "didn't do that anymore." Lundvall recalled bringing Whitney Houston in as a potential signee. Krasnow passed. Ditto Stevie Ray Vaughan. Lundvall realized that Krasnow did not want Lundvall to sign anyone, just to do marketing. Krasnow felt that Bruce wasn't working as a president. He was behaving like an A&R guy whose love was jazz and blues. Bob isolated Bruce, who felt it.

Meeting at an RIAA function, Capitol/EMI head Bhaskar Menon approached Lundvall, discreetly inquiring about his availability to start either pop or a jazz label or both on the East Coast. Capitol owned the venerable jazz label Blue Note, which was offered to Lundvall to supervise. "We can use you," said Menon. Then, continuing in his artful phrasing, Bhaskar explained, "We have no catchment area on the East Coast."

After a private trip to Los Angeles over the weekend, Lundvall met with Goldman and Horowitz, who'd asked Lundvall to extend his contract. Elektra was working, heading toward profitability. Horowitz said he didn't want Lundvall to leave, but in the end, he'd left the decision up to Krasnow. Bruce returned to the office. He told Bob about the Capitol opportunity. Krasnow answered what Lundvall expected: "Man, you gotta do this! This is great for you!"

And that was it. Exit Lundvall. He was not replaced.

By 1983, Linda Baker had put in four years in Detroit's branch sales office, moved up from covering secondary markets (the boonies) to the city. Her energy, love of music, and resourcefulness had made her a promotion woman and the one to whom many in our Detroit office turned first. Her diary noted: ". . . early on in the Talking Heads' career, when Jerry Harrison, David Byrne, and I get kicked out of a deli for throwing gefilte fish onto the next booth, freaking out an older woman customer . . ."

That November, she was introduced to Peter Gabriel. They hit it off immediately. "We had a riot," Linda later recalled. "We talked over the phone a lot at first, and then later spent time throughout 1983, me visiting him while on his tour of the *Security* album featuring 'Shock the Monkey.' Peter, who was separated from his wife, and I spent time together throughout the Midwest. I just remember the *huge* crowd adoration and *me*, knowing that I was the only one he was going to spend the night with. We 'dated' for about eighteen months. I went to England in August to visit him and bicycle around England and Scotland, my first trip to Europe at age twenty-five.

"I also got lots of attention during that year from John Wetton [the singer of Asia] and also dated John Illsley, bassist for Dire Straits, who were a very *hot* band then. So, it was certainly a pretty great dream for me, a girl from the Midwest, not related to anyone famous or rich—only to be from the same small town as Madonna!—to be hanging with the rich and famous musicians as buds, etc."

Unlike the CFOs, Linda Baker was not thinking numbers. Linda still remembers her rock-star era as the best part of working in the record business, come what may.

Since Atari's collapse, Bert Wasserman had made peace with WCI's bankers but, even for bankers, these men felt sweaty to the palm. Warner Communications hadn't the cash to meet "certain financial covenants." The banks insisted that, until WCI could pull its debt to under $700 million, the cost of borrowing would have to rocket. Credit lines got reduced and collateralized by the stock of the movie, records, and publishing divisions. Stock dividends were limited. Investments had to be okayed by the banks. Atari got dumped off to Jack Tramiel for no cash, just warrants. Panavision, then run by Jac Holzman, sold off for $52 million. The Franklin Mint, sold for $96 million plus $66 million in debt. Corporate staff was cut a whopping 65 percent, often by Bob Morgado. Company debt was cut about 33 percent. No stockholders' meeting was convened.

As part of its continuing bail-out from the Atari collapse, WCI put up for sale its interest in MTV. Among the interested buyers: David Horowitz + Bob Pittman + Boston Ventures, a funding bank. Time, Inc., too, bid for the Warner Amex Cable property. Ultimately, WCI sold its stake in Showtime/The Movie Channel, as well as its two-thirds interest in MTV Networks to Viacom International. WCI got cash—$500 million—plus warrants for future purchases of Viacom stock. Herb Siegel, the white knight from Chris-Craft who thought having even one company plane was lavish, loved that half a billion.

To the record labels, *who* owned MTV didn't matter. What did matter was the cost of making song videos, which now was up to six-figure huge. Labels tried selling copies of these music videotapes. Only hits by Madonna and Prince sold.

Meanwhile, getting videos *onto* MTV got harder. The music channel had grown picky. Artists, too, started rejecting $100,000 videos after they'd been finished. Label heads asked, "Why spend all this money for videos that never play on TV?"

Under fire for the cost of promo video clips being produced, Jeff Ayeroff of WBR's Creative Service's went on the defensive: "If you want to go through and do a *mea culpa* about how badly we've handled videos as a creative entity, how insensitive we've been to our artists, and how we've delivered so much crap that we don't like how it looks, that's one thing. But to say that video doesn't work for us is foolish, because it can and does."

Ayeroff thought that an older generation of record-business executives, who grew up selling records without video, was freaking at this new approach to marketing. He complained about the previous generation's record executives. "Anybody who sits and stares at budgets all day long is driving with the brakes on, not with the gas pedal. What you have to do is take your shots. The fact that I would do a hundred-twenty-thousand-dollar clip on A-Ha—four million albums later, who's going to tell me I'm wrong?"

By 1985, now with twenty-five million subscribers, when it came to promoting singles, MTV was a six-hundred-pound gorilla. It had clout like never before. Before MTV, before television concerts like Live Aid, small-town audiences just didn't see much of this kind of thing, not in Fargo, where the Stones had never rolled, where radio was hicky-wishy-washy. Then, suddenly, there *it* is, on TV!—*all* day *all* night! Fargoites saw moving chest hair, torsos they had only before imagined, rock bodies like Mick Jagger, Phil Collins, Dire Straits, Elton John, U2, Eric Clapton, Metallica, Twisted Sister. Fargo's youth ogled crotch-grabbing, four-inch tongues, girls in chains. They could not get enough of it. What's more, they bought it, at $18.98 apiece.

The Warner Record Group had survived overselling, the killer Atari, and a dozen Plagues. The CD and MTV had made our world juicier than ever. Underlying weaknesses in the business had been well covered by a "double the price" rise in the CD and the euphoric product demos by MTV. I kept trying to throw away that "Beyond Our Control" list I'd made on the plane, but it just would not disappear. Our business's weaknesses getting covered by CD-MTV was a relief but in a few years we'd realize that our business still stood upon underlying weaknesses. We were selling fewer "units" every year. Not a good sign.

For now, however, the Eighties was the decade to rake it in. Just one more thing to fix. Crucially, our promotion forces were finding themselves powerless when it came to getting "station adds" on their new records unless we dealt with men who behaved like extortionists.

Significant Releases

1984

Atlantic: Laura Branigan (*Self Control,* including "Lucky One") • Julian Lennon (*Valotte,* including "Too Late for Goodbyes") • Ratt (*Out of the Cellar,* including "Round and Round") • Twisted Sister (*Stay Hungry,* including "We're Not Gonna Take It")
Atco: INXS ("The Swing")

Elektra: Peabo Bryson ("If Ever You're in My Arms Again") • Lindsey Buckingham (*Go Insane*) • The Cars (*Heartbeat City,* including "Drive," "Hello Again," "Magic," and "You Might Think") • Howard Jones (*New Song*) • Patrice Rushen (*Now*)
Asylum: Teddy Pendergrass (*Love Language,* including "Hold Me") • Linda Ronstadt (*Lush Life*)
Megaforce: Metallica (*Ride the Lightning*)
Solar: Midnight Star ("Operator") • Shalamar (*Heart Break*)

Warner Bros.: Dio (*The Last in Line*) • John Fogerty ("The Old Man Down the Road") • Honeymoon Suite ("Feel It Again") • Al Jarreau (*High Crime*) • Chaka Khan (*I Feel for You*) • Christine McVie ("Got a Hold on Me") • Prince (*Purple Rain,* including "I Would Die 4 U," "Let's Go Crazy," "Take Me With U," and "When Doves Cry") • Sheila E. ("In the Glamorous Life") • Rod Stewart (*Camouflage,* including "Infatuation" and "Some Guys Have All the Luck") • The Time (*Ice Cream Castle,* including "Jungle Love") • Van Halen (*1984,* including "Jump," "I'll Wait," and "Panama") • ZZ Top ("Legs")
Full Moon: Chicago (*17,* including "Along Comes a Woman," "Hard Habit to Break," "Stay the Night," and "You're the Inspiration")
Geffen: Berlin (*Love Life,* including "No More Words") • Sammy Hagar (*VOA,* including "I Can't Drive") • Don Henley (*Building the Perfect Beast,* including "All She Wants to Do Is Dance," "Boys of Summer," and "Sunset Grill") • Elton John (*Breaking Hearts,* including "Sad Songs" and "Who Wears These Shoes") • Donna Summer ("There Goes My Baby") • Wang Chung (*Points on the Curve,* including "Dance Hall Days") • Whitesnake (*Slide It In*)
Qwest: Frank Sinatra (*L.A. Is My Lady*)
Sire: Madonna (*Like a Virgin,* including "Angel," "Dress You Up," and "Material Girl") • The Pretenders (*Learning to Crawl,* including "Back on the Chain Gang," "Middle of the Road," and "Show Me") • Talking Heads (*Stop Making Sense*)
Slash: Los Lobos (*How Will the Wolf Survive?*)

25

Just one layer below Icon Level at the WCI labels (Ertegun, Ostin) worked younger talent. Within Warner Bros. Records, president Lenny Waronker, attorney Dave Berman, accountant Murray Gitlin, and marketing chief Russ Thyret (pronounced "Thigh-RET").

Eddie Rosenblatt, vice-president of marketing, had known Russ Thyret since 1968, when Russ worked in a Sunset Strip record store. When Eddie joined WBR in 1972, Russ, whom Eddie referred to as "The Soul Man," joined Eddie as his promotion director. The son of a cop, Russ exuded firm belief with little doubt, a mix that magnetized his troops.

Russ now entrusted sales management to traditionalist Lou Dennis. Lou, too, knew things "absolutely." For any occasion, in fact, Lou had a pre-developed operating rule. He knew that conference rooms should be kept at sixty degrees Fahrenheit, to keep audiences awake. If a price raise was made—say, $9.98 for a double cassette—Lou always had a reason ready, like "Whatta you mean? The first two hundred thousand units will have a ten-by-twenty-inch booklet!" Even at breakfast time, Lou never waffled.

With Lou performing keel duty for WBR's marketing ship, Russ Thyret became its sails: At heart, Russ was a promotion man. Like some guy running a Crusade, Russ could hold high a cassette, shout "Storm the charts!" and hordes of believers charged along behind him.

But now, in New York and Burbank, promotion executives like Russ faced a more difficult madness than the party life they'd led for years. At the outset of the music business, the song plugger's job had been to get ball-room orchestras to play publishers' new songs. Pluggers had paid for such play discreetly, either with cash in an envelope, not in a naked palm, or with copyright credit (giving a percentage of the songwriter income right to the bandleader who played the song). It was how the economy worked, back into the 1920s and even before. (Who's to say the Sirens of Ancient Greece weren't greased?)

When radio found a larger audience, people no longer had to show up in dance halls to hear the latest. For song publishers, radio became the short-cut, doing a song plugger's weeks-long job in an hour. With the arrival of all-music radio, how often you got a record played made or unmade your life. By the mid-Eighties, promotion was forced to follow harsh new rules of picks-to-play, set by radio program directors.

National record pickers—men who put out expensive weekly tip sheets to help disc jockeys learn what was happening in other towns, reviewing at the skinny level what the larger trade magazines like *Billboard* lacked in "street sense"—these men had become "factors" in the 1970s.

First such a factor was a sport named Kal Rudman. An ex-DJ himself, Rudman was five feet six, two hundred pounds, and known therefore as "the round mound of sound." He was also known for having no chair in his office; he worked at a lectern. He had learned early in life the appeal of being chauffeur-driven in a cream-colored Caddy. He'd started a national, weekly tip sheet called *The Friday Morning Quarterback*, which came out mimeographed and stapled. It took ads, and the records in the ads, often enough, turned out to be Kal's Pix of the Week. While Kal's sheet hardly guaranteed a hit record, a different guarantee got associated with it. Without an ad, Kal's sheet could ignore a label. Getting ignored by *The Quarterback* was poor business. Labels bought ads.

Rudman was, in spirit, the father of the sons who became the thing called The Network.

By the 1980s, program directors had begun listening less to our promotion men. More often, PDs were picking records urged on them by others— by nationally tuned-in, independent promotion men. These new power figures muscled their ways into the smaller world of our one-bagger promo men and women. Six to twelve of these "indie" promoters took charge of American radio. They named themselves The Network. To put it simply, without retaining a Network guy, a label's singles got too little play and so did not sell. To get a *real* hit, label guys like Thyret needed to hire The Network, like it or not, and, as time went by, pay The Network more and more. For labels, their staff promotion men and women became, at the worst, an expensive excess.

Old-time promo men—ours and every label's—could no longer deliver the kind of playlist "adds" they once had. They grew to dread their Thursday conference calls when, with their peers from other cities listening in, they had only promises, not adds to list. For a label promo man not to get an add it was like a car salesman going dry, week after week.

Record promotion had changed drastically. Program directors at Contemporary Hit Radio played it safe: They wanted only real, proven hits. New singles were neither real nor proven. Each week a program director was faced with a choice like a judge in the Miss America quarter finals, maybe, when two hundred attractive new singles were paraded before him by ten or more good-buddy label reps, all of whom wanted to know if there was anything the program director would like. What PDs liked most were their jobs. Those depended on their station's ratings. Radio played what listeners wanted, not what record companies wanted. PDs played it safe.

One way to distinguish safe records was to pick mostly from those that were getting labels' full attention, nationwide: displays hung in stores, national tours by the artists, a new album, too. The word used was "priority." Labels often put out, say, six new singles a week. Secretly, so as not to offend its artists, a label had a secret "priority" list, a piece of paper hidden, its existence deniable. Thyret had one but could not admit it. The best way a radio program director learned which single was a *real* priority was asking one of those Network consultants, some guy who had no label ax to grind, who was being paid by all labels. PDs learned to trust Network guys when it came to adding to that week's playlist the, say, three or five new records out of the week's new two hundred. The singles on the Network's "paid to push" list became the industry's priorities.

During the 1980s, record labels began bidding for the services, on a record-by-record basis, of Network guys. A "station add" in St. Louis might cost a label seventy-five dollars that week. Next week, moving that single up, another seventy-five dollars. And how many stations were there, times how many singles? As the Network's services became more crucial, their prices moved up, up to a hundred thousand, maybe two hundred thousand dollars per record, depending on the quantity of "adds" delivered. Hiring the Network guys cost labels a bundle. Then two bundles. Then ten.

The Network could not deliver a hit if the record lacked pop appeal but it could *prevent* an appealing record from getting its share of airplay.

Of the Network men, two stood out. In Los Angeles, it was Joe Isgro. From the East (Cherry Hill, New Jersey), it was Fred DiSipio. For no other reason than the size of my office at WBR, both had individually come to visit me, each time escorted by Thyret. We small-talked. Behind both Isgro and DiSipio, during their separate visits, stood ox-shouldered bodyguards making sure I did no harm to their bosses' Bijan blazers.

Isgro shone, with shirts of black silk and jewelry of gold tonnage. He sounded like he'd seen *The Godfather* once too often. His pencil-thin mustache reminded me of Jack Warner's. He greased back his hair and, in the macho manner of the Eighties, looked like he'd been too busy to shave. Mr. Isgro lived up in the hills above our San Fernando Valley in one of those architectural sprawls whose decor ran to marble floors and lampshades preserved in their original plastic wrappers. Most important, Joe Isgro had no sense of humor, so our visit was short and blessedly superficial.

DiSipio, in contrast, was a bit nerdy, nasal, and short. His massive "security dude" who stood behind him: Big Mike. On meeting him, I called him "Mr. Michael," later worrying that I'd sounded like Tiny Tim. The industry line about Big Mike was that when he went into a restaurant, they didn't give him a menu, they gave him an estimate.

The Network worked. Payola was part of it. Program directors, some of them, got rewarded in cash, sometimes through pseudonym-registered post-office boxes. Whatever it took. Monthly birthday cards, whatever. Costs of Network services to record labels ran from CBS (the most thankful, spending over $10 million a year on Network consultants), down next to MCA, on down to the WCI labels (no purists we, at about $5 million a year). These millions cut sharply into the profits our labels brought back to October meetings with Bert Wasserman. The budget line item designated "radio promotion" grew like a goiter, and just as visibly.

By 1980, amid the industry's hard times (the death of disco, the commercial impotence of New Wave music, the birth of little else), David Horowitz had tried persuading his labels to "kill this expense." He estimated that this Network of around twelve promotion representatives collected upward of seventy-five thousand dollar to one hundred fifty thousand dollars for handling just one record. Multiply that by how many singles?

The label heads knew the math but were not sure that boycotting the Network would be effective. They had experienced the Network's power. Horowitz knew that *some* label had to say no first. So . . . ours first.

In November 1980, the Warner labels announced that they were unilaterally discontinuing the use of independent promo men. Unsaid was our hope that this would provide other labels with a rallying point.

The reactions to our initiative came fast: "Not cutting back," said RSO's Al Coury. "Everyone needs help now and then," said MCA. "No plans whatsoever," said Capitol. Our competition crowded in through the door we'd tried to shut.

CBS's joining our ban was critical. At first, Walter Yetnikoff's label announced, "We do not follow the lead of Warner Bros. or any other label." Then CBS did join the ban. The Network fought back, proving first to Columbia, then to Warner, that it could stunt sales. CBS caved. Warner stood there, noble as Don Quixote, and just as out of it.

Indie promotion had been costly, but the loss of radio play began costing even more dearly. Then one Network rep, asking anonymity, said that though he was no longer working WB product, he was still on retainer at Atlantic/Atco, was doing "special projects" for Elektra, and had lost no other accounts. A face-saving ploy—not paying the Network directly, yet letting the label's *acts* get "marketing advances" so *they* could hire the Network—started being used. By 1981, WCI's ban was over. The costs (and adds) continued.

Over the next years, Thyret, a practical evangelist, hid the cost of indie promotion. A year's budget would be set, and Russ, no skinflint at promotion, still came in under, for ten months. Once October's budget review got past Corporate's budget meetings, there'd resound an "oops" from the promo area, where Russ would—"oops"—discover a forgotten drawer in his desk, crammed with payables to the Network. Still, the year had gone well. A year's going well forgave much else.

Except, perhaps, the cost of maintaining two promotion forces, when one of them—Russ's own—was having little effect on PDs.

Maybe I'd just had it with rock concerts, but in autumn 1985 my elder son, Chris, coming down from Sarah Lawrence College, met me in Manhattan for the weekend. I picked the evening's concert; this one, I told him, was "a must." We went to the Upper East Side, to an expensive nitery, and caught Count Basie and his big band. Basie was old. He was rolled up to the piano by wheelchair. But I told Chris, this is what I *do:* I preserve music. I guess I just wanted to bond once more with Basie, with his white-haired black-faced band playing from sheet music that looked like it'd survived the Civil War. And I wanted Chris to hear it, before it was too late. I kept nudging my son. "Hear that?" *I* could hear that: articulate swing singing by good Joe Williams, who intoned melody, shaped phrasing, and I could understand the lyrics, something I guess I'd missed when singers started to yell, twenty years back. I hoped Chris could hear what I heard, and I hoped that, to him, Basie did not get filed next to Bach.

A month later, I took him to hear Woody Herman atop the Rainbow Roof, and Mr. Herman came by our table and shook Chris's hand. A month later, Chris called me in California to tell me that, using his own money, he'd gone down to the Village to hear Oscar Peterson. I felt I had been a good father.

Knowing she had cancer, Thelma Walker retired in 1984. She relocated to the South of France, only to die within the year. Her spirit lives on in these listings. For 1984: Warner Bros. 33 + Atlantic 21 + Elektra/Asylum 11 = WEA got 65 onto the charts.

Privately, Steve Ross discussed with Walter Yetnikoff—of all people— the possibility of his moving over to the Warner Music Group. Back in 1984, in the midst of the PolyGram merger fight, Steve had turned to Elliott Goldman, asking that he study replacing Ahmet by hiring Yetnikoff to run Atlantic. Yetnikoff was sounding out a package with WCI, one that would include not only himself but also Peter Guber and Jon Peters, movie men that Walter wanted to work with. Goldman, however, concentrated on Yet-nikoff as a soloist, suggesting a five-year deal for $500,000 a year, plus a $1 million signing bonus. This didn't fly. Yetnikoff had been using Warner's in-terest in him to buoy his renegotiation with CBS. He eventually re-upped

there for $475,000 a year, plus a $250,000 signing bonus. What made his renewal sweet, however, was CBS allowing him to dabble up to 10 percent of
his time in the movies.

Through all this, Atlantic Records was told nothing about Corporate's
feelings toward its performance. The decline of Atlantic's market share went
noticed at WCI. When Atlantic issued a seven-album set—the best of Atlantic's R&B records, going back to 1947—the set sold fifteen thousand
copies. Ben E. King decided, "I think the saddest thing I've ever seen happen is the black music section of Atlantic disappear almost completely.
Somewhere along the way, somebody stopped paying attention." In 1985,
Atlantic slipped again. The count became Warner Bros. 44 + Atlantic 19 +
Elektra 14 = WEA's 77.

Courtney Ross and husband, WCI board member Beverly Sills and husband,
and Evelyn Ostin and husband flew in the Wicky Bird to WCI's Acapulco
Villa Eden, a sprawl of a hilltop estate reserved for VIPs of WCI. Villa Eden
resembled a small but oh so elite tropical hotel, with a view of Acapulco
Harbor that reminded guests of the view overlooking Hong Kong harbor—
breathtaking. To resuscitate guests, the villa had a staff of ten. Tennis courts,
of course; the villa ran up a bill for twenty-four thousand dollars for tennis
shoes alone. For Mexico, the villa was incomparable, with satellite TV
dishes, a playhouse to screen movies, a pool whose luminescent water ri-
valed Capri's but with added underwater speakers playing Record Group
music. Over dinner, Ross confessed to the others his relief at having caught
in time some pancreatic cancer. He'd had the surgery. All he needed now
were periodic blood tests. Mo noticed how relieved Steve appeared. It had
been caught; it was over; he was now in great shape. Over a world-class
salad dressing and a universe-class sunset, the conversation drifted on at the
edge of the Pacific.

By now, Elliott Goldman, in the Horowitz spot, felt the powerlesness of his
staff job: Nobody to command. No future within WEA International. Blaming "corporate politics," Goldman quit. Ross replaced him with Bob Morgado, head of his cost-cutting rescue squad during the Atari crisis. Morgado
told me he felt "only loosely in charge," put there, in Ross's way, as "some
mysterious character." Bob was an activist, hands-on. Ross knew that. As
Morgado recalled, Steve's instructions to him went something like this: "I
don't know what has to be done there. I know we have a sort of a good company, but I don't think we're doing as much as we can be doing. Go figure
it out."

From the outset, Ostin regarded Morgado warily, especially after Bob
had confessed to Mo that he deep down was a politician, and that meant

to him that he "needed power." Mo regarded Bob's words as ominous bragging.

Morgado felt his first concern should be Atlantic Records. But Ahmet stood there, blocking that doorway. He made no invitations for Bob to do any fixing. Morgado turned to what he called his "area of greatest opportunity"—probably a euphemism for "least-defended fortress"—WEA International. To Morgado, Nesuhi's International had felt loose, undirected, and indifferent. WEA Spain was a case in point, a company that, not understanding it was supposed to distribute Warner Home Video videos, had just left cartons of *Superman* sitting on its loading dock in the rain for months.

Quickly, in May, Ramon Lopez was promoted to co-CEO alongside Nesuhi, who lied to *Billboard* about how much he endorsed the appointment: "Maybe I will be traveling a little less, but my duties remain the same. In fact, I have just renewed my contract." The truth was that Nesuhi always grew WEA International slowly, laissez-faire in his own, autocratic way. He'd given Lopez little authority.

Morgado viewed Nesuhi as a dinosaur, and a slow one at that. Within a year, at a meeting including both Mo and Ahmet, the power circle in Records decided that it would be better to let Ramon just take over. Who was to tell Nesuhi? Ahmet could not. He had no answer if his brother would ever ask him, "With all your power, you couldn't stop this?" The telling fell to Mo, who walked over to Nesuhi's office to break the news. After Nesuhi announced his resignation at a meeting in Venice of twenty-five WEA managing directors, Lopez became WEA International's full-time chief.

Nesuhi moved to the twenty-ninth floor at 75 Rock, into offices next to Morgado's, back to record more jazz. Atlantic revived one of its old label names, East West,[119] so that brother Nesuhi could once again stand in the studio with gentlemen like the Modern Jazz Quartet.[120] Not now to make money, but instead to Do Good. As if a lesson to the lawyers and tin ears who jumped into music in the Seventies, Nesuhi Ertegun went back to what always counted most: to making music, but doing it now in a world that had changed, when other executives couldn't tell E-Flat from a hole. In retirement, Nesuhi chose to stay in Manhattan and save for us fine music on disc.

---

[119]East West had been a label-on-the-shelf for several incarnations at Atlantic, most recently in the 1950s to serve producers Lee Hazelwood and Lester Sill, when it released two dozen singles over two years, but only one hit: "Weekend," by the Kingsmen.

[120]Atlantic for many years indulged music both the Erteguns adored, and not just jazz. "Cabaret music," a form of singing that involves good-voiced singers (Bobby Short, Mabel Mercer, early Bette Midler) and exquisite songs (Noël Coward, Cole Porter) persisted at Atlantic, unnoticed, uncharted, and relished by the few. The survival of cabaret at Atlantic I can credit only to Ahmet, who after all these years still loved great songs by great singers.

In the words of Bob Morgado, "He was on my payroll and sat on my floor. He was with me and, unfortunately, a year later his contract was canceled."

Nesuhi concentrated on leading IFPI, the International Federation of Phonograph Industries. He became the industry's leading fighter against music thieves, its Pirate Killer. He did more than any other person to clean up whole countries: Hong Kong, Singapore, Egypt, even Turkey joined the legit world records community. For IFPI, Nesuhi kept busy, wheedling Korean bureaucrats into coughing up some royalties.

"Nesuhi traveled even more," his wife, Selma, told me. "He was afraid people would forget who he was."

Five years after the first WCI-led Record Group ban against the Network had flopped, the cost of paying DiSipio, Isgro, and Company had suffocated poorer labels unable to afford their high rates. Yetnikoff, using his CBS checkbook to crush commoner labels, was rumored to be paying almost $13 million a year for Network services (*Rolling Stone* had it at $17 million). Then, in 1986, a different network, NBC, televised on its nightly news a seven-minute investigative report. I was home, just watching TV, when there on Channel Four were Network guys I had met, Isgro and DiSipio in New York reportedly meeting a don. "Cash, cars, expensive watches, drugs, and nights with women are being provided," NBC said, describing "the new payola." I checked the door locks on my trophy house. The next morning, NBC's seven minutes had grown into a front-page scandal. Quickly, the RIAA announced its companies' views, denying that we in records had any involvement with bent-nosed nasties. U.S. Attorney General Rudy Giuliani and L.A.'s Organized Crime Strike Force (doncha love it!) sent out subpoenas. Tennessee's Senator Al Gore said he was going to investigate these payola and promotional practices in the record industry.[121] Record labels rushed to disassociate themselves from any use of the Network. Within seven days, a full and complete ban against using the Network arose, solid as a Berlin Wall. It was the end of an era of amazing grease.

In follow-up video bites, Isgro, with his two English hulks visible over his shoulder, stood there, looking stunned. He said stunned things, like "Where is my crime?" I was inclined to believe him. He'd just been scuffling in a business that accepted scufflers. Scuffling, wasn't that American? Wasn't this simply the way things worked?

---

[121]Earlier that the same year, Senator Al's wife, Tipper, heard her daughter listening to Prince's "Darling Nikki," which included the lines "I met a girl named Nikki / I guess you could say she was a sex fiend / I met her in a hotel lobby masturbating with a magazine." This experience helped Mrs. Gore found a media watchdog group called the Parents Music Resource Center, which initiated a Senate hearing on potentially harmful lyrics. Performers who testified were John Denver, Frank Zappa, and Twisted Sister's Dee Snider.

Label promotion returned to feeling like itself, more and more.[122] Prince came along and became a Thyret "must." Nowhere was Thyret's charisma more evident than in WEA's annual mass weekends at Miami's Diplomat Hotel. And this was the year. The Network was in retreat. Our label promo forces were back onstage, once more kings and queens of radio promo.

As in most years, before Labor Day, many in the record group flew to Miami, first class. They'd deplane at MIA, step outdoors, and experience instant humidity, like standing in the last half of an automatic car wash. In three minutes flat, as wet air engulfed them, they became too slippery to hug, too wet to grip. Wondering which Mad Financial Controller, what worshiper of de Sade, had chosen Miami in August, they found their suitcases and hopped into cabs. Cabs to the Diplomat were driven by sleep-deprived Cuban exiles who drove harrowing routes, as if they knew that life was cheap.

The Dip lobby was *Miami Vice* and it was Ricky Ricardo. On lobby tables posed sculptures of black cats, big ones, left there, like yard-sale rejects from Haiti. Paisley carpets and drapes, as if chosen by some blind Iranian decorator, clashed. Anything white had turned yellow with stain, long, long before.

Waiting in the lobby for their luggage, sales and promo people high-fived one another moistly. Then conventioneers would head upstairs, hoping for a room away from the elevators, preferably on a middle floor to avoid the noise of lobby revels below and the all-nighter suites above. In each room, air conditioners hummed but produced no wind, simply re-breathing 1950s air.

One purpose of a Warner Music Group convention was to inspire the troops over the fall's upcoming albums. To that end, label and distribution people sat in huge rooms, where for three days and 190 new albums, video depictions of each assaulted their gradually dimming sense organs. Veterans brought a sweater; sure as Lou, it'd be sixty degrees in there. Before the first hour was over, it all sounded one way: loud.

Speakers spoke.

- Chairman Steve Ross flew in to kiss Henry Droz on the cheek.
- Milton Berle appeared to thank the crowd on behalf of his nephew Marshall, who managed Ratt. Berle did shtick: spilling wine on the

---

[122]Mo promoted Russ Thyret up to senior VP of Warners. Asked about it for the press, Thyret casually commented that his job would stay pretty much what it had been, with "just less time for fishing." The next day, Music Vision, run by Network promotion power Dennis Lavinthol, installed a wading pool in our company's lobby, with two large live fish.

fly of his tan Brioni suit, followed by fifteen minutes of farce. The oldies in the audience loved it. The kids squirmed.

• After first apologizing for my poorly matched clothes (my wife and I had just separated), I then demonstrated for the convention how an audio signal from a new CD-ROM could turn on a margarita blender. *Ga-zshu-ooo,* the blender started, creating massive applause. Boy, was I ever tech! As seven hundred cheered, I scurried back to my seat.

• Sheldon Vogel, weary of such new digital-disc forms—our "CD + something" configurations—announced Atlantic's own new, CD antipiracy technology. Vogel named it CD-IUD.

At breaks, the multithousand audience moved rapidly from sixty degrees to ninety-eight degrees. Thawing out at poolside was favored. Forget the Atlantic Ocean; that was seaweed and jellyfish. Poolside, women wore lipstick.

At one end of the pool rose a cavern of man-made rocks enclosing a gods-made bar. Under thatch, WEA hearties drank tropical pink and sky blue cocktails, fast as they could. Following enough of these, and to piss off hotel security, promotion men and women scrambled up the rocks, to the top of the waterfall. As if in some silent movie, one good-looking couple came out of the hotel, stopped poolside, stripped, continued walking into the ocean for a swim, returned across the beach, put their clothes on, and walked away, with no comment.

Record artists had been flown in. Over in the corner, Roger Daltrey dressed in nothing but a black Speedo, great physique, the girls agog, their red lips open. Simply Red's Mick Hucknall did laps, his gold-red hair locked up with a barrette. Record stars like Daltrey, Hucknall, and, over the years, so many more, flew down to the Dip because promotion men and women had gathered there, and promotion was the way these artists and musicians got heard, sold, and jets.

Rock stars hung and talked as equals to promo people like Dallas's Paul Poulos, whom Elektra's Mike Bone affectionately termed "a madman." To get records played, Poulos had recently sent pig heads, real ones, out to stations with notes reading, "Don't be a pighead. Add the record." He'd done it for "I Still Believe" by the Call, and for "Object of My Desire" by Star Point—two records, two pig heads, two adds. Poulos heard his boss Mike's frustration over WDVE, Pittsburgh, not going for the Call single. Poulos figured, "Why not?" Though it wasn't his territory, Poulos sent a pig's head and a note via five-day UPS to WDVE's program director, Greg Gillespie. This time, Poulos's note read, "Play the Call, or be slaughtered!!"

After five-day UPS, the box turned more than a little smelly when Gillespie's secretary opened it. The sight of a rotting pig's head made her throw up over much of the station's lobby. Gillespie wrote this note to Elektra:

From what I have been able to ascertain, Mike Bone orchestrated this ploy on a recent Elektra promotion conference call. The entire Elektra field staff was urged to send me a note regarding my ability to hear a hit record . . . I called Mike Bone this morning to inform him that no one at WDVE will take a call from an Elektra employee, that no Elektra employees will be allowed to enter our offices, and that WDVE should be removed from all Elektra mailing lists, as we have no further use for your product. In short, our business relationships are now completely severed.

Poulos was praised by Bone because promotion men were part of the record-business chain, out there to get attenton to get records played.

During the day, WEA's convention lived inside the Dip's main ballroom. When the sun set, unnoticed, and product videos ended, the delegates threw off their leashes, heading up to their rooms. When Atlantic promotion man Lou Sicurezza came back to his room, his key would not work. Security drilled a hole through the lock. Everything in Lou's room was upside down, superglued to the ceiling. With a guy last-named Sicurezza, the jokers should not have screwed around. Lou was not a forgive-and-forget type.

Dinner: Industrial-strength servings of Miami Mystery Meat were the norm, so the hotel's dinners got ducked. Duckers ran into town on some VIP's expense account. At dinner at Joe's Stone Crabs, people asked Sicurezza what he thought of their prank. Lou dumped on it: "Nah. Cute, but done before." Cabbing back to the Dip, when Lou got out, forty pounds of cheesecake dropped from the hotel portico, trapping him like Mafia cement shoes. Lou was asked, "Well, Lou, *that* original enough for you?" Lou muttered *omertà*.

After dinner came live shows by Iggy Pop, Aerosmith, Natalie Cole. Upstairs, Mick Hucknall trashed his suite, then explained to WEA, "It's okay, I can do this, because I'm a star and stars do these things."

Midnight, after the show, began WEA's Animal House of Style. Mingling parties challenged the resources of room service, ending when the clock read Blurrrrr.

Past midnight. Two wings to the Dip: the newer wing and the moldier wing. In the newer wing, it was all-night poker in George Rossi's suite. In the mildew wing was Blood Alley, where an elitist clique hung together, pushing away inhibition with credit cards, wearing black T-shirts with dripping red letters, executives acting like depraved teenagers, exotically excited, wiping their bloody noses on white curtains.

One inebriate ran the hallways in nothing but a towel, carrying a blow-up shark pool toy, initiating the greeting "Fins up!" He pounded on girls' doors, offering them his shark. Others settled him down. Phones rang at two in the morning. Lou Sicurezza again, yelling, "Get over to my suite for a meeting, and bring your phone book." Everyone tossed phone books into the whirling blades of the air duct seven floors down, the pages flying up into the sky. A few thousand in damages, but not out of one's own pocket.

Your phone rang at three. It was the topless waitress from the topless doughnut shop calling and promising "sexual favors" when you got there; at the door, she was naked and took you into the bedroom, where a promotion meeting began.

Your phone rang again at four, and it was up to the suite again, where they'd invented a new one: tossing melons off the balcony, trying to bull's-eye a pool lamp down below, and it was the great guys, like Mick Jones from Foreigner, guitar guys from Winger, promo guys. Security comes to stop you again.

Back to your room at five, only there's some guy from Elektra passed out on your bed, having thrown up in the tableside drawer, ugh, get another room quick! Try to sleep.

At six, down the hall, they ran a smoke machine, the kind rock bands have. The alarm bell went off, half-dressed people came out of half-neat rooms, evacuating. Security came charging once more.

At seven, roaming the lobby, Russ Thyret approached friends, trying to *buy* some sleep . . . from anybody. Nobody had any to sell. "Did you ever try to score some . . . sleep?" he moaned. "In this joint, it's a valuable commodity! If I'd tried to buy some yesterday, I could've bought whatever I needed. But today it's not available. I'll pay top dollar for one stinkin' hour of quality sleep! Anybody interested in selling me some?"

Then, after seventy-two hours in Miami, promotion and sales people headed back home. Those who had been doing the Dip for many a year thought of conventions there the way real people thought of Thanksgiving back home, that good. For them, it was a time when, maybe they didn't realize it, life would get no better.

Warner's Rick Wietsma, riding away, looked back at the sagging hotel and thought, "The best thing that happened at the Diplomat was we all avoided Legionnaires' disease." Those from Blood Alley flew back home wearing sunglasses.

Branch supervision of promo expenses was stepped up. Actual receipts for freebies had to be stapled to the expense form. New employees signed papers pledging "no heavy drugs." The word "grease" became a word about hamburgers. Our label-promotion men and women once again felt like crucial people, once again worthy to drop melons down the air ducts of the Diplomat.

Linda Baker had been promoted and was now, fully fledged, a WEA promotion woman. She had never told her WEA bosses that she knew how to type. Raised Catholic, she once had prayed in a football huddle backstage with some frightened nineteen- and twenty-year-old, Irish Catholic kids before they went onstage at Harpo's in Detroit. In 1987, a few years later, Linda stood with those same boys backstage, watching them—U2—play America's largest stadiums as the biggest new band in the world. "That's when it was really best to work for a label and be in the business," she recalled.

WEA moved Linda to handle Washington radio stations. There, one day, she dressed up in her never-to-be-used wedding gown, saved from her-wedding-that-never-happened, to promote Honeymoon Suite's "Feel It Again," carrying around a triple-tier wedding cake with a fake robot hand moving out of it. It was enough to get play out of B104's Steve Kingston. And she, like most in promotion those days, without any Network, thank you, could get adds. She was happy again.

Significant Releases

1985

Atlantic: Phil Collins (*No Jacket Required,* including "Don't Lose My Number," "One More Night," "Sussudio," "Take Me Home," and "Hang in Long Enough") • The Firm • Foreigner (*Agent Provocateur,* including "I Want to Know What Love Is" and "That Was Yesterday") • INXS (*Listen Like Thieves,* including "What You Need") • Mike + the Mechanics ("All I Need Is a Miracle" and "Silent Running (On Dangerous Ground)") • Ratt (*Invasion of Your Privacy*) • Twisted Sister (*Come Out and Play*) • *St. Elmo's Fire* and *White Nights* soundtracks
Atco: Pete Townshend (*White City,* including "Face the Face") • Yes (*9012 Live - The Solos*)
Duck: Eric Clapton (*Behind the Sun,* including "Forever Man")
Es Paranza: Robert Plant (*Shaken 'n' Stirred*)
Modern: Stevie Nicks (*Rock a Little,* including "I Can't Wait" and "Talk to Me")

Elektra: The Cars (*Greatest Hits,* including "Tonight She Comes") • The Cure (*The Head on the Door*) • Dokken (*Under Lock and Key*) • Howard Jones (*Dream Into Action,* including "Life in One Day," "No One Is to Blame," and "Things Can Only Get Better") • Mötley Crüe (*Theatre of Pain,* including "Smokin' in the Boys Room") • Starpoint ("Object of My Desire")

Warner Bros.: A-Ha (*Hunting High and Low,* including "Sun Always Shines on T.V." and "Take on Me") • Dio (*Sacred Heart*) • Dire Straits (*Brothers in Arms,* including "Money for Nothing," "So Far Away," and "Walk of Life") • The Dream Academy ("Life in a Northern Town") • John Fogerty (*Centerfield*) • David Lee Roth (*Crazy From the Heat,* including "California Girls" and "Just a Gigolo/I Ain't Got Nobody") • Scritti Politti ("Perfect Way") • ZZ Top (*Afterburner,* including "Rough Boy," "Sleeping Bag," and "Stages")

Geffen: Aerosmith (*Done with Mirrors*) • Elton John (*Ice on Fire*, including "Nikita" and "Wrap Her Up")
Paisley Park: Prince (*Around the World in a Day*, including "Pop Life" and "Raspberry Beret") • Sheila E. ("Love Bizarre")
Sire: Talking Heads (*Little Creatures*)

1986

Atlantic: AC/DC (*Who Made Who*) • The Firm (*Mean Business*) • Genesis (*Invisible Touch*, including "In Too Deep," "Land of Confusion," "Throwing It All Away," and "Tonight, Tonight, Tonight") • Julian Lennon (*The Secret Value of Daydreaming*) • Gloria Loring ("Friends and Lovers") • Nushooz (*Poolside*, including "I Can't Wait" and "Point of No Return") • Stacey Q (*Better Than Heaven*, including "Two of Hearts") • *Stand by Me* soundtrack
Duck: Eric Clapton (*August*)
Island: Steve Winwood (*Back in the High Life*, including "Higher Love," "Finer Things," and "Freedom Overspill")

Elektra: Anita Baker (*Rapture*, including "Sweet Love") • Georgia Satellites ("Keep Your Hands to Yourself") • Howard Jones ("You Know I Love You . . . Don't You?") • Metallica (*Master of Puppets*) • Benjamin Orr ("Stay the Night") • Simply Red (*Picture Book*, including "Holding Back the Years")
Asylum: Jackson Browne (*Lives in the Balance*, including "For America") • Linda Ronstadt (*For Sentimental Reasons*)
Solar: Midnight Star (*Headlines*)

Warner Bros.: Peter Cetera ("Glory of Love" and "Next Time I Fall") • Chicago (*18*, including "Will You Still Love Me?" and "If She Would Have Been Faithful" • Club Nouveau ("Lean on Me") • John Fogerty (*Eye of the Zombie*) • Miles Davis (*Tutu*) • David Lee Roth (*Eat 'Em and Smile*) • Paul Simon (*Graceland*, including "You Can Call Me Al") • Van Halen (*5150*, including "Dreams," "Love Walks In," and "Why Can't This Be Love")
Geffen: Berlin ("Take My Breath Away") • Peter Gabriel (*So*, including "Big Time," "In Your Eyes," and "Sledgehammer") • Ric Ocasek (*This Side of Paradise*, including "Emotion in Motion") • Wang Chung (*Mosaic*, including "Everybody Have Fun Tonight" and "Let's Go") • Neil Young (*Landing on Water*)
Paisley Park: Prince (*Parade*, including "Kiss")
Qwest: The Color Purple soundtrack
Sire: Madonna (*True Blue*, including "La Isla Bonita," "Live to Tell," "Papa Don't Preach," and "True Blue") • The Pretenders ("Don't Get Me Wrong") • Talking Heads (*True Stories*)
Slash: Violent Femmes (*The Blind Leading the Naked*)
Tommy Boy: Force M.D.'s ("Tender Love")

26

LOOKING over his new domain, a more pleasing prospect than the disaster that had been Atari, Bob Morgado kept analyzing the companies in his music division. He saw three labels being run "imperially" by Ertegun, Krasnow, and Ostin. None of the three had any next-in-line being groomed. (The same lack of succession grooming was true of Steve Ross and Morgado himself.) The labels' lack of leader-depth deeply vexed Morgado, he said. The label heads, however, slowly began believing that "succession" was some cover-up that allowed Bob to fire Steve-devoted guys so that he could name new Bob-devoted followers. No, one of his jobs, Bob insisted, was to make sure the casting of his division was correct.

He also saw a huge imbalance. The Thelma Walker Memorial Tally for 1987: Warner Bros. 48 + Atlantic 16 + Elektra 9 = WEA total: 73. Two out of three hits coming from Burbank.

Beyond the three labels and distribution (America under Droz, elsewhere now under Lopez), Morgado's domain also included Warner's music publishing, run by Chuck Kaye, who worked autonomously, profitably, and candidly. "I don't think Bob at first even knew much about publishing. Our numbers were small compared to the other divisions, so we maybe talked three times at first," Chuck reflected. "In the early years, I hardly remembered him, other than some guy who slouched in his chair at meetings and said nothing."

Of all these top men, only the newcomer Lopez was flexible and seemed happy with Morgado's involvement. Of the six biggest division heads reporting to Morgado, Lopez was the only one who didn't have a "what's your name again, kid?" attitude toward his boss.

Morgado wasn't the only one who talked about the group's successor problem. In mid-1988, Joe Smith, by then back in the business running Capitol Records, told *Playboy*, "The fascination is that in the Top Ten a year from now there will be three names we never heard of today. And we'll wonder whatever happened to some of the names in the Top Twenty. What's con-

stant is the executives. Ahmet Ertegun is a star. David Geffen is a star. Walter Yetnikoff's a star. Stars burn out . . ." And, Smith added sadly, his generation had failed to recruit the next generation of leaders, blaming that on
faults like drugs in the work culture and on a younger generation that behaved with a different work ethic.

Allied with Lopez, the broad-faced, often-smiling Morgado focused on
International. Together, they bought market share, beginning in 1988 with
German classical-music company Teldec. That elevated WEA/German's
market share from 10 to 20 percent.

When Morgado decided to hand the American distribution rights for
Teldec over to Elektra, I was stumped, since Elektra already had Nonesuch,
so . . . why another classical label there? Bob had earlier told me that he'd
been trying to strengthen the labels where they were lacking. So I asked
him, "Why Elektra? Why not to Warner Bros.?" Morgado answered simply,
"Mo already has enough."

I visited Teldec in Germany. The company and its people reminded me of
what I liked about the record business: music. Teldec's employees smoked
too much—in one meeting I had to ask for an "air break"—but these Teldec-
ers were men and women who, on their own, would walk to Sunday-morning
chamber-music recitals, there to sit in bare and chilly rooms wearing handed-
down scarves, to sit with eyes closed to hear each hush of the music, to feel
at times the slowness of the music, to transcend for an hour the big-business
expectations that had descended upon their lives with America's purchase of
their company. People like me.

Classical music scratched my CD-development itch. I wanted to add on-
screen explanations of what Bach was doing at a particular moment, like "hear
the oboes echo the string theme." It was a new technology we called
CD+Graphics, and, when I explained to Morgado and Lopez that JVC wanted
to make the players for our CD+G discs, the two men had yippeed, a performance little seen in Sunday-morning concerts where no one dared to cough.

Lopez and Morgado kept saying buy-buy. Their check writing became
fervid. WEA International made a long-term exclusive marketing deal with
France's classical label, Erato Disques. Each added deal was, for Lopez and
Morgado, a win. I was in Morgado's office when Ramon told him of still
another addition, like picking up a company in Norway. At the news, Morgado and Lopez high-fived. To me, their leap—I could not imagine Mo or
Ahmet high-fiving—revealed an odd broadening within our business. Suddenly, here was this Portuguese Hawaiian (Morgado) jumping up to slap
the palm of this tall, Castilian Spaniard (Lopez). Ethnic broadening, I
thought. While a mere thirty stories down on the curb below, black street
musicians continued to drum on overturned paint cans, picking up tourist
dollars.

Then, while busy with international growth, into the lap of Bob Morgado fell an acquisition the size of a fertilized cow.

Since the collapse of the Warner merger, PolyGram Records had been deep in cash trouble. PolyGram's 1984 American head, the gentle, music-involved Gunther Hensler, put up for sale the company's crown cow: Chappell-Intersong, Europe's music-publishing giant. PolyGram sold its giant for $100 million to a consort of buyers led by Freddy Bienstock (successfully the second husband of Miriam Abramson). The hundred mill helped to turn around PolyGram's fate. (PolyGram chief Jan Timmer soon thereafter moved Hensler into a narrower job: head of classical music, and put Warner's Dick Asher in charge of PolyGram's U.S. operations. The sudden move stunned Hensler.) Now, in the world of music publishing, two titans faced each other: Warner Music Publishing (biggest in America) and Chappell (biggest in the world). Their leaderships had experienced more rivalries than Notre Dame football.

And now, having held on to Chappell for two full years, Bienstock and Backers were ready to see what the market would bear.

Warner Music Publishing head Chuck Kaye had come into publishing from his family; his stepfather (Lester Sill) and stepbrother were also music publishers. Tall, warm, and athletic, Kaye entered publishing in the early 1960s, age twenty, always running his publishing show, first for Screen Gems, then Phil Spector's Philles Records, then over to A&M's Almo/Irving and Rondor Music. By 1980, when David Geffen had started Geffen Records, Chuck had also begun Geffen-Kaye publishing. One year later, 1981, he came in as the new head of Warner Music Publishing. The first morning, in its offices up on Sunset Boulevard, Chuck found an out-of-date company of thirty employees "all somehow related to each other." He brought in new talent: accountant Les Bider for legal and business affairs, Jay Morgenstern as his general manager.

Chuck had gone out to find new copyrights. He'd made innovative deals with WBR and Elektra, sharing publishing proceeds with the record labels for acts the labels steered to him: 25 percent to the label, 25 percent to Warner Music, and 50 percent to the singer/songwriter, often based on a more generous mechanical rate of, say, a penny over the minimum rate. It was fresh lucre for the labels. It brought a windfall of new copyrights to Warner publishing. During the Atari bonanza years, Kaye's publishing had grown its own bonanza: 20th Century–Fox Music, plus Madonna, Michael Jackson, Whitesnake, Mötley Crüe, Vangelis, and on and on.

Kaye heard the buzz: Chappell was back "in play." He realized that buying, owning a Warner + Chappell, would be the kind of deal that, overnight, would put Warner into the biggest league in publishing, bigger than Number

One. More like Number God. Kaye called Steve Ross and pitched: We should buy Chappell, even though its price, in two years, might have gone up from $100 million to $150 million. Steve told Kaye, "Give me fifteen minutes, then call me right back." Chuck called his financial aide, Les Bider, into his Sunset Strip office to witness the callback. "This," he told Bider, "could be historic."

Quickly, Steve decided that WCI should be all ears.[123] Kaye and Bider flew to New York, threw the pitch, and the powers of Corporate picked up the phone to call Chappell's owner/negotiator, Freddy Bienstock. Bienstock had worked starting at age fourteen as a mailroom "counter boy" for Chappell's Max Dreyfus, called "Pruneface," one assumes due to wrinkling. Dreyfus was one of the brothers who'd sold Warner Bros. their publishing empire back in the late Twenties. The price then: $4 million. Bienstock had later become the publishing rep for the Aberbach brothers' Hill & Range, the publisher most suited to supply Elvis Presley his songs; Bienstock's job was to record demos—dubs—of the songs that sounded Presley-like. He'd handed Elvis "Don't Be Cruel." He'd bought Hill & Range in 1966, then scooped up more and more copyrights into his own company, Carlin Music, which became Britain's top publisher eleven years in a row. One difference: In America, record companies had the power; in Britain, publishers still ruled. Bienstock and his backers acquired more and more, even the New York Times Music Publishing Company in 1977, adding its five thousand copyrights. Then he'd bought Chappell, from a needy seller, with turnaround in mind.

As head of Music for WCI, Morgado was brought in to make the deal. Kaye hated it when Morgado smiled at him and joked, "I guess I'll have to get involved with this silly business of yours." While Kaye and Bider roamed the world, figuring how to fit Chappell and Warner's operations together, Ross, Wasserman, Morgado and his new Mergers and Acquisitions executive, Paul Vidich, negotiated with Bienstock.

After months of talks, in May 1987, Warner Music bought 100 percent of the world's largest music publisher. What two years earlier had cost Bienstock's consortium $100 million now cost WCI $285 million, or $712.50 per song. Adding Chappell's revenues (about $100 million a year) to Warner Music's revenues (about $50 million a year) created a publisher four times the size of America's next largest. Chappell added 400,000 copyrights to Warner Bros. Music's 300,000 copyrights, adding up to GEE,000. Through this acquisition, songs by Cole Porter now snuggled with songs by Bananarama.

---

[123]WCI already had a second-party share of Chappell via an investment it had earlier made in Boston Ventures, one of Freddy Bienstock's backers when he'd acquired Chappell a couple of years earlier. WCI effectively would, in small part, be buying Chappell from itself.

Kaye got set to run the resulting Warner/Chappell. He spent the first months of '87 amalgamating the two companies, concentrating on Australia, France, Holland, and Scandinavia. Kaye's itinerant, handle-things-himself, "disappearing" style annoyed Morgado, who now believed that Warner/Chappell demanded more than Chuck's one-guy, "boutique" management.

Gradually, and then with a rush, Kaye recognized he was being left out of talks. Morgado had taken over. He was making operating decisions that Chuck always had made, that his contract guaranteed were his to make. On the side, Chuck was being wooed by a Japanese company to start up music publishing for them in the United States, so he felt secure. But he wanted it the way it always had been—his. He asked for a meeting with Steve. It took place at the Bel-Air Hotel, Hollywood provider of swans-in-your-lake, private cottages, and *bonnets du* cash. Just Steve, his PR head Geoff Holmes, Chuck, and (at Steve's request) Mo Ostin. "What's going on?" asked Steve. Chuck was, as he usually is, sure of what he wanted. He complained about being ostracized. Ross looked over Chuck's wish list. On it: Report to Steve. Ross took the list and told him, "Chuck, don't make a decision. Don't go with the Japanese. I'll make sure that this gets fixed. I want you to come to New York next week, and we'll arrange a meeting." Leaving the Bel-Air, Mo expressed his amazement at how strongly Chuck had come on.

For that follow-up four-man meeting, Chuck flew in to New York to meet with Steve, Morgado, and Marty Payson. He walked into the room, only to be told, "Steve can't make it." At that moment, Kaye knew that his career at WCI was over. With his bosses, as shrinks would phrase it, Chuck had a "character conflict." Having had a $50 million funding offer from Japan to start a new publishing company, he resigned. Morgado pointed to Warner Music's financial officer, Les Bider, to take over the publishing empire.

The next year, Warner/Chappell Music Publishing acquired Birch Tree Music Group, including the song "Happy Birthday." Around dinner tables everywhere, before blowing out candles, celebrants would raise their voices in song, violating copyright law.[124]

"The consumer is voting with his pocketbook!" enthused massive mass merchant David Lieberman, all abubble over the faster-than-wished-for decline of the LP. By February 1987, the LP was down to about 8 to 11 percent of total rack industry sales. And the CD's sales had climbed from 1984's $10 million to 1986's $100 million.

---

[124]A dozen years later, ASCAP would demand that the Girl Scouts pay fees for singing "Happy Birthday" around campfires. ASCAP got laughed at and retreated back into the woods.

The forms of digital sound erupted. Amid all of them—and there were a dozen—lurked the record business's greatest villain, a disc called CD-R. The R stood for "recordable." Philips, still a foreigner (America had next to no electronics business), had come to market with the first machines capable of recording (copying) digital sound at home. The villain's tool's disguise was not great, other than its price: $6,995 each. CD-R was hardly a consumer item. So shrug. Yet the loosing of CD-R meant consumers could now copy CDs as simply as cassettes. It was only a question of cost now. CD-R cost about $6,500 too much to worry about. It went largely ignored in 1987, amid the business's shower of cash and confusion of new technologies.

The crowd of CD-plus-something-elses obscured the CD-R. Hardware makers scratched for CD-Cousins. On came: the CD-3 (a three-inch single, except you had to fit a collar around it to play in five-inch trays). "Cassingles," a term registered by MCA's IRS label, which killed that form; CD-V, for music videos on five-inch discs; CD-Interactive, which Jan Timmer of Philips spent several hundred million dollars to promote; CD+Graphics, which scrawled clunky words onto an attached video screen; DAT, another scary one—digital audiotape—and the RIAA threatened to sue the first company who sold such a recorder in America.

Without the law on its side, the record "industry" was at the mercy of expensively, perfectly copied sound, sound truly good as the original. It just, so far, cost $6,995. We knew to fight commercial piracy, but no one had solved "home disc–ing." We knew how plush was our catbird seat, how tech was simply machinery that meant nothing without our hits. This pride and oversight would prove expensive.

March 1987 sales at Warner's included 26 percent of America's hit singles. Our music was getting gobbled up by radio faster than peeled shrimp at a plumbers' convention. It was the biggest single month in WEA history. With clamor like that, who had time to worry about what R stood for?

At the year's WEA convention, Atlantic's Ahmet made one of his short, stylish speeches of thanks to his distributors: "Thank you for all the work you did on the flops as well as the hits." Sixteen words, then he sat down. Atlantic had been active now for forty years, as had its surviving leader. The label threw itself a fortieth-anniversary party. Madison Square Garden was barely big enough to hold the twelve-hour celebration show. A crowd of twenty thousand attended. Jerry Wexler, across town with WBR, did not, would not attend. Led Zeppelin reunited for the occasion. The show went on till one-forty in the morning, when the birthday cake candles were extinguished.

Later in the year for Atlantic, Ahmet and Jerry both were inducted into the Rock and Roll Hall of Fame, which Ahmet had cofounded. So were the Coasters, Clyde McPhatter, Aretha Franklin, and Joe Turner. That one Wexler attended.

Inside Atlantic, however, after twenty years at the label, Dave Glew had turned unhappy with his role and rewards. He felt he'd peaked at the top of the sales mountain. CDs were up to 70 percent of everything. Glew recalled, "The windfall profits were absolutely amazing. Return ratios were as low as they'd ever been. When you're selling something at sixteen ninety-eight with no returns, that covers up for the one hundred thousand records you were shipping and taking back ninety thousand."

Deep down, Dave knew he could do more than just market records, had told his bosses that, but he'd persuaded no one up top that he could do more. Finally, he decided. Unable to locate Ahmet, Glew wandered around on the morning of his resignation, trying to figure out to whom he could resign. When Glew found Sheldon Vogel, Shelly was not surprised. "Ahmet had always made it clear to Dave that he'd never be higher than he is now. When it came to carving up the bonus, Dave was not treated as one of the upper echelon."

By two-thirty that afternoon, when Ertegun did come to the office, the word was out. Glew moved over to run Epic Records, which evaluated his talent differently, giving him room to grow.

Into Glew's place stepped Mark Shulman, who reported to president Doug Morris, who in turn reported to Sheldon Vogel, who in turn reported to Ahmet Ertegun, who in turn reported to the IRS, but afternoons only.

Teenage singer Debbie Gibson signed with Atlantic. She was publicized as a dance-hall diva, a Madonna killer. She said exactly the right thing: "I'm very driven, even though I don't drive." Miss Gibson walked her twelve-inch single into radio stations herself.

After a rumored possible dismantling the year before, Elektra had came back with top albums. "With only twenty or thirty releases a year," Bob Krasnow said, "there's a lot of pressure for each album to succeed. But we don't have expectations that are overreaching for each record. It's a high-wire act, but we've chosen this path. You need nerves of steel to run a company like this." By October, Elektra had three of the Top Ten albums: *Tracy Chapman*, the *Cocktail* soundtrack, and Metallica's *. . . And Justice for All*.

Mötley Crüe's *Girls, Girls, Girls* shipped 1.2 million copies on its first day. To commemorate that fact, three Crüe-members in mini-attire, net stockings, and advertising sashes invaded Henry Droz's office to pose all over the man. Droz, quick to recover, commented, "I haven't had a business meeting like this since Detroit's Pontchartrain Hotel in 1968."

Mike "Pig Head" Bone left Elektra to take on the presidency of

Chrysalis Records.[125] To fill Bone's spot, Krasnow promoted Hale Milgrim (marketing) and Dave Urso (promotion), both from within the company. Each label was acting its own way: Atlantic, frugally run by Shelly, but otherwise preoccupied in open-till-dawn clubs from South Beach to North London; Elektra, a determined outsider among labels, issuing nothing to be ashamed of later, thus remaining boutique size; and third, Warner Bros., the ocean liner of labels, fully staffed, in every sense now, a major. *The* major.

This major reported to General Mo, perhaps the best executive at listening to others' opinions ever found in the record business, his ears tuned not only to musical hooks but also to sharp people ranging from Paul Simon to his Nashville head, Jim Ed Norman. Ostin still asked dozens of people his questions. Then, once each of those dozens would answer, Mo would test that answer with some contrary viewpoint, just to hear what this answerer would stand up for.

Ostin's greatest compliment about someone was "very smart." He collected and preserved smart people, often contracting them, supporting them, saving them in his buildings' offices, sometimes letting them overstay. But to argue against Mo's final choices, you ran great odds.

Mo Ostin passed most tests successfully. His greatest test—to spend last year's profits to build the next's better company—had paid off most successfully. The year 1987 turned into WBR's most profitable yet. He was at the top of his game, had a one-on-one relationship with Steve that made someone like Morgado worthy of treating politely, but not worthy of being bossed by. Mo, everyone knew, had Steve. And vice versa.

Mo planned for even more. He reactivated Reprise as a label, invested in its full, promotion-artist roster operation, even people answering the phone just saying, "Reprise."

"If you set up another label," Mo explained, "you're giving shots to people who might not otherwise be able to grow with the company because other slots are filled. We've got incredible stability of personnel here, with very, very little turnover."

---

[125]Bone was infamous in the record business, and in another life he could have made good money as a bucking bronco. Among all else, he became known for: promising to shave his head if his company broke Sinéad O'Connor (it got shaved); sending out dead rats to promote Boomtown Rats albums; sued for sexually harassing a female assistant at Island Records (he settled out of court); after that, he became the "little too hot to handle" top executive of three record companies in three years (Island, Mercury, and Arista); appearing at a record industry fund-raiser with his body painted yellow (the band was called Yello); necking passionately with the winner of a Miss Heavy Metal Atlanta contest, only to learn later that the girl he was kissing and feeling up was a guy. I hope Mike's still at it.

*   *   *

At its annual sales meeting, WEA presented the year's hit artists with gold records. Elektra's Bob Krasnow, an artist when it came to tasteful excess, announced that gold-record plaques commemorating Tracy Chapman's *Tracy Chapman* were being shipped to *all* members of the Elektra and WEA market teams. Next up, Atlantic Records presented *all* members of the WEA marketing staffs with multiplatinum awards. Then, at the closing-night banquet, forty-three more gold records were handed out to WEA staffers. After seeing the photo coverage of this meeting in the trades, Joe Smith sent Henry Droz this note: "The parking attendant at Chuck's Steak House and the busboy at Hampton's are disturbed that they didn't get a chance to pose with you. I assured them that they were the only two left and you'd get to it soon."[126]

By midyear of '88, WEA-distributed labels had captured a 44.4 percent share of the *Billboard* Top Pop Albums chart, way up from '87's 33.2 percent. CBS, the runner-up, had dropped like a prom gown, to a 14.2 percent share. That stat—44.4 percent—glowed above us, headier than a halo.

At a San Francisco WEA International meeting of its managing directors, Morgado proclaimed from the stage, "We're knocking on the door of becoming a two-billion-dollar company. The company's unit sales have increased by thirty-three percent over the past two years. The Record Group's earnings for the first half of 1988 are expected to exceed *total* annual earnings for any year prior to 1986." He showed pride and thought he should get some of the credit for those percentages. Under his term in office, money came in as never before.

Intent on more, Bob Morgado added cardboard to the WCI music group, buying a longtime printer to the Warner labels, Ivy Hill.[127] WCI recouped the cost of Ivy Hill in the next two years.

In 1987, Sony (at the urging of Walter Yetnikoff) bought CBS Records, for $2 billion. CBS attorney Allen Grubman called the sale "the year the record

[126]Though no longer in the Warner music area, Joe continued as part of our lives, if only for his work emceeing industry functions, piercing egos. At tuxedo-rich events, Smith introduced Ahmet Ertegun by asking, "You know why there's so much anti-Semitism in the world? Because Turks don't travel." After that, Smith looked over at Sire's Seymour Stein and announced, "Seymour Stein is to the record business what surfing is to Kansas."

[127]Ivy Hill's long relationship with Warners went back to Manhattan in 1914, when letterpress operator Jack Gordon established the Gordon Press, Thirty-seventh Street between Eighth and Ninth Avenues. Like the Warners, Jack Gordon and his brothers had come from Poland. Gordon Press serviced the movie industry, printing nickelodeon programs and posters. Its first customers included United Artists, Goldwyn Pictures, 20th Century–Fox, Paramount, and Warner Bros. Gordon's pinochle-game buddies include Gene Picker Loew, who had theaters, and Jack Warner. Jack Warner once offered Gordon a piece of Warner Bros. in exchange for annoying invoices. Gordon passed.

business was bar mitzvahed." David Geffen, now but two years away from owning all of his label, just loved the sound of that price. By the end of 1988, *Billboard*'s Top Pop albums were led—one, two, three, four—by WCI's record labels.[128] • In 1988, for the first time, at the top of the "Recorded Music and Music Publishing" column in the Annual Report was printed a new name:

Warner Music Group
Robert J. Morgado

Under every other name on the page appeared some title, like president or CEO. Under Morgado's name, in respect to Mo and others, Steve Ross said no title should appear. Yes, he was there, this said, but no, his authority was unclear.

In two years, Morgado had increased market share for WEA International. He had manipulated Chappell's merger into Warner Music and had created a bloodless transition from Chuck Kaye to Les Bider. He had acquired Ivy Hill. His record group was at an all-time high atop the corporation and against competing labels. He felt he had accomplished good changes, though he told the 75 Rockers there was so much more to be fixed. Since my dashing demo of Margarita blending via digital sound cues, I had been asked by Bob Morgado if I'd rejoin the Warner Music Group full time. It sounded like home to me, and on the first day of 1988 a new company called Warner New Music was invented, for me to run. Our mandate was vague. Morgado's after-signing-me advice was simple: "Try not to lose too much money."

I was never really good at that. It reminded me of my parents' advice during my early childhood in the Great Depression, when, faced with diners' jukeboxes, they'd cautioned me not to put a nickel in. "We do not waste money so foolishly," they'd told me, "and finish your tuna fish." Other money wasters, they'd told me, were comic books at a dime each. It's a wonder I had any childhood at all.

Morgado, however, wasn't talking tuna. He meant what he told me.

In WCI's Annual Report, a new mantra was intoned: worldwide growth . . . internationalism . . . globalization. In the report, where front-of-the-book positioning had always meant who gets the most tickets to ride the Wicky Bird, now was stationed WEA International. Our tallest child had outgrown even its American parents.

The year's numbers were displayed with intent to overwhelm, the way *nouveau* collectors overwhelm guests with their shelves of Steuben glass. Looking over those double-digit growth numbers—the gross and the net of

---

[128]WEA-distributed U2's *Rattle and Hum*, Anita Baker's *Giving You the Best That I Got*, Guns n' Roses' *Appetite for Destruction*, and the *Cocktail* soundtrack.

them—who knows, maybe Steve Ross felt content about the Film numbers. And the Music numbers? Even contenter. Who knows, maybe Ross pondered the smallness of WCI's Publishing division.

	Revenue	Profit
Music	$2,040,000,000	$319,000,000
Film	1,571,000,000	203,000,000
Cable	456,400,000	75,000,000
Publishing	138,700,000	10,500,000
Total	$4,206,100,000	$607,500,000

WCI, now post-Atari, felt full of fuel. Ross felt that same urge again: No stalling! Keep this car moving up the hill.

He assembled charts, numbers, and visions on paper. With marriage on his mind, he skirted the skaters down in Rockefeller Plaza, over to a neighbor skyscraper, aimed at the headquarters of a publishing company, one itself under possible siege from different outsiders wanting to scoop it up for themselves. Steve knew what sieges felt like.

Tall as a white knight, Steve strolled into the Time-Life Building.

Significant Releases

1987

Atlantic: Foreigner (*Inside Information,* including "I Don't Want to Live Without You" and "Say You Will") • Debbie Gibson (*Out of the Blue,* including "Foolish Beat," "Only in My Dreams," "Shake Your Love," and "Staying Together") • Lou Gramm ("Midnight Blue") • INXS (*Kick,* including "Devil Inside," "Need You Tonight," "Never Tear Us Apart," and "New Sensation") • Levert ("Casanova") • The System (*Don't Disturb This Groove*) • White Lion (*Pride,* including "Wait" and "When the Children Cry")
Atco: Yes (*Big Generator,* including "Love Will Find a Way")
Island: Steve Winwood (*Chronicles,* including "Valerie")

Elektra: The Cars (*Door to Door,* including "You Are the Girl") • The Cure (*Kiss Me, Kiss Me, Kiss Me*) • Dokken (*Back for the Attack*) • Metallica (*The $5.98 E.P.: Garage Days Re-Revisited*) • Mötley Crüe (*Girls, Girls, Girls*) • Linda Ronstadt (*Canciones de Mi Padre*) • Simply Red (*Men and Women,* including "Right Thing") • 10,000 Maniacs (*In My Tribe*)

Warner Bros.: Atlantic Starr (*All in the Name of Love,* including "Always") • Dio (*Dream Evil*) • Fleetwood Mac (*Tango in the Night,* including "Big Love," "Everywhere," "Little Lies," and "Seven Wonders") • Dolly Parton, Linda Ronstadt, Emmylou Harris (*Trio*) • The Isley Brothers (*Smooth Sailin'*) • The Jesus & Mary Chain (*Darklands*) • Randy Travis (*Always & Forever*) • Hank Williams, Jr. (*Born to Boogie*)
Reprise: Roger (*Unlimited,* including "I Want to Be Your Man") • Dwight Yoakam (*Hillbilly Deluxe*)
Def Jam: L. L. Cool J: (*Bigger and Deffer*)

Dark Horse: George Harrison (*Cloud Nine,* including "When We Was Fab" and "Got My Mind Set on You")

Full Moon: Chicago ("I Don't Wanna Live Without Your Love")

Geffen: Aerosmith (*Permanent Vacation,* including "Angel," "Dude (Looks Like a Lady)," and "Rag Doll") • Cher ("I Found Someone" and "We All Sleep Alone") • Guns n' Roses (*Appetite for Destruction,* including "Paradise City," "Sweet Child o' Mine," and "Welcome to the Jungle") • Sammy Hagar (*Give to Live*) • Elton John ("I'm Still Standing") • Robbie Robertson • Tesla (*Mechanical Resonance*) • Whitesnake ("Here I Go Again" and "Is This Love") • Neil Young (*Life*)

Paisley Park: Prince (*Sign 'O' the Times,* including "I Could Never Take the Place of Your Man" and "U Got the Look") • Sheila E. (*Sheila E.*)

Qwest: New Order (*Substance*)

Sire: The Cult (*Electric*) • Ice-T (*Rhyme Pays*) • Madonna (*Who's That Girl,* including "Causing a Commotion") • The Pretenders (*The Singles*) • The Smiths (*Louder Than Bombs* and *Strangeways, Here We Come*)

Slash: Los Lobos (*La Bamba,* including "Come On Let's Go")

Tommy Boy: Force M.D.'s (*Touch and Go*)

1988

Atlantic: AC/DC (*Blow Up Your Video*) • Bad Company (*Dangerous Age*) • Crosby, Stills, Nash & Young (*American Dream*) • The Escape Club ("Wild Wild West") • Mike + the Mechanics (*Living Years*) • Ratt (*Reach for the Sky*) • Winger ("Headed for a Break" and "Seventeen")

Atco: Sweet Sensation ("Hooked on You")

Virgin: Paula Abdul (*Forever Your Girl,* including "Cold Hearted," "(It's Just) The Way That You Love Me," "Opposites Attract," and "Straight Up") • Steve Winwood (*Roll With It,* including "Don't You Know What the Night Can Do?" and "Holding On")

Elektra: Anita Baker (*Giving You the Best That I Got,* including "Just Because") • Beach Boys ("Kokomo") • Tracy Chapman ("Fast Car") • Dokken (*Beast From the East*) • Metallica (. . . *And Justice for All*) • Teddy Pendergrass ("Joy") • The Sugarcubes (*Life's Too Good*) • *Cocktail* soundtrack

Musician: Gipsy Kings (*Gipsy Kings*)

Nonesuch/Explorer: Bulgarian State Female Vocal Choir (*Le Mystère des Voix Bulgares*)

Vintertnacht: Keith Sweat (*Make It Last Forever,* including "I Want Her")

Warner Bros.: Al B. Sure (*In Effect Mode,* including "Nite and Day") • BulletBoys • Fleetwood Mac (*Greatest Hits*) • Sam Kinison (*Have You Seen Me Lately?*) • Little Feat (*Let It Roll*) • Randy Newman (*Land of Dreams*) • R.E.M. (*Green,* including "Stand") • David Lee Roth (*Skyscraper,* including "Just Like Paradise") • Rod Stewart (*Out of Order,* including "Crazy About Her," "Forever Young," "Lost in You," and "My Heart Can't Tell You No") • Randy Travis (*Old 8 &10* • Van Halen (*OU812,* including "Finish What Ya Started" and "When It's Love") • Karyn White ("Secret Rendezvous," "Romantic," "The Way You Love Me," and "Superwoman") • *Colors* soundtrack

Reprise: Chicago (*19,* including "I Don't Wanna Live Without Your Love," "Look Away," "What Kind of Man Would I Be?" and "You're Not Alone") • Al Jarreau (*Heart's Horizon*) • Dwight Yoakam (*Buenas Noches from a Lonely Room*) • Neil Young & the Bluenotes ("This Note's for You")

Es Paranza: Robert Plant (*Now and Zen,* including "Tall Cool One")

Full Moon: Peter Cetera ("One Good Woman")
Geffen: Edie Brickell & New Bohemians (*Shooting Rubberbands at the Stars,* including "What I Am") • Danny Elfman (*Beetlejuice* soundtrack) • Guns n' Roses (*G n' R Lies,* including "Patience") • Kylie Minogue ("The Loco-Motion") • Jimmy Page (*Outrider*) • Siouxsie and the Banshees (*Peepshow*)
Paisley Park: Prince (*Lovesexy,* including "Alphabet St.")
Sire: Erasure (*Innocents,* including "Chains of Love" and "Little Respect") • Ice-T ("Power") • k.d. lang (*Shadowland*) • Morrissey (*Viva Hate*) • Talking Heads (*Naked*)
Tommy Boy: Information Society ("What's on Your Mind (Pure Energy)")
Wilbury: Traveling Wilburys (*Volume One*)

27

ACROSS the 169 strides from his door to their door, Ross carried a portfolio of bullet points, ballistic charts, and intercontinental seductions. The portfolio highlighted a deal already worked out in Ross's mind and printed in detail on executive-thick stationery. Steve loved this deal the way other men love Mom. His stroll ended up in the offices of Time, Inc.'s Dick Munro, Nick Nicholas, and Gerald ("Jerry") Levin (pronounced Le-VIN)—the three men who, in that order of pecking, ran Time. Time was much more than a magazine; it was an empire of magazines, from *People* to *Sports Illustrated.* It also owned HBO and other cable habits.

Ross was not heading into some blind date. There had been introductory meetings, starting a few weeks earlier when Nick Nicholas had met with Ross in his Park Avenue aerie.

Steve's audience of three listened. The Time men had been worrying that they'd gotten stuck in a world of print while the rest of the world had turned to video. Of the three, Chairman and CEO Dick Munro had the personality of the Dean of Humanities, a peacemaker. He was about to retire. A deal with Warner would place an exclamation mark at the end of his career. Dick relied on Time's president, Nick Nicholas, for drive, for firing people, for exterminating stalled divisions. Nick was to take over Time. He was tough, wore wide-lensed rimless glasses. He considered Time's leadership as mostly smoothy-WASPy (anti-Semitic, to be candid about it) intellectuals, guys who might manage a war but would never dirty their hands by shooting actual guns. Nick did not believe that martinis belonged on expense accounts. The third man, Jerry, was the house brain, Time's vision-of-the-future guy, short, a cut-rate dresser, with a puffy little mustache but a head full of useful facts. With Ross, who needed no Number Two or Three guys at WCI, Time's three leaders agreed to a painless, no-debt merger of the two companies. They speculated about Turner Broadcasting's adding to that whole, too; both companies already owned pieces of Ted Turner's empire. For both companies, Warner and Time, this merger would be what Jerry Levin called "a Transforming Transaction," one that would vault them into the 1990s.

The two companies figured they would compute the relative worths of their stocks and then, after a fair evaluation of each, put both stocks into one new company and merge their balance sheets. That method avoided having to pay either taxes to the government or sale profits to their shareholders. Warner shareholders would get .465 new shares of Time Warner. The combined company would be worth $15 billion on the stock market and, being Debt Lite, could sprint ahead of its rivals. Then the new Time Warner could launch an acquisition rampage. As deals go, it was ideal.

On March 4, 1989 WCI and Time wrote up their merger agreement. Time needed to know CEO succession: Who would be the new company's Numbers One and Two? Steve's "you have my word of honor" ended up with Munro and Ross as co-CEOs. They took Steve at his word. He was taller, he showed no self-greed, and was rich already. One Warner executive had told me, "Look at the bottom of Steve's shoes. He never walks. To get to '21' across the street, he gets carried."

Time's Board, many of them Ivy Leaguers who wore lace-up shoes and avoided things unsavory, okayed the deal, despite muttered misgivings over Ross's mildly tainted past, the one peopled with bent-nosed guys in a money-laundering scandal at the Westchester Premier Theater that'd made nasty headlines for Ross back in the Seventies. Nevertheless, the vote went, as one Time board member later put it, "Mafia twelve, Whiffenpoofs nothing."

The deal and the vote outraged Time, Inc.'s stockholders, who saw it (with justification) as an unprecedented enrichment of WCI's management, with a razzle-dazzle of stock-option payoffs and, once that *kaching* had *kachunged*, a "double dip" of fresh new stock options put in place, given WCI's new evaluation, all the older ones having been cashed in for huge gains.

Not only Time stockholders yelled. Martin Davis, the leader of Paramount, who'd also been hankering for Time, objected, too. Davis said, "Forget merging. I'll *buy* Time." Instead of new stock, Davis offered Time's shareholders first $175 a share, than an even sweeter $200 a share—$10.7 billion—to buy Time.

On the top floors of Rockefeller Center towers, in frustration at Paramount's move, doors went *slam slam slam*. Davis's offer ruined the clean, no-debt TW deal. To do better than Paramount's offer, Time could no longer simply merge with WCI. Time's shareholders, expecting a shower of Paramount cash, wouldn't stand for a marriage with no dowry. Time would now have to *buy* WCI, and to buy it would mean Time's having to borrow well *over* $10.7 billion to pay off everyone.[129] All that debt made the merger profoundly worse. At this point, Ross's attorney, Arthur Liman, cautioned Steve, "Steve, do you *really* want this? A *co*-CEO, a different board, a

---

[129]Atari-era white knight Herb Siegel alone profited by more than $2.3 billion in cash and stock from the buyout of his 19 percent share in Warner.

different culture?" Not to mention this new TW starting out life with over $16 billion in debt?

Time was feeling trapped, nearly choiceless. It had either to buy (Warners) or be bought (by Paramount). The revised deal would load Time Warner with huge debt, which would for years restrict its freedom to go-go globally. It would take the best of its cash cows, from *People* to Prince, just to keep ahead of the interest payments. Interest would cost the company $3 million a day. Even for dreamers like Ross or Levin, facing another $3 million to pay along with each morning's toothbrushing, just to keep *even,* had to make it scary looking in that mirror.

For Ross and his rubber-stamp board, however, the payoff was personally more tempting than eternal life.[130] Warner's stock options became to WCI what Madonna became to the tabloids: undeniably seductive. Five hundred Warner executives were paid, in cash, a total of $680 million, the largest acquisition payment ever made. Then, right away, they received their new options pegged at $38 a share. Twenty percent of the new TW stock was reserved for stock-option plans. Ross' take was $193 million. The movie studio's Bob Daly and Terry Semel made $50 million apiece. Wasserman and Payson each made $20 million. The thirty law firms handling the buyout made $76 million. Four investment-advisory firms made more than $60 million. Don't overlook $29 million in "miscellaneous."

In the end, suitor Paramount was left out of the wedding. The January 10, 1990 nuptials plunged the merged company into $16 billion in total debt, before the two even *began* sharing one morning mirror. The honeymoon focused on two agendas: getting out of debt and keeping some of TW's executives, like HBO's Michael Fuchs and WB Pictures' Daly and Semel, from killing each other. Fuchs would say, "Why can't HBO make movies?" WB Studios' Daly and Semel said, "Because *we* make the movies."

Daly and Semel, like the record execs, had long known Steve, worked for Steve, trusted Steve, and, as Morgado had already experienced, nothing could get in the way of that. Ross reassured Daly and Semel that he'd be up top for years, planning, dreaming, and absolutely there for them. Stock-option cash-ins for Warner execs felt better than a four-hour massage; Morgado, for instance, got $16 million for his stock options as the deal closed.

To begin digging out of debt, this new conglomerate first pondered what it could sell. Nicholas led. His list of "what might go" included Warner/Chappell, Hasbro, Chris-Craft Industries, Viacom, Franklin Mint,

---

[130]Former senator/governor Abe Ribicoff, appointed to the WCI board as one of Herb Siegel's votes had left the board in 1987, saying "I have never in my life been with a board so subservient to the chairman or the CEO. I couldn't take it anymore. I think Steve Ross's contract is one of the most outrageous things that has ever happened. Nobody is worth that kind of money. You have a bunch of myrmidons on the board completely manipulated by Steve Ross, stooges to give Steve Ross anything he wanted."

CVN, Atari, Scott-Foresman publishing, Warner Cable, and even their percentages of Turner Broadcasting. In July 1991, Nicholas, on Ross's recommendation, secretly tried creating a joint venture between Warner Music and MCA Music, for which Time Warner would get $3 or $4 billion. None of us in Records knew about the talks. The deal went nowhere, although Steve judiciously kept even its concept secret from the heads of his Records division. It was Steve acting like Dad to his collected (and even adopted) divisions, while Nicholas acted like a "how much can we sell our kids for?" business manager. His process was one way to the bottom line. Steve's, which leaned more toward mergers and opportunities, was a second way. Their two different attitudes produced tension between Ross and his heir designate.

Ross sought friendlier ways of getting out of debt: new investments from new partners. He traveled the world to find investors wanting minority interests in his hard-built company—to France, to Germany, even to the sultan of Brunei—to whittle $16 billion down to single digits. After two years, pacing through long nights, sweating a bit in meetings, Ross came up with nothing even close. He realized only $1 billion, that from selling part of Warner Bros. Studios to Japan's C. Itoh and Toshiba.

It felt odd to see Steve exhibit strain.

While vacationing at Villa Eden, David Geffen told his deal-making attorney, Allen Grubman, the time had come—again—to cash in his record label. Back home, David let out the word, big time, that Geffen Records could be, for the right price, had.

Adding static during Ross's investor-seeking travels were phone calls from David, reminding Steve that for years he'd told David that when it came time to buy Geffen Records, he'd be ready. David, upset that Steve had merged Warner with Time without first telling him, was not ready to do Steve any price favors. Geffen Records was by now as hot as any company Steve had. After those icicle-hot first five years, Geffen's A&R gurus had found big-hair hard rock—from Whitesnake to Guns n' Roses. Once again, Geffen was out front.

Pressured for cash, Ross turned the Geffen buyout issue over to his deal-wizard, Ed Aboodi, and to Morgado, assuming that some deal would somehow happen. Aboodi and Morgado urged David *not* to sell but to sign up for seven more years of WEA distribution. Their offer left David underwhelmed. Next, Ed and Bob offered David $75 million in option money toward a buyout of the label four years hence, when cash would be easier.

David knew that even for an option, $75 million was trivial. Both *The Wall Street Journal* and the *Los Angeles Times* reported that Geffen Records was being sold to EMI for about $700 million. (Not accurate, but why squash such a helpful rumor?) Warner Bros. Records was willing to buy too, but hardly at the numbers now being asked. Lower, "in the three-hundred- or four-hundred-million-dollar million range," recalled Murray Gitlin. Then, when the sale of Geffen Records to EMI lost momentum, it was MCA calling up David to say, "We'll buy." David told them, "Send me an offer, and I'll get right back to you."

MCA's two-page offer arrived on a waxy fax. It made Geffen and his execs transcend reality: $545 million. Still Geffen hesitated, considering how to make that number grow. "Now what if . . . ?" David conjectured. Label president Ed Rosenblatt, strong of voice, came right at Geffen: "David, just say yes. This . . . is payday."

"From the deal point of view, there was no one that felt we should pay that price for him," Marty Payson, then Time Warner exec VP, told me. "What I do know is that, had Steve not at this stage have other fish to fry and been distracted, had Steve worked his old magic, catering to David, talking to him about this, it is conceivable that David would have taken a lesser deal to stay in the family."

Geffen opted for payday. His label moved to MCA, sold for $545 million in MCA stock. To WEA, losing the Geffen label—with hit artists like Guns n' Roses, Don Henley, Aerosmith, Whitesnake, Tesla, and Cher—would hurt. Over at Sony Records, Jerry Greenberg observed, "The kids grew up and left home. But what a home!"

Geffen was pleased to be out. He'd told Rosenblatt the difference between now and when he'd started Asylum was that now "I don't like the music, and I don't like the people."

For the year 1988, Time Warner lost $256 million. Three men with a J. in their names signed the annual report:

J. Richard Munro	Co-Chairman and Co-CEO
Steven J. Ross	Co-Chairman and Co-CEO
N. J. Nicholas, Jr.	President

Growing from here would not be easy. Still, the Warner Music Group, all by itself, had become—get this now—the Largest Record Company in the Whole World.

By March 1989, Time Warner's recorded-music division hit the financial pages more often than the entertainment pages. Dean Witter Reynolds analyst Fred Anschel said, "The record division is the engine of the whole company, and it's a huge cash generator."

WEA's performance on the charts had gone up like the Washington Monument. On the *Billboard* charts for Best Selling Albums, WEA had eight of the Top Ten, twenty-five of the Top Forty, forty-four of the Top 100, seventy-five of the Top 200—stats unprecedented in record-business history. WEA captured 26.4 percent of the Top Black Albums and 23.6 percent of the Top Country Albums, both Number Ones in *those* fields. *Billboard* ran this headline: IT'S WEA BY A MILE.

During the 1980s, WEA International's profit had grown, on average, 30 percent a year. The Warner Music Group's revenues had grown 179 percent in the last five years. Revenues for the year were $2.545 billion, over which $500 billion was take-home profit. (To pay off Time Warner's debt, that amount would still require thirty-two straight years.)

To the newly combined TW management, having seen the Morgado-era growth in international sales, how to manage Music was a no-brainer (administratively, that is): just new contracts for its executives. It was time for *more* Bob. When Morgado pointed out that his contract as Music CEO conflicted with Ostin's "reports only to Steve Ross" contract, a side letter (a clarifying document) was created. Now co-executive VP at Time Warner, attorney Marty Payson drafted the side letter, telling Morgado that he *really* was the boss, Mo's contract notwithstanding. Morgado got it in writing.

He went to work. He had no reason to look back; Ross, he knew, wouldn't second guess him. As Bob once described life with Steve, "You know there'll never be scapegoats. He just wants to know, how do we fix things and move forward?"

In 1989, Waxie Maxie Silverman died at age seventy-nine; his was the store that had adopted the Erteguns in Washington and first staked them. Pete Marino, the San Francisco WB promo man who shocked Maui and freed the doves, then gone on to his own Channel 20 show, died of skin cancer in private. Also this year, Nesuhi Ertegun died. His memorial service filled a concert hall and brought together figures who adored the past, from Dennis Goodman to the Modern Jazz Quartet. It produced a memorial album—as if a few CDs could help.

A new logo was stuck above the doors at 75 Rockefeller Center, home now of a new corporation named Time Warner. The logo had no letters. It was all symbol, combining lines for an eye and ear, for sight and sound. In bronze, it o'erstood the Time Warner building's ever-revolving doorways.

Into the lobby, visitors passed by guards who looked, it felt to me, like they were on assassin alert. Above, on elevators to the double-digit floors, up there, worked the new TW team.

On lower floors were the New York offices of its labels, Atlantic, Elektra, and Warner Bros. On still another floor, the U.S. offices of "Warner Music International," renamed from WEA International. WMI accounted for 55 percent of the music that Warner Music Group sold. That old name, WEA, now was in America only.

I didn't much ponder it then, but looking back, the building felt worse than corporatized. It felt governmental, a windowless world. For you to get to an actual window, some receptionist first had to check your pass. Only then could you enter offices that had windows (which would not open), where executives worked for a company with $16 billion of debt. One could not imagine ever finding there a portable swimming pool with two fish in it.

That year's Big Decision—to sell WCI at a cost of $16 billion—was the day Records itself got the blues. This $16 billion in debt was much worse than the post-Atari crunch. It preoccupied Steve, who became less involved with his division heads, men who often had every right to feel like Ruth Brown, sitting for hours in the lobby, unable to get through.

As much as possible, the debt crisis was kept away from the Music Group's investment decisions. We no longer had the *pleasure* of making gobs of money to smooth our days and nights. Now we *needed* to make gobs.

For Morgado and others in New York, the answer to "the debt problem" was made clear by Wasserman. There was only one solution: "Grow the businesses, you drop to zero on your debt. If the businesses are run properly, if the cash flows are monitored and spent prudently . . ."

As never before at the Music Group, making money became a bigger priority than making hit music.

Back again at the steamy Diplomat, WEA convened for the Nineties, celebrating the first billion-dollar year by any record company. At the age of eighteen, WEA brimmed with adult confidence but, talking teen, called its chart share "awesome." Year to date, its labels had 52.3 percent of the Top Ten charts and 36.8 percent of the Top 200. Astonished at these stats, Droz did his Jack Benny, slapping his own cheek. A fourth day got added to the convention, there was so much music to show off. As Henry warned on opening morning, "Music acts can happen at any time. Do not be surprised if a knock on your door will be followed by a live performance."

It was the Summer of Piece and Love. At the stations that played it, 2 Live Crew's "Me So Horny" became 1989's "most requested."[131]

Whatever market-share percentages mean, in those words I recalled from Joe Smith, "It's better you should win than lose." Warners *had* won, the full year showing its combined chart share in the 40 percent range and the follower, CBS, down around 16. Yetnikoff's label had frozen and was not breaking acts like the Warner labels' Debbie Gibson and Anita Baker. Walter had blamed CBS management—"the goy upstairs"—for strangling his funds. He then checked into Minnesota's Hazelden clinic.

Since Sony's buyout of CBS Records in early January for $2 billion, Warners had outsold its rival almost by double: $1.05 billion to $650 million. Warner's profit margins doubled CBS's, 16 percent to 8 percent. Secu-

---

[131]In response to the naughtiness, two men from Miami formed a group they called 2 Live Jews, which in 1990 issued the album *As Kosher As They Want to Be*. It included rap songs such as "Shake Your Tuchas," "Young Jews Be Proud," and "J.A.P. Rap."

rities analyst Lisbeth Barron of McKinley Allsopp figured the "Warner labels are run by men who understand that the most important thing in this business is relationships, that you need to spend a certain amount of money to maintain those relationships. [CBS President Laurence] Tisch didn't get that. Steve Ross understands that better than anybody."

Over at RCA Records, its head, Bob Buziak, said, "It's amazing what's happening, just amazing. They're gobbling up market share like Pac-Man." By March, *Los Angeles Times* reporter William Knoedelseder analyzed the Record divisions of WCI: "All together, the four label chiefs have logged nearly 100 years of experience in the Warner organization, a stunning statistic in the notoriously itinerant record business." The *Times* then got David Geffen's opinion: "It's a credit to Steve Ross' genius that he's managed to keep these people for so long. People don't leave Warner to go elsewhere; there's no step up from here."

Knoedelseder's article continued:

Overseeing the activities of [the Warner labels'] headstrong executives—as well as 8,000 other record division employees worldwide, is Robert Morgado, 37, a corporate executive vice president whose three years as head of the records group coincides with the division's dramatic growth.

"Morgado deserves more credit than he'll ever get publicly because his style is so low-key compared to the others," said a colleague.

In the article, Morgado analyzed it thus: "We do have personalities out there. My job is to keep creating the environment in which they can perform. You have to encourage the spirit of independence, but the bottom line is, you can't let chance totally guide the outcome. You have to create a collective whole. The pieces have to add together, the investments and attitudes have to mesh, and you have to have a corporate strategy that makes sense.

"I'm not involved in the day-to-day acquisition of talent—that's their job. The day-to-day acquisition of companies, that's my job, creating values and assets."

Despite Morgado's determination to rule his Records Group, the heads of the three U.S. labels listened to him but would not nod. The U.S. labels were hot, and hot meant "hands off." Their rule was the same: You can't get along without guys with good ears.

Elektra's Bob Krasnow was as outspoken as any about the need for creative label heads. *Manhattan, Inc.*, a magazine more likely to interview "suits," asked to interview Bob. What the hell, Krasnow thought, I own many remarkably good suits. From his newly remodeled offices, Bob did not pussyfoot: "The real problem in America today is a creative problem.

You always read about the same thing, that people would rather buy assets than create them. That's a disgusting idea, and I have nothing but contempt for those people."

Krasnow ran Elektra like an edgy wildcatter. He expected loyalty. When Joe Smith, now running Capitol Records, beckoned to Elektra's senior VP Hale Milgrim to come over to Capitol, Milgrim first consulted Krasnow about it, asking to be president of Elektra, or else he'd have to leave. "Don't be talking to other people when you're working for me," Krasnow told Milgrim, "because you'll talk yourself right out of a job." Bob immediately sent off a cease-and-desist letter to Smith; then, within a day or two, Krasnow told Elektra staffers that Hale was leaving. Milgrim was stunned. It was Friday the thirteenth of October, and nobody would talk to him. Krasnow told Milgrim, "This is all about music. Executives come and go. No one turns horseshit into ice cream. You think you're such a fucking genius, go be a fucking genius."

With the success of Sire's Madonna, the exec who'd said yes to her record career, Seymour Stein, was feeling underenriched. His deal with Warner Bros. Records gave him half a point (five cents for every ten dollars' worth sold). Seymour felt this was unfair. He decided to ask for more. His attitude met with financial and legal astonishment from execs like Murray Gitlin, who believed that if you have a contract, you abide by the contract. "There are others," Murray conceded, "who believe that, 'Hey, what's a contract?' And, if you're successful, you tear it up and write a new one. I have to say, I fought Seymour on that."

Seymour, word had it, had sent his resignation notice to Ostin, who publicly denied it. Seymour turned sour as grapefruit marmalade. Ostin's denial went on a bit too long. It read, "If we were to receive such a notice, it would not be accepted as he is currently under long-term contract . . . We love Seymour . . ." The issue of profit bonuses, which was at the heart of Seymour's plea, kept rising. Seymour filed, then withdrew, a federal-court suit against Warners. He threatened to move to another label. Ostin stood by Stein's contract. Morgado argued that to lose Stein would be wrong. Positions froze. Marty Payson finally stepped in to mediate; he urged Mo to relent. Mo relented, and Seymour got his better deal. The announcement of it came, surprisingly, not from Warner Bros. Records. "We are very pleased," Morgado announced, "with the outcome, and from everything I know from my personal conversations with Seymour, he is pleased."

Not helping Warner Music's cash cow was the exit stampede of distributed labels whose eyes had got big over big bucks in the market. In 1990, Virgin was sold. Island left, sold to PolyGram for $300 million. Geffen was gone to MCA. Those labels had meant large numbers for WEA, and for Atlantic and

Warner Bros. Records. At the end of 1989, WEA had a 40.4 percent chart share. But by halfway through 1991, that chart share dropped 12 percent, mainly because Geffen and Island were gone. Warner's label heads rushed to sign new distributees.

Ostin, searching for a Geffen-like entrepreneur, had turned to a Geffen rival, diminuitive Irving Azoff, ready to start his own, appropriately named Giant Records. Irv, as he was known before he became Irving, was in my Top Ten of Laughable Louts; he'd once put his attitude this way: "I never met an asshole in the record business I didn't like." I felt the same way about Irv. Long an artist manager, he was another master of the telephone, handling that instrument's twelve keys the way Cliburn handled eighty-eight. Azoff worked the front row at Lakers games. In 1983, Irving had taken over MCA Records as a fourth job, while maintaining his own current and conflicting businesses: Front Line Management (managing the Eagles), Facilities Merchandising (rock T-shirts and arena souvenir items), and Full Moon Records (Chicago, Joe Walsh). Three years later, he sold almost all that to MCA for $15.7 million.

Irving decided there was only one place to turn: "If you look at the independent labels—Geffen, Asylum, Sire, Island, Virgin—those are all WEA." From his temporary offices on the MCA lot, Azoff made a label deal to be financed by Warner Bros. Records. For a few days, Giant grew faster than a bean pole. Its leader kept busy, even in this era when all phones had cords: lunch with Ostin; calls from Geffen, Rosenblatt. From Henry Droz, a telegram: "We're so elated, we opened a bottle of champagne. Unfortunately, it had to be Korbel, because Time Warner's in a lot of debt."

Often labels were co-ventures, with Warner putting up all the risk capital but deriving only half the possible profits, on a when-and-if basis. But if you wanted high-profile record producers these days, it was the price you paid.

Rich Fitzgerald was made VP and director of promotion of Reprise and given a staff of twenty-five, including Linda Baker, named national promotion manager for the reactivated label. In her new job, Linda noticed, "The difference between regional and national promotion is more Excedrin. More money but more headaches. You go from the freedom of being out on the road to being in the office."

The artist-roster pickings for Reprise, at first, were slim. Unknown acts like Simon F., the BoDeans, the Dream Academy, Taja Seville, Rosie Flores, Roger Troutman, Dwight Yoakam. Many of the new Reprise staff had begun regretting their choice, leaving WBR. In Reprise's first years, the label had nothing but stiffs. Then, finally, a nibble. Reprise hit with Roger Troutman of Zapp's "I Want to Be Your Man."

For Linda, life in records was less fun now. Tied to her desk, she spent hours on the phone trying to get through to radio programmers who were overwhelmed by calls from what Linda called "amoeba-splitting and reproducing" start-up labels. Within the Burbank HQ, Linda realized she was a smaller fish. This wasn't like Cleveland or Detroit or Washington, let alone London. Backstage passes meant little now, shared with wannabes, with rich kids from Beverly Hills. Hanging backstage, once a turn-on, grew tedious, political. A child of rock, Linda hated rap and hip-hop.

She missed being in her car with the cassette player cranked up, toking on a joint with a music director who liked her records much more in a pot-hazy, radio-rowdy car. Dollars for promotional tchotchkes had dried up; their efficacy was unprovable. Conference calls with field-promotion execs, such as she'd once been, now grew heated. Linda knew of more than a couple of local promo types who, after a harsh call, had to cry to relieve the stress.

The free-spirited buzz of rock that had turned up her passion and exuberance was gone. Linda began listening to talk radio, then no radio at all. She stopped listening to CDs at home. She felt herself changing, wising up at age thirty-four. She had spent fifteen years, "my entire adult life," promoting WB/R songs, making good money, a nice redwood house, BMW, gardener, Jacuzzi, but she felt empty. She dreaded Mondays and Tuesdays, which were radio-playlist "add days." She discovered that Prozac was becoming a promo-goddess drug of choice. By 1992, she was diagnosed with chronic fatigue syndrome and stayed out for four months, till she got a call saying that Reprise had to bring in someone to replace her. She felt betrayed, abandoned, and relieved, no longer "in the greatest amusement park of life." She moved to Maui, spending the next decade trying to learn who she was.

In an earlier structuring of Atlantic Records, Chairman Ahmet had given the label's Number Two position to his longtime organization man, Sheldon Vogel. Shelly embodied Atlantic's no-nonsense business approach, doing it since the 1960s, from the day he'd moved up from Barneys, a clothier.

Sheldon could negotiate. He liked to. At Atlantic, however, negotiation had become a secondary art. Primary was signing talent that sold. With Bob Morgado's focus on more-more, Doug Morris became, in his nine years as president at Atlantic, the more-more man, Shelly Vogel the for-less man. Vogel was famous for not doing favors, as well as for his refreshing common sense.

In 1989, to strengthen Atlantic, with Morgado's backing, Ahmet had upped Doug Morris from president to his new chief operating officer, third in command behind Ahmet and Shelly. Morris had been with Atlantic since the early Seventies.

Just out of Columbia University and an army stint in France, Doug had hung around mid-Sixties Atlantic A&R, gofering for producers Arif Mardin,

Nesuhi Ertegun, and Bert Berns, fetching Berns's check, getting it over to the bank, bringing Bert back his cash. Morris went on to write songs like "Sweet Talkin' Guy" for the Chiffons, then moved on to a VP/GM role at Laurie Records. He and partner Dick Vanderbilt started Big Tree Records in 1970, funded by Ampex, which needed music to sell its tapes. (Al Grossman's Bearsville was also backed by Ampex.) When Ampex went out in 1972, Big Tree went over to Bell Records. When Bell Records dissolved in 1974, Morris was back at Atlantic for distribution.

By 1978, Atlantic had bought and absorbed Big Tree, made Doug president of Atco, and, in 1981, made him president of Atlantic. Doug had credentials. In announcing Doug's appointment, Ahmet made it clear that Doug "understands the realities of the business, promotion, artists, lawyers, and Turks." Ahmet, though he kept his titles, turned over management of Atlantic to Morris. "You know those people who don't want to delegate authority?" Ahmet commented later. "I'm one of those people who loves to give up almost all authority if someone else is willing to do the work." Ahmet continued to travel the world.

Reading the press announcement of Morris's new title stunned Vogel. His name was not even mentioned in it. "I raised hell about that," Vogel told me. "Doug was a problem for me from the moment he came in. When he became president, he did interviews with the trades. They all came out the same: He would be running the show. One of the trades even asked, 'Well, what about Vogel?' And his response was something like 'Well Vogel has been a good, loyal fellow. We'll have a place for him.' "

Furious, Shelly found Ahmet to ask, "Ahmet, is *he* Number Two or am *I* Number Two? Let's get this straightened out."

"Well, you are," replied Ahmet.

"That's not the way this reads." The next day another press release came out, clarifying Two vs. Three. Doug told Shelly, "It was all taken out of context. I never said that." Shelly watched the following week, in *Cash Box*, when it said the same thing. "They misread you also, huh?" he asked Doug.

In theory, it was Vogel who had the final say. He did the numbers, he ran the office, taught Morgado how things worked, but did not make the final *final* judgment, only the financial judgment. When Doug objected to Vogel's analysis, he could (though seldom did) go to Ahmet. Doug trod lightly.

Morgado supported Doug Morris, the signer. The joke went that Morgado—not Ahmet and not Doug—was Atlantic's chairman. As jokes go, it was so-so.

Ultimately, the freeze between Morris and Vogel grew big as a berg. Morris, regarding himself a street fighter, told Vogel, "You'll never beat me." Vogel's private remarks, his departmental complaints, all had come back to Doug's ears. "Sheldon," Doug said, "you don't understand it, but the walls have ears. You can't breathe without my knowing it."

Later, when Shelly approached Ahmet about the conflict, Ahmet looked blank for a moment. He must have felt caught, but he had to say it: "Doug is going to win this one, and you'd better make your peace with him." Vogel complained, "I can't work for that motherfucker." In this new Atlantic, Ahmet paused, then told the truth: "If you want to stay, I can't support you. You're on your own." Hearing and seeing that, Shelly, who'd worked for Ahmet for decades, regretted just one thing. That he understood.

Vogel knew better than to keep appealing to Ahmet, whom he saw, he once told me, as "out of touch for the past ten years." Shelly recognized that Ahmet now needed Doug more. "Like all of us," Shelly told me, "Ahmet was looking for his future. Regardless of the money he has, Ahmet's job is very important to him, for his social contacts, this office, this title is very important to him. Whether he *does* anything or not is not important." He praised Ahmet's "genius for staying in the middle so he doesn't get on anybody's side. He doesn't get in anybody's way. He's certainly a good figurehead. But he's never on the wrong side of anybody."

From Morris's viewpoint, when he needed financial counsel, he found another colleague: Vogel's assistant, Mel Lewinter. He had been working with Mel for months. Finally, Morgado called Vogel up to his office to tell him, "You're going to be reporting to Doug." Vogel guessed that Morgado thought he had Doug Morris in his pocket. Returning downstairs, Vogel told Morris, "I see you've won the battle." Morris, relieved at not having Vogel, whom he saw as resistant to the record business's new economics, any longer standing in his deal-making way, answered, "I didn't win the battle, I won the war."

"Okay, you've won the war. So what do you want? You want me to leave? You want me to stay?"

"Mel Lewinter's going to be my financial person," Doug answered, "but if you want to, we can keep you on, and you can go negotiate deals with other ventures, whatever."

"Okay," Vogel answered, "I'll try."

Later, Lewinter came to Vogel's office and heard that Vogel was going "to give it a try." Within five minutes, Morgado called Vogel, gave him a two-year contract extension, and moved him out of Atlantic, up to Corporate level to oversee the Group financials. Up there, Vogel moved to a corner office on Morgado's floor high above Atlantic, becoming the first of Morgado's about-to-grow, Corporate staff.

Atlantic had just experienced a bad 1989. Its aging hair bands were over. The year following, Morgado met with Ahmet and told him, bluntly, that "Atlantic isn't cutting it." Time for still another management change. At Morgado's firm insistence, Ahmet agreed to share his chairman/CEO position with Doug. "I felt that it couldn't work at Atlantic," Morgado later told me, "unless it worked *with* Ahmet. It had to be somebody that Ahmet would accept, unless I took Ahmet out. Since I didn't want to do that, the best shot that I had was Doug, because Ahmet would step aside for that." In 1990, Doug Morris gained titular equality with Ahmet. Succession had become fact.

Morris reached out first for new executives. He brought in artist manager Val Azzoli, first giving him the title "Minister Without Portfolio." The two men had known one another since the early 1980s, when Morris had tried to sign the Azzoli-managed group Rush. The idea was to change the profile of Atlantic.

Azzoli showed up for work and found a phone and a rented desk, period. Doug was in California. Val walked into Mel Lewinter's office next door and asked, "So?" Mel answered, "Work it out." Azzoli took charge of the Metal and Alternative Music departments.

East West as a label name had been around Atlantic since 1957. Most recently, it had been the name of the late Nesuhi Ertegun's jazz label. Atlantic launched still another version of East West Records: East West America, with up-from-the-ranks Sylvia Rhone—where within Atlantic she had successfully grown acts such as En Vogue and Pantera—as its president.

Next, Doug Morris brought in longtime pal, the rap-attuned, baseball-capped Jimmy Iovine, to discuss distribution of *his* new label, Interscope. Talks became interrupted when Iovine took on a partner: Marshall Field's grandson Ted Field. Learning from the free-to-move-out-leaving-nothing-behind departures of the Geffen and Island labels that year, Morgado insisted to Field and Iovine, "We invest. We own a percentage of the label." At first, the own-a-piece approach failed. Later, after checking the alternatives, Field and Iovine came back for WEA distribution. Atlantic Records afforded what it could of the Interscope buy-in's cost, with Morgado's corporate funds covering the remaining part to own 25 percent of Interscope.

It was December 1990. Four stories below, on Fifty-second Street, the Salvation Army stationed its bell ringers, looking for hits. Jimmy Iovine's ears were elsewhere, over in Rap Land.

Morgado's strong hand helped steer Atlantic. He focused on profits. In the future, Morgado would lift several expenses off Atlantic's P&L, items like Ahmet's salary, paying off Vogel's contract, and Atlantic's investments in Interscope. To Ostin, whose Warner Bros. Records enjoyed no such leniency, this was dirty corporate pool, just designed to make Atlantic look better than it deserved.

Beyond Bob Morgado's reach, for now, lay Elektra as well as those "West Coast" companies, as Bob lumped them, showing little admiration when he lumped. "West" meant Warner Special Projects, WEA Distribution, and Warner Bros. Records.

About the last of these, Bob had once told Chuck Kaye, "I just don't get why Mo is such a big deal. I mean, all he has to do is sign three acts a year, and everybody falls apart." Later that day, Chuck called Mo to tell him what Morgado had said. Mo put the hush on Chuck with his reply: "Don't worry. I report to Steve."

Significant Releases
1989

Atlantic: Phil Collins (. . . *But Seriously,* including "Another Day in Paradise," "Do You Remember?" "I Wish It Would Rain Down," and "Something Happened on the Way to Heaven") • Debbie Gibson (*Electric Youth,* including "Lost in Your Eyes" and "No More Rhyme") • Lou Gramm ("Just Between You and Me") • Kix ("Don't Close Your Eyes") • Bette Midler (*Beaches,* including "Wind Beneath My Wings") • Rush (*Presto*) • Skid Row (*Skid Row,* including "18 and Life" and "I Remember You") • Donna Summer ("This Time I Know It's for Real") • Pete Townshend (*The Iron Man*) • Winger ("Headed for a Heartbreak")
Atco: Enuff Z'Nuff ("Fly High Michelle")
Delicious Vinyl: Tone-Lōc (*Lōc-ed After Dark,* including "Funky Cold Medina" and "Wild Thing") • Young M.C. ("Bust a Move")
Duck: Eric Clapton (*Journeyman*)
Modern: Stevie Nicks (*The Other Side of the Mirror,* including "Rooms on Fire")

Elektra: Jackson Browne (*World in Motion*) • Tracy Chapman (*Crossroads*) • The Cure (*Disintegration,* including "Love Song") • Deee-Lite ("Groove Is in the Heart") • Mötley Crüe (*Dr. Feelgood,* including "Don't Go Away Mad (Just Go Away)," "Without You," and "Kickstart My Heart") • Aaron Neville ("Don't Know Much") • Simply Red (*A New Flame,* including "If You Don't Know Me by Now") • 10,000 Maniacs (*Blind Man's Zoo*)

Warner Bros.: Elvis Costello (*Spike,* including "Veronica") • *Batman* soundtrack • Maze Featuring Frankie Beverly (*Silky Soul*) • R.E.M. ("Stand") • Rod Stewart (*Storyteller,* including "Downtown Train" and "This Old Heart of Mine") • Randy Travis ("No Holdin' Back")
Reprise: The B-52's (*Cosmic Thing,* including "Love Shack" and "Roam") • Chris Isaak (*Heart Shaped World,* including "Wicked Game") • Neil Young (*Freedom*)
Cold Chillin': Biz Markie ("Just a Friend") • Big Daddy Kane (*It's a Big Daddy Thing*)
Def American: Andrew Dice Clay (*Dice*)
Geffen: Aerosmith (*Pump,* including "Janie's Got a Gun," "Love in an Elevator," and "What It Takes") • Cher (*Heart of Stone,* including "If I Could Turn Back Time" and "Just Like Jesse James") • Enya (*Watermark,* including "Orinoco Flow (Sail Away))" • Don Henley (*The End of the Innocence,* including "Heart of the Matter," "Last Worthless Evening," and "New York Minute") • Tesla (*The Great Radio Controversy,* including "Love Song") • Whitesnake (*Slip of the Tongue*)
Paisley Park: Prince & the New Power Generation (*Batman,* including "Batdance" and "Party Man")
Qwest: New Order (*Technique*)
Sire: The Cult (*Sonic Temple*) • Ice-T (*Freedom of Speech . . . Just Watch What You Say*) • k.d. lang and the Reclines (*Absolute Torch and Twang*) • Madonna (*Like a Prayer,* including "Cherish," "Express Yourself," "Keep It Together," "Like a Prayer," and "Oh Father") • Lou Reed (*New York*)
Tommy Boy: De La Soul (*3 Feet High and Rising,* including "Me Myself and I")

1990

Atlantic: Phil Collins (*Serious Hits . . . Live!*) • Crosby, Stills & Nash (*Live It Up*) • En Vogue (*Born to Sing,* including "Hold On") • INXS (*X,* including "Disappear" and "Suicide Blonde") • Led Zeppelin (*#18*) • Bette Midler (*Some Nice People's Lives,* including "From a Distance") • Alannah Myles ("Black Velvet" and "Love Is") • Ratt (*Detonator*) • Winger (*In the Heart of the Young,* including "Miles Away")

Atco: AC/DC (*The Razor's Edge*) • Bad Company ("If You Needed Somebody" and "Walk Through Fire") • Soho ("Hippychick")

Def Jam: L.L. Cool J ("Mama Said Knock You Out")

Es Paranza: Robert Plant (*Manic Nirvana*)

Luke: 2 Live Crew (*As Nasty As They Wanna Be*)

Vintertnacht: Keith Sweat (*I'll Give All My Love to You,* including "Make You Sweat")

Virgin: Paula Abdul (*Shut Up and Dance*)

Elektra: The Cure (*Mixed Up*) • Deee-Lite (*World Clique,* including "Groove Is in the Heart") • Aaron Neville "(*All My Life*)"

Warner Bros.: Al B. Sure (*Private Times . . . and the Whole 9!*) • Jane Child ("Don't Wanna Fall in Love") • Damn Yankees ("High Enough") • Fleetwood Mac (*Behind the Mask*) • James Ingram ("I Don't Have the Heart") • Jane's Addiction (*Ritual de lo Habitual*) • Monie Love ("It's a Shame (My Sister)" • Paul Simon (*The Rhythm of the Saints*) • Rod Stewart ("Downtown Train") • Randy Travis (*Heroes and Friends*) • ZZ Top (*Recycler*) •

Reprise: Neil Young (*Ragged Glory*)

Cold Chillin': Big Daddy Kane (*Taste of Chocolate*) • Biz Markie ("Just a Friend")

Def American: The Black Crowes (*Shake Your Money Maker*) • Andrew Dice Clay (*The Day the Laughter Died*)

Geffen: Edie Brickell & New Bohemians (*Ghost of a Dog*) • The Simpsons (*Sing the Blues*) • Tesla (*Five Man Acoustical Jam,* including "Signs")

Paisley Park: Prince (*Graffiti Bridge,* including "Thieves in the Temple") • The Time ("Jerk Out")

Sire: Depeche Mode (*Violator,* including "Personal Jesus," "Policy of Truth," and "Enjoy the Silence") • Madonna (*I'm Breathless,* including "Vogue" and "Hanky Panky," and *The Immaculate Collection,* including "Crazy for You," "Justify My Love," and "Rescue Me") • Tommy Page (*Paintings in the Mind,* including "I'll Be Your Everything") • The Pretenders (*Packed!*) • *Dick Tracy* soundtrack

Tommy Boy: Digital Underground (*Sex Packets,* including "The Humpty Dance") • Kyper (*Tic-Tac-Toe*)

Wilbury: Traveling Wilburys (*Volume Three*)

28

THE top troika of the new Time Warner—Munro, Ross, and Nicholas—turned to their "seconds" to start the merger's motor. From the Warner side, those charged included Ed Aboodi and Bob Morgado, two of Ross's foremost "go to" guys. Aboodi and Ross were hardly rivals; Morgado had invested in and become a director of Ed Aboodi's off-campus Berkshire Bank. Along with Bert Wasserman and Marty Payson, Aboodi and Morgado had worked collegially on projects like negotiating for Geffen Records and other tourniquet jobs.

Time's Jerry Levin and Warner's Bob Morgado got to know each other while co-managing an introductory three-day confab for Warner and Time's executives. It took place in Time's version of Acapulco: the pink and palatial Lyford Cay Club, on New Providence Island in the Bahamas. Seventy top executives from the combined companies flew in for the bicultural sizing-up. Levin and Morgado set up the project together. Each found the other strong in the Doing Department. At the meet, executives tried to please, in an interesting fashion: WCI's dressed up, wore coats and ties. Time's dressed down to sport shirts and golf pants in either lime or tomato. Wandering verandas together, Time, Inc.–ers tried out new self-descriptors. They thought up names like "TWinks." One Time executive even suggested the term "TWERPS," for *T*ime *W*arner *E*mployees *R*ealizing *P*ersonal *S*uccess.

Back in Manhattan, up near Steve's barbershop and the gym, the top four floors of the new Time Warner were upgraded. Enough cherry paneling was used to endanger America's forests. The executive dining room (reachable off the twenty-ninth floor by a private elevator after passing a sweet woman and unobtrusive spy cams) was for lunches of filet de schmooze in its large room, plus executive-niche dining rooms for six. The cuisine was *haute* as hell there, yet in emergencies, catsup could be found. Nick Nicholas and Jerry Levin had much on their plates, as they said in this room, and were pleased not to have the record business to contend with. They knew little about records and, to keep stirring the culinary metaphors, had bigger fish to fry.

They were relieved to have Morgado, a man who, when he worked as secretary to Governor Carey, had made $80,000 a year, but had since come up in the world. He was getting known for his accomplishments: the invigorating and profit-growing he'd done with Music's International division (now in seventy countries); with Atlantic's label deals; and with his willingness to expand the record group with two dozen sprouting companies.

From the windows of the executive dining room, Morgado could look at downtown Manhattan and, just beyond, to Burbank, a place still on his Fix-It list. While just up the street, there was Elektra with the other Bob: Krasnow.

Having grabbed the reins, like John Wayne atop a stage coach, Morgado entered show business. He backed records-related startups, buying into companies as if he were just tossing dimes on a roulette table. He used his desk-always-neat mergers-and-acquisitions VP Paul Vidich to strategize and negotiate acquisitions. Inspired to shop, like Phil Rose's wife Gwen visiting the Sherman Oaks mall, Morgado bought and bought.[132]

In the early 1990s, the thirty-first floor's Warner Music Group bought all or part of two dozen new companies: Music Choice, offering digital cable radio channels; Music Sound Exchange, for direct marketing through (a) Time Warner Direct Entertainment's Music & Gifts by Mail (catalogue albums to over-thirty-fives) and (b) a "Stamp Sheet" direct marketer (selling cassettes to women over fifty-five); NVC, an English publisher of classical music videos; Track Marketing, selling music through concert promotions; Ticketmaster U.K., for London shows; Personics (later Warner Custom Music) to create custom cassettes in record stores; Warner Interactive, for video games, plus distribution for Accolade and Inscape Games; Warner Interactive International; Warner Music Cable, for alternatives to MTV around the world, including Viva (German language), Channel V (Asian), and Ya TV (Latin American); Warner Music Enterprises, for informercials; New Country Music Service; Music Magazines (titles like *Radio Aahs, HuH, BBC Music,* and *Jazziz,* each with a promo CD inside); Rock Video Monthly, for a music video by "cutting-edge, alternative rock artists"; Warner Vision, the successor to Atlantic's A∗Vision.

For the year, the Warner Music group edged up its gross, enough to prove the claim it had "done better" eight years in a row. Despite losing distribution of Geffen, Island, and overseas MCA, the gross had inched up from $558 million to $560 million, with profits edging up from $256 million to $260 million. The big face-saver was income from WMG's 50 percent ownership in Columbia House. The record club had been picked up

---

[132]Phil Rose had once vowed that, upon his death, he wanted his ashes buried under the walkway of the Sherman Oaks Galleria, halfway between Bullocks and Broadway. "It's the only way," Phil said, "I'll be sure Gwen visits me after I'm dead."

cheap when Yetnikoff, now running Sony Records (ex-Columbia) rashly stole Jon Peters and Peter Guber, then under binding contract to WB Studios, to head his new Sony Pictures. Sony had to pay for stealing the pair. Cost: Half its record club fell into the WMG's hands. Columbia House provided sweat-free income—$50, $60, or $70 million—every year thereafter, sometimes a bonanza of income that would mean the difference between a year of P or L.

Two years earlier, at the beginning of my own company, Warner New Media, I'd become the corporation's version of Epcot Center West. We housed ourselves in tasty, tenth-floor offices overlooking the studio. When Steve Ross and others came across a new tech idea, they'd often sent the idea-man out to our offices in Burbank. It was thus that we'd had the diplomatic challenges of nodding with interest at such fliers as Mick Fleetwood, there in our offices demonstrating his Body Drum, a leather vest strapped across his chest, wires dangling from it, and when he slapped his chest parts, different drum sounds emerging from speakers. Then there was actor Richard Dreyfuss and his concept that each different note in the scale stood for a different color (C Sharp equals magenta, for instance), so we should add that to our CDs, and when their music would play, people could watch evolving colors on your TV screen.

In short, I got to play again. We thought more highly of our own ideas, and were called upon to show them off to corporate and its friends and co-investors.

In the elevator up to our tenth-floor offices, Ross led his new TW troop, including Nicholas and Levin, Bob Pittman (back at Warners for a year here), Steve's secretary, Carmen, and his business confidant, Aboodi. For Steve, it was not a comfortable ride. Despite his "I'm okay" verdict of five years earlier, cancer cells had begun to spread into the fat surrounding his prostate gland, entering the lymph nodes in his pelvis and bloodstream, landing in the bones near his spinal cord. Steve had learned that such cancer is rarely curable.

As Steve moved into our demo area, I noticed some pain on his face. "My back," he told me, "not to worry." He winced. His jowls sagged. To sit, for him, was an effort.

For two hours we demonstrated our new devices, I talking, with a dandy lass named Kim in her mini pressing the remote. We showed our interactive-CD video of *The Magic Flute*, which displayed graphics translating the opera for you on your TV screen, in your choice of languages with full CD sound. Then we showed an example of interactive magazine publishing called *Desert Storm*, created with *Time* magazine's delightful managing editor, Dick Duncan. We finished with our major invention, one we called the *Megillah*, because this one *did it all*: It was a new kind of TV channel (or laser disc) where viewers at home could choose their own live camera shots as they watched, say, Channel 15. During a basketball game, any viewer could cut to different camera angles while the game and its audio rolled on uninterrupted; could watch a movie in one of sixteen different audio tracks, Spanish to Swahili; could watch a movie in G or PG or X form, at his choice; and could display all kinds of text overlays and subtitles (we did not use computer terms then) as the TV rolled on. By the end of the demo, many congratulations and pats followed. They stayed till seven, loved it, hardly knew what to make of it all.

When they were on their way out, I pointed out a photo of mine that I'd hung over our receptionist's desk. I asked them all if they knew who the guy in the photo was. They stared, but no one knew. "Jack Warner," I answered. "Oh." They nodded. Then they left. All that was missing was any business plan from them or us on what to do with our inventions. Steve said he'd send Spielberg up for a look.[133]

The next week, I got a congratulations duffel bag filled with Bugs Bunny and other Warner merchandise, plus a note from Steve wishing me well. His note ended with a typed "Best Wishes," but Steve, as he often had, crossed out "Best Wishes" and wrote in "Much Love, Steve." He was off to France, flying the world, looking for investors, and little more seen by us.

With Morgado's supporting checkbook, Morris had begun diversifying Atlantic. He renamed it the Atlantic *Group*. He'd started A∗Vision to create/distribute important videos like *Buns of Steel*. He'd started Time Warner Audio Books to get into spoken cassettes. He'd made new label deals—Big Beat and Third Stone Records. Atlantic Nashville had been incorporated. With all that investment cost, and with East West under Sylvia Rhone, 1991 turned out as Atlantic's first money-losing year since 1948.

Curly-haired (like Orphan Annie's, but black) Val Azzoli had been hanging in with the specialist groups at Atlantic: the country group, the jazz, the alternative, the metal, the dance. Val believed that Atlantic's approach to marketing was "just a lot of dead weight. Don't forget, Atlantic's idea of breaking records was the following: sign the band, get it on the radio, and WEA sells the records. We became a smaller, more agile company. Because the world is changing." Any band Azzoli had managed had made it without radio. Doug found Azzoli's ideas intriguing. Eight-months-there Val Azzoli became Atlantic's senior VP for marketing. He created a Product Development Department, doing what an account exec does at an ad agency. When Val came into Atlantic, the press department numbered three. Now it numbered fifteen. Val was changing the way a label worked records. Azzoli

---

[133]Nicely enough, Ross cronies like Steven Spielberg and Quincy Jones, came by for the same demo, all sent by Steve. No one was ever sent by the Time, Inc.–ers. I'd neglected to hang a reception room photo of Henry Luce.

cut into Atlantic's mini-divisions, eliminating forty-five jobs. On that Friday, people walked around Atlantic afraid to meet each other's eyes, fear on their faces.

Morris had two new flailing side-labels on his hands, old Atco and his newest, Sylvia Rhone's East-West. He merged Atco into East-West, Rhone taking over both. East-West distributed Interscope.

Looking for more vigor, Doug got another artist manager, Danny Goldberg, to set up a West Coast office for Atlantic "with a goal to create a different type of energy there," as Azzoli put it. Goldberg, an outspoken liberal and an artist manager whose beliefs attracted clients as diverse as Bonnie Raitt, Nirvana, and Manhattan Transfer, joined Morris. Goldberg became the magnet for alternative bands. When such bands came in, Azzoli had the new Atlantic machine to sell them.

Amid the turmoil, Ahmet continued, with profile lowered, as cochairman, a man who twenty years earlier had been lovingly described as "a white corporate executive who really *does* have some black best friends . . . a millionaire fat-cat who, when the revolution comes, will probably be allowed to keep at least one of his chauffeurs." Over the next years, with his office on a different floor than Atlantic's, he attended label-head meetings and spoke witty brevities at conventions. His bio would add that, in the decade to come, he was responsible for signing the Three Tenors.

The Warner labels kept trying to be black, for the same reason they tried to be country and folk and jazz and Christian and classical. When 1991's fall program was announced, WEA came up with another nifty theme: " 'Tis the Season." The black-music area insisted on getting its own slogan: "It's a Rap Thing."

At the convention, Chicago woman Oprah Winfrey showed up to dance to a Prince performance. WEA's Top Two albums—by Natalie Cole and Color Me Badd—got drawled off by guest Randy Travis, who, in thanks for his own sales, gave Droz a Gibson guitar with a plaque reading THANKS 13 MILLION. Droz summed up quickly how things had changed: "In the past five years, sales exceeded the total of the first fifteen years. In a given month this year, our sales exceed the entire sales of our first year." He totaled up the listening time of all records sold by Warner labels over that past twenty years: to listen to all would take 139,840 years.[134]

The Chicago convention filled with music. Labels had nights. Atlantic's began with John Lee Hooker and ended with the metal band Kix. Its leader, Steve Whiteman, looked his role: a screaming blond in a black shirt and silver scarf; chiseled cheeks; heavy gold rings and an amulet; knees pulsating in black elastic pants. He threw buckets of confetti and cash out at the audi-

---

[134]It's late at night, so my math might be wobbly, but I multiplied this and it came out to 1,737,422,600 albums.

ence, pressed his mike stand overhead, then fell on his knees. "Doug Morris is here!" Whiteman screamed. "Second time he's seen us in ten years. Doug, he hung with us for ten fuckin' years. That's a man!"

Kix performed its first—and last—gold single, "Blow My Fuse." It all sounded trite, tired, even a bit like one of those Golden Oldie concerts starring Frankie Avalon or Herman's Hermits. Kix then dropped from sight, joining the record business's unending passage to the passé.

Arena rock, to make too simple a statement, had dominated the 1980s, but was aweary in the 1990s. Heavy metal gasped last breaths. No longer did hair bands dominate; speed metal and grunge had happened. I was relieved to learn this, ever since one day taking my younger son, T. Guy, to a concert that excited him, making me the good and hip dad. The star was one of our acts, Metallica, I think, but we arrived a bit too early, driving there in the blue Mercedes, to see a formerly edgy, formerly anti-"all of this shit" band, now turned to making money from fans who arrived for its concerts in pickup trucks and RVs, looking like they didn't have jobs. Out in the parking lot, we walked through a pre-audience that drank beer, wore T-shirts that said FUCK This or That. They called each other "dude," and their arm veins had blue spots. They judged good beer not by taste but by quantity downed. Both sexes shaved their heads or put stickum on to make porcupine hair.

Inside the arena, women pulled up their tops to wag their boobs for the video cameras. T. Guy, age fifteen, pretended boredom, but his eyes were on alert. Anonymous announcements boomed out urgings to us fifteen thousand tailgaters, exciting us about concession stands where, for my son T. Guy I bought a "once in a lifetime" souvenir T-shirt (twenty-five dollars per memory). Other announcements made clear the night's three prohibitions: booze, smoking, and concealed weapons. We felt so much safer. Audience nudity was not warned about. When we went backstage for a brief "this guy's important" visit, we passed a guard who was telling two groupies, also wanting backstage, "If you want to ball the star, you've got to ball me first." I felt blessed to show our two laminated VIP passes and be let through. T. Guy met the bass player, and the two of them bounced fists.

It began. The bands came on with a blast, bared to the waist. It was all about young people feeling power, worshiping body bulges, their ears and bones beaten by booming bass. Flashpots exploded, and strobes robbed it all of continuity. Dozens of down spots flashed in sync, red as hell. Out front, the audience had seats and disdained dancing. Instead, down in front of our best seats, a crowd on its feet countercircled in the pit, hard-skipping into each other like bumper cars, elbows out, in a mosh. *Slam-slam-slam-slam.* Beat the crap out of each other. Guitarists with sweat-matted hair dived from stage toward us, caught by the moshers and born aloft like some saint's statue in Spain, only one that wiggled. I looked over at T. Guy. He looked cool and less excited than before, because he'd been backstage with the stars and wore his laminated backstage pass. Guitars onstage were jerked off. Guys around us played air guitar. For my son, it was a whole lot better than a visit to Oz.

He was impressed with me, but I wasn't. On the way home, so I'd feel part of all this, I told T. Guy that, to re-sign with Elektra Records, Metallica had to be paid $35 million.

"Awesome, dude."

But now, as WEA's convention was making clear, despite concerns over bad taste, a next thing—rap and hip-hop—had worked its way off the streets and into the awareness of the Warner labels, giving us one more chance to sell black music. Back in 1987, trying to get themselves into the rap market, both Atlantic and Warner Bros. Records wanted to distribute New York label Cold Chillin' Records. WBR's Benny Medina—new in black A&R for WBR—moved in fast. He got the deal. WBR's deal with the Cold Chillin' label began paying off: Biz Markie's first album, *Goin' Off*, had got off, as had the soundtrack to *Colors;* WBR's black-music head, Benny Medina, told *Billboard*, "When you're dealing with rap, I think one of the great luxuries is that we know that the public's going to find it before the industry does." WEA execs learned how 2 Spell 4U.

Rap had become 9 percent of the records sold, about $70 million worth. Despite little or no airplay, rap acts started dominating the charts. Atlantic's new label, Interscope, put up $10 million to bankroll Death Row Records, a label founded by rap producers Dr. Dre and Suge Knight, two young African-Americans from Compton, California, both with entrepreneurial criminal records. Since starting his label, Knight had been twice arrested on battery and weapons charges. Death Row pushed hard-core hip-hop into the mainstream with its rap song "Nuthin' but a 'G' Thang."

Rock hits became fewer. R.E.M. became the first rock band to reach Number One on the charts in over eighteen months. Nineteen months before that, it had been Metallica. In between, where had rock gone? Neil Young told where: "Remember when you used to watch TV in the Sixties and you'd see Perry Como in a cashmere sweater? That's what rock & roll is becoming. It's your parents' music."

"Black music is the pop music of the Nineties," insisted Elektra's black-music exec Ruben Rodriguez. "At major companies, you look at the bottom line. Fifty percent of what's in the Top Ten is black artists or black music. The money is there."

By 1991, black music spoke up loud through black artists who no longer sang "Shimmy shimmy ko ko pop." They had more to say. *Rhyme Pays,* Sire's 1987 debut album by Ice-T, became the first record to carry a parental warning sticker under the Parental Music Resource Center plan. For a few years, stickers worked. But in 1992, the ruckus got too big to hide behind a sticker. Ice-T cut a rap track about killing brutal cops.

Ice-T represented Southern California ruff rap, coming to the map after New York's rap. Ice-T's Southern California was a Southern California we never even drove through: those flat 150 blocks stretching from beat-down Compton over to industrial Long Beach, no buildings over two stories. Gangsta rap's vocabulary had new rhymes for words like "gatts," "ho's," and "crack." It was the new Southern California sound, as real to its audience as had been the Beach Boys and the Eagles to theirs. Ice-T rapped about poverty, hopelessness, and guns.

Because of Ice-T's new record, the Combined Law Enforcement Association of Texas (CLEAT) called for a boycott of Time Warner. Obediently, at least fourteen hundred record outlets pulled his *Body Count* off their shelves.

At 1992's Time Warner stock holders' meeting at the Regent Beverly Wilshire, Jerry Levin withstood five hours of pleas from over twenty testifiers. Stockholder Charlton Heston stunned the audience by quoting Ice-T:

> *I got my twelve-gauge sawed off*
> *I got my headlights turned off*
> *I'm 'bout to bust some shots off*
> *I'm 'bout to dust some cops off.*
> *Cop Killer, better you than me.*
> *Cop Killer, fuck police brutality!*

Levin struggled to maintain order in the meeting. Heston asked Levin, "Were that song entitled 'Fag Killer,' or if the lyrics read, 'Die Die Die Kike Die,' would you still sell that album?" Following Heston, a complete silence befell the audience as two police officers described their ordeals after having been shot in the face—one of them by a twelve-gauge shotgun—and blinded. Police unions threatened to sell their Time Warner stock.

Levin stood firm in defense of *Body Count*. "It will stay on the market," Levin promised. "What would it profit anyone if, in the name of pleasing everyone, the country's leading media and entertainment company ceased to risk saying anything worth listening to?" Later that afternoon, Ice-T was seen passing the hotel pickets in his car and was photographed giving them the finger.

The next day, picketers marched with signs reading TIME WARNER PUTS PROFITS OVER POLICE LIVES. As Time Warner stood firm, one older hand knew why. Capitol head Joe Smith figured "the money that Time Warner stands to make on the Ice-T record is so insignificant in the overall picture. When you realize that this giant, multibillion-dollar corporation is taking a free-speech stand on a record that barely sold a few hundred thousand copies, there can be only one reason why they're holding their ground. It's a matter of principle."

Ice-T defended *his* record business qualifications: "I've got a phone, answering machine, TV set, computer, hand grenade—everything you need to run a business in Los Angeles." He deleted "Cop Killer" from his album, replacing it with a new cut, "Freedom of Speech," in which Ice-T made his point with vengeance:

> *Think I give a fuck about some silly bitch named Gore?*[135]
> *Yo, PMRC, here we go, war! . . .*
> *The sticker on the record—it what makes 'em sell gold*
> *Can't you see that, you alcoholic idiots*
> *The more you try to suppress us, the larger we get*

When Ice-T came to Burbank with his next album—*Home Invasion*— its cover painting showed a white teenager listening to rap on his Walkman, with Malcolm X's autobiography next to him. The kid's thought bubble depicted scenes of the 'hood: space burglars invading, a white man getting assaulted, a white doll being groped. It *was* deliberately in your face.

Despite Corporate's freedom-of-speech stand, others knew elsewise. Marty Payson felt that Ice-T "was beginning to hurt the corporation, more than an embarrassment. Adversaries of this type of music began to boycott the products of the company, whether it was cable, or Six Flags . . . it became dangerous.

"This is not a First Amendment issue," Payson insisted. "With the publishing business, we *select* what we publish. We're not stifling them. The movie company doesn't put out X-rated product." I was up in Boston showing off our new *Desert Storm* at Mac World, and my own righteousness got tempered when *Time* magazine's Dick Duncan pointed out there was more to this. "Well, at *Time*," Dick said, "when it comes time to publish, we also consider good taste."

Ice-T's cover was debated over and over within WBR. "You were trying to defend something you believed in," recalled Murray Gitlin, "but it was a losing situation. The public was really against you." Even when Lenny and Mo met with TW's Board on this issue, no one told them to get rid of Ice-T. Mo told Ice-T it planned to change his album cover to a solid, noncontrover-

---

[135]MCA's Irving Azoff had, a couple of years earlier, invited the crusader-against-naughtiness Tipper Gore, once a drummer in her high-school rock band and fervent follower of the Grateful Dead, to meet with Hollywood. The record-industry folks talked back, telling Tipper Gore that she was off base. "I know they think I'm a prudish, uptight, sex-disliking Washington housewife with nothing better to do than eat bonbons all day," she said.

sial blue. The hassle would not be worth it. Either that, or he was free to leave the label. "Ice-T was a terrific artist who spoke the truth," Ostin felt. "But the corporation got so thin-skinned after the incident at the shareholders' meeting. In the end, Ice-T decided to leave because he could not allow tampering with his work. And I can't blame him—considering the climate." Ice-T would soon make a great deal with Priority Records anyway, and he knew it would be better that way, for everyone.

Not long after Warner Bros. Records and Ice-T parted ways, other labels followed suit. After a revolt by MCA's female employees, MCA withdrew FU2's single, "No Head, No Backstage Pass." The cover of San Francisco rapper Paris's album showed a man with an automatic weapon, ready to ambush President George H. W. Bush. WEA never released Paris; it came out on Scarface Records. Tommy Boy dropped its contract with Almighty RSO after the group's "One in the Chamba" was noticed by police organizations.

Sheldon Vogel, now upstairs as the WMG's corporate CFO, complained to Morgado that he had no authority and handed Morgado a resignation letter. Morgado tore it up: "Unacceptable." Morgado now thought of Vogel, once a valuable tutor, as a conscientious objector to what he saw as Bob's financially bad deals. Within three months, Vogel was replaced by CFO Jerry Gold. Remembering how it went, Time Warner's CFO, Bert Wasserman, said "Morgado wouldn't let [Vogel] have any authority or do anything. Morgado wanted to make all the decisions. Shelly was also a penny-pincher. He'd sometimes rather lose an artist than take a little risk."

Vogel went in to meet his replacement. At first, Gold felt like saying "don't blame me" and started to apologize, explaining he was now making three times what he'd been making in his last job. Shelly stopped him: "Jerry, don't apologize. I'm happy to leave. Here's what you have to know. If you want to keep this job, you've got to have no independent thoughts. If you can do that, you can get along fine."

Constantly quarreling with Morgado, CFO Bert himself had problems with Morgado's hard-charge style. Frothing, Bert would call out, "Let's get Jerry Levin down here!" When Jerry would come in, he'd find Bob and Bert loudly debating. He'd listen for about ten minutes, then say, "Fellas, you gotta solve these problems," and out he would walk.

Looking around for new investments, Morgado became interested in Rhino, a label that had made its living out of repackaging leftovers, after beginning as a morally fair-minded Los Angeles record store. In 1977, Rhino's store manager, Harold Bronson, had even boycotted CBS for charging an extra two dollars ($8.98 list) for Barbra Streisand's *A Star Is Born* soundtrack. In the store, he'd put up a wordy proclamation:

Please join with us in boycotting the new Barbra Streisand album, *A Star Is Born*, as Columbia has seen fit to charge an additional two dollars for this album just because they believe there are enough suckers out there who will pay such outrageous money for a piece of vinyl. If we allow them to get away with this travesty, pretty soon you'll be paying six to seven dollars for all single albums. Please convince anyone you know to pass over this album under any circumstance.

By now, however, Rhino had grown savvy about repackaging label-neglected acts and anthologizing great swaths of neglected music. Morgado wanted just such a label to exploit the Warner group's catalogues. To buy Rhino, Morgado once again used Atlantic, the only label that was making him feel welcome. "It became clear to me that Atlantic was the one to do it," Bob told me. Atlantic was his-glad-to-cooperate label. "Atlantic was somewhat supportive, but when Rhino pushed the deal a little over the edge, Atlantic became a little touchy. So I bought it." In a nearly-no-cash deal, Morgado took the risk on Rhino and acquired 50 percent immediately.

"The people who were running Atlantic weren't risk takers in that way," observed Morgado's new CFO, Jerry Gold. "They might be risk takers when it comes to signing artists, but business deals make them nervous." Morgado asked Atlantic to monitor Rhino, and if there were losses, he'd move them off Atlantic's P&L so the label wouldn't have to bear them. "I don't think he could have asked Krasnow," Gold speculated, "and certainly couldn't have asked Mo to do this. He felt he could go to Doug and say, 'Help me with this. I think it is important, and I'll cover you.' It was sort of odd that we had to shove it down Doug's throat."

Rhino, being run in squeeze-a-nickel fashion by Richard Foos and Harold Bronson, began to repackage Atlantic's heritage albums, from Ruth Brown forward.

Such favorite-son deals more and more angered Ostin and Krasnow, who steadily played by the rules of risk to their own bottom lines, without Morgado's insurance-backed deals. They saw Atlantic being favored with protection, which their labels never received.

Music-business brass turned out in October 1991 for an AMC Cancer Research Center charity dinner honoring Bob Morgado, with "You Gotta Have Friends" as its theme. Tables filled the towering glass atrium of the Wintergarden of New York's World Financial Center. The take was over $2 million.

When it came to charisma, Bob Morgado never made anybody's Top 100. Many people talked about his political side, remembered him as Steve's hatchet man, despite his easy smile, acknowledged his successes, and distrusted his ambitions. He had intellect, he had gall, he had drive, he produced results, but he'd be a tough picnic date. Perhaps it was all Bob's time spent in politics, where to screw is human. Perhaps it was all that time fixing Steve's messes, where to fire was salvation.

Ostin debated whether to attend; Morgado, he felt, was best kept three thousand miles away. Finally, Mo was there, but in late and out early. It was an odd evening, in a fifty-foot-high, glass-walled hall that echoed amplified speakers so the evening's speeches sounded like shortwave from London.

A thousand, in tuxes and fine gowns, digesting baked salmon, listened as Sammy Cahn sang spritz lyrics worthy of a Morgado roast. Morgado's ex-boss, former New York Governor Hugh Carey, quoted Bob's favorite lines of poetry, "If it were not for hope, the heart would break."[136]

Steve Ross walked in slowly. When he sat at table Number One, it took him a while to find a comfortable position. As familiar faces came by to greet him, he shook hands but did not rise. His cancer was pressing against his lower spine. For the pain, he took Percodan. The cancer in his bones leached calcium into his blood. This night would be Steve's final public appearance.

On the way home, I remember reading in the *New York Post* a splashy report about how Krasnow and his wife, Sandy, had split up. I rode a cab back uptown, not knowing what to think of it all, why the evening felt so drafty.

For the year 1991, the Atlantic Group stumbled from fourth to ninth place on the charts, its share slipping from 1990's 7.6 percent to 1991's 4.3 percent. In Time Warner's Annual Report, under his name a title now was added:

> *Warner Music Group*
> Robert J. Morgado
> *Chairman*

Seeing that, Ostin flew in to New York to talk to Ross. Ross blamed it on Nicholas. He told Mo "not to worry."

Significant Releases

1991

Atlantic: The Escape Club ("I'll Be There") • Roberta Flack (*Set the Night to Music*) • Genesis (*We Can't Dance,* including "Hold on My Heart," "I Can't Dance," "No Son of Mine," and "Jesus He Knows Me") • Bette Midler (*For the Boys*) • Mr. Big (*Lean Into It,* including "To Be With You") • Rude Boys ("Written All Over Your Face") • Rush (*Roll the Bones*) • Skid Row (*Slave to the Grind*)

---

[136]By Thomas Fuller, 1732.

East West: Gerald Levert (*Private Line*) • Simply Red ("Something Got Me Started")
Interscope: Gerardo (*Mo' Ritmo,* including "Rico Suave" and "We Want the Funk") •
Marky Mark ("Good Vibrations" and "Wildside")
Modern: Stevie Nicks (*Timespace*)
Nothing/TVT: Nine Inch Nails (*Broken*)
Virgin: Paula Abdul (*Spellbound*) • Lenny Kravitz (*Mama Said*)

Elektra: Natalie Cole (*Unforgettable With Love*) • Metallica ("Enter Sandman") •
Mötley Crüe (*Decade of Decadence—'81–'91,* including "Home Sweet Home
'91") • Aaron Neville ("Everybody Plays the Fool") • Teddy Pendergrass (*Truly
Blessed*) • Keith Sweat (*Keep It Comin'*)

Warner Bros.: Elvis Costello (*Mighty Like a Rose*) • Dire Straits (*On Every Street*) •
James Ingram ("Baby, Come to Me," "One Hundred Ways," and "Somewhere Out
There") • Red Hot Chili Peppers (*Blood Sugar Sex Magik,* including "Under the
Bridge") • REM (*Out of time*) • Paul Simon (*Concert in the Park*) • Rod Stewart
(*Vagabond Heart,* including "Broken Arrow," "Motown Song," and "Rhythm of My
Heart") • Randy Travis (*High Lonesome*) • Travis Tritt (*It's All About to Change*) • Van
Halen (*For Unlawful Carnal Knowledge,* including "Top of the World") • Karyn White
("Romantic" and "Way I Feel About You")
Reprise: Chicago (*Twenty 1*) • Enya (*Shepherd Moons*)
Cold Chillin': Biz Markie (*I Need a Haircut*) • Big Daddy Kane (*Prince of Darkness*)
Def American: Andrew Dice Clay (*Dice Rules*) • Slayer (*Live—Decade of
Aggression*)
Duck/Reprise: Eric Clapton (*24 Nights*)
Geffen: Cher (*Love Hurts,* including "Love and Understanding") • Joni Mitchell
(*Night Ride Home*) • Siouxsie and the Banshees ("Kiss Them for Me")
Giant: Color Me Badd (*C.M.B.,* including "All 4 Love," "I Adore Mi Amor," "I Wanna
Sex You Up," "Slow Motion," and "Thinkin' Back") • *New Jack City* soundtrack • Tara
Kemp ("Hold You Tight" and "Piece of My Heart")
Paisley Park: Prince (*Diamonds and Pearls,* including "Cream," "Gett Off," and
"Money Don't Matter 2 Night")
Qwest: Tevin Campbell (*T.E.V.I.N.,* including "Round and Round" and "Tell Me What
You Want Me to Do") • Keith Washington (*Make Time for Love*) • *Boyz N the Hood*
soundtrack
Sire: Erasure (*Chorus*) • Ice-T (*O.G. Original Gangster,* including "Body Count" and
"New Jack Hustler (Nino's Theme)") • Morrissey (*Kill Uncle*) • Seal ("Crazy")
Slash: Violent Femmes (*Violent Femmes*)
Tommy Boy: De La Soul (*De La Soul Is Dead*) • Digital Underground (*This Is an E.P.
Release*) • Naughty by Nature ("O.P.P.") • *Club MTV Party to Go*

29

WHILE Bob Morgado was signing deals like a new label chief, hoping one in twenty of his new acts made it big, bigger labels like Warner Bros. felt another kind of squeeze, and her name was Madonna. A material lady indeed, she wanted more than royalties.

More than ever before, in 1992, to extend the contracts of major artists like Madonna, labels had to come up with Joint Ventures. Such fifty/fifty deals often commanded advance payments the size of city budgets. The contract terms of the old "standard" deal now read as quaint as a malt-shop menu.

Record contracts from the 1920s had come from a *different* record business, when producers and song publishers had been the key men. Then, when a record company had a song and needed a record, it would either hire some singer (not called an artist) or use one already under contract. If the singer asked for royalties, that question got an "Okay, but." It'd go, "Okay, but for you to get royalties, you'll first have to repay your recording costs out of your royalty percentage." This came to be known as "cost recoupment." Recoupment of costs by labels were the reason that singers like Ruth Brown got royalties only if a mighty high tide of sales surged in.

In the 1990s-style joint-venture deals, the artist *became* equal partner in a new label. In referring to Madonna and her manager, Freddy DeMann, Murray Gitlin said, "Her new joint-venture label [Maverick] now has its own staff, its own set off offices, and Madonna's own people. Now we have to *share* all the profitability with the joint-venture label."

For years, artists *appeared* to have "their own" labels, whether it was Led Zeppelin's Swan Song or Prince's Paisley Park. But mostly those artist labels had been trips not to the bank but for the ego. The artists got little or no equity. On her records for Sire, Madonna had been earning 18 percent royalties. On that contract, she had four albums to go yet. Madonna wanted more pay for her work. Mo could not see any reason to change now, given four albums to go.

Freddy DeMann, a distinguished sort in his fifties, who had paid decades of dues, had endured his share of shrieking, half-hour phone tirades. He considered a manager's job to be much more than an endurance contest for ears. He wanted to help Madonna build careers beyond just records. He told her, "This is our moment, our time to do it." In all modesty, Madonna concurred. DeMann assembled gunslingers. Like this was the first half hour of *The Magnificent Seven*, DeMann saddled up attorney Allen Grubman, agent Michael Ovitz, provocateur Madonna, and himself. This foursome created a Big Presentation with a glitzy video, then flew to New York. In 75 Rock's lobby, the posse strode past HBO's Michael Fuchs, who looked at the killer squad and, at the foot of the elevators, said, "Oh, boy, there is some *thing* going on. You guys aren't just here to visit."

Upstairs, around Steve's blond-and-umber art deco conference table, waited the executive brass: Ross, Nicholas, Levin, Morgado, and Ostin. Madonna, dressed as and acting like a businesswoman, presented her wish list like a pro. It ranged across Time Warner's freshly spread divisions, encompassing everything this side of *Martha Stewart Living:* It was books and movies, merchandising rights, television, music publishing, and in particular her own record company, Maverick. A complexity of negotiations eventually took place, six months' worth, projecting Madonna's work over a seven- to eleven-year deal.

When it was done, Madonna would get an advance of $5 million for every album, against a 20 percent royalty. Warner got an added three albums from Madonna at that rate, now seven in all. Most important, Maverick became a joint venture with Time Warner. Maverick Records *owned* 50 percent of the label's masters. HBO's Michael Fuchs put up over $2 million for two HBO concert specials. Madonna got merchandising rights. Madonna got Warner Books to issue her compilation of erotic photos/poems/stuff, to be called *Sex.*

Madonna opened Maverick Records and eventually it paid off: Its young "ears" exec, Guy Oseary, had his share of failures, but made two signings that pulled the label beyond egoism. In 1993 he signed Candlebox, and two years later, Alanis Morissette, whose first CD sold well over ten million copies. Warner Bros. Records, accustomed to 80 percent, got 50 percent.

Two years later, at the party to introduce *Sex,* Jerry Levin arrived dressed for the occasion in a WB baseball jacket. Entering, he saw an actress bent over to receive a tattoo on her butt. He saw transvestites gyrating upon pedestals in leather corsets. He saw Madonna herself, led around on a leash 'til she bumped into Jerry, one bewildered-looking executive. Others from the *Time* background, who had in their careers reported on world catastrophes, had seen it all, from Crimean mass rape to the Salk vaccine, seen it then been able to golf a round each Sunday, felt disgust. "*Sex* was a low point in publishing," Marty Payson opined. "Everyone associated with the company was embarrassed about that." Madonna's companion album, *Erotica*, became the most-returned in WEA memory.

Still, this was the emergence of a woman in the rock business. A woman had emerged, complaining of a glass ceiling where, heretofore, there'd been a mirrored one. Through her book, even blowjobs had now been commercialized and mass marketed.

Another woman from another era resisted mass marketing and held to the more personal traditions that had made America what it is. Cynthia Plaster Caster, now forty-six, sued to recover her casts of celebrity pricks which, in 1971, she had stored in the home of Frank Zappa's manager, Herb Cohen. Cohen had kept the statuettes for two decades, and now refused to return them. Cynthia sued Herb for $1 million; Herb countersued for $2 million. "It's more like a child custody battle," Cynthia explained endearingly. "These things aren't just pieces of plaster to me, they're like my little children. Each one holds precious memories for me."

Since the 1960s, Cynthia had moved to Chicago, where she less frequently plastered. Ever the artist, for Christmas, Cynthia sent out a photo card of her front yard, where, instead of forming a snowman, she formed another erect snow sculpture.

"What Cynthia did is as much a part of rock lore," wrote important rock groupie and GTOs leader Pamela Des Barres in her book *I'm With the Band: Confessions of a Groupie*, "as what any record producer or engineer or manager did. A hundred years from now, when people look back on the Sixties, Cynthia will be remembered as an important pop artist."

The L.A. Superior Court judge ruled that Cynthia Plaster Caster could recover her casts of the aroused and famous.

In a business dominated by retail selling of discs and tapes, the plague of "home taping/piracy" had continued. Records had been taped, by amateurs, swap-meeters, and Asian pros; had been oversold, shipped back, and remaindered; sampled by other artists; killed off by better disc forms; copied off radio play—all affecting the number of recorded "units" sold. CDs had started out at high list prices, then slowly stepped down in price. Now CDs by star acts got pushed back up one more dollar, to $16.98 list price, first by Garth Brooks on Capitol. Tower Records' Russ Solomon expounded, "It only takes one word to sum up this price increase: greed!"

Generally, the press could not understand $16.98. Why? reporters asked. Costs for pressing CDs had gone way down; record companies already charged $3 more for the same music on CD as on cassette. In fact, there were no answers based on cost. The $16.98 price was all based on how much profit record labels (and their royalty cohorts, the artists) could squeeze out of one sale. The cost of a record had jumped (although, in the United States, it was less than in Japan, where a single compact disc was often $25). No clamor was really raised over CD pricing. Record labels behaved like business-school models, getting "as much as the market will bear."

The increased price of $16.98 brought one more self-inflicted Plague: used CDs, bought back and resold by stores. Retail prices for preowned CDs ranged from $1 to $9. Record labels got nothing for resold CDs but were helpless about it, owing to a legal doctrine called "First Sale," which meant that after a seller first sold its copies, that first seller has no further rights to collect from subsequent sales.

Bad enough when it was just little shops selling used CDs. By 1992, Wherehouse Entertainment became the first major-major record chain to advertise that it sold used CDs. The markup on used CDs (100 percent) versus that on the average album (30 percent) fascinated some retailers. Record labels got little sympathy. "The record companies have backed consumers and store owners up against the wall with these ridiculous CD prices," wrote Erik Flannigan in the *Ice* newsletter. "I don't know what the record companies expect." Record companies refused to pay for ads placed by retailers who resold CDs. It was like trying to stop a flood by standing in the middle of the Mississippi, waving your arms.

New laws were passed to kill old Plagues, usually after it was too late to do much good. In 1992 came the Audio Home Audio Recording Act, which charged pennies for digital audio tape sales, paid into a fund to be split by record companies, their artists, publishers, and songwriters. In 1995 came a Digital Performance Right in Sound Recordings Act to fight subscription services over the Internet. All missed their targets.

"I definitely think we are at the end of an era," stated David Geffen. "The big change is that all the companies have put these numbers guys in charge. It's starting to be like the movie industry now. All that's left now in the movie world is a bunch of faceless conglomerates, and the result is that there aren't many good movies being made anymore, are there? I'm afraid it won't be long before the music industry ends up the same way."

Financial commentators, however, preferred suits to artists. Merrill Lynch's Harold Vogel said, in his best Greenspanese, "The record business is much better off now than it ever was. If the conglomerates didn't have the numbers people riding herd over the industry, the banks and stock market would not have enough confidence in what's going on to supply the enormous amounts of capital these companies need to operate on a global basis."

Still, there was nostalgia for the careless stuff that went on in lower-numbered decades. Joe Smith, knew that the "pizzazz is gone in the record business, and we miss it.

"In the Eighties, you could negotiate a deal at the Forum during intermission, sign it during a time-out, and sometimes close it in the time it took the ball to get passed from one side of the court to the other. Nobody ever had to ask anybody's permission.

"That's all gone now. You can't make any deal without first checking with somebody in London or Tokyo or Holland or Frankfurt. Everything has to fit into some giant plan. There are reporting avenues and channels that did not exist before."

In August 1992, I was standing at the MacWorld convention in Boston, showing off what Warner New Media was working on—CD multimedia projects, mostly—when a young man with a video camera walked up. He made videos for Steve, he told me, "so Mr. Ross can keep up with the business," which Steve was now doing from his home in East Hampton, Long Island, overlooking Georgica Pond, where he was, the video maker said, recuperating. For his camera, I ad-libbed a few minutes to Steve and pointed to twelve different projects I hoped would be part of his future. After the tech demo, I paused, then looked into the camera and ended with "Much Love, Stan." I trust he saw the video; I'll never know.

Within a month or so, I folded my own tent, resigned, and moved on from Warner New Media. Corporate, it had said, wanted my company to turn a profit, and I had no clue how our inventions would conquer the world. That, I left to others.

Warner New Media proved me correct: There was no market for "multimedia discs." As if to prove it, new leaders from Corporate jumped in and, in only twelve months, more than tripled the company's five-year losses. Within a couple more years, WNM, renamed Time Warner Interactive, was folded when Corporate fired Geoff Holmes, who'd headed up the division. In that folding, our early, ambitious projects became just a blip, but a creative blip that I remember with fondness.

I retired without a parade or tribute dinner, sneaking out with an inch-and-a-half notice by Irv Lichtman's "Bulletin" on page 94 of *Billboard*, October 17:

Retiring after thirty-three years with the Time Warner music division, the last eight as president/CEO of Warner New Media, Stan Cornyn has, with wit, humor, and wisdom, told the music industry of the day radio died, of its glorious past and its exciting technological future. He made Warner Bros.' jolly label ads the envy of the industry. He also delivered that rare kind of speech at industry gatherings: He stated important things that managed to make their points without pontification. Cornyn is retiring to pursue, he says, "pure creativity." *Bulletin* wishes Cornyn lots of flowing juices.

(The above commercial has been included just in case my sons ever read this book.)

After 33 years driving in to work in Burbank, it was over. Within 1992, my wife and I divorced, I retired, and dyed my hair all white (sic). I moved to a serene-to-a-fault, 4BR/3BA lakeside home thirty minutes to the west. The silence was scary. I'd ride around the lake in my silent (electric motor) boat, which I'd named Athanasius Kircher for the medieval inventor of the rocket bird. That took thirty minutes. Life became less than challenging. I felt no inclination to get back into records or, in fact, ever again face pulling on the panty hose to head in for work. I was sub-sixty, retired, and supposed to be enjoying my Platinum Years.

At Corporate, a leadership unease had gone on for two years. Ross, while debilitated by cancer,[137] had realized that his successor, Nick Nicholas, believed that thrifty business management was an end more than a means. He was miscast for WCI divisions used to an adoring father figure in Steve. Nicholas's short-term visions were wrong (Steve presumed) for the new Time Warner. Ross found Jerry Levin more his kind of visionary. Nicholas was paid to leave in February 1992. With Munro and Nicholas both out, Ross and Levin became the two leaders.

At a Time Warner board of directors retreat, a two-man committee was appointed to slim down the Time Warner board, which, with twenty-one members, was viewed as "unwieldy." The two men were former Time chairman Richard Munro and former Warner director Hugh Culverhouse, chosen, I presumed, because he owned the Tampa Bay Buccaneers (and liked Steve).

Ross had been unable to eat or drink for months. He'd been flown to Los Angeles, where he underwent eleven hours of desperation surgery at USC's Cancer Hospital. Too weak to disturb, he played no role in the revamping of the Time Warner board. He died on December 20, 1992, expectedly when you thought about it, but shocking to the heart nonetheless.

In that same day, the board—via a phone poll—dropped six directors from its staff. Among those dropped were two longtime Ross men: Marty Payson, who was forced to resign as vice chairman of Time Warner and did it "in a pique," according to the *Los Angeles Times*; and CFO/executive VP Bert Wasserman. Board-free, Wasserman continued in his job, now at the pleasure of his new boss, Jerry Levin.

Less than a month later, the Time Warner board affirmed that Jerry

---

[137]Nicholas and Levin were aware Steve's cancer had recurred and that his case was probably hopeless. Doctors agreed on that.

would be chairman, CEO, and president, with no Number Two. On the twenty-ninth floor, only one office was occupied: Levin's. The *New York Times* asked Levin about a chief operating officer, his Number Two, to which Levin answered he'd decided against that, saying Time Warner did not need "bureaucratic overlay."

Pausing for 1.5 paragraphs to acknowledge the loss of Steve Ross, 1992's Time Warner Annual Report made an awkward, somewhat curt tribute: "The most reliable and immediate measure of our ability to carry out this creative mission is the performance of our businesses." And then went on.

The Annual Report now was signed by one person:

Gerald M. Levin
Chairman and Chief Executive Officer

Or, as Dick Munro said to other directors, "We *bought* this goddamn company!" Or, as Bette Midler once put it, "You're only as good as your last two and a half minutes."

Steve Ross's memory was not easily erased. A series of all-star memorial services commemorated an executive who put relationships first, a powerful man who made others feel they were the only ones in the room with him. As Beverly Sills put it, "He knew how to share curtain calls." He'd proudly passed out Batman pins like they were photos of his kids. He'd preferred a company where longtimers were not fired but, preserving their dignity, given other jobs within the family. As Mo described Ross at a memorial service on the Warner lot, "He treated his executives like artists."

In TW's Annual Report, where in 1990 Robert Morgado had been listed without title in the Warner Music Group column, where in 1991 he had been listed with the title of chairman, in 1992 it read:

Warner Music Group
Robert J. Morgado
Chairman and CEO

Morgado and his new boss Jerry Levin had read the same chapter of *Profit Growth for Dummies*. They believed that the Warner Music Group would not grow without entering new businesses: direct marketing, record clubs, tours. "Jerry figured," Wasserman told me, "that to get double-digit growth out of Records, coming out of an eight-hundred-million-dollars base, it wasn't going to happen in the United States only. Whether or not it could happen around the globe, we weren't sure. Some of it happened with the CD. Jerry was looking for *other* avenues of growth. I told him I thought the way Morgado was acting was harmful. Jerry brushed it aside. 'He sees the future,' he told me."

The struggle between Ostin and Morgado now became more noticeable. Morgado the suit got bad press. Music people told how he'd just showed up at their gates one day, a little like Attila. They found him an unemotional executive, one who talked funny, used terms like "leveraging" and "vertical integration," terms that sounded to people who had dedicated their lives to records, night and day, like they came from the mouth of "the demon himself." Morgado, used to constant fights between Democrats and Republicans in his old career, found all this grumbling, all this name-calling, irrelevant to getting *his* job done.

Mo Ostin and Bob Morgado tried working out their differences over a neo-Italian dinner with Jerry Levin at Primavera, Eighty-first and Second, where Mo had often dined with Paul Simon and Mike Nichols. Levin's recommendation was no more detailed than "try to work this stuff out." To which Mo, truthfully, told Jerry in front of Bob, "I don't trust this man." To which Jerry replied, "Bob has to make decisions. They may not appear to be right from your perspective. We want to keep an open communication."

As Mo left the dinner, he considered how Levin was unlike Ross. Both could be aloof and apart, but the difference was that when something was about to explode, Steve would smother it with affection and twenty pounds of love. Levin, instead, though bright, sure, and Ross's equal as a manipulator, was less of a hugger, harder to read, an introvert. Mo recognized another thing: This was a different corporation now.

Significant Releases

1992

Atlantic: INXS (*Welcome to Wherever You Are,* including "Not Enough Time") • Tracy Lawrence (*Sticks and Stones*) • Led Zeppelin (*Remasters*)
Atco: AC/DC (*Live*) • Pantera (*Vulgar Display of Power*)
East-West: Das EFX (*Dead Serious*) • En Vogue (*Funky Divas,* including "Free Your Mind," "Give It Up, Turn It Loose," "Giving Him Something He Can Feel," and "My Lovin' (You're Never Gonna Get It)") • Gerald Levert ("Baby Hold On to Me")
Interscope: 2Pac (*2Pacalypse Now*)

Elektra: Tracy Chapman (*Matters of the Heart*) • The Cure (*Wish,* including "Friday I'm in Love" and "High") • Grand Puba (*Reel to Reel*) • Pete Rock & C.L. Smooth (*Mecca and the Soul Brother*)

Warner Bros.: Al B. Sure! (*Sexy Versus*) • Damn Yankees (*Don't Tread,* including "Where You Goin' Now") • R.E.M. (*Automatic for the People*) • Randy Travis (*Greatest Hits*) • Travis Tritt (*T-R-O-U-B-L-E*) • ZZ Top (*Greatest Hits*)
Reprise: Atlantic Starr ("Masterpiece") • The B-52's (*Good Stuff*) • Black Sabbath (*Dehumanizer*) • Eric Clapton (*Rush* soundtrack, including "Tears in Heaven") • Neil Young (*Harvest Moon*) • *Wayne's World* soundtrack

Duck: Eric Clapton (*Unplugged,* including "Layla")

Sire: • David Byrne (*Uh-Oh*) • k.d. lang (*Ingenue,* including "Constant Craving") • Madonna (*Erotica,* including "Deeper and Deeper") • Ministry (*Psalm 69*) • Morrissey (*Your Arsenal*) • Lou Reed (*Magic and Loss*)

Cold Chillin': Kool G Rap & D.J. Polo (*Live and Let Die*)

Def American: The Black Crowes (*The Southern Harmony and Musical Companion*) • Danzig (*III—How the Gods Kill*)

Giant: Jade ("Don't Walk Away")

Paisley Park: ⚥

Slash: Faith No More (*Angel Dust*)

Tommy Boy: House of Pain ("Jump Around")

30

ELEKTRA had become a successful and daring label with a diverse roster including 10,000 Maniacs, Anita Baker, Tracy Chapman, and Metallica. Bob Krasnow fought for his vision: a record company with, as he'd put it, "ethical culture," which I took to mean quality acts that bring critical respect to a label. From his office looking across at St. Patrick's Cathedral, Krasnow avoided "soundalikes," and pursued originals. He'd gone after Grandmaster Flash and the Furious Five in 1982, long before rap became a good bet. He knew fresh style, down to the handcrafted desk ("no nails"), worthy of a place in the Museum of Modern Art, that stood in the corner of his office. Krasnow's ego rebelled at dumb *drek*.

At 1992's WEA convention, each of the major labels had its morning. On Elektra's morning, Krasnow, sitting in the front row, looking like a model for *GQ,* waited with his staff to take the stage. Before turning the day over to Elektra, that day's emcee, WEA manager Fran Aliberte broke the ice. He put onstage a comedy duo that sang "Fudge Packers in the Sky," about stopping at a restaurant on the interstate and getting hit on by "a homo." In the darkened auditorium, Krasnow's voice yelled out, "Who the fuck did this? This is *our* day. Get this piece of shit off the stage."

Krasnow stormed into the lobby in search of any distribution exec he thought responsible for booking those country jokers on Elektra's stage. He demanded the WEA guy get these guys *off.* The kid pled, "Why me?" Krasnow passed his promo head Mike Bone on the way back in, yelling at him, "You're from down South, so fuck you, too." Bone got a closeup of Krasnow's well-manicured finger. Inside, Elektra staff members cowered in fear. East West's Sylvia Rhone laughed 'til she wept. Elektra accounting mensch Aaron Levy finally calmed down his boss. At the dinner that evening, Henry Droz, in recapping the day, mentioned that Krasnow that very morning had fired three people who didn't even work for him.

Not many there knew that Bob Krasnow had contracted lymphoma, a form of cancer requiring operations, recuperation. Whatever thoughts

Morgado now had about modernizing the leadership of Elektra Records, he put to one side. This was hardly the time.

Henry Droz, now sixty-six years old, was feeling pooped, and maybe looking it. He also refused to be a yes-man to Morgado. On a trip to New York, he and Bob got down to gold tacks. Morgado had been particularly frustrated with the California operations, and thought of Henry as "a Mo guy." Morgado was now moving faster on more fronts, like a one-star general who's been told (or only knew how) to charge up that hill and damn any cannons. To him, systems and re-organizations were more important than the people who'd run his companies. Impatience was a virtue; delays be damned.

He had a list of new efficiencies proposed by Andersen Consulting, a massive company filled with experts who try to keep on consulting to clients as long as the clients will pay for it. To Andersen-ize, however, given the strong managers of Warner's companies, was going to take some persuading. "People get set in their ways. These companies were acquired separately," CFO Jerry Gold told me. "Someplace there was always some obstacle telling us, 'We are not going to do this.' " Implicitly, Gold meant that Henry Droz was of the old school. When the 30th Floor wanted something changed, Henry had smiled, nodded . . . but had not jumped.

Morgado and Droz talked retirement. They even made a list of candidates for Henry's job. Gold had criteria for the new president of WEA: "When Bob and I were picking a replacement for Henry," Jerry told me, "it was very important in my mind to find an executive who was open to a fresh look at things, who didn't have an immediate tie to the old system."

George Rossi, Droz's number two, was thought of as lovably cranky, but not groomed for what the new job would require. After some thought about Morgado's criteria, Droz suggested Dave Mount, a former WEA video manager who'd gone out on his own and done well.

Mount had entered WEA in 1975 as the L.A. branch's kid-in-the-cage. He'd work in a fenced and locked area doling out concert tickets, T-shirts, and other goodies. From there, he'd worked his way up. While field sales manager out of Los Angeles, he'd gotten his MBA from Pepperdine University. (Applauding at commencement was Dave's father, Ernie Mount, once "dean of the replacement needle business" as sales manager at Fidelitone in Chicago.)

In the early Eighties, as WEA fitfully distributed Atari, Mount had been put in charge, lasting as long as Atari, and then tossed out. He'd moved over to Live Video, and by 1991, worked his way up to become president of Live Home Video. The next year, Live needed cash, like maybe a $20 million advance. With Live's distribution deal through MCA expiring, Mount shopped for a new, cash-full distributor. Over lunch, Mount and Droz had renewed their relationship and cut the deal.

Alerted by Morgado, Time Warner's corporate headhunter, the memorably named Warren Wasp called Mount, telling him of a job opening: head of WEA. Bob Morgado, Jerry Gold, and Henry Droz each met with Dave.

"Dave came out of the old WEA system," recalled Gold, "but he wasn't tied to the old system. David was very senior executive, a smart guy with the right personality for this, but he wasn't caught up in the corporate personality. That is why we picked him over some of the other candidates." Gold's phrase "the corporate personality" and his comments on how it must have disturbed the 30th Floor Gang tells much about what was going on in 1993.

Following Droz's three-day stay in a hospital (severe bronchitis), Morgado flew out to the West Coast personally to make some changes. The first involved a small unit called Warner Special Projects, run by third-generation record man Mickey Kapp.[138] Within Warner, Kapp had started at Elektra, then set up Warner Special Products to license Warner label songs to companies for anything from movies to General Motors spots. Kapp had grown WSP by creating its own TV-retail–sold albums, and getting into market research and technology watch for the group.

Over a patio breakfast at Beverly Hills' Peninsula Hotel, Morgado told Kapp that he was just too old; Kapp felt he was sixty-two and terrific. Morgado answered he should plan to retire from Warner Special Products before the end of the year, and that Kapp's replacement would be WSP's longtime financial head, Tony Pipitone. Bob advised him not to take it personally, however, as others of WEA's first generation of management would be getting the same message. It was part of Morgado's "succession plan," which, he told Kapp with careless ease, would also, by the end of the year, involve Krasnow and Ostin.

Kapp wasted no time in calling Mo to tell him of the conversation. A few nights later, seeing Krasnow dining at Cicada in Los Angeles with two friends, Mickey also told them about his talk with Morgado and the succession plan. Good to know the news, though likely to flatten one's soufflé.

Morgado met with Dave Mount, determined to set off in a new direction, and told him, "This is what we're going to start to think about." Mount was open to the plan. On the evening of June first, Morgado informed Droz that his choice was Dave Mount. Gold saw "Henry as quite pleased with our selection." Others saw Henry as passive in his acceptance. To whom could he complain? Morgado introduced Mount to the record labels; it took three days. Inside WEA, people right away resented being run by an outsider, even one they'd known.

---

[138]Generation one was grandfather Meyer Kapp's Music Store at 2846 North Madison in Chicago. Generation two were Jack and Dave Kapp of Brunswick and then Decca and Kapp Records.

On August third, 1993, *Billboard* ran an Executive Suite notice: David Mount would replace Henry Droz in December. At WEA's August sales meeting in Vancouver (the theme being "Together We Make It Happen"), Dave Mount attended as Incoming WEA Copresident.

In September, Mount moved up to Burbank, joining Droz as co-president while they toured the branches. After twenty-one years with WEA, Henry Droz tossed his business cards in the waste basket and family photos into his attaché case, with three months' wait 'til it was time to leave. He refused any plans for a farewell party. He told Morgado, "Bob, you can call a party, but I won't show up."

On Droz's last day in the office, just before Thanksgiving, an all–home office farewell lunch had been arranged on WEA's ground floor. Droz attended, then, halfway through, eased out of the building, barely saying good-bye, never intending to return. He walked to his car and drove alone to his home. Like Louis Armstrong that night in Detroit, he just went home, his day spent, now over and done with. "Henry kind of faded out of the picture," Mount told me. "He didn't want a big-deal farewell, and probably didn't want to quit."[139]

Having "back office" staffs, one per label, to handle somewhat mechanical functions—like ordering records and packages—made no sense in the Morgado-ized Warner Music regime, ever searching for efficiencies, ever searching for group profits.

Morgado assigned the efficiency priority to his new CFO, Jerry Gold. People whose life work was organizing—people often good with numbers and flowcharts and common sense, combined with a lack of love for the way it's always been done—began to fill the thirtieth floor at 75 Rock, headquarters for the Warner Music Group. They found themselves faced with preestablished businesses, like printing companies and CD plants that had been earlier bought by WCI, then left on their own. A most obvious fact showed up. If a WEA label went outside to a non-Warner pressing plant—not its own—it could buy a CD for ten cents cheaper.

Andersen Consulting found cobwebs. At WEA's Specialty Records in Olyphant, Pennsylvania, the pressing plant had 143 maintenance people on payroll. Of these, 30 worked in heating/air-conditioning. "When's the last time the air-conditioning went down?" Good question. Thirty people had to think back a ways.

The Thirtieth-Floor Gang saw a better objective, and that was not how *many* of a record your company could manufacture. The better goal was to get the *right* record to the *right* place at the *right* time. That meant making

---

[139]Within a couple of years, Henry Droz became head of Universal Music's own distribution system.

fewer records and fewer jackets, to control the waste of it all. Control returns. Which meant to hell with those individual companies' quantity-base bonus checks. "Efficiency-wise," Jerry Gold put it, "the problem is that we *have* three companies, but they really are *one* company. Let's make them one company."

It meant more. It meant that thirty people in heating/air-conditioning would be out of work.

The report from Andersen Consulting confirmed what Gold and Ric Weitsma already knew: Operations were costing too much, particularly when Dad's in the hole $16 billion. Given the gravitas of Andersen Consulting, changes—like direct shipping from the plant to stores, bypassing branches—got going. Branches spent more time selling, less time handling labels' whims.

"None of these things were revolutionary," Ric Weitsma told me. A veteran of the consulting business, Ric had taken over manufacturing in Burbank years before. Shelly Vogel had brought Ric from WBR to Corporate to handle combined order service (discs, jacket ordering) for the combined labels. To run it all from New York took one staff as large as (or larger than) the three separate staffs had, but still, it kind of maybe made sense. Ric had been around long enough to know the history. "Originally, in 1971 to 1980, we didn't have manufacturing. We just had the branches. There was a certain commonsense awkwardness to the way we were doing things: Make something at the factory. Put it on a rack. Take it out of the rack. Ship it to the branches. The branches take it out. They ship it to the customer. From the viewpoint of today, there's some extra handling going on."

Andersen Consulting's report took oneness one step further. What if manufacturing were not three companies (branches, manufacturing, printing) but all *one* organization, all with *one* goal? Changes were made, as never before. Bar codes and SoundScan (accurate sales counting) turned the record business from hype to tight. The three labels, once baronies, found that unity made them a little richer in the end.

To administer all these efficiencies took, of course, more and more efficiency administrators. Morgado's corporate staff had grown to more than two hundred.

The contrast in how much somebody got paid, the difference between people in plants and people up in Rockefeller Center, became front-page embarrassment. Contractual platinum parachutes for corporate executives certainly looked obscene. Lifetime paychecks had been assured some, whether the guy worked for the company or had been fired (Nicholas was guaranteed $500,000 a year for life). In the merger year, Ross had cashed in for $200 million and 1.8 million new stock options. Workers in the Olyphant pressing plant got pink-slipped with two weeks' notice.

Aware of his own future, Ross had bargained for a "golden coffin" clause in his contract: not only for $7.9 million life insurance plus, but also, for three years after his death, his heirs would receive his full salary and bonuses; and till the year 2002, Ross's heirs could exercise his 7.2 million stock options. One compensation expert was of the opinion that "executives rewarded this way act like blind dogs in a sausage factory."

Inside the Warner Music Group's National Returns Center in Chicago, the glamour of the record business was measured in RPH efficiencies: refurbishments per hour. Workers without parachutes were paid on an hourly basis. The fewer workers per day, the better. On an average day, 150,000 CDs and cassettes were dumped onto the center's "in" docks, to be fixed up, like new, before tomorrow arrived, and with it, 150,000 more.

While Mick and Jerry were lolling in Bali, while Bob and Jerry were bouncing in stock-option heaven, Larry and Crew sweated in RPH Land, their hands moving at the speed of light.

The computers at Chicago's Returns Center knew every box of albums being returned before it reached the dock. Its computers noted that an RA (return authorization) was on its way from a branch. The carton came in on a pallet. Raymond Reach Trucks carried the return pallets to the Holding Area, where at one of thirty-eight Detail Check-in Workstations, people making $8.70 an hour opened the box, a mess of rejects with different titles, and started figuring how many could be recycled. A Symbol Technologies scanner, using a Computer Identics Wedge, scanned bar codes. The albums went into one of three color-coded tote boxes: red for audiocassettes, gray for videocassettes, blue for CDs. The tote boxes rolled down a Rapistan Conveyor, finding their way by reflective tape and photo sensors. A pair of spinning wheels from Everhard Machinery burned shrink wrap in two without harming the jewel box. Rubber fingers pulled away the shrink wrap. A vacuum sucked up the trash. A Scandia machine re-shrink-wrapped. The albums then cascaded into Dorner Manufacturing's Sortation Machine, with four to seven bar-code-label scanners from Computer Identics to rescan the UPC labels, finding, no matter which side was up, which of 22,000 Stock Keeping Units (SKUs) this one was. The bar codes moved freshened product onto one of ten different aisles, where Label-Aire machines affixed new, preprinted labels like FEATURING THE HIT SINGLE (SOMETHING OR OTHER). A Walk Sequence Sorter accumulated albums into twenty-CD loaves. When a $7.90-an-hour person called a Filer saw a light go on at the end of the Accumulation Aisle, he or she picked up the loaf and put it with other loaves like it, until a carton of identical loaves was filled. A Zebra Technologies Labeler printed the carton's contents. The National Returns Center's own In-House Random Locator System told where the carton should to be put, with partial pallets going on the lower racks, full pallets on the top racks. This process took two days from "in the door" to "ready to resell" at full price. Unusable returns were ground to dust by hand, by Grinders who also made $7.90 per hour.

Average corporate-executive salaries in the Music Group were now in the millions of dollars. Shelly Vogel noticed that Mel Lewinter, once his assistant in finance at Atlantic, where he'd made $300,000 a year, now made $2 million a year under Doug Morris. That seemed unfair, especially when these same people flew in to make places like Olyphant's pressing plant and Chicago's Returns Center more efficient, getting rid of $7.90 people who for their whole lives had put up with dull jobs, had never enjoyed a drug-mad evening of pushing a piano out a top-floor window, and who had to buy their own records in stores, while they knew that those guys in suits got theirs free.

In 1993, as the snow flurries began falling, the Warner Music Group, still using the WCI logo once characterized by Jac Holzman as two and a half turds in a punch bowl,[140] moved its income up from $585 million to $643 million. Good money. CD prices had gone up again, the $13.98s becoming $15.98s.

Down below the counting house, there was once more ice in Rockefeller's rink, the air was brisk, the exhaust from parked limos puffed snowy white. Budget meetings, a ritual as winter dawned, reconvened.

For 1993, the Warner Music Group made more money than in 1992: The group's EBITDA (an accounting term whose "EBI" means "earnings *before* interest," a convenient accounting lingo in these debt-burdensome years; "TDA" stands for "taxes, depreciation, and amortization") edged up from $3.214 million to $3.334 million. Of the year 1993, the nearly forgotten Thelma Walker's totals would show a vigorous upsurge by Atlantic: Atlantic 37 + Elektra 12 + Warner Bros. 38 = 87 made the charts.

Staffers at Warner Bros. and Elektra Records watched Morgado. They coined a new name for him: "The Smilin' Hawaiian." They read publicity splashes about the new Atlantic Records, but none for Warner or Elektra. *Billboard* ran an effusive cover story on Atlantic, something unusual even for a trade magazine that constantly puts out issues with ad-laden salutes to 'most anybody. *Billboard* made more "salutes" than a buck private. But this salute to Atlantic had come out of nowhere. Why? the Warner and Elektra labels wondered. The magazine explained how the Atlantic Group's revenues were up 55 percent in two years. To Mo, the article felt unfair, as well as less than spontaneous.

Atlantic kept signing labels: Select Records (the Jerky Boys), Mammoth (Seven Mary Three), and Gerard Cosloy's Matador (Liz Phair). Phil

---

[140]Earlier, other interpretations of the logo had arisen. In Jerry Greenberg's office, they'd been referred to as "two reds and a bennie."

Collins, having appeared on albums selling 57 million copies, signed a new worldwide recording, publishing, and distribution agreement with WMG companies. Rhino began originating its own albums with its Forward label for Atlantic. Mick Jagger returned to Atlantic, but solo, without his wrinkly friends, posing for the trades between Ahmet Ertegun and Doug Morris, his signers. In April-May-June-July, Atlantic's market share outpointed Warner's.

This new label style—deprecated by Warners and Elektra as "Atlantification"—sat poorly both with Krasnow's "boutique" approach as well as with Ostin's "all service, career artists" approach. Atlantic, it seemed, was being run in a more M.B.A.-like way, defining an album's markets and how to sell to them. To Warner and Elektra this was manipulative, impersonal, and cheap. To Atlantic, it felt like it was working.

Whether to extend Ostin's contract rose up to a Corporate-agenda item. Time was approaching for renewal talks. Morgado wanted a change: If he really was running the Warner Music Group, he argued, it made no sense to have *part* of that group—Mo Ostin—independent of his control, reporting to a preoccupied Jerry Levin.

David Geffen, Barbra Steisand, Michael Ovitz, Paul Simon, Clint Eastwood, and other entertainment icons wrote personal letters to Jerry Levin, each with a similar message: "Do not lose Mo." Levin answered that he had no intention of losing Mo. Neither had he any intention of losing Morgado, whose view he also accepted: that Elektra and Warner Bros. were far from maximizing profits.

As part of Mo's contract talks, Corporate asked for the succession plan at Warner Bros. To Ostin, this "who's your Number Two?" and "succession" business increasingly looked like some bad excuse for something else. Morgado had no Number Two. Nor did Levin, who'd earlier brushed that topic aside as "too much bureaucracy." Morgado and Levin both structured their own areas to resemble one cherry sitting atop a very wide pancake. Still, Ostin recommended that Lenny Waronker be moved up as co–chief executive of WBR in two years, in 1995. Mo also proposed, as part of the extension, that he'd continue to report directly to Time Warner's chairman, Levin. With that on the table, Mo took the Concorde off to London for a week of business, promising to return through New York for reaction to his proposal.

An issue of major contention had crystallized. It was now Morgado vs. Ostin. Morgado was determined to end the final music baronies that Ross had nurtured. Morgado stated his case: "Some people don't do well with their own transition, their own mortality. Mo was difficult because he could not deal with the idea that somebody in his own company could be equal to him. It's very human, I understand that. But then he turned *me* into the issue.

And to me . . . well, it's all really *bullshit,* frankly. To me, this is ultimately about how companies handle changes in their executive management."

On Ostin's return from England, Levin told Mo he could not accept Mo's reportage clause. Levin's reasoning: In no other division of Time Warner was such an unconventional structure allowed. Levin then gave Morgado the green light to impose his "strategic plan" on Mo. When I asked others about this later, Marty Payson observed, "You have to look at the press comments Levin made. In the press he said, 'Mo is too old.' One of the things Morgado had said was that we need young blood . . . and Levin publicly endorsed that, rightly or wrongly. He ultimately has to have responsibility for what happened to the music business. I do know, in fact, that Levin endorsed these moves."

Having told Mo that dual reportage wouldn't work anymore (and at Corporate, Levin was not alone in that opinion), Jerry offered Mo a new contract, to run three years. For the first eighteen months, Ostin would continue as chairman and CEO. For the second eighteen, Ostin would be chairman and Lenny Waronker would be CEO. Ostin would report to Morgado.

Unable to sign the document, Mo stuck it in a drawer. He continued, doing what he knew how to do: run Warner Bros. Records.

Despite David Geffen's comment—"What do you want with a fifty-year-old folksinger?"—Ostin re-signed Joni Mitchell to Reprise, twenty-three years after she had left for Asylum, then Geffen. Joni and Mo met and dealt in Peppone's, a red-leather-booths Brentwood restaurant known for its combination of lively pasta and deathly cholesterol. Joni Mitchell warned Ostin, "I'm fifty. I'm not going to run around all day and night promoting. I had two records dropped while I was at Geffen." Ostin picked up the dinner check. He still knew talent when he heard it.

Selected Releases

1993

Atlantic: Phil Collins (*Both Sides*) • Genesis (*Live The Way We Walk*) • Mick Jagger (*Wandering Spirit*) • Tracy Lawrence (*Alibis*) • John Michael Montgomery (*Life's a Dance*) • Rush (*Counterparts*) • Stone Temple Pilots (*Core*)

East-West: Das EFX (*Straight Up Sewaside*) • En Vogue (*Runaway Love*) • Snow (*12 Inches of Snow,* including "Informer")

Es Paranza: Robert Plant (*Fate of Nations*)

Interscope: Four Non Blondes (*Bigger, Better, Faster, More!*) • Primus (*Pork Soda*) • 2Pac (*Strictly 4 My N.I.G.G.A.Z.,* including "I Get Around" and "Keep Ya Head Up")

Death Row: Dr. Dre ("Nuthin' But a 'G' Thang" and "Dre Day") • Snoop Doggy Dogg (*Doggy Style,* including "What's My Name" and "Gin & Juice")

Elektra: Brand Nubian (*In God We Trust*) • Jackson Browne (*I'm Alive*) • Natalie Cole (*Take a Look*) • Metallica (*Live Shit: Binge & Purge*) • 10,000 Maniacs (*MTV Unplugged,* including "Because the Night")

Warner Bros.: Ray Charles (*My World*) • Vince Neil (*Exposed*) • Porno for Pyros • Rod Stewart (*Unplugged . . . and Seated*) • Van Halen (*Live: Right Here. Right Now*)
Reprise: Earth, Wind & Fire (*Millennium*) • Donald Fagen (*Kamakiriad*) • Chris Isaak (*San Francisco Days*) • Dwight Yoakam (*This Time*) • Neil Young (*Unplugged*) • Zapp & Roger (*All the Greatest Hits*)
Giant: Jade (*Jade to the Max,* including "Don't Walk Away") • Various Artists: *Common Thread: The Songs of the Eagles*
Maverick: Candlebox
Paisley Park: Prince (*The Hits/The B Sides*)
Qwest: Tevin Campbell (*I'm Ready,* including "Can We Talk") • New Order (*Republic*)
Sire: Depeche Mode (*Songs of Faith and Devotion*)
Tommy Boy: K7 ("Come Baby Come") • Naughty by Nature (*19 Naughty III,* including "Hip Hop Hooray")

31

IN 1994, their ages were: Ahmet Ertegun, seventy-one. Mo Ostin, sixty-seven. Bob Krasnow, fifty-nine. Jerry Levin, fifty-five. Doug Morris, fifty-four. Lenny Waronker, fifty-two. Seymour Stein, fifty-two. Bob Morgado, fifty. Danny Goldberg, forty-four. Sylvia Rhone, forty-two. Jimmy Iovine, forty-one. Val Azzoli, thirty-nine. Dr. Dre, twenty-nine.

That February, the year banged open with a massive California earthquake that first jolted, then crushed WEA's San Fernando Valley warehouse. At five in the morning, WEA employee Jac Lee drove to the warehouse in Chatsworth, where he found computers still dancing on the floor. With his flashlight, Lee saw overturned furniture, toppled file cabinets, glass everywhere. "Beirut," he thought.

The roof was blown half off, north and south walls were cracked, and rain had begun. Six inches of water flooded the floor. Branch manager Brent Gordon bought socks, boxes of socks, for his warehouse staff to work in, helping to keep dry. Then pullovers to keep out the February cold coming in through the opened roof.

Aftershocks rocked for three days, leaving the warehousers staring at teetering tons overhead. Lee lived in his car. After three days of cleanup, it was worse. The main staircase: cracked. Every steel beam needed rewelding. That meant noise, like living for a week in a dentist's chair. Repairmen were contracted to work all night, till the neighbors complained to the police.

Jac Lee did not have time to read the newspapers to find out what else was going on in places like New York, up at 75 Rock, or in Montreux, Switzerland.

In summer 1994, Warner Music International's convention met on Lake Geneva's edge, in Montreux. It is a narrow-streeted, Old World-y village, where you can buy anything from Rolexes to eight-foot alpine horns. Appetizers always included fondue. Montreux's unofficial mayor was a longtime

Warner/Swiss favorite, the ever-boyish, knows-everyone Claude Nobs, who also produced the town's July jazz festivals.

For 1994's convention, Warner Music International head Ramon Lopez had made it clear: This year's would be a "no spouses, no dates" gathering. Elektra chairman Bob Krasnow decided such a rule did not apply to him. He arrived in Montreux with a date and a half, a gorgeous Miss U.S.A. type, to the impatience of many there. Bob was asked not to include her at the functions. The first night—a Lake Geneva boat ride—Bob brought Miss. She became, for impatient execs like Lopez and Morgado, Strike One.

Strike Two: The next morning, during International's "numbers presentation," when Elektra's results looked bad on the slide "Breakthrough of New Acts Overseas," Krasnow publicly berated Cynthia, his head of International. "Outside in the lobby, Bob started screaming at her," remembered her boss, Aaron Levy. "The poor girl was hysterical. People were running to look for me to get him to get inside and quiet down. By the time I arrived, poor Cynthia was just sitting there crying her eyes out."

Strike Three: At the first luncheon meeting, the topic was "Pacific Rim Markets," and Krasnow insulted the Japanese at his lunch table. "I gotta be what I am," Krasnow told me a year later. "I don't care if I self-destruct. I gotta say things that are on my mind."

Away from Krasnow, Lopez held quiet conversations with Morgado, his CFO Jerry Gold, and others, debating how to handle Krasnow's disruptiveness. Levy, watching it all, realized that Morgado just couldn't handle it anymore. Lopez and Morgado asked Krasnow to leave the convention, taking his beauty queen with him.

As Elektra's Number Two, Aaron Levy figured that Krasnow would be next to leave, not just from Montreux but from the Music Group, too. He knew that his boss was feeling a lot of physical pain and psychological pressure after his operation, knew he no longer gave a damn. "He just got to be a nasty piece of work at the end. He is a good guy in many ways, and I think something snapped in him, and he just became too big for his own sake. He made a lot of enemies among the other labels. When we would have our international meetings, he would point out some managing director and say things in front of the whole group about his lack of ability. Bob was very direct. Very. He was not a diplomat. In the beginning, he was polite. But at the end, after the disease, no, not at all."

On his flight back to New York, Morgado expressed his frustration to his key staff, especially Gold and his legal head, the once-hippie-like Fred Wistow. He believed that his mandate was to revitalize his too-fat labels, which he'd accomplished with Atlantic, and from Levin down, he'd heard applause. He had only Elektra and Warner Bros. now standing in the way of a full new house of young, driven executives. But when he'd brought up revitalizing with Elektra or Warners, their doors got slammed in his face.

Struggling with the U.S. labels, Morgado realized that he would never get respect as "a music guy." He was the suit, the hatchet guy, the mistrusted, occasionally elevated from Smilin' to the rank of "The Lyin' Hawaiian." Bob's solution: Find a music guy to shut these labels up.

Morgado liked end runs like this. Creating a "Warner Music–U.S.," an umbrella for the three labels. That would mean he could still run the whole show, be involved in International, but the perception would be that a music guy, someone who could tell E-flat from E-mail, would interface with the U.S. fiefdoms. Morgado knew which E-flat guy to pick, too. Wistow learned in a staff meeting of Morgado's plan to promote Doug Morris from Atlantic to head this new U.S. Music Group. Wistow scribbled a word on a piece of paper and handed it to Morgado: "Frankenstein." Morgado understood the Morris-Monster risk, but, remembering how Morris and he had worked together in reforming Atlantic, he felt sure he'd have Doug in his pocket.

Morgado took his plan to Jerry Levin, who had problems of his own. Time Warner's stock was trading near its low for the year, which was hardly when one liked to meet analysts, but was, also, when one needed to mingle with them. Washington was bearing down on TW's cable rates. Jerry's agenda of problems left him preoccupied. He didn't communicate as once he had, with jokes and a light air. In learning how to charge at a problem, he'd forgotten how to stroll. One observer thought maybe Jerry was just plain numb. In Jerry's state, Mo Ostin was hardly a top issue.

Levin agreed to the Morris promotion. The plan would clearly dilute the power of Ostin, Krasnow, and other top executives. "I wanted Doug to work with them," Morgado explained. "I didn't know what the problem was. Did they have the wrong A&R people? I thought Doug would have a better spin."

In an afternoon meeting, just after America once again celebrated its independence, Morgado called Krasnow to explain this new setup, "Warner Music–U.S.," and how Krasnow would now be reporting to a kinsman, a *music* exec, Doug Morris. The news smacked Krasnow full in the face. He called Ostin in London, who flew back to New York to confront Morgado on this new issue. Mo learned that the new setup would begin later that summer and that absolutely only five people knew about it: Levin, Morgado, Morris, Krasnow, and Ostin himself. Morgado told Mo not to worry, because under this new setup, for Mo it was to be business as usual. Ostin listened, said he understood, but did not assent.

Arriving in Aspen the next day, Ostin's son Michael asked his dad if he'd heard: Morris to head U.S. operations. Mo was stunned that the word was out. "The word" was traced, from Irv Azoff, who'd heard it from Geffen, who'd . . . Mo felt bitter toward Morgado's assurance of confidentiality. "Another lie," Ostin added to his list.

Meanwhile, Krasnow said he needed more time, and talked to his attorneys. He knew better than to explode and quit, thus breaking his contract. He phoned Morgado to say he thought he could make it work. "And, on the other end of the phone, there was dead silence," Krasnow recalled, "because this is the last thing the guy wanted to hear." When Krasnow suggested, "Why don't I meet with Doug Morris," he was not given that chance.

The news went full-bore public. From Morgado's offices came a press release announcing that Atlantic Group cochairman and co-CEO Doug Morris would step up to be the new president and chief operating officer of a new holding company for the American labels. The job would give Doug power over his fellow label heads, including Ostin and Krasnow. For Morris, running American WEA was the good dream, not only for himself but also for the three labels. He wanted to run them as they'd grown up—as music labels, not corporate growths.

With Morris running America from Bangor to bikinis, what was left for Morgado to run? Well, try Warner/Chappell, Warner Music International, Special Products, Direct Marketing, his bunch of new-technology companies, as well as WEA, the U.S. manufacturing and distribution arm of Warner Music. Morgado also held on to Mount's operation, conceding to the press only that "Dave Mount will work very closely with Doug on the selling and scheduling of releases, and in fact will take his direction on that from Doug." And, of course, Morris would also report to Morgado.

Bob Krasnow's calm acceptance of reporting to Morris had left him where Morgado and Morris did not want him: in Elektra's chairman's chair. The label was down to one Top Ten album, Keith Sweat's *Get Up on It*. Hardly enough.

In a role he called "as a friend of the court," Ahmet Ertegun phoned to ask Krasnow if he'd like some other job in the company and to say that Morris could ensure it, anything Bob wanted. Listening, Bob sensed what he called "Ahmet's hand" behind this maneuvering. "I have always said," Bob told me, "and I would say it to his face, he is a manipulative fucking guy." When I asked Krasnow about Ahmet's lack of power in all this, Bob saw it differently: "Ahmet is too smart ever to be powerless. Ahmet always has a place. I mean, who told me that I was out?"

Morgado and Morris offered Krasnow a product deal, a label deal. But now Krasnow just sat, wanting to get paid off. It was no longer a matter of cancer; those treatments had worked. It was no longer a matter of principle or of art. It was a matter of buyout. To willingly rise from his contractual chair, Krasnow was reported to have settled for $7 million.

In his new job, Doug Morris debated who he'd get to replace himself at the Atlantic Group. Ahmet had briefly been soloing as chairman of the company, but for almost fifty years, solo had never been Ertegun's forte. Ertegun reported to Morris now. He was treated like a member of the House of Lords: He looked good in robes but ruled no empire.

Morris settled on Atlantic's Los Angeles head, Danny Goldberg. Goldberg would not become co-CEO with Ahmet, only president. Goldberg moved wife and children to New York. His style was the antithesis of flash. He wore no gold chains. He was neither bald nor ponytailed. He'd brought to Atlantic alternative acts like Stone Temple Pilots and Liz Phair, so he had good ears. He talked humbly. He shared Morris's worries over too much corporatizing.

Doug quickly moved on to Elektra. Krasnow's personal effects would be boxed and out of the office by July 13. Within a week, Doug named Krasnow's successor: Sylvia Rhone, formerly chairwoman and CEO of Atlantic's East West Records. Sylvia would command both labels, Elektra and East West. And five days later, Sylvia Rhone, a twenty-year veteran of the music business and the first black woman to head a major label (there had been other black women who'd earlier run R&B labels), sat herself down in Krasnow's chair.

Sylvia had been raised in Harlem. After finishing an undergrad degree at the University of Pennsylvania, then a master's from Wharton, she'd first worked in international lending at Bankers Trust, but found the atmosphere there too inhospitable: "I wore pants to work, and all eyebrows turned up. No one actually said anything, but they made it clear that what I'd done was unacceptable." In 1974, at age twenty-two, she took a major pay cut and moved to work for Art Kass at Buddah Records, in promotion. In 1980, Sylvia became Elektra, as its Northeast regional promotion manager/special markets. Five years later, she was over at Atlantic. Hank Caldwell, Atlantic's black-music head and by now Atlantic's legacy when it came to promoting R&B records, had searched for the best man to be head of national promotion for Atlantic. "She got the job," Hank said, "because she was the most qualified person I interviewed." Three years later, she became senior VP. Then, two years later, CEO and copresident of East West Records. By 1991, at forty-one, she'd become solo head of East West then added Atco Records when that label's head was let go.

Her signing credentials were real. She'd nabbed En Vogue. She'd even told the *Los Angeles Times* "eventually, that sexist good ol' boy school of thought will go the way of the dinosaur. It'll take us a few years to accomplish it, but hey, I'm up for the fight."

Bringing her East West label with her to Elektra from Atlantic would help strengthen her new label's Chart Lite. Sylvia first saw herself as chairwoman over two labels that would "coexist, side by side, independently." She'd spoken too fast. Three months later, she oversaw the firing of forty staff members, and nobody was talking about two separate label staffs. With two of his own new label heads in chairs, Morris had no inclination to push around the third, Mo Ostin, who still, in his heart, reported to Steve.

Each year, financier Herbert Allen threw a retreat for media executives in Sun Valley. Invitation only, and no one turned it down. This was big time. At 1994's lawn-and-tent party, David Geffen stopped Jerry Levin walking past David's filled-with-importants lunch table. "You're making a terrible mistake," David told him. "Mo is the single most important music executive in the world. I compete with him every day, and he still beats our brains in more often than not. Jerry, this is *not* a good idea for you." Levin listened, nodded, and moved on.

For months, Mo's Levin-Morgado-drafted contract lay gathering disgust in his desk drawer, while he listened to other offers and to his own allegiances. Several times during this, Ostin's worst year since the sale of Reprise, he and I had lunch. He had suggested to WBR's head of advertising that he wished today's ads had the spunk of our old ads, so his current head of Creative Services, Jeff Gold, called me up to write more ads. Why not? I began visits to my old building but told Gold I had one condition: I did not want to wait in the lobby like some stranger till I got fetched upstairs. Jeff accommodated my ego.

Up on the top floor, some people recognized me, waved, and came over to talk. Within thirty seconds, each of them would whisper roughly the same thing—"It's not like it used to be"—and then describe how the company had to justify all expenses against expected revenues. Meanly, I'd recall 1969, flying all twenty of us in Creative Services up to San Francisco for dinner and a Dead concert, staying over, for the hell of it, then back to work the next morning, the company paying for it all.

Anyway, I wrote some new ads, but only one ever got published. The company's caution shocked me; they even checked out one of my ads with the lead singer's mother, who killed it. I loved that ad.[141] Like others, it went as underappreciated as lyonaise potatoes.

When Mo and I would lunch, we'd discuss the pressures he felt, and his options. He'd insist that he wasn't through with the record business. He talked about being courted by other companies, about starting a new label, and he checked with me three times during the year that I was "still available." I saw Mo as ever the realist, the smart man, but I also saw him sad. He'd put in over thirty years in the Number One chair at WBR, and now *he* looked as underappreciated as lyonaise potatoes.

The choice for Ostin was hardly easy. He'd thought it over and over and over, in the car rides from his Pacific Palisades home, driven by Jimmy Rowe,

---

[141]If you'd like a copy, e-mail me at exploding@cornyn.com.

who'd decades earlier worked as our after-hours janitor in the old machine-shop building. Now, driving Mo each day, Jimmy became a bit of Mo's mirror on life. Each morning, Mo would alight from his car, say something to parking-lot guard Howard Washington (who tended a ten-by-three-foot flower garden near his guard shack), then walk into a building he'd made affordable, seeing a future without these connections to his past life.

On August 15, after having met with Levin to work out "plans for continuity, succession, and a transition," Mo announced that he would leave Warner Bros. Records when his contract expired. Four more months. As Mo put it, simply, "When I came to the realization that I *could* let go—which was very, very painful for me, after all the years I had put in—and I addressed the idea of leaving, I almost felt a sense of relief." Levin and Morgado asked Mo to stay as chairman emeritus, an Ertegun-like position. He turned that down, too.

Both sides had become stuck on stubborn. Mo held on to his independence, while Morgado held on to his need to manage a company he viewed as covered with barnacles. In the end, Levin had allowed it all to end for Mo by making no choice. He had simply backed his division head, banking on Morgado the Younger to invigorate Burbank as earlier he had done downstairs at Atlantic.

Krasnow, who still could not fathom Mo's being out at Warner Bros. Records, when asked by inquiring reporters, turned the question around to ask about Morgado: "How did all of this happen? Why would a man burn down the most beautiful house on the block with all the beautiful stuff still in it? Why?" Artists like R.E.M. threatened to jump ship. Inside 75 Rock, now increasingly populated by the Time-inclined, Mo was well liked but part of "the Steve era."

Ostin fought press reportage that described WBR as an "old folks' home for aging superstars." "That's just a bad rap created by our competitors," Mo told people, "to create misperceptions about how vital this company is. I think it's really unfair. Everyone knows we are the prime competitor anytime it comes time to sign new acts . . . If you look at the charts and study our profit performance over the years, we are by far the most consistent and stable company on the block."

Ostin sent a letter to all employees of Warner Bros. Records. The letter read, in part, "I am neither resigning nor retiring. I am however moving on . . ."

Lenny Waronker was announced successor to Mo as CEO (although not as chairman).[142] To preserve his stock options and bonuses, Mo chose to re-

---

[142]"Chairman of the Board" was a baloney title in the record group. Anywhere below the top of Time Warner, there existed no boards to chair. "Chairman of the Board" just got stuck onto titles to puff them huger. Once one person got a chairmanship, then all others needed to get one, too.

main tied to Time Warner for a whole year, through early August of '95, vaguely labeled a consultant. Actually, the extra seven months were a negotiated period of "noncompete" time bought by TW to keep Mo off the market.

Three days later, WEA opened its sales meeting, this time in Nashville, and on August 18, both Mo and his successor, Lenny, addressed the convention. Ostin talked about others: "There comes a point in every man's life when he realizes that in order to reach for the stars, he must stand on the shoulders of giants. I've known some giants in my time. To name one, I realized that I'd have to name them all. And if I did that, we'd probably be here for the next thirty-one years. But then I thought, 'What the hell. It's my speech. I can take all day if I want. What are they going to do? Fire me?' "

Mo covered his life debts, from Norman Granz, who gave Ostin his first job in the music business, through Sinatra and on. The audience sat still, watching Mo, a halting orator, struggle through his last speech to them, covering emotion with too-long sips from a plastic Evian bottle.

Mo spoke of a common history, one clearly, for the many before him, now over. The audience reacted like fans of the home team who in this, the final game of the series, saw their team fall behind in the first quarter, see the score get worse, until the final buzzer, when the stands fall silent. Everybody in the auditorium had Mo as his or her home team; nobody now expected last-minute miracles. Atlantic's new chief, Danny Goldberg, told friends in the press, "It was a very emotional event. Everybody was crying."

A photo was posed, one to show the old guard and new guard together, however uncomfortably. While looking into the lens, Morgado offered a possible caption: "All the generations of Warner Music." To which Mo forced a smile. Lenny, as usual, murmured his "This just doesn't feel right" commentary, then blurted, "I can't believe this!" To which Atlantic's Goldberg added the spin, "Yeah, isn't it great!"

A month later, *Business Week* ran a story that astounded, then maddened the executives in Burbank. They felt as if 75 Rock, now overflowing with spin-the-press publicity experts like Morgado's Margaret Wade, a tall New Orleans *belle dame,* had set this up. (In the center of the page was a photo of Morgado, looming over "his cardboard-cutout pals the Three Tenors".) The story pointed out that Atlantic had overtaken WBR in U.S. market share. A table, from SoundScan statistics, illustrated—a bit vaguely, with no real numbers attached—this ratio change:

> 1993: Warner Bros.: about 9.5% 1994: Warner Bros.: about 8.3%
> 1993: Atlantic: about 7.75% 1994: Atlantic: about 9.2%

The article and its chart infuriated Mo Ostin. Traditionally, between the WEA labels, there had never been any public breakout of number differences. This article pointed accusatory fingers, using sentences such as "Unlike Ostin, who carried on a notorious rivalry with Sony's predecessor company, CBS Records, Morgado has an array of joint ventures with Sony."

Ostin, feeling screwed over, started setting the record straighter: "Except for the first six months of this year, Warner has consistently outperformed Atlantic in market share and profit contribution. And, since we're in a business of the arts, one also has to look at the quality of the music you put out. If you look at the Grammy Awards as one example and compare Warner and Atlantic, that will tell you a lot. Just no contest."

Even now, with Mo as lame-duck chairman, little attempt was made to patch up the split between Rockefeller Center and Burbank. Morgado's office looked forward to working with Waronker.

That autumn, Lenny became upset that Seymour Stein, who'd for years headed Warner's Sire label, had been hearing from Morris how good it would be for Seymour to sign on as president with Rhone's new Elektra label in New York. No one mentioned to Lenny that he'd be losing Seymour; he'd read it in the paper. Despite Seymour's often-trying behavior, he was very much "a record man" (polite term for a record geek in his fifties), one who knew B sides and chart positions going back to the 1950s and, as such, one of Lenny's "us" crowd. The kind you keep around. For Lenny to hear secondhand, after the fact, that Seymour was "being moved to Elektra," struck Warner's new CEO-to-be as very, very odd.

Publicly, Lenny dismissed this stripping of authority, but it was hard to believe that 75 Rock had simply forgotten to tell him. Lenny already had reservations over taking Mo's job. Actually, his persona was one of *always* having deep second thoughts. Even when it came to choosing from a taco-stand menu, Lenny would shake his head in dismay. To sit in Mo's chair, however, that was a major taco. Mornings Lenny woke up upset over driving into work at a label where he foresaw clashes. Morris, his boss-to-be, was already pushing for faster roster cuts than agreed to by Lenny—who still felt bad over earlier cutting Bonnie Raitt and Van Morrison from the label. Pressure was also applied to trim Warner Bros. Records' staff.

Lenny took a call from Morgado, one designed to pep him up, *keep* him in the Number One chair. Later, when Doug learned about this call of encouragement, he pondered. Why was Bob Morgado making this call? Weren't the U.S. labels *his,* not Morgado's? Doug believed that the U.S. *was* his to run. It's what his title and contract said.

To Lenny, Corporate loomed large. As he later put it, Lenny, like Mo, had found WBR's East Coast business lords "unbelievably arrogant." It felt like a fleet of bulldozers was revving up out there, ready to rumble through

Burbank. The knot in his stomach changed his mind. In the studio, Lenny knew, when something doesn't feel right, "you either fix it or get rid of it."

Lenny Waronker, on October 24, after two months as the Chairman Presumptive to Warner Bros. Records, rejected Time Warner's offer of Ostin's job. He simply said that he, like Mo, would leave WBR when his contract expired.

Within "the industry," as record people now called themselves, this mayhem, this slaughter felt like some Sega shoot-em-up. After all those good years, when violent change had at most meant a Steinway getting shoved out a penthouse window, we searched for reasons. This felt like clan warfare, like the king's off in somewhere like Croatia, out of touch, and the barons are having at each other.

It seemed as if each morning's *Times* carried another astonishment. People you knew asked a yearlong series of questions without answers. Why position Doug over Mo? Why not Mo over all the United States? Now Krasnow's gone, too? Sylvia who? Why Danny for Atlantic? What's happened to Ahmet? Mo quitting? Lenny for sure? Seymour moving? Morgado did what? And, finally, where *is* this Levin guy?

Significant Releases

1994

Atlantic: Tori Amos (*Under the Pink*) • Brandy ("I Wanna Be Down" and "Baby") • Carreras, Domingo, and Pavarotti (*The Three Tenors*) • Collective Soul (*Hints Allegations and Things Left Unsaid*) • Hootie and the Blowfish (*Cracked Rear View,* including "Hold My Hand," "Let Her Cry," and "Only Wanna Be with You") • Tracy Lawrence (*I See It Now*) • John Michael Montgomery (*Kickin' It Up*) • Jimmy Page & Robert Plant (*Unledded: No Quarter*) • Stone Temple Pilots (*Purple*)
East-West: Dream Theater (*Awake*) • Gerald Levert (*Groove On*) • Pantera (*Far Beyond Driven*)
Blitzz: All-4-One ("I Swear" and "So Much in Love")
Interscope: Blackstreet ("Before I Let You Go") • Thug Life (*Volume One*) • *The Crow* soundtrack
DeathRow: Above the Rim soundtrack • *Murder Was the Case* soundtrack
Nothing/TVT: Nine Inch Nails (*The Downward Spiral*) • *Natural Born Killers* soundtrack
Matador: Liz Phair (*Whip-Smart*)
Select: The Jerky Boys (*The Jerky Boys 2*)

Elektra: Anita Baker (*Rhythm of Love*) • Natalie Cole (*Holly & Ivy*) • Mötley Crüe • Phish (*Hoist*) • Keith Sweat (*Get Up on It*)

Warner Bros.: Elvis Costello (*Brutal Youth*) • Jeff Foxworthy (*You Might Be a Redneck If . . .*) • Faith Hill (*Take Me As I Am*) • Little Texas (*Kick a Little*) • Tom Petty (*Wildflowers,* including "You Don't Know How It Feels") • Prince (*Come* and *The Black Album*) • R.E.M. (*Monster*) • Travis Tritt (*Ten Feet Tall and Bulletproof*)

Reprise: Green Day (*Dookie,* including "When I Come Around") • Joni Mitchell (*Turbulent Indigo*) • Neil Young and Crazy Horse (*Sleeps With Angels*)

American: The Black Crowes (*Amorica*) • Johnny Cash (*American Recordings*) • Danzig (*Danzig 4*)

Rhyme Cartel: Sir Mix-a-Lot (*Chief Boot Knocka*) • Slayer (*Divine Intervention*)

Duck: Eric Clapton (*From the Cradle*)

Giant: Hammer (*The Funky Headhunter*) • Big Head Todd & the Monsters (*Strategem*)

Maverick: Madonna (*Bedtime Stories*)

Mute: Erasure (*I Say I Say I Say*)

32

INTERSCOPE Records started business with Atlantic's buy for $15 million of 25 percent ownership in the label. The label tottered at its start in 1989 (acts like Marky Mark), but by 1994 had become a rampage of pop hits. Looking black (from its Death Row gangsta-rap releases) and evil (from Nothing Records' industrial and ghoul rock by Nine Inch Nails and Marilyn Manson), Interscope appealed to the Nineties rebel teens.

Doug Morris had bet on Jimmy Iovine. It was as if Interscope's music head, Iovine, knew something others knew not. Iovine made astonishing alliances, signing musicians beyond what most labels thought of as any good. It was as if Iovine had majored in Adult Music Rejection. Teens—70 percent of them white—ate up Interscope's albums. Death Row's rap riveted their attention like summer monster movies. The Interscope-distributed label, formed in 1992 by Suge (pronounced "Shoog") Knight and Andre ("Dr. Dre") Young, specialized in scary-looking black acts. Fans expected gangsta rap to be performed by real gangsters; Interscope's acts assumed the role. They acted tough, huge, and tattooed, with hands the size of hubcaps, on which they wore gold rings fat as lemons.

Interscope releases were what pop music had been for fifty years: music that was much louder, shocking, parentally revolting, offensive to solid citizens, and a gold mine. Iovine showed his ears. One level lower were black-music expert John McClain (who made the label's deal with Death Row)[143] and the label's eventual president, Tom Whalley.[144]

Ted, Jimmy, John, and Tom made Midas look like some piker. Iovine

---

[143]When he left Interscope, McClain went to A&M Records to vitalize that label's "urban" division. A&M was then sold to MCA/Universal. As, later, was Interscope. Parking places presumably rejoined.

[144]In the early 1980s, Whalley had given up teaching to join Warner Bros. Records in its mailroom. He worked his way up to talent scout in WBR's A&R department. By the mid-1980s, however, he'd left for Capitol, running its "talent" division, signing, among others, Bonnie Raitt with more to come.

pushed the virtue of small: "The concept of a big record company is totally antiquated," he told acts. "They're dinosaurs. I break two artists in a year, and so does a company with five hundred million dollars in billings. So if you're a new artist, where are you going to go? Where you know you're not going to get lost."

Whatever Interscope touched, it seemed to turn many times platinum. Acts like 2Pac Shakur and 4 Non Blondes got followed by more and rowdier. Acts like the provocative Snoop Doggy Dogg and Dr. Dre had sold $350 million worth of albums for Atlantic. To many, including members of Time Warner's Board, what these acts rapped and stood for offended them deeply.

Up to now, Time Warner's defense to things like that had been three words: Freedom of Speech. By now, however, the patience of the upper floors at Time Warner was thinning.

Five years after its birth, in 1994, Interscope's contract called for other record companies to compete against Atlantic in buying a second 25 percent, with Atlantic able to match the top bid. Morris, not wanting Interscope to walk over to PolyGram or Sony, told Interscope to begin getting its bids. Up on the thirtieth, he told Morgado and Jerry Gold how important Interscope was, how talented an A&R head Jimmy Iovine was. But the price had become high enough to make Morris nervous. He thought the bidding for the next 25 percent of Interscope might begin around $300 million. A bit like a favorite son wheedling more allowance out of Dad, he told Morgado, "If we want to keep Interscope, we've got to give them more money. But we can't bear it alone. We're talking all the risk."

The bids coming back were huge. Doug got nervous about matching them, saying "Yeah, maybe we should *sell* it." Gold looked at Doug and said, "Wait a second, you just finished explaining that [Jimmy] was the greatest A&R executive that came down the pike except for maybe Mo himself, and you don't want to step up to the investment?" Privately, Morgado worried about Doug's ability to captain all of the U.S. decisions.

Without consulting Morris, Morgado moved in. He did not agree to let Interscope solicit price-setting bids and looked into sending cease-and-desist notices to competing record-company executives, demanding they stop approaching Interscope with buyout offers. When Morgado made his move, Morris wondered what had hit him.

A couple of days after Lenny's "not me" call, Morgado spoke calmly to Wall Street analysts. He recognized the headlines about personnel firings by saying, "Change, particularly when it involves an element of surprise, can be unsettling."

The session held little more drama, the analysts caring little about moralities.

For his profits, Morgado accepted Wall Street's congratulations for the big growth in International, now accounting for 57 percent of the Music Group's billing. It was a helluva morning, with WEA up over 20 percent of the U.S. market share, and new acts breaking.

When Morris and his intimates read Morgado's quotes in the papers the next morning, they went apeshit. Look at those charts!: Snoop Doggy Dogg, R.E.M., Green Day, Eric Clapton dominating the *Billboard* Top Ten. This was *our* work, it was our American labels' work, not Bob's, but Morgado was grabbing all the credit.

Having lunch with the Warner U.S. Group that day, Dave Mount saw Morris's CFO, Mel Lewinter, carrying the *Daily News* with its picture of Morgado, talking about the Warner Music Group's worldwide performance. "Mel, Danny, and Doug were going crazy over it," Mount saw. "They were nuts. I mean, this article was not about the U.S., this was about the *whole* thing. But they were seeing Morgado taking credit. Danny saying, 'You see, they treat you like shit!' Doug needed to be patted on the back a lot."

Upon Morris's demand, Jerry Levin met with him and Morgado that afternoon at four to restore order and better define Morris's turf. Doug yelled about interference: how about Morgado's pep call to Lenny, and how about the Wall Street analysts' slight. Morris had been head of U.S. music for three months. He had not signed his contract. Levin listened for five minutes, then left, saying, "You guys'll just have to figure this out, or I'll have to step in and settle it myself."

Another shouting match followed, one described to me by a bystander as Doug acting the absolute animal, losing control even if he knew he shouldn't, screaming at the top of his lungs, going nuts, turning purple, orange. Workers three hundred yards away heard about it, vividly. Morgado, just as strong but three notches less loud, refused to be pushed out of the action. In frustration, Morris said, "Maybe I should go back to running Atlantic." Doug felt cheated, and his righteous staff fed into his rages.

Morgado used his rank and kept hands on. Finding someone to replace Waronker was up next. Morgado suggested Rob Dickins, since 1971 head of Warner Music in London, a good record man but (in his own words) a tough lunch. Over dinner, however, I'd always found Dickins more relaxed. At Mirabelle's, a fading but tony English restaurant, I'd once marveled at his ability to hang a spoon from his nose tip.

Morris, never a Dickins doter, asked Rob to fly in from his spot as chairman of Warner Music–UK. In New York, the wiry, engaging, and in-your-face young Englishman said yes, he was interested in the Burbank job. In talking it through, Morris warned him: Warner Bros. Records was not a place where Dickins's reputedly arrogant and imperious style would work beneficially.

Morris went on to explain *his* vision of the job to Dickins. "When he talked about the job," Rob recalled, "he didn't make it terribly attractive. Doug wanted to run Warner Bros., and he wanted me to be a label manager. I said in my *past* experience, Warners didn't run like that. Doug wanted joint appointments of any key executives, with me reporting to him every single day. I thought, 'That's Atlantification, isn't it?' "

Time Warner's *Entertainment Weekly* magazine was preparing its 1994 list of "The Power 101" in show business. On October 19, the day before the issue was to go to press, its editors had the Morgado-Morris team appearing together, at Number Nineteen. (Lenny Waronker was fifty-ninth.) Morgado's press handler, Margaret Wade, saw Morgado and Morris together in one box, picked up her phone, and took it upon herself to chastise the magazine, calling the teaming (at least) "inappropriate." Phone calls flurried at the editors, who finally just said "Screw it" and, around midnight, deleted anything about Morris. The new draft of their "Power 101" page, with Morgado doing a solo, got faxed over to Doug, who saw his deletion and was heard to shout, "What is *this?!*" Danny Goldberg, breathless, exclaimed "What an embarrassment!" When Morris's office called *Entertainment Weekly* to ask why, the magazine just said, "Call Morgado's office." On the phone, Doug had a screaming argument with Wade. Too late.

Morris chafed even more. He believed that Wade's moves were all at Morgado's command (which they were not). She told Doug, "In the future, oral press needs to be approved by Corporate."

"I'll speak with whoever the hell I want to," Doug replied.

Doug, heady, his self-esteem pumped up by his staff, like some eight-story-high figure floating down toward Macy's on Thanksgiving Day, felt he deserved his title's authority, no ropes attached. He obsessed. "Every day," Val Azzoli recalled with a full sigh, "every lunch."

Morris had moved on, beyond accepting Morgado's ideas (as he'd done at Atlantic) to defying his boss's input in his new job. Behind this change, four people I talked with described Goldberg as Doug's Iago, a man who only simulated true contact with people, the man behind, nudging him, pointing out to Doug, "You have a title, but not power."

Morgado's group saw Morris's group acting upstarty, like Rhode Island developing its own foreign policy. At a Waldorf black-tie dinner arranged by the law firm Paul Weiss, the Morris and Morgado groups sat at tables side by side. The Morris group refused to shake hands with the Morgado group. Rebuffed, the Morgado group found one common spirit, namely, "Well, fuck Doug Morris." They believed that Doug was completely inflated with his new fame, and they speculated about his need for a larger penis. They saw Danny as "Super Machiavelli." One table member told me how the Morris squad lived: "Every day, when these guys get up, they look in the mirror and ask themselves, 'How are we going to get Morgado today?' " Both tables now had their own press reps working their cell phones. The Morris-vs.-Morgado battle got waged in magazines and newspapers. Doug Morris's music group felt it was getting treated like ice cubes in men's urinals.

On October 26, Morgado called Doug at home to say he accepted Morris's offer to go back to running Atlantic. No more title; no more head of Warner Music–U.S.

In the middle of the night in London, Rob Dickins answered his phone. It was Morgado, telling him he that he and Jerry Levin had met, and the Warner Bros. Records job was his. Dickins was to fly in immediately.

Before midnight, Morgado again phoned Morris, telling him that he'd just chosen Dickins to replace Lenny atop Warner Bros. Records. At midnight, Doug started calling his Atlantic bunch into a next-morning group meeting at the home of Atlantic's A∗Vision's head, Stuart Hersch, overlooking Central Park from the west. Doug wanted a once-and-for-all united stand. Or else.

After he got the call to meet next morning, Azzoli told his wife, "Get ready. This could be my last day."

The next morning, before heading for Heathrow, Dickins told friends he'd got it. He rode the Concorde to Manhattan, seated next to Steve Stewart, manager of the Stone Temple Pilots. In good spirits, Rob and Steve talked about real estate near Burbank. Dickins checked into the Carlyle Hotel. There, he waited for Morgado to phone, awaited the contract, ready for the press conference.

Two dozen blocks downtown and across chilly Central Park, the Atlantic-Elektra bunch met in secret to declare war. Convened were Danny Goldberg, Ahmet Ertegun, Mel Lewinter, Val Azzoli, Ina Lea Maibach (attorney and exec VP of Atlantic), Jason Flom (Atlantic senior VP of A&R), Tony O'Brien (Atlantic's new CFO), and Sylvia Rhone. Their language was born out of outrage: "Who *is* this *geek* from *politics* who's trying to ruin our business!" They agreed on the threat from Morgado, determined their U.S. division would survive. They talked about a mass march on management. (It would be an awkward march, climbing straight up, since management worked 260 feet of stairs above Atlantic's offices.) Each in that apartment paced, all cell phones firing. The meeting's agenda came down to "what we'll do if Doug gets fired." A mass exodus was proposed.

Such a walkout was the kind of spectacle that Jerry Levin certainly did not need. Ahmet tried to make peace in a complex situation. He called Mo, telling him what was going on that morning, the uniting of record guys against this suit, Morgado, and wanting Mo's support, telling him, "You can have it back, Mo, just like it was before." Doug called Lenny with the same message: "Come back, and we'll ride our horses back to victory."

Ostin chose not to think all that over again. He had decided, he told Ahmet, and he was out. He'd heard all the options and just said no.

Morris had not come to that powwow. That morning, he'd been called to meet with Bob Morgado. In Morgado's office, Morris calmly outlined a plan for better working conditions between the two. Actually, it turned into a nearly sane hour. Doug talked through his grievance list, which started with *real* autonomy, his insistence on working with U.S. artists and labels without shots coming across his bow from the frigate *Morgado*. He complained about Morgado's call to Dickins. Bob listened, thanked, and gave no promise. Rob Dickins had arrived in New York, Bob revealed, ready to be crowned head of Warner Bros. Records. At the meeting, Morgado reviewed *his* latest thinking, which was that Morris should return to Atlantic, to run that. And there it ended.

Morris reached his comrades' gathering about eleven and told them, "Not good. It went awful." He expected the Dickins's appointment to be announced momentarily. Azzoli, like the others, was surprised. They knew Doug as a guy who could always talk his way out of anything. The group decided to go into the office, to let dust settle. Dickins continued to sit. Morris and Azzoli had lunch, then Azzoli called his wife to tell her, "It's not looking good." Doug called Jerry Levin, asking him to meet at Morgado's at two. Ertegun, wanting less than total mayhem, called Morgado, telling of his concern. Levin once again went to visit Morgado. Bob and Jerry, neither a man with a record or CD or cassette player in his office, talked the same language. Jerry asked about this rumor of the impending walkout.

Believing that Morris was behaving more touchily than a Tuscan tenor, Morgado told Levin his view: Morris was a runaway executive. Levin nodded, commiserating about how his own hands were full with his Time Warner board, worrying over corporate image. The press was all over Warner's Record division, headlining how R.E.M. and Neil Young were both ready to leave the label. Needing calm, Jerry suggested delay. He told Bob, "Look, you've got the gun. You've got the bullets. You're the one who can call the moment. Just don't pull the trigger now. Not now."

Given that assurance, as Levin moved out his door, Morgado called Doug, reconstituting the meeting. Doug, along with Ahmet, showed up to learn the future. For the next three hours, Morgado stunned them. He gave in to nearly every item on Morris's list. Previously vague boundaries got hammered into razor-sharp walls. Although he still reported to Morgado, Morris would rule the North American companies. Agreed. Morris told Morgado that Dickins would *not* get the Warner job; rather, Danny Goldberg would. Agreed. Morris wanted a new title: chairman and CEO of Warner Music–U.S. Agreed. It was reminiscent of those years that Morgado himself had been patient, had waited for his own full job title to show up in the Annual Report list. The three hours ended with champagne in tall, thin, truly crystal glasses: Morgado, Morris, Goldberg, Lewinter, Rhone, and— stopping by for the photo op—Levin.

At five-thirty, Morris rode the elevator back down to Atlantic's offices. "How'd it go?" he was asked. "Great!" answered Morris. He outlined the new setup, starring Doug's Atlantic troops, now heading all three labels. The list:

- Doug Morris—Chairman/CEO of the Warner Music Group–U.S.
- Val Azzoli—President of Atlantic
- Danny Goldberg—Chairman of Warner Bros. Records.
- Sylvia Rhone—Chairman of Elektra/East-West

America was totally Morris, W + E + A. Amazement. Chins dropped. Azzoli headed home to report to his wife: "The same day I almost get fired, I end up the president of Atlantic Records." But riding home, Azzoli pieced it out, how Morgado was a corporate guy, a corporate fighter who didn't get there by marrying the chairman's daughter . . . same could be said of Doug . . . so you have two powerful guys that don't forget . . . and that's a very uncomfortable situation."

At nine that evening, Dickins, still sitting in his room at the Carlyle, got a call from Morgado's office. He learned that Morris had vetoed his appointment. Hanging up, Dickins went from fear to sorrow to fury to London.

Morris took control, though Morgado was, technically, still the boss, still had Morris reporting to him. It was not a solution. It was, however, what Levin needed: pacification. Like people clobbered on the head by construction cranes, Doug's angry rebels suddenly quieted down. It was the day after. Morris told the press, "What I really want to do is try and soothe these waters." He claimed the whole thing was "overblown."

Mel Lewinter, Doug's finance man, was named president of Warner Music–U.S. More photos to pose for. As one executive mentioned, "Those smiles, those hugs, the making good, all covered just one inning in a nightmare ballgame. Morgado," he said, "is powerful and will not soon forget. He has been defanged but not declawed."

On October 31, Jerry Levin appointed his own Number Two: Richard Parsons, whom Morgado described as "a friend of twenty-two years." Reports that Morgado was going to leave the company were, Bob said, "absurd beyond belief."

The same day, Danny Goldberg's appointment to head Warner Bros. Records was announced. As CEO and chairman of WBR, he flew quickly to Burbank to calm the shaken, to soothe the nerve damaged. With Waronker and Ostin still running WBR till the end of the year, Goldberg stayed out of the way while still meeting the executives he wanted for *his* management team, to make them offers, getting them to sign contracts. Through November and December, Goldberg lived in a hotel, worked out of a temporary office, and met exec after exec until his own day of management—January 1, 1995—became official. No executive talent was lost, with Goldberg signing WBR's leading execs to whopper (million-plus-per-year) contracts.[145] Danny hoped to bring in, as his Number Two, as his president, Virgin Records' Phil Quartararo, even though Phil still had a long-term contact.

The feeling among Warner acts was less "whoopee" than the press spin indicated. One artist's manager, stunned at Dickins' treatment, said, "In terms of corporate guff, this particular situation has produced more than I can ever remember. It's quite evident that the people in senior management don't know what they're doing, and they don't care about their artists." The British music press speculated that Dickins might leave Warner to start up a label for the new SKG (Spielberg-Katzenberg-Geffen) venture. By now, Mo told me, he and Lenny were also thinking about heading toward SKG, with Mo insisting that his impending contract with SKG stated that he was reporting to the SKG board, not to David Geffen directly. The talks, clearly, had advanced to that stage.

The *Los Angeles Times* that Thanksgiving ran a list of show-business "Reasons to Be Thankful." It included a paragraph headed "Be Thankful That You're Not Robert Morgado":

> Here's one of the industry's great ironies. Morgado spent much of his career as Warner Music Group chief trying to gain control over Warner Records, the industry gem that was independently managed by Mo Ostin. But Morgado's Machiavellian moves ultimately cost him dearly. The realignment at Warner set off an executive revolt, which resulted in Doug Morris' becoming domestic music czar. Morgado was left with international.

Morgado, too, moved ahead, keynoting a music-video conference in November, referring to the upheaval as "a synergy-driven stunt to increase the circulation of *Time* magazine." He joked, admitting that the tumult at Warner made "Bosnia look like Shangri-la."

On December 5, 1994, Doug Morris signed his contact as chairman and CEO of Warner Music–U.S., a contract to last until December 31, 1999.

Mo Ostin, preparing to leave his lifelong swivel chair, ruminated, "In this business, the company should never underestimate the power of its artists. But look, at Warners we've seen Frank Sinatra retire. We've seen Jimi Hendrix die. We've seen the Who break up and James Taylor leave the label.

---

[145] I think it only honorable to point out that I once made more money per week than Mo Ostin. It was around 1960, when I made $525 a month, but Mo made only $100 a week. I also believe I may have peaked too early.

And the company continues to grow and prosper. So what is the common thread? It's management. And while artists are what a music company is made up of, management has some real value—and it should never be underestimated."

WBR's employees gathered that December 11 at Chasen's restaurant. The party was dedicated not to Santa but to Ostin and his years at WBR. More liquor per capita was drunk that evening than in any party in the history of the label. Bar none.

The night turned into what seemed like a compulsive-huggers reunion, peopled by a tribe—management—convinced it had followed the right instincts, seen an era closing, people wanting one last hug before the walls crashed down. Russ Thyret spoke emotionally from the podium, blaming "the flu" for his less-than-100-percent-coherent speech. He recalled a plane ride earlier that year from the Nashville WEA sales meeting into a private airport and the feeling of those five or six men after they walked down the ramp, standing that night on the airstrip: that all their careers were heading for oblivion. That night, Thyret was able to tell Ostin, "Mo, I love you. And I owe you my life."

Lenny Waronker arranged for ladies to line up before the podium, holding up letter cards reading M-O-O-S-T-I-N. Lenny decided what each of the seven letters stood for, like "O Number Two" stood for "Oh, shit, I can't believe he's really leaving."

Ostin spoke last. He thought back over his memories. Like losing out on signing the Buffalo Springfield, followed by his elation at signing Neil Young. Sitting with Marilyn Monroe and Liz Taylor for *Sinatra at the Sands*. Staying up till four-thirty in the morning persuading (and in the end failing to convince) James Taylor to stay at WBR. Chasing Sex Pistols' manager Malcolm McLaren into a sex and bondage shop. The company plane and front-row Laker tickets, no longer his.

Ostin told, finally, of his father, never a successful man, at age seventy-five, heading back with his son to visit Brooklyn. The father and son traveled Ostin style that time: the WCI jet, backstage to meet Randy Newman and Ry Cooder, the first-class suite at the Carlyle, best reached by limo. Ostin recalled how his father, after all this deluxeness, finally turned to his son to ask, "Morris, what is it exactly that you do?"

And how Mo had answered, "Pop, I have the best job in the world."

Surveying the fallen of major record-business colleagues—Mo Ostin, Lenny Waronker, Henry Droz, Bob Krasnow, Nesuhi Ertegun, Chuck Kaye, and others—the head of rival empire Capitol/EMI, Charles Koppelman, just shook his head. "They broke up the Yankees."

33

Bob Morgado, even with his mouth bound by duct tape, still enraged the Doug Morris camp. They had achieved their victory, which they defined as music people running the Music division (in America, at least). Still, every path Morgado walked, they probed for land mines. Call it paranoia or call it caution, Morris's warriors still worked together, still plotted against suit-ism together. They felt like Colonials under George III.

Among the Morris clan's key members were Goldberg, a longtime fighter for civil liberties and thus maybe the most righteous of them all; financial head Lewinter; video head Stuart Hersch; legal exec Ina Maibach; and their "tell our side to the press" doctor, publicist Ken Sunshine. It was a well tailored, righteous group.

Distribution head Dave Mount saw Doug's fever build: "Instead of people saying to Doug, 'Hey, Morgado just did this deal *for* Warner Music–U.S. It's real great. You two have to work together' . . . someone would say, 'You're smarter than Morgado.' And I guess, in the back of Doug's mind, instead of doing the job for a year or so and being successful at it, he remembered the past too well."

Sunshine (and, to some degree, Goldberg) overdid telling reporters inside stuff, slanting their side. Articles describing the advance of Warner Music–U.S. against Corporate's suits got printed, with Morris marching through Corporate with the same immodesty that had been pioneered by Krasnow, Geffen, and Napoleon.

In the first months of 1995, Morgado kept quiet. He took a public trouncing, especially in magazines. *Vanity Fair* created the first of two major stories that year covering the Music Group's changes, calling it "the juiciest, most emotional entertainment business story the media had fought over in years." Looking at Morgado, the magazine characterized him as an "executive whose clumsy execution of Machiavellian principles suggests that he may have read only the Cliff's Notes to *The Prince*."

After New Year's Day, 1996, the day after the Bowls, Danny Goldberg took over at Warner Bros. Records for real. He planned to run the Burbank label from Manhattan. He later explained to me that the Goldbergs had moved enough, especially the year before, from California to Manhattan to run Atlantic. "I'd just uprooted my wife [Rosemary Carroll], who had her own law practice out of California, to New York. I'd just found a New York school for my kid . . ."

As Goldberg assumed the chairmanship, an array of its executives was spread before him. The list of vice presidents was a stunner. WBR had sixty-eight VPs (or higher). Put sixty-eight VPs into one weekly meeting, that meeting got to be called "Korea," it went on so long.[146] Cut the VP list or not? Quickly, Goldberg eliminated two from the roster. Sixty-six.

Goldberg created a pair of vice chairmen to run things in Burbank: Russ Thyret and business-affairs head Dave Altschul. He emphasized that the company would be, once again, two labels: Warner Bros. Records, led by Steve Baker, plus Reprise, led by Sire's general manager, Howie Klein. From the outside, people got confused by the multileveled executive wedding cake and said sass like, "Now they've got *five* guys doing Mo's job."

Goldberg, having hitched golden tethers to his chosen company leaders, knew that his next threat might be an exodus of Mo-loving artists. To control roster damage, artists were re-signed with generosity. Neil Young's manager, Elliott Roberts, negotiated a five-album deal worth $25 million, including a signing bonus of $5 million and a per-album guarantee of twice the $2 to $3 million that Neil had been willing to accept before Mo left.

Burbank did not crumble. SoundScan reports were solid: Green Day was Top Ten, and WBR had R.E.M., Tom Petty, Madonna, and Van Halen, all making *kaching*.

With stability in view, on January 24 Goldberg and Morris officially convened the whole WBR crew on the open patio of the building. After being introduced by Thyret, Morris told the hundreds, "It's very hard for me to believe that Melvin Lewinter and myself represent the dreaded Corporate. But believe me, our goal is one of support, certainly not interference. With that, I wish you the best year ever. Thank you very much."

While Doug was speaking, Danny covertly shook up a new Coke can. Taking the microphone, he pulled the tab and got a geyser of foam. It was a "regular guy" move. Goldberg thanked Thyret, thanked head of human relations/company "mom" Jean Lumley, thanked Doug Morris and Mel Lewinter. He apologized for the people he did not mention and said, "No symbolism to that. No shoe is going to drop."

---

[146]I had once planned to list all sixty-eight in this footnote, but my publisher explained how many trees it would cost to print them all. If, however, you would like the full list, e-mail me at exploding@cornyn.com

Saying he felt like the Forrest Gump of the record business, Goldberg discussed all the WBR rumors about mass firings and other insensitivities, how most stuff he'd heard was not true. He went on about how he was, like they, all music, how he was no "high-tech guy," how he was afraid even to log on to AOL.

Now unmentioned around Warner Bros. Records was Lenny Waronker, president emeritus. He worked on projects out of sight, like the soundtrack to Clint Eastwood's *Bridges of Madison County*, Randy Newman's *Faust*, and the Brian Wilson–Van Dyke Parks collaboration, *Orange Crate Art*. The decisions Lenny currently made were personal.

As total chairman of Time Warner, Jerry Levin enjoyed, I presume, his reputation as a strategist for the company's future. Fair enough, except when the chairman was so focused upon the future—issues like cable wiring that leads to as many homes as do phone lines—that he had too little time for the company's present. Out in the field, or even on floors lower than Jerry's, that got to be the perception about him. His executives less and less frequently came to him with their problems. He was a figure up in his own strategy-intent world, with less charisma than his title would bear.

Still, Jerry was chairman and thus on the A List for any good fete. That spring, the Music Group's Grammy afterparty took place at an old department store on Los Angeles's equally retro Wilshire Boulevard. There, Goldberg refused to have his picture taken with Levin, country artist Faith Hill, and Morgado because, he told the group, "I won't have my picture taken with Morgado. It's out of respect for Mo." That effrontery was deliberate. Levin was within earshot. A mustache twitched. A moment to remember.

At a time when Warner Bros. Records was having its best year, Morgado was being publicly tagged—by the industry press and by most people in records—for the loss of Ostin. Morris complained, again publicly, that Morgado's record clubs were stealing sales from American retailers, costing Doug's labels millions in lost sales, while Morgado, who oversaw the Music Group's 50 percent of Columbia House, got the credit. (Hardly the case; music clubs were fast losing ground.)

Levin had been absorbed with a full buy out of Ted Turner's cable business, another huge step up, adding Turner's cable to Warner's cable and Time's HBO, led by Michael Fuchs. Adding Turner Cable would fill Jerry's world with three companies—Time, Warner, and Turner—with the accompanying CEO congestion.

Wall Street remained skeptical. "I think the chairman is in very tenuous shape," wrote some VP at State Street Research. "His choice of people, ability to run partnerships and technological vision have been lacking." Never tested as a leader of men, only as a leader of ideas, Jerry's engine seemed to sputter. He'd left the handling of their divisions to others—like Daly and Semel at the Studio; Fuchs at HBO; Morgado at Music.

Huge stockholders[147] swore like bears because Time Warner's stock had for six years, despite two bull markets, sat at relatively the same value. Through it all, Jerry focused on his strategy, which came down to getting two-way cable highways built into America's living rooms. He was like a records man fixing a distribution system, not worrying about making hits. Jerry fixated privately, inscrutably, taking risks, confident, surviving in the jungle, moving aloofly over divisional execs' power fights—guys like Fuchs, Morgado, Ostin, Morris, then multiply those guys by four or five other divisions (Print, Cable, Movies, Publishing). Jerry stood above, making it tough to get a nod from him.

But a disturbing corporate buzz had begun: that Morgado might be fumbling, unpardonably, having lost key talent like Mo, Lenny, Krasnow, and those other guys. Levin, who had endorsed each and all of Morgado's moves, got more curious about the mess in the press. Turning from utter trust, he began to speculate. Too much static scratched in Levin's ears. He checked around, listening more to others beyond Morgado, like Morris, like Goldberg, who still complained that Bob's actions jeopardized Warner Music. Jerry remembered the letters and calls from Ostin's supporters from the year before. He remembered Geffen's line in Sun Valley: "You're making a terrible mistake."

At Levin's request, Ostin met with him at Time Warner's Acapulco hacienda. From six to nine that evening, Jerry told Mo he was prepared to do almost anything to get Mo to come back, and he listed perquisites that Time Warner executives got. Mo just answered that he'd been through all this before and still had his Morgado problem. Jerry said he'd "get to that," then went on talking about other things, making Mo feel like an insider, revealing to Mo that Morgado was going to be fired even before Morgado knew it. Jerry said his staff had looked at company after company, executives at every major record company, and had ended up with Mo atop the list. Mo asked who'd be replacing Morgado, heard the name Michael Fuchs, whom he knew only casually. Mo didn't say it, but to himself, he couldn't see the logic of another outsider like Fuchs coming in. Jerry asked Mo to keep all of this "under his hat." Mo flew home, actually feeling positive.

In early May, Levin fired Morgado over lunch, basing his decision upon constant complaints from Morris and other Record Group executives about Morgado's continued interference with the U.S. Music Group operations.

---

[147]Major stockholders included Seagram/MCA's Edgar Bronfman, Jr., owning 14.9 percent, and yearning to be bigger in the record business. Others of size were Gordon Crawford of Capital Research Company (9 percent); and even ex-knight, Herb Siegel. A restive bunch.

Levin, who'd earlier fired other Warner insiders—men like Wasserman, Payson, and Aboodi—told Morgado that "of all the people that served me at your level, you are the one I trusted and who had the best long-range strategic vision." Morgado was spared having to pick up the lunch check. He took the news like a political pro. His life was not tied to any one office, or even to Time Warner. Whenever I later asked Bob anything about losing his job, he showed no hint of humiliation or devastation. He understood why Jerry had done him in. This was a high-stakes game. Where once execs like Morgado had scattered dimes on the roulette table, now the table was much larger, and on it, Morgado and the rest found themselves to *be* dimes as well.

Having informed Morgado he'd been terminated, Levin next took the elevator down to the third floor to tell Doug he no longer had his old boss, Bob. It would instead be new boss Michael Fuchs. Levin also told Morris "not to worry. Someday you'll be CEO." Morris's first reaction was disbelief. Despite all the yelling, he'd liked and respected Morgado. He even had lunch with Bob the next day, and Doug told him that, if he could go back eighteen months, he might not have done what he did.

To observers, it was like tacking a happy ending onto *King Lear.* Bob knew how politicians can yell and scream, but once the vote's in, they join together, hold each other's hand aloft, for the greater cause.

As Morgado and Morris rose from the lunch table, they shook hands and could hardly believe it was over.

It was not.

Firing Morgado had not happened in a few flippant minutes. Two weeks before lunch with Morgado, Levin had told colleagues and HBO chairman Michael Fuchs, a twenty-year Time Inc. vet that he, Fuchs, would be overseeing the Music Group, too—double chairmanships. The added responsibilities, even if they were not fully hands-on, gratified Fuchs, who'd been feeling stale after two decades at HBO. Levin also told his board that Morgado would be leaving because he'd alienated many of the company's music executives. The board seemed relieved; they, too, had read those articles.

Or, as Marty Payson, now retired, later nailed it for me, "Time Warner is like studying the Kremlin." Marty was referring to another battleground, one uphill from the Record Group's, but filling just as fast with fallen comrades. In Corporate, gone were Ross, Payson, Wasserman, Aboodi, Morgado—men who'd built WCI. The survivors on the field were men of use, like Fuchs, Joe Collins in Cable, Daly and Semel in Pictures. Time Warner clearly was indifferent to tenure.

Morgado's contractual parachute cost Time Warner a stunning $60 million. By my rough estimate, that amount equaled the cost for twelve hundred man-years worked by people paid normal amounts. Bob's colleagues, however, told me he was not driven to riches.[148] Still, $60 million may have had a calming effect.

Bob also had his facts to console himself: He'd come into the Music Group when its revenues were under $1 billion, and five years later, he left when they were up close to $4 billion.[149] Some people might say "well done." Few chose to speak such words; instead, the memory stuck of Yankees he'd broken up.

Morgado gave or was asked for few interviews, but summed up his view this way: "I had a responsibility to a public company. I think some of the people on the music side thought they only had a responsibility to themselves." One observer close to him told me, "Bob Morgado made two mistakes: He trusted the wrong guy, and he underestimated Mo and people's loyalty to Mo." Maybe, I wisely decided. After all, Bob was not a career music guy. To him, this was only like losing some election: You get on with your life. Anyway, Morgado never could understand why people would want to work until they're seventy years old.

Michael Fuchs's experience as a company builder was strong but had little to do with music. Years before, Fuchs had started out as an entertainment lawyer; he'd once represented Carly Simon. He then worked at the William Morris Agency. But for the past two decades, he had been a Time, Inc.–er, joining its pay-satellite service, HBO, back in 1976. Within eight years, Fuchs had become HBO's chairman. He'd overseen its growth, from 600,000 subscribers in 1976 to 30 million in 1995. Most important, he was a man whose character Levin could use: Fuchs was a take-charge type who specialized, more than Morgado ever did, in a hands-on, puppet-strings approach to managing divisions.

Levin also knew that, assuming his talks to make Turner Cable + Warner Cable + HBO + Warner Bros. Studios worked, some edgy ego mixes would be involved. Fuchs in Cable had butted heads repeatedly with Bob Daly and Terry Semel in Studio. On a smaller scale, Fuchs figured HBO's comedy specials could be turned into record albums. No to that one, too. But now, adding Music under his command, that was seen by observers like the *New York Times* as catapulting Fuchs "into a position of power at Time Warner second only to Mr. Levin himself."

---

[148]Earlier at Warners, they pointed out, he had already given up the company's courtside seats for the Knicks and Rangers, a gesture in corporate humility that even Mahatma Gandhi would have high-fived.

[149]Of 1993's $3.33 billion, International was 37 percent, U.S. was 25 percent, Direct Marketing was 15 percent, Manufacturing was 12 percent, Warner/Chappell was 10 percent, and 1 percent was "other." Even in giving up the U.S. to Morris, Morgado still stirred 75 percent of the pot.

Fuchs's first agenda item was to meet with Doug Morris, to agree about what Doug's future would now hold—a graduation from overseeing the American labels to overseeing the world for Warner. "Either I must promote you or you can walk from your contract," Fuchs assured him. Fuchs didn't want to run record labels. He saw himself with a larger Corporate job, now chairman of both HBO *and* Music. "I am here to put out fires," he told Doug.

Morris's group found Fuchs embraceable as an army tank. Morris became even more than outraged over being passed over to head the Group, at having to answer to still another of these nonmusical, suit guys. Believing it should be he in the Morgado chair now, he told people, "They fired Morgado, but they dissed me." He didn't hide his feelings. In a meeting with Fuchs, the Morris clan again threatened to take all the music talent and just leave. It was not the sort of threatening that works on a Fuchs.

Fuchs's press release said he was counting on Doug Morris to help him guide the record sector. "I may be in the Cable TV Hall of Fame," he said, "but I doubt if I will ever get invited to join the Rock and Roll Hall of Fame. But with Doug Morris and his team, I believe we've got the best record executives in the world on board—and I plan to consult with them regularly and count on their advice."

Morgado called Fuchs, asking if he could help in the transition. Two days later, Fuchs and Morgado broke pasta, orange juice, and mineral water in the executive dining room.

Fuchs assured Morgado that he could handle Doug. They spoke also about Danny Goldberg, called "a smart man, but there's some connection loose there." Their opinion: Goldberg had Morris's ear, working as his *consigliere*. Over lunch, both men agreed that Morris was not to be trusted. But Fuchs wanted to keep Morris, needing to give the music guys their space while Fuchs worked on supramusical matters.

When Madonna's press executive, Liz Rosenberg, told her diva that she should now meet the new chairman, Michael Fuchs, Madonna complained, "Again? I have to meet a new chairman again?"

A week later, Fuchs sketched out a new, expanded role for Morris. It included power in the international area, a new title, and a promotion. On May 15, he put it into a letter: Morris would be promoted to president and CEO of the worldwide music division in a month, on June 25. If not, he'd be free of his contract. They began negotiations for the new contract. Morris's autonomy clause—only Morris could hire or fire an employee in the U.S. end of music—was, to Fuchs, completely unacceptable. With Fuchs, "autonomy" was an ugly word. Negotiations ground on.

Independently, Fuchs started exploring reorganization, evaluating executive talent. He hired a twenty-year Bronx friend, the ubiquitous attorney Mickey Rudin, to recommend repairs. Rudin knew the past, and he knew Ostin.

*   *   *

By 1995, Atlantic's ownership of Interscope had hit 50 percent, but the label had become to Time Warner an utter embarrassment. When Fuchs got his nod, it was like Levin might have said, just as Michael was heading out the door, "Oh, and see what you can do about this Interscope thing. The board's on my back about it." Snoop Doggy Dogg had been accused of murder. 2Pac had been convicted of sexual abuse. Dr. Dre was a drunk driver. And Interscope had been asking, "Do we have a deal or don't we have a deal?"

If rap had sold like Ravel or Ruth Brown, this issue undoubtedly would have never made it onto the main screen. Instead, Interscope's signings of various rap and gangsta-rap artists meant hundreds of millions of dollars to Atlantic, comforting manna, though hardly from heaven. Morris, especially, hoped that the political right's agitators would just fold their megaphones and shut the fuck up. The board just wanted out, even if it meant losing Interscope's gross sales, about $145 million.

To artists like Quincy Jones, who was by now a fully-fledged Autumn Chicken, this was all nonsense. Q could recall all the way back to the evils of jitterbugging. As he told it, "My whole life I've been totally surrounded with a whole pot of gumbo. We ate all of it. That's the way it is now. I just feel that rap has come out of a very organic place, a youth culture that felt disenfranchised, who said, 'The hell with it. You won't let us in, we'll start our own.' It's not so much unlike bebop, in essence. It's the newest musical black baby."

As she'd done for a couple of years, at May 1996's stockholders' meeting, stockholder (ten shares) C. DeLores Tucker of the National Political Congress of Black Women rose to her feet. She knew only contempt for rap's violent, woman-bashing lyrics. Her tirade ran longer than "In-a-gadda-da-vida," over seventeen minutes, according to those audience members in charge of timing. At the end of her speech, about a third of the packed audience broke into applause. Among the applauders: Time Warner board member Henry Luce III, son of Time, Inc.'s founder. Levin replied that he had asked his record-label chief to develop standards for labeling potentially offensive material. That meant Fuchs, who was now stuck between rap and a hard place.

When Iovine refused to let Time Warner hear the contents of its next album—Tha Dogg Pound's *Dogg Food*—Fuchs refused to release it, saying Atlantic would release Interscope albums on a "record-by-record basis." Iovine felt stymied. "What were we going to do if Time Warner refuses to put out one of our records?"

To get out of the Interscope deal, Fuchs had to contend with formidable record-business attorney Allen Grubman, someone who could outstare even him. Meeting Fuchs, Grubman spoke right up: "I represent forty-eight of the top fifty people in the record business," he said. "You don't renege on a deal. You don't do business that way. This is too small a business to act that way."

Iovine understood Fuchs's impasse: "The problem for Time Warner was they had no control over what records we put out. When you're a company as big as that, you need a certain stability. We come in there and do anything we want, and Time Warner couldn't be in business with a company like that."

For those of you who have been through as much marriage counseling as I have, you can see that Death Row, Interscope, and the Time Warner board had reached the "just give it up" point. Fuchs knew it. Interscope knew it. "If it was just about money," as Iovine said, "we could have stayed at Time Warner. If we'd agreed to change our contract with them, we could have sold the second half of our company to them for a minimum of two hundred million dollars." Instead, Interscope went out onto the free market.

For the three U.S. label heads (unfamiliarly called Val, Sylvia, and Danny), all Morris appointees, adjusting from Morgado's political style to Fuchs's military style felt tough as squeezing into old wedding clothes. Both Morgado and Fuchs were good at business, both smart. CFO Jerry Gold saw a difference: "Bob was much more the strategist and the future planner. He gave more responsibility and authority to the people who worked for him. Michael came from a world where HBO was just that: *one* big thing, way more centralized as an organization, much more of the decision making reviewed (if not made) at the center."

Fuchs believed that the entire Music Group's local authority had gone too far, so he centralized control. The first rule became this: When in doubt, check with Michael. The second rule: When not in doubt, keep Michael informed. Division heads started reporting to him, a regal rite Morgado had never enjoyed. To varying degrees (Rhone being the most resistant), Fuchs got it his way, and much of "the garbage" (to use Jerry Gold's word for elbowing) went away. Now, all people know their reporting lines. An absolute rush of cooperation followed.

"Michael comes in, says, 'I'm Michael the King,' and there is none of this bullshit," Gold recalled. "There was a lot of frustration for me, being the CFO, getting my wrist slapped. It wasn't any fun, and we were trying not to make the [WMG politics] controversy worse. Trying to get it calmed down."

Fuchs looked at his org chart—Who Reports to Whom—and realized it could work, perhaps better, without Morris on it. Morris's supporters, Fuchs was finding, were mostly his old Atlantic staff now running the American labels. There was a soft buzz about the Morris group's being in touch with Universal's Edgar Bronfman, Jr. (who owned about 15 percent of TW's stock), speculation about some possible mass move over to Universal's label, about Doug's legal exec, Ina Maibach, being wired to Bronfman.

Not really into slow growth, Fuchs ended that long list of Morgado's start-up (money-losing) ventures, including Warner Music Enterprises. Closing all those old distribution ventures cost one more bundle, but Michael saw that hoping for that kind of growth would cost two. *Ka-chunk.*

When Time Warner issued its third-quarter report, it did its best to bury the Warner Music Group's financial cleanup costs. Crawling through the prose of the earnings report, one could spot an "<85>," signifying that $85 million had been deducted as an "other charge" against the Music Group's earnings of $142 million. That $85 million was used to cover the recent costs of terminated executives, starting with Morgado but extending on through the long, long list of those killed-off new ventures recently funded by Morgado.

Fuchs flew to Positano, Italy, for Warner Music International's division meeting. No reason for you to be there, Michael had told Doug; this is International. Amid bowls of the freshest cioppino money could buy, while the seacoast hill town bared its breasts for tourism, Fuchs listened to International's 37 percent of the executive pie. "Morris?" asked the pie, "Why him?" Ramon Lopez saw little reason to move one step down the ladder and report to Morris.

On his return, Fuchs met with Levin to share his conclusions: Morris was more than divisive to the whole group; he might be fiddling with plans for a management coup that could reach even as high as Levin himself. At Warner Bros. Records, many execs (other than Danny) saw Morris as a slasher of overhead. International saw no reason to report to him. Fuchs decided, with Levin's support, to drop Morris. Maybe, they speculated, they really could get Mo back to run it all for them?

Doug's autonomy ideal for his Record people was already a fading reality. He just didn't know that yet. Like so many first-date promises, that month-earlier letter that Fuchs had given Morris now seemed to lie. Fuchs realized that delegating it all to Morris was "completely unacceptable." Five days back from Italy, Fuchs called Doug to come over to HBO. Doug rode over, ready to top off his deal to become head of it all. He was mistaken. Fuchs handed Doug a press release. Up top, it read:

DOUG MORRIS RELIEVED OF RESPONSIBILITIES AT
WARNER MUSIC GROUP

NEW YORK, June 21, 1995—Michael Fuchs, Chairman, Warner Music Group, announced today that Doug Morris has been relieved of his responsibilities as chairman and CEO of Warner Music U.S. effective immediately. "I have made a careful but difficult decision which I strongly believe is in the best interest of the growth and stability of the entire Music Group," said Fuchs . . .

"Michael's decision has my full and complete support. He is dedicated to creating an environment where artists thrive and employees do their best work. I expect him to take this business to even greater heights," said Gerald M. Levin, Chairman and CEO of Time Warner.

The Fuchs monologue continued: Morris, with four full years left on his contract, would get a buyout. Mel Lewinter, Ina Maibach, and Ken Sunshine would probably go, too.

Doug was followed back to his office ten blocks uptown by security guards, who stood outside his door, like Black Belts in Humiliation, watching as Doug packed up personal items, then walked him down to the lobby, past the newsstand, and to the revolving doors onto Fifty-second Street.

Watching it, Val Azzoli commented, "was hell. Everybody here was terrified for our jobs. You see, Doug is a great music guy, and he touched all of our lives. He was like the big papa bear who protected us from all the horrible corporate evil out there. When Doug got blown out, we were like a bunch of innocent cubs huddled around the cave, terrified, looking at each other, saying, 'Hey, *now* who's going to go out and get the food?"

The answer arrived in next morning's papers. Fuchs's story was this:

"For the past six weeks, everybody has been asking me, 'What are you going to do? You're not a music guy. You can't pick hits.' But my goal is to get this organization in shape. That's what I bring to the party and I'm damn good at it. Warner Music might be a good company now, but you come talk to me in a year. I guarantee that I'm going to make it better."

If there was a moment when music vs. money collided, it was Morris & Company's uprising. They'd bet on talent. They'd got Morgado out. Then, in ambition, in anger, they'd overbet, and they'd failed.

Azzoli, Rhone, and Goldberg now found themselves reporting to Fuchs, as did International, Warner/Chappell, and WEA. For senior staff, Fuchs turned to Morgado holdovers Jerry Gold and attorney Fred Wistow. The next day, Fuchs told them, "This is not 1970, and I was not going to live under the old rules. This is 1995. And what used to work in the old days does not work anymore. My job is to unify this awesome company, and I'm going to build an effective organization." His goal: to top WMG's current 21.1 percent market share. That sounded familiar.

Rumors buzzed like killer bees. Would they get Mo back at Warner Bros.? was the buzziest. It felt as if Goldberg was already considered a goner. In mid-July, the hot spec (this takes patience to believe) was that once again Rob Dickins was being considered to run Warner Bros. Records. The Concorde stood at the ready.

Hearing about Morris's fate, the National Political Congress of Black Women—C. DeLores again—whooped it up. "The firing of Doug Morris is a major victory for those of us who asked Time Warner chairman Gerald Levin to stop putting out pornographic music. We asked Mr. Levin to take control and this was his first response. Doug Morris was the biggest supporter of this smut at the company, and now he's gone. I predict that Interscope Records will fall next—and after that, Danny Goldberg will get the boot."

The next Thursday, Morris learned that the platinum parachute earlier enjoyed by Morgado and other corporate heads was not to be his. Instead, he was being fired "for cause," meaning Atlantic had been caught being naughty, and his contract was voided. Time Warner leaked Morris's contract to the public. Everyone learned that he had already received about $10 million that year. Learned that his contract had given Doug $5.5 million as a bonus for signing, an annual salary ($750,000) and bonus guarantee of almost $4 million a year, stock options, a deferred-compensation package, a personal chauffeur, and "access to corporate aircraft." Tough to feel pity for Doug, which was the point behind leaking the contract.

Then Corporate stated its case. Late in 1994, the papers had briefly splashed a story about an Atlantic "scandal" involving stolen CDs. Such a scandal was, at its roots, no big deal. Scams—stories of records being sold by promotion men and by radio stations, of branch back doors left unlocked, of freebies used for favors—all had been going on before Ahmet was a pup. But with Warner Music going front page, such everyday practices got blown up too big, especially the skimming of CDs. Reports said that more than twenty thousand ($150,000 worth) of CDs were missing. Then running Warner Music–U.S., Doug Morris had cleaned up the mess by firing ten Atlantic employees, led by Atlantic vet Nick Maria, who were "believed to be involved." The "for cause" part was that, during his anointment process into the Warner Music–U.S., Morris had never told Corporate about this incident.

Stunned, Doug filed a $50 million breach-of-contract lawsuit. According to the suit, that $50 million was meant to compensate Morris for four years of his contract yet unserved: for the salary, benefits, bonuses, stock options. Salary alone was worth about $20 million. So $50 million seemed more like it, since Morgado had gotten about $60 million, Krasnow had gotten $7 million, and Mo and Lenny, it was estimated, had shared $8 million. And what about how much Time's Nick Nicholas and Dick Munro got for going out *their* doors?

On Morris's leaving without a go-away bundle, one Warner employee reflected that "they gave everybody a turkey, and then they ran out of turkeys, right? It felt creepy that they had to go after Morris personally." But the sympathy was far from universal.

Levin, who'd earlier heard directly from the Morris camp its intention to walk if it didn't get its way, presented Time Warner's case at a very off-the-record lunch with *Time* magazine's editors. He confided to them that Morris and his colleagues *had* been in the process of a coup, which could not be tolerated, and Fuchs had fired Morris with his complete support. When asked about the fate of other key Music Group executives, Levin said, "Once you cut the head off, you see how the body behaves."

The effect of Morris's being fired was deep agony at Atlantic. "The bad news is Doug was a very well loved chairman," Val Azzoli told me. "He was a real people person. It affected everybody. Every day you're talking to people in the business for four hours on the phone. Every day you're thinking, 'Am I going to get fired?' You think this way. Every day the managers calling me, going, 'What the hell's going on?' I'm spending eight hours in the day talking about it."

The next week, Warner Music filed papers with the New York State Supreme Court explaining that Morris had been fired for "improper sales practices" and that he was "well aware of the underlying reasons for his termination." Warner lawyers sought to recover more than $10 million that Morris had been paid since signing his contract the December before.

Fuchs and the Time Warner legal department had decided that deluxe parachutes did not fit the others near this case. On June 30, Mel Lewinter (president and COO of Warner Music–U.S.) and Ina Lea Maibach (its exec VP) were called into Fuchs' office and told to take a thirty-day leave of absence.

On August 1, Lewinter returned from the thirty days off. He, too, was fired "for cause." Lewinter, too, was followed back to his office at headquarters by four security guards, who stood in his office with an attorney watching Mel pack and exit. Reading about it over breakfast, Bert Wasserman thought, "It was difficult for me to hear. It's hard to say to a guy, 'You can't go up to your office. There's a security team up there.' I grew up with Mel. We all have our faults, but he was part of the team."

Word was that the remaining executives at Warner Music–U.S. would soon be fired and the unit disbanded. A week later, Lewinter sued Time Warner for $15 million, claiming he'd been wrongfully fired by Fuchs, despite having a contract with four years yet to run. "Mel is outraged," his attorney, Edward Shapiro, proclaimed, as lawyers are paid to proclaim. "It is shameful for a respected executive to be treated so shabbily after twenty-five years of loyal service."

At the U.S. labels, an eerie silence fell, which Goldberg described: "The phones just seemed to stop ringing. Nothing, you wait. One afternoon, Russ Thyret and I just went to the movies together."

Having cleared away the people Fuchs and Levin believed were political agitators, or most of them, it was now time for Fuchs to get a handle on this business. He continued to focus his diagnosis on the three labels. He set up CEO meetings, watched how people acted, met with "little people," and remembered what they told him. He saw a diffusion of executive bullshit. Bullshit is seldom tidy.

At one meeting with senior music execs, Fuchs told them, "You guys are lucky to have me. I'm management's equivalent of Michael Jordan," which inspired one of the assembled music men to whisper, "Sure, but don't tell the schmuck that this is baseball." Other execs felt that Fuchs was smart but could use at least thirty days in charm school.

At Fuchs's request/order, Danny Goldberg canceled his appearance opposite Bob Dole on *Face the Nation* to discuss freedom of rap. Through summer months, tension grew between Fuchs and outspoken and self-assured Sylvia Rhone, who neither kissed ass nor took shit. I was told that because of her long and close relationship with Doug, she would not have been happy with anyone who fired him. Speculation began that she would not last.

That August, Nick Maria (like nine others at Atlantic, all fired with zero as their parachutes) shared a table at "21" with Fuchs. Maria cooperated with Time Warner in building the "for cause" case against Morris and Lewinter. Time Warner promised not to press any charges against Nick, paid him a $200,000 severance package, and, aptly enough, added a comprehensive health-benefit plan.

34

ONE of Fuchs and Levin's first ideas was to move Ostin, who at this time was still "on hold," up to a "senior position" in the Music Group. When Fuchs offered Ostin the entire Music Group to run, Mo asked him, "Shouldn't you have an alternative plan?" to which Fuchs answered, "That's why I'm here. I'd like to make you vice chairman of the entire Music Group, or even its cochairman." In this new job, Ostin would relocate to the East Coast.

A series of meetings followed. Mo flew to New York to make sure about the proposal. Mickey Rudin, on retainer to Fuchs, rode beside Mo. Fuchs and Levin proposed Mo take it over, all of it, despite Bob Krasnow's advice: "Forget it, Mo, there's no *there* there anymore."

On the plane ride back to California, Rudin was an enthusiast for the deal, so much so that Mo finally stopped him, saying, "Wait a minute, aren't you supposed to be representing *me?*" Mo sensed in all this a bit of hard sell. Rudin, actually trying to represent both parties, was torn between the two, and quickly stepped out of the marriage-making business. From California, Mo phoned Fuchs and asked, in his clearest manner, if they as cochairmen were to disagree, "Which of us has the final say?" Fuchs replied, "I'd be happy to be cochairman with you. But if we came to an impasse . . . well, I will still have my duties to Corporate." That reply told Mo the fact: He would not be in charge the way he needed to be. It also made his decision a no.

Two weeks after firing Morris, Fuchs informed Danny Goldberg he could get "a friendly contract settlement" if "no comment" became his answer to prying questions from the press. The exit negotiation took about a month, and $5 million was said to be the offer. Goldberg immediately dropped from view to avoid reporters' phone calls.

A year later, a cooled-down Goldberg still refused reporters' phone calls. He told me, "If I had to do it over again, I would have been a bit more diplomatic in some of my utterances. I got caught up in Doug's fight with Morgado."

Fuchs, having learned that he could not have Mo Ostin back in the fold, considered others he knew to take Goldberg's place, like Les Bider at Warner/Chappell, like Tom Ross at CAA. Time was ticking. The weather was getting sweltery, so the year's Record Group convention must be imminent. On instinct, Fuchs chose WBR's next chairman, promoting from within. "When we were in meetings, Russ [Thyret] was the one who did all the talking," Fuchs later told me. A few days before the WMG's annual blowout in Washington, D.C., WBR vice chairman Russ Thyret accepted the position of Warner Bros. Records' head, with contract terms to be decided later.

Reaction to Russ was positive, and Ostin's endorsement didn't hurt: "This is a great choice and an excellent move toward bringing everyone together and restoring stability. Russ is a total record man—brilliant, experienced, and well rounded in every aspect. I love the guy."

The appointment calmed a demoralized division. Russ himself was elated. Asked about rap, Thyret said, "My watch starts today. I'll stand up for the music that we produce under my watch."

With Goldberg leaving the company, Neil Young's manager, the ever-observant Elliott Roberts, just shrugged: "These changes affect the artists surprisingly little. Though you may miss some people on a personal level, they have very little to do with your records when you hand them in. In our case, all the people at the lower levels who worked on the records are still there. The loss is in the paranoia that seeps through a company when it goes through this transition."

A couple of days later, WEA's operating head, George Rossi, opened the August convention—"G'morning, God bless"—in the sweltering heat of Washington. Following his "Robert, roll it!" command to Bob Moering came a ten-minute video parade of recent hot songs.

Dave Mount at the podium looked pleased, content, and professionally laundered. He threaded one-liners through his opening remarks, saying with a sigh, "As Nietzsche put it, 'That which does not kill me makes me stronger.' "

Mount was addressing a larger crowd than in years earlier. WEA had been blended into a new company, called WMMD that contained WEA, WEA Manufacturing, Ivy Hill, and Ric Weitsma's Operations unit of Warner Music. Mount now ran that conglomeration. After citing achievements of the year past, Mount then suggested that the largest problem the people in this auditorium faced was the name of the new organization: Warner Media Manufacturing and Distribution. Too long, not catchy. "So I've come up with a new name for the company," Dave announced. "With great fanfare, I would like to propose that our new name be Distributors of Audio Visual Entertainment. Or, more appropriately, DAVE.

"Now, think about it, when people ask, 'Who do you work for?' you can just say, 'I work for DAVE.' "

Next up was someone who believed everyone worked for Michael. On the podium, Fuchs looked at ease with himself and his position, still communicated bossness in his manner. He wore a suit but had removed his necktie. One Midwest sales head whispered to the guy next to him, "Isn't that Mr. Stay-Puft?"

Fuchs rambled but used notes. He told about going to see Alanis Morissette the night before at New York nightclub Tramps, then over to a reception at Flowers to meet her. "She's very nice. Tells me she's heard I'm the greatest record executive ever. And then says, 'Thanks for coming, Mr. Ertegun.' " Then, turning serious, Fuchs ran long over his allotted ten minutes, using precept words about his beliefs for the Music Group, like "unification," "leadership," "synergy," "loyalty," "good citizenship," "fun," "winning," "family." "We will win, and we will win big. Trust me; I do not lose. I never have, and there are too many winners here to ruin my streak."

As I watched Fuchs at the mike, an odd realization came to me: that this man had never known the joy of having some bigger-than-life bandleader step on his hand.

Making his address in his forty-seventh year as head of Atlantic Records, Ahmet mounted the stage uneasily, limping from a shattered pelvis and three hip operations. Still, his cane was, you bet, gold handled. He wore custom shoes by John Lobb of London, said to cost three thousand dollars a pair, so much you hoped Ahmet had shoe insurance. Summarizing his formula for success in this business, his speech, as always, was brief: "There's hard work; there's understanding music and songs and how they work with public taste; and there's luck."

Ertegun then turned the mike over to his new cochair Val Azzoli, who had stayed up til two o'clock the night before, rehearsing his speech, while the stage crew grabbed five thousand dollars worth of overtime. Azzoli, dressed in a pinstripe suit, his black hair curling and cascading around his face, spoke of his latest boss: "Michael has been very supportive. He just told me, 'Hey, Val, it's your company. You run it your way.' " He noted that Atlantic (with Rhino and Curb and other sublabels) was now the Number One label in the country. Its profits had tripled.

Sylvia Rhone was introduced, a bit amazingly, as "our company chair with the longest tenure." She gave an energetic speech, recalling at one point an exchange of business axioms between her and Fuchs: "Michael and I were talking the other day about the music business, and I figured it would be a good move to quote a little Vince Lombardi to him, you know, that rah-rah line about 'Winning isn't everything; it's the *only* thing.' But right back at me comes another great Lombardi line. Michael said to me, 'That's good to hear, because if you're not fired *up* with enthusiasm, you'll be *fired* with enthusiasm.'

"I *heard* that can happen around here."

As usual, loud music videos blared, pounding out the climaxes from up-coming CDs. The parade of new acts went on for days. New labels, new products poured over the audience like cement over Jimmy Hoffa. No longer was it just rock or pop. Country Music just *had* to get its few hours, too. Over the past several years, first at WB, then at Atlantic, WMG's country divisions had bitten major pieces out of the Nashville cookie. Early in '95, 40 percent (or eight out of the Top Twenty) of the top country albums were shipped by WEA: Tim McGraw, Jeff Foxworthy, Clay Walker, Sawyer Brown, Neal McCoy, John Michael Montgomery, David Ball, and Hank Williams, Jr. pushed Granddad's Acuff types off the charts. And Elektra wasn't trying hard yet.

As the presentations boomed on, out in the lobby, WEA's Nick Massi, after thirty years of wanting to, walked up to Ahmet Ertegun, not too close to the shoes, and got his picture taken with Ertegun. Massi told about *his* father who'd played in Vic Faraci's Big Band, about how his parents lived across the street from Vic and Barb Faraci; how there are about six different guys named Vic Faraci in that particular neighborhood in Chicago; told how in the Faraci family, they only use three different names: Vic, Sam, and Peter, even if you were a girl.

In response, Ertegun reminisced, "Chicago? I remember a night that Jerry and I . . ." Relief to both men came just in talking about the more comfortable past, no matter how trivial. The mood that day in Washington seemed often to yearn for the years before. Dave Mount walked by, heard saying "Jerry Sharell told me how *old* he felt, finding the Cars in the Rhino collection." There was, at that moment, the relief of having survived the slaughter.

By the end of September, negotiations to separate Interscope Records from Time Warner were completed. Label owners Ted Field and Jimmy Iovine promised to pay Time Warner (about) $115 million dollars for TW's 50 percent of the label (the same $115 million that TW had, over the past five years, paid to get the half ownership). Within two months, Field started asking prospective suitors for $125 million for only 25 percent of the label.

Distribution of Interscope albums "on a record-by-record business" would continue at WEA through March 31, 1996. 2Pac's *All Eyez on Me* was hot, but the moral issue overruled all. Fuchs announced that WEA was passing on Dogg Pound's new album, too.[150] Gangsta rap, though proclaimed done with and tired, continued to sell well, just not through Warner's record

---

[150]Warner Publishing, thanks to a $4 million advance, continued to profit from all the publishing of Death Row on the basis (a) of nobody's saying no to such a deal and (b) the belief, in Michael Fuchs's words, that "owning publishing was about Time Warner making money, not about what we put in front of our children."

labels. Huge (315 pounds) Suge Knight decided to issue it on Halloween because "they're all so scared of it." People bought it. "Tha Dogg Pound record is in the stores," said Suge. "So what did DeLores Tucker accomplish?"[151]

Tupac became the first artist to debut at Number One on the charts while serving a jail sentence for sexual assault.

Soon thereafter, Interscope's reclaimed 50 percent was quickly sold to the needy: MCA, for $200 million.

Atlantic, having lost Interscope's revenues, went after new sources fast. Azzoli signed new label deals: Tag, Big Beat, Celtic Heartbeat, Mesa/Bluemoon, Jason Flom's Lava. All were like signing a small flock of artists, each "label" having a small staff. They were not fifty/fifty joint ventures, still more like eighty/twenty, so Atlantic "can make money off of ten records, as opposed to twenty records." Atlantic's nonexclusive deal with country-oriented Curb Records Azzoli called "the biggest move of market share in the record business this year."

Hootie and the Blowfish's *Cracked Rear View* had become the best-selling debut album in Atlantic's history. The *New York Times* gave credit to Atlantic's Tim Sommers, who'd signed the dark-horse band. Ahmet Ertegun was asked, "Who *really* signed Hootie?" "The answer is," Ahmet said, "Atlantic Records signed the band. There are seven different people, all claiming credit. The truth is, it started down in research, when they saw some activity on a regional record."

Ertegun's blow to the cult of the ego made sense. Atlantic had a staff whose job was watching minor-station playlists, alert for another act like Hootie, then moving in to sign up ready-made hits. Rather than become Atlantic "house producers" on salary, such producers now created their own labels, which Atlantic just distributed. Under Azzoli, Atlantic made its money as a marketer.

Azzoli's Atlantic was a changed label caught between the high cost of talent and the high expectation for profits. Val's focus was signaled by a change of verb. Used to be, Atlantic would "release" albums, then chose airplay; now, it "marketed" albums. Meeting with Azzoli in his big-for-Manhattan office, with its NASA-size sound system, I heard from him that "the way WEA was set up, with all these different profit centers, everyone was making money off our dime before we were. We would spend—I'll just pick a number—a million dollars and we'd recoup our million dollars in royalties. The problem is, [WEA printer] Ivy Hill is making money. WEA

---

[151]Later, when C. DeLores Tucker was asked why she didn't yell at MCA's stockholder meetings, she explained that MCA was foreign owned. In fact, MCA's owner, Seagram, was based up in Canada. Sony was based in Japan. EMI was based in England. PolyGram was based in Holland. BMG was based in Germany.

distributing is making money from record number one. Warner/Chappell is making money. We didn't make any. So we stopped and said, 'Wait a minute! What's wrong with this picture? We lost five million dollars and everyone else made ten?' "

Azzoli adapted. It was hardly like "the old days," but then, in the mid-Nineties, there was not enough time to behave like in the old days, when the older Atlantic had gone walking into clubs, listened for talent, signed it, chose songs for it, then recorded it with on-staff producers. Under Azzoli, a label head had to do more than *hear* the music. He needed to know how to sell.

Atlantic announced a new division "geared specifically toward marketing its releases to gay and lesbian record buyers," with noted music journalist Peter Galvin as his VP of Product Development/Gay Markets.

If you're driving north from Hollywood, the freeway exit to Warner Bros. Records is Barham Boulevard, the one that Mo Ostin took when Reprise married Warner Bros. Records, back in the Sixties. But if you missed the Barham exit, the very next exit—two minutes, even if you're driving a pre-owned—led to MCA Records, on the Universal Studios lot, where music head Al Teller and Edgar Bronfman, Jr., had already accumulated start-up labels by Doug Morris (Rising Tide Records) and Bob Krasnow (Krasnow Entertainment). MCA itself, however, was not an esteemed label. Even with Bronfman's passion for music, some said that MCA still stood for Music Cemetery of America.

Mo became free of his noncompete deal in August 1995. Lenny had negotiated his own exit for the same date. Mo's son Michael, a valued A&R man at WBR, had not signed a new contract with the label the previous October, when it had been offered him by Goldberg. All three were free, but could not, till the calendar page turned, officially sign with DreamWorks/SKG Records.

The clock ticked toward August 10, the day of an expected "Warnerization" of DreamWorks. The clock ticked again till DreamWorks joined Krasnow's and Morris's labels, all to be distributed by MCA, that one ramp to the north. For them, Bugs Bunny was out, and some big shark was in.

Within four months, on November 16, Doug Morris became head of MCA's record group, replacing Al Teller.[152] "Do I have a weird life or what?" Morris asked industry analyst Chuck Philips of the *Los Angeles Times,* who was able to get him on the phone. "All I can say is that this has been a very strange year."

Jerry Levin continued getting slammed in the press. Year-end critics had a field day over the past twelve months at Warner. The *Los Angeles Times'*

---

[152]Al Teller's severance deal was $20 million.

Philips wrote, "Nothing was more dramatic than what happened at the Warner Music Group, where seven top executives were fired in a corporate bloodbath—all under the watch of the *Times'* Pop Eye column's loser of the year, Time Warner Chairman Gerald Levin, which described him thus: 'He is the man Time Warner shareholders have to thank for virtually dismantling in eighteen months what others had spent thirty years building into the world's most successful record company'."

Being pulled apart in more pieces than a medieval heretic, Levin was still heavily wooing Ted Turner to sell Time Warner his cable company. It became Jerry's fixation. Disney had bought ABC, and Turner's reaction was "I want to see what it's like to be *big* for a while." But Turner was no pushover. He remembered the past years clearly, getting beaten up in his boardroom by Time's Fuchs, who (because of Time and Warner's 20 percent owners' share of Turner Cable) sat on Turner's board. Only the last year, in a talk at the National Press Club, had Turner—accurately tagged as "The Mouth of the South"—described Time Warner's constant vetoes of his plans as rituals of clitoridectomy.

Then, on September 22, Time Warner announced its $7.5 billion "merger" with Turner Broadcasting. Not cash, but paper—about 10 percent of TW's stock—enough to buy most of Montana.[153] Speculation had it that Fuchs would be the guy overseeing the new combine—Turner Cable + HBO. But not Music. Major shareholder Gordon Crawford had let that one drop in a phone call to Fuchs.

The question of where Music would fit into this new setup got tossed around like a Mexican flapjack. Studio heads Daly and Semel hated how Levin had treated their Burbank-lot pal, Mo Ostin. Fuchs's moving up into Corporate made them wary up to their armpits. They'd read those "heir apparent" news items and choked at the thought of reporting to Fuchs. They'd talked about quitting Time Warner. Semel's contract had an escape clause, and he'd been noticed talking to potential employers, included Bronfman at MCA. As Fuchs rose nearer to step two at Time Warner, the somewhat temperamental studio chief Bob Daly, who'd been known to walk down the Warner back lot's dusty Western Street at high noon, unsnapped *his* holsters.

Jerry Levin needed no more anger in his daily Daly life. He asked what would it take to calm down Daly and Semel, so the Turner deal could close. In October, Levin signed up Daly and Semel for five more years. One press account put the cost at $150 million, give or take a leg.

The deal gave Daly and Semel a division called Entertainment, including WB Studio *and* the Warner Music Group. The deal would send Fuchs

---

[153]Turner, now employed, saw his salary go up to $111 million for five years' work, in contrast to his $7 million for the previous five. Turner looked upon his job as vice chairman of TW as "not much of a job."

back to HBO. Fuchs, who'd been assuming a bigger future for himself at TW, exploded. A loud Fuchs now stood in Jerry's way.

Worrying by Levin seemed excusable. *Variety*'s good columnist and editor-in-chief, Peter Bart, wrote that "Michael was going crazy. He's not a lot of laughs even when he's not going crazy, but now he was going crazy." Fuchs complained to the Time Warner board. Levin, telling colleagues that "anyone who put his own interests ahead of the company's would be steam-rollered," told Fuchs to be quiet.

After being locked up with the TW board all morning, at two on the afternoon of November 16, 1995, Levin summoned Fuchs up from HBO to his book-lined conference room on the twenty-ninth. Fuchs saw on Jerry what he called his "game face." Jerry pulled out some paper and drew a triangle, starting to describe the new setup with Turner in it. Fuchs stopped him and asked, "Is there a press release you want to show me?" The question was stiletto quick.

Levin slid the release across for Fuchs to read. It was over in two minutes. Having been in charge of Warner Music for 195 days, Fuchs could ride back the eight blocks down to HBO without security guards. From his wide, open office, he glanced across at the Bryant Park treetops' few leaves. It was late in the year. He went home that night feeling the loss. He awoke the next morning feeling the comfort of a severance to last 312 weeks, one that would cost Time Warner $60 million. What else he thought was nobody's business.

One top Warner Music exec sang, "Ding-dong, the witch is dead." Few in the entertainment industry were privately surprised that the Bad Boy of HBO, with his Napoleonic strut, had fallen. His end came not because of his rule over the Music Group. "You could see this coming," said one Wall Street source. "Fuchs burned bridges with Jerry and with the board by fighting city hall. The cumulative damage couldn't be reversed."

The day after Fuchs's dismissal, Sylvia Rhone, who had repeatedly distanced herself from the strong-minded Fuchs, treated her entire staff to sixteen-inch pizzas. To those who asked, Sylvia said she was merely celebrating Thanksgiving a week early.

Significant Labels in the Warner Music Group

1995

Warner Bros. Records: Reprise • American Recordings • Giant • Maverick • Qwest • Warner Nashville • Reprise Nashville • Warner Alliance • Warner/Reprise Home Video • Tommy Boy

Bestsellers: Coolio • Enya • Goo Goo Dolls • Jeff Foxworthy • Green Day • Faith Hill • Chris Isaak • Quincy Jones • Madonna • Alanis Morissette • Tom Petty • Seal • Rod Stewart • Travis Tritt • Van Halen • Clay Walker • Dwight Yoakam • Neil Young

The Atlantic Group: Atlantic • Atlantic Classics • Atlantic Jazz • Atlantic Nashville • Amphetamine Reptile • Big Beat • Celtic Heartbeat • Code Blue • Curb • Holiday • Lava • Mammoth • Mesa/Bluemoon • Modern • 143 • Rhino • Tag
Bestsellers: All-4-One • *Batman Forever* • Brandy • Collective Soul • Everything But the Girl • Hootie & the Blowfish • Junior M.A.F.I.A. • Tracy Lawrence • Neal McCoy • Tim McGraw • Bette Midler • John Michael Montgomery • Jimmy Page & Robert Plant • Sawyer Brown • The Three Tenors • Hank Williams, Jr.

Elektra Entertainment Group: Elektra • Asylum • East-West • Sire
Bestsellers: Natalie Merchant • AC/DC • Better Than Ezra • Metallica • Rembrandts • Adina Howard • Gerald & Eddie Levert • Bryan White • Björk • Phish • Tracy Chapman • Das EFX • Kut Klose • Silk

35

THREE weeks before Michael Fuchs was given the golden gate, the two men about to take his place—longtime movie guys, Warner Bros. Studios' Bob Daly and Terry Semel—had known they would take over. Jerry had told them so. For years they ran the studio with the same flamboyance that most studio heads flambéd. Bob and Terry lived on the same block in Bel Air. They car pooled. They finished each other's sentences. Their goal was to run Records in the same Steve Ross, hands-off, supportive style.

Despite the Morgado-Fuchs management mayhem, WMG albums had kept on selling. Alanis Morissette's *Jagged Little Pill* had produced about $200 million so far. But to others, Bob and Terry had described Music's last two years as being "behind the Iron Curtain." With calm restored, they knew that the Warner Music Group could get back to happy days to double-digited corporate applause, and, who knows, maybe even to that opening spot in the Annual Report.

How wrong their beliefs, their hopes were. What Bob and Terry did not realize was—what most people did not realize was—how much the business had changed.

On November 16, 1995, Time Warner's newly chosen president, Dick Parsons, had phoned the heads of the Music Group. He described how their corporation was reorganizing, changing from a five- to a three-division structure. Three meant that two of the divisions—Movies and Records— would be combined into one lump, called Entertainment. In this new setup, there would be, unfortunately, no role for Michael Fuchs. One by one, Parsons told them that Fuchs was out.

Almost immediately, each division head's phone rang a second time, Daly and Semel calling. Their voices soothed like Steve's used to. They talked about giving the divisions "more autonomy." No more "this week's earthquake."

"Have you *heard?*" and "You won't believe *this* one!" became the day's Number One and Two Top Phone Shrieks. The press leaped upon the story like an old lover on some long-lost mistress. Calming quotes got shoved into press releases, like Daly's "Jerry streamlined the company, and there was a fallout. The fallout was Michael Fuchs, and that is unfortunate."

In 1996, Bob Daly was fifty-nine years old, and Terry Semel was fifty-three. Age, however, was no longer an issue. Adding Music to Movies, Daly and Semel now ran a $10 billion a year empire, give or take. Lots of things to cross-merchandise, now that previously separate divisions co-sat at meetings. "For those into hip-hop, we could sell them Bugs Bunny boxers. Get it?" Warner's Records division had been merged back into Warner Bros. Studios, whence it had come.

The *Los Angeles Times:* "Was what happened in the virtual destruction of Time Warner's music division anything short of a scandal? By the time the dust had cleared, most of the men who had steered the company's labels to huge profits had been fired by a team of corporate players that itself was soon given the pink slip—with severance pay exceeding an estimated $100 million." Jac Holzman, looking at the WMG battlefield, said, "What happened in Music was a clear example of Jerry's lack of vision, weak people skills, and unwillingness to make hard choices. And the result was he ended up like a badminton bird going from one polarized decision to another."

That December, the Music Group's New Yorkers celebrated Christmas at Roseland Ballroom. Thirteen hundred people arrived, most wearing either red ties or bangles. Some wore both. Daly and Semel made a little seasonal speech together, though most of the partiers talked through it, with a been-there, heard-that disregard. For all involved, the new year could not come soon enough.

Daly's and Semel's offices were at Warner Bros. Pictures. Daly, the elder, had Jack L. Warner's office: Enter through copper-and-aluminum art deco double doors, then four steps down. There was J.L.'s fireplace. The room was lighter in color now; J.L. had kept it Old World dark, I remembered. A window wall to the south now brought in the sun.

An oval metal table piled with scripts. No CD player, no speakers. More double doors to a bar/refrig/glasses on three-quarter-inch, green-edged glass shelves. Sofa and chairs you fully sank in with a *woomf.* Fruit, and a tray of carrots and celery. *Rolling Stone's Images of Rock & Roll* on the coffee table. Phones at both ends of the sofa. Persian carpet. Beige walls, with tortoiseshell sconces. Carved elephant.

I'd returned to this office where, thirty-six years earlier, for WBR's 1959 slide-film show of new albums, I'd managed to get Jack Warner to speak into my tape machine: "This is Jack Warner. I was there in the beginning." He'd read my script correctly, like Orson Welles. "Thanks, Chief," and I was out of there.

Now I was in that room because WEA Distributing had asked me to write a book for its twenty-fifth anniversary. Writing that history had become harder than I'd expected. Previously relaxed friends whom I interviewed now turned rigid handling any but Nerf-ball questions. Ahmet, for instance, got halfway through one interview, then asked me, "Why do you want to know *that?*" Which made me feel like some bad guy. I waved him "no problem" and asked him no more. After I sent a letter of fact checks to Mickey Rudin, he sent me one of his famous vile letters, telling me how he'd turned down millions in advances for a book on his life and wasn't gone to tell me things for *free.* I'd sent six questions to Ramon Lopez in London; he wrote back saying he did not feel like answering even one of them but, next time he was in town, let's be sure to have dinner. It was eerie. For the first time, I felt real tension in people I'd relaxed with for decades.[154]

I'd come to DalyandSemel—it was to their credit that it was hard to separate them—to ask my "what happened next?" questions. They, too, were guarded and answered me with honeyed sentences. How they'd run Music? Daly depicted things like they'd been under David Horowitz, and under "early" Bob Morgado. "We're basically businesspeople, who don't come from the world of music . . ." Terry jumped in to add, "But who do come from the world of entertainment and who've worked with talent for many years, and with creative executives."

They explained how monthly CEO meetings would continue with Azzoli and Ertegun, Rhone, Thyret, Mount, Bider, Lopez, and two Music Group corporate managers, Jerry Gold and Fred Wistow. Meeting agendas, if any, would be loose. Just moving around the table and bringing each other up to date.

Daly and Semel talked, as do all businessmen with a public company, about growth. "The biggest single growth is Asia, followed by Latin America. Cable and satellite all over the place, particularly in the next year or two. That's the one business that was started a couple of years ago that has a really good future. Unfortunately, we arrived at a time where there's a lot of red ink."

Low on their chart of growth was the American market, where WEA had been, except for one *Thriller* year, Number One for the last twenty-five.

"The cultures of the studio and the Warner Music Group are very similar," Daly kept pointing out. "The attitudes of the people and the way we are treated, so similar."

---

[154]That WEA book, called *Footprints*, never appeared. I'd written it gently, I thought. Then I was told it was viewed as "inappropriate" and "too inflamatory" and "not what we need right now." They were probably right; I hadn't sensed the tension of the workers in the group and had tried just telling the facts. Dave Mount wanted the book printed, and he'd paid for it. From above his head, he got overruled.

To which Terry added the clincher: "We all come from the same roots—Warner Communications."

I asked my most daring question, which was about Daly's girlfriend: "Will Carol Bayer Sager be signing with Warner Bros.?" I expected a laugh. I could see it in their eyes: Interview over.

Daly and Semel had worked quickly to make sure the Music Group's leaders, already well fed, now felt well relaxed. Rhone had assured the duo of her willingness to stick around, which felt good. Elektra had delivered hits by Natalie Merchant, Adina Howard, Ol' Dirty Bastard, and Better Than Ezra. She was the only label chief who'd made her numbers by mid-'95. She said, "There I was, dislodged from the individuals who had been my mentors and thrown into the fire with a boss who was confrontational. After what we went through here, I think I could deal with just about anything corporate America has to dish out."

Val Azzoli, who later said he'd several times felt minutes away from quitting his dream job, was assured he would be promoted to a par with Ertegun, Thyret, and Rhone, becoming cochair and co-CEO of Atlantic. With his appointment, Azzoli's old title—president—was left vacant.

Despite all the turmoil of recent years, *SoundScan* observed that Warner's Music Group had "not only maintained their preeminent position this year, they have increased their market share at a juncture when the majors are losing market share. This is a very healthy business." In fact, describing the business as healthy was about as accurate as describing Wichita as a resort. Without realizing—and no one did—how big the business's changes were—and that just getting back to the Steve Ross style might not be all that was needed, Bob, Terry, and the Music Group smiled smiles of relief and strode off toward the Emerald City.

As 1996 opened, worry rose high whether Warner Bros.' hit acts would follow Mo and Lenny out the door. To get R.E.M.—a money act since 1988's *Green*—into a new contract became a mission. When Ostin and Waronker's future at the label had been wavering, R.E.M. had loudly proclaimed its intention to walk. Now the group was free to sign elsewhere. Maneuvering to sign R.E.M. were not only DreamWorks but also Sony, Capitol, and Outpost.

That earlier proclamation was forgotten. With Russ there, R.E.M. felt no problem with Warner Bros. Post-Mo, they found 3300 Warner Boulevard the same; same faces. At home in Athens, Georgia, R.E.M. studied its pile of offers, then talked to California lawyer Don Passman, who was used to this sort of Signing Super Bowl; he'd done a bunch. For two consecutive fourteen-hour days, in one room, R.E.M.'s manager, Bertis Downs, and Passman came up with a price so big it crushed the lungs and felt up the wallets of the other side's negotiators, Warner Bros. Records' new president,

Steve Baker, and financial head, Dave Altschul. Daly and Semel's instructions: "anything within reason."

For its twenty-fifth-anniversary convention in mid-1996, WEA met in Anaheim, in a hotel across from Disneyland, where, to comfort the mobs, hallways were twenty feet wide. Opening night, I stood against the wall as, once again, the parade of hits videoed by. The thousands in the room watched as they were praised, once again, for breaking those hits.[155] Eventually, Thyret got up to introduce Warner Bros. albums. During his speech, Bertis Downs walked out onstage and handed Thyret a telegram. Thyret read it aloud: "We've always said we'll only do this as long as it's still fun, and right now, it feels like we're just getting started, so let's keep going. R.E.M." Around me, two thousand employees of WEA leaped up and whooped. Some cried. That mess-up in Corporate was not about them. This proved it. Thyret cried onstage, too, cried from relief, from validation.

The cost would soon emerge: R.E.M., it was said, had made an $80 million deal. The deal's fine print made such an estimate, Bob Daly answered, "ridiculous." The front side gave up $10 million advances for each of five albums; plus another $20 million advance on royalties for a sweetening on R.E.M.'s six-album catalogue; a 24 percent royalty (about $2.50 per record); and, when the deal was over, R.E.M. would get its albums back about the year members of R.E.M. would be nearing their fiftieth birthdays.

Russ was not alone in his relief that morning in Anaheim. Dave Mount's new manufacturing/distribution complex (still called WMMD) had, by 1996, been built up to handle a truly titanium-size future. It could make up to 300 million CDs a year; more than 250 million audiocassettes; more than 16 million VHS tapes. Vinyl records, even. All it took was 5,500 employees in manufacturing, packaging, and distribution, now working for this guy Dave. And the biggest mistake a guy like Dave could make would be to ever, *ever* run out of capacity.

But in the cities inside America, the pizzazz was off the rose. On six hundred streets across the land, people this year had stopped, looked into familiar store windows, seen suddenly empty floors, and wondered, "Where'd it go?" Stores, once stacked with CDs, now bare. Retailers had been "consolidating," a nice word. By May 1996, the business had again hit a wall. Sales flat as a Triscuit. A $12 billion industry had stalled at $12 billion. Retailers were living not off sales but off collecting labels' subsidies for ads and for discounts given them for front-of-the-store product placement.

---

[155]When the lights came up, I had no clue where to sit. I'd been invited as some Golden Oldie. I just plunked down at an empty table for ten. From onstage, Dave Mount saw me, asked me to stand up, and promised everyone a copy of the WEA-history book still to come, so I waved, and that was that.

In searching for answers, the industry pointed out that CDs as LP replacements had long lost their buoying power. Poor sales results were blamed on what some called "aging icons" like Rod Stewart, Phil Collins, and Bon Jovi, now presumably running out of breath. The Red Hot Chili Peppers, Lenny Kravitz, Candlebox, Blind Melon, and the Spin Doctors all sold under expectations. Even R.E.M.'s *New Adventures in Hi-Fi* turned out sluggish, selling 25 percent of what the group's 1994 *Monster* had sold. Fearless Russ Solomon, owner of the Tower Records chain, looked at his oversupply of yellow-and-red shopping bags and commented, "Optimism is not the prevailing mood in the music market these days."

Discount houses like Best Buy and Circuit City stole sales from retail chains Tower and Wherehouse (just as they, a quarter century earlier, had cut down mom-and-pop retailers). If you ran a records-mostly store, that hardly helped the retail slump go away. Even Ralphs Grocery stores announced they were going to sell records. These new guys didn't care if the CDs they sold made them profits. Best Buy bought the Top 100 CDs from manufacturers for about $10 each, then sold them for $9.98. That way, they creamed the top 10 percent of the retail business, trusting that their loss on CDs would lure in shoppers to buy their microwaves and fax machines. Turned out it did. Why should consumers pay $16.98 for a CD when they could pay $9.98 at Circuit City (144 stores)? WEA worried over possibly having up to $1 billion in returns sitting out there on shelves, a mound so huge it made even Richard Simmons's legendary piles look teeny.

The Warner Music Group's concern was for the welfare of its back-catalogue business, the CDs not found where only the Top 100 Loss Leaders got sold. If the Best Buys of the world killed off the Wherehouses of the world, catalogue would be beyond reach. In November's Top Pop Catalogue Albums chart, WEA had 30 percent (fifteen of the chart's Top Fifty). Losing those sales . . . ouch.

To stop this, Warner and other record companies set a "minimum advertised price," or MAP. They told stores that undercut the MAP that they'd get no money for ads. It did not help.[156] Bankruptcies faced WEA's all-star team: Warehouse, Camelot, Wax Works, Strawberries, Peppermint-Starship.

On July 27, 1997, the *New York Times* summed up the future of music retailing: "Investors may want to stick to this industry's relatively short-term opportunities." What those opportunities were, the *Times* didn't say, but if you made your living selling browser boxes, the trend was hardly encouraging.

---

[156]They were right. It took until 2000, but the Federal Trade Commission busted all the majors for this price fixing, saying the labels had overcharged buyers $500 million over four years.

As the months passed, Val Azzoli got quoted in *Business Week:* "It's not about market share now, it's about bottom-line profits."

In 1996, the record industry released almost 30,000 albums. One newsletter counted that it'd gotten 710 new albums in one week. Fewer than 2 percent of the 30,000 sold more than 50,000 copies. Azzoli complained, "We have too much money chasing too few acts. At this rate, we're going to blow our brains out." Hootie went twelve times platinum. Metallica and Green Day, both eight times. Alanis, five times. Upcoming was Hootie's next, *Fairweather Johnson*. Val described the phenomenon: "This is why everyone wants to be in the record industry. It only cost us one hundred twenty-five thousand dollars to sign Hootie and the Blowfish. Where else are you going to get a return on your investment like that?"

In 1997, reality took its toll. Sales moved like slugs, and, worse, every new signing went for naught. Thyret appointed Virgin's now-available Phil Quartararo as WBR's president. Phil Q, as he was called, was a strong administrator (Russ Thyret was far better at hugging; given an all-industry hugfest, Russ would come in Number Two, behind only Quincy Jones). Phil Q would run things, Russ said, but would not move into that Number Two office next to Russ, the one that Lenny's interior decoration had botched. Office Number Two remained empty.

Cuts began. Tommy Boy was sold back to Tom Silverman. Irv Azoff's Giant was shrunk (new name: Revolution) and represented. Distribution of Rick Rubin's American Records went to Sony.

Atlantic, too, made cuts of its Matador, Mammoth, and Celtic Heartbeat label deals. Azzoli had learned their cost: "I would rather make a hundred percent of the money rather than fifty percent of the money."

At Warner Bros. Records, people cutting began in 1997. Over a hundred midlevel executives in the New York and Nashville offices, out. Gone were people who had little to show for their time in the record business except maybe some souvenir T-shirts hanging in their closets.

The idea of two fully servicing labels seemed over. Howie Klein continued to run Reprise, but its departments got "consolidated" in Burbank. Even his Number Two exec, Rich Fitzgerald, was moved over to become WBR's head of marketing. As Phil Q put it, "There's Warner Bros Records, and then there is a sidecar called Reprise."

When Phil Q became president of the WBR label, ex–WBR president Steve Baker left in January 1996; his own Number Two, Jeff Gold, had been let go earlier. Another forty-five from the home office, out, including twenty-year vets. The industry winced over the fate of old friends. Even Ted Templeman, who'd come from Autumn Records and given the label the Doobie Brothers and Van Halen, cut. These things hurt.

*   *   *

Artists became more public with their protests about the Advance vs. Deductions choke hold. If an artist got a signing advance of, say, a million dollars, that million was often the last money the artist would see. Advances behaved like borrowing from a hip bank. In the end, hip or no, every bank is still a bank.

In the 1990s, record contracts had grown tighter-fisted than ever. New clauses held back more money more ways than recording sessions costs. In the Eighties and Nineties, new deductions grew like gophers in the spring, munching away at the roots of greenery. Clause Two—Promotion Cost Deduction—grew to include the label's costs for tour support, videos, most marketing (posters, ads, parties), indie promoter fees. Standard contracts now had a Clause Three, called New Technology Deduction, born during the CD start-up when manufacturing costs had been higher. The clause had lingered. Through it, record labels (not just Warner's) took out another 15 to 25 percent from royalties.

Artists who wanted out had to fight their way out. And as they left, they wanted to take their recorded masters with them. As Prince put it, "If you don't own your masters, your master owns you." But masters remained locked behind clauses. The angriest of the artists muttered words like those journalist Hunter Thompson once wrote: "The music business is a cruel and shallow money trench, a long plastic hallway where thieves and pimps run free, and good men die like dogs. There's also a negative side."

It felt like a long, long time since Frank Zappa had organized his artists' parade down Warner Boulevard, to thank us. In anger, Prince shaved "Slave" on his cheek and changed his name to something looking like a door knocker.

Artists, especially those without hits, not only felt enslaved, they also felt like stoop labor.

One such act, Ani DiFranco, an independent with her own label, Righteous Babe, was making $4.25 for each record, triple the $1.25 that Atlantic's Hootie and the Blowfish made[157] and even double Michael Jackson's $2 an album at Epic. How'd she do it? "The good news is that if you are disgustingly sincere and terribly diligent, there are ways for any serious artist to operate outside the corporate structure," she answered. Ms. DiFranco skipped Schwarzenegger-size mass media buys, created her own packaging, spent zero on tip-sheet ads, and produced her records for under $20,000. It could still be done. She owned her own masters and publishing. "The way I feel about it," she once said, "[is] if I can play music and pay my rent, I'll be happy and doing well on the planet."

---

[157]Hootie did not do badly, since Atlantic sold twenty times more copies than DiFranco did.

Such economics contrasted dramatically with the major labels', whose contracts paid artists differently:

Suggested List Price/CD	$15.98
Less Cost of Manufacturing/Packaging	<u>4.00</u>
	$11.98
Less Free-Goods Deduction	<u>1.80</u>
	$10.18
Less CD New-Tech Cost	<u>2.04</u>
	$8.14
Paid Artist at 15% Royalty	<u>$1.22</u>

Other diminishments—for independent producers (2 to 3 percent), for record-club sales, and for international sales—cut into the $1.22.

In 1996, Prince and Warner Bros. Records finally gave up on each other. Prince's lawyer, Londell McMillan, reflected, "You see what's going on in this industry and you have to ask yourself, is this artist the kind of mercurial crazy some people say, or is he the wise one who understands where he fits at the start of a new century?"

The heads of the Warner labels, even with corporate chaos off their backs, still confronted this mess of a market. Stores closing, artists rebelling, acts expensively bombing, and digital piracy gophering away at sales. CD burners cost $299 now, not $2999.

The Internet felt like just one more of those fuzzy new techno things. Depending on what you wanted, it was: a big chat room, a place to show covers of new albums, a place to send and receive messages, and too slow.

The Internet grew fast, though, moved from chat rooms to record collecting without having to pay. Downloading CD songs became increasingly quicker as net pipelines widened. A few artists, nerdlike, questioned what they called "A2L2B"—a business model that stood for "Artists to Labels to Buyers." With the Internet, they felt it could be simple as pay, could be "A2B." Who needs an "L"?

Record companies rallied around a cure, called "encryption." That meant, "You can't decode this record's data unless you pay the label first." I thought back to the early Eighties, when I'd memorized a simple sentence my own tech teacher, Al McPherson, had told me about digitized music: "If it's digital, no matter what *we* add to the digits, some other guy can figure out how to take that away. Once digitized music is out there, it can just keep on getting passed around, copied, for free." From that day, I became suspicious of any "encryption" program. Later I read a good variation: "Anything that a forty-one-year-old thinks up, a fourteen-year-old can undo."

Every one of the twentieth century's albums was already out there, as writers now put it, like the genie out of the bottle, albums that had never been encrypted, fully in the hands of "fourteen-year-olds."

Fighting off freely shared CD tracks made the record labels and their RIAA appear to music fans about as comforting as Bill Gates dressed in a casual sweater. Customers saw through it. Record labels were behaving just corporate branches, in this for the money.

Unlike in the Sixties and Seventies, when labels were part of The Movement, when executives had grown the beards and marched the march, in the late Nineties, those big labels headed by big egos marched in a world different from artists struggling from gig to gig on minivan tours.

In 1997, Val Azzoli said, "We met this really talented kid last year who told us a story about how a certain executive tried to sign him over breakfast at this fancy restaurant. Apparently, the executive blabbed the whole meal about how amazing he was and how he had basically invented the music business. When the executive got done, the kid said he asked him if he had any questions. And the kid said, 'Yeah, just one. Is it all right if I leave?' "

Significant Releases

1996

Atlantic: Tori Amos (*Boys for Pele*) • Phil Collins (*Dance Into the Light*) • Hootie & the Blowfish (*Fairweather Johnson*) • Jewel (*Pieces of You*, including "Who Will Save Your Soul" and "You Were Meant For Me") • Tracy Lawrence (*Time Marches On*) • Donna Lewis (*Now in a Minute*) • John Michael Montgomery (*What I Do The Best*) • Rush (*Test for Echo*) • Stone Temple Pilots (*Tiny Music . . . Songs from the Vatican Gift Shop*)
Big Beat: Lil' Kim (*Hard Core*) • Quad City DJ's ("C'Mon n' Ride It (The Train)")
Blackground: Aaliyah (*One in a Million*)
Curb: Tim McGraw ("She Never Lets It Get to Her Heart") • LeAnn Rimes (*Blue*)
Celtic Heartbeat: Bill Whelan (*Riverdance*)

Elektra: Björk (*Telegram*) • Tracy Chapman (*New Beginning*, including "Give Me One Reason") • Metallica (*Load*) • Natalie Merchant ("Jealousy") • Phish (*Billy Breathes*) • Busta Rhymes (*The Coming*) • Keith Sweat (*Keith Sweat*)
Asylum: Kevin Sharp (*Measure of a Man*) • Bryan White (*Between Now and Forever*)
Fiction: The Cure (*Wild Mood Swings*)

Warner Bros.: Jeff Foxworthy (*Crank It Up—The Music Album*) • Faith Hill ("Someone Else's Dream") • Tom Petty and the Heartbreakers (*She's the One*) • Adam Sandler (*What the Hell Happened to Me?*) • R.E.M. (*New Adventures in Hi-Fi*) • Van Halen (*Best Of, Volume 1*) • *Evita* soundtrack
Warner Sunset: *Space Jam* soundtrack
Reprise: Enya (*The Memory of Trees*) • *Phenomenon* soundtrack
Sire: Spacehog (*Resident Alien*)
Maverick: Alanis Morissette ("Ironic")
Giant: Clay Walker ("Hypnotize the Moon")

Tommy Boy: Coolio) ("1,2,3,4 Sumpin' New") • *ESPN Presents Jock Jams Volume 2*
WEA Latina: Luis Miguel (*Nada Es Igual*)

1997

Atlantic: Collective Soul (*Disciplined Breakdown*) • Jewel ("Foolish Games") • Tracy
Lawrence (*The Coast Is Clear*) • Duncan Sheik
Be!: Aaliyah ("The One I Gave My Heart To") • Magod and Timbaland (*Welcome
to Our World*)
Big Beat: Changing Faces (*All Day, All Night*)
Curb: Tim McGraw (*Everywhere*) • Tim McGraw with Faith Hill ("It's Your Love") •
LeAnn Rimes (*You Light Up My Life—Inspirational Songs* and *Unchained
Melody/The Early Years*)
Lava: Matchbox 20 (*Yourself or Someone Like You,* including "Push" and "3 AM") •
Sugar Ray (*Floored,* including "Fly")

Elektra: Björk (*Homogenic*) • The Doors (*The Doors Box Set*) • Missy "Misdemeanor"
Elliott (*Supa Dupa Fly*) • Metallica (*Reload*) • Mötley Crüe (*Generation Swine*) •
Busta Rhymes (*When Disaster Strikes*) • Third Eye Blind (including "Semi-Charmed
Life")
Asylum: Lila McCann (*Lila*) • Bryan White (*The Right Place*)

Warner Bros.: Bill Engvall (*Here's Your Sign*) • John Fogerty (*Blue Moon Swamp*) •
Madonna ("Don't Cry For Me Argentina") • Loreena McKennitt (*The Book of Se-
crets*) • *Private Parts* soundtrack
Warner Sunset: Monica ("For You I Will") • *Batman & Robin* soundtrack
Reprise: Barenaked Ladies (*Rock Spectacle*) • Chicago (*The Heart of Chicago
1967–1997*) • Fleetwood Mac (*The Dance*)
Mute: Depeche Mode (*Ultra*)
Maverick: Prodigy (*The Fat of the Land,* including "Firestarter")
Tommy Boy: Coolio (*My Soul*) • *ESPN Presents Jock Jams Volume 3* • *MTV: Party to
Go '98* • *Nothing to Lose* soundtrack
WEA Latina: Luis Miguel (*Romances*)

36

AFTER Dave Mount had added printing and manufacturing to his distribution duties, his head of distribution remained the agreeably crusty man that Henry Droz had relied upon, the unpretentious George Rossi, famous for answering each phone call with variations on "Morning, God Bless" followed by a cigarette cough.

I'd once asked Rossi what he liked about his job. "My best moments are—still—seeing a record happen," he told me. "From my Decca days, from Bill Haley and 'Rock Around the Clock' and Webb Pierce's 'There Stands the Glass'—just seeing a record happen. 'Jingle Bell Rock.'

"Through the years, you have all of those new artists. The thrill of taking an artist and seeing that record break. Seeing that artist become a superstar, that's the record business. That's the business.

"From the retailer's perspective, it's changed a little. I think they look upon the music not so much as music but as a business. Today, it's a SKU number. It sells or it doesn't sell. But there are less and less of the people today who care if the record sells.

"It scares me."

Sales had slumped, nationally and internationally, but especially for the Warner Music Group. Daly and Semel kept talking about the future, not today.

Universal's Music Group, however, led by Iovine and Morris, whooped it up, with Interscope at one point Numbers One, Two, Three, and Four on the charts with Bush, Snoop Doggy Dogg, No Doubt, and Makaveli. Universal now had Henry Droz over there, too, heading distribution.

Career artists guaranteed no hits. But for Warner Music International, America's hip-hop and its newer, training-bra acts like Jewel were sales mysteries. In Europe, only two 1997 Warner Music albums ever made it to Top Twenty. Both were soundtracks: *Space Jam* and *Evita*.

Russ Thyret confessed, in a most apt phrase, that after all the turmoil over Ice-T, his label had become gun-shy about rap. The WMG labels, particularly Warner Bros., had turned their backs on the music that new record buyers craved most: hip-hop and rap. In so doing, the three labels had turned their backs on their customers. It was like years before, when rock & roll, folk rock, and singer/songwriters had come in. If a label just put out "better" albums by the King Sisters, Trini Lopez, and Connie Stevens, it was in danger of sterility.

Some of 1997's music execs questioned if rap was even music. To them, rap sounded like rough-spoken Hallmark cards making proclamations of 'tude. Rhythm, even just bass and drums, was in. Songs were for oldies.

Atlantic found itself in the forefront of the woman's movement. It had hits with hot trotters like Brandy, Jewel, and Junior M.A.F.I.A's "explicit" Lil' Kim, who cautioned us, "please all these haters tryin' to get up all in my grill . . . for nuthin'! this queen bee gots them mad skillz to show and the fresh rymes to flow continuously . . . ya'll just jealous i'm rackin' up cristal and plantinum while all ya'll pigeons be chasin' pennies wit ur scrubs." Lil' Kim was the Media Momma for Biggie Smalls (a.k.a. Notorious B.I.G.). She rapped sexually charged lines, rhyming 'bout sexual freedom over sweat-dripping *thudda-thuddas*. Lil' Kim was all about sex:

> I used to be scared of the dick
> Now I throw lips to the shit, handle it like a real bitch

The public knew what it wanted and bought it, with or without stickers. Prohibiting rap made as much sense as had prohibiting gin.

By now, Daly and Semel's hands-off policy to their record divisions had become more tactile. Returns were high. Profits were low. Abusive spritzes from Ted Turner had grown more frequent.[158] With Warner Music's share of market slipping each year, with profits plummeting, Bob and Terry ran low on excuses.

As Daly and Semel knew, down on Wall Street, "numbers" meant more than tunes. In 1999, Wall Streeters glancing at the WMG numbers just shrugged. When it came to Time Warner, Wall Street now treated the Music/Entertainment division like a rounding error. To the Street, the music business looked lower than pork bellies. Warner's part looked near zero.

To me, all this seemed too bad to be true. On a trip to New York, I lunched with a Wall Street analyst, an acquaintance of mine. I'd called ahead, asking him to explain why, so suddenly, Warners was bums. To get my answer, we met in a packed downtown trattoria. He had a professionally

---

[158]Turner had the habit earlier illustrated by Bob Krasnow: He overdid self-expression. When Turner's son, who worked in Turner's cable company, asked his dad what would happen to him in the merger with Warner, Turner answered, "I guess you're toast."

trimmed ponytail and loved investing, as he put it, in companies that held some "unfair advantage" in their market. Over a basket of multiseeded breads and oil, he leaned forward to talk about his heroes, guys who had "BSD." That one stopped me. I figured the D would be for "digital," but . . . "What's BSD mean?" I asked.

"Big swinging dicks."

Conveniently, that segued to my subject. "So what about the record business?"

"No growth," he answered, and ordered off a tall menu in which nouns like "steak" and "halibut" were buried beneath modifiers like "free-range" and "ginger reduction." Taking our pasta orders, the waiter sincerely wished us *"Bon appétit"* and slithered off.

My counselor had brought to lunch a small pile of Time Warner's Annual Reports. Once our Riccards had been sipped, he showed me what BSD guys looked for, that he called EBITA, what we used to call "Profits."

He first showed me 1996's TW Annual Report, which talked a lot about the value of "branding." He explained that meant "you put out more Superman CDs." The Music Group appeared on page twelve, equivalent to finishing fifth in the Derby.

About Music, the report's writers had claimed "outstanding achievements by Music Group artists were a bright spot in what was *a difficult year* [visualize him punching his finger at the italicized words] throughout the music business. *Adverse market conditions* were characterized by *ongoing weakness* in the retail sector that is expected to continue through 1997. Warner Music Group has responded with a series of initiatives designed to increase efficiencies and reduce costs . . ."

"Okay," he told me, brushing crumbs off my cuff, "now watch this!"

He pulled out the next one: 1997's report. It showed Music moved *back* nine pages, to page twenty-one, part of Daly and Semel's Entertainment group. Levin had been made to say that "*except* for the Music Group, which continued to restructure in the face of internal and external challenges . . ." Later on, Daly was quoted: "We had a weaker release schedule than in past years, partly because a number of our major stars pushed back their album release dates from '97 to '98. We always have slippage, but rarely at the level we felt in 1997. Our catalogue sales were *down, too,* which really speaks to an industry-wide problem, and we had a *decline* in our direct-marketing operations.[159] On top of that, we've had to deal with all the negatives that accrue from *flat markets, sluggish economies,* and currency fluctuation in various parts of the world. This mix made it a difficult year."

He nodded at me in a way I can only describe as shrewdly. While a

---

[159]Columbia House, half owned by Warner, had gone down and down.

waiter gave too much importance to decrumbing our table, my tutor, ready with an air of wisdom, found his next dog ears in 1998's report. "Where's your Music *now?*" he asked.

Page twenty-nine, I saw, nestled inside Entertainment. He had underlined "the continuing recovery of the U.S. retail music business and a growing presence overseas, Warner Music Group regained its positive momentum . . . accounted for 23 of the year's 100 best-selling albums . . . share of U.S. album sales was 19.8 percent." I felt good, even if Music was finished off in just two skimpy columns. The report named no executives. Later in the book came a different story: "Revenues *decreased* to $3.691 billion . . . EBITA *decreased* to $467 million from $653 million." Uttering the phrase "cappuccino Florentine," he nodded at the waiter and picked up his final report.

The one for 1999 seemed seriously short. Now, no division executives at all were pictured. Music was stuck back at page twenty-nine, but even the names Daly and Semel were gone, without explanation. Music was down to 9 percent of TW's EBITA. In the back pages, an explanation went, "While our Music business declined 8 percent during the year, all of our other established businesses delivered solid, double-digit EBITA growth."

My host looked over at me and exercised his eyebrows. "When analysts meet with Jerry now," he said, "music is not something he likes to talk about." For five years, TW had been saying "Wait till." Back to the report, he pointed out where TW's Richard Parsons explained "adverse economic conditions in Japan, German, and Brazil, three of the five major international markets" and where Jerry added "some slippage" to that, because major performers—Madonna, Alanis, Jewel—had not shown. Or, as the report's next sentence quoted Jerry, "Not enough of our big horses were out there."

I asked my friend if he thought, under the circumstances, he could pay for lunch. He was a friend indeed.

I saw it clearly. The continuing decline of the Warner Music Group's performance had handed Wall Street the yawns. An analyst at some Dutch financial conglom called Barings had written, "Given that the entire music division represents only 10 percent of the company's cash flow, one would have to argue that the division is practically worthless."

People in the record business, when interviewed by the press, talked more and more off the record. There was all that corporate debt still to pay off. One who spoke said, "There was a time when everyone in the business would sit around and talk enthusiastically about all the great music being made, no matter what label it was on . . . John Lennon . . . Curtis Mayfield . . . Velvet Underground . . . Joni Mitchell. Today all anyone talks about are growth projections."

SIGNIFICANT PERFORMANCES BY WARNER MUSIC GROUP
(IN MILLIONS OF DOLLARS)

	Revenues	Ebita
1995	$4,196	$595
1996	$3,949	$653
1997	$3,691	$467
1998	$4,025	$493
1999	$3,834	$452

My analyst lunch had been enlightening, but writing this chapter has made me feel very sad.

For five years, Daly and Semel had done an admirable job of steadying the Record Group's boat. They were like the last of Steve Ross' management in the corporation and, true to their words, they behaved that way. The two heads of the Entertainment Group would not, however, change their ways; they were in charge. They prevented Corporate's meddling with their executives.

At meetings among the TW *machers*, Jerry Levin and Ted Turner had grown increasingly critical about the "old" way Daly and Semel ran things, their extravagances with stars, their rich deals, and, recently, their iffy profits. That double-digit growth the corporation kept expecting remained single, at best.

New York's backing for Daly and Semel felt weaker. Their worldwide cash flow in the past three years had fallen by 57.2 percent. Such performance invited killer criticism. Ted Turner, owning 11 percent of TW and responsible for 92 percent of TW's outrageous comments, pushed for financial discipline at Daly and Semel's picture and record companies.

By midyear, Time Warner's market share had dropped another step, from 19.7 percent down to 18.3 percent. Sales of new albums had fallen to 14.7 percent. In the Corporation Market-Share Charts, WEA had dropped to *third* place, behind both Universal and the independents.

Daly's and Semel's contracts were to expire on the last day of the century. The July before, it came time to talk about the next term. Jerry Levin told them he wanted a next term, but on better conditions: that the music division be controlled by others; that their annual pay (said to be about $25 million each) be reined in; that they'd get fewer stock options; and that operations at Warner Bros., including private jets, round-the-clock nannies, and gifts of new Range Rovers to their executives—all that outdated, Steve Ross stuff—now lingering only in Burbank at WB and WBR—would come to a halt. This was a new millennium on the way. Audiences had had it with Clint Eastwood and Kevin Costner was Corporate's stance. Rather than movie or recording stars, Jerry envisioned an enterprise constructed of cable and phone wires, thought about reaching many rooms in most homes, about fat pipes. Own the pipes and what flows through them. Whether that was Clint or Kevin, Metallica or Lil' Kim, was old, twentieth-century kind of stuff.

Jerry restructured. His president, Richard Parsons, became lord over Bob and Terry's realms, lowering Entertainment one more degree of separation. Daly and Semel, once barons, were reduced to duke size. They saw the signs. They hardly needed their jobs. One source said Semel had put away $500 million now, while Daly, suffering the same as I from California's community-property laws, had a lesser, $300 million's worth. He had my sympathy.

On Bastille Day 1999, Daly and Semel returned by Time Warner jet from a showbiz wedding in Venice (the Italian one). They met with Jerry and gave him their simple message: "We're through." It was clear, clean, monosyllabic. Levin, it was said, cried at the loss, perhaps in frustration over all these egos that had kept exploding all over his buttoned-down plans. But by August, Levin was telling the press that TW was searching for "music management on the front line, concentrating twenty-four hours a day."

Journalists speculated on who'd take over: Val? Sylvia? Russ? Dave? Parsons, TW's president, would choose, but it looked like the next-in-charge would be someone from within music. Daly, still believing that the upside in Music lay outside American's markets, considered a newcomer from International, an ex–PolyGram exec named Roger Ames. As for Daly and Semel, as one fellow in records reflected, "They were both nice guys, and they didn't think much about music, mostly left us alone. But it *would* be nice to get someone from music back in charge."

Not since Jack L. Warner had the Music division been run by anyone who could sing.

In 1999, music strove to be Y2K compliant. Woodstock was restaged, at a hundred fifty bucks a ticket, plus service fees. The call from the mud pits of "Peace" and "Love" changed to the call from the mosh pit: "Show us your tits."

In 1999, Ice-T sold merchandise via *http://www.mcicet.com*. At an industry convention, he advised record artists that when their labels insisted that they sign away the Web-site rights, they should tell the labels to "eat a bowl of dicks."

That ex–PolyGram executive being pursued by Time Warner was Roger Ames. He had been born in Trinidad, and he was now forty-nine. He'd spent his adulthood in records, starting (along with Ramon Lopez) at EMI UK in 1975. Over to PolyGram in 1979. There, in 1983, he'd restarted PolyGram's London label, gotten part ownership of it, and recast what had once been a hi-fi label as a new-acts label, starring Echo & the Bunnymen and Orbital.

By 1996, Ames was president of PolyGram's music group, but when Universal bought PolyGram, he was out of a job. The English press speculated that Ames would end up working as Number Two for his decades-long buddy, Lopez.

By the end of August, Dick Parsons had named Ames to replace Daly and Semel. His London label became attached to Seymour's Sire Group, turning the result into London/Sire, killing two birds with one Stein. Parsons, listing Ames's good qualities, included that he was "well respected in the investment community." The HQ of the Warner Music Group was moved back to New York.

Bob and Terry slid into the shadows. They had settled the waters in the Music Group when morale was lower than a codfish in Death Valley, but as the music business was changing, perhaps profoundly, they'd done little to reposition the group.

By the end of 1999, the group had fallen again, down among the five corporate giants to Number Four.

Ames was faced with a declining set of labels, fourth down and a mile to go in an industry assailed by recording artists demanding a new kind of fair share, with buyers preferring records more fairly priced or freely traded, with a marketing system some looked upon as dated as an Edison cylinder, and with corporate owners who thought in quarters of years. In passing on hip-hop, rap, and teen acts, the Warner labels had missed high tides.

The record business is like a moving sidewalk. People can step on it for a while, until either it or they run out of patience, and the time comes to step off. Never doubt, it keeps on moving, with or without you. But what, who, had caused the Warner Group to slip from Number One to Number Four?

I remembered back to when I'd been asked to pitch this book to various publishers, how one of them, staring me straight in the knees, asked me, "So who is the villain in your book?" I answered what I believed then, which was "Nobody."

Still, I wondered, why *had* all this happened? This book had a deadline, but I was determined to sift through the clues of this mystery. Who really was this book's villain? To catch him, I turned to a mighty coven of detectives, about seven fellow executives who had been through the record business but who now were on a different label. They were members of the Montecito Book Club.

Significant Releases

1998

Atlantic: Tori Amos (*From the Choirgirl Hotel*) • Brandy (*Never S-a-y Never,* including Brandy & Monica ("The Boy Is Mine")) • Phil Collins (*Hits*) • Hootie & the Blowfish

(*Musical Chairs*) • Jewel (*Spirit*) • Jimmy Page & Robert Plant (*Walking into Clarks-dale*) • The Three Tenors (*The Three Tenors—Paris 1998*) • *Great Expectations* soundtrack
Curb: Jo Dee Messina (*I'm Alright*) • LeAnn Rimes (*Sittin' on Top of the World*)

Elektra: Metallica (*Garage Inc.*) • Natalie Merchant (*Ophelia*) • Flipmode Squad (*The Imperial*) • Busta Rhymes ("Dangerous") • Keith Sweat (*Still in the Game*) • *The X-Files* soundtrack
East West: Gerald Levert (*Love & Consequences*)

Warner Bros.: Cher (*Believe*) • Goo Goo Dolls (*Dizzy Up the Girl*, including "Iris" and "Slide") • Faith Hill (*Faith*, including "This Kiss") • R.E.M. (*Up*) • Seal (*Human Being*) • Van Halen (*Van Halen 3*) • *City of Angels* soundtrack
Blackground: *Dr. Doolittle* soundtrack
Reprise: Barenaked Ladies (*Stunt*) • John Fogerty (*Premonition*) • Frank Sinatra (*The Very Best of Frank Sinatra*)
Maverick: Madonna (*Ray of Light*) • *The Wedding Singer* soundtrack
Tommy Boy: Everlast (*Whitey Ford Sings the Blues*)

1999

Atlantic Recording Corporation: Tori Amos (*To Venus and Back*) • Brandy ("Almost Doesn't Count") • Buena Vista Social Club (*Buena Vista Social Club*) • Collective Soul (*Dosage*) • The Corrs (*Talk on Corners*) • Jewel (*Joy: A Holiday Collection*) • Kid Rock (*Devil Without a Cause*) • Edwin McCain (*Messenger*) • Tim McGraw (*A Place in the Sun*) • LeAnn Rimes (*LeAnn Rimes*) • Stone Temple Pilots (*No. 4*) • Sugar Ray (*14:59*, including "Every Morning")

Elektra Entertainment Group Inc.: Missy "Misdemeanor" Elliott (*Da Real World*) • Gerald Levert ("Taking Everything") • Metallica (*S&M*) • Ol' Dirty Bastard (*Nigga Please*) • Phish (*Hampton Comes Alive*) • Busta Rhymes (*E.L.E. Extinction Level Event * The Final World Front*) • Linda Ronstadt & Emmylou Harris (*Western Wall/The Tucson Sessions*) • Trio (*Trio II*) • Third Eye Blind (*Blue*)

Warner Bros. Records Inc.: Eric Benét (*A Day in the Life*) • Eric Clapton (*Blues*) • Faith Hill (*Breathe*) • Alanis Morissette (*MTV Unplugged*) • Orgy (*Candyass*) • Red Hot Chili Peppers (*Californication*, including "Scar Tissue") • Static-X (*Wisconsin Death Trip*) • *Austin Powers: The Spy Who Shagged Me* soundtrack

37

"**V**ILLAIN?" that publisher had asked me. I had a bookful of clues. They begged to be chased down. As in *The Magnificent Seven*, I rounded up seven sleuths to find out What Had Gone Wrong and Who'd Done It. I'd moved up to Santa Barbara/Montecito, abandoning my lake and boat to take up residence with a lass named Meg, a marathon runner without a Hollywood bone in her. On our first date, I made it clear I'd had enough of divorcing, and she just looked at me puzzled, and said "Fine, fine." I realized that, with Meg, I'd never need to call Allen Grubman. She and I stuck fast. I only hope you've done as well. Meg and I had begun traveling to odd spots, I dabbling again with writing what you're reading.

Getting toward the end of this book, I remembered that publisher's "villain?" challenge and turned to my Book Club sleuths. The Montecito Book Club was a group I'd been welcomed into by other retireds and semiretireds, all homing now in Santa Barbara and all from the record business.

One such couple—Eddie and Bobbie Rosenblatt—had begun herding this book club into once-a-month evenings. Entrance fee was that everybody had to read an agreed-upon chosen book, then convene to discuss it over informal meals. This requirement had proved a little rigorous for some, but the hardy and semiliterate stuck. They would become my posse.

I worried that we book-club oldies resembled those other old record guys of the Sixties, those guys I'd noticed in Manhattan hanging out in wood-paneled bars, sipping at four-thirty in the afternoon, shaking their heads over the spectacle of us energized youngsters zipping around in our Nehru jackets, ruining what had been a good business, one where singers sang the songs that were handed to them, when albums cost nine hours in the studio.

Were *we* now geezers? Had I been guilty of believing that this would be a complete book, but really ended up with only a chapter in a longer history? Was it possible the record business might move on and on, like that airport walkway, without us?

When I got in my stew over *why* the Warner Music Group, once so enjoyable, had sunk so, I brought my kettle to the Montecito Book Club, who would be delighted to speculate with me. Anyway, this was more fun than reading those assigned novels, the slow kind that took one full page just to evoke how, one winter's morn, the icicles dropped from sagging branches like . . . The kind our club's guru, Mary Sheldon, called "chick books."

My seven samurai included Eddie; Chuck Kaye, who had, in my mind, been the First Little Indian of the Warner decimation; Jeff Barry, who'd written eminently catchy songs ("Doo Wah Ditty" and "Da Do Ron Ron") before Dylan forever ruined music with meaningful words; two showbiz lawyers, both named David (Braun and Gersh).

Most intriguing to me, a less-famous fellow who stretched even further back in the business than I: Bones Howe, who'd been engineering and producing records in the 1950s. In the 1960s, Warner Bros. Records enjoyed his work with the Routers, the Marketts, and the Association. For the last-mentioned group, which had opened 1967's Monterey Pop Festival, Bones Howe had produced a wondrous sound. For other labels, he'd recorded the 5th Dimension, Jerry Lee Lewis, even the Turtles and the Monkees, and then made the turn: to exec VP of Columbia Pictures. Since then, Bones had done well enough to have a Montecito estate with eleven oak trees in its big front yard. But now he had time on his hands, which annoyed him. He composed a list of his sayings—Poor Bones' Almanac—and I like especially two lines from it:

- The reward for success is that you get to do it again.
- If you stay active in this business, you never retire. It retires you.

I began with Bones, who believed that "what killed our business" was all the alternative radio stations. Bones loved Top Forty. "Boss radio!" he blurted. "I mean, remember KHJ, with boss jocks like the Real Don Steele doing the music? Remember," Bones said unstoppably, "in the KHJ lobby, there was that girl, always ready for *whatever*? Remember her? Remember her name? Amazing Grace!"

Against every nasty instinct in me, I tried to control Bones's flying reminiscences. I wanted us clue searchers to snoop back only through Warner history, fitting together bits of the past into this jigsaw of *Exploding*. The whys.

For my first clue, I asked Bones Howe and our two ladies out for the appropriately named T-bones and gin at the Plow and Angel. I was not prepared for how flatly Bones would condemn his old profession, now that it was mid-Y2K. "Things die," he told me flatly, like I was acting too hopeful. "The business started as a bunch of individuals but ended as a bunch of corporations. Companies may buy their ways back to Number One, but it'll never be like it was. That time can't be repeated."

I asked him, "Maybe *we're* old farts, now? Maybe twenty-year-olds, getting into the business, they're as turned on as we were back then?"

Bones wouldn't buy it. "No label has the patience. Either you make it on your first album now or you're out. That's just wrong. You can never tell an artist by the first one. If Bob Dylan were starting out today," he said, looking at me over the top of his glasses, "he'd have to start selling through the Internet."

Looking at him straight through my bifocals, I nodded. "It's like," I added, "if Shakespeare didn't write a hit first time out, he'd have been toast? Back to teaching in Stratford."

Being a detective felt more like being an undertaker. At the end, we split the check. Thanks to the 1960s, we both could afford to. I decided to poll the whole club with my first "What happened?"

The book club's first answer was the one that surfaced most often in my researching: that Time Warner had killed off its best executives, losing Droz, Kaye, Ostin, Morris, Krasnow, Nesuhi, Waronker, Vogel, Goldberg, and a couple of suits named Morgado and Fuchs. I told them how I'd talked with Dave Glew, now a hit exec at Epic, where he'd mentioned coming across a photo of the Warner Music heads, ten of them, and how suddenly he realized only two were still there.

But losing these men, however painful, was no proof that their loss ruined other things. Of all those on the list, only Doug Morris had quickly found a new sweet spot at MCA. The others? At WEA, Dave Mount became as funny as Henry. His amalgam of distribution-manufacturing-printing was working. Hard to tell where International would have gone if Nesuhi had stayed on, but at least during the early Morgado/Lopez years, it had indeed grown nicely. Which brought us to the three labels. Were they doing things worse now? That question stopped the posse for one evening. Round the fire, we downed our Chinese chicken salads and Merlot, while coyotes howled in the blue hills above.

We argued it out. It was hard to make sure judgments. Would Ostin and Waronker have done better than Thyret and crew? (After five years at DreamWorks, they'd turned nicely hot.) Would Krasnow have done better at Elektra than Sylvia? Had Atlantic, in losing Morris, done worse under Azzoli? Hard to prove.

So it may *not* have been the people explosion after all. But if not people, then what? One of the detectives offered, I thought, the best explanation: Our universe got derailed whenever, in our lives, the money became more important than music.

We came up with three instances:

- Steve Ross, when merging Warner with Time, mostly in the end, at that Critical Moment when Arthur Liman stopped Steve for one beat and asked him, "You *really* want to do this?" Steve could have pulled back and saved what he had. But Steve had gone for the Big Payoff. The result created a burden of debt that from then on made cash more critical than better records.
- Then there were Levin and Morgado, intent on building profits at the cost of people. Was it *all* just about "more"? Morgado, Levin, Fuchs—all had the big vision of a 1990s music empire. In pursuing the vision, they'd tossed people out of office who behaved more slowly, followed other values—tossed out like they'd just lost some election. Small but profitable had become impossible to be.
- And third, there was the decision by Levin, Fuchs, and the stockholders, who ultimately caved in to "moral" pressure, confusing that with what the American public wanted to hear. TW management got scared that Ice-T and Interscope might bring down Western Civilization. They forgot that Jerry Garcia and the Fugs and MC5 never brought down Western Civ (just as most of *us* often forgot that tons of people thought that Donny and Marie were good to listen to).

What we had accomplished in '69 we had forgotten by '99. When money changed from being a wondrous shower and became ruler over all, everything suffered. Swarms of suits had, in the end, endorsed greed over boogie. Chuck Kaye put it one way: "In the music business, bigger is not necessarily better. In fact, I believe smaller is actually better."

As usual, Eddie could sum it up the shortest: "The suits won."

All those turning points had come from powerful men born without music instincts, intent on money. They should have stood back. Their three solutions, when combined, had broken the heart of Warner Music, best as we all could guess. It was only at Warners that those three deeds piled up. The other big labels also had their own suits aplenty. But those other companies, Numbers Two and under, seemed to keep following the instinctive ears of music-passionate geeks and kept their suit guys in the background. They let their music geeks rule.

In south Las Vegas, there's a bowling alley called "13 Strikes," where, on weekends, twin brothers Arnie and Kenny Gatto have been making recordings of bowling pins bashing together. Random smashings of pins, overdubbed one atop the other, without pause, recorded by mikes suspended right above the pins, where it's intolerably loud. I talked to the Gatto brothers by phone. They spoke passionately about their work, their art, their records. Arnie and Kenny had grown disgusted with hip-hop ("Cute? It's just shit," to quote exactly). They also were contemptuous of rap, saying that

dudes forcing words to rhyme was "phony-phony." Although no actual people formed their bowling-pin "group," Arnie and Kenny had made up a
name: "The Puke Pins." They put Puke Pins recordings on the Net, and have
sold Puke Pins CDs, ones they'd burned themselves, outside Vegas school-
yards. They were making a living.

I had so much I could tell the Gatto boys. Then I realized: the gulf.
Arnie and Kenny had never seen a vinyl record, nor owned a record player,
nor even known what "You sound like a broken record" means. In their
lives, MTV had always existed, and Michael Jackson had always been white.

When I mentioned I'd been in the record business, at Warner Bros., Artie
and Kenny showed no sign of being impressed. They did not ask if I could introduce them to anybody. About the record business, they had no questions,
but when we got back to Puke Pins, they talked fast again about the rush
of noise. I could hear their passion about being in "the record business." I
asked them what the name of their label was. "Static!" they both yelled.

The second puzzle facing the Montecito Book Club was harder: Why was
the entire record *business*—not just Warners—going downhill, the record
clubs down more than 50 percent, hit artists selling fewer units, the whole
industry getting obsessed with kids sharing digital discs, for free, over the
Internet. Had we, sellers of records, had we all lost our way? Was this a different, more profound kind of Exploding, called Imploding?

Like Bones, admitting now to "nearly seventy," the rest of us, too, had
acted as the bridge between the music makers and the public, preserving
music for the people. We'd gotten good (and a little rich) at it. Soberly, the
Montecito Book Club had to admit, when you looked at music and the public that way, we all had been glorified middlemen. Could be, and there's no
rule that middlemen should earn money forever. Our business, therefore,
was not to be defined just as stores, we agreed, nor just as music (think spoken; think video); not even by any tangible configuration (grooves or pits),
not as radio (programmed-by-others), not jukeboxes (pay-per-listen). All
those forms of our business today have come and may, in the future, go.
Companies and executives, too, they come and go. Discs and tapes may
come and go. What survives is getting people the music they want when
they want it.

The book club still loved that part, though felt dispensible about it.

Much more history is unfolding, with a fresh cast of characters, however. Not entirely, however. There's Ahmet, still out there, walking slow, as
he once put it, patiently listening for some artist who moves you and who
will make you very rich. Ahmet, overshadowed now, walking slow with a
snazzy bamboo cane, in shoes, I'd guess, worth thirteen thousand dollars
apiece.

Index